FROMMER'S
DOLLARWISE
NORTHWEST

INCLUDING OREGON, WASHINGTON, VANCOUVER/VICTORIA, SUN VALLEY, & CRUISES TO ALASKA

MARYLYN SPRINGER
AND DONALD SCHULTZ

1989–1990

Published by Prentice Hall Trade Division
A Division of Simon & Schuster, Inc.
Gulf + Western Building
One Gulf + Western Plaza
New York, NY 10023

ISBN 0-13-217837-0

ISSN 0884-0253

Text Design: Levavi & Levavi, Inc.
Manufactured in the United States of America

CONTENTS

MAPS

INTRODUCTION

DOLLARWISE
NORTHWEST

□ □ □

1. WHY THE NORTHWEST
2. WEATHER OR NOT
3. WHO LIVES HERE?
4. A CAPSULE HISTORY
5. WHAT'S HAPPENING TODAY
6. VISITOR INFORMATION
7. FROMMER'S DOLLARWISE TRAVEL CLUB

Giant redwoods that were mere seedlings when Columbus set sail soar into the stratosphere, their branches spreading into an emerald sky-curtain pierced only by the most determined sunbeams. Silvery waters crash and tinkle, curling seductively around boulder barriers, then torrenting over golden cliffs worn sheer by relentless cascades. Lashing seas splutter and spume over monolithic crags and spill between towering dunes that ripple along the shoreline.

1. WHY THE NORTHWEST
Welcome to the nation's Northwest territory, a land sometimes fanciful, sometimes farcical, occasionally fanatical—and everywhere so punch-gut beautiful it leaves you gasping at the sheer majesty of it all.

Through this land twist some of the nation's most awesome rivers: the mighty Columbia carving out a massive gorge; the swirling Salmon, tearing so determinedly downstream that it's called the River of No Return; the racing, rapids-strewn waters of the Deschutes, the Klamath, the John Day.

Over it all loom nature's most dramatic productions, mile-high, snow-topped, volcanic sentinels that float eerily on the horizon, rearing up suddenly before you in drop-jaw splendor. Their spiky spires speak of cataclysmic discord, of rumbling, blasting explosions that once tore across this land, ripping open gashes that would become gorges, baring flatlands that would one day appear before you as mile after rolling mile of flower-kissed meadows, slumbering away the centuries in the shadow of forests deep and dark.

This magnificence, this tangible evidence of nature's might and rights, is America's Northwest territory, a land tucked way up in the return-address corner of the nation, an environmentalist's Disneyland, nirvana for nature lovers.

Yet there are more than natural wonders here. Carved from the wilderness are glittering cities, man-made forests of steel and glass. But here even those citadels of chic modernity are softened by nature, muted by forest parks, winding rivers, and always on the horizon, the snow-capped reminders of this kingdom of nature.

Once, and still, a rough-and-tumble land, this northwest corner of the continent is a place of legend, of Indian totem tales and Paul Bunyan-esque characters, of buried treasure and visible treasures.

It is a place you come expecting to be awed, only to discover that even your wildest expectations of geographic grandeur pale amid the real splendor of these snow-crowned massifs and sweeping seascapes.

It is a land that touches you, humbles you, and finally forces you to face the inevitability of your very small role in a massive geologic play that has been on stage for incalculable ages. It is humbling, yet soothing, scenery—a snow-clad, sapphire-laked, pine-trimmed promise of much to be seen and done.

It is a land of terrible beauty, a series of vistas so stunning in impact, so awesome in timeless immutability that everyone who comes here leaves a different person.

Across this land passed a vivid part of American history, a part that survives so visibly it seems to have happened only yesterday. You may be riding on a superhighway, but just over there you can touch deep ruts left by wagon trains that only a century ago followed each other down the famed Oregon Trail, toddling along in line like so many ducklings behind mama.

Along dramatic cliffs cut by the rushing waters of the Columbia River, trees of immense girth still bear rope burns inflicted by early settlers as they carefully lowered wagons packed with treasured stove and favorite doll, hand-carved chair and hand-me-down lamp.

WHO LIVES HERE: Up here in the corner of the continent, people live close to their history and love it. They live close to their land and love it. They know the liabilities of this, their chosen land, and they know their own limitations. They laugh at both. You hear the jokes right after you hear the first hello:

"We get so much rain here that we call it the Pacific North*wet*."

"We don't tan, we rust."

"Northwest natives have webbed feet."

"If you fall off a bike in the Northwest, you drown."

"If the sun shines for more than three days up here, we get nervous—there must be *something* wrong."

That "we got it—let's love it" stance is characteristic of these Northwest dwellers, and it is just that quirky perversity that shaped the history of this rugged corner of the nation. When others would surely quit, Northwesterners hold on with tenacity that would do a bulldog proud. Their determined stubbornness is as classically implacable as the monolithic rocks that rear up along their coast line.

These are tough people occupying land that is quite civilized now, but was plenty tough and demanding when they took it on a century ago. It was a land in which native Indian tribes fought brave and bitter battles to retain what had been theirs for so many centuries, slaying many of these hardy newcomers, and dying themselves, in a vain attempt to stop a tide that would not be quelled.

Because dangers and deprivations were many and companions few in those rugged early days, friendships were by necessity quickly made and highly valued. That is still true today. When road repairs back up traffic on a mountain highway, drivers clamber out of their cars and come on over for a chat, very much as they must once have done along the original Oregon Trail. By the time traffic is moving again, you've been invited over for dinner.

Today's Northwest is a land of red-checked lumberman's jackets, of karma candy and tofu soufflé, of hikers who stroll, singing, as rain pours down on them, and of bicyclists who go for an afternoon spin up the side of an 8,000-foot mountain.

SPACES AND PLACES: This is a land in which a village of more than 1,000 people calls itself a city. It is, therefore, a land with many cities but very few, shall we say, metropolises. Drive five miles or so from dead center of nearly any major metropolitan area of the Northwest and you're in a vast wilderness of pine, mountain, pasture, and pacificity.

As determined as they are to keep their cities growing, however, these Northwesterners are just as determined not to exchange past for progress. Up this way history is as serious a subject as religion—and frequently a great deal more controversial. People love every historic stick of their towns, and in these days of backlash from the Age of Plastic they love those sticks even more. Throughout the Northwest, hundreds of millions of dollars have been spent to restore what was once uprooted to make way for the Progress of the '50s, whatever that was.

In Seattle whimsical architecture in Pioneer Square has been primped and polished. At the city's funky Pike Place Market, clinical, if soul-less, revamp was fought so ferociously that even the fighters seemed surprised at the intensity of their feeling for this picturesque decades-old marketplace. In the Washington village of Port Townsend, a whole *town* is a museum of fabulous Victorian architecture.

In Portland ornate, burbling drinking fountains, gift of a '30s lumber millionaire who worried that Prohibition was frustrating Portlanders, have been cleaned, painted, and put back in operation. Blocks of iron-fronted Portland buildings, second-largest collection of such antique constructions in the nation, have been carefully restored to their former beauty.

In Vancouver an imposing old copper-roofed hotel is still the most refined place in town for afternoon tea. At the city's eerily evocative museum of native Indian life, huge totems and mammoth native construction projects fill a classic museum that is the finest of its kind in the world.

In Victoria, history-worship started long ago and never ebbed. When you see this town you may think they knew they were making history even as they were making it, so slavishly do they dedicate themselves to re-creation of life in Merry Olde England here. Mob-capped waitresses serve you in a massive and ornate Victorian home, so breezily painted it seems to have stepped right out of a coloring book. A whole English village is re-created before your wondering eyes and teatime is as elaborate a ritual here as it is in Britain.

YESTERDAYS . . . : In the Northwest every town has a historical museum, no matter how few historic treasures have been found to put in it. Out here, anything more than ten years old is likely to qualify as antique, so keep a good grip on your children. So many museums are there, in fact, that towns seem to be one-upping each other. One tiny two-street village in Washington has no fewer than five museums, including one dedicated to the history of seeds!

Still, as you wander these museums, huge and tiny, you cannot help but be touched by delicate reminders of how we were: lace-trimmed handkerchiefs; 600-piece, Gold Rush–wealth chandeliers; sternly simple, handmade pioneer furniture; elaborately elegant parlor clocks inset with a thousand tiny pieces of wood.

Faded old photographs are particularly poignant: Indians sitting proud and grim, their world crumbling around them even as they posed; pioneer families with lined and sunburned faces looking as if they'd like to, please, just get on with it; pioneer children in knickers merrily romping about a one-room school-house that would be attended by their children and their grandchildren.

What lost secrets might be recovered if all the separate treasures of these museums could be catalogued and combined! Yet half the fun of touring the Northwest is seeing each one of these history-recorders working so hard to salute its ancestors with these very personalized displays of their treasures.

No, you won't find Disneyland and trained dolphins, sequined chorus lines and glitzy casinos here. You will, however, find history lifted from dry old books and brought to life in the most intriguing ways.

At Fort Clatsop near Astoria, park rangers dressed in meticulously researched and painstakingly replicated buckskins outline for you the miserable winter of 1805 when Lewis and Clark camped out here but couldn't get an hour's sleep free from flea-infested bedding, soaked by days of never-ending rain. Even Sacajawea plays her part at this fort, whose buildings have been reconstructed from plans drawn by the explorers on a piece of rawhide.

South of Portland an annual summer theater production focuses each year on just one of the many dramatic events that occurred in the settling of the West.

In a village in southwestern Oregon, you can watch Hamlet and Lady Macbeth agonize on the boards of a delightful outdoor amphitheater, a Tudor-style reproduction of an Elizabethan theater, and delight in the talents of a repertory company that has won one of the nation's most coveted drama awards.

And in another charming pastoral village lined with Gold Rush–era buildings, you can attend performances of a dance and music festival presented on the rolling green lawns of an early settler's beautiful home.

Let it also be known that all is not rugged frontier. Operas, symphonies, and theaters play to packed houses in every major city and many small towns as well.

. . . AND TODAY: If modernity is what you seek, Seattle, Portland, Vancouver, and Victoria stand ready with the finest in down-home cookin' or nouvelle cuisine, created with a bounty of wonderful seafood scooped from these seas, fruits and vegetables fresh from farms and berry patches.

Shops in Vancouver, and Victoria brim with luxurious furs and glittering jewels. In Portland and Seattle stunningly renovated department stores and huge high-rise shopping complexes outfitted with carousels and ice rinks beckon.

You will find less tinsel in the Northwest than in most other parts of the country. No tawdry, honky-tonk strips, no rootin'-tootin' Disneylands, little that is false and practically nothing pretentious.

For beneath the sleek sophistication of Vancouver, the busy commercial life of Portland, the easy blend of bigtown-smalltown in Seattle lies an ingenuousness, an innocence that is not easily beguiled, but is quite beguiling.

Secretly, and sometimes not so secretly, those who inhabit the Pacific Northwest march to the beat of a very different drummer, although ostensibly they are careful to keep pace with the rest of the world.

Up here they think they have a message for the rest of the nation, but, perversely, they care little whether you hear or understand it. Unspoken but deeply felt, that message is one that has been passed on to them across generations, an age-old bequest from those who stayed doggedly on here, despite every kind of suffering, despite grief, misery, exhaustion, and not infrequently, death.

It is a message of challenge and response, of faith in the collective power of individual initiative built on unfathomable, unplumbable reserves of hope and courage. It is a message sensed more than spoken and felt more forcefully here than perhaps anywhere else in the nation, if only because beneath its surface sophistication this land is still so new, so little changed by changing times.

2. WEATHER OR NOT

Okay, let's get what you really want to know right up front here.

Does it rain? In a word, yes. In several words, yes but not as much as the interminable jokes would suggest.

What precipitation does fall from above is the debatable gift of the warm Japan Current that rolls up along the coastline. Its heated waters rise to create clouds that scud merrily across the skies until they reach the massive snow-clad peaks of the long Cascade Mountain backbone of the Pacific Northwest.

Unable to top towering peaks, those clouds dump on the Northwest. Happily, most of that water falls in the least popular visitor seasons. Summers, when most people visit here, are generally not only very warm but quite dry as well.

Even when it does rain, it rains not with terrifying claps of thunder and vicious force, but softly, gently. Armed with an umbrella—many hotels even stock loaners—and a light raincoat, you won't be held back by this California dew and may hardly even notice the precipitation.

Seattle, in fact, sponsors its big celebration of the year, Seafair, in July, swearing Nature never rains on that parade.

Claims to aridity notwithstanding, July and August see the least rain of any months of the year. More than 22 of Seattle's average of just 71 cloudless days occur in those summer months.

Throughout the Northwest, October, November, and December get the most rainfall. In winter Nature pulls out all the stops. Exciting windstorms along the coast have actually become what may be the only storms in the nation people actually go out of their way to see.

Coastal villages in Oregon and Washington are visited all winter long by romantic types who sit by the fireplace featured in many hostelries and toast each other happily as the weather rages across the sea, kicking up interesting driftwood, valuable agate jewels, and colorful glass floats that have bobbed all the way here from the nets of Japanese fishermen.

TEMPERATURES: As for temperatures, well that's the good news. Those same warm currents that dump on the Northwest more than its fair share of rainy days also keep this part of the nation warm in winter and cool in summer.

Temperatures very rarely drop below 32° in winter, hovering in the 40s on the average, and rarely top 75 or so in summer months. When snow does occasionally fall in Seattle or Vancouver, people are flabbergasted and mill around in a quandry of indecision whether to go out or stay in, leave cars or drive them home, break dates or keep them.

Snow? Hardly ever in the sea-level towns of Victoria, Vancouver, Seattle, and Portland, but *always* high on spectacular mountains that float like eerie white spectres over Northwest metropolises. Which means, of course, that you can finish afternoon tea, pick up your skis, and be schussing before sundown. So close are ski-worthy mountains to Seattle, Portland, and Vancouver that residents routinely go skiing after work and get home in time for the 11 p.m. news.

On the other side of that towering Cascades range, geography is another story entirely. Unprotected by warm coastal breezes, the "other" side of the mountains—Spokane and Walla Walla in Washington; Bend, Ontario, and Pendleton in Oregon—has greater extremes of hot and cold. Here it's warmer and sunnier in summer, colder in winter.

At the first sign of spring, damp Seattle residents head for the Tri-Cities to dry out, Portlanders seek the sun in Bend. They are not disappointed, for Ole Sol shines unremittingly in summer east of the Cascades and is very, very warm, often raising temperatures to the 90s.

So toasty is the climate that eastern Washington and towns near Portland grow fat and sassy grapes that swell in the sun, are harvested in fall, and finally become increasingly noteworthy Oregon and Washington wines.

Cold winds off the mountains make winter temperatures in eastern Washington and Oregon colder than those of their neighbors on the west side of the Cascades, but chilly breezes bring with them the absolute promise of snow for skiing, snowmobiling, tobogganing, and fireside chats.

MOUNTAINS OF THE NORTHWEST: Those lofty peaks affect the land forms too. On the west coast of Washington, Oregon, and British Columbia, you will find deep green forests, even lush rain forests where fir trees grow 300 feet tall and wider than a basketball player is tall. On the east side of the mountains, vast deserts stretch for mile after seemingly endless mile, their undulating golden curves broken only by countless clumps of sagebrush and the weird forms of mechanical irrigation equipment.

Never does the Pacific Northwest let you forget the power, the majesty, and the geological impact of its mountains. Even if for a moment you cannot see one of the spectacular blue-and-white and green-and-gray montages of color and light soaring to the sky, you can always see the havoc wreaked over the ages by these volcanic sentinels.

These are, after all, mountains very new in the scheme of things, born just short eons ago by volcanic upheaval. Mount Mazama, which created Oregon's deep-blue Crater Lake; Mount St. Helens, which just a few years ago showed the world what nature can do; towering Mount Rainier, Mount Baker, Mount Hood, lovely Three Sisters, Mount Adams, and Mount Garibaldi in British Columbia—all are Cascade Range monoliths that form part of a circle of volcanoes known as the "Ring of Fire."

In Idaho near Sun Valley, a bizarre and eerie sight called National Lava Rocks Monument stretches for miles before your wondering eyes. Tossed up by ancient upheaval and looking for all the world like the moon, it is a desolate, forbidding, craggy landscape of volcanic monsters rising to haunt the horizon.

At Mount St. Helens words are inadequate to convey how petty mankind's worries seem. Who are we, compared to explosive natural forces that can fell everything in their path, dropping like pick-up-sticks thousands of trees so huge only three of them can fit on the back of a logging truck?

3. WHO LIVES HERE?

Dwelling as they do amid this spectacular scenery, those who live here can be as unusual and as dramatic as the geography around them.

They are isolationists by geographical accident, iconoclasts by choice and experience, neither overcome nor unimpressed by the trappings of success.

A conglomeration of all kinds of people mixing in remarkably tranquil ethnic interplay, the Northwest is home to folks who are quick to measure you up but slow to rule you out.

Eccentricity has been elevated to an art form here, its definition expanded to the widest possible interpretations. To call someone "a little weird" is to deliver a judgment bordering on compliment.

In some Northwest places—Eugene, Oregon, is one of them—it is possible that there is no word in the local language for odd. Anything goes here, so long as it doesn't interfere with *everyone's* enjoyment of this place or—and this is very important—with the environment, personal or biological.

That word "environment" has more shades of meaning in the Northwest than perhaps anywhere else on earth. It also causes more battles here than anywhere else on earth. Not one tree, not one old building, no matter how innocuous, not one river, not one plot of land may be changed one whit without a challenge.

Nature lovers up here are not in the least loathe to go to battle. To say "Sierra Club" in these parts is to utter words akin to prayer—or to mouth the worst of profanities. A favorite loggers' bumper sticker reads: "Sierra Club, Kiss My Ax."

Health is more than a concern, it's a cult. Vegetarianism is so widely practiced you'll see carrot cake and tofu soufflé on the most exclusive gourmet menus. Outdoor sports are pursued with religious fervor so intense that in one city a rent-a-doberman service provides canine companionship to nervous runners.

People speak their own language up here, big mouthfuls of spluttery syllables hereafter to be known as Northwest-speak. Try these around your tongue: Mukilteo, Cathlamet, Duckabush, Humptulips, Kalaloch, Siskiyou, Sequim, Snohomish, Skykomish, Snoqualmie, Wallowa, Willamette. If you think you've got those pronunciations right, you haven't.

While linguistic nightmares are a challenge to today's visitor, less tongue-twisting, but far more humbling, monickers are clear testimony to challenges past: Deadman's Gulch, Tombstone Prairie, Pull and Be Damned Road.

Cussed individualists all, these Pacific Northwesterners make their own rules when those they've got don't seem to be working. People in one small town got so mad when the county seat was moved to a neighboring village, they just up and refused to surrender the county records. Which meant that government officials in the new county seat had to come skulking into town in the dead of night, break into the courthouse, and steal the records! And that's just what they did. Of course.

4. A CAPSULE HISTORY

It is really quite impossible to separate your exploration of the Northwest from history, and who would want to? History, architecture, and geology are inextricably tied here. That's why you'll find that we have included much of the history that has shaped this corner of the world right in our discussion of each region and of what to see and do there. But to give you a general idea of just what happened here over the years, here's a brief rundown of Northwest historical highlights.

EARLY DAYS: The first Europeans to get a good look at this land were Spanish sailors who sailed up here from Mexico. None of them stayed around too long, but they did lay claim to the land and leave some Spanish names behind: Cape Blanco, for the chalk-white cliffs they saw along the coast of Oregon; Heceta (pronounced "Heh-*sea*-tah") Head after one of their captains; Lopez, Fidalgo, Guemes. Those names are about all the mark Spanish travelers left here, however, and that nationality had only a minimal effect on activities up this way.

Other nations began showing an interest in the Northwest also. The Russians moved from Siberia, to Alaska, and down the coast to what is now Northern California, all for the fabulous, fur-bearing sea otters. But the ones to leave the most-noticeable stamp were the British. Sir Francis Drake was the first to come, sometime around 1580, if only to skirt the coast and then turn back south when the fog became too thick. Next was the equally famous Capt. James Cook, who took a brief look at things hereabouts in 1778 on the same voyage that gave England claim to Hawaii. Cook, however, seems not to have been too impressed: along the coast of Oregon, he dubbed one forbidding promontory Cape

Foulweather. It was left up to Capt. George Vancouver and his right-hand man, Peter Puget, to explore the coastline of this northwest corner of the continent.

But by any standards Drake, Cook, and Vancouver were latter-day explorers. Native American Indians had settled here more than 12,000 years earlier, probably walking across a natural land bridge over the Bering Strait to move in here with mastodons and whales.

Paddling ocean-going canoes, coastal tribes hunted whales and seals that you will still see blowing and romping off the shores today as they plow their way north to Alaska on an annual migratory trek of 8,000 miles.

In the rivers Indians dipped long-handled nets to pull up hundreds of salmon headed upstream for spawning grounds. You can still see them fishing that way today, generations later.

For coastal Indians, home was a long communal building made of logs and called a longhouse. Several families lived together in each longhouse.

Inland tribes traveled by horse, the unintended gift of the Spanish, riding and raising fine Appaloosas as well as tamed wild horses. They hunted for a living and lived in tepees (sometimes spelled tipis) that could be folded up and moved easily as the game migrated.

Their languages differed too. Coastal Indians spoke softer sounds like Suquamish, Shohomish, and Duckabush, while inland tribes mouthed harsher syllables—Spokane, Yakima, Cayuse.

A fluke of nature has preserved in amazing detail an awesome record of ancient Indian life. Nearly 500 years ago a Makah Indian village on the northwestern tip of Washington's Olympic Peninsula was buried in a mudslide. More than 60,000 artifacts have been recovered and are on display, everything from baskets to harpoons, canoes and beaded cloaks, even an entire longhouse. Museums in Spokane and Yakima, in Vancouver and Seattle are also fascinating places to see the art and artifacts of these earliest of Northwest residents.

Although much has changed for these peoples, they have in recent years worked hard to preserve their heritage. You can see traditional Indian folk music and dancing at many Northwest festivals. For a list of them, contact the United Indians of All Tribes office, Discovery Park, Daybreak Star Art Center, Box 9910, Seattle, WA 98199 (tel. 206/285-4425).

Back to Captain Vancouver, who arrived in the Northwest only to find that an American captain named Robert Gray was sailing his ship on the same waters. Gray and Vancouver talked things over and decided to divvy it all up: Vancouver sailed north to discover Vancouver Island, home of British Columbia's capital city of Victoria, and mainland British Columbia, where his name graces the largest city in the province. His pal Puget loaned his name to Puget Sound.

Meanwhile, Gray sailed south to discover Gray's Harbor, now a popular fishing and clamming ground in Washington. In a search for the fabled Northwest Passage, Gray also managed to discover the Columbia River and thereby laid American claim to what would come to be known as the Northwest Territory.

EXPLORING THE NORTHWEST TERRITORY: About 13 years after Gray and Vancouver sailed the waters blue, the president of the U.S., Thomas Jefferson, called two rough-and-ready fellows into his office and sent them on an errand. If the U.S. was ever going to get its westward push going in the right direction, he told them, the nation needed a waterway to the Pacific, an inland passage, and it needed to know what on earth was out there in the northwestern wilds.

Charged with President Jefferson's instructions, Meriweather Lewis and William Clark set out from St. Louis and had some pretty rough days until they met an Indian maiden named Sacajawea. She traveled with them, helping them find their way to the coast and keeping them alive through months and months of grueling and dangerous overland travel. Lewis and Clark's detailed reports on what they found here spurred the settlement of the Northwest.

While nationalistic types had been trooping around trying to raise their colors on Northwest land, early entrepreneurs were already making their own kinds of claims. Furs, and consequently riches, were what these fiercely competitive traders and trappers were after and they got them. Trading posts in the region were established by the North West Co., which built Spokane House in 1810, the first building erected by a white man in Washington. North West's bitter rivals, Hudson's Bay Co., arrived. Millionaire John Jacob Astor turned up in 1811 with his Pacific Fur Co., which sent two parties out west, one overland on what was to become the Oregon Trail, the other by sea around Cape Horn. They settled at Astoria, first commercial outpost in Oregon.

American furriers didn't stay too long, however: they left when the War of 1812 broke out and were replaced in Astoria by the Canadian North West Co. Once again, that powerful Hudson's Bay Co. won over all of them and was the only company to retain fur-trading rights in the region.

THE PIG WAR: Britain and the U.S. didn't get along too well in those days, but in the Northwest they somehow managed to tolerate each other. For many years the region was occupied by both nations. In 1846 they got together and Britain's occupation began at the 49th parallel, today the Canadian border.

While they were trying to work it all out, Americans and British almost went to war over a pig! Seems both sides were laying claim to the San Juan Islands in Puget Sound. Their "I want it, you can't have it" battling went on until both sides were downright irritable about the whole thing. One day in 1859 a pig of British origin (we'd hesitate to say British pig) mistook the agreed-upon boundaries and stepped into an American potato patch. An annoyed American potato farmer shot the pig. British soldiers protested their unexpected pork chops and everybody got very angry—so angry, in fact, that both nations called up the troops and got ready to fight. Reason, which is not often a winner in nationalistic disputes, won this round, ending quickly the nation's most ludicrous contretemps, the Pig War.

THE SETTLERS COME WEST: By the middle of the 1800s the only European settlers in the Northwest were some trappers, most of them French-Canadians, some Catholic missionaries who had followed them, soldiers who had drawn the short straw, and a few adventurers who trickled in alone or with families.

Then in the middle years of the 1800s, pure economic need for more land, added to glowing reports of beautiful western scenery, was enough to convince many eastern families to make the trek westward.

They came in covered wagons, smaller even than the famed Conestoga wagons, which were too large to negotiate this journey. They came on horseback and on foot, following a trail that led them along rivers where the going was easier, through forests and over mountains where it was anything but easy.

At first just a few wagons came through Oregon and across to the Columbia River Gorge. There, after a difficult portage, they sailed down the river to Portland and on to the Willamette Valley.

Soon, however, the trickle of wagons had become a flood, with so many passing through that their wheels have left a lasting rut in the ground near Umatilla, Oregon, and at the Whitman Mission Historic Site just west of Walla Walla, Washington.

They settled in and held on, despite storms, Indian attacks, fires, and floods.

Slowly they built tiny settlements into big cities. Although the region was isolated for many years by its far-northwest location, construction of the Northern Pacific Railroad in 1883, discovery of gold and silver, and generous land-subsidy programs doubled the population in just five years.

Eventually the two regions split into separate Washington and Oregon Territories, later becoming states, while Vancouver joined Canada to become a province.

5. WHAT'S HAPPENING TODAY

Today the Pacific Northwest is providing much more to the nation than gorgeous scenery.

THE REGION'S ECONOMY: Oregon is one of the nation's most vital sources of lumber. Nearly half the land is forested. Lumber for plywood, pulp, and paper has been for more than half a century a major factor in the economic life of the two million people who live in this state.

East of the Oregon Cascades, wheat is the prime crop, making Portland one of the nation's most important wheat-export harbors. It is likely that apples, peaches, berries, beets, or potatoes at your grocery came from the Willamette and Hood River Valleys.

Sheep raised here encouraged skilled weavers, and Oregon's Pendleton wools have achieved worldwide fame.

In Washington agriculture supports the state's four million residents, thanks to an elaborate irrigation program. Washington apples are famous throughout the nation, and that state produces more apples than any other in the U.S. Cherries, peaches, pears, and plums are grown here along with all kinds of vegetables. In southeastern Washington near Walla Walla, wheat is king, its golden stalks rolling over hundreds of thousands of acres.

Aircraft construction, primarily by Boeing, plays a major role in the region's economy, while dairy and beef farming, lumbering, and fishing play secondary parts.

PEOPLE OF THE NORTHWEST: While you might expect the Northwest to be settled by Back Bay Bostonians and Canadians with roots 27 miles long, you would be wrong.

There is a fascinating ethnic mix of nationalities. Chinese laborers lured here to work on railroad construction projects settled in Vancouver, which now has the second-largest Chinatown in North America. Scandinavian settlers moved into all parts of the Northwest, perhaps seeking dramatic scenery similar to their mountainous homelands. Many became part of the lumbering industry in Oregon or moved into communities near Seattle. Slavs and Ukrainians celebrate mass in a Russian Orthodox church in the foothills of Mount Rainier and Japanese settlers occupy fascinatingly exotic neighborhoods in Portland and Seattle. In Jordan Valley in southwestern Washington there's even a small community of jai-alai–playing Basque settlers!

SOME MISCELLANY: The capital of Washington is Olympia; of Oregon, Salem. Victoria is the capital of British Columbia. Washington's nickname is the Evergreen State while Oregon boasts the monicker Beaver State. British Columbia's motto is "Beautiful Columbia."

Oregon, Washington, and British Columbia are on Pacific Standard or Daylight Time.

The telephone area code in Oregon is 503; in Washington the area code is

206 west of the Cascades and 509 in central and eastern Washington; in western Vancouver and Victoria, the area code is 604.

6. VISITOR INFORMATION

There are many people waiting to greet you in the Northwest, which has one of the most complete and efficient visitor information network systems in the nation.

IDAHO: You can call the **Idaho Travel Counsel** (208/334-2470, or toll free 800/635-7820) or write to them at State House, Room 108, Boise, ID 83720, to get information on travel and tourism in that state.

Those interested in specific activities might find the following addresses and telephone numbers useful:

State parks: **Idaho Department of Parks & Recreation,** 2177 Warm Springs Ave., Boise, ID 83720 (tel. 208/334-2154).

Fish and game: **Idaho Department of Fish & Game,** 600 S. Walnut, Boise, ID 83707 (tel. 208/334-3700).

Highway information: **Idaho Department of Transportation,** 3311 W. State, Boise, ID 83707 (tel. 208/334-3664).

Historic sites and museums: **Idaho State Historical Society,** 610 N. Julia Davis Dr., Boise, ID 83707 (tel. 208/334-2120).

Rockhounding and mining: **Idaho Bureau of Mines and Geology,** Morrill Hall, Room 332, University of Idaho, Moscow, ID 83843 (tel. 208/885-7991).

Fly-in recreation areas: **Aeronautics & Public Transportation Division,** 3843 Rickenbacker, Boise, ID 83705 (tel. 208/334-3183).

The "Vacation Planner" brochure available from the Idaho Travel Counsel lists names and addresses of the U.S. national forests in Idaho and provides a good deal of other useful facts about the state.

OREGON: In Oregon folks at the **Tourism Division of the Oregon Department of Economic Development,** 595 Cottage St. NE, Salem, OR 97310 (tel. 503/378-3451, or toll free 800/547-7842, 800/223-3306 in Oregon), will be happy to answer all your questions and arm you with plenty of brochures.

Oregon operates **information centers** near its state borders at Seaside, Lakeview, Brookings, Klamath Falls, Ontario, Portland, the Siskiyou Rest Area south of Ashland, and Umatilla, and in Goldendale, Washington.

Information gazebos located along main highway arteries—I-5, I-84, U.S. 101, and U.S. 97—offer written information supplemented with pictures of scenic and recreational attractions and commercial establishments. They are unstaffed but allow calls for reservations and information.

Oregon State Parks and Recreation Division, 525 Trade St. SE, Salem, OR 97310 (tel. 503/378-6305), has detailed information on reservations and facilities at all state campgrounds, and a toll-free number in Oregon (tel. 800/452-5687) for campsite reservations.

The **U.S. Forest Service,** 319 S.W. Pine St. (P.O. Box 3623), Portland, OR 97208 (tel. 503/221-2877), oversees activities in the forests, while the **U.S. Fish and Wildlife Service,** 506 S.W. Mill, Portland, OR 97207 (tel. 503/229-5403), can fill you in on licensing requirements and good hunting and fishing grounds.

WASHINGTON: In Washington the **Tourism Division of the Department of Trade and Economic Development,** General Administration Bldg., Olympia, WA 98504 (tel. 206/586-2102 or 206/586-2088), has its tourism information facilities down to a science. They know everything about their state and will be happy to answer questions on everything from golf to guided tours. For a free travel guide, call toll free 800/544-1800.

If you're driving into Washington, you'll find state-operated **border information centers** at Oroville, Vancouver, Megler, and Blaine, Washington, and at Maryhill and Umatilla in Oregon. There is also an information center at Sea-Tac International Airport.

The **Washington State Parks and Recreation Commission,** Interpretive Services, 7150 Cleanwater Lane, KY-11, Olympia, WA 98504 (tel. 206/753-2027), can guide you through the state's more than 100 parks.

Information on Washington's national parks and forests is available from the **Outdoor Recreation Information Center,** 1018 First Ave., Seattle, WA 98104 (tel. 206/442-0170), and the **National Park Service,** Pacific Northwest Regional Office, Westin Bldg., Room 1920, 2001 Sixth Ave., Seattle, WA 98121 (tel. 206/442-4830). They can fill you in on reservations and facilities at campgrounds and picnic areas in all national forests and parks.

Saltwater and salmon fishing information is available from the **Department of Fisheries,** 115 General Administration Bldg., AX-11, Olympia, WA 98504 (tel. 206/753-6600). For seasonal and limit information for freshwater fishing and hunting, contact the **Department of Wildlife,** 600 N. Capitol Way, GJ-11, Olympia, WA 98504 (tel. 206/753-5700). For saltwater fishing license information, call 206/586-1425 in Seattle; for freshwater fishing license information, 206/753-5719 in Olympia.

The **Pacific Northwest Ski Association** (division of the U.S. Ski Association), P.O. Box 68010, Seattle, WA 98188 (tel. 206/246-3614), has all the details on skiing in the Northwest.

BRITISH COLUMBIA: Tourism British Columbia now operates 145 InfoCenters across the province and will whizz you out a package of information on the province if you call them toll free at 800/663-6000. You can also write for information to Tourism British Columbia, Parliament Buildings, Victoria, BC V8V 1X4 (tel. 604/387-1642), but you're likely to get the information more quickly by calling the toll-free number. In Vancouver the Tourism British Columbia office is at 1055 Dunsmuir St., Bentall Four Bldg., Vancouver, BC V6E 4C8 (tel. 604/682-2222 or 604/683-2000). If you're traveling by car, there's a convenient InfoCenter in Whiterock, about 25 miles south of the city at 15047 Marine Dr. (tel. 604/536-6844).

For information on sports events, contact **Sport BC,** 1760 Broadway, Vancouver, BC V6Z 2C6 (tel. 604/737-3000), an umbrella organization representing amateur sports groups there. BC's **Outdoor Recreation Council,** Suite 170, 1200 Hornby St., Vancouver, BC V6Z 2E2, also can fill you in on sports activities in the region.

If you're looking for train or ferry schedules, contact **B.C. Rail** at B.C. Rail Passenger Department, P.O. Box 8770, Vancouver, BC V6B 4X6 (tel. 604/984-5246); or **British Columbia Ferries,** at 1112 Fort St., Victoria, BC V8V 4V2 (tel. 604/669-1211, or 604/685-1021 for schedule information).

British Columbia's parks are one of the province's prides. For details on national parks, contact **Environment Canada,** Parks, Western Region, P.O. Box 2989, Station M, Calgary, AB T2P 3H8. Provincial park information is available from the **Ministry of Environment and Parks,** Parks and Outdoor Recreation Division, 4000 Seymour Pl., Victoria, BC V8V 1X5.

DOLLARWISE—WHAT IT MEANS: In brief, this is a guidebook giving specific details—including prices—about the Northwest's hotels, motels, restaurants, bars, cafés, sightseeing attractions, nightlife, and tours. Establishments in many price ranges have been documented and described. No restaurant, hotel, motel, nightclub, store, or café paid to be mentioned in this book.

Unfortunately, although every effort was made to be as accurate as possible, remember that prices do change, and they rarely go downward. When checking into a hotel, always inquire about the rate and agree on it. That policy can save much embarrassment and disappointment when it comes time to settle the tab. If the prices quoted are not the same as those mentioned in this book, remember that our prices reflect those in effect at the time this edition was researched.

This guide is revised cover to cover every other year. But even in a book that appears with such frequency, establishments do change their décor, their name, their management, their type of service, a fact in our fast-moving world that leads to the next major point—

AN INVITATION TO READERS: Like all the books in the "Dollarwise" series, *Dollarwise Northwest* hopes to maintain a continuing dialogue between its authors and its readers, for your comments and suggestions can be a great aid to other readers.

Therefore, if you come across a particularly appealing accommodation, restaurant, store, or bargain, please don't keep it to yourself. Comments about existing listings are also very helpful. So send your comments or finds—and yes, those inevitable complaints that always arise—to Marylyn Springer and Donald Schultz, c/o Frommer Books, Prentice Hall Press, One Gulf + Western Plaza, New York, NY 10023.

7. FROMMER'S DOLLARWISE TRAVEL CLUB—HOW TO SAVE MONEY ON ALL YOUR TRAVELS

In this book we'll be looking at how to get your money's worth in the Northwest, but there is a "device" for saving money and determining value on *all* your trips. It's the popular, international Frommer's Dollarwise Travel Club, now in its 28th successful year of operation. The club was formed at the urging of numerous readers of the $-A-Day and Dollarwise Guides, who felt that such an organization could provide continuing travel information and a sense of community to value-minded travelers in all parts of the world. And so it does!

In keeping with the budget concept, the annual membership fee is low and is immediately exceeded by the value of your benefits. Upon receipt of $18 (U.S. residents), or $20 U.S. by check drawn on a U.S. bank or via international postal money order in U.S. funds (Canadian, Mexican, and other foreign residents) to cover one year's membership, we will send all new members the following items.

(1) Any *two* of the following books
Please designate in your letter which two you wish to receive:

Frommer's™ $-A-Day® Guides
Europe on $30 a Day
Australia on $30 a Day
Eastern Europe on $25 a Day
England on $40 a Day
Greece (including Istanbul and Turkey's Aegean Coast) on $30 a Day
Hawaii on $50 a Day
India on $25 a Day
Ireland on $35 a Day
Israel on $30 & $35 a Day
Mexico (plus Belize and Guatemala) on $25 a Day
New York on $50 a Day

New Zealand on $40 a Day
Scandinavia on $60 a Day
Scotland and Wales on $40 a Day
South America on $30 a Day
Spain and Morocco (plus the Canary Is.) on $40 a Day
Turkey on $25 a Day
Washington, D.C., & Historic Virginia on $40 a Day
($-A-Day Guides document hundreds of budget accommodations and facilities, helping you get the most for your travel dollars.)

Frommer's™ Dollarwise® Guides

Australia (avail. July 1989)
Austria and Hungary
Belgium, Holland, & Luxembourg
Bermuda and The Bahamas
Brazil
Canada
Caribbean
Egypt
England and Scotland
France
Germany
Italy
Japan and Hong Kong
Portugal, Madeira, and the Azores
South Pacific
Switzerland and Liechtenstein
Alaska
California and Las Vegas
Florida
Mid-Atlantic States
New England
New York State
Northwest
Skiing USA—East
Skiing USA—West
Southeast and New Orleans
Southeast Asia (avail. July 1989)
Southwest
Texas
USA

(Dollarwise Guides discuss accommodations and facilities in all price ranges, with emphasis on the medium-priced.)

Frommer's™ Touring Guides

Australia
Egypt
Florence
London
Paris
Scotland
Thailand
Venice

(These new, color illustrated guides include walking tours, cultural and historic sites, and other vital travel information.)

Gault Millau
Chicago (avail. April 1989)
France (avail. July 1989)
Italy (avail. July 1989)
Los Angeles
New England (avail. April 1989)
New York
San Francisco
Washington, D.C.

(Irreverent, savvy, and comprehensive, each of these renowned guides candidly reviews over 1,000 restaurants, hotels, shops, nightspots, museums, and sights.)

Serious Shopper's Guides
Italy
London
Los Angeles
Paris

(Practical and comprehensive, each of these handsomely illustrated guides lists hundreds of stores, selling everything from antiques to wine, conveniently organized alphabetically by category.)

A Shopper's Guide to the Caribbean
(Two experienced Caribbean hands guide you through this shopper's paradise, offering witty insights and helpful tips on the wares and emporia of more than 25 islands.)

Beat the High Cost of Travel
(This practical guide details how to save money on absolutely all travel items—accommodations, transportation, dining, sightseeing, shopping, taxes, and more. Includes special budget information for seniors, students, singles, and families.)

Bed & Breakfast—North America
(This guide contains a directory of over 150 organizations that offer bed & breakfast referrals and reservations throughout North America. The scenic attractions, and major schools and universities near the homes of each are also listed.)

Dollarwise Cruises
(This complete guide covers all the basics of cruising—ports of call, costs, fly-cruise package bargains, cabin selection booking, embarkation and debarkation and describes in detail over 60 or so ships cruising the waters of Alaska, the Caribbean, Mexico, Hawaii, Panama, Canada, and the United States.)

Dollarwise Skiing Europe
(Describes top ski resorts in Austria, France, Italy, and Switzerland. Illustrated with maps of each resort area. Includes supplement on Argentinian resorts.)

Frommer's Belgium
(Arthur Frommer unlocks the treasures of a country overlooked by most travelers to Europe. Discover the medieval charm, modern sophistication, and natural beauty of this quintessentially European county.)

Guide to Honeymoon Destinations
(A special guide for that most romantic trip of your life, with full details on planning and choosing the destination that will be just right in the U.S. [California, New England, Hawaii, Florida, New York, South Carolina, etc.], Canada, Mexico, and the Caribbean.)

Marilyn Wood's Wonderful Weekends
(This very selective guide covers the best mini-vacation destinations within a 200-mile radius of New York City. It describes special country inns and other accommodations, restaurants, picnic spots, sights, and activities—all the information needed for a two- or three-day stay.)

Manhattan's Outdoor Sculpture
(A total guide, fully illustrated with black and white photos, to more than 300 sculptures and monuments that grace Manhattan's plazas, parks, and other public spaces.)

Motorist's Phrase Book
(A practical phrase book in French, German, and Spanish designed specifically for the English-speaking motorist touring abroad.)

Paris Rendez-Vous
(An amusing and *au courant* guide to the best meeting places in Paris, organized for hour-to-hour use: from power breakfasts and fun brunches, through tea at four or cocktails at five, to romantic dinners and dancing 'til dawn.)

Swap and Go—Home Exchanging Made Easy
(Two veteran home exchangers explain in detail all the money-saving benefits of a home exchange, and then describe precisely how to do it. Also includes information on home rentals and many tips on low-cost travel.)

The Candy Apple: New York for Kids
(A spirited guide to the wonders of the Big Apple by a savvy New York grandmother with a kid's-eye view to fun. Indispensable for visitors and residents alike.)

The New World of Travel
(From America's #1 travel expert, Arthur Frommer, an annual sourcebook with the hottest news and latest trends that's guaranteed to change the way you travel —and save you hundreds of dollars. Jam-packed with alternative new modes of travel that will lead you to vacations that cater to the mind, the spirit, and a sense of thrift.)

Travel Diary and Record Book
(A 96-page diary for personal travel notes plus a section for such vital data as passport and traveler's check numbers, itinerary, postcard list, special people and places to visit, and a reference section with temperature and conversion charts, and world maps with distance zones.)

Where to Stay USA
(By the Council on International Educational Exchange, this extraordinary guide is the first to list accommodations in all 50 states that cost anywhere from $3 to $30 per night.)

(2) Any one of Frommer's™ City Guides

Amsterdam
Athens
Atlantic City and Cape May
Boston
Cancún, Cozumel, and the Yucatán
Chicago (avail. July 1989)
Dublin and Ireland
Hawaii
Las Vegas
Lisbon, Madrid, and Costa del Sol
London
Los Angeles
Mexico City and Acapulco
Minneapolis and St. Paul
Montréal and Québec City
New Orleans
New York
Orlando, Disney World, and EPCOT
Paris
Philadelphia
Rio
Rome
San Francisco
Santa Fe and Taos (avail. April 1989)
Sydney
Washington, D.C.

(Pocket-size guides to hotels, restaurants, nightspots, and sightseeing attractions covering all price ranges.)

(3) A one-year subscription to *The Dollarwise® Traveler*

This quarterly eight-page tabloid newspaper keeps you up to date on fastbreaking developments in low-cost travel in all parts of the world bringing you the latest money-saving information—the kind of information you'd have to pay $35 a year to obtain elsewhere. This consumer-conscious publication also features columns of special interest to readers: **Hospitality Exchange** (members all over the world who are willing to provide hospitality to other members as they pass through their home cities); **Share-a-Trip** (offers and requests from members for travel companions who can share costs and help avoid the burdensome single supplement); and **Readers Ask . . . Readers Reply** (travel questions from members to which other members reply with authentic firsthand information).

(4) Your personal membership card

Membership entitles you to purchase through the club all Frommer publications for a third to a half off their regular retail prices during the term of your membership.

So why not join this hardy band of international budgeteers and participate in its exchange of travel information and hospitality? Simply send your name and address, together with your annual membership fee of $18 (U.S. residents) or $20 U.S. (Canadian, Mexican, and other foreign residents), by check drawn on a U.S. bank or via international postal money order in U.S. funds to: Frommer's

Dollarwise Travel Club, Inc., Gulf + Western Building, One Gulf + Western Plaza, New York, NY 10023. And please remember to specify which *two* of the books in section (1) and which *one* in section (2) you wish to receive in your initial pack age of members' benefits. Or, if you prefer, use the order form at the end of the book and enclose $18 or $20 in U.S. currency.

> Once you are a member, there is no obligation to buy additional books. No books will be mailed to you without your specific order.

CHAPTER I

GETTING TO AND AROUND THE NORTHWEST

□ □ □

1. GETTING THERE
2. GETTING AROUND

Like you, perhaps, we have memories of landing in some pretty unusual spots after some quite harrowing experiences. It is our great pleasure to tell you that you need fear no donkey rides or skiff landings in the Pacific Northwest. Getting here is simple and comfortable.

In these days of fierce competition between airlines, buses, rental-car companies, trains, and even trucks, life could hardly be better for the consumer. As transportation entities vie for your dollar, your buying power increases. That's the good news.

Now the bad news: Trying to find your way to the best bargains through the maze of fares, tours, packages, and optional extras is like trying to play Lewis and Clark without a *Sacajawea*: you may succeed, but you'll spend weeks wandering in the wilderness.

If there was ever a day when your friendly, local travel agents really earned their keep, that time is now. These days most of them are, by necessity, experts at computer operations and so can quickly race through fares and schedules to put together your trip with amazing speed—and at amazing savings. It won't cost you a cent to pick the willing brains of these walking computers, who spend all their time on and off duty studying tariffs, hotels, car rentals, and tour packages so they'll be ready for your questions. Sure, you'll still have to make the big decisions on how much time and money you want to spend seeing the beauties of the Northwest, but with an agent's help that planning can be easy—and just looking at the pictures and dreaming a little is almost as much fun as the trip.

1. GETTING THERE

To give you an idea how you can escape to this land of dramatic gorges and towering peaks—and how much it will cost—here's a look at air, train, and bus fares, and even a glance at what you can expect to spend traveling by automobile. Here comes the disclaimer, however: we wouldn't guarantee the price of snow-cones tomorrow, much less airline fares! So don't blame us if the prices you are quoted for air or train fares differ from those you read here. If there's one thing we *can* guarantee, it's that those prices will be different—but, wonder of wonders, they may even be lower!

BY AIR: Some muggy summer day when your thoughts turn to long and chilly, you can enter the miraculous silver bird and emerge a few hours later to don a pair of skis and schuss off down some feathery Northwest mountainside, then slip into a swimsuit and splash the day away. Such is the glory of the Wright brothers' invention and such is the glory of the Northwest.

Such is the glory of airline competition that air fares may be the only things that are now actually lower in price than they were a decade ago! In the shattering wake of deregulation, fierce airline competition has led to many different kinds of fares—APEX, super-APEX, chicken-feed fares, peanut fares, no-frills fares, excursion fares, half fares, discounted fares, cheaper fares for flying to a designated airline hub city and then flying on from there, frequent flyer fares—fares, fares, and more fares. So many are there, in fact, that it is possible you could take a plane some day and find every person on it paying a different amount for a seat. Ever optimistic, we're holding out for the penultimate in special fares, the no-fare fare.

While we're all waiting for that magic moment, however, you should be aware of a few airline dictums that have changed little over the years. Here they are:

(1) If you can plan your trip well in advance, say a month or so, you can probably save money. That "probably" disclaimer is necessary since it is entirely possible that the airline will drop fares suddenly after you've purchased your ticket, but if they do your travel agent can help you get a better deal. Most of the time, however, the best bargains go to those who book and pay early for their tickets.

(2) If you're willing to travel on unpopular days—weekdays rather than weekends or holidays—and at off-peak hours (usually the wee a.m. or late-night hours), you're likely to save money.

(3) You'll find that the more you are willing to reveal to your travel agent, the more you are likely to save. By that we mean, age, travel companions, destination, budget, willingness to fly nondirect (with one or more stops and/or plane changes) to your destination.

(4) That item 3 naturally brings us to this (4): if you don't already have a travel agent with whom you do business, get one. Good travel agents work very hard for a living and will beat their computer fingers to the bone in an attempt to find you the cheapest fare if you indicate that's what you want. Those computers, with fares lined up in rows like so many sentinels waiting to be investigated, drive agents crazy but they also keep them current on fares in a way you never could accomplish by reading the Sunday travel section of your newspaper.

Once you've booked your ticket to this scenically glamorous land up in the return-address corner of the nation, you might also check to see if the airline on which you'll be traveling has a package plan that includes rental car, hotels, attraction-admission discounts, or sightseeing tours. Many do. Here again, a good travel agent will be able to outline what budgetwise bargains are lurking out there.

A *good* travel agent, and we're stressing good here purposely, will also help you look around to see if you might combine "legs" of a ticket (for example, flying from New York to Minneapolis and changing planes to Seattle) to take advantage of budget fares offered by two or more different airlines. How well a travel agent responds to your requests for a serious search for a low price can help you determine how "good" that travel agent is for you.

It won't hurt to keep close touch on airline rates as well. It costs nothing to give the line a call to try to ferret out prices so you know whether an agent's deal is a good one.

BY TRAIN: As train enthusiasts, we are thrilled to tell you that very good and interesting **Amtrak** and **VIA Rail** service exists to the Pacific Northwest. Amtrak has daily service that begins in Chicago and makes its way across the top of the nation through Minnesota, North Dakota, Montana, and into Sandpoint, Idaho, where you can alight for a Sun Valley or Coeur d'Alene visit, then travel on to Spokane, Portland, or Seattle. We'd certainly recommend a visit to Sun Valley—and for that matter to other sections of Idaho, which is one of the nation's best-kept scenic secrets. (We should point out, however, that you will need to rent a car or arrange some other kind of transportation to get from this Idaho train stop to Sun Valley and other points in that lovely state.) Allot a few days for these Idaho diversions as this is a big state.

Called the *Empire Builder,* this train has through cars from Chicago all the way to Portland. It splits in Spokane, with one train stopping in Pasco, Wishram, Bingen–White Salmon, and Vancouver before going on to Portland. That other half of the train makes stops in Washington at Ephrata, Wenatchee, Everett, and Edmonds before it reaches Seattle.

Another Amtrak streaker, this one called *The Pioneer,* connects Chicago with Salt Lake City through Denver and then goes on to the Idaho cities of Boise and Shoshone, where you can hop off for a stay at Sun Valley. From there the train shoots up the eastern side of Oregon, stopping in the Oregon cities of Ontario, Baker, La Grande, Pendleton, Hinkle, The Dalles, Hood River, and Cascade Locks on its way to Portland. When it pulls out of Portland, it goes on to Washington, stopping at Vancouver, Kelso-Longview, Centralia, East Olympia, Tacoma, and ending at Seattle.

Finally *The Coast Starlight*—don't these trains have wonderful names?—connects Los Angeles, San Jose, San Francisco, and Oakland to cities in Oregon and Washington. Stops on that run up to the Pacific Northwest are in the Oregon cities of Klamath Falls, Chemult, Eugene, Albany, Salem, and Portland, and the Washington towns of Vancouver, Kelso-Longview, Centralia, Tacoma, and Seattle. If you're bound for Vancouver, B.C., you can get off in Seattle, Washington, where a connecting bus picks up Vancouver-bound passengers.

A dedicated bus offers connecting motor-coach service between the VIA Rail Canada stop at Sandman Inn in downtown Vancouver and Seattle.

Amtrak can be reached toll free at 800/USA-RAIL (800/872-7245).

Amtrak has a zone fare program offering substantial savings on ticket fares. Called **All Aboard America fares,** the price structure offers maximum prices of $299 round trip for trips that travel across three zones of the country, say, from New York to Seattle. Fares from Chicago and Houston to the West Coast are $239 round trip. Trips from Los Angeles to Seattle are in one zone and cost just $159 round trip.

Seating is in coach seats, and certain restrictions apply to the tickets: all travel must be completed within 45 days; only a limited number of special-fare seats are available on each train, so once they are sold out, you will have to change your plans, catch another train on a different date, and pay a higher fare. Fares for children 2 to 11 on the All Aboard program are half price; sleeping-accommodation fares are added to the rail fare.

Round-trip excursions fares are less than two one-way tickets, but may not be available during holiday seasons and other peak travel periods. Special low promotional fares also are often offered during off-peak travel seasons. Be sure to ask Amtrak ticket or reservations agents if any promotional fares are available.

If several members of a family are traveling together, Amtrak offers a dis-

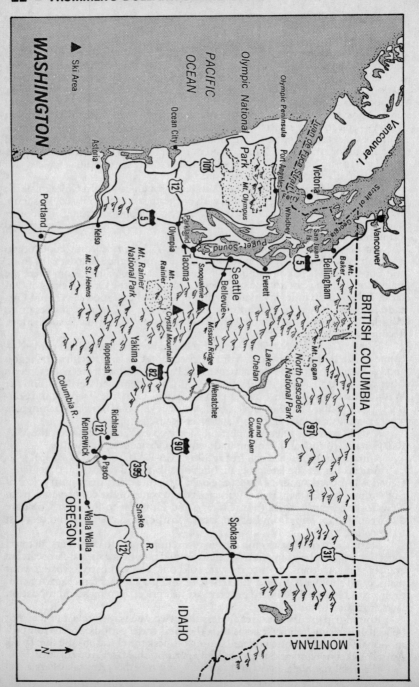

counted family fare: one adult pays the regular coach fare, spouse and children 12 to 21 pay half that fare, and children 2 to 11 pay 25% of the fare. Children under 2 ride free if they share a seat with a family member.

Amtrak also offers a 25% discount to travelers 65 or older.

Sleeper cars are comparatively expensive. An economy bedroom for one person is $153 from Los Angeles to Portland. A larger "deluxe" bedroom with shower for two adults is $315 one way.

All the trains traveling the routes we have outlined for you have restaurant and lounge cars serving three full meals and snacks so you don't have to scrunch up in your seat all day. That cross-country trip from Chicago to Seattle takes two days!

In Canada, VIA Rail trains end at Vancouver after a thrilling run through the Canadian Rockies and across the Cascades. What a trip!

Since the advent of Amtrak's All Aboard America fares, the company has been offering travelers the special reduced-rate fare in addition to its former one-way/round-trip excursion prices. All Aboard America fares are sometimes lower than the railroad's published one-way fares. Here's a look, then, at what you'll pay for a cross-country train ride. Keep in mind that money-saving package programs and discounts are often offered, so ask Amtrak or VIA Rail representatives to explain all their offers carefully.

To	From (one-way/round-trip All Aboard America fares)			
	New York	Chicago	Los Angeles	Houston
Seattle	$299/$299	$254/$239	$164/$159	$239/$239
Portland	$299/$299	$254/$239	$151/$159	$239/$239
Spokane	$299/$299	$254/$239	$199/$159	$239/$239

BY BUS: Greyhound will get you here from everywhere, and it often sponsors family deals or special passes that offer you great dollarwise deals. Buses stop in just about every little village in the Pacific Northwest, often picking up and dropping off passengers at the local drugstore or grocer's shop. Express buses have cut the time a bus trip takes, but you should still figure five days or more to get from Chicago or New York to the Northwest.

To stay competitive with other forms of transportation, Greyhound has now established advance-purchase discounts that can drop the price of even cross-country travel to as little as $59 one way, $139 round trip. Like airline fares, discount bus fares may have restrictions on how long you can stay or when you can go and still receive the special fare. That $59 one-way fare, by the way, applies to tickets purchased 30 days in advance. Several other similar plans are available. Holiday travel may be excluded from some special prices.

To give you a basis for comparison between other methods of transportation and the bus, here are some examples of unrestricted fares to the Northwest on Greyhound.

To	From (one-way/round-trip)			
	New York	Chicago	Los Angeles	Houston
Seattle	$139/$258	$153/$199	$139/$264	$139/$219
Portland	$139/$258	$153/$199	$127/$241	$139/$219
Vancouver	$139/$258	$174/$330	$161/$306	$139/$219

Greyhound has another money-saver called **Ameripass**, which offers you a seven-day pass good for travel anywhere in the U.S. or Canada for $189. Longer passes are $249 for 15 days and $349 for 30 days of travel. Some local affiliates of Greyhound also accept the Ameripass. Call local stations for schedule information.

BY CAR: By far the most popular way to get to the Northwest is by car or recreational vehicle. It is a wonderful trip, no matter what your starting point. If you're planning on driving, we'd suggest you join the American Automobile Association, which charges about $46 as an annual fee, but for that it will plot out your entire trip on a series of maps—free—and arm you with booklets on where to stay and what to see across the country. AAA has offices in every major city in the U.S. AAA, by the way, now estimates that driving costs for a family of four including hotel, meals, gasoline, and other car costs run $170 a day, plus $7.40 for each 100 miles.

2. GETTING AROUND

BY AIR: Airlines operating between cities in the Pacific Northwest include Alaska Airlines, Harbor, Horizon, Pacific, San Juan Airlines flying to the San Juan Islands, and Western Airlines.

Alaska Airlines, Northwest, United, and Western connect the region to Alaska.

BY TRAIN: As we mentioned above, **Amtrak** trains (tel. toll free 800/USA-RAIL or 800/872-7245) connect many towns in Washington and Oregon, while Canada's **VIA Rail** (tel. toll free 800/USA-RAIL for the Canada desk of Amtrak; in Canada toll-free numbers vary according to the region from which you are calling) runs from eastern Canada to Vancouver. A small local train also runs from Victoria on Vancouver Island to Nananimo.

Sample one-way/round-trip fares are: Portland to Seattle, $25.50/$38.50; Seattle to Spokane, $60/$76; Pendleton to Portland, $32.50/$49; Seattle to Tacoma, $7.25/$11; Eugene to Portland, $22/$33.

All Aboard America fares, which break the nation into eastern, western, and central regions, offer fares of $159 for travel within just one of those regions, the Pacific Northwest, for instance. Three stops are permitted in 45 days with that fare.

BY BUS: Buses make it easy for you to get around within these states, so we've listed the telephone numbers and station addresses in most major cities in our discussion of those cities.

Some typical one-way fares on Greyhound are: Seattle to Spokane, $31; Seattle to Portland, $23; Seattle to Vancouver, $20. Round-trip tickets are slightly less than double the one-way fares.

BY CAR: With all that space at its command, the Pacific Northwest has filled it with plenty of major expressways and loads of small backroads that offer delightful scenery.

Because so many people travel the Northwest by car, their own or a rented car, we have arranged chapters in a way we think will make it easy for you to follow a route through the entire Northwest. That route starts in Seattle, makes a loop through the Cascades, then heads west to Spokane and Sun Valley, Idaho. From there you can drive down to Boise to pick up I-84, the old Oregon Trail, which takes you up the eastern side of Oregon and along the Columbia River Gorge into Portland.

Then it's on south alongside the Cascades through the Willamette Valley

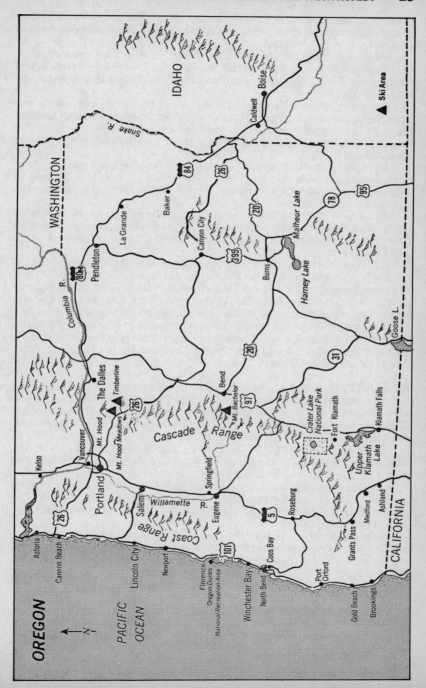

towns of Eugene and Salem to some interesting activities in southwestern Oregon, then through the giant redwood forests and north along the much-traveled Oregon coast and into Washington.

Once in Washington, you can visit that state's lonely, wave-swept coastline then head north to tour the lush rain forests of the Olympic Peninsula before returning to Seattle. Then it's on to Vancouver, via Victoria or vice versa—by land or by sea.

The major north-south Interstate highway is I-5, which runs all the way from the California border to the Canadian border, where it becomes Canadian Hwy. 99 into Vancouver. The trip from Seattle to Portland takes about 3½ hours; from Seattle to the Canadian border, about 2 hours. Add another hour to get to Vancouver.

In Washington the major east-west artery is I-90, which zips you from Seattle to Spokane in about five hours. A branch from that road, U.S. 82, goes to Yakima in about three hours of driving. From Seattle to the Washington beaches is about a three-hour drive.

In Oregon the major artery traversing the eastern part of the state from north to south is I-84, which comes in from Boise through Ontario, Baker, La Grande, and on to Pendleton. There it runs west to follow the Columbia Gorge into Portland.

The main north-south arteries on the eastern side of Oregon are I-5, connecting Portland, Salem, Eugene, and Medford at the southern edge of the state; and along the coast, U.S. 101 runs from Crescent City in California straight up the coastline connecting Coos Bay, Florence, Newport, Lincoln City, Cannon Beach, Seaview, and Astoria to Washington's coast and the Olympic Peninsula.

Representative driving times in Oregon are: Boise to Pendleton, 4½ hours; Pendleton to Portland, 4 hours; along the coast from Astoria to Crescent City, 10 hours; Portland to Salem, 1 hour; Portland to Bend, 4 hours; Eugene to Bend, 3 hours; Portland to Medford, 5 hours.

BY FERRY: Washington State Ferries travel on the nation's most scenic—and least crowded—highways! For a complete list of ferry departure and arrival points and times, contact the **Washington State Department of Transportation,** Washington State Ferries, Pier 52, Seattle, WA 98104 (tel. 206/464-6400, or toll free 800/542-0810 in Washington).

Black Ball Transport, 10777 Main St., 106 Surrey Bldg., Bellevue, WA 98004 (tel. 206/622-2222), can provide you with information on the ferry that travels between Port Angeles and Victoria.

Princess Marguerite, a ferry that operates between Seattle and Victoria each day, can be reached for schedules and rates at Seattle Terminal, Pier 69, 2700 Alaskan Way, Seattle, WA 98121 (tel. 206/441-5560, or for auto reservations, 206/441-8100).

British Columbia also has a ferry system for transportation across its many miles of water. Contact them at **British Columbia Ferries,** 1112 Fort St., Victoria, BC V8V 4V2 (tel. 604/669-1211, or for schedule information, 604/685-1021).

CHAPTER II

SEATTLE

□ □ □

If the Pacific Northwest were choosing a capital city, Seattle would win the toss. This is the hub of the Northwest, an art and theater capital, a shipping and transportation nucleus, center for big business and monkey business.

If there's one thing you can say for this brash and brazen city, it's got pluck. With every reason to fail and practically none to succeed, Seattle has succeeded beyond even its wildest dreams. As for its pioneers, well, they always knew Seattle was destined for greatness, they just never figured it would take so long. So convinced were they that their hodgepodge collection of clapboard huts and muddy thoroughfares would one day rival any city, they first named it New York–Soon!

From that determined, if a tad utopian, embryo sprang this sprawling urban mass of 1.5 million people and just about as many buildings. Its growth has been an odd juxtaposition of events melding into a montage that exemplifies Seattle's never-say-die spirit.

That unquenchable spirit is, in fact, what makes this place so interesting for visitors. On a visit here, you will see easily the magnificent natural beauty that drew those early settlers here—snow-capped peaks hovering over the city, emerald forests just outside town, lordly expanses of water. With just a bit more effort you will discover what kept them here in the face of all odds and what keeps them here today, despite some often-dreary weather and through some bleak times.

Seattle-ites, you see, are now and always have been strong, stubborn, occasionally a little silly, but never, never stodgy. Things and people sometimes move slowly here, but once they get going . . . well, get out of the way.

1. INTRODUCTION

A CITY RISES: People have been underestimating Seattle for a couple of centuries now. Spanish sailors from Mexico are believed to have passed this way first, but they were only looking. English Capt. James Cook and a couple of French explorers charted Puget Sound, but they didn't stay either. As for Lewis and Clark, they skipped Seattle altogether, ending their long overland journey on the coasts of Oregon. It took a tenacious powerhouse called the Hudson's Bay Company to see the value of Seattle and move in here. They hung on for many a year, profiting from the fur trade but sending potential settlers packing.

Finally presidential candidate James Polk got behind the slogan of "54–40 or fight," and managed to make the first of many deals on this land. Britain and the U.S. agreed that the U.S.-Canadian border would begin at the 49th Parallel, where it remains today.

When the dust settled, a 19-year-old Iowan named John Holgate came up to take a look around this untrammeled territory. He liked its mountains, its emerald-green forests, and its dramatic harbor views and brought the family. A year later some of Washington's other "first families"—the Collinses, Van Asselts, Maples, and Hanfords—moved in.

One story of Seattle's earliest days has it that in 1851 three adventurous pioneers—David Denny, John Low, and Lee Terry—brought all their possessions and families all the way from Illinois, across the plains to Portland. Then they walked 175 miles or so to Seattle to have a look. Not bad, they decided. So they sent word back to wives and children to come on up. After a miserable schooner trip the families disembarked on a miserable strip of land in a miserable rainstorm. Cold and wet and . . . well, miserable, those tired pioneer wives took one look at the only habitation around—a cabin with no roof—and just sat down on the riverbank and sobbed. So much for the joys of the pioneer life.

But with true Seattle grit, they stayed. They also discovered that somebody already lived here—a short, stocky, silver-haired, 65-year-old tribal chieftain, by marriage the head of not just one but two tribes, the Suquamish and the Duwamish. His name: Sealth.

Now Sealth may not have been wise in the ways of the white man, but he was a quick study. He and his tribe bowed to the inevitable and welcomed the early arrivals. When the time came to be rewarded for his help to the settlers, the chief, called Seattle by the newcomers, asked for financial remuneration. Otherwise, the chief warned, after his death his spirit would do a backflip each time the name Seattle was mentioned. A deal was struck around the campfire one night, and Seattle became Seattle, while Chief Seattle and his spirit became $16,000 richer!

Seattle and his tribe earned whatever they got from the settlers. In 1855 bellicose Indians from tribes east of the Cascades focused their animosity on the residents of Seattle. Puget Sound Indians warned settlers of an impending Indian attack on the small settlement. A rapid retreat to a stockade was effected, and a warship arrived in the nick of time to repel the Indians with the ship's cannons. That attack lasted only one day and was never repeated, but fear of another Indian uprising discouraged many a would-be Seattle settler.

One day the city fathers, and we do mean fathers in this case, looked around and discovered something vital was missing from this city by the sea—women! There just weren't enough to go around. So in true Seattle style all the fellows got together, each potential hubby kicked in some beef jerky and a couple of coins, and they sent the most silver-tongued of the lot off on a trip back East to New England. His orders: Don't come back without feminine companionship.

Asa Mercer, who had never suspected his job as first president of the territorial university would one day include this kind of recruitment, did his duty. Eleven daring lasses defied convention and returned to Seattle with him. Encouraged, Mercer went back East on a second trip. This time, however, newspaper editors got wind of this strange recruitment effort and wondered aloud just what this Seattle slickster had in mind.

Poor Asa was only able to lure west another 36 unmarried women and a dozen or so Civil War widows. That was enough, however, for Mercer to win himself a permanent place in the hearts of male Seattle—and a bride as well. Today many of Seattle's best-known families are descendants of those early lasses, known as "Mercer Girls."

By 1878 the streets of Seattle were still rutted seas of mud, kept gooey by the rain that falls here despite the most potent incantations of the chamber of commerce. Shops were nothing more than tents; fancy shops were boxy, thrown-together clapboard structures with canvas signs strung out over the city's creaky wooden sidewalks. Village youngsters with no place to go roamed the streets. Settlers finally got a schoolhouse in 1869, only to have so many youngsters turn up on opening day that an overwhelmed teacher, all by herself with that mob, sent the youngest ones home to "ripen a while."

Supplies were few and hard to come by. Tiny craft called the "mosquito fleet" were vital transportation in watery Seattle. Coal was abundant and profitable but had to be shoveled into a tiny railroad car, hauled by barge across Lake Washington, rolled across a portage track, put aboard another barge to cross Lake Union, and finally hauled to storage bins at the foot of Pike Street.

Seattle needed a railroad. In 1873 when the Northern Pacific Railroad, the era's kingmakers, tracked on to Tacoma, Seattle built its own railroad and named it the Seattle and Walla Walla Railroad. Although tracks never reached Walla Walla, the railroad did so well that seven years later the Great Northern Railroad eyed its success and laid tracks to Seattle. Today every regional railroad ends here.

Life in Seattle was rough and tumble in those days. At one point, brawling and violence had gotten so bad, and the police and courts so impotent, that Seattle-ites rebelled. When a popular merchant was robbed and murdered, vigilantes went looking for the two killers. They found them. When police and courts didn't take action, the mob beat up police officers, kidnapped the murderers and another local tough guy, and lynched all three from a tree next to founding father Henry Yesler's house.

Four years later in 1886 the city faced another crisis, an ethnic dispute with Chinese immigrants who had been hired as cheap help by the railroads. When low-paid Chinese immigrants began to displace local workers, a mob turned on the Chinese community and tried to force them onto a ship bound for San Francisco. Army troops quelled a riot, but in the aftermath of violence most Chinese left Seattle.

Despite its difficulties, Seattle put together a chamber of commerce way back in 1882. A year later the city had become the largest metropolis in the Northwest Territory and even had an opera house!

For a decade in the 1880s business boomed. Seattle's population increased a whopping 1,200%, growing from a tiny frontier village of 3,500 to a big frontier village of 43,000.

At the end of that decade, on June 6, 1889, the dream went up in smoke. A glue pot boiled over in a cabinet shop at 1st and Madison Streets, and fire, dreaded enemy of early settlers, swept through the city. To make matters worse, the fire chief was out fishing, and his bewildered assistant hemmed and hawed long enough to let block after block go up in flame. Every pier in the city was destroyed. Flames flickered all night long, and the next morning 116 acres of Seattle had burned.

But Seattle was indomitable. Shopkeepers brushed themselves off, bought a few yards of canvas, propped up a tent, wrote their names on the front, and laughed disaster off with signs that read "Our business is intense." In fact, most everybody in town agreed the fire might have been a godsend. Now there wouldn't be any arguing—a favorite Seattle sport—over the removal of some of the city's old, rat-infested, buildings.

A CITY REBUILDS: Seattle rebuilt quickly in the boom that accompanied the turn of the century. A new opera house was built, a symphony orchestra formed, an art museum constructed in 1930, and with a little assist from Pittsburgh millionaire Andrew Carnegie, a library was built.

Even fate played into Seattle's hands. In the summer of 1897 an Alaska steamer pulled into port weighed down with a ton of gold and the world's most famous rush was on. Seattle was a natural gateway to the Gold Rush, and city entrepreneurs quickly found their place in the pursuit. Why sweat in the goldfields when you could make money selling to those who want to sweat in the goldfields?

Saloons, restaurants, equipment shops, general stores and hardware stores, assayers and banks. Think of a product in those booming days, and someone had just opened a shop in Seattle to sell it. In four years at the turn of the century, more than $175 million in gold crossed the counters of the local assay office. Plenty remained here.

With typical perversity, the town that profited from the thirst of gold miners went dry in 1916, four years before the rest of the country ever heard of Prohibition! Not ones to deny themselves much, Seattle-ites continued to be supplied with hooch by a local police lieutenant named Roy Olmstead, who remains a Seattle folk hero.

Two world wars were as tragic in Seattle as they were throughout the nation, but this city profited from the arrival of a fledgling firm named Boeing Aero Products Company, which was to become massive Boeing Aircraft, now a major economic force in Washington. Seattle's prominence as a seaport also grew in those grim days of troop and supply ships.

Seattle has always been architecture-conscious. Its first skyscraper, the 41-story Smith Tower, soared heavenward in 1914. When the city ruled that downtown rejuvenation was in order, it decided that upgrade should take architectural form. Thus was born Century 21 Exposition, better known as the 1962 World's Fair. At that fair was born Seattle's symbol and its landmark—the rotating, futuristic Space Needle.

Seattle's fair was successful in other ways. Not only did the city make money, it also ended up with an opera house, science center, coliseum, arena, a raft of theaters, fountains, statues, playgrounds, and a zippy monorail.

These days Chief Seattle's name is mentioned more and more often in more and more powerful places around the nation and the world. It seems likely the chief's spirit, like metropolitan, cosmopolitan Seattle, is spinning quite happily.

2. GETTING THERE AND GETTING AROUND

GETTING THERE: Biggest star in the Northwest airline firmament is **Seattle-Tacoma International Airport** (tel. 206/433-4604), Sea-Tac for short. All major international and national air carriers serve the airport, among them Alaska, American, American West, Air BC, Braniff, British Airways, Canadian Coastal, Continental, Delta, Eastern, Finnair, Harbor, Hawaiian, Horizon, Japan, Mexicana, Northwest, Pan American, Piedmont, San Juan, SAS, Thai, Trans

World, United, and USAir. So no matter where you are, the Pacific Northwest makes it easy for you to come on out and enjoy.

Amtrak trains make several stops a day at their King Street Station a few blocks from the waterfront, at Third Avenue South and South King Street (tel. 206/464-1930), coming in from California, Idaho, and points east through Spokane.

Greyhound makes a special effort to serve Seattle and environs well. Buses arrive from all parts of the country at Greyhound's station at Eighth Avenue and Stewart Street (tel. 206/624-3456).

Traveling by car any distance on the Pacific Coast means using the "freeway" system. The single most important auto artery of that system leaves Blaine, Washington, on the British Columbia border, zooms south through downtown Seattle and Tacoma past Olympia. It heads south through Portland and Eugene, over the California border, skirts San Francisco by dodging east to Sacramento then plunges on down to Los Angeles and San Diego before coming to a full stop at Tijuana, Mexico. It is the U.S. 1 of America's West Coast—I-5, backbone of the West Coast's freeway system.

From the east, the most frequently used stretch of concrete is I-90, which comes from Spokane and crosses the Cascade Mountains into Seattle over Lake Washington from Bellevue. Both these highways have reverse lanes in use during morning and evening rush hours.

SEATTLE BY SEA: The **Washington State Ferries** are America's largest ferry system. They cruise the Puget Sound waters and sail from Anacortes to the San Juan Islands and Sidney, British Columbia. Daily service to Seattle from the **Olympic Peninsula, via Bremerton and Bainbridge Island,** is provided throughout the year. In West Seattle state ferries leave Fauntleroy Pier for **Vashon Island** and **Southworth.** Service is also available from Seattle to **Edmons** and **Kingston.**

You may write for Washington State Ferry schedules and rates at Washington State Ferries, Washington State Department of Transportation Marine Division, Colman Dock, Seattle, WA 98104 (tel. 206/464-6400, or toll free 800/542-0810 in Washington).

Coho Ferry, a private ferry service operated by Black Ball Transport, Inc., sails between Port Angeles, Washington, and Victoria, British Columbia, Canada. Crossing time is one hour and 35 minutes. For their ferry schedule and rates, contact Black Ball Transport, Inc., 106 Surrey Bldg., Bellevue, WA 98004 (tel. 206/622-2222 or 206/457-4491).

From May to October, the British Columbia Steamship Company provides daily round-trip ferry service between Seattle's Pier 69 and Victoria, B.C., via the 332-foot cruise ship the *Princess Marguerite.* It is a luxury cruise liner that handles automobiles, motorcycles, and bicycles. For their schedule and rates, contact the *Princess Marguerite,* Seattle Terminal, Pier 69, 2700 Alaskan Way, Seattle, WA 98121 (tel. 206/441-5560). Reservations advised.

Ferries operated by **British Columbia Ferries,** 1112 Fort St., Victoria, BC V8V 4V2 (tel. 604/669-1211, or for schedule information, 604/685-1021, or 206/441-6865 in Seattle), also have service connecting Washington and British Columbia.

GETTING AROUND: Driving into Seattle from Sea-Tac Airport (about 14 miles to city center) is a fairly straightforward maneuver. From the airport complex drive straight out the exit to the Wash. 99 North turnoff. This road goes right through the center of the city and, although slower than I-5, will afford you

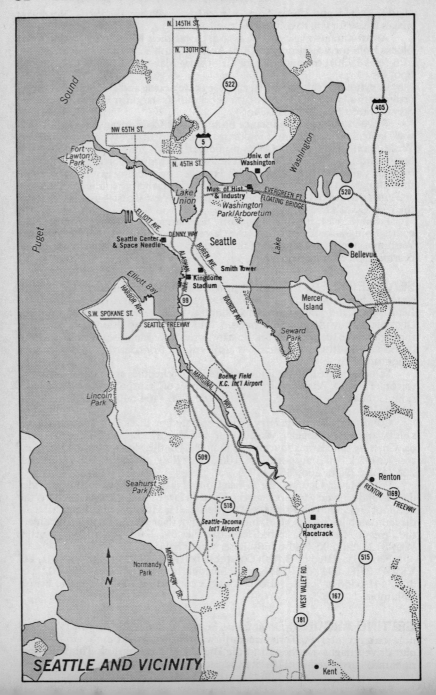

SEATTLE AND VICINITY

an opportunity to locate your destination with less frustration than high-speed thoroughfares.

Gray Line operates express airport buses at 30-minute intervals to most of the larger downtown hotels at fares of $9 for adults and $3.50 for children under 12. For information concerning pickup points, call 206/626-6088.

Seattle's **Metro buses** go everywhere for little—often no!—cost. They operate to and from all points in the Seattle area including Sea-Tac Airport. Peak-hour fares are 65¢ or $1, depending on how many of the city's two zones you cross. Other times, fares are 55¢ or 85¢. Children under 5 ride free with an adult, and older youngsters pay only a one-zone fare no matter how far they travel. You pay (exact change required) when you board the bus traveling toward downtown, when you get off traveling out of town. Transfers are available. For route information, telephone 206/447-4800.

Metro's no. 174 or 194 bus goes to and from the airport every 30 minutes, traveling into town along Fourth Avenue and charging a two-zone fare for the ride to downtown. On the way out of town to the airport, the bus travels a route that takes it along Ninth Avenue and Steward Street. Allow at least 45 minutes for the trip.

If you're going farther than midtown from the airport, the **Suburban Airporter** will take you to accommodations in the surrounding suburbs for fares starting at $7. For exact destinations and fares, telephone 206/455-2353.

Rental Cars

Rental cars are a good value in most of the Northwest. For our money there's no better deal in town than **Budget Rent-A-Car,** which has offices at Sea-Tac Airport (tel. 206/682-8989); in downtown Seattle, at Fourth and Columbia (tel. 206/682-8989) and at Westlake and Virginia Streets (tel. 206/448-4859); in the university district at 6000 Roosevelt Way NE (tel. 206/525-5300); and at 17808 Pacific Hwy. South (tel. 206/244-4008).

Why are we praising Budget? Well, for openers they are always competitively priced and often offer special deals you can't find at other companies. Equally important, however, in Seattle Budget owns all the 300 Diamond Parking lots in town, and when you rent from Budget, your parking is free at a Diamond lot. In Seattle, where parking spaces are as rare as moon rocks and almost as pricey, that free-parking offer alone can save you a bundle.

That same deal is offered on rentals in Portland and Spokane. No matter where you rent the car, you get free parking in all those metropolitan areas. All the company's cars offer unlimited mileage, and Budget has special Thursday-to-Monday weekend rates of $21 a day for economy or compact cars with a two-day minimum. Prices drop according to demand and competition, but at last check weekly rentals began at $179 a week with seven-day notice. You can even rent a spiffy Lincoln town car from the company for $277 a week or $45 daily. Free shuttle service to hotels too.

Although Budget has the most rental-office locations of any rental-car company in Washington, other major rental-car companies have offices in Seattle, including **Avis,** 1919 5th St. (tel. 206/448-1700), or at the airport (tel. 206/433-5231); **Hertz,** 722 Pike St. (tel. 206/682-5050), or at the airport (tel. 206/433-5264); and **National,** 1942 Westlake (tel. 206/622-3355), or at the airport (tel. 206/433-5501).

Public Transportation

Best news on public transportation is Seattle's **"Magic Carpet"** free bus service, which is available in the main part of the downtown area, from the water to Sixth Avenue and from Jackson Street on the south to Battery Street on the north, or roughly from Seattle Center to Pioneer Square. For information on routes, call the 24-hour information line (tel. 206/447-4800) or stop into the company's offices at 821 Second Ave. at Marion Street.

Metro's **One-Day Visitors Pass** is more good news for travelers. For $2.50 you can travel on all bus routes, take a free ride around Seattle's colorful harbor on the vintage Waterfront Streetcar, and enjoy discounts at hundreds of shops and attractions around town. Pick up passes and Seattle public transportation information at the **Metro Customer Assistance Office,** Exchange Bldg., 821 Second Ave., Seattle, WA 98104 (tel. 206/447-4800).

The easiest and most interesting way to get to Seattle Center from downtown is aboard the **monorail,** which begins at Fourth and Pine and covers the 1.2-mile stretch in 90 seconds. Monorail fare is 60¢, and it glides from 10 a.m. to midnight Sunday through Thursday, to 12:30 a.m. on Friday and Saturday.

Taxis

Cabs operating in Seattle include **Yellow Cab** (tel. 206/622-6500), **Farwest Taxi** (tel. 206/622-1717), and **Gray Top Cab** (tel. 206/622-4949). Hailing a cab is frowned upon, but service is quick by telephone, and cab stands are numerous. The fare is $1 at the flag drop, $1.20 for each mile.

ORIENTATION: Seattle directions sound complicated but are actually pretty simple once you get the hang of it. You'll find that most of the addresses you, as a touring visitor, are looking for are in the downtown section, which is really quite simple to negotiate. Outlying districts are a bit more complex.

Downtown Seattle

Downtown Seattle begins at the waterfront and is bounded roughly by Denny Way on the north, Yesler Way on the south, Broadway (which parallels I-5) on the east, and the harbor on the west.

The major expressway through the downtown area is I-5, which borders the eastern edge, running along Sixth Avenue. I-90 enters the city about a mile south of downtown. These two highways have reverse lanes in effect during morning and evening rush hours. Motoring through the city is further eased by many one-way downtown streets. Traffic lights are synchronized on Fourth Avenue northbound and on Second Avenue southbound.

Nearly all **streets** in the downtown section have names, for instance, Virginia, Leonora, Seneca, or Spring Street. **Avenues,** on the other hand, generally have "number" names: Second, Third, or Fourth Avenue. Downtown roadways do not carry a north, south, east, or west designation. Many hotels and restaurants help you out, however, by using as their official address two street designations—for instance, the Warwick Hotel, Fourth and Leonora, which translates to Fourth Avenue and Leonora Street. So if you don't see the words "Avenue" and "Street"—and you will often see addresses stated as something like Fourth and Leonora—it is safe to assume that a name (Leonora) indicates a street, a number (Fourth) indicates an avenue.

Avenues always run from north to south, streets east to west—or as close to those directions as they can come in a city that curves around its harbor and lakes.

One more note: Wash. 99, which before the construction of I-5 was a main roadway through town, takes on three different names as it passes scenically along the city's rustic waterfront. From south to north it's called Marginal Way South, Alaskan Way South, and finally on the north end of town, Aurora Avenue North. Wash. 99 is also called Pacific Highway.

Outside Downtown

Now for those outlying districts. In areas outside the downtown district, **avenues** also run north-south, but may be designated either by name or by number. Similarly, **streets,** which run east-west just as they do downtown, may be either numbered (such as 1st Street) or named (for instance, Columbia Street).

Addresses outside the central downtown area may be (but aren't always) further pinpointed with **directional designators** like North, South, East, and West, or a combination of those (Northeast, Northwest, Southeast, and Southwest). Note that these directional designators precede the names of streets (and may be abbreviated in this guide as N., S., E., W., or N.E., N.W., S.E., or S.W.) as in South Washington Street, but they follow the names of avenues (where only the abbreviations NE, NW, SE, and SW will be used in this guide) as in Sixth Avenue South.

Roughly, streets and avenues south of East Yesler Way carry a "South" designation. Similarly, streets east of Broadway and north of East Yesler Way carry an "East" tag (for instance, East Union Street or 11th Avenue East). On the north end of town similar designations appear north of Denny Way (for instance, Ninth Avenue North) and west of Queen Anne Avenue, where "West" designations begin.

You'll find the University of Washington and environs, known as the **University District** in the northeast section of town, bounded roughly by I-5 on the west, 36th Avenue NE on the east, N.E. 45th Street on the north, and waters of Portage and Union Bays on the south.

Bellevue, across Lake Washington east of Seattle, does indeed have a belle view, so has become a very large and chic suburb with a population of 73,000. Its "downtown" is a 12-square-block area bordered on the north by N.E. 12th Street, on the south by Main Street, on the west by 100th Avenue NE, and on the east by 112th Avenue NE.

Sea-Tac International Airport is south of Seattle between South 154th and South 188th Streets off Wash. 99 or I-5. Wash. 99's other name, Pacific Highway, is used in addresses of hotels and motels near the airport.

3. TOURIST AND USEFUL INFORMATION

TOURIST INFORMATION: Here are some telephone numbers and addresses that will cut down the frustrations of finding things you need and want in a city unfamiliar to you.

No matter what your purpose in being in town, the people over at the **Seattle–King County Convention and Visitors Bureau** will be able to help with advice and literature to make your trip more successful. Contact them at 666 Stewart St., Seattle, WA 98101 (tel. 206/447-4240). The bureau also has a **Visitor Information Center** at Sea-Tac International Airport on the baggage-claim level (tel. 206/433-5217). Or if you're in Bellevue, stop at the **East King County Convention and Visitors Bureau,** Lincoln Center, Suite 111, Bldg. 515, 116th Ave. NE, Bellevue, WA 98004 (tel. 206/455-1926).

For more in-depth information about the city and its infrastructure, stop by the **Seattle Chamber of Commerce,** 1200 One Union Square, Sixth Avenue and University Street, Seattle, WA 98104 (tel. 206/461-7200).

USEFUL INFORMATION: For police, fire, or medical emergency, dial 911. . . . Seattle **telephone area code** is 206. . . . For one-hour color-print film development and five-hour enlargement service, call on **Olympic Camera Center,** 1319 Fourth Ave. (tel. 206/623-1070). . . . For minor **medical needs,** call the Mason Clinic, Fourth Avenue and University Street (tel. 206/223-6490), or the Virginia Mason Medical Center in Virginia Mason Hospital, emergency room open 24 hours (tel. 206/583-6433 or 624-1144). The hospital is at 1006 Spring St. . . . For **bus information,** call 206/447-4800. . . . For Washington state **ferry information,** call 206/464-6400. . . . Seattle is located 125 miles from the Pacific Ocean, 128 miles from the Canadian border, and is closer to Tokyo and London than is San Francisco. . . . About 34 inches of **rain** falls here each year, but very little snow. . . . The population is 525,000 in Seattle, more than a million in King County. . . . A 24-hour gas station is at Huston's Arco Mini Mart, which also has groceries, ice, and firewood (tel. 206/525-1234).

4. WHERE TO STAY

Seattle's hotel options are clustered in three general areas—near the airport, downtown, and at the university. It seems to us that for the pleasure traveler, downtown locations are best, simply because they're the closest to most of the things you'll want to see in this bustling city. Downtown locations cost more, generally, but we've located a few budgetwise stops too. If you're budget-conscious, you'll find more dollar-saving accommodations north of town, at the airport and sometimes in the university section, although you'll have to add the cost of transportation to room rates. Here's a look at the hotels, categorized first by location and then by price:

DOWNTOWN HOTELS: In Seattle downtown hotels are clustered rather close together, so if you're not too laden down with luggage and/or are driving, you can easily look at several, then make your choice. Naturally they also all have the advantage of being close to most of the things you'll want to see in this lovely waterside city. We've divided your choices into luxury, medium-priced, and budget choices.

Luxury Hotels

The **Alexis Hotel,** 1007 First Ave. (at Madison Street), Seattle, WA 98104 (tel. 206/624-4844, or toll free 800/426-7033), gets our vote for one of the most beautiful and elegant hotels in Seattle—or anywhere else. Near Pioneer Square, the Alexis is listed on the National Register of Historic Places. Constructed in 1911, the building fell into disrepair for many years before it was totally revamped.

Now the hotel opens onto a long lobby lined with deep square armchairs offset by light-green carpeting. Colors and furnishings are evocative of the art deco era: pale pastels, rounded lines, curving furnishings. Peek and peer around and you'll find a myriad of details like a lion carved into cement. In a central courtyard clever designers filled a former airshaft with plants.

Rooms are a study in delicate colors, peaches and blues, offset by creamy white moldings and beams, handsome polished wood furniture, writing desk, tiny lamps, fresh roses. You'll find special soaps and lotions, and you are remembered in the evening with turn-down service and chocolate. They'll shine your shoes here, deliver a morning paper to your door, treat you to a continental breakfast.

There's a small steamroom and two rooftop tennis courts. If you want to impress someone with your contemporary good taste, this is the place to do it. For all this pampering you pay $125 single, $145 double, $180 for twin rooms or parlor suites, and $240 for an executive suite, $260 for one with fireplace.

Lovely custom here: Gratuities are *included* in the room rate for baggage handling.

There's more good news: the Alexis's dramatic dining room is considered one of the best restaurants in the city. Its chef is among the most innovative in the Northwest (see "Where to Dine"), if not the country.

Our vote for the most beautiful old-world hotel in Seattle is the **Sorrento,** 900 Madison St., Seattle, WA 98104 (tel. 206/622-6400, or toll free 800/426-1265 in the continental U.S., Alaska, and Hawaii; collect calls are accepted from Canada, and from within Washington). You can't miss the building: it's on the corner of Terry and Madison and has two red-brick wings trimmed at the roofline with white columns. Wings flair out from a rounded corner to circle a brick courtyard. From a distance there's nothing awe-inspiring about this small hillside hotel, but once you pass its tall gates into the fountain-centered courtyard, you'll begin to discover how sybaritic life must have been before cookie-cutter motels caught the American imagination.

In the small lobby there's a certain hush, as well there should be. Once a decrepit home for low-income residents, the Sorrento is today as primped and polished as a dowager millionairess. Fabulous Honduran mahogany beams and paneling, uncovered from beneath layers of white paint, are polished and glowing in their original splendor. Every room in this elegant, small 76-room hotel is lovely, but the prettiest of them all is the octagonal sitting room you'll see as you enter the lobby. A massive central pillar is topped by clever lighting enclosed in an ornately carved dome, from which ceiling beams radiate like sunbeams. Around this central pillar is a tapestry-covered banquette in muted shades of green and rose, colors that are picked up in other furnishings in the room. Every one of the eight walls in this unusual room is of floor-to-ceiling, glowing mahogany paneling. The focus of attention is a forest-green tiled fireplace with a French country ceramic mural above it. During the Sorrento's down days, this fireplace was hidden by a plastered plywood panel! Two clever gentlemen who bought the building studied early drawings of it and discovered that behind the plaster was a Charles Rookwood–designed fireplace, one of only three remaining in this country, one of only ten in the world.

But the new owners did much much more with this building than just discover a fireplace. In a residence that at one time had nearly 150 rooms, they broke through walls and refinished and refurbished to create 76 exquisite dwellings, each different and each filled with antiques (some of them from the old Olympic Hotel here), original artwork, goosedown pillows, and furnishings that are as much a delight to live in as to look at. When you stay in one of these lovely rooms, you'll find a mint on your pillow at night, fluffy towels, fancy soaps in your bathroom, and a copy of the *Wall Street Journal* or *USA Today* at the door in the morning. Should you splurge for a suite, elegant French doors open into a separate bedroom. The ratio of guests to workers here is about as close as you can get to one to one, including a charming bellman who knows the history of the Sorrento, the hotel in which his parents honeymooned in 1937!

Do you get the idea we love this place? Good, then you get the idea. More than half the Sorrento's rooms are suites, and on the top floor are two spectacular penthouses. All rooms have televisions and refrigerators; some have stereos.

Just off that octagonal room is an equally impressive Hunt Club Bar and dining room, both of which are paneled wall to wall and trimmed in stained glass. All in all, this is one very beautiful place to call home.

Rates at the Sorrento start at $95 for deluxe rooms and $150 for suites, and run from $250 for executive suites. Weekend rates are $90 for deluxe rooms and $110 for one-bedroom suites, including breakfast.

As long as we're giving awards here, our prize for most accommodating hotel we've ever experienced goes to Seattle's **Warwick Hotel,** Fourth and Leonora, Seattle, WA 98121 (tel. 206/443-4300, or toll free 800/426-9280 outside Washington). What could be nicer than a free ride anywhere you want to go in the city—and a ride back? All you do is tell a bellman where you're headed, then hop in the courtesy transportation and off you go. So popular is this particular service that some suburban dwellers book a room here for a celebratory weekend, then go out to local nightspots, secure in the knowledge that they won't have to drive home later.

While that was to us the most outstanding part of the hotel's service, a smiling willingness to help with *anything* at all didn't hurt a bit: we needed some office supplies unavailable at the desk, but lo and behold, a few minutes later up came a bellman delivering just what we needed! He'd taken the trouble to search a little-used storeroom on his own when he overheard what we were seeking.

In the small bilevel lobby cushy chairs and couches are pulled up around a welcoming fire. In a small lounge nearby hot hors d'oeuvres appear at happy hour, while in the moderately priced brass-railed dining room, hearty steaks and succulent local seafood are served. A small sidewalk café–deli offers pastries, sandwiches, and espresso to revive flagging spirits.

In your room you'll find a chrome-and-leather tilt-back chair with a hassock to ease tired muscles, an attractive russet décor, and the most elaborate marble-lined bathroom we've ever seen. Peppermint-shaped soaps and a basket of toiletries round out the sybaritism. Suites have wet bars, great views, balconies, and king-size or double beds.

You can relax in a sauna here or swim in a heated indoor pool, splash in a whirlpool, or work out in an exercise room. They'll even provide you with a jogger's map of downtown Seattle. Location is great too: right downtown, steps away from the Pike Place Market, the monorail, and downtown shops and restaurants.

Rates at the Warwick are $125 to $145 single, $150 to $170 double, with highest rates for deluxe accommodations. A third person sharing a room is $15. Suites with living room, bar, and a whirlpool spa by the master bedroom begin at $325.

Once upon a time long ago, Seattle's Olympic Hotel suffered a fate about like that of many other Seattle hostelries: age and lack of concern left their marks. Then along came saviors who turned this magnificent 1920 structure into a breathtakingly beautiful spot now called the **Four Seasons Olympic Hotel,** 411 University St., Seattle, WA 98101 (tel. 206/621-1700, or toll free 800/223-8772, 800/821-8106 in Washington, 800/268-6282 in Canada). If there's one single word to describe this 450-room hotel, it's "dramatic." In the massive lobby walls soar two stories, enclosing a second-floor mezzanine trimmed with ornately carved wood moldings and railings. At one end of the lobby a few wide stairs lead to the Georgian Room, a dining room with a soaring two-story ceiling from which hangs a giant crystal chandelier. On Sunday the peach décor here is backdrop to a fabulously elaborate brunch buffet, adorned by ice carvings and served to an elegant crowd.

You'll find acres of marble in this Italian Renaissance architecture, beautifully carved woods, shimmering chandeliers, an alluring peach and forest-green décor. Add to that every kind of cosseting service: one-hour pressing, complimentary shoe shines, indoor swimming pool, whirlpool, sauna and health club, 24-hour room service, twice-daily maid service, same-day laundry and valet services, valet parking, the finest shops, and robes in every room. Whew!

While you're waiting for your car to be brought around, you can lounge on taupe leather couches, and when lunchtime rolls around you can dine in the glittering Garden Court where full-grown trees reach for the high ceilings. Tiny streams sparkle as they flow around the room.

Four Seasons Olympic's 450 guest rooms are big going on bigger. All are decorated in soft contemporary shades, with high ceilings and lovely furnishings including armoires that hide televisions, and some even have adjoining sitting rooms reached through tall French doors perfect for the sweeping entrance, Bette Davis style. For casual moments, Shucker's offers oyster bar service and a range of beef and seafood dishes.

Rates range from $160 to $235 double for rooms, depending on size, while those bedroom/sitting room combinations with the French doors are $210 to $235. You can save money on weekends (Friday through Sunday nights), when rates range from $95 to $155, and small suites are $155. Single travelers pay $20 less for most rooms.

Seattle dwellers call the twin towers of the **Westin Hotel,** 1900 Fifth Ave., Seattle, WA 98111 (tel. 206/624-7400, or toll free 800/228-3000), their corn cobs, but they also call them a beautiful new addition to this city. Contemporary as a new penny, this hotel features three restaurants ranging from the flotsam and jetsam of Trader Vic's to the elegance and élan of the Palm Court. For dancing and cocktails, try Fitzgerald's on Fifth.

Rooms here range from beautifully tailored basic guest rooms with television hidden away in a wardrobe/wall unit to massive bilevel suites. In the lobby a pianist plays as you sip afternoon tea or cocktails. All around you is the polished marble of the lobby and under your feet is a custom-made carpet with ribbons of color streaming across it.

Westin Hotel prices are $135 for rooms with a limited view. Prices rise to $185 to $200 for rooms with a panoramic view and drop to $165 double for rooms with a city view. Children under 18 are free in their parents' room.

The Sheraton Corporation decided that Seattle had all the ingredients of an up-and-coming city, so they opened here with the **Seattle Sheraton,** Sixth Avenue and Pike Street, Seattle, WA 98111 (tel. 206/621-9000, or toll free 800/325-3535, 800/268-9330 in western Canada).

When Sheraton moved in, it did so with 900 rooms in a triangular building that also includes 43 elegant suites in its 35 stories. There's a view of the city from every room in the hotel, and from some you can see Mount Rainier, the Olympic Mountains, and the Cascades, as well as Puget Sound. Way up top there's a rooftop swimming pool and exercise equipment.

In the large lobby you'll find an unusual ceiling treatment—hundreds of tiny colored strings looped from the ceiling pick up the colors of a fiber wall hanging. Nearby a sunken lounge called Banners provides a spot for an intimate or late-night drink, light lunches, and snacks, including fish and chips and an interesting appetizer called shrimp martini, shrimp steamed in guess what?

Nearby is Fuller's Dining Room, another highly rated Seattle restaurant featuring continental cuisine, the likes of duckling with gooseberry and peppercorn sauce or sirloin steak with coubise sauce, in the $15 to $20 price range. The Sheraton also has a coffeeshop with lunch for $5 to $7, dinner for $10 to $12, and an irresistible $6.25 dessert buffet.

The rooms are decorated in contemporary shades of rust and beige with bedspreads in a handsome large geometric design. Rates are $151 to $181 double, with suites beginning at $192; single travelers get a $20 break on the price. Weekend packages and other kinds of special programs can save you money.

Holiday Inn has arrived in downtown Seattle with one of its new upmarket hotels called **Holiday Inn Crowne Plaza,** Sixth and Seneca, Seattle, WA 98101 (tel. 206/464-1980, or toll free 800/HOLIDAY). The lobby here rises four stories and is filled with plants. A mezzanine café offers all three meals, and on sunny days tables move outside into the International Plaza. A more formal dining room offers lots of fresh regional seafood and whatever beautiful fruit and vegetables the chef finds in the market that day, and all for prices in the $8 to $14 range for lunch and $12 to $25 for dinner.

Rooms at the front of this new hotel have a pretty view of Freeway Park and a fountain across the way. A very contemporary building of straight-up glass, Holiday Inn Crowne Plaza is located conveniently close to town, just up the hill from the ferry terminal. You'll find 420 spacious and attractive rooms with modern décor and all the extras from room service to same-day laundry and valet help, in-room movies, and choice of room with king-size beds or two doubles. A concierge will arrange dining, cars, tickets, and the like, and someone will deliver a morning newspaper to your room. Health club facilities are available.

Rates are $145 double on regular guest-room floors and $185 double on concierge floors. Singles pay $20 to $30 less. A special weekend rate is on a space-available basis.

The **Seattle Hilton,** 60 University St., Seattle, WA 98101 (tel. 206/624-0500, or toll free 800/426-0535, 800/542-7700 in Washington), is one of Hilton's less showy properties, and, we'd guess, one of its smaller ones. In true Washington style they greet you with a big silver bowl full of apples at the lobby desk. A small coffeeshop called McCully's has a cozy libations corner that beckons the thirsty with travertine tables.

Rooms here are quite spacious and in 1986 the hotel underwent a major refurbishing. All the usual Hilton accoutrements prevail, however, including special soaps and lotions in the bath, televisions, and plenty of space. You can have rooms with one double bed, two double beds, or king-size beds, and there are some suites available. For dining the Hilton offers the Top of the Hilton Restaurant.

Rates are $108 to $118 double, about $15 less single, with one- and two-bedroom suites available for prices starting at $180. Extra persons are $10. On weekends you can save a bundle: rooms are $70 daily Friday and Saturday, single or double!

If you're looking for a room with a view, you could hardly do better than the **Stouffer Madison Hotel,** 515 Madison St. (at Fifth Avenue), Seattle, WA 98111 (tel. 206/583-0300, or toll free 800/HOTELS-1). Perched up on a hill, the Madison occupies quite serene surroundings with lovely views over the city and waterfront. Although it's right in the heart of the downtown area, there's a park outside the door. Opened not long ago, this star in the Seattle firmament is operated by Stouffer Hotels and has 554 rooms decorated in soft contemporary colors and fabrics. Some rooms have a small sitting area, even handcrafted cabinets trimmed in brass. Forest green is the color scheme in the public rooms, from the long canopy at the entrance to the bellman's uniform. Travertine walls and floors and etched glass add elegant touches. Amenities include a gym, a sauna, and a big, heated indoor swimming pool. A garage houses your car. Rates are $114 to $169 double; $134 to $189 double on the club level.

For dining and sipping, the Lobby Court Lounge is an informal spot for cocktails and lunch, while up a flight via escalator the Maxwell Café beckons. On the 28th floor the beautiful split-level, brass-trimmed Prego restaurant reigns, with entree prices in the $12 to $17 range.

Medium-Priced Hotels

Mayflower Park Hotel, 405 Olive Way, Seattle, WA 98101 (tel. 206/623-8700, or toll free 800/426-5100, 800/562-4504 in Washington), is a delightful close-in hotel (just around the corner from the monorail) that offers a charming combination of old-world and contemporary living.

In a spacious lobby you'll find stained-glass panels inset over the reception desk and beamed ceilings. An ornate wrought-iron balustrade with a polished wood handrail along the stairs leads to a mezzanine sitting room fitted out with wing chairs and an old fireplace. On a cream-colored ceramic floor is a handsome forest-green and beige carpet rimmed with groupings of dark-green velvet chairs and couches. A low cocktail table holds a giant glass globe filled with fresh flowers.

Just off the lobby is Oliver's, a gorgeous high-ceilinged cocktail lounge filled with light that pours through ceiling-high small-paned arched windows. Potted ficus trees shade marble-topped tables and contemporary furnishings. The management is proud of the Clipper Restaurant with its award-winning design of tall windows and gold-and-white décor accented with seafoam and brass. Guests dine amid fresh flowers and greenery on Northwest cuisine specialties and pastries baked here.

In the guest rooms you'll find contemporary colors and designs: brass lamps, white pleated shades, burgundy armchairs, beige and burgundy bedspreads in a geometric print, a writing desk and chair, plush carpeting, and dark-wood headboard. Rates at the Mayflower Park, which has direct access to Westchester Mall and the monorail linking downtown Seattle to Seattle Center, are $72 to $85 for double rooms, $120 to $165 for suites, and $64 to $78 single.

In the medium-priced bracket, the **Hotel Seattle,** 315 Seneca St., Seattle, WA 98101 (tel. 206/623-5110), is a good if not glamorous choice. Rooms here are of medium size, dolled up in sometimes attractive, sometimes a bit florid, wallpaper with bedspreads in a coordinating print. Burgundy-carpeted stairs lead to a comfortable upper-level lobby with wing chairs and a lovely antique cabinet. Downstairs, Bernard's provides gemütlich atmosphere and Bavarian wiener-schnitzel-style meals.

The Hotel Seattle's not a fancy place, but it's a comfortable one that's kept clean and neat. Prices are comfortable too: $54 to $58 for a room with one or two double beds; extra persons are $6.

Another conveniently located and conveniently priced stopping spot is the **Regency Motor Inn,** 2200 Fifth Ave., Seattle, WA 98121 (tel. 206/441-9785), where an unimposing exterior houses a raft of freshly decorated rooms. You enter a spacious lobby outfitted in dark-wood furniture with a faintly Mediterranean look and dark-velvet upholstery.

In your room you'll find cheerier-than-average motel furnishings, two double beds with brightly colored spreads, nice carpeting, and attractive wood headboards with a faintly Federalist air about them. Modern baths are tiled and have a shower and tub separate from a small dressing area with sink. Rates here are $47 for a room with one double bed and $57 for one with two beds.

We debated just where in this book to put a small new hotel called the **Inn at the Market,** 86 Pine St., Seattle, WA 98101 (tel. 206/443-3600, or toll free 800/446-4484). The Inn at the Market, you see, likes to think of itself as presenting the ambience of a bed-and-breakfast without the breakfast. A charming hotel right at the marketplace, this lovely addition to Seattle is decorated in cozy country French style with lots of chintz and prints. There are plenty of restaurants nearby and the inn has a coffee pot and imported coffee in each room, along with a refrigerator you can stock with goodies from irresistible stands at Pike Place Market.

A welcome addition to this elegantly charming spot is the Campagne Restaurant, where the kitchen offers such tempters as Snohomish veal with garlic and basil, baked shoalwater oysters with chives and cream, and seafood sausage stuffed with Alaskan salmon and scallops. With this location smack in the middle of the Pike Place Market area, they've got a treasure trove of produce at their doorstep and use it to succulent advantage.

The Inn at the Market also offers complimentary limousine service in the downtown area and has an lounge with an amusing name, the Gravity Bar, serving freshly squeezed juices and room service for breakfast. For sinners, the Café Dilettante & Chocolatier is nearby—just follow the aroma of espresso.

The Inn at the Market has 65 rooms, handmade furniture, and a delightful lobby fireplace. Rates are $85 to $145 double, depending on the view from your ceiling-high bay window. Singles are priced about $10 to $15 less, and higher-priced suites also are available.

An ornate canopy shades the entrance to the **Pacific Plaza Hotel,** Fourth Avenue at Spring Street, Seattle, WA 98104 (tel. 206/623-3900, or toll free 800/426-1165, 800/732-1235 in Washington; in Canada, call 604/222-9286 in Vancouver, 604/383-1216 in Victoria). Up a few stairs from the entrance and registration desk, secreted away in a corner of the building, is an attractive sitting room.

You can peek down over a mezzanine wall to the Red Robin Restaurant below or step into a tiny adjoining coffeeshop with high-backed wooden booths. The Red Robin Lounge is a cozy spot just inside the door.

Rooms in this 166-room hotel feature attractive carpets and contemporary décor in muted colors. Some have a small couch in a sitting area off to one side of the room. Recently redecorated, the Pacific Plaza is an old hotel but one that is working hard to keep up-to-date.

Downstairs that Red Robin Restaurant is downright gorgeous, done up in deep burgundy and trimmed with lots of brass, wood, and etched glass that creates a contemporary Victorian look. High ceilings and arched windows, some bearing painted parrots, add to that atmosphere. Prices are in the moderate range, about $10 to $12 for dinner entrees.

Rates at the hotel are $58 for a double bed, $66 for twin beds, and $70 for a king-size sleeper. Call for weekend specials.

Another budgetwise hotel in downtown Seattle is the **Kennedy,** 1100 Fifth Ave., Seattle, WA 98101 (tel. 206/623-6175). Some rooms, like no. 990 and others in the same vertical stack, have big windows offering a smashing view of downtown Seattle and Puget Sound beyond.

Friendly workers preside over a small but attractive lobby outfitted in rose-colored carpeting. They'll be happy to show you a room here, and when they do, you'll discover medium-size quarters with modern baths, often some rather startlingly colorful décor. Plastic-cushioned chairs in many rooms are a bit of an incongruous touch. Management at this quite convenient in-town hotel goes out of its way to help you out with such small things as an iron and ironing board, lint brush, sewing kit, extra pillows and blankets, razors, Alka-Seltzer, after shave, shoe polish, shampoo, Band-Aids, just about anything you can dream up, right down to a jigsaw puzzle—and specifically requests you not to tip for these services. They even deliver a newspaper to your door six days a week, and if you'd like to read it in bed, they'll bring along a continental breakfast.

Rates at the Kennedy are a very reasonable $45 double, $2 less for a single, and $6 more for a room with two double beds. A few suites are available from $60. Additional persons sharing a room are $5. Some rooms also have kitchens, and for those you pay an additional $7. Continental breakfast is included in these prices. The Kennedy also valet-parks your car and has two movie channels to amuse you.

Another motor hotel in the downtown area is the **Towne Centre / Days Inn Motor Hotel,** 2205 Seventh Ave., Seattle, WA 98121 (tel. 206/448-3434, or toll free 800/648-6440). You won't find it fancy here, but rooms are serviceable and offer free local phone calls, no charge for cribs or for children under 16, free parking, color television, even no-smoking guest rooms. The Towne Centre is a four-story building along a rather lackluster downtown street. It is, however, within reasonable walking distance of many Seattle amusements.

In the hotel is a small restaurant and lounge called the Greenhouse, which features dinner prices in the $10 to $15 range. The Towne Centre charges $53 double for a room with king- or queen-size bed, $56 for a room with two double beds, and $60 to $75 for a parlor suite. Single travelers will pay about $6 less in each category. Additional persons sharing a room are $7.

One street farther north are two other mid-priced, center-city motels, the **Travelodge Downtown,** 2213 Eighth Ave., Seattle, WA 98121 (tel. 206/624-6300, or toll free 800/255-3050); and **Best Western Loyal Inn,** 2301 Eighth Ave., Seattle, WA 98121 (tel. 206/682-0200, or toll free 800/528-1234). Of the two the Best Western is the snappier, but either provides standard motel accommodations for prices of $54 double for a room with a queen-size bed, $62 for two beds at the Travelodge; $54 to $58 double at the Best Western Loyal Inn.

One final option: an apartment hotel. We haven't seen this one yet, but have heard about it from customers pleased with what two renovators have done to refurbish the **Baker Apartments and Guest House,** 700 E. Mercer St., Seattle, WA 98102 (tel. 206/323-5909). Once occupying a turn-of-the-century house, the Baker recently moved itself—lock, stock, and claw-footed bathtubs—to two new buildings, one a contemporary spot, the other a Spanish-style manse. This new "old" Baker, as they like to call their complex, occupies a pleasant spot in a quiet residential setting near one of the city's historic districts and right around the corner from a fashionable shopping boulevard. Here you can stroll among imposing old mansions and get a close look at some of the region's history.

Each apartment has a fully equipped kitchen with everything right down to wine glasses. Furnishings are an eclectic array of valuable period pieces and what the owners laughingly call "collectibles, Early Attic and Rehabbed Art Deco . . . livable and sometimes laughable, but comfortable." Brochures for the Baker are a mini-tome on things to see and do in Seattle, and how to get there to do them. So here you have your choice of a studio or one-bedroom apartment in a contemporary building or in a 1920s atmosphere. Both have televisions, telephones, and antique pieces, although the more contemporary building has more contemporary furnishings.

Rates are $60 to $70 a day for a one-bedroom apartment and studios are $50 to $55. To reach the Baker, take I-5 to exit 168A southbound (Roanoke Street) or exit 166 northbound (Olive Way). It's right off Broadway, one of the main thoroughfares near Lake Union, at Mercer Street.

Budget Hotels

If a quite inexpensive room is your goal and you don't mind the most basic of furnishings, put the **Pacific Hotel,** Fourth Avenue and Marion Street, Seattle, WA 98104 (tel. 206/622-3985), on your list. Located in the free-bus-service zone, this quite antique hostelry still shows some of the features that must once have made it a very handsome place. You'll find marble stairways and an attractively homey, old-fashioned lobby with a fireplace and some comfortable chairs. There are a couple of stained-glass windows and a tiny landscaped courtyard. Management here is very friendly and will be happy to show you a room so you can decide whether or not this is for you. As for those rooms: they're small and rather haphazardly decorated; some have private bath, some don't.

If you peek around a few corners you'll see marble columns here and there. Décor is the simplest of simple, but rooms are clean. Pacific's central location is a boon. Rooms without bath are $21 single, $24 double; rooms with bath are $27 single, $30 double. Beat that!

In Seattle the **YMCA**, 909 Fourth Ave., Seattle, WA 98104 (tel. 206/382-5000), offers rooms with or without private bath and with color television or without. It also accepts both couples and singles, men or women, charging just $30 a day for a small but serviceable double room with television, bath down the hall.

A big and spotlessly clean lobby greets you here as do two delightful young ladies, weekend helpers, who gigglingly informed us that the hotel "has very nice help at the front—especially on weekends." True. What's more, the Y is in an excellent central location across the street from some very posh real estate. In fact the Y's building is also a handsome ornate structure of red brick. Rooms are simply decorated with Danish modern furniture. Very clean, however. You'll also feel quite secure here since a room key is needed to operate the elevator.

Single rooms are just $27.25 a day, with the top rate for a double with bath and television at $32.75. Included are use of exercise facilities, tax, laundry facilities, maid service, and in-room phones with free local calls. You'll also find a barbershop and tailor shop here. The YMCA is just two blocks from the airport bus terminal, quite close to Pioneer Square and the waterfront.

At the **YWCA**, 1118 Fifth Ave., Seattle, WA 98101 (tel. 206/447-4888), it's women only. The rooms are spartan—no phone or TV—but so is the price: just $21 per person without bath, $26 with bath. A tad rough around the edges, the YWCA is, however, clean, and rooms provide simple but basic comforts. What it lacks in room décor it makes up in central location. There's also a small restaurant and deli here, and a health and fitness center. For a small additional fee you can use the swimming pool, sauna, and weight-training equipment.

American Youth Hostels operates inexpensive lodging for hostel members, who are mostly, but not exclusively, young people and students. In Seattle the youth hostel in 1987 moved from its temporary quarters at the YMCA to a new building called the **Seattle International Hostel**, 84 Union St., Seattle, WA 98101 (tel. 206/622-5443). This hostel occupies the former 1915 Old Longshoreman's Hall once known as the "Ellis Island of the Pacific." Youth hostel members pay $10 if they bring their own sheets, $16 if you rent one of their sheets. The nonmember rate is $19. To reach the hostel, take bus 174 to Pine Street and First Avenue, walk two blocks south on First to Union, then one block west to Western, where you'll find the hostel on the corner.

There are other youth hostels in the state at Almira, Ashford, Blaine, Carnation, Chinook, at Friday Harbor and on Orcas Island in the San Juan Islands, Nordland, Port Townsend, and Vashon Island. American Youth Hostels annually publishes a directory of hostels in the U.S. For a copy of that and information on becoming a hostel member, contact American Youth Hostels, P.O. Box 37613, Washington, DC 20013.

NEAR THE UNIVERSITY: In this part of town you'll find some very good budgetwise choices.

If you've got a student in the family or just want to take a look at a beautiful college campus, you might want to spend some time at the **Meany Tower Hotel**, 4507 Brooklyn Ave. NE, Seattle, WA 98105 (tel. 206/634-2000, or toll free 800/648-6400). The hotel is just off I-5, right in the middle of Seattle's University of Washington district, not far from town but not walking distance either.

Every one of the 155 rooms at this tall, recently remodeled hotel is a corner room with wide double-bay windows that offer some lovely views of the city and of the snow-clad mountain that floats in the distance like a whitewashed mirage. Meany Tower Hotel provides direct courtesy-car service to and from the

Airporter Terminal, and there's a beauty salon, gift shop, and services for business travelers. Children under 16 are free.

To get there, take the N.E. 45th Street exit from I-5 and go four blocks east. Rates are $82 to $86 double, and begin at about $10 less single.

Nendels University Plaza Hotel, 400 N.E. 45th St., Seattle, WA 98105 (tel. 206/634-0100, or toll free 800/547-0106), in Seattle's university district, three miles north of downtown; get off I-5 at exit 169 or take Wash. 99 to 45th Street. They have a restaurant and a cocktail lounge; parking is free. The garden swimming pool, open from April to October, is heated. Transportation to and from Sea-Tac Airport is available.

Rates at the Plaza are $65 double; extra people sharing the room are $8 each, and children under 12 are free.

College Inn, 4000 University Way NE, Seattle, WA 98105 (tel. 206/633-4441), is a lovely bed-and-breakfast where you will have to forgo a private bathroom, but you'll be treated to a continental breakfast served in a renovated 1909 Tudor-style building. A very cozy place, the College Inn features dramatic burgundy carpeting as background to antique furnishings and fluffy comforters. The price is right too: $32 to $35 single or $40 to $48 double, including continental breakfast.

IN THE AIRPORT AREA: In Seattle, as in most cities, hotels located close to the airport largely serve business travelers who need a place they can get into and out of fast to make plane connections (and perhaps to catch a few extra winks they'd have to spend on the road if they chose a hotel farther from the airplanes).

Business travelers tend to demand what they pay for, so you can expect good service and well-planned serviceable rooms in these hotels. Airport hotels are located about 15 miles from the downtown area.

Luxury Leaders

The **Airport Hilton** is just opposite Seattle-Tacoma International Airport, 17620 Pacific Hwy. South, Seattle, WA 98188 (tel. 206/244-4800; or tollfree 800/445-8667). That's quite a convenient location, particularly if you plan to do some of your touring by plane.

This Hilton offers all the amenities travelers have come to expect from this successful chain. Lush gardens are a delight in summer, as is the big, heated, outdoor swimming pool and the covered whirlpool. Rooms, which cost $104 to $128 double for rooms with one or two double beds, are spacious and recently decorated with quiet contemporary furnishings and have radios, color TVs, and air conditioning for warm summer days. They'll pick you up at the airport in a van and deliver you back there when you have to leave at no charge. Free parking too.

One dining room overlooks a poolside garden area. There's a coffeeshop and a more formal restaurant called Buckwell's, where you can dine on quite good steaks and seafood in the $15 range for entrees, plus some special treats like venison, duckling, and blackberry soufflé. Buckwell's is open every day from 6 a.m. to 11:30 p.m. You'll also find a cozy Cabaret Lounge here with entertainment Tuesday through Saturday.

Red Lion Inn/Sea-Tac, at 18740 Pacific Hwy. South, Seattle, WA 98188 (tel. 206/246-8600, or toll free 800/547-8010), is another hotel located conveniently near the airport—just opposite it, in fact. Quite a large hotel, the Red Lion has glass elevators that run up the outside of the building. If you like balconies, this airport-area hotel may be just your cuppa.

Behind the balconies are handsomely decorated rooms with cable TVs, radios, telephones of course, and combination or shower baths. The Red Lion has

850 rooms, and if you're in the mood for a splurge, it has several very showy suites. There's free parking if you drive in, and complimentary transportation to the airport if you fly here. For relaxing—and warm enough—days there's a heated swimming pool. Showiest part of this hotel, however, is Maxi's Restaurant, a rooftop aerie sporting a grand view and an equally grand menu ranging from rack of lamb to Grand Marnier soufflés plus a scrumptious Sunday brunch. Dinner entrees are in the $15 to $20 range. Entertainment and dancing here too, so reservations are a good idea. Rates are $110 to $126 double.

At the **Hyatt Seattle,** 17001 Pacific Hwy. South, Seattle, WA 98188 (tel. 206/244-6000, or toll free 800/228-9000), you can slip into a sauna, then cool off a bit in a heated swimming pool. Like others in this upmarket chain, this Hyatt features 350 very contemporary and spacious quarters with in-room movies. Complimentary transportation gets you here from the airport next door. Rates are $120 for hotel rooms, $135 for the fancy Regency Club, which features concierge service, morning newspapers, and continental breakfast. You'll dine at pretty and intimate Hugo's Rotisserie, which sports a big salad bar and three different preparations of salmon, or at an attractive coffeeshop where a greenhouse atmosphere prevails. Evenings there's entertainment at Hugo's Bistro.

Marriott Hotels, 3201 S. 176th St., Seattle, WA 98188 (tel. 206/241-2000, or toll free 800/228-9290), is represented here with 462 rooms just opposite the airport. All the usual amenities are provided by Marriott, including movies, radios, televisions, and big handsome rooms. When you're exhausted after a long day of sightseeing, you can ease the pain in a heated indoor pool or in the hotel's saunas or whirlpool. Or you can work up a little suffering in Marriott's health club gymnasium. Again, there's free airport transport here plus a good-looking dining room where prices are in a reasonable $20 range and a cocktail lounge.

Rates at the Marriott Hotel are $116 to $126 year round, $10 additional for extra persons.

Holiday Inn Renton Inn, 800 Rainier Ave. South, Renton, WA 98055 (tel. 206/226-7700, or toll free 800/HOLIDAY), is spiffy-looking these days following a top-to-bottom renovation. At this brightly decorated Seattle property you'll find 188 rooms, complete with movies, radios, and attractive décor. For fun, there's a heated indoor pool, saunas, whirlpool, and health club. Airport transportation is complimentary and the hotel also can arrange for you to get to a nearby shopping center and to the racetrack. There's a coffeeshop, the 360°-view Penthouse Lounge, and Brandy's dining room, open from breakfast at 6 a.m. to 11 p.m. daily with prices in the $15 range for dinner entrees. Rates at the inn are $76 to $95 double.

Medium-Priced Choices

Best Western Airport Executel, 20717 Pacific Hwy. South, Seattle, WA 98188 (tel. 206/878-1814), has 150 rooms in a multistory building, a few of them with balconies, all of them attractively decorated. A few rooms have refrigerators, and all have cable TV, in-room movies, and radios. Rates are $67 to $80, and extra persons sharing the room with you are $6 each. Best Western is about one mile from the airport.

An unusual spot in the airport area is the **Continental Court Motor Hotel,** 17223 32nd Ave. South, Seattle, WA 98188 (tel. 206/241-1500). At this quite large property, about two blocks east of the airport, you'll find 330 units, about half of them very large, two-bedroom accommodations offering all the comforts of home and perhaps some comforts even home doesn't have! Fireplaces, for instance—about a third of the motel's rooms have them and many add a pretty view of the hotel's 30 acres of landscaped grounds and pool. Many quarters have full kitchen facilities including a stove, a refrigerator, even a dishwasher. Free airport limo service too.

You can rent space here by the day, week, or month at rates of $35 to $40 double, $5 for an extra person, and no charge for children under 5 in the same room with their parents.

Nendels Sea-Tac, 16838 Pacific Hwy. South, Seattle, WA 98188 (tel. 206/248-0901, or toll free 800/547-0106), will fix you up with a complimentary continental breakfast to stave off early-morning hunger pangs. This motel's located just opposite the airport and some of its rooms have balconies. Airport transportation is free. No restaurant here, but there is one right next door. Rates are $54 double year round.

Quality Inn at Sea-Tac, 3000 S. 176th St., Seattle, WA 98188 (tel. 206/246-9110, or toll free 800/228-5151), was once known as the Jet Inn, attesting to its proximity to the airport just across the road. By now you probably know what to expect from Quality Inns: efficient service, predictable but good-quality furnishings, and reasonable mid-bracket prices. You'll find that all here in this 221-room hotel, which features two swimming pools, one outdoor and one indoor. You can also perspire off a few calories in a sauna and swoosh around in a whirlpool. Airport transportation is free here too. You'll dine in an attractive dining room or coffeeshop open from 6 a.m. to 10 p.m. In a cocktail lounge you can sip a few to the sounds of a piano player. Rates are $57 to $61 most of the year, about $5 higher in summer months.

Budget Spots

The **Airporter Inn Motel,** 14845 Pacific Hwy. South, Seattle, WA 98188 (tel. 206/248-1061), is about a mile north of the airport but does have airport transportation. A medium-size motel with 72 units, the Airporter Inn features air conditioning in only 40 of its units, so be sure to ask for one of those if you figure the weather will be warm. A restaurant next door will see to your hunger pangs. No pool or recreational facilities here, however. Rates at the Airporter are $26 or $29 year round, and extra persons sharing a room are $3 each.

Sandstone Town & Country Inn, 19225 Pacific Hwy. South, Seattle, WA 98188 (tel. 206/824-1350), is a comparatively small hotel with just 98 rooms simply but adequately furnished. A few have kitchens and a few are two-bedroom units, good if you're traveling with the family. Transportation to the airport, which is just a mile away, is free, and there's a small restaurant here open 24 hours. Rates are $44 double for a room with one double bed, $48 for one with two doubles.

Another money-saver in the area is **Sea-Tac Crest Motor Inn,** 18845 Pacific Hwy. South, Seattle, WA 98188 (tel. 206/433-0999), a quite small motor inn with just 35 standard rooms. Once again, free airport transportation. No pool or restaurant here, but the motor inn serves you a life-sustaining pastries-and-coffee breakfast free. Rates are $38 to $48 double year round.

CAMPING: Fifteen miles south of Seattle, you'll find **Seattle South KOA,** 5801 S. 212th St., Kent, WA 98032 (tel. 206/872-8652), just four miles from Sea-Tac International Airport and close to the Seattle bus line. Seattle South offers a lovely mountain-view setting, level pull-through sites, and a heated pool. There's a shopping mall nearby. To get to the campground, take I-5 to Wash. 188 (exit 152), then follow Orillia Road to the campground. Rates are $17.50 double, with full hookup.

BED-AND-BREAKFAST OPTIONS: The **Pacific Bed & Breakfast Agency,** 701 N.W. 60th St., Seattle, WA 98107 (tel. 206/784-0539), offers rooms in everything from Victorian mansions to waterfront or hillside homes. Breakfast is always included in rates that range from $25 to $40 single, $35 to $65 double. Among the choices is an English Tudor home with a view of the Sound and Mount Rainier, a deluxe condo close to downtown, a colonial home overlooking Puget Sound, a fully equipped apartment near Seattle Center, and a Victorian home with antique furnishings and a wrap-around sunporch. If you send them $2, they'll send you a directory listing the 85 or so homes in Seattle, on Whidbey Island and the San Juan Islands, and in British Columbia and Oregon.

Another B&B reservation service in the Northwest is **Traveller's Bed and Breakfast,** P.O. Box 492, Mercer Island, WA 98040 (tel. 206/232-2345). A friendly, helpful British operator of this reservations service also will help you find your way through the ferry system and can even help you plan an itinerary through the Northwest. Bed-and-breakfast operations listed by this service are in what they call "more deluxe" homes in Oregon, Vancouver, Victoria, and Washington, and range in price from $45 to $100. All are inspected by Traveller's before they are recommended. A directory of the properties is available for $5.

Condominium reservations services include **The Hotel Alternative,** 555 116th Ave. NE, Suite 201, Bellevue, WA 98004 (tel. 206/454-2800); and **Homefires Condominium Rentals, Inc.,** 855 106th Ave. NE, Bellevue, WA 98004 (tel. 206/454-7888).

Just north of Seattle off I-5 is the small town of Edmonds, where an old-fashioned trolley chugs you off to local boutiques, restaurants, museums, and galleries. Diversions include the occasional sight of a sea lion, an underwater garden for hearty scuba-divers, some pleasant waterfront dining-and-drinking establishments, and easy access to ferries headed for the Olympic Peninsula.

Our newlywed friends Wendy and Steve loved a guesthouse there called **Pinkham's Pillow,** 22202 Third Ave. South, Edmonds, WA 98020 (tel. 206/774-3406). We haven't seen this one yet, but we trust that high-flying duo for accurate reports. Rooms here are all named after females—Lacey, Joy, Melissa, Adria, and Shannon—and are decorated in soft pastels, brass beds, lace coverlets, and pretty floral wallpapers. Two rooms have private baths in the room; the rest have a private bath across the hall. Rates range from $45 to $65 daily.

5. WHERE TO DINE

Gourmets used to snicker at the mention of Seattle, but these days the laugh's on them. As the city has grown in size and sophistication, the quality of its restaurants has improved so much that even California critics, long convinced that gastronomy ended at their state line, are now heralding Seattle's chefs!

What amazes us most about Seattle as well as the rest of the Pacific Northwest is prices: restaurant prices that make Seattle residents blanch are common numbers to the rest of the country. Best of the rest in Seattle are charging à la carte prices in the $12 to $15 range, tops, but by far the most common prices are in the $10 to $12 range and very often less. Here's a look at some of the city's favorite dining spots, divided by specialties.

SEATTLE SPECIALTIES: In recent years Seattle has emerged as a most innovative culinary capital of the Northwest. With an awesome array of the freshest ingredients available from sea, mountains, and forests, Seattle's chefs are gaining nationwide attention for their unusual preparations focusing on the region's bounty.

That bounty might include such treats as grilled ling cod with a jalapeño-plum sauce, venison grilled with juniper berries, Puget Beauty strawberries, Shoalwater Bay or Oregon or Belon flat oysters from Westcott Bay in the San Juan Islands, Dungeness crab, wind-dried salmon, wild mushrooms, broiled salmon with gooseberry-and-dill sauce, rack of lamb with chestnut-and-pear sauce, mussels in lovage mayonnaise, rhubarb sorbet with rhubarb compôte or a Yakima peach and rose-geranium sorbet. If we've not gotten your undivided attention, here are some of the best-known restaurants specializing in new and interesting combinations of Northwest produce.

You'll find **Café Sport,** 2020 Western Ave. (tel. 206/443-6000), at the north end of Pike Place Market close to an awesome variety of tempting produce. Seafood is the specialty here in this casual but stylish dining room, where prices fall in the $13 to $20 bracket for dinner. Café Sport is open from 7 a.m. to 10 p.m. daily (from 9 a.m. on weekends).

Restaurant LeGourmand, 425 N.W. Market St. (tel. 206/784-3463), is one of Seattle's acclaimed restaurants, begun by two Northwest chefs who have made quite a name for themselves up this way. You'll find an amazing variety of Northwest treats on the menu at this restaurant, which is open from 5:30 to 10 p.m. Wednesday through Saturday. Fixed-price dinners range from $18 to $25.

Chez Shea, 94 Pike St., Suite 34, in the Pike Place Market (tel. 206/467-9990), is, as you might guess, the creation of a lass named Shea, Sandra Shea, to be exact. Here you have a view of Puget Sound as you dine on elegantly presented culinary triumphs, once again featuring the Northwest's bountiful produce. Chez Shea is small and quite popular, so reservations are essential here. Chez Shea is open daily except Monday from 6 to 10 p.m. and the price of a four-course fixed-price dinner is $29.

We couldn't decide whether to put **Dominique's Place,** 1927 43rd St. East (tel. 206/329-6620), here or to list it under French cuisine, but finally the restaurant's marriage to foods of the Northwest prevailed and here they are. Often lauded as one of the best—if not *the* best saucier—in Seattle, Dominique learned to cook in France and all the treasures of the Pacific Northwest appear here with an irresistibly French flavor. Dominique's is open weekdays from 11:30 a.m. to 2:30 p.m. for lunch and daily from 5 to 10 p.m. for dinner. Entrees fall in the $10 to $18 bracket.

At **Green Lake Grill,** 7850 Green Lake Drive North (tel. 206/522-3490), chef Karl Beckley teams a variety of unusual Northwest ingredients with his own quite stunning skills in the kitchen to come up with things like watercress-and-walnut salads, corn-and-oyster pancakes, a seafood stew with Cajun spices, wonderful baby vegetables, up to and including steamed young cattails. Traditional favorites, like a veal-and-peppercorn pâté, remain favorites with the crowd that frequents this place. Entrees are in the $12 to $17 price range, and the restaurant is open from 11:30 a.m. to midnight weekdays, and from at 5 p.m. weekends.

It's hard to imagine a sunnier, happier atmosphere than a summer afternoon on the flower-bedecked patio at **Rover's,** 2808 E. Madison St. (tel. 206/325-7442). From the kitchen pours some outstanding Northwest cuisine skillfully blended with French touches. Such innovative treats as sea scallops with wilted wild greens, a duck salad, Penn Cove mussels with caviar-and-crayfish sauce, salmon with oyster sauce, grilled rabbit with pine nuts, and some to-die-for white or bittersweet chocolate mousses are created here. You'll pay $15 to $18 for entrees and hours are 11:30 a.m. to 2 p.m. weekdays and 5:30 to 11 p.m. daily; closed Sunday.

A POTPOURRI OF ETHNIC COOKERY: Labuznik, 1924 First Ave. (tel. 206/441-8899), is a Czech word for those who love food and that about tells the story of this fine restaurant. Owner Peter Cipra, a Czech, uses the best basic ingredients, preparing each diner's selection individually—so individually, in fact, that he refuses to prepare more than three entree choices per table, so group diners have to get together on what to sample. What you order hardly matters here, however, since so many things are so good. You need never fear leaving hungry either: selections are usually accompanied by red cabbage, sauerkraut, and bread dumplings! Among the favorite choices in this serene restaurant are roast pork or duck and veal Orloff, or for dainty diners, pastas and innovative sandwiches. You can dine outside or in at this spot which attracts after-theater noshers in search of Labuznik's sinful post-prandial sweets. Dinner entrees are in the $13 to $25 range, including soup or salad. The restaurant is open from 5:30 to 10 p.m. Tuesday through Saturday. The outdoor café opens an hour earlier.

On a sunny day, Seattle gets a little crazy. If you want to see how crazy, hie yourself down to Pike Place Market and look up to the balcony of **Copacabana,** Triangle Bldg., Pike Place Market (tel. 206/622-6359), where throngs of sunseekers will have turned pale epidermis up to absorb rays as they absorb some good, solid Bolivian food. Right on the main street of the market, this second-floor spot offers paella Thursday through Sunday, and some interesting variations on familiar Latin favorites: spicy pastry-clad meat-and-vegetable combinations called saltenas, pork cubes called fritanga, and shrimp soup. You'd have to work hard to spend more than $10 for dinner here. The Copacabana is open from 11 a.m. to 10 p.m. Monday through Saturday and 10 a.m. to 5 p.m. on Sunday.

If you've never tried a Trader Vic's, now is the time. This **Trader Vic's,** in the Westin Hotel, 1900 Fifth Ave. (tel. 206/624-8520), is a maze of rooms filled with masses of palm fronds, glass fishing floats, and South Seas décor. Refreshingly polite, waiters scurry about to serve you good Chinese and Polynesian specialties with efficiency and good humor. In a back room, cooks labor over two huge brick Chinese ovens from which pour beautifully baked meats, accompanied by masterfully cooked vegetables and, if you like, by amazingly elaborate cocktails. Burgers are not something the restaurant brags about, but we encountered some wonderful ones on a late-evening visit. Entree prices are in the $15 to $20 range, and you can expect the bill to mount rather rapidly if you succumb to the appetizer and libation temptations here. Trader Vic's is open from 11:30 a.m. to 2 p.m. and 5:30 to 10:30 p.m. Monday through Saturday, from 5:30 to 10 p.m. on Sunday for dinner only.

Once you've discovered the exotic flavors of Indian food, you will never be able to go long without it. If you're suffering a tandoori attack in Seattle, head for **India House,** 4737 Roosevelt Way NE (tel. 206/632-5072). Those who can't make up their minds or want to sample everything can feast on thali dinners, which offer you a taste of several dishes. Beginners and/or those negative on fiery flavors should start slowly with something like butter chicken, a light medley of chicken, butter, cream, and spices, or add cucumber raita for cooling. They'll be happy to tame any dish down or up to your taste here—just ask. India House is a bit of a distance from downtown, out in the university district, but easy enough to get to on I-5. Prices are quite low as they usually are in Indian restaurants: $8 to $13 for entrees, perhaps a few dollars more for extras like breads and marvelously exotic desserts. Open from 5 to 10 p.m. daily for dinner, to 11 p.m. weekends.

There may not be anything as satisfying as a cheery atmosphere and some stick-to-the-ribs cooking on a cold or rainy night which does, we must admit, occasionally occur here. On a night like that, try the **Austrian,** 2355 Tenth Ave. East (tel. 206/322-8028). Wienerschnitzel is a big slab of tender veal; goulash is topped with dumplings and sour cream; soups are filling as they're meant to be; Bavarian sausages are round and firm and fully packed. When you eat here, you *eat.* Décor in this upstairs/downstairs spot is half formal Austrian, half gemütlich beer hall. The Austrian is open for dinner daily except Monday from 5 to 11 p.m. Prices are as satisfying as the food: $9 to $16 for entrees.

Moroccan cuisine? **Mamounia,** 1556 Olive Way (tel. 206/329-3886), is Seattle's favored Moroccan spot, complete to midnight-at-the-oasis atmosphere.

A five-course dinner here, including such choices as couscous, lamb with honey and prunes, or lemon-adorned chicken plus breads, soups, salad, a pastilla pie of chicken, nuts, a touch of cinnamon entree and honey-flavored, deep-fried chabbakia, and mint tea, is $13.50. Hours are 5 to 10 p.m. daily except Monday.

ITALIAN: One could hardly find a more propitious spot for a restaurant than Pike Place Market, where the produce is so blue ribbon we defy you to stop by there without buying anything. That's likely the reason **Il Bistro,** Pike Place Market (tel. 206/682-3049), settled here and why you'll find so many of Seattle's discerning diners camped out in this restaurant. A simple spot that limits its décor to white linen and fresh flowers. Il Bistro specializes in Italian flavors, things like cioppino, unusual sald greens, fresh pastas, very good veal and lamb, even pheasant. Chef Frank D'Aquila comes from a wine-making family and uses his background to come up with unusual wine vinegars that are part and parcel of many selections. Prices are in the $12 to $17 range à la carte, but the temptations are many, so figure on impulse-purchase extras. Il Bistro's in the Main Arcade and is open for dinner daily from 5:30 p.m. to midnight.

Another very big hit in Seattle is the **1904 Restaurant and Bar,** 1904 Fourth Ave. (tel. 206/682-4141), a spot convenient to many downtown hotels including the Westin and the Warwick. Hi-tech décor here makes interesting use of glass blocks and hard-edge substances attractive to a chic crowd that gathers to partake of unusual pasta creations, ravioli in various preparations, seafood, light delicacies like carpaccio with mustard sauce, fresh oysters, or steamed mussels, pâtés, and an antipasto platter. Prices are in the $8 to $15 range for most things, another reason for its popularity. Lunch is served from 11:30 a.m. to 2:30 p.m. weekdays; dinner, from 5:30 p.m. to midnight daily except Sunday.

FRENCH: Nothing could get us out of Seattle without a stop at the **Café Alexis,** in the Alexis Hotel, First and Madison (tel. 206/624-4844). Not only is the restaurant a lovely place, outfitted in handsome furnishings, but the food is a wondrous combination of the best of nouvelle culinary techniques combined with the best of the Northwest's bounteous produce. A bilevel dining spot so cleverly designed you hardly know there's anyone else there, the dining room features tall windows rising to high ceilings with ornate moldings. Curving lines are echoes of the art deco era that has influenced the design here. On the table: dramatic black-rimmed Fitz & Floyd china, cut-glass goblets, and shining silver.

As for dinner, savor these thoughts: Whidbey Island mussels steamed with riesling and herbs, salmon filet with ginger chutney, trout salad with avocado-mint dressing, rock fish grilled over fruitwood, roast rack of lamb with rosemary glaze, a greens-of-spring cream soup, a salad of most unusual greens— fiddlehead fern, for instance. Chef Jerry Traumfeld has acquired considerable fame for top culinary talents that produce delicate creations like those at prices in the $12 to $20 range for entrees. Figure $60 to $70 for two, including drinks. Hours are 6:30 to 10 a.m., 11:30 a.m. to 2 p.m., and 5:30 to 10 p.m. daily, later on weekends.

Ask anybody to recommend a restaurant in Seattle and chances are a significant proportion of answers will be Jacques Boiroux's **Le Tastevin,** 19 W. Harrison (tel. 206/283-0991). A resident of toney Lower Queen Anne Hill, Le Tastevin provides atmosphere equal to the neighborhood and food that's among the best in the Northwest. For intimate evenings seek a table among the wine racks, then dine on Villeroy & Boch china playing backdrop to mouthwatering bouillabaisse or scallops unfettered by anything heavier than a touch of tomato.

Le Tastevin has such a stunning wine list that for five years the restaurant has been listed among the 20 best wine cellars in the *world* by a wine magazine, and the fine culinary skills of the chef recently won the restaurant accolades from *Pacific Northwest* magazine as Seattle's best restaurant.

Light dinners, designed for the pre-theater crowd, are in the $14 to $16 price range, à la carte entree items are $15 to $20, and the restaurant is open for lunch from 11 a.m. to 2:30 p.m. weekdays and for dinner from 5 to 11 p.m. daily except Sunday.

A stately hostess showed us the **Palm Court,** Westin Hotel, Fifth Avenue and Westlake Street (tel. 206/624-7400), with such charm and elegance that we were enticed into an evening there. Just as well she was so beguiling, for what followed was a memorable evening among forests of greenery, unobtrusive service, and culinary delights melding Northwest ingredients with innovative nouvelle culinary skills. You dine here in one of a winding series of multilevel, glassed-in rooms, shiny as a greenhouse at lunch, glittery as a cityscape at dinner.

Pâtés are outstanding, salads imaginative, and combinations of flavors that sometimes take nouvelle to bizarre new heights are at other times wondrously inventive. If you're new to the peach-and-lobster combos typical of nouvelle cuisine, stick to something like duck with a port sauce or lamb with cherries. No use shocking the palate into a coma. Halibut with a creamy lobster sauce is top-flight, as is breast of duckling with mushroom mousse and port sauce. A pricey spot as hotel restaurants always seem to be, the Palm Court, decorated in soft shades of russet and peach, sports à la carte prices in the $15 to $25 range for entrees and is open from 11:30 a.m. to 2 p.m. weekdays for lunch, from 6 to 10:30 p.m. daily for dinner.

More good news here for those in search of light dining: the Alexis has opened a lounge-dining room combination serving light meals like a Caesar salad, chili topped with sour cream and cheddar and accompanied by hot flour tortillas, a turkey avocado sandwich, or a spinach salad for $5 or less. It's called the Bookstore and is open from 11:30 a.m. to midnight daily, later on weekends.

Nouvelle cuisine is featured at **Fuller's,** in the Sheraton Hotel, Sixth and Pike (tel. 206/621-9000), so if you've fallen for those unusual color and flavor combinations, Fuller's should be on your list. Tucked away near the quiet lobby bar of the bustling Sheraton Hotel, Fuller's is a subdued spot named after a local art museum supporter and featuring the work of Northwest artists. Among the unusual flavors you'll find blended here with consummate skill are green peppercorns and cassis atop game, and apples united with duck. Despite our earlier ravings about low prices, this one is pricey: in the $16 to $23 range for entrees. Open from 5:30 to 10:30 p.m. daily except Sunday.

Maximilien-in-the-Market, 81 A Pike St. (tel. 206/682-7270), is a pretty little café right in the middle of Pike Place Market. Maximilien is the creation of prize-winning chef François Kissel, who uses whatever looks best in the market to create innovative selections from breakfast to lunch and dinner. You can even order fresh apple cider pressed from Washington apples. Hours are 7:30 a.m. to 10 p.m. Monday through Saturday, and 9:30 a.m. to 4 p.m. on Sunday for brunch, and prices are in the $12 to $17 range for dinner.

BEEF/CONTINENTAL: Sooner or later everybody who matters goes to **Henry's Off Broadway,** 1705 E. Olive Way (tel. 206/329-8063). They go there to (1) see, (2) be seen, or (3) both. Because you certainly qualify as beautiful people, you will want to hie on over to the elegance of glittering crystal and glowing chandeliers here too. Never know when you might make a good connection. While you're examining this glitterati atmosphere, you may indulge in some quite good food that stays well within the bounds of cookery familiar to and loved by American diners.

Henry's wins raves for seafood but also produces top-notch steaks, veal, and a specialty, rack of lamb Dijon. Accolades for the pastas too. An oyster bar in the lounge is a popular meeting place and features good nibblies to munch while you watch. Naturally you pay the piper for this kind of mingling: prices are in the $14 to $23 range for entrees. Open weekdays for lunch from 11:30 a.m. to 2 p.m. and for dinner daily from 5:30 to 10 p.m. Entertainment and espresso until postmidnight hours Tuesday through Saturday. Reservations wise.

The Other Place, 319 Union St. (tel. 206/623-7340), second creation of Seattle restaurant operator Robert Rosellini, is one of our favorites as much for its sophisticated, cosmopolitan atmosphere as for its very good food. Somewhere along the way Rosellini decided that if you can't buy what you want, raise it yourself. That's why the restaurant now has an interest in a game farm and a fishing operation. À la carte entrees are in the $11 to $16 range. A bilevel dining room decorated with tasteful restraint, the Other Place has a quite extensive list of offerings, with many selections made or served with fruit and nuts, two of the restaurant's favorite ingredients. Most meats are butchered right here "and deployed throughout the menu in a poetic way," an employee assured us. Poetry notwithstanding, freshness and quality are a sure thing. The Other Place is open from 11 a.m. to 3 p.m. weekdays for lunch, from 5 p.m. to midnight for dinner daily except Sunday.

Rosellini's first and lasting fame came from his creation of **Rosellini's Four-Ten,** Fourth and Wall (tel. 206/624-5464), an equally satisfying spot. As at the Other Place, you will find a chic crowd dining in a sophisticated, multiroom restaurant whose long suits are top-quality fresh ingredients and some unusual game offerings. You'll be pleased at either of these two fine restaurants. This one is open from 11 a.m. to midnight weekdays and from 5 p.m. to midnight on Saturday; closed Sunday. Prices are similar.

By now you know how we feel about the Sorrento Hotel, so it should come as no surprise that we are also enthusiastic about its restaurant, the **Hunt Club,** 900 Madison St. (tel. 206/622-6400). A paneled beauty glowing with polish and good taste, the room is a study in intimate low lighting and serene simplicity. At lunch salads reign supreme; at dinner a long list of fresh seafood takes over. Prices are in the $8 to $15.50 range. The restaurant is open from 7 to 11 a.m. for breakfast, 11 a.m. to 2 p.m. for lunch, and 5:30 to 10 p.m. for dinner daily; Sunday brunch begins at 7 a.m. and stuffs to 2:30 p.m.

Canlis, 2576 Aurora Ave. North (tel. 206/283-3313), is still as pricey as it has always been but that does not negate the value of the place. Many have come to rely on the delightful service provided by Japanese waitresses in pretty kimonos, its healthy steaks, and fresh, delicate cooked seafood. Nothing changes much at Canlis, and perhaps that's just as well because this legendary Seattle restaurant has a lock on the audience to which it appeals. That audience, by the way, is likely to turn up here in diamonds, certainly with jacket and tie. Dedicated to the old favorites that have snared diners for many a decade now, Canlis specializes in blue-ribbon steaks broiled over charcoal, frosty martinis, big lamb chops, swordfish or dolphin, onion rings, shoestring potatoes, and tableside-tossed Caesar salad with a minty twist. A family-owned operation, the Canlis began way back in 1947 on Waikiki, opening to serve the Seattle hungry in 1950 when the family lived above the restaurant in a penthouse that is now a chic dining room. A new addition to this quite chic dining spot is a piano bar where a French pianist plays and warbles for diners. You dine here overlooking Lake Union in a very attractive newly renovated setting of copper, natural stone, wood, and glass. The dining area was enlarged to take advantage of a magnificent view of Lake Union and city lights. The wine list, rated in the top 100 in the United States, is still growing. Prices are in the $16 to $30 range for entrees on an à la carte menu. Canlis is open from 5:30 to 11:30 p.m. daily except Sunday.

By now everybody knows about **Benihana of Tokyo,** IBM Plaza, Fifth and University (tel. 206/682-4686), a top-flight steak-and-seafood house in which nimble-fingered Japanese cooks cut, chop, cook, and flip giant peppermills around with Olympic agility. It doesn't hurt that Benihana begins with the best beef, the freshest shrimp and vegetables, cooking them right before your wondering eyes. Prices for a complete dinner are in the $10 to $20 range and the restaurant is open from 11:30 a.m. to 2 p.m. weekdays for lunch and 5:30 to 10 p.m. daily, an hour later on weekends. There is entertainment in the lounge on Saturday.

Lively crowds of all ages pack **Jake O'Shaughnessey's** history-filled dining and drinking hall at First Avenue North and Mercer Street (tel. 206/285-1897). Story has it, in fact, that a singing bartender was what put this place on the Seattle map. A big maze of a place, Jake's is a household word in Seattle, as much for its pubby, memorabilia-packed atmosphere as for its solid good cooking. Good times roll in the big bar at front where they have frothing Guinness stout on tap and lay claim to the world's largest collection of single-malt whiskies. In the dining room waitresses in long dresses and frilly aprons serve up the house specialty, prime rib roasted in rock salt, a terrific alder-roasted salmon, and a good Puget Sound stew of lobster, oysters, clams, cod, salmon, scallops, snapper, shrimp, and Dungeness crab. You'll pay $10 to $18 for dinner entrees, which are served here daily from 5 p.m. Reservations taken.

Jake's creators went on from their hugely successful beginnings to create two more restaurants in Seattle. Next came **F. X. McRory's Steak, Chop, and Oyster House,** 419 Occidental St. South (tel. 206/623-4800), another healthy-eater spot featuring slabs of pork chop, fresh fish, oyster stew, thick steaks, and the like. Here, as at Jake's, the fish comes from the restaurant's own fishing operation, so fresh is a given—no fish more than five days out of the water, they say.

McRory's is right down the way from the Kingdome and is packed during events there. No reservations, but you can while away the wait trying some of the bar's imported hops, which include, on tap, ale, porter, steam, stout, and goodness knows what others—a pubber's heaven. Prices are in the $10 to $17 range and the restaurant is open from 11:30 a.m. to 2 p.m. for lunch weekdays, from 5 to 11 p.m. for dinner, later on weekends.

Third star in the Jake-McRory firmament is **Leschi Lakecafe,** 102 Lakeside Ave. (tel. 206/328-2233), which does indeed occupy a lakeside spot next to a marina. From a window at front is dispensed a creditable fish-and-chips combo, while inside crowds feast on burgers, shakes, salads, and pub grub. Prices are in the same range as the other restaurants: figure $5 to $7 or so for lunch and $7 to $16 for dinner. Lots of suds on tap here too. Leschi is open daily from 11:30 a.m. to 2 p.m. for lunch, 5 to 10 p.m. for dinner.

In a hundred years we couldn't think of a better name than **McCormick's Fish House & Bar** for McCormick's Fish House & Bar, 722 Fourth Ave. (tel. 206/682-3900). McCormick's exactly matches the picture that name conjures up to us: merrily Irish, brass rails, wood tables, white-coated no-nonsense waiters, and food short on fancy touches, long on simple goodness. Seafood fans will find such an extensive menu here that even instant decision-makers will find such an extensive menu here that even instant decision-makers will be nonplussed. We've consumed sizable quantities of seafood but found plenty of surprises here: things like calico scallops, Manila clams, and sablefish. On the daily fresh fish list were what seemed an endless selection of sea treasures, simply but excellently prepared. Oyster fans should have a go at the oyster combination, which features those bivalves baked three ways, with shrimp cream sauce, with spinach and cheese, and with tomato, bacon, and cheese.

They pack 'em in at this bilevel dining room from early to late but always seem to find one more spot for a seafood-starved soul. McCormick's is a casual spot frequented for its lively bar as well as for its amazing selection of seafood. Prices are quite reasonable and a marvelously efficient waiter named Bill can be as adorable as a warm puppy. McCormick's serves lunch from 11 a.m. to 3 p.m. weekdays and dinner from 5 to 11 p.m. daily. Prices are in the $12 to $17 range.

If you'd like to dine way up in the air, the Space Needle is the answer. At the **Emerald Suite Restaurant** you'll find entree prices in the $18 to $28 range at dinner, $10 to $15 for lunch. On the menu here are a strip steak with Pernod sauce and gold raisins, as well as pheasant roasted with bacon and cognac atop a bed of colored cabbage.

Part of the revolving platform occupied by the Emerald Suite is allocated to a slightly less expensive restaurant, simply called the **Space Needle restaurant,** where lunch is in the $8 to $12 range; dinner, about $15 to $25. On this menu are salmon prepared three different ways and fried tiger prawns rémoulade, among others.

You ride to the top of Seattle's Space Needle free when you dine at one of its two revolving restaurants. Both restaurants can be reached by telephoning 206/ 443-2100. Lunch is served from 11 a.m. to 3 p.m. daily. Dinner hours Sunday through Thursday are 5 to 11 p.m., to midnight on Friday and Saturday. Sunday brunch is on from 8 a.m. to 3 p.m. You'll find the Space Needle in Seattle Center at Fifth and First Avenues North.

VIEWS . . . AND MORE: An enthusiastic English authority on Northwest crafts enthusiastically turned us toward **Cutters Bay House,** 2001 Western Ave., in the Market Place (tel. 206/448-4884), a recommendation for which we are grateful. Cutter's Bay thinks pink in its décor and thinks fresh and creative in its menu, which offers reproductions of some of the favored dishes from restaurants across the nation and hand-shaken margaritas! Seafoods and pastas are the favorite choices here as the restaurant works really hard on those. That is not to say, however, that anything gets short shrift.

Cutter's is open from 11 a.m. to 2 a.m. daily, later when the crowd encourages. Midnight munchers and late lunchers will find most any offering served any time of day. You'll pay $7 to $13 for main selections here, resulting in an evening made even more pleasant at the bottom line.

Daniel's, 200 Lake Washington Blvd. (tel. 206/329-4191), is a very pretty place with a great view of sailboats skimming across Lake Washington. A big copper chandelier dangles from a beamed ceiling, and the tables are onyx! Specialties of the house are aged steaks, lamb chops, milk-fed veal, and some good seafood selections. Top it off with strawberries dipped in chocolate and filled with Grand Marnier. Prices are in the $12 to $20 range for à la carte dinner entrees, and the restaurant is open from 5 p.m. to midnight daily.

Another room with a view is **Benjamin's,** 10655 N.E. 4th St., in the Seattle Trust Building, Bellevue (tel. 206/454-8255), which opened more than ten years ago in an aerie atop one of the tallest buildings in that hilly Bellevue section overlooking Seattle. Mount Rainier floats in the distance as you dine in a chic contemporary décor with lots of mirrors, tile, and tropical cane furnishings.

You'll have more than 50 entrees to choose from here, including an interesting chicken sesame salad, pastas and Italian veal preparations, steaks, and stir-fried vegetables with prawns. Benjamin's is open for lunch Monday through Friday from 11:30 a.m. to 4 p.m., to 3 p.m. on Saturday. Dinner entrees are served nightly from 4:30 p.m. to midnight for prices in the $9 to $17 range. Try Sunday brunch from 10 a.m. to 2 p.m.

The **Market Café,** in the Westin Hotel, 1900 Fifth Ave. (tel. 206/728-1000), has more than 50 kinds of American and imported beer, wines, salads, and sandwiches. A variety of dinner specials include salmon filet, steamed mussels, and steaks from $11.50 to $16. Parking is free when you dine here from 5 to 9 p.m. daily, and there's an 80-item Sunday brunch from 11 a.m. to 2 p.m.

You never know when a hunger pang is going to strike, so it's good to know that **Thirteen Coins,** 125 Boren Ave. (tel. 206/682-2513), is open around the clock every day. Chefs flip, flame, and sauté right in front of you at this spot, which has no fewer than 128 items on its menu. Everything from omelets to salads to steaks and salmon here, for prices in the $10 to $15 range for entrees. Thirteen Coins, which also has a restaurant with piano lounge at 18000 Pacific Hwy. South (tel. 206/243-9500), is named after a Latin American good luck wish.

Red Robin Burger and Spirits Emporium, Fourth Avenue at Spring Street (tel. 206/447-1909), has half a dozen restaurants in Seattle. One convenient— and pretty—one is in the Pacific Plaza Hotel. Brass, etched glass, burgundy décor, and a Victorian look combine to produce an attractive and intimate dining spot at which you can dine on steaks, salads, chicken, and seafood, as well as 28 different kinds of burgers. Prices in the $5 to $8 range are attractive too. The Emporium is open from 11 a.m. to midnight daily. Great Victoriana bar here too.

In **Pike Place Market** you'll find lots of restaurants, small and large, expensive and cheap. We've already mentioned a few of the more elaborate restaurants, so here are a few other good spots to feed while grazing among the goodies: **LoPriore's Pasta Bar,** in Post Alley (tel. 206/442-9400), is a tiny walkup spot with the irresistible scent of rich tomato sauce wafting about, where you have a choice of four toppings and several kinds of pastas plus good salads for prices that won't top $5; **Au Gavroche** (tel. 206/624-2222), a sinful pastry shop; **Rasa Malaysia** (tel. 206/624-8388), which features spicy Malaysian curries and other exotic flavors for prices in the $5 to $7 range or less and has a second restaurant in the university district at 4300 University Way (tel. 206/545-7878).

A former owner of a successful restaurant called Simon's in the fall of 1988 opened a whole bevy of restaurants in the **1021 Third Avenue Building** at the same address. Among the options are the **Brooklyn Café, Estelle's Delicatessen, Mel's Market,** and **Joelle's Espresso Bar,** each pretty self-explanatory, we think. We haven't checked all these out yet, but if you're in the area—and it's a quite central area—you might stop by and see what's happening there.

6. AFTER DARK

Here, as everywhere, today's hysterically popular nightspot is tomorrow's yawner. We've tried to select a few places that have long-standing popularity in the hopes that we won't hear the place is defunct. To discover the trendier-than-thou spot today, seek out a copy of *Seattle Guide* or check the pages of the *Seattle Post-Intelligencer's* entertainment section.

McCormick's, 722 Fourth Ave. (tel. 206/682-3900), as we mentioned earlier, is a meeting spot for the up-and-coming pinstripe-suit set, youthful but meaningful, if you know what we mean. Cocktail hour is best here.

When they've reached what the McCormick's crowd is reaching for, they go to the **Garden Court** at the Four Seasons Olympic Hotel, 411 University St. (tel. 206/621-1700), to view their competition.

In the Westin Hotel, 1900 Fifth Ave. (tel. 206/624-7400), you'll find many an elbow bending along the edges of the 65-foot marble bar at **Fitzgerald's On Fifth.** Jazz buffs make their way to **Jazz Alley,** in the United Air Lines Building, Sixth and Leonore (tel. 206/441-9729), where someone's always jammin'.

If you could use a good laugh, giggle on over to the **Comedy Underground,** 222 S. Main St. (tel. 206/628-0303), where tomorrow's Robin Williams and Bob Hope are struggling to keep the yucks going. Now in its seventh year, the club offers stand-up comedy seven nights a week. Monday is "open mike" night when anyone who's got a joke is welcome to tell it. You'll find the club downstairs at Swannies Restaurant near the Kingdome. Shows are at 9 p.m. every night, with an extra show at 11 p.m. on Friday and Saturday. Give them a call to find out who's playing. Cover is $3 to $7.

The **Edgewater Inn,** Pier 67 (tel. 206/624-7000), has entertainment and dancing with a panoramic view Wednesday through Saturday.

7. WHAT TO SEE AND DO

SEATTLE SIGHTS: If there's one place every single person who comes to Seattle goes, it's the city's landmark and love, the **Space Needle.** Rising 605 feet—61 stories—into the air, the Space Needle anchored the 1962 World's Fair and can be seen from wherever you are in Seattle. What many people don't realize until they visit here is that the futuristic Needle is just the hub of the vast complex of buildings known as **Seattle Center,** which includes the Seattle Art Museum Pavilion, the Pacific Science Center, an amusement park, the Northwest Crafts Center, and 75 acres of gardens. If you bring the youngsters here in the morning, don't plan to get them out again until well into dinner hour.

Rides up to the top of the world on the Needle (tel. 206/443-2100) take 43 seconds at ten miles an hour and cost $3.75 for adults, $2 for children 6 to 12, free for children under 5. An observation deck one-third of a mile up in the sky is open from 9 a.m. to midnight daily. Once up there you can dine at the Space Needle Restaurant and Lounge. See "Where to Dine" for more information on these spots.

Last year a million people discovered the **Pacific Science Center,** 200 Second Ave. North (tel. 206/443-2001, or 443-2860 for IMAX information). They experimented on 50 computers, discovered the stars in the planetarium, and compared their own talents with such greats as inventor Buckminster Fuller, scientist Jonas Salk, and anthropologist Margaret Mead. They wandered through six buildings and played at 200 hands-on exhibits and displays designed to illustrate how the world works.

When the brain tired, they headed for one of two theaters to indulge in the sensual enjoyment of a laser light show or the huge world of IMAX, where movies are bigger than life—shown on a screen as tall as a three-story building.

Exhibits are open every day except Thanksgiving, Christmas Eve, and Christmas Day. Admission is $5 for adults, $4 for juniors ages 6 to 17, and $1 for preschoolers ages 3 to 5.

All of this—plus an internationally themed collection of walk-up food purveyors called Center House, and a branch of the Seattle Art Museum—is in buildings that housed the 1962 World's Fair, an event that put the final legitimatizing touch on Seattle's expansion into a major metropolis. Unlike some World's Fair cities, this one had the good sense to capitalize on all those leftover buildings.

Seattle Center is bounded by Fifth and First Avenues North, Mercer Street, and Denny Way. It is open from 11 a.m. and closes at various hours depending on what's going on at this busy park. Call 206/625-4234 to find out what's happening when you're here.

Most interesting way to get here, by the way, is on the monorail, which zips nonstop from Fourth Avenue and Pine Street to Seattle Center and back again, covering the 1.2-mile stretch in 90 seconds! Fare for the monorail, which is open from 10 a.m. to midnight Sunday through Thursday, to 12:30 a.m. on Friday and Saturday, is 60¢.

Seattle operates a free bus (see "Getting Around") that runs from about four

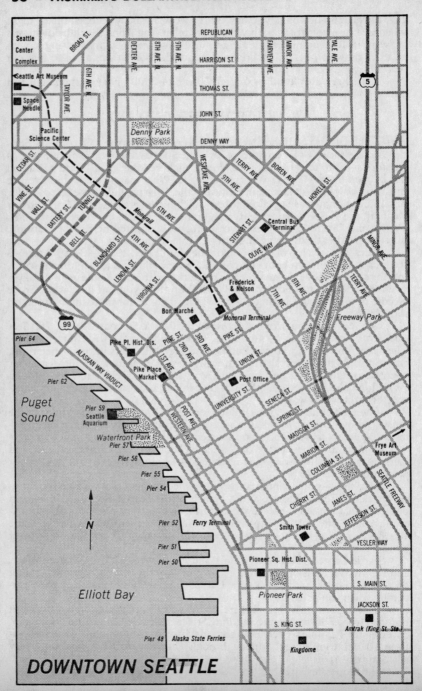

DOWNTOWN SEATTLE

blocks south of Seattle Center along Alaskan Way, with stops at the Seattle Aquarium, near Pike Place Market, and waterfront sites, to Pioneer Square. Pike Place Public Market is as much something to see as it is a shopping spot.

One of the city's prides is **Freeway Park.** A most innovative use of urban space, this collection of greenery and waterfalls is built right over the top of the state's major north-south artery, the I-5 expressway. So skillfully is this unusual green space put together that you really can't tell you're sitting atop an expressway. Much-photographed Freeway Park is between Sixth and Boren and Hubble and Spring Streets.

Combine an open fire with a fat salmon and you've got a good dinner and an entertaining evening at Seattle's **Tillicum Village.** Tillicum Indians, master woodcarvers and basket weavers, have lived on the north coast for many many generations and now exhibit the highlights of their culture at their village on Blake Island, birthplace of Chief Seattle.

Trips to the village begin with a cruise across Puget Sound and a narrated tour of Seattle's harbor. Once there a sumptuous dinner begins with savory steamed clams, moves on to a tossed salad and relishes. Dinner culminates in salmon right out of the sound, split, held steady by a backing of sticks attached to a pole, and then baked over an open alder fire—all in traditional Indian style. After dinner, villagers perform Indian dances in full costume. All of this takes place in an Indian longhouse, a replica of ancient dwellings of Northwest Coast Indians. On display are numerous craft and cultural items and pieces by a resident woodcarver.

Boat-trip departure times for Tillicum Village at Blake Island Marine State Park vary according to season. During the summer months departures are usually Monday through Saturday at 11:30 a.m., 4:30 p.m., and 6:30 p.m.; Sunday departures are at 1:30 and 4:30 p.m. It's a good idea to contact **Tillicum Village & Tours, Inc.,** 2366 Eastlake Ave. East (tel. 206/329-5700), for the latest information and departure times.

The cost for the four- to five-hour trip, dinner, and show is $29 for adults, $26 for senior citizens, $5 to $12 for children under 12, and free for toddlers ages 3 and 4. Tours leave from Pier 56 at the foot of Seneca Street.

For an eagle's-eye view of Seattle, book a trip on Lake Union Air, 1100 Westlake Ave. North (tel. 206/284-0300), which leaves from Lake Union daily on 30-minute flights. Fare is $25 per person.

Seattle lays claim to the world's first **floating concrete bridges.** You won't have any floating sensation as you roll over these floaters, which are known as the Lake Washington Floating Bridge (I-90), connecting Seattle with Mercer Island, and Evergreen Point Bridge (Wash. 520), connecting Seattle with Bellevue and Kirkland.

The Japanese art of teatime is an age-old ritual filled with secret meaning. To find out just what this tea thing is all about, stop by the **Japanese Garden,** at the south end of the University of Washington's Washington Park Arboretum just north of East Madison at 1502 Lake Washington Blvd. East (tel. 206/684-4725 or 644-4075). You will see students of the tea ceremony learn which gestures are wise and which are most decidedly not. Admission is $1.50 for adults, 75¢ for children 6 to 18. The gardens are open daily from 11 a.m. to 6 p.m. June through August, from 10 a.m. to 4 p.m. other months (closed December through March).

You'll always find a crowd at the **Seattle Aquarium,** Pier 59, Waterfront Park down the Pike Street Hillclimb (tel. 206/386-4300 or 625-4357). Among the interesting things you'll see here are a touch-tank where you can handle sea stars and sea anemones, an underwater dome in which you can watch salmon going on about their business, an otter pool with some adorable otter pups, and a coral reef and tidal pool artificially controlled so you can see how tidal-basin creatures live as their tidal home appears and disappears.

Admission is $3.25 for adults, $1.50 for youngsters 13 to 18, and 75¢ for younger children; those under 6 are free. Hours are 10 a.m. to 7 p.m. daily from May 30 to early September. In other months the aquarium closes at 5 p.m. daily.

The **Omnidome Theater,** Pier 59 next to the Seattle Aquarium (tel. 206/ 622-1868), is another huge-screen theater. Sit down in comfortable lean-back seats and watch the current offering of *The Eruption of Mount St. Helens,* among others. You'll soar by helicopter into the mountain's crater, see closeups of the actual eruption in progress and the devastating results.

Omnidome operates daily from 10 a.m. to midnight May to October, closing at 6 p.m. in other months. Ticket prices are $5 for adults, $4 for seniors and youths, and $3 for children 6 to 12. Combination tickets with Seattle Aquarium are available at discount prices.

William Boeing of Boeing Aircraft fame got his start in Seattle in a red barn that grew to become the **Museum of Flight,** Boeing Field, 9404 E. Marginal Way South (tel. 206/764-5707). Through pictures, 34 planes, and reproductions of early aircraft, you'll learn a little about early construction techniques. It's open from 10 a.m. to 5 p.m. daily (to 9 p.m. on Thursday and Friday), and admission is $4 for adults, $3 for children 12 or older, $2 for those 6 to 12.

Boeing also conducts free tours of the **Boeing Assembly Plant,** located next door to the Snohomish County Airport about 30 miles north of Seattle. A 5,500-square-foot facility, the $600,000 Visitor Tour Center features a 100-seat theater, souvenir shop, viewing area for handicapped customers, and a glassed-in lobby with a terrific view out over the aircraft assembly line. This is the world's largest building by volume, with about 300 million cubic feet of space. Just the section where they rivet wing panels on 747s is bigger than a football field. Tours are on a first-come, first-served basis at 9 a.m. and 12:30 p.m. Monday through Friday, with two extra tours in summer. Great as it would be for the kids, children under 12 are not admitted. For information, contact Boeing Aircraft, P.O. Box 3707, Seattle, WA 98124 (tel. 206/237-1710).

Seattle's top-flight zoo, called **Woodland Park Zoological Gardens,** has done away with cages and housed the animals in natural surroundings. Giraffes lope about an "African Savanna" and the nation's best gorilla exhibit occupies a tree-lined meadow. Admission prices are $3 for adults and $1.50 for children 6 to 17. The park is located at 5500 Phinney Ave. North, between Phinney and Aurora Avenues and between 50th and 59th Streets North (tel. 206/789-7919). The zoo is open from 8:30 a.m. to dusk April to October, closing earlier in other months. The story of Seattle's big Oriental and Asian community is told at **Wing Luke Asian Museum,** 417 Seventh Ave. South (tel. 206/623-5124). Through Asian-American history and culture and Asian folk art, the museum works to bridge the gap between the Asian and non-Asian communities. Exhibits detail Asian immigration to the Pacific Northwest, the work of Asian-American artists, and Asian folk art.

The museum is open Tuesday through Friday from 11 a.m. to 4:30 p.m., on Saturday and Sunday from noon to 4:30 p.m. Admission is $1.50 for adults, 50¢ for children.

Although still known as Chinatown, Seattle's Oriental community now is mostly Japanese. Here tiny shops sell preserved quail eggs, exotic lychee nuts, dried ginseng, woks, Hapi coats, sandals, kimonos, chopsticks, and a boggling array of unusual produce. Today the city likes to call the region, bounded roughly by Fifth and Eighth Avenues South between South Washington and South Weller, the **International District.**

Begin your exploration with a visit to **Nippon Kan Theater,** 628 S. Washington St. (tel. 206/624-6342), a restored building listed on the National Register of Historic Places, where you can get a multimedia introduction to the district. Tickets are $2 and reservations are required. You can get a map outlining a walking tour of the region here too.

The **Hiram M. Chittenden Locks** and the **Lake Washington Ship Canal Visitor Center,** both located at 3015 54th St. (tel. 206/783-7059), make a great place for a day's outing. Watch fish leap up ladders past viewing windows as they head back to spawning streams. These locks were built to link Puget Sound with Lakes Union and Washington and, in the process, to make shallow bay waters navigable. Summer hours for the visitor center are 11 a.m. to 8 p.m. daily; in winter the center is open Thursday through Monday from 11 a.m. to 5 p.m. The grounds, however, are open daily throughout the year from 7 a.m. to 9 p.m. Admission to both facilities is free.

Probably the smallest national park—and certainly the only one indoors—is the **Klondike Gold Rush National Historic Park,** 117 S. Main St. (tel. 206/442-7220). Part of the park includes historic structures from Skagway and on the Chilkoot and White Pass Trails. Rangers show a series of films on the discovery of gold in the Canadian Klondike strike of 1897–1898. More than 100,000 miners streamed through Seattle on their way to the gold mines. Park hours are 9 a.m. to 5:30 p.m. daily, year round. Free admission.

ODDITIES: Totem poles have fascinated mankind for generations, from the Indians who carved them to modern visitors who gaze up at them in awe. These ancient poles were not, as is often thought, a focus of worship but actually a kind of tribal storybook, name plate, welcome mat, tombstone, billboard, and perhaps even status symbol!

Figures on the poles are symbols, representing characters and events in tribal folklore or history. Most common of the symbols is Raven, a tricky fellow, who spent his time creating the earth and its people and bamboozling the forces of nature.

You'll see one of Seattle's most-visited totem poles looming over **Pioneer Square.** This 50-foot hemlock pole, brought here from a Tlingit village during the Yukon Gold Rush and put up in 1899, is a most unusual totem: it honors a woman called Chief-of-All-Women at a time when most tribal chieftains were men! The totem you see today is a replica of the original.

Researchers think totem poles originated as support pillars inside and later were constructed outside the house to tell visitors the name and history of those who lived there.

A totem at **Pacific Science Center's Sea Monster House** features a carved whale with Raven on its tail. Grizzly bears on totems inside the house indicate a powerful family. Other totems are at the **Thomas Burke Memorial Museum** on the University of Washington campus and at **Daybreak Star Arts Center** in Discovery Park at 36th Street West and West Government Way.

Totems are read from the top down, but the message was not always what one wanted to read: one of the four totems at the Burke Memorial Museum at the University of Washington is a "ridicule pole," put up to tell the world who owed you a debt. This one reminds a debtor that he has failed to pay a marriage debt. That not-very-subtle reminder seems to have worked: the pole was found to have been unearthed, turned around, and adorned with three copper pieces indicating the debtor had paid up!

The **Kingdome** is a sports arena of gargantuan proportions. Tours of this 250-foot-tall arena with a 660-foot-diameter dome take place Monday through

Saturday at 11 a.m., 1 p.m., and 3 p.m. from mid-June to mid-September. Admission is $2.50 for adults, $1.25 for children. You'll find the stadium at 201 S. King St. (tel. 206/340-2128 for information or to verify tour availability).

One of the weirder "sights" in Seattle is a spot called **Ye Olde Curiosity Shop,** a kind of Ripley's believe-it-or-not collection of oddities from shrunken heads to the Lord's Prayer engraved on a grain of rice. Where else could you find a 67-pound snail, a ten-foot rattlesnake skin, and fleas in dresses? Honest. This is a shopper's paradise with everything from Oriental cloisonné to ivory carvings, Indian and Eskimo art, Mexican onyx, you name it.

Ye Olde Curiosity Shop is at 601 Pier 54, Alaskan Way, Space 100 (tel. 206/682-5844), and admission is free. Originally opened in 1899 by lifelong curiosity seeker Joe Standley, this weird and wonderful shop is now operated by the fourth generation of his family. Open 9 a.m. to 6 p.m. daily.

TOURS: When fire destroyed much of Seattle in 1889, the city just cleaned up the rubble and built on top of it—10 to 35 feet on top of it, in fact. That's why Bill Speidel, who calls himself a "historical gossip columnist," operates **Bill Speidel's Underground Tours.**

Tour-goers meet in a restored 1892 saloon called Doc Maynard's Public House, in the Pioneer Building at First Avenue and James Street. After a little orientation, you go underground to explore brick buildings and meet some of the colorful characters who built this city. In recent years the attraction has revamped its walkways, improved lighting, added old, enlarged photographs of Seattle to the underground walkways so you can see things as they were while you walk. Rest easy, history buffs, they've kept the cobwebs. Tours leave hourly from 9 a.m. to 6 p.m. June to September, with a reduced schedule in winter. Tickets are $4 for adults, $2 for children 6 to 12, and reservations are necessary. Bill Speidel's Tours operates at 610 First Ave. (tel. 206/682-1511, or 682-1164 for information, 682-4646 for reservations; phones are open 24 hours).

You can tour the district on your own above ground by heading down to First Avenue and James Street and just wandering around from there. A totem pole marks the center of the district and provides an unmistakable landmark.

If you want to do it yourself, you can buy a book called *The Compleat Browsers Guide to Pioneer Square* at Elliott Bay Book Co., First Avenue and Main Street (tel. 206/624-6600).

Rainier Brewing Co., 3100 Airport Way South (tel. 206/621-2600), a historic brewery, offers free tours of its facility from 1 to 6 p.m. weekdays.

One of the loveliest ways to spend a sunny summer day is out on Puget Sound aboard a harbor tour put together by **Seattle Harbor Tours,** Pier 55, Suite 201 (tel. 206/623-1445). Tours begin in April on weekends only at 12:15, 1:45, and 3:15 p.m. In May the same hourly schedule prevails every day. June through September the daily schedule is 11 a.m. and 12:15, 1:45, 3:15, and 4:30 p.m.; in October the May schedule again prevails. Tickets to your day on Puget Sound are $6.50 for adults and $3 for children aged 5 to 11; students aged 12 to 18 pay $6.

Another harbor tour operating in the sparkling waters around Seattle is **Major Marine Tours,** 6049 Seaview Ave. NW (tel. 206/783-8873). Major Marine operates two different kinds of water trips, including a daily fishing trip departing year round from Pier 54 with a guaranteed eatable fish catch or you get a free pass to try again. Price for those trips is $39 per person. Major Marine also operates hourly tours from Pier 54 from June through September aboard a 100-foot Coast Guard vessel. A barbecued-chicken picnic lunch is included in the price of $6.50 for adults, $5.50 for senior citizens, and $4 for children under 12.

Gray Line Tours 720 S. Forest St. (tel. 206/624-5813, or toll free 800/426-7532), operates much of what rolls on big bus wheels in Seattle, everything from airport-town transportation to a fascinating variety of tours. A subsidiary of Holland American Cruise Line, whose ships tour Alaska in summer, Gray Line has tours around the city and to such garden spots as the San Juan Islands, the Tillicum Village Salmon Bake, Victoria, Mount Rainier National Park, Vancouver, and Whistler Resort, a favorite British Columbia ski and summer resort. Gray Line has discovery tours that visit floating bridges, the tranquil beauty of the University of Washington campus, and salmon fish ladders, among other stops, plus a boat trip across Puget Sound at $29 for adults, $14.50 for children under 12. Gray Line also operates a trolley that whizzes and clangs around the sights of downtown Seattle for $2 per person.

Tillicum Village and Tours, 2366 Eastlake Ave. East (tel. 206/329-5700), operates Tillicum Village, believed to have been the birthplace of Chief Seattle, at Blake Island State Park, eight miles from downtown Seattle. On display here are an Indian communal longhouse, totem poles, and a wide variety of things Indian. A resident woodworker demonstrates how he creates masterpieces of carving art from cedar and alder trees. Best known of the activities at the village is a four-hour harbor tour that takes you to the village, where you're treated to a salmon bake. Hours vary widely by season, with trips taking place on a regular, although changing, schedule from May to mid-October and irregularly, depending on the weather, in other months. Price of the tour, which includes a stunning display of costumed Indian dancing, is $29 for adults, $26 for senior citizens, $5 to $13 for children depending on age; under 3, free. June through August there's a Hiker's Special tour in daylight hours that gives walkers an additional couple of hours to explore Blake Island, which is also a state park.

To learn the history of the 80-year-old **Pike Place Market,** turn up at 10 a.m. on Saturday in summer at the Pike Place Market Management Office of Preservation and Development (tel. 206/682-7453), at the south end of the market. You'll find the office by going to Don and Joe's Meat Market and down one flight of stairs. Knowledgeable folks will take you on a walking tour of the market for a donation of $3.50 for adults, $2.50 for children. Call ahead.

For closeup views of the spectacular Northwest, talk to Harry Ellis, owner/operator of **Adventure Outdoors.** Small groups of 12 or fewer embark on van tours of the mountains and beaches designed to introduce you to "the real Northwest." Call him at 206/842-3189 or write 5354 Ruby Pl. NE, Bainbridge Island, WA 98110. Ellis's trips have become quite popular and he's added trips to Alaska which have gotten widespread coverage. Ellis now uses a deluxe custom van with captain's chairs, stereo, air conditioning, blinds, and curtains on day trips that include a stop in an alpine meadow or on the beach for a salmon barbecue. Ellis knows and loves the Northwest, and his enthusiasm for his chosen land is infectious. Prices vary widely so it's best to give him a call and outline what you're interested in seeing.

ARTISTIC AND CULTURAL PURSUITS: From July to September the city sponsors a **free summer concert** series at various locations and often at noon, so lunching workers can enjoy too. Folks at the Seattle–King County Convention and Visitors Bureau can tell you what's playing when.

The **Seattle Art Museum** has two branches in town, the major facility at Volunteer Park, 15th Street East and East Prospect Street (tel. 206/447-4710), and one at Seattle Center (tel. 206/447-4796). Both have lauded collections of Asian art and African works as well as the work of artists from the Pacific Northwest.

At the University of Washington campus the **Henry Gallery** (tel. 206/543-2280) features artists of the region and major shows.

Among the top purveyors of Eskimo and Indian art and craft are **The Lega-**

cy, 1003 First Ave. (tel. 206/624-6350), and **Stonington Gallery,** First Avenue and Leonora Street (tel. 206/621-1108) in Pioneer Square.

Film fans can revel in the city's **May film festival.** Seattle Center is home to the **Pacific Northwest Ballet** (tel. 206/447-4655), the **Seattle Symphony** (tel. 206/447-4736), and **Seattle Opera** (tel. 206/447-4711), the first American company to present a season series in English!

Touring dance companies and other dance programs are presented by **Discover Dance,** performed at various locations in Seattle (tel. 206/282-1880), and **On the Boards** (tel. 206/325-7901), which goes on the boards at Washington Hall Performance Gallery, University of Washington.

Tune in on the tinkling sounds of a chamber orchestra at the **Seattle Chamber Music Festival,** a three-week midsummer program at Lakeside School, 14050 1st St. NE (tel. 206/282-1807).

Thanks to Seattle residents' all-consuming interest in theater, Seattle does not lack. **A Contemporary Theater (ACT),** First Avenue West and Roy Street West (tel. 206/285-5110), performs year round. May through November is the main season of six plays with an annual presentation of Dickens's *A Christmas Carol* in December, a season of three plays for young audiences from February through April, and special musical offerings at various times of the year.

The **Seattle Repertory Theater,** called The Rep, recently moved into the $9.4-million Bagley Wright Theater in Seattle Center (tel. 206/447-4764). It features both American and English plays.

MusicComedy Northwest produces Broadway's best at Seattle Center Playhouse (tel. 206/325-3633); **Intiman** theater, in the Seattle Center (tel. 206/587-5766), features classic American and European plays. The **Fifth Avenue Theater,** 1308 Fifth Ave. (tel. 206/625-1900), offers touring Broadway shows in an Oriental movie hall modeled after Peking's Imperial Palace.

SPECIAL EVENTS: Among the biggest of Seattle's celebrations is **Seafair,** a multitude of events spread over three weeks in July and August. Many of the city's ethnic groups take part in the festivities with displays of native costume and dance. Best loved of those is the Bon Odori, a street parade of Japanese dancers.

In February, Pioneer Square celebrates the **Pioneer Square Gallery Walk,** which focuses on the district's art galleries.

A festival with the chuckly name of **Bumbershoot** occurs on the Labor Day holiday and comes complete with art festival, rock concerts, and book sales. It got that name, so Seattle dwellers say, because it always rains on Labor Day.

In May, Memorial Day specifically, some interesting crafts and folklore are revealed at the **Northwest Folklife Festival.**

Jazz musicians jam in August when the city welcomes the **Kool Jazz Festival** that draws the top names in jazz. There's even a jazz hotline telling what's jamming where—call 206/624-JASS.

8. SPORTS

Sports fans should head straight for the **Kingdome,** 201 S. King St. (tel. 206/628-3311), where most of the city's sporting events take place.

PROFESSIONAL SPORTS: If it's baseball you're seeking, the **Seattle Mariners** play April through November. For information on playing dates and times, check the *Seattle Post-Intelligencer* or *Seattle Times,* or call the team at 206/628-3555. Tickets are $5 to $10.

The Kingdome is also the spot to see the **Seattle Seahawks** (tel. 206/827-9766), the city's pro football team. Tickets are hard to get and vary widely in price.

The basketball team is called the **Seattle Supersonics** (tel. 206/281-5850), and plays at the Kingdome.

Shuttle and direct bus service are available to Kingdome sporting events. Fare is 60¢. For schedules, call 206/447-4800.

HORSE RACING: If parimutuel sports are more your speed, you can find plenty of speed at **Longacres Racecourse** (tel. 206/226-3131) in Renton, a small town about 11 miles south of Seattle. Longacres is an elegantly pretty thoroughbred race course with a dozen restaurants ranging from tables on a covered terrace at the final turn to a three-story Paddock Club with reserved table seating (tel. 206/251-8717).

On 200 acres of ground here you'll find a historic clubhouse lounge, an interesting equine art collection, and free Saturday-morning workouts and free jockey-led tours of the stables on some weekends (tel. 206/226-3131). Admission to the track is $3 for grandstand seats, $5 for the clubhouse, and the season runs from April through October with racing Wednesday through Saturday.

Direct bus service is available to the track from various points in Seattle (tel. 206/447-4800). If you're driving, take I-5 south to exit 157, 156, or 154A. Longacres is at 1621 S. W. 16th St., and spreads between West Valley Road South on the East and West Valley Freeway South on the west, between I-405 on the north and S. W. 27th Street on the south. Open from 11 a.m., with post time at 12:45 p.m. weekends and holidays, 2:45 p.m. weekdays in April, an hour later May through mid-August, varying after that.

A SCENIC TRAIL: Walkers, joggers, and bicyclists in search of a scenic playground take to the 12.5-mile **Burke-Gilman Trail**, which follows a former railroad spur line. The trail begins at Gas Works Park at North Northlake Way and Meridian Street North and ends at Kenmore Logboom Park in Kenmore. A map of the trail is available from the Seattle Department of Parks and Recreation, 100 Dexter Ave. North (tel. 206/625-4671).

BICYCLING: You can rent bicycles from **Gregg's Greenlake Cycle**, 7007 Woodlawn NE (tel. 206/523-1822), for $3 to $4 an hour. All kinds of bikes from tandem tourers to mountain bicycles are available at daily rates ranging from $7 to $20.

HIKING: To rent hiking equipment—tents, boots, everything—go to **Rei Co-op**, 1525 11th St. (tel. 206/323-8333). Prices vary widely depending on how much and what kind of equipment you need.

SKATING: Gregg's rents roller skates too, at $2 an hour, for rolling adventures along Green Lake. Ice skating? **Highland Ice Arena**, 18005 Aurora Ave. (tel. 206/546-2431).

PUBLIC FACILITIES: The Seattle Department of Parks and Recreation, 100 Dexter Ave., can also help you find swimming pools, indoor and out, tennis courts, and golf courses near you, and will be happy to outline all the city's many recreational facilities. Among the **indoor swimming pools** are Ballard Pool, 15th Avenue NW and N.W. 67th Street (tel. 206/783-7176), and Evans Pool, Latona Avenue NE and East Green Lake Drive North (tel. 206/625-4258).

Among the many **tennis courts** in the city are those at Broadway Playfield,

11th Avenue East and East Pine Street, and Discovery Park, 36th Avenue West and West Government Way.

Public golf courses in the Seattle area include the 27-hole Jackson Park municipal golf course, 1000 N.E. 135th St. (tel. 206/363-4747); the 27-hole Jefferson Park municipal golf course, 4101 Beacon Ave. (tel. 206/762-4513); the 18-hole Tyee Valley Golf Club, 2401 S. 192nd St. (tel. 206/878-3540); and the 18-hole West Seattle Golf Course, 4470 35th Ave. SW (tel. 206/932-9792). All are open daily and greens fees are in the $9 to $15 range.

WATER SPORTS: You can catch some monsters in these salt waters. If you'd like to try your luck, **Major Fishing Charters** (tel. 206/783-8873) will take you out onto the seas. They're docked at Ray's Boathouse, Seaview Avenue NW and N.W. Market Street, just north of the Ballard Locks on Lake Union. Price is $39, including tackle, if needed, and trips are six hours long, beginning at 6 a.m. and 2 p.m.

To some of us, a trip to the **beach** is sport. If you're one of those, try the silica at Discovery Park, where you can romp on two miles of Puget Sound beaches. Discovery Park is at West Government Way and 36th Street West. Other beaches are found around Lake Washington in Madrona, Matthews, Pritchard, Seward, Madison, and Mount Baker Parks.

With its many bays, inlets, locks, and lakes, Seattle is a great place to rent a boat and go **sailing** into the sunset. Boats of all sizes are available at Green Lake Boat Rentals, 7201 E. Greenlake Dr. North (tel. 206/527-0171), for fishing boats, canoes, and rowboats; Ledger Marine Charters, 101 Nickerson St. (tel. 206/283-6160), for sailboats; Sailboat Charters and Rentals Unlimited, 1046 Westlake Ave. North (tel. 206/283-4664); and Ray's Boat House, 6049 Seaview Ave. NW (tel. 206/783-9779). Prices vary according to boat size.

SKIING: If you're here in winter, a scenic hour's drive will get you to three ski areas at Snoqualmie Pass; if you have a weekend you might want to try runs farther away at Skykomish or Mount Baker.

At **Snoqualmie Pass,** ski runs at Alpental, Ski Acres, and Snoqualmie Summit offer interchangeable tickets so you can ski them all from November through April for a daily lift price of $19. A shuttle-bus service connects all three on weekends and is free to ticket holders. Lifts are open from 9 a.m. to 10:30 p.m. daily, with some holiday closings. Alpental and Snoqualimie Summit are closed Monday; Ski Acres is closed Tuesday.

It's a 45-mile drive east on I-90 to Snoqualmie Pass ski areas so it's a good idea to check on slope conditions and special events before making the trek out there: call 206/236-1600 or the office at 206/232-8182. Details on ski lessons, equipment rental, and slopes are available from **Ski Lifts, Inc.,** 3020 77th Ave. SE, Mercer Island, WA 98040.

At **Alpental** (tel. 206/434-6112 weekends) you'll find 15 runs from beginner to star, with four chair lifts, four rope tows, and a platter pull. Top is 5,400 feet with a vertical drop of 2,200. There's a ski school for the uninitiated and a cafeteria to stave off starvation.

Ski Acres (tel. 206/434-6671 weekends) has seven chair lifts and six rope tows, a ski school, equipment rentals, a cross-country center, a cafeteria, and even a nursery. One of its four trails is 1¼ miles long and the top here is 3,880 feet with a vertical drop of 960 feet.

Six double-chair lifts, two triples, and five rope tows rise to the head of 15 slopes and trails at **Snoqualmie Summit.** Chair lift top elevation is 3,900 feet with a vertical drop of 900. Ski patrol, ski school, rentals, and restaurant here too.

Stevens Pass near Skykomish is 78 miles from Seattle west on U.S. 2, and has six double- and six triple-chair lifts operating from late November to mid-April, from 9 a.m. to 10 p.m. daily. The top is at 5,800 feet, with an 1,800-foot vertical drop and 1,125 acres of skiing. Write to this one at P.O. Box 98, Leavenworth, WA 98826 (tel. 206/973-2441; ski report hot-line 206/634-1645).

A ski trip to **Mount Baker** makes a nice weekend excursion from Seattle. You'll find the mountain and its new day lodge about 56 miles from Bellingham, which is about 90 miles north of Seattle. Mount Baker is open from late October to mid-May and has six double-chair lifts, rope tows, and bowl skiing, and its longest run is 6,500 feet. You can ski daily here to January 3 and on Friday, Saturday, Sunday, and holidays to May 14. For information on facilities, write 1017 Iowa St., Bellingham, WA 98226 (tel. 206/734-6771).

Prices at lifts depend on how long a season the ski area anticipates it will have. Exact lift prices are rarely available until the first snow, but you can expect them to be in the $19- to $25-a-day vicinity.

9. SHOPPING

Top of the list is **Pike Place Market,** a fascinating hillside marketplace that assaults the senses—pleasurably—with a mélange of color, sound, and smell. Short of designer fashions, one cannot imagine what you could want that is not sold here: flowers by the bushel basket, vegetables and fruit fresh off the farm, fish and meat, Dungeness crabs just plucked from the sea, specialty coffees and imported teas, intriguing ethnic restaurants and shops.

This is no new hyped-up spot created to draw the tourists. Seattle's beloved market has been around for generations, since 1907 in fact, and its warren of buildings is a fascinating architectural mixture. In the 1970s when some officious types decided the market ought to move for "progress," residents rose to battle and fought fiercely. The market remains.

Interesting anecdotes with downright wonderful photographs of the market in its earliest days are chronicled in a fascinating history called *The Pike Place Market: People, Politics, and Produce,* authored by Alice Shorett and Murray Morgan and published by Pacific Search Press, Seattle.

Best loved of our market treasures is a delightful wooden box carefully carved from a cross-section of plum tree. These hunks of native hardwoods are left in their natural shape by artists Paul Richards and Teri Peynado, who follow the form of the wood to hollow out the interior, add a drawer or an interior tray and lid. The end product is not only a handsome hunk of wood hand-rubbed with tung oil and wax on the outside, walnut oil on the inside, but also an intricate creation that's as useful as it is intriguingly beautiful.

These artful creations are among the most unusual woodcraft you'll find anywhere and sell for quite reasonable prices, ranging from $7 to $150 but averaging about $15 to $30. We loved these so much we wrote to the duo in search of another and discovered that Teri and Paul, who have been showing in the market for 13 years, often mail their creations to far-away customers. You'll find the artists in the market on Monday, Wednesday, Friday, and Saturday.

Their work is also on display at the Northwest Gallery of Fine Woodworking in Pioneer Square, 202 First Ave. South (tel. 625-0542). The address for the company, called **Bizarre Boxes,** is P.O. Box 10426-S, Pike Place Station, Seattle, WA 98101 (tel. 206/281-TREE).

Another tempting spot in the market is **Made in Washington,** an intriguing compilation of genuine craftwork, not the junky souvenirs you'll find in many city gift shops. The shop, operated by Gillian and Jack Mathews, is in Post Alley between Pike and Pine (tel. 206/467-0788). You can buy smoked salmon, preserves, pickles, hazelnuts, wine, and books on Washington here too.

If you'd like to take home some of that unmatchable Pacific Northwest salmon or other seafood, folks at **Pure Food fish market** will pack it in an odorless, dripless, waterproof container you can take on a plane or in a car. They'll even deliver to your hotel room. Call Sol Amon, one of a crowd of Amons who have run this operation for more than 75 years, at 206/622-5765. They're open Monday through Saturday from 8 a.m. to 6 p.m. on the upper level.

Pike Place is open from practically dawn to practically dusk or whenever the customers dwindle, every day but Sunday. Explore all the corners, including the usually missed section below the produce stalls, where all kinds of cast-off treasures, even some antiques, are sold. Nose into everything—no one will mind. You'll find the market covering the streets from Pike to Virginia Streets between First Avenue and Pike Place. Lower market shops are on Western Avenue.

There are still more **shops along the city's waterfront.** To get there from Pike Place Market, find the big market clock at the foot of Pike Street and you'll find a new footbridge and elevator right under it.

Two colorful **trolley cars** nobody thought would catch on did and still run, many years after they were dreamed up by a local politician. Their renovation and lively paint job cost $3 million. You can ride them along the waterfront drive, Alaskan Way, from Pier 70 to Pioneer Square. Fare is 60¢ and cars run every 20 to 30 minutes (tel. 206/447-4800).

Pioneer Square, Seattle's original "downtown," is interesting historically and for the trendy array of shops and art galleries here. Start at **Grand Central Arcade,** a delightful spot in which to while away a few hours with espresso and croissants as glassy-eyed shoppers amble by (or to stash nonshoppers). From there the shops extend out along 1st Street South and South Main Street, offering art galleries, antique shops, and some alluring bookstores as well as craft shops and avant-garde fashion shops.

Pioneer Square, by the way, was the site of pioneer Henry Yesler's "Skid Road," a monicker it got from its use as a log skid that rolled logs between the mill and the waterfront.

Pioneer Square's red-brick architecture and its plethora of ornate architectural furbelows make it a great ogling spot before, after, or during the shopping.

Favored department store through the Northwest is **Bon Marché,** called "The Bon" by absolutely everyone. In downtown Seattle it's at Fourth and Pine (tel. 206/344-2121).

Nordstrom's, Fifth and Pine (tel. 206/628-2111), is another favorite large department store, as is **Frederick & Nelson,** Fifth and Pine (tel. 206/682-5500). **I. Magnin** is at Sixth and Pine (tel. 206/682-6111).

You'll find those stores and many more downtown in the main shopping areas bounded by Second and Sixth Avenues and University Street and Olive Way.

You can watch artists doing their art and craft work at **Northwest Crafts Center** at Seattle Center.

International shops are the specialty in the university district which, naturally enough, has some good bookstores, imported treasures, and clothing boutiques along University Way, nicknamed "The Ave."

Rainier Square has a Ralph Lauren Polo Shop. Enough said? The square's at 13th and 5th Avenues. Another occupant is the original **Eddie Bauer** store, the sporting goods company that sells boat shoes no preppy would be without, at Fifth and Union (tel. 206/622-2766). And, heaven forbid we should forget, **Brooks Brothers,** 1401 Fourth Ave. (tel. 206/624-4400). And **Abercrombie and Fitch** in the Four Seasons Olympic Hotel, 421 University St. (tel. 206/623-2175).

Piers 51, 52, 56, 57, and 59 have shops and restaurants in an interesting waterside location worth the stroll whether or not you buy anything (see Ye Olde Curiosity Shop, above).

If you prefer **shopping malls** you'll find **Northgate** on the north side of the city at exit 173–Northgate Way, First Avenue NE or northbound exit 103rd Avenue NE from I-5. Bon Marché, J. C. Penney, and Nordstrom department stores are the mainstays here.

On the south side of the city, **Southcenter** has more than 125 shops, fountains, and suspended mobiles. Take Southcenter Boulevard exit from I-5 and turn left at the light.

CHAPTER III

WASHINGTON'S CASCADE MOUNTAIN LOOP

□ □ □

1. ORIENTATION

2. WHIDBEY ISLAND AND THE SAN JUAN ISLANDS TO THE NORTHERN CASCADES

3. WINTHROP AND WENATCHEE

4. CENTRAL AND SOUTHERN CASCADES

5. WASHINGTON APPLE COUNTRY: YAKIMA

From the mountains to the valleys to the oceans white with foam . . . all that and even a little desert can be yours on a downright awesome trip through Washington's majestic Cascade Mountains.

Wonder and weather-maker, these mountains shape the land they crown, both scenically and meteorologically, causing the drizzle that keeps eastern Washington emerald green, but blocking rainclouds to create in western Washington a land of sagebrush at your feet, snow on the horizon.

Paralleling the Pacific from California to British Columbia, the Cascades lavish scenic treasures on the traveler. No one could be prouder of that spectacular mountain greenery scenery than Washingtonians who are well aware that they are blessed with the most prominent promontories in the West.

Connecting peaks and pasturelands, Washington's roadways cross and recross the Cascades, offering you the chance to travel on a looping journey through the most breathtakingly beautiful sectors of the Cascade Range.

Dubbed the Cascade Loop, this scenic circular trip begins north of Seattle to take you on a fantastic journey past misty, windswept islands, across rolling foothills and steep-sided canyons, through alpine passes garlanded in wildflowers, to vast stretches of dusty desert dotted with silvery sagebrush.

Here as in few places in the world you can travel through both geologic and historic time, from 20th-century Washington to the 19th-century American West, with touches of old New England and Bavaria thrown in as extras; from Pacific seascapes done in water colors to Pacific landscapes rippling in the rainbow hues of tulip fields.

On you go from lush forests and alpine lakes to stark sage and lonely desert, where ingenuity and irrigation have teamed up to create America's apple capital. Along the way you meet gold-mining towns of yesteryear, where talk of that glittery metal is little abated among hopeful souls who still seek underground riches.

You'll meet towns with intriguing names like Sedro Woolley, Concrete, Index, Goldbar, and Diablo. You can travel up scenically dramatic 60-mile-long Lake Chelan, a fjord-like sparkler in the eastern Cascades, to Stehekin, a village so isolated it's reachable only on foot or by boat or small plane.

At North Cascades National Park you will meet 505,000 acres that encompass some of America's most breathtaking mountain scenery: waterfalls, jagged peaks, dense forests, and flower-trimmed mountain meadows, an endless panorama of stunning vistas. Get off the road and walk a few feet along a mountain trail and you will be rewarded with views of glacially sculpted valleys, icy peaks, and snowfields.

1. ORIENTATION

In this day of rapid transit, you can cross the Cascades by bus, train, air, and expressway, but we recommend—urge—an unhurried drive along some roads less traveled, roads on which you can *experience* the majesty of the Cascades, find your own pace, stop when wonderment overcomes. Take time to fall in love with a quiet village, a mountain lake, a singing stream; to picnic deep in primeval forest or stroll streets turned out in alpine furbelows or Old West shoot-'em-up style.

So convinced are we that this is the way to go that we're saying whatever the cost, rent a car if you must, but get out here on these scenically dramatic byways for a look at how the Northwest got this way and why it remains one of the most picturesque corners of this nation.

Although there are several east-west routes across the Cascades, one is our special favorite, a looping drive across the northern Cascades, through parts of central Washington, returning by a southerly route that cuts across another section of the Cascades and travels through Snoqualmie National Forest. We'll have to admit we aren't the first to find these roads: a group called the Cascade Loop Association has published a 50¢ booklet outlining parts of this drive. Write for one to the Cascade Loop Assn., P.O. Box 3245, Wenatchee, WA 98801 (tel. 509/662-3888).

So get out a map—we'd suggest the *Official Washington State Highway Map and Guide,* available from the Washington State Department of Transportation, Transportation Administration Bldg., Olympia, WA 98504 (tel. 206/753-2150). To keep on track through these backroads and byways, you might outline this loop route with a highlighter.

Start from Seattle on I-5 and head north to Mukilteo for a ferry ride to Whidbey Island. From there head for Burlington, where you turn east on Wash. 20. This northern Cascades portion of your route stretches to the town of Mazama, 118 miles to the east.

A journey down the eastern slopes and across the sagebrush of eastern Washington begins east of Mazama and continues to Wenatchee, 109 miles to the south. Your route changes just beyond Twisp, 24 miles south of Mazama. Here Wash. 20 swings east, and Wash. 153, your new route, goes south toward Carlton. Just outside Pateros, Wash. 153 joins U.S. 97, which you will follow from there, turning south toward Azwell and Chelan. Stay on U.S. 97 to the outskirts of Wenatchee, where you head west. At Wenatchee a side trip to the orchards of Yakima Valley is fun.

Snoqualmie Forest is a highlight of the third leg of our trip, which recrosses the Cascades right through this massive national forest. Note that after turning west at Wenatchee toward Leavenworth, U.S. 97 is joined by U.S. 2. When you leave Leavenworth, stay on U.S. 2 across the Cascades into the town of Everett, on the Pacific coast, where you rejoin I-5. Everett is 29 miles north of Seattle, where your trip began.

Back in Seattle your odometer will show you've traveled 512 miles, but we'll bet you that all your "oohs" and "aahs" will have totaled a number lots higher than that!

You can join this loop drive at any point, driving over from Spokane, for instance, or up from Yakima. If you're on a fly/drive holiday, you can fly into Seattle, Spokane (see Chapter IV), or Pangborn Field in Wenatchee (tel. 509/884-5715), which is served by Cascade Airways.

2. WHIDBEY ISLAND AND THE SAN JUAN ISLANDS TO THE NORTHERN CASCADES

Let's begin this fascinating trip right at water level, visiting a rustic rural enclave called Whidbey Island, once the dwelling spot of Indians and early settlers.

To get to Whidbey Island, take I-5 from Seattle to exit 189, heading for a town with the guttural Indian name of Mukilteo (pronounced "Muck-ill-*tay*-o"). While its name sounds like something you should sprinkle on your lawn, this small town is quite a pretty little place, built on a bluff that drops down to the sea where the cheery, chugging ferryboat awaits.

If you arrive in Mukilteo at dining time, try **Arnie's,** 714 2nd St. (tel. 206/745-0601), a big, blue-and-white building perched over the ferry docks. A bank of windows offers a great view of the comings and goings in Puget Sound and several dining rooms offer a woodsy retreat from the day. The fare leans toward plenty of good steaks, supplemented by some seafood selections. You might also await the ferryboat in the downstairs bar, which features a tranquil sea view too. Prices are in the $10 to $15 range and hours are 11 a.m. to 2 p.m. for lunch weekdays, 9:30 a.m. to 2 p.m. for Sunday brunch, and 4:30 to 9:30 p.m. for dinner Sunday through Thursday, later on weekends and in the lounge.

(If you are following the Cascade loop in an opposite direction from the one we've outlined, you can traverse Whidbey Island from north to south by departing I-5 at Mount Vernon, where you take Wash. 20 to Deception Pass and Oak Harbor to begin the down-island trek on Wash. 20/525.)

You can get here from Port Townsend too, on a ferry that docks on a long flat strip of seashore in the center of the island at Keystone.

WHIDBEY ISLAND: We love this place so much we almost kept it all to ourselves. But we just couldn't deprive you of the joys of discovering for yourself what a delightful bit of pastoral joy lurks on this island minutes away from Seattle's fast track.

Although you can drive the 50-mile length of Whidbey in an hour, we suggest you allot a few days to relax here, to become part of the easy, *mañana* atmosphere of the place and to explore some fascinating wooded backroads where life seems little changed in pace since Victorian days. In the telephone book you even find a few recipes!

Whidbey is truly a vacation island where the what-to-see-and-dos are limited to a few antique shops and some dramatic scenery, small rustic cafés, and waterside watering spots. It's a wonderful place to walk, bicycle, and just generally hang out, as they say, letting the world go by.

Surprisingly, Whidbey seems to have remained largely undiscovered by

Seattle-ites, who ought to be coming here in droves but seem to visit only in trickles. Perhaps proximity breeds overlook.

However, weekend visits to the island are popular getaways for travelers from Seattle, Port Angeles, and many other spots connected by ferry to the island, so be sure to have reservations if you're planning a weekend visit here.

For information about the island, contact the cheerful, friendly folks at any one of three chambers of commerce: the **Langley Chamber of Commerce,** 220 1st St., Langley, WA 98260 (tel. 206/321-6765); the **Central Whidbey Chamber of Commerce,** 5 Main St., Coupville, WA 98239 (tel. 206/678-5434); or the **Greater Oak Harbor Chamber of Commerce,** 2506 Wash. 20, Oak Harbor, WA 98277 (tel. 206/675-3535).

Here's a look at the island's most interesting places.

Langley

After 20 minutes of scenic ferryboat ride from Mukilteo, you land at Clinton following a tranquil journey that seems all too short. Your first sight of Whidbey Island is a lovely one, the tiny town of Clinton.

Don't set off on the main road, Wash. 20/525, across the island just yet. Instead turn off at Wilkinson, Langley, or Coles Roads to get to Langley, a postcard-pretty spot on a cliff overlooking the sea, frothing and bubbling across the beach below. Langley itself stretches out along a single street that dips its way past rustic watering holes and surprisingly chic little shops.

You might start your exploration of the island in Langley by stopping for a while at the **Whidbey Inn,** 106 1st St. (P.O. Box 156), Langley, WA 98260 (tel. 206/221-7115). One could hardly find a more beautiful location, high over Puget Sound, and the inn itself will steal your heart. Below your high perch, the sound is visible from your balcony; inside are soft colors, an antique armoire, a comfortable wing chair, marble-topped tables, polished wood floors, quite contemporary bathrooms. Each morning breakfast is delivered to your door, so you can sip coffee on the balcony or in the tiny side garden. For this glamour and comfort you pay $70 to $110 double.

Just a few streets away the scenery turns from rugged to pastoral. In the middle of that tranquility is **Caroline's Country Cottage,** 215 6th St. (P.O. Box 459), Langley, WA 98260 (tel. 206/221-8709). Here owner Caroline Satterberg herself will greet you at her handsomely decorated home that's cozy as an oyster shell but twice as pretty. Trimmed throughout with lovely light wood, the former farmhouse has been redone with delicate artistry that has also managed to create several contemporary nests, each with its own small bath screened off from the room but sharing a window view over rolling lawns. Soothing pale green and rose hues, polished cottons, and brass beds team up to create an atmosphere both cozy and sophisticated.

Caroline will be happy to fill you in on her chosen Northwest corner and guide you to some good restaurants. Rates at this bed-and-breakfast manor are $80 double, and include full breakfast served in a sunny, handsome dining room, use of a hot tub, and an evening of wine and hors d'oeuvres.

As you're exploring Langley, stop in at the **Dog House Tavern,** a western-façade watering spot frequented by just about everyone in town. Shops of interest include **Islandesign Interiors,** 111 1st St. (tel. 206/321-5121), for home furnishings; and **Whidbey Island Antiques,** Anthes Emporium, Anthes Avenue (tel. 206/221-2393), or **Virginia's,** 206 W. 1st St. (tel. 206/221-7797), for antiques.

Freeland

Next stop up the island is the village of Freeland, where a local bakery called

Boulangerie de l'île, Harborview and Main Streets (tel. 206/321-6282), wins rave reviews from local residents, who go here to pick up great French breads and deli treats that form the basis of a picnic in Deception Bay, a spot of dramatic beauty up at the end of the island (more on that below in our look at Oak Harbor). Freeland is so small it hardly qualifies even as a village, just a cluster of homes spread out along the cliffs to take best advantage of the view.

One awesome place to spend a day or two here is called **Cliff House,** 5440 S. Windmill Rd., Freeland, WA 98249 (tel. 206/321-1566), where you rent not a bedroom but a whole house! Most months of the year Cliff House's friendly owners move themselves into a garage apartment and rent this architectural wonder to romantic souls who revel in its dramatic 30-foot-tall atrium, its massive stone fireplace and surrounding sunken living room, its loft bedroom and private bath, kitchen, and handsome décor accenting modern art and Indian basketry.

You begin sinking into the atmosphere the minute you turn into an almost-hidden driveway that winds for some distance through 13 acres of deep forest that are part of the grounds of this architectural-award-winning house. Occupying a perch of gaspable beauty, the house overlooks the sea, where you can watch whales blowing by in winter and sometimes see sea lions on their northward migration.

Clamber down a couple sets of stairs and you're on a rugged beach. Nap in a hammock. Paddle in a hot whirlpool. Fantastic! The price for a setting that will renew you for weeks is $185 per night (with a two-night minimum), including breakfast and sole use of the whole house. Reservations vital far in advance.

Cliff House now also has a lovely little cottage, Seacliff Cottage, which shares the same spectacular views of forest and beach but is quite a private little enclave, separated from the main house by plenty of trees. Seacliff Cottage rents for $110 a night with a two-night minimum. No children or pets, however.

Greenbank

Here is yet another little wide spot in the road, but one that offers a tempting place to spend an atmospheric day or two. That place is Greenbank, home of **Guest House Cottages,** 835 E. Christenson Rd., Greenbank, WA 98523 (tel. 206/678-3115). Although the name isn't strong on romantic overtones, the place is. Once an aging farm, the grounds here have grown under the loving craftsmanship of owners to include a sleekly modern two-story log guesthouse with soaring stone fireplace and tall windows overlooking a small pond and five rustic but handsomely decorated cottages. The newly built Tennesee Cottage is filled with chintz and calico, television, compact kitchen, fireplace, skylights, a Jacuzzi bathtub for two, and a long front porch with rockers.

Whether you choose that imposing log house under the firs, the small front cottage near the main house, or one of the several cottages tucked into the forested grounds here, you will be treated to a country breakfast tray all done up in calico frills and homemade jams, cereal, eggs, toast, fresh croissants, cheese, coffee, and orange juice.

Accommodations range from the lovely Wildflower Suite in the main farmhouse at $75 double, to one of several fully equipped log cabins with stained glass, sleeping loft, fireplace, and oak furnishings, to the farm cottage where a small deck makes a lovely place for morning coffee. Cottages are $85, and that great guesthouse—a perfect honeymoon retreat—with skylights, stone fireplace, and down comforters, is $150 double. Tennessee Cottage is $125 double.

Coupeville

A jam-packed shop with antiques spilling out the door and onto a dock kind of sets the tone for this bohemian cluster of historic, false-front, Old West–look buildings and furbelowed Victorian beauties, one of which is painted a delightful shade of peach!

As you walk the single "downtown" street here you look way down and out across a smashing view of the sea. If it's lunchtime, you can pop into **Knead and Feed,** 4 Front St. (tel. 206/678-5431), where you can watch the sea roiling around below the windows. Inside, irresistible smells of home-baked breads are abetted by steaming soups and fresh local blackberries baked in a pie. Hours are 11 a.m. to 3 p.m. weekdays (closed Tuesday) and 10 a.m. to 4 p.m. on Saturday and Sunday.

There is something so relaxing, so appealing, so unpretentious, and in-tune-with-nature about this town that we can tell you you're going to want to stay.

To get into the Victorian spirit of the island, you might try to find a space in a Victorian farmhouse, a new addition to the island's restored-home roster: the **Col. Crockett Farm,** 1012 S. Fort Casey Rd., Coupeville, WA 98239 (tel. 206/678-3711). We admit we haven't yet seen this recently restored spot, but we hear from those who have that a smashingly lovely restoration has been done here to create a lovely five-room bed-and-breakfast inn. Built in 1855, the farmhouse now features a library, a formal dining room with individual tables, and lots of lacy touches in five bedrooms that all have private baths. Rates are $55 to $70.

Before evening rolls around and your appetite begins to make its presence known, call **Rosie's Garden Restaurant,** 606 N. Main St. (tel. 206/678-3989), which got its name from a fortuitous combination of events: the owner's name and a lovely rose garden. Operated by Rosie and Michael Anter, this restaurant replaces their former effort, a wonder called Michael's Your Place Restaurant. Two very, very good cooks, the Anters offer lovingly prepared delicacies like prime rib Oscar topped with crab and béarnaise sauce; fresh poached salmon cooked in wine and herbs with a hollandaise sauce; a fruits de mer combination of local seafoods; Penn Cove mussels steamed in wine, garlic, basil, and cream; baked oysters Rockefeller; freshly baked pies; and a changing array of delectable desserts—have we got your attention? This is first-rate cooking that ought not to be missed. Prices are in the $12 to $15 range for most selections, and hours are 11 a.m. to 2 p.m. weekdays for lunch and 6 to 9 p.m. daily for dinner, from 10 a.m. to 2 p.m. for brunch on Sunday. You'll find the restaurant in a tiny shopping arcade called Mariners Court.

Coupeville is home to a long-time inn, the **Captain Whidbey Inn,** 2072 W. Captain Whidbey Inn Rd., Coupeville, WA 98239 (tel. 206/678-4097), which has been around since 1907 and is quite a snug enclave overlooking a small cove. You have your choice here of shared-bath rooms in the cozy lodge, quarters in a small two-story strip of comfortably decorated rooms overlooking the cove, or in a couple of large but spartan cottages. Those motel rooms are the best bet, but no matter which you choose you have full run of the inn's popular rustic dining room and comfortable bar, a library, and a cozy nook before the fireplace. Rates range from $65 for inn rooms with bath down the hall, to $85 double for quarters overlooking the lagoon, and $95 for private cottages.

Even if you don't stay here, you can drop in for dinner. Make reservations—this is a favorite island dining room. You'll dine on simply cooked but very fresh seafood like salmon or local mussels, or good steaks, served with fresh salads and vegetables, and home-baked pies. Prices are in the $12 to $20 range for entrees, and hours are noon to 2 p.m. for lunch and 6 to 8 p.m. for dinner. Open daily.

You'll find two or three well-stocked antique shops in town, including

Mitchell's Antiques, 6 Front St. (tel. 206/678-5519), where the owner is one of the Northwest's foremost collectors and authorities on Haviland china, and **Salmagundi Antiques,** 12 Front St. (tel. 206/678-5888), which features Oriental antiques from Thailand and China, as well as American antiques, at quite reasonable prices. Salmagundi now carries more than 186 different styles of Victorian lampshades, beginning at $32.50 for Chinese silk shades. G. A. Lloyd, owner of Salmagundi, also has a Historic Register 1890 Victorian farm two miles south of Coupeville. It's filled with antiques too, and the company ships to anywhere in the world and has a monthly mailing that lists what's available. On Front Street, you'll also see a shop filled with beautiful wools and weaving looms.

While you're here, be sure to take a look at the **Alexander Blockhouse** on Front Street. Built in the 1850s to shield residents from Indian attacks, it is amazingly well preserved. **Fort Casey,** a bluff-top fort with gun mounts and nice beach, is three miles south of town.

Oak Harbor

A comparatively busy spot of shops and fast-food restaurants, Oak Harbor is the least tranquil spot on the island, but it is a good place to stock up on supplies for a picnic lunch in nearby **Deception Pass.** That pass is a narrow neck of water through which tides roar with swirling intensity, creating whirlpools and eddies that roil around jagged rocks. Swimming is out of the question here, but this makes a lovely place to picnic or spend some time just watching nature at work.

Dutch settlers landed here years ago. Their influence is honored at **Auld Holland Inn,** 2837 N. Wash. 20, Oak Harbor, WA 98277 (tel. 206/675-2288), a bright and cheerfully kitschy motel you certainly can't miss: it has a big windmill over the office. Some very pleasant people run Auld Holland Inn and have turned the top floor of this standard motel into really lovely rooms, with a striped half-canopy over the beds and a few antiques scattered about. Auld Holland also has a restaurant offering $12 to $17 dinners to its guests and other visitors too. Rates at the inn are $38 to $65 double.

LaConner

Technically, lovely little LaConner is not part of Whidbey, but it's so close we're including it here to be sure you don't miss this charming and historic village. Another town that thrived until left behind by the railroad's move inland, LaConner is actually on the mainland just south of Wash. 20. Two roads marked with signs to LaConner and to the neighboring Swinomish Indian Reservation will get you there.

Settled in 1867 by trading-post entrepreneur John Conner, who named the town after his wife, Louisa A. Conner, the town stretches out alongside the Swinomish Slough, a very picturesque place that has lured many a Northwest artist and photographer.

On weekends antique-searchers pour into town in search of bargains offered by a handful of shops here. On quieter weekdays you can sink into the atmosphere of old Victorian homes—one hillside home has a widow's walk that must have offered a view all the way to China.

You can, in fact, sink into the spirit of things in rather considerable style at **LaConner Country Inn,** Old Town, LaConner, WA 98257 (tel. 206/466-3101). A faintly Tudor feeling created by a second floor that overhangs the first is teamed with the country look of cozy wing armchairs in a library and guest rooms with fireplaces and brass beds.

An English pub is a pleasant place to while away some time, and the restaurant here is quite good, serving such delicacies as veal in puff pastry with artichoke hearts, mushrooms, and a cream sauce, or prawns in a dill sauce, or four-peppercorn steak, featuring black, red, white, and green peppercorns. Prices are in the $12 to $17 range, including soup or salad, vegetables, and freshly baked sourdough bread.

There are just 28 rooms here, so reservations are mandatory, particularly on summer weekends. Rates range from $65 double for a room downstairs to $83 upstairs, where beamed ceilings add still more rustic flavor. Continental breakfast is included. No charge for children under 12 sharing a room; older extras are $5.

If you're here for lunch or breakfast, **Calico Cupboard,** 720 S. 1st St. (tel. 206/466-4451), makes a wonderful way to break the day. Waitresses dressed in frilly long dresses zip about the pretty blue-and-white country-décor dining room, serving hearty, additive-free meals of homemade soups, crispy salads, and thick sandwiches on fat slices of bread baked in the restaurant's next-door bakery. At breakfast only the most iron-willed will be able to resist crumbly coffee cakes, steaming cinnamon rolls, pecan breads, and the wonderful fruit pies on display in the bakery cases. Prices are very reasonably in the $4 to $8 range for most things, and hours are 8 a.m. to 5 p.m. daily.

Evenings the place to combine some local color with local flavors is **Swinomish Longhouse,** 952 Moorage Way (tel. 206/466-4444). Owned and run by the Swinomish tribe, this intriguing silvery-gray, weathered-wood longhouse overlooks the waters of the slough. You watch as cooks labor in a glass-enclosed kitchen, grilling salmon over alder logs.

Salmon, the specialty, is supplemented by seafood fettuccine, fish and chips, steaks, and scallops, all for prices in the $12 to $15 range. The Indian fried bread is worth a try. Hours here are 11 a.m. to 10 p.m. daily (from 10 a.m. on Sunday).

One more good spot in town is the **Black Swan Café,** 1st and Washington Streets (tel. 206/466-3040), where two very talented cooks are at work whipping up a changing array of specialties, including ravioli made from tomato pasta, several fine veal preparations, and some unusual treats like rabbit in garlic-and-walnut sauce and white salmon herbed with marjoram.

Locally grown fruit, including some sensational raspberries, is incorporated into wonderful desserts. Prices are in the $11 to $17 range for dinner, served from 5 to 9 p.m. daily.

LaConner has several interesting museums and historic sites, but the best of them is lovely **Gaches Mansion,** 703 2nd St., at the top of the hill (tel. 206/466-4288). This beautiful Victorian mansion, gutted by fire years ago, has been lovingly restored by local residents. The noted Valley Museum of Northwest Art is on the second floor. Gaches Mansion is now open for tours from 1 to 5 p.m. Friday through Sunday, closing an hour earlier in winter. Admission is $1.

Friends recently told us about a spot called **Downey House,** 1880 Chilberg Rd., LaConner, WA 98527 (tel. 206/466-3207). We haven't seen it yet, but based on their raves you might want to take a look at this historic homestead. Owners here trace their heritage back to pioneer days and have furnished their home in an upscale version of pioneer homes. Special touches include a masonry wood stove and bake oven and a hot tub. Overlooking the tranquil Skagit Valley, this inn bills itself as a bed-and-breakfast, but one with a touch that is downright irresistible to us: they offer—they promise—bed, breakfast, and blackberry pie. Do you need other reasons? There are five guest rooms here, some with shared bath, some with private facilities. Rates are $50 to $60 for shared bath, $75 for private bath.

In mid-April the town features a **LaConner Home Tour,** during which private homes and historic sites are open for viewing, and you can also get a look at the riotous colors of huge **tulip farms** in bloom. Call 206/466-4288 for festival information.

SAN JUAN ISLANDS: Just because a place is small and quiet doesn't mean it wants to stay that way. When we put this travel guide together for the first time, we had the temerity to neglect a mention of the San Juan Islands, thinking them small, remote, and difficult enough to reach that the average Northwest explorer just wouldn't make the effort required to visit them. Whew, did we get blistered!

We'd hardly started happily reading the letters of travelers who tried and approved our choices of dining spots and stopping places in the Northwest, when the first few "What happened to the San Juan Islands?" letters began to arrive. It didn't take us long to discover that while there may not be many travelers headed for the San Juan Islands, those who do are very vocal in their enthusiasm for this cluster of seaswept islets just off the coast of Washington. So here is a look at the San Juan Islands.

Even the die-hard San Juan–lovers will admit that **getting there** is not the easiest thing in the world to do. There are, however, two ways to do it: you can fly here from Seattle aboard San Juan, Otter, or Lake Union Airlines, which connect the islands to the mainland and to each other; or you can drive up to Anacortes on Fidalgo Island, just north of Whidbey Island, board one of those lumbering, big Washington State Ferries, and sail off across Rosario Strait on one of the most scenic cruises in the nation.

Gray Line, a Seattle-based tour company that covers the waterfront both literally and figuratively, also has tours to the islands. You depart from Seattle and journey to Semiahmoo Resort near Blaine, Washington, where you board one of the line's sightseeing tour boats for a 3½-hour journey through the islands. A major stop on the tour is a visit to a wildlife refuge where seals and sea lions snore in the sun. Tours depart June through mid-September. Information on the trips is available from the company at 300 Elliott Ave. West, Seattle, WA 98119 (tel. 206/626-5208, or toll-free 800/426-7532). Fares for the trip are $56 for adults, $27 for children 5 through 12.

Waiting for you out there in Puget Sound are no fewer than 192 emerald islands, only four of them developed enough to welcome the casual traveler: Orcas, Lopez, Shaw, and San Juan. If you want to see more than those four, you can charter or rent a boat and get out there on the water and chase down all the other 188.

If you should want to stay overnight in Anacortes, Beverly and Winfred Stocker recently opened a bed-and-breakfast there called **Burrow's Bay.** It's quite close to the San Juan Island ferry at 4911 MacBeth Dr., Anacortes, WA 98221 (tel. 206/293-4792). Rates are $75 double for the one available room, which includes sitting room, separate bedroom, private bath, fireplace, television, and private deck and entry.

Here's a look at the four major islands and what you'll find there.

Orcas Island

Orcas Island is the largest of the four, a picturesque place crowned by one very lovely antique hotel called Rosario. It takes about 90 minutes to get to the island by ferry from Anacortes, a much shorter time to get there on San Juan Airlines, which flies in here from Port Townsend, Seattle, Port Angeles, or Bellingham.

A highlight of the island is **Moran State Park,** a 5,000-acre park that offers camping, fishing, biking, hiking, swimming, and boating. Over it all looms Mount Constitution, a 2,409-foot peak. Reservations are required for campsites here between June and September. Required deposit fees range from $4 to $11. You can contact park rangers for reservations at Star Route Box 22, Eastsound, WA 98245 (tel. 206/376-2326).

Popular hikes in the park are from Mountain Lake to Twin Lakes, about 2 ½ miles, and from Mount Constitution Summit to Twin Lakes, 1 ½ miles, much of it straight up—or down. It's worth the effort, however, for a look at some lovely waterfalls and gorgeous scenery.

Up at the summit of Mount Constitution you'll find the island's best-loved landmark, a 50-year-old stone tower that crowns a quite amazing view—in the distance are the Olympic Mountains, the Cascades, Mount Baker, the Canadian island of Victoria, the Washington state coastline, Vancouver in British Columbia, and on a clear day, Mount Rainier.

Photographers will love this island which has a refreshing and innocent rusticity that's quite appealing. Discover it by just strolling the streets here, exploring nooks and crannies, visiting with local shopkeepers and chatting with the island's 2,700 residents. More than the usual number of artists and craft workers seem to have settled here, so shopping is interesting. Just steps away from anywhere is the freshest of fresh Northwest seafood, served, along with Northwest lamb and beef, in small, cozy restaurants whose proprietors as likely as not will pull up a chair and join you for a chat.

Queen of island resorts is the sprawling **Rosario Resort and Spa,** Eastsound, WA 98245 (tel. 206/376-2222, or toll free 800/562-8820 in Washington). Centered around the 1905 Moran mansion, the resort is on the National Register of Historic Places and has some spectacular accommodations in waterfront or hillside villas overlooking Cascade Bay. There's lots of romantic atmosphere here—from balconies with smashing views out over the water to cozy fireplaces ideal for cuddling on a cool evening.

Rooms have televisions, films, handsome furnishings, and all the comforts, including, in 43 of them, kitchens. There are three heated pools to splash in, a beach, whirlpools, rental boats and canoes, a marina, fishing facilities, windsurfing, tennis courts, nature trails, a children's playground, rental mopeds and sailboats, even a health club.

Fine fare is served in the resort's dining room every day, but the Sunday champagne brunch gets particular raves. Friday night there's a seafood buffet. Hours at the three resort restaurants are 7:30 to 11 a.m., noon to 2 p.m., and 6 to 10 p.m. daily. Prices fall in the $10 to $15 range for dinner entrees.

One final classy touch here: Every afternoon there's an organ concert in the music room of the mansion. Rates at the resort are $85 to $165 double.

Other resorts on the island include: **Turtleback Farm Inn,** Crow Valley Road (Rte. 1, Box 650), Eastsound, WA 98245 (tel. 206/376-4914), a charmingly restored 1800s farmhouse surrounded by 80 acres of pastoral scenery, where rates are $75 to $110 double; **Landmark Inn,** Main Street (Rte. 1, Box A7), Eastsound, WA 98245 (tel. 206/376-2423), which offers one- and two-bedroom suites with living room and kitchen, private balcony, fireplace, and great views of the water for rates of $60 to $75 double, depending on season; and **Deer Harbor Resort & Marina,** P.O. Box 17, Deer Harbor, WA 98243 (tel. 206/376-4420), a 29-unit hotel with rooms and cottages, many with fireplaces and good sea views, plus a heated indoor pool, beach, whirlpool, hot tubs, dining room, and playground, for $48 to $120, depending on size and elaborateness of accommodations.

San Juan Island

Friday Harbor is the center of things on this island, very likely because this is where the plane, the boats, the ferry, and anyone who's coming here from anywhere lands. This island is the site of that weird war we mentioned back in the opening chapter of the book—the Pig War! That battle occurred when the British and Americans, always a little testy with each other in those days of territorial disputes, verged on fisticuffs, or worse, one day when a British-owned pig ventured into an American cabbage patch. The only casualty of the short-lived war, however, was the porker, which ended up as a platterful of bilateral pork chops!

That 1859 war is commemorated in **San Juan Island National Historic Park,** still neatly divided into an English camp and an American camp. Here you can see an old blockhouse in the English camp, and in the American camp, get a look at the restored quarters of the camp's laundress and one of its officers. There are plenty of beaches and picnic grounds to play on too. Grounds are open from sunrise to sunset daily all year, but the buildings are closed in the winter months. Hunting and camping are not permitted, but anything else goes. You can reach park rangers at San Juan Island National Historical Park, P.O. Box 429, Friday Harbor, WA 98250 (tel. 206/378-2240).

Another diversion: The University of Washington Research and Teaching Laboratory (tel. 206/378-2165) offers guided tours of its display tanks and an **aquarium** on Wednesday and Saturday from 2 to 4 p.m. in July and August. It's free.

Sports of all variety abound here, from fishing and swimming to golf at the nine-hole San Juan Golf & Country Club, bicycling, and hiking.

Perhaps the best-known local sport, however, is **whale watching,** best pursued at Lime Kiln State Park, about ten miles west of Friday Harbor. Orca whales (also known by the somewhat less appealing name of killer whales) and minke whales splash around these waters in many months of the year.

You can learn a whale of a lesson about those whales at the **Whale Museum,** 62 1st St. (tel. 206/378-4710), paddling about inside one of the town's oldest buildings. The museum includes a complete skeleton of a baby gray whale and an adult orca whale and compares them to human skeletal systems. Exhibits tell you all about the biology, behavior, even the strange sounds emitted by the wailing whales. Hours are 10 a.m. to 5 p.m. daily from June to October, same hours Wednesday through Monday the rest of the year. Admission is $3 for adults, $1 for children over 12, and 50¢ for younger children.

If you're staying over here, the island's poshest resort is **Roche Harbor Resort,** P.O. Box 1, Roche Harbor, WA 98250 (tel. 206/378-2155), a stunning spot that combines both history and hospitality. Located in a village that once supported the largest lime works west of the Mississippi, Roche Harbor Resort centers around the Hotel De Haro, a Victorian wonderland of towers and turrets winding around a yellow-brick road made in local kilns. Accommodations are in the hotel, in charming company-town cottages, and in chic Lagoon Park or Westpoint condominiums. Tennis, golf, bicycling, hiking, fishing, and boating are all at the doorstep, and there's dancing and dining in candlelit historic surroundings as well—a very romantic place indeed.

Roche Harbor Inn, the resort's restaurant, is open for all three meals and specializes in local seafood but has plenty of beef and poultry choices available in the $10 to $15 range for dinner.

Rates at the resort are $48 double for rooms with shared bath, $65 to $85 for atmospheric suites with private baths (Teddy Roosevelt stayed in one with a fireplace and balcony), $100 and up for condominium units, $75 and $85 for cottages accommodating four or six. Roche Harbor's Hotel De Haro closes from November to about May, but its condominium accommodations remain open in winter when prices drop 15% to 25%.

The Orcas Island Historical Museum in Eastsound (tel. 206/376-4849 or 376-2316) is good for a look into the lives of early pioneers who settled here in the late 1800s. It's open June through August from 1 to 4 p.m. Monday through Saturday, and asks only for a donation.

When hunger strikes, head for the **Duck Soup Inn,** Roche Harbor Road, Friday Harbor (tel. 206/378-4878). Not only the name is intriguing: the cooking here is exemplary too. You'll pay $15 to $20 for dinner. Hours at Duck Soup are 1 p.m. to 10 p.m. daily.

Lopez Island

Much more sparsely populated than San Juan or Orcas Island, Lopez is home to two parks much loved by campers and one of the few good swimming beaches in the San Juan Islands, at Spencer Spit (notice we didn't say anything about warm water). Bicyclers flock to this island to ride the comparatively flat 50 miles of road on the island, and fishing fanatics drop hook, line, and sinker in the trout-filled waters of Hummel Lake.

There's just one resort on the island: **Islander Lopez Lodge,** on Fisherman Bay on the west side of the island (P.O. Box 197), Lopez Island, WA 98261 (tel. 206/468-2233). The Islander Lopez has two large lodges equipped with living room, kitchen, fireplace, and beds for 6 or 12, and about 30 other rooms, plus a hot tub, pool, marina, playground, restaurant, and lounge with entertainment. Rates are $40 to $75 double year round.

Shaw Island

Population: Very small. Activities: Few. Accommodations: None except a six-unit campground at Indian Cove. Scenery: Forests. Fresh water: None. Living: Rough. If you like seclusion and survival training—a great place.

FROM SEDRO WOOLLEY TO NEWHALEM: On we go now from these islands and the nearby tranquil sea-level cities to the heights.

From LaConner, return to Wash. 20; turn east through Burlington to begin the mountain-scenery section of this varied-terrain tour. Suddenly the Hudson's Bay Company of history books takes on meaning: the West's 17th-century trade roots were here in the Skagit River Valley. Your route east along the valley keeps the river on your right as you travel through Sedro Woolley— an early sawmill owner's egotistical combination of the Spanish word for cedar and his own name—on to Lyman, Hamilton, and Concrete (a town named for limestone deposits nearby).

Between Concrete and Marblemount is a 1,500-acre sanctuary for bald eagles. A highway turnout just east of Concrete is the most rewarding spot to view these magnificent birds.

Much of this leg you'll drive in the shadow of Mount Baker, a 10,778-foot peak that's snow-capped year round. You'll see its snowy head 20 miles to the north. In summer or winter, it's a favorite playground for hiking, weekend skiing, and just looking.

Washington Hwy. 20 divides North Cascades National Park into north and south units and leads you through one of the densest pine forests in the world. At Rockport your route swings to a more northerly direction. Now you're in "dam" country. Gorge, Diablo, and Ross Dams follow in quick succession east of Newhalem. These harness the Skagit River to produce more than 550,000 kilowatts of electric power.

A fascinating stop along the way here is at Diablo, where the Seattle City Light Company, the folks who keep the lights on in Seattle, operate a boat tour up the Skagit River to Diablo Dam. Exploration begins with a ride on an incline railroad up Sourdough Mountain to Diablo Dam, then by boat, on the most amazingly green water you'll ever see, to Ross Dam. In four hours Skagit tours give visitors an entertaining look at local history, technology, and natural beauty. Tour arrangements are made with **Seattle City Light Skagit Tours,** 1015 Third Ave., Room 809, Seattle, WA 98104 (tel. 206/386-1234 or 684-3030). Trips leave Diablo at 11 a.m., 1 p.m., and 3:30 p.m. daily except Tuesday and Wednesday. Tour tickets, including an all-you-can-eat chicken dinner served family style, are $18 for adults and $15 for children ages 6 to 12. Tours operate from late June to Labor Day.

Newhalem is the beginning of a 75-mile strip of wilderness without gas stations or restaurants. Fifty-nine miles east of Rockport and climbing, you'll reach Rainy Pass at 4,860 feet, and five miles farther, Washington Pass at 5,477 feet. Two vista points between the passes have pull-off areas so you can get a close look at the Cascades as they roll away to the north and south.

A third viewpoint just east of Washington Pass awaits with all the alpine splendor for which the Cascades are famous. Follow "Scenic Viewpoint" signs to a parking lot. A few steps along a paved walkway bring you to the overlook: Liberty Bell peak rises tall and craggy in front of you and to the north the Pasayten Wilderness, wild and mysterious, a sight to haunt you as you begin the long descent into the Methow River Valley (natives say "Met-ao").

Now the forest thins to reveal craggy cliffs as the lush green of the rainy side of the Cascades gives way to sagebrush and sand. The desert begins.

3. WINTHROP AND WENATCHEE

As Wash. 20 swings south from Mazama, land forms change. Here begins a broad and open land of big vistas teamed with a western frontier atmosphere! Welcome to the Methow Valley.

Thirteen miles down the road is Winthrop, an Old West town that transports you back 100 years with its time-warp Main Street. Rows of false-fronted buildings, wooden sidewalks, and old-fashioned street lights hark back to the 1890s, when a mining boom brought many settlers to the area.

WINTHROP: Seems that things were kind of slow in Winthrop, so the city fathers (and presumably mothers) decided to, shall we say, enhance history a bit. They created wild, wild Winthrop right from the ground up, an O. K. Corral lookalike. Didn't we tell you that you never know *what* to expect in the Pacific Northwest? Up went the Old West false fronts and out came bright new signs renaming everything in town in keeping with this new old image.

It worked. On summer and, for that matter, on winter weekends crowds throng in here to soak up a bit of this Old West theme, to hang out in Three-Fingered Jack's or the Duck Brand Cantina, shop at the Last Trading Post or Wood 'n Wampum.

Lest you think this is a crass grab at the wallet, let it be known that Winthrop really does have a history. Occupied for many summers by Indians, who came here in the warm months to fish for salmon in the Methow River, the town was first settled in 1883 by a Scotsman named James Ramsey. He was almost talked out of the move by Indians who told him there was so much snow here in winter that it took two summers to thaw!

In 1891 the town's best-known ancestor, Guy Waring, opened the Methow Trading Company and a post office. A couple of years later just about everything in town burned down but was rebuilt. In 1897 Waring built himself a new house, now the Shafer Museum. Somewhere along the way Waring invited a friend named Owen Wister to come and visit him. Wister came, saw, and went on to write a book called *The Virginian* about his western experiences.

Despite its location in the 1,000-foot foothills of the Cascades, Winthrop is treated to 300 days of sunshine a year, which makes it a pleasant place to swim, fish, hunt, ride an innertube down the river, or hike the mountains in warm weather. In winter the sun stays around but temperatures plummet to an average of 19°, making the town a lively winter playground, patiently waiting for a long-planned ski lift to get off the ground. In the meantime snowmobiling and cross-country skiing are favorite sports.

If you've ever pictured yourself an urban cowhand, this is the place to try out your swagger. **Winthrop Information Center,** Main Street (P.O. Box 402), Winthrop, WA 98862 (tel. 509/996-2125), can fill you in on local activities, and in winter you can get a report on highway pass conditions by calling 509/663-5151.

If you're staying over here, **Sun Mountain Lodge,** P.O. Box 1000, Winthrop, WA 98862 (tel. 509/996-2211, or toll free 800/572-0493), is a study in stone and massive beams, occupying a wondrous site overlooking the Cascades. Nine miles west of Winthrop, Sun Mountain Lodge has just 50 rooms, two of them suites with fireplace. Sun Mountain keeps you busy with riding trips, a heated pool that is open all year, tennis courts, hiking expeditions, and in winter, skiing at Loup Loup about half an hour's drive away. A good dining room here adds to the inn's appeal, serving up well-loved prime rib, steaks, poultry, and seafood. Rates at the lodge are $60 to $80 double, $100 for suites.

The **Virginian Motel,** North Cascade Hwy. (P.O. Box 237), Winthrop, WA 98862 (tel. 509/996-2535), is as well known for its restaurant as for the log structure that houses 40 nicely decorated quarters, including a few with fireplace. There's a heated swimming pool here too.

All meals are available at that restaurant we mentioned, but specialties of the house are good steaks and chops, some interesting pasta dishes like fettuccine with prosciutto or pesto, and seafood preparations like oysters Florentine, and snapper parmesan, all for prices in the $10 to $15 range for entrees. Rates at the Virginian are $41.50 to $54.50 double.

For dining, we've already mentioned two of the 18 places in town, but let us add that the **Winthrop Palace Hotel,** Main Street (tel. 509/996-2245), provides hearty slabs of steak, plenty of homemade soups and baked goods, and breakfasts that could keep you for a couple of days. Dinner entree prices are in the $10 to $15 range and hours are 8 a.m. to 10 p.m. daily.

Duck Brand Cantina, in the Coates Building, Riverside Avenue (tel. 509/996-2192), and **Three-Fingered Jack's Tavern,** Main Street (tel. 509/996-2411), are popular watering holes serving simple fare. At last check Duck Brand was purveying Italian and Mexican treats, while Three-Fingered Jack was passing out pizza, hot spiced wine, nachos, and hamburgers. Hours are 11 a.m. to whenever things slow down.

As for what to do here, sports are the major pursuit, so we'll concentrate on those. Everything's on Main Street in this small town, by the way.

Several guides operate in the area offering country pack trips, rafting journeys, and skiing. Among those companies are **North Cascade Safari** (tel. 509/996-2350), specializing in pack trips by horseback; **Chewack Riding Stables** (tel. 509/996-2497), also specializing in equestrian activities; **Methow Valley Guides** (tel. 509/996-2507), offering rafting trips and high-country skiing expeditions; **Rocking Horse Ranch** (tel. 509/996-2768), sponsoring two-day trips into the backcountry; and **Rendezvous Outfitters** (tel. 509/997-0822), teaching skiing and offering a wilderness ski hut.

Racers in innertubes, canoes, and rafts tear down the Methow on a 12-mile river race in early July and in mid-September the city hosts an **antique auto rally and rodeo.** In mid-January annual **Dog Sled Races** draw nearly 100 sled teams from all over the West.

Be sure to visit the **Shafer Museum,** a few steps from downtown and housed in the Guy Waring Log Cabin built in 1897. Exhibits drawn from the upper Methow's early days include furniture, tools, old bicycles, and carriages.

STEHEKIN AND LAKE CHELAN: Travel 59 miles farther, and another jewel of the Cascades glistens into view. Lake Chelan traces a 60-mile-long finger into the very heart of the mountains. The result is a Norwegian fjord with mountains sloping to water's edge—steep cliffs, water cascades, mountain goats, and at its head, far into the mountains and far beyond the last road to outside, the old village of Stehekin, now a park concession. There are only two ways to get to Stehekin: fly in or take the *Lady of the Lake,* a cruise boat which leaves Chelan docks each morning at 8:30 a.m. from April 15 to mid-October for an all-day round trip. The fare is $19 for adults, $9.50 for children 6 to 11; younger children, free. For information, call 509/682-4584 or 682-2224. Schedules vary from November to April.

At Lake Chelan is a paradise for the smallfry: a massive complex called **Slidewaters** offers a veritable maze of swooping slides, hot tubs, and other spluttery fun. Admission is $8.50 for adults and $5.50 for children under 7. You'll find this slippy-slidy park open from 10 a.m. to dusk Memorial Day through Labor Day. Look for the slides just off U.S. 97 at Prospect Street and Waterslide Drive (tel. 509/682-5751).

For longer stays here you can get more information on what to do and see by contacting the **Lake Chelan Chamber of Commerce,** P.O. Box 216, Lake Chelan, WA 98816 (tel. 509/682-2022, or toll free 800/4CHELAN in Washington).

WENATCHEE: Thirty-nine miles along the banks of the Columbia River you arrive at Wenatchee, self-proclaimed Apple Capital of the World.

Wenatchee traces its roots to 1811, when fur traders came to trap and trade with the Indians. Paddlewheelers once steamed up the Columbia to Chelan and all the way down to Portland before dams made river traffic impossible.

Wenatchee is a betwixt-and-between spot, with alpine meadows and towering mountains on one side, arid deserts on the other.

Between all that geological drama lies this bustling market town of 42,000 people. Western Washington dwellers race over here to "the other side" to soak up an abundance of sunshine in summer and head this direction in winter to ski fluffy powder on the eastern side of the Cascades at Mission Ridge.

Getting There

You can fly into Pangborn Field on United Airlines. The **Greyhound bus** stops at the station at 301 1st St. (tel. 509/662-2183). **Amtrak** pulls into its station at the foot of Kittitas Street twice daily.

Rental cars are available from **Hertz** at Pangborn Field (tel. 509/662-6134), or from **Alpine Motors,** 132 N. Wenatchee Ave. (tel. 509/663-0587), in downtown Wenatchee.

Travelers driving in from the north will find that the final leg of their journey will be on U.S. 2, while those from the south and east will arrive on Wash. 28. U.S. 2 runs from Wenatchee on the east to Everett on the west.

Visitor Information

Wenatchee Area Visitor and Convention Bureau, 2 S. Chelan Ave., (P.O. Box 850), Wenatchee, WA 98807 (tel. 509/662-4774, or toll free 800/57-APPLE in Washington), is housed in the historic Carnegie Building.

Where to Stay

The **Chieftain Motel**, 105 N. Wenatchee Ave., Wenatchee, WA 98801 (tel. 509/663-8141), lures many a summer visitor with a big pool that is a welcome sight on hot summer days.

Attractively decorated rooms are in a good-looking, wood-sided, two-story building with glass doors opening onto private balconies. Rooms dubbed "executive" are extra large and have queen-size beds and a sitting area. Televisions, of course, and telephones. Rates are $42 to $47 double.

You'll find a dining room here togged out in red and black and a bar called the Pow Wow Room. There is entertainment almost every night.

What to See and Do

If you have even the tiniest interest in gardens, you must not miss the **Ohme Gardens,** perched on a rock bluff overlooking the Wenatchee Valley. The nine-acre grounds are ranked among the leading gardens in America. Sixty years in the making, the once-barren hillside is now an alpine wonderland.

Wild alpine flowers bloom here each spring, to the in-unison gasps of flower fanciers. From here you can see the Wenatchee River curling merrily along the valley, ogle the Cascades rising in snow-capped splendor, and even watch the Columbia River coursing to the sea. Located three miles north of Wenatchee off U.S. 97, the gardens are open daily April 15 through October 15 from 9 a.m. to dusk. Admission is $3 for adults and $1.50 for children 7 to 18.

Dam fans will want to detour to **Rocky Reach Dam,** seven miles north on U.S. 97/2, where 15 acres of lawns and gardens offer you plenty of places to curl up and stare at the concrete. At the visitor center you can stare down a salmon heading upstream to its last gala evening and visit the Gallery of Electricity. Admission is free and the exhibits are open daily from dawn to dark.

Mission Ridge points out that it is the region's premier downhill skiing facility, with 31 runs. Certainly it has all the appearance of premier: four chair lifts and three rope tows get you up to 33 groomed trails more than two miles long and powder bowls. There's a ski school here too. Information on facilities is available from the Mission Ridge office (tel. 509/663-6543) or the Wenatchee Area Visitor and Convention Bureau (tel. 509/662-4774, or toll free 800/57-APPLE in Washington). Mission Ridge is 13 miles southwest of Wenatchee: follow the west bank of the Columbia out of town to the Old Stagecoach Road and turn west at the fork toward Appleyard to Mission Park.

You can always be sure of snow, here, thanks to snowmaking equipment. Lift prices are $18 a day for adults, $13 for children 7 to 13, free for under-7s. Half days are $13 for adults, $10 for children, and the rope tow is free. Some days and nights two-for-one prices are offered and three- to five-day passes are available.

Mission Ridge is open daily (including holidays) from December 10 through Easter Sunday, earlier and later if there's snow. Overnight facilities are not available, but there is a lodge with a sundeck, cafeteria, and snack spot. Skiing from 9 a.m. to 4 p.m. Wednesday through Sunday and 5 to 10 p.m. five nights a week. Get a snow report by calling 509/663-7631.

Special Events

Apples are as sweet to the cash register out this way as they are to the tooth, so naturally the city honors them with a **Washington State Apple Blossom Festival** in early May. The festival is capped by a colorful **Apple Blossom Parade** on the first Saturday in May.

Sports

We've already mentioned swimming, but there are sundry other sports possible at **Lake Chelan**—boating, diving, baseball, and whatever else for which you have imagination and equipment.

Golfers have a choice of courses, including **Crescent Bar Island Golf Course,** about 20 miles south of Wenatchee on Wash. 28 (tel. 509/787-1511); **Rock Island Golf Course,** 314 Saunders Rd., Rock Island (about 9 ½ miles southeast of the city off Wash. 28), a nine-hole course (tel. 509/884-2806); **Three Lakes Golf,** five miles south of Wenatchee on West Malaga Road, an 18-hole, 5,354-yard course; and at Lake Chelan, the **Lake Chelan Golf Course,** an 18-hole, 6,300-yard challenge (tel. 509/682-5421).

Hockey players and ice skaters can get out on the blades on two sheets of ice at **Wenatchee Ice Rink,** 5th Street at Worthen (tel. 509/662-7731).

Finally at **Douglas County Park** there are bumper boats to amuse the youngsters—and perhaps the not-so-young-sters. Open daily May through September from 9 a.m. to dusk.

If you've outrun all the runs at Mission Ridge, hop on over to **Echo Valley** at Chelan and see what's happening with the schussing crowd there.

Arts

Who could resist a theater called Laughing Horse? We couldn't, and we're glad we didn't. That snickering equine provides you with a summer full of repertory theater with plays ranging from mystery to comedy. Performances of the **Laughing Horse Summer Theater** are at the Tower Theater in McConnell Hall on the Central Washington University campus, at 14th Avenue in Ellensburg (tel. 509/963-3400), and begin at 8 p.m. Tuesday through Saturday (dark Sunday and Monday), from the beginning of July to mid-August.

Take the Old Stagecoach Road south out of Wenatchee for a historic drive to Ellensburg. A season ticket to all four plays is $19.50, and individual admissions are $5.50 to $6.50. You can write the theater at P.O. Box 1412, Ellensburg, WA 98926.

Shopping

In downtown Wenatchee you'll find free parking in the shopping district near the Convention Center at 121 N. Wenatchee Ave.

At **Mission Square,** 2nd Street and Mission Avenue, an eclectic assortment of shops and boutiques beckons, and at **Wenatchee Valley Mall** there are 47 stores full of treasures (it's across the bridge in East Wenatchee).

Valley North Mall is a king-size shopping center with 25 acres of stores and parking. It is in north Wenatchee at Valley Mall Parkway.

A new shopping area in town is a cunning spot: it's a group of houses togged out to look like a Victorian village. That, in fact, is the name of this spot, **Victorian Village,** at 611 Mission St.

4. CENTRAL AND SOUTHERN CASCADES

It's time to hold tight to your incredulity now. About 7 miles west on U.S. 2 is a town right out of the 1880s, and 12 miles down the road is a U.S. Bavaria!

When their lumber-based economies waned in the 1960s, tiny Cashmere and Leavenworth knew they were headed for the big ghost town in the sky. A Washingtonian give up? Never. Cashmere decided early America suited it best, while Leavenworth transformed itself into a bustling little alpine village with quaint shops and galleries.

Nestled in the foothills, Leavenworth is Bavarian Village. From architecture to foods, crafts, and festivals, Leavenworth's success with this innovative reconstruction project is downright amazing. Between the downtown areas of these two old, nearly forgotten, railroad towns runs the Wenatchee River, on which a leisurely rafting trip makes a pleasant Cascades experience.

LEAVENWORTH: Leavenworth looms up in the middle of the road like a Bavarian mirage! One minute you're driving through mountains, streams, and little settlements; the next you're in a forest of chalets, carved shutters, ornate wall paintings, and lederhosen.

What happened here in the town with the "jail name" was a little crazy and a lot canny. Leavenworth, you see, was an uninteresting little burg, lined with motels, a few shops, and a couple of gas stations. When the citizenry sought to make the town a more inviting, tourist-worthy spot, one canny couple suggested, "Why not make ourselves a Bavarian village here in the mountains?"

Not everyone in town thought this alpine approach was such a terrific idea. At first. But as time went on and bank balances went down, it seemed worth a try. Little by little the townspeople worked together to iron out their differences over this instant-village plan. Loans were floated, craftspeople came from Europe, flowers were planted, and *voilà!*—instant Austria.

Today what those Washingtonians have created is nothing short of wonderful. Huge pots of flowers in all the colors of the rainbow are scattered about the streets. Wooden signs and shutters are ornately carved and painted. There's a delightful shop that sells nothing but delicate little music boxes, another that's filled with wooden Christmas ornaments and intriguing wooden toys. Every place in town—even the Chinese restaurant—has its flowery, shuttered Austrian front.

The idea worked. On any day you'll find the town jammed with delighted visitors drinking in the effervescent mood of the place. Cash registers ring merrily and Leavenworth is, these days, very, very happy. We think you'll be just as happy when you discover this unusual oasis in the middle of the Cascades.

Even the local newspaper's Bavarian: it's called *Sonnenschein* ("Sunshine" to the rest of us). In summer the town's a study in rainbow-hued blossoms, popping out everywhere you look, from sidewalk barrels to balcony boxes. At Christmas the village becomes a wonderland of sparkling lights twinkling from rooflines and rimming the town's central gazebo. Handbell ringers and a costumed Bavarian band play throughout the year and are always on hand for the town's three major festivals: the **Maifest** on the second weekend of May, the week-long **Washington State Autumn Leaf Festival** beginning the last weekend of September, and the **Christmas Lighting Festival** on the first and second Saturdays in December, when even Scrooge turns up in Leavenworth.

Getting Around

U.S. 2 runs right through the middle of town, although Main, Front, and Commercial Streets, on the south side of the highway, are the primary shopping spots. Most of the motels are located right along U.S. 2, although a few small hotels are tucked in above shops and restaurants.

If somehow you got here without a car, you can get yourself some wheels for local exploring at **Mike's Moped Rental,** on U.S. 2 at 268 Sholtz St. (tel. 509/548-5590). Rates are $3.50 an hour or about $16 a day.

Bicycle Rental (tel. 509/548-4381 or 548-7325) delivers bikes to you, so they're not telling their street address. You can call them for reservation and delivery any day from 6 a.m. to 9 p.m. A deposit of $10 is required, and bike-rental rates are $12.50 a day for one bike, $20 a day for two; half day, $7.50.

Tourist Information

The friendly **Leavenworth Chamber of Commerce** folks at a teensy corner office with lace curtains will be happy to provide you with all the material you need to have a real alpine adventure during your stay in town. You'll find the chamber on U.S. 2 (P.O. Box 327), Leavenworth, WA 98826 (tel. 509/548-5807).

Where to Stay

If you love the place so much you don't want to leave (and that's a good possibility), you have a variety of interesting choices.

Some hostelries are just simple motels with a bright and beautiful façade. Most, however, have gone all-out with carved furniture, antique painted pieces, and frilly curtains to reproduce that Bavarian *gemütlichkeit*. There's even a bed-and-breakfast *pensione* in a chalet!

We might as well start with a hotel named after the Austrian national anthem: **Edelweiss Hotel and Restaurant,** 843 Front St., Leavenworth, WA 98826 (tel. 509/548-7015). Decked out with little balconies, beamed eaves, flower boxes, and colorful wall paintings, the Edelweiss has four rooms with baths (nos. 1, 3, 4, and 12). Those are the four prettiest too, one with white French provincial furniture and décor, a triangular balcony with glass doors, and a smashing view of the mountains. All the rooms are on the second floor, with the hotel's cozy little restaurant downstairs. Rates for rooms with bath are $31.50 to $38; those without baths are $18.75 for a room with single bed and $19.25 to $23.75 (all including tax) for a room with double bed; for one with two doubles and shared bath you'll pay $33.75. Baths and showers are quite near rooms without in-room bathing facilities.

A similar hotel a few steps away is the **Hotel Europa,** 833 Front St., Leavenworth, WA 98826 (tel. 509/548-5221). Here you'll find a few rooms with pretty, antique-looking, high headboards—one is red trimmed with tiny painted flowers—and, sometimes, a view out over Front Street. Once again the hotel is on the second floor, the restaurant at ground level. A couple of units here have kitchens too. A room with a view is $47 (as are rooms with kitchen facilities), and rooms without scenery are $36, all including tax and continental breakfast. There's a swimming pool here too.

Yet another spot on the same street is the **Tyrolean Inn,** 633 Front St., Leavenworth, WA 98826 (tel. 509/568-5455). Above a lounge and a large, comfortable restaurant you'll find rather basic rooms, most with Jacuzzis, with views of the town and mountains. The restaurant serves Bavarian entrees buffet style in the $10 price range. Rates at the inn rise from $40 double to $75 for suites, and $5 for additional persons. Off-peak-season rates are discounted 20%.

The **Enzian Motor Inn,** 590 U.S. 2, Leavenworth, WA 98826 (tel. 509/548-5269, or toll free 800/223-8511 in Washington), takes its Bavarian commitment so seriously it hides its air conditioning units with flower boxes! A new motor inn, the Enzian is bright as a new penny from the tan wood siding to the elaborate alpine architecture. You'll find 57 rooms here, all with queen-size beds plus some suites with Jacuzzis and fireplaces. Furnishings were imported from Austria to create the contemporary but cozily Austrian atmosphere you'll find at this sprawling hostelry. Continental breakfast, served in a very cozy little loft over the lobby, is included in the motor inn's rates of $56, single or double, for a room with one bed, $59 for one with two beds. Executive suites with king-size beds and honeymoon-anniversary suites with Jacuzzi and fireplace are higher.

If you've ever wondered what a real European pension is like, wonder no more. Stop in at the **Haus Rohrbach Pension**, 12882 Ranger Rd., Leavenworth, WA 98826 (tel. 509/548-7024), and you will see one in action. Cuddled up to the base of Tumwater Mountain, the lodge is a study in flower-bedecked alpine architecture. Rooms have charming names like Windsong, Dayspring, Alpenglow, and Wildflower, and all are adorned with fresh flowers and candy. Six rooms have beautiful views and the rest have just very, very pretty views. Six rooms also now have private bath and two rooms on each floor share a bath. Evenings, the pension serves apple, berry, or peanut-butter pie or Schwarzwalder kirsch torte, and the inn makes its own salsas, jams, preserves, and sauces with produce from its own gardens. Country crafts are available here too. Breakfast is served on a big deck overlooking still more views. Some rooms here share bathrooms, and some are quite small, but the neat, clean atmosphere of the place makes up for shortcomings. Rates range from $60 to $80 double.

River's Edge Lodge, 8401 U.S. 2, Leavenworth, WA 98826 (tel. 509/548-7612), is geographically irresistible: a cluster of 23 rooms right on the edge of the Wenatchee River, so close to the water you could just about dangle a hook out your window. Rooms are simply but attractively decorated; some have kitchens and all have free coffee. Rates are $40 double.

CAMPING. Outdoor folks will find a cozy camping spot tucked in among the pines at **Pine Village KOA Campground**, 11401 River Bend Dr., Leavenworth, WA 98826 (tel. 509/548-7709). In the shadow of 7,000-foot mountains you can frolic in a heated swimming pool. Rates for three are $20 for full hookup, and $2 to $4 a day for extra persons.

Where to Eat

Restaurants are tucked away in many a nook and cranny of this nook-and-cranny-filled town.

The **Edelweiss,** in the Edelweiss Hotel and Restaurant, 843 Front St. (tel. 509/548-7015), is open for all meals, and at dinner German specialties are the order of the day. Fondue is available too, and the apple strudel is terrific. Prices are in the $10 to $14 range, including salad bar, potato, and vegetable. Try the restaurant's scaloni, billed as a combination of scallops and abalone. Hours are 7 a.m. to 10 p.m.

The **Tyrolean Inn,** 633 Front St. (tel. 509/548-5455), is open daily from 7 a.m. to 10 p.m. and on weekends features a Bier Garten specializing in that rib-sticking German fare and plenty of suds. Steaks and seafoods are the mainstays other days, when prices are in the $10 to $14 range for entrees.

Katzenjammers Steak & Seafood, 221 8th St. (tel. 509/548-5826), is a lively spot where visitors gather to chow down on steaks, prime rib, and seafood in the $10 to $12 price range. It's open from 11 a.m. to 10 p.m.

Café Christa, upstairs at 801 Front St. (tel. 509/548-5074), offers a pretty mountain view. German cooking is the specialty here, so step right up for wienerschnitzel and sauerkraut at delightful prices in the $10 to $15 range. Café hours are 11 a.m. to 10 p.m.

What to See and Do

This *town* is what to see and do! Leavenworth itself is a lovely place to explore, to look closely at the transformation these townspeople have created—American ingenuity at its best.

Beyond that, in winter cross-country skiing is a favorite pastime in these parts. You can buy or **rent ski equipment** and get all the info on where and how to go about your trek at **Der Sportsman,** Front Street (tel. 509/548-5623).

Cross-country skiing treks are operated from the **Haus Rohrbach Pension** (see "Where to Stay"), where touring, instructions, and rentals are overseen by Liv Nurman. There's a pool and hot tub there too, in case newly discovered muscles need a soak.

At the **Leavenworth Golf Club** (tel. 509/548-7267), golfers can duff around a picturesque 18-hole course at a horseshoe bend of the Wenatchee River. The course is 5,695 yards long and is open daily until the diehards begin to lose the little white orb in the snowbanks.

Northern Wilderness Company, P.O. Box 265, Leavenworth, WA 98826 (tel. 509/548-4583), offers statewide **river-rafting trips** that splash down the Wenatchee and the Methow Rivers, among others. Trips vary in price according to length.

Also in the rafting game, **Leavenworth Quiet Water Outfitters and Guides,** 21588 Wash. 209, Leavenworth, WA 98826 (tel. 509/763-3733), offers one- and two-day trips for $35 to $45 per person, and also rents canoes. **Wenatchee Whitewater,** P.O. Box 12, Cashmere, WA 98815 (tel. 509/782-2254), has a roster of eight different river trips ranging from a two-hour meander downriver at $22 per adult, to a three-day Methow/white-water trip for $240 per person.

Late spring, by the way, is prime time for big waves that challenge experienced wave-jumpers, while summer is for the toes-over-the-side-of-the-raft crowd; fall is fine for drift fishing and innertube "train" rides.

Shopping

In case you haven't been listening, Leavenworth itself is one big boutique, filled with a variety of smaller boutiques. Everybody sells something here, but all the somethings are something you're likely to want: wooden toys, antiques, local pottery, handmade candles and homemade candies, colorful Christmas ornaments, country fabrics, gingham and calico things by the billions.

If we had to pick one shop—a terrifying thought—we'd have to give the nod to **Die Musik Box,** a tiny shop filled with the sound of music playing on dozens of music boxes, no two alike. If there's a song written that they don't have—unlikely—they'll get it. This tuneful trading post is at 837 Front St. (tel. 509/548-4101). And don't buy the one with the tiny Austrian girls twirling on the top—we're coming back for that one! Open from 10 a.m. to 6 p.m. daily. If you can't wait to get there to buy, you can write for a catalog that pictures the most popular of the store's tinklers.

Groceries may be the last thing you'd consider shopping for on your vacation, but perhaps the thought of fat grapes, juicy peaches, bing cherries right off the tree . . . have we got your attention? Then stop for a look at **Prey's Fruit Barn,** a mile and a half east of Leavenworth (tel. 509/548-5771). Cold juice and spicy ciders are among the goodies. Open July through November from 9 a.m. to 5 p.m., sometimes later.

GOLD BAR, STARTUP, SULTAN, AND SNOHOMISH: Leaving Leavenworth you begin a climb to **Stevens Pass,** 4,061 feet up and 36 miles west. Here thin vegetation gives way abruptly as you reach the pass and a dense forest trumpets the arrival of logging territory. **Vista points** on either side of the pass give you a chance to wonder how those westbound pioneers got through these trees. Look closely through the new growth trees and you will see four- to six-

foot-diameter stumps of the original virgin forest that tested the stamina, skill, and imagination of the men and women who made that trek.

Over the pass this four-lane highway begins the long descent to Skykomish, then to Index, about 25 miles away. From the **Mount Index lookout** you'll see Mount Index rising 5,979 feet to the southwest, as well as **Sunset Falls** and **Eagle Falls.**

The next three towns, Goldbar, Startup, and Sultan, all began life in Gold Rush days, and some of the oldtimers will be able to tell you where to find a few traces.

That town name, **Startup,** would make more sense to you if you were heading east instead of west—the highway "starts up" there, beginning its climb to the pass from this village. Before leaving Startup, stop by **Skykomish State Salmon Hatchery,** located just east of town. Open to the public year round (from 9 a.m. to 5 p.m. daily; free), the hatchery will give you an idea of what it takes to keep salmon on your table.

One last lookout, about four miles west of Sultan, gives you a last look at the mighty Cascades. From here to Everett on the Pacific coast, rolling, heavily timbered hills give way to dairyland and vegetable farms.

In **Snohomish,** the state's antiques capital, the streets are lined with gorgeous old Victorian-era mansions. Walking-tour maps of the city, which is these days a happy hunting ground for antique seekers, are available from the **Snohomish Chamber of Commerce** adjacent to the Blackman Historic Museum (P.O. Box 135), Snohomish, WA 98290 (tel. 206/568-2526). Antique shops by the dozen are on 1st Street and at Star Center Mall, 829 2nd St., which has more than 150 shops open daily from 10 a.m. to 5 p.m.

The Salish Lodge, 37807 S.E. Snoqualmie Falls City Rd. (P.O. Box 1109), Snoqualmie, WA 98065 (tel. 206/888-2556, or toll free 800/826-6124), is the latest creation of the folks who dreamed up the Oregon coast's legendary landmark, Salishan. What they have done here at this historic Snoqualmie property is just as cozy and cosmopolitan as you would expect. Occupying a just slightly spectacular site above Snoqualmie Falls, Salish Lodge offers 91 rooms, complete, they said in their early ads, with "running water." If you've ever wanted to live on the edge without any of the fear that normally accompanies that kind of living, this place is your nirvana.

Drama reigns outside here in the magnificent falls pouring over a massive cliff. Inside, a cozy country-inn atmosphere abetted by a wood-burning fireplace in your room, puffy comforters, and polished woods, surrounds you in snugness. There are few inns in the Northwest with such dramatic scenery, both interior and exterior. Rates are $150 to $165 double for rooms with two doubles or a king-size bed, whirlpool tub, small refrigerator, and remote-control television. If you'd like to share this joy with 20 close friends, you can fit all those easily into a parlor suite that rents for $400 a night.

John D. Rockefeller thought enough of **Everett** to lead a group of eastern investors to begin development of the town in 1891. **Boeing Aircraft** moved in here, locating its 747/767 assembly plant at Pain Field, at I-5 exit 189 west. By volume it is the largest building in the world. Tours are free, weekdays from 10 a.m. to 4 p.m.

The last portion of your trip is the easy 29-mile glide down I-5 to Seattle.

5. WASHINGTON'S APPLE COUNTRY: YAKIMA

Although Yakima is well off the Cascade loop, it is so popular with Washington sunseekers that we're including it here, in case you're a sunseeker, too.

That sun we're talking about does more than just warm western Washington's rain-weary residents. It also turns this region into the state's most fruitful valley. On a visit here you'll drive through mile after mile of apple and cherry groves and pass by plenty of tempting fruit stands.

GETTING THERE: Horizon, PSA, and United Airlines fly into **Yakima Municipal Airport** (tel. 509/575-6149).
 Greyhound buses stop at 602 E. Yakima Ave. (tel. 509/457-5135) and bring visitors here from many parts of the state and the nation.

TOURIST INFORMATION: Information seekers should head straight for the **Yakima Valley Visitors and Convention Bureau,** 10 N. 8th St., Yakima, WA 98907 (tel. 509/575-1300), where workers will be happy to answer your questions.
 Two other information sources are the **Greater Yakima Chamber of Commerce,** P.O. Box 1490, Yakima, WA 98907 (tel. 509/248-2021); and the **Yakima Motel Association,** 1300 N. 1st St., Yakima, WA 98901 (tel. 509/248-6666).

USEFUL INFORMATION: For **police emergencies,** call 509/248-1010. . . . For **minor medical emergencies,** call or go to Westside Medi-Center, 40th and Tieton Dr. (tel. 509/965-1770), where someone will be on hand to help from 7:30 a.m. to 11:30 p.m. every day of the year. . . . To discover whether the sun will shine today, call for the **weather** at 509/453-8934. . . . If you're here at a time of year when there's reason to wonder about the **road conditions in mountain passes,** call 509/575-2606 for the latest word. . . . Alpine Automotive Service has **24-hour road service** and both diesel and nondiesel gasoline at 213 S. Third Ave. (tel. 509/248-9921). . . . **Tiger Bin Mini Mart** at 1808 N. 1st. (tel. 509/248-9421), has gas and packaged snacks night and day. . . . Send your cleaning to **Frank Wear Cleaners,** 106 S. Third Ave. (tel. 509/248-0310), for quick service.

WHERE TO STAY: You won't find a plethora of hotels in this agricultural center, but there is one very large motor inn and quite a line-up of smaller motels.
 Top of the line in Yakima is the **Towne Plaza,** at North 7th Street and East Yakima Avenue, Yakima, WA 98901 (tel. 509/248-5900, or toll free 800/572-9181). This resort sprawls right in the middle of town, as the name might suggest. You're greeted in a two-story lobby that winds around and around, finally leading you to three restaurants, two lounges, 155 guest rooms, a beauty shop, gift shop, and two swimming pools. At this almost-a-city motor inn, spacious rooms have colorful spreads and carpets and sliding doors onto a balcony or terrace, many of them overlooking a curving swimming pool. You can expect to pay $48 to $62 double for a room with a double queen-size, or king-size, bed. Suites with a bar are $85 to $145.
 At the end of a long day, you can plunk down in a sauna or leap into a heated pool at the **Comfort Inn Mesa Motel,** 1700 N. 1st St., Yakima, WA 98901 (tel. 509/248-5650). Located just a few blocks off the main Wash. 82 thoroughfare, this wood-sided, two-story motor inn with a shingled mansard roof offers newly renovated rooms with simple but attractive furnishings. The Mesa treats you to a complimentary continental breakfast and has a free airport courtesy car. Rates are $44.50 to $48.50 double.

WHERE TO DINE: The **Red Robin,** Nob Hill Plaza, Nob Hill Boulevard (tel. 509/575-1575), rises with the sparrows and closes with the nightowls. In this good-looking coffeeshop brightened by skylights and lined with greenery you'll find good, simply prepared food suited to all the family. Red Robin wakens at 11 a.m. and finally flags at midnight daily. Prices are quite reasonable, in the $10 to $15 range for dinner. There are 29 kinds of burgers here!

If you're shopping at Yakima Mall, take a breather at **The Market Place** (tel. 509/457-7170). Chow on sinful pastries, or sip specialty teas or espresso while you contemplate just how badly you need that gorgeous. . . .

For a change of pace and a return to days of yesteryear, stop by the **Heritage Inn Restaurant** at the Yakima Indian Nation Cultural Center, about 20 miles south of Yakima on U.S. 97 north of Toppenish (tel. 509/865-2551). Specializing in seafood and steak, the Heritage Inn also serves up Indian fried bread, Columbia River sturgeon, buffalo steak, and lighter meals like salmon nuggets and fries (where else but in the Northwest would you find that one?). Huckleberry pie winds it up. Prices are in the $7 to $10 bracket or less, and there are frequent specials. The Heritage Inn is open 8 a.m. to 5 p.m.

A comparative newcomer in town is the **Greystone Restaurant,** in the Lund Bldg. a 5 N. Front St. (tel. 509/248-9801). Built at the turn of the century as the Alfalfa Saloon, the Greystone comes complete with well-aged stone walls, an antique mirrored bar, and ceiling fans. Pastas are made right here, as are the crackers, but the menu includes a wide range of beef, chicken, and seafood selections. Prices are in the $10 to $15 range and this atmospheric restaurant is open from 6 to 10 p.m. daily except Monday; the lounge opens at 4 p.m. daily except Monday and shuts when the last reveler disappears.

One of the most respected restaurants in the Northwest is right here in Yakima: **Gasperetti's Gourmet,** 1013 N. 1st St. (tel. 509/248-0628). Pouring out top-quality Italian cuisine featuring fresh fish of the region, specialty veals, and delicate pastas, Gasperetti's also has an impressive list of local and imported wines. You'll pay $10 to $15 for dinner at this mainstay of central Washington dining, open from 5:45 to 10:30 p.m. Tuesday through Saturday.

Several times voted the best restaurant in central Washington, **Birchfield Manor,** Birchfield Road (tel. 509/452-1960), is a massively showy old 23-room farmhouse that has been lovingly restored and filled with antiques. Everything here is carefully prepared and elegantly presented. Continental cuisine is the order of the day, as are seven-course fixed-price meals that begin with soup and unusual breads, followed by equally unusual salads, often beef or pork entrees straight from the fields of eastern Washington topped with imaginative sauces, fresh local vegetables, coffee, and dessert. Figure about three hours and $25 per person, plus wine, for the whole gustatory shebang. Birchfield Manor has seatings at 7 p.m. on Friday, 6 and 9 p.m. on Saturday, and 6 p.m. on Sunday only.

Yakima has quite a large Mexican population so you'll find some of the best Mexican food in the Northwest right here. One of the places to begin looking is **Santiago's,** 111 E. Yakima Ave. (tel. 509/453-1644). You can pull up a margarita here and tuck into some innovative treatment of south-of-the-border specialties. Santiago's prices are in the $10 bracket or less, and the restaurant is open from 11 a.m. to 2:30 p.m. and 5 to 8:30 p.m. daily.

NIGHTLIFE: Even if you don't have a chance to attend one of the entertaining events at the **Capitol Theatre,** 19 S. 3rd St. (tel. 509/575-6267 for tours), stop by for a look at this lovingly restored 1920 structure. Don't miss the hand-painted ceilings. A variety of entertainment goes on the boards here year round at a variety of prices.

Try out Grant's Scottish Ale, a local brew at the **Brewery Pub,** a cozy spot at 25½ N. Front St. (tel. 509/575-1900). Wednesday is live music night, everything from classical to country. On quieter evenings dart players turn up for private tournaments, light meals, and plenty of what the name suggests. The Brewery Pub is open from 11 a.m. to 11 p.m. daily.

WHAT TO SEE AND DO: Clang-clanging **trolley cars** ride the rails in Yakima on summer weekends from 11 a.m. to 3 p.m. Every Saturday and Sunday from early May to mid-October cars leave on the hour from Fourth Avenue and Pine. The 45-minute trip takes you past orchards, across the Naches River, along the Yakima Ridge through Selah Gap, past "convicts" cave to the Selah Civic Center and return. To find out when and where the trolleys are going, call Yakima Interurban Lines Association at 509/575-1700. Offices are at 10 N. 8th St.

Yakima Indians gave their name to this city ages ago and will explain how it all came about at the **Yakima Indian Nation Cultural Center,** a half mile north of Toppenish on U.S. 97, which is 20 miles south of Yakima on U.S. 97 (tel. 509/865-2800). Dioramas and exhibits at this top-rated center outline the history of the Yakimas. You'll also get to look at a tepee and an Indian winter lodge. A gift shop here offers a variety of crafts created by Yakima and other Indian tribes.

In spring and autumn it's open daily from 10 a.m. to 6 p.m.; summer hours are 9 a.m. to 9 p.m. Admission is free on Monday; other days it's $5 for a family group of five or more or $2 for adults and $1 for seniors.

One more interesting Indian activity here: **salmon fishing.** Only Indians are permitted to fish the area just below Sunnyside Irrigation Dam, where the salmon run in the last week of April and the first week of May. You'll find the dam three miles south of Union Gap on Wash. 12. Watching is free.

Those early soldiers did all right by themselves, as you will see on a visit to **Fort Simcoe,** a cornerstone of Fort Simcoe State Park, 28 miles west of Toppenish at the end of Wash. 220 (tel. 509/874-2372). Here five buildings constructed in 1856 remain to prove that there *was* life—and a pretty good one —on army posts before the slab-sided concrete monsters the army now uses. Open daily during daylight hours and free. Tours are available Wednesday through Sunday.

The 38,000 square feet of exhibit space at the **Yakima Valley Museum,** 2105 Tieton Dr. (tel. 509/248-0747), is almost exclusively devoted to local history. A hands-on section is a special delight for children—and we saw quite a few adults ringing the schoolbell and grinding coffee too! Plains and plateau Indian artifact exhibits, a general store and post office, blacksmith shop, rock and mineral collection, and a most comprehensive horse-drawn wagon collection keep young and old amused and bemused. Hours are 10 a.m. to 5 p.m. Wednesday through Friday and noon to 5 p.m. on Saturday and Sunday. Admission is $5 per family or $2.50 for adults, $1.25 for seniors and students.

Yakima Valley Museum also operates the **H. M. Gilbert Homeplace,** 2109 W. Yakima Ave. (tel. 509/452-1461), a delightful turn-of-the-century farmhouse listed on the National Register of Historic Places. The homeplace is open April through December on Friday from 10 a.m. to 3 p.m. for tours and tea. Admission is $3 per person.

For a wine tour, call **Robinson Valley Wine Tours** at 509/457-7522. They'll hit the highlights of this vintage-conscious country and wheel you home.

For general tours of the area, try **Sunshine Valley Tours,** 4602 Glenmoor Circle (tel. 509/966-4863), or **Yakima Valley Bus Tours,** 2505 W. Yakima Ave. (tel. 509/248-3707). Tour prices are about $12.

The **Yakima Brewing and Malting Company, Inc.,** produces those golden suds at 25 N. Front St. (tel. 509/575-1900), and will take you on tours of their factory. After you've seen how it's done, stop in next door to sample the brew at the Brewery Pub, which also features some good pub grub at prices in the $3 to $5 range.

Crunch! Apples are big business out this way. To find out just what they can do with those toothsome orbs—and sample a few—stop at Tree Top, at the corner of 2nd and Railroad, in the nearby village of Selah (tel. 509/697-6151), about a mile north of I-82, where you will find another "est" superlative: the largest apple-processing plant in the world. They'll even give you a sample of their juice products. Free.

Archeologists and historians will want to have a look at **Indian Rocks,** where ancient Indians painted pictures of what was most familiar to them—the sun—and the most unfamiliar—their gods. You can see them at Naches Highway and Powerhouse Road, but you'll have to traverse a path and staircase. Free and open anytime.

Kids will love **Applewood Park,** where you ride a pulley and visit a water castle—by swimming to it! It's in Naches, which you reach via Wash. 12 west. Free.

Now here's something you can't do just anywhere: feed the elks! There's an **elk-feeding station** on the road to White Pass (that's Wash. 12 west). Look for the fork in the road after you pass the sign, walk a path in, and grab a handful of food to feed those horned and hungry fellows. Free and a springtime event.

SPECIAL EVENTS: Horses are almost as important out here in the farmland as they were when the pioneers first rode them through town. In June you can see an **All Indian Rodeo** and a statewide horse competition in White Swan, an **Arabian Horse Show,** a high school rodeo, and **Indian pow-wows.**

The **Central Washington State Fair and Rodeo** is a rip-roaring event that takes place each September. Head for the fairgrounds at Fair Avenue and Nob Hill Road, where tractor races will be going strong. Admission is $6 for adults, $4 for children 6 to 12; under 6, free.

SPORTS: They keep busy out here on the plains so you need have no fear of flab. If you want to work the muscles in traditional workout style, head for **Nordic Nautilus,** 306 E. Chestnut (tel. 509/248-6000), where the barbells lie.

For tennis, racquetball, saunas, exercise classes, Jacuzzis, handball, and a BLT to go with it, try the **Yakima Athletic Club,** 2501 Racquet Lane (tel. 509/453-6521).

Yakima's **YMCA** is at East Yakima Avenue and Naches Street (tel. 509/248-1202).

Two **golf courses** in the region offer 9 or 18 holes. Fisher Park, the 9-hole course, is at South 40th Street and Arlington Avenue (tel. 509/575-6075); while Sun Tides, the 18-holer, is at 2215 Pence Rd. (tel. 509/966-9065). Greens fees are $12 to $15.

In winter Yakima snow fans head for **White Pass,** 51 miles west of Yakima on U.S. 12, for tobogganing, sledding, and cross-country skiing, plus a restaurant and cafeteria. Lift fees are $17 a day and you can reach White Pass Ski Area by asking the telephone operator to dial White Pass no. 1.

If you'd rather watch than participate, rev your engine and get on over to the **Yakima Speedway,** 1600 Pacific (tel. 509/248-0647), to watch the checkered flag drop on NASCAR race cars. Admission is $5.

Horse fans will lose no time hieing themselves over to **Yakima Meadows,** Yakima Meadows (tel. 509/248-3920), where the like-minded will put their fivers on velvety noses from mid-February through May and from the end of August through November. This is weekends-only thoroughbred, and occasionally quarterhorse, racing. Any seat in the house is under $5.

Seventeen **parks** around and about offer you everything from playground equipment for the youngsters to tennis courts, horseshoe pits, and basketball courts.

Carrot's Rafting Rentals, 1107 Fruitvale Blvd. (tel. 509/248-3529), can get you out into the rivers and streams on your very own inflatable. Carrot's has rental equipment and will help you pick a river to float.

SHOPPING: Fifth Avenue Village, 104-106 N. Fifth Ave., is a cluster of quaint country shops. Diana Schmidt, artist and entrepreneur, operates the **Storefront Art Studio,** a watercolor print outlet and artists' space which she shares with EGGraphics, a graphic design service. **Gallery Gage** showcases local artists' work, a frame shop, and a print and poster outlet. Ann Stohl operates **Fabric & Folkart,** while **Stained Glass** is the creation of Carolyn Bowman and **Fabric Fantasies** is the handiwork of Suzanne Milliron. Open Monday through Saturday.

The **Yakima Mall** in downtown Yakima (tel. 509/457-5105) is anchored by four department stores and wedges about 70 boutiques in between. **Valley Mall** at 2515 Main St., in nearby Union Gap (tel. 509/453-8233), has 44 specialty shops and four department stores.

For souvenirs and craftwork and interesting Scandinavian creations, look in at **Scandia House,** 910 Summitview, Summitview Center (tel. 509/248-2838). Ruth Johnson specializes in northern European imports like crystal, glassware, pewter, and jewelry.

Yesterday's Village and Farmer's Market, 15 W. Yakima Ave. (tel. 509/457-4981), has more than 150 shops stocked with crafts, dolls, toys, plants, handcrafted creations, glassware, books, paintings, and all kinds of restaurants ranging from the Village Sweet Shop to Dearzele's German Sausage and Casa de Carlos Tacos. Yesterday's Village is open daily.

A similarly down-home shopping spot with a *real* difference is **Track 29 Specialty Shops,** 1 W. Yakima Ave. (tel. 509/457-2929), a re-creation of a '20s-era town in a cluster of 21 old railroad cars. Track 29 is an ambitious effort on the part of one man, John Edwards, a train lover who has re-created the train generation right here on tracks that in 1885 were the stomping grounds of the Northern Pacific Railroad.

CHAPTER IV

SPOKANE AND THE COULEE DAM

□ □ □

These days Spokane calls itself the Lilac City.

How the city's early settlers would have snorted at that delicate delineation! Certainly those purple blossoms thrive here, their scent permeating the spring air, their frothy hues a delight to the eye. But in the early days of this city the only scents in evidence were tannic acid and rawhide, and the only color of note was not purple but silver.

Welcome to the Inland Empire, once a rough, tough-talking spot settled by fur trappers and traders, fellows who never came closer to a lilac than a once-every-few-months shave and haircut, followed, on special occasions *perhaps,* by a splash of lilac water.

Those same tough fellows hung 18 Indians who got in their way, stringing them up on gallows erected at a spot that still bears the name Hangman's Creek. Dressed in buckskin and buckram, they panned gold right in the middle of town on the Spokane River. And they came here to toast their success or drown their sorrows, depending on the tide of their triumph in the silver of fabulously rich Coeur D'Alene mines.

In those days it took tough to keep going, and if there's one thing you can say for Spokane, it keeps going, no matter what the setback. First the fur industry brought riches to Spokane, then it petered out, but that didn't stop this spunky town. It just turned to the forests for lumber and to the fields for grain, milling both right here alongside the waterwheel-turning cascades of the Spokane River.

One day in 1889 the whole town went up in flames, destroying every stick of this little colony of a thousand or so hardy souls. Finis for Spokane? Certainly not. Just one day after flames turned the city to charcoal, a train laden with building materials pulled into town and Spokane was back in business.

Shops made of a few logs and a lot of canvas opened their flaps for business. Bricks still hot from the flames were relaid on ground still smoldering—and that, thank you very much, was that. Just one year later there were 200 buildings in Spokane where none had been, and some of those new edifices were a soaring five and six stories tall!

Spokane. Boomtown. By 1910, just 20 years after that destructive blaze, more than 135,000 people strode through the streets of this metropolis. In 20 more years Spokane was the biggest city between Minneapolis and Seattle, home to 250,000 people.

Many a silver lining meant that the rich got richer at an amazing pace in Spokane. Millionaire miners went first class. They built huge homes boasting all the humility of Le Petit Trianon and elaborate gardens fancy as those of an English manor house.

But that Age of Elegance ended here, as it did everywhere in the world. It was followed by decades of deprivation. By the time the middle years of the 20th century arrived Spokane had reached a seedy low. As one local put it: "If the Eisenhower years were sleepy elsewhere in the country, in Spokane they were comatose."

Was Spokane dying? Not on your life. With nothing more to offer than a sad collection of buildings once dubbed Depression-era dreary, Spokane stumped for—and won—selection as the site of the 1974 World Exposition.

To prepare for the fair Spokane ripped up hundreds of acres of decrepit railroad tracks, covered the land with grass, built fanciful futuristic pavilions, and opened every empty space in town to more than five million visitors.

When the dust cleared, Spokane had constructed a sleek opera house and convention center, a serene park that stretches its rolling lawns out alongside the river, and a clever contemporary skywalk system that connects downtown shops so you can walk all over town, inside, above ground, without braving the elements.

Spokane is rightfully proud of those architectural highlights, particularly its Riverside Park, which has proven to be a popular, green gathering-spot that has united the city as few other projects could.

Life and times are still very conservative in Spokane, which remains a quintessentially Midwest town that just happens to be in the Far West. Here you'll see cowboy boots and ten-gallon hats worn by wheat farmers who have come to party on this urban island in the ceaseless roll of prairie wheatland that stretches from horizon to horizon a few miles south of town. Talk here is a lot more likely to include commodity prices than clever puns, and wallets boast pictures of a new tractor right next to those of a new toddler.

On the opposite end of the spectrum you'll meet a town with its own special kinds of pretensions—and its own inimitable interpretation of them: at a fancy polo club luncheon, socialites dressed in wide-brimmed hats and long lacy dresses casually shucked their shoes to tread barefoot across a lawn mowed with scissors and a ruler.

A musical tribute to America that warbles "From the mountains to the prairies . . ." could have been inspired by Spokane. Minutes from downtown the slopes of Mount Spokane rise 6,000 feet. At the city's edge begin the vast rolling lands of Palouse Prairie, where topsoil 200 feet deep nurtures boundless acres of winter wheat.

If an outdoor life is what you seek, you could hardly do better. Spokane is gateway to 12 national parks and 15 national forests, home to 76 lakes and enough white-water rivers to keep you swimming and rafting for a year. Skiers travel only 30 minutes from town to the slopes of Mount Spokane. If you can't ski outdoors, you can ski inside! A facility called Magic Mountain is one of only 20 indoor skiing facilities in the nation.

Quite a place, Spokane, a city whose motto is one both phonetically helpful and historically accurate: "Yes you can . . . in Spokane."

1. GETTING THERE AND GETTING AROUND

GETTING THERE: Several airlines serve Spokane International Airport (tel. 509/624-3218) from various points around the state and nation. Included among those are Alaska, Horizon, Northwest, and United.

Campus Link (tel. 208/882-1223) will transport you to Pullman and Moscow for $27 one way and $42 round trip.

Amtrak rolls into town at West 221 1st St. (tel. 509/624-5144).

Greyhound Bus Lines stops here at West 1125 Sprague Ave. (tel. 509/624-5251).

Numerous roads track into and through Spokane, Washington's eastern gateway. From the north two major highways cross city limits, **U.S. 2** and **U.S. 395,** which join to become Division Street, a thoroughfare dividing the city east from west. **I-90** comes out of Post Falls, Idaho, from the east and cuts through Spokane downtown, then swings southwest out of the city.

To get to the downtown area and most hotels, I-90 exit 280B is convenient. Travelers from the south and southwest will come in on I-90 or U.S. 195, which joins I-90 at the southwestern edge of the city. Coastal Washingtonians use U.S. 2, which also joins I-90 in Spokane.

GETTING AROUND: All the usual transportation modes apply to Spokane in abundance.

Budget Rent-A-Car, a very price-conscious operation, has offices downtown at North 228 Browne St. (tel. 509/838-1434) and at the airport (tel. 509/838-8662). Other rental-car companies in town include **American International,** West 430 First Ave. (tel. 509/624-3322); **Avis,** at Spokane International (tel. 509/747-8081); **Dollar Rent A Car,** at the airport (tel. 509/747-2191); **Hertz,** at the airport (tel. 509/747-3101); and **National,** also at the airport (tel. 509/624-8995).

Spokane Transit Authority operates buses (tel. 509/328-RIDE) that travel through the valley for fares of 60¢ for adults or children older than 6. Express buses are 75¢.

Checker Cab (tel. 509/624-4171) and **Yellow Cab** (tel. 509/624-4321) are two of the cab companies operating in the city. Fares are $1.75 at flag drop plus $1.70 a mile.

Spokane is an easy city to drive in. **Sprague Avenue** divides the city north from south and **Division Street** east from west. All streets are named, usually after presidents or Spokane historical figures. Avenues north of Sprague are named, but avenues south of Sprague are numbered consecutively. The core of downtown lies between Division Street and Monroe Street, between First Avenue and Spokane Falls Boulevard.

Most Spokane addresses indicate the direction of travel *first,* for example, West 609 Spokane Falls Blvd.

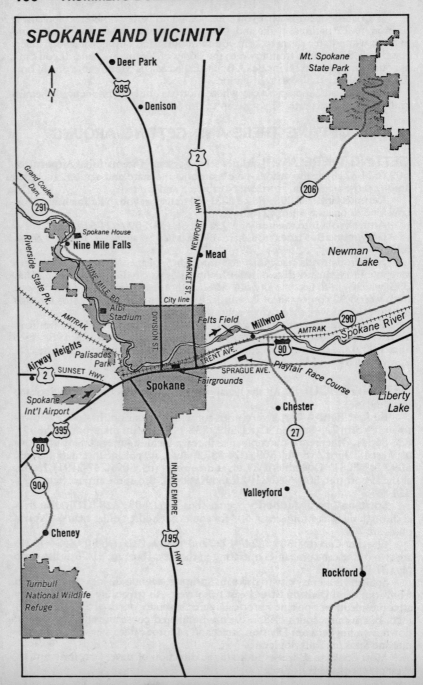

SPOKANE AND VICINITY

2. TOURIST AND USEFUL INFORMATION

TOURIST INFORMATION: The staff at the **Spokane Regional Convention and Visitors Bureau,** West 926 Sprague Ave., Spokane, WA 99204 (tel. 509/747-3230), will be happy to help you with information on anything from the nearest hot-dog stand to a snow report.

The **Spokane Valley Convention and Visitors Bureau** is at East 10303 Sprague Ave., Spokane, WA 99206 (tel. 509/924-4994).

The **Spokane Chamber of Commerce** is located at 1020 Riverside Ave. (tel. 509/624-1393).

USEFUL INFORMATION: For **police or emergency medical** help, dial 911 . . . For **weather** report, call 509/624-8905 . . . For information on condition of mountain passes and **road conditions,** call 509/456-6333 . . . For one-hour **film processing,** call Crazy Bear, North 3180 Division St. (tel. 509/325-1559) . . . **Western Union** is at South 110 Madison St. (tel. 509/456-8870) . . . For dental help, call **Dental Referral Service** (tel. 509/624-9993) . . . To find a **doctor** in the city, call Health Line at 509/624-2171 . . . You'll find a coin-operated laundry at **Empire Cleaners and Laundry,** West 1305 14th St. (tel. 509/624-8518) . . . **Halpin's Pharmacy,** East 11406 Sprague Ave. (tel. 509/928-9500), is open to 10 p.m. daily . . . For veterinary emergencies, call **Pet Emergency Clinic,** East 21 Mission St. (tel. 509/326-6670) . . . Lee's Union **gas** station, Third Avenue and Stevens Street (tel. 509/624-9834), is open to 7 p.m. daily.

3. WHERE TO STAY

Spokane has one antique hotel once so large and impressive that the city is said to have grown around the hotel! Most hostelries, however, are modest in both amenities and price. Spokane is, in fact, such a moderately priced city that you can stay in a top hotel for about half of what you'd pay for similar quarters in Seattle or Portland. While Spokane has a large population, most of the city's hotels are located in or near downtown and quite close to most of the things you will want to see.

LUXURY HOTELS: In Spokane you can live in one of the city's top hotels for prices in the $60 to $80 range.

With 400 rooms, two restaurants, and a very lively bar, the **Sheraton-Spokane Hotel,** North 322 Spokane Falls Court, Spokane, WA 99220 (tel. 509/455-9600, or toll free 800/456-9601), is one of the largest hotels in Spokane and also one of the most conveniently located, next door to the city's dramatic opera house, the Agricultural Trade Center, and the showy Riverfront Park, site of the 1974 World's Fair. As in other Sheraton hotels, the rooms are large and attractively decorated in contemporary colors and fabrics. Executive suites have a small sitting area with chairs, table, and couch, and often a pretty view over downtown or the river. All rooms have large bathrooms equipped with the little extras that make life comfortable for forgetful types: shampoos, showercaps, and in some suites, even a hairdryer and coffee maker.

Downstairs, residents and visitors mingle in Mrs. Greenthumb's Garden Café, an intriguing 1881 restaurant with boxcar booths, and J.J.'s Lounge, a hot spot of local nightlife. There's a swimming pool recently covered and heated so you can swim in this sunny city most of the year. Rooms range from $59 to $85, higher for suites.

Cavanaugh's Inn at the Park, West 303 N. River Dr., Spokane, WA 99201 (tel. 509/326-8000, or toll free 800/THE INNS), is a very showy hotel right on the river overlooking downtown Spokane. In the lobby you'll see a five-story atrium streaking skyward. Outside a snappy swimming pool sports a small island in the middle and a tumble of rocks secreting a water slide that's a big hit with the youngsters.

An Atrium Café and Deli is filled with potted palms illuminated by a sky-light. Winters the fireplace is lighted. For more formal dining Windows of the Seasons Restaurant overlooks the river and a twinkling cityscape. The Park Place Lounge swings nightly with musical entertainment. On the roof cantilevered walls of glass in Cesare's Lounge afford panoramic views of the mountains and Riverfront Park while floor-to-ceiling mirrors reflect the romance and glamour of this see-and-be-seen spot.

A recent executive wing added 85 deluxe suites and rooms bringing total accommodations to 270, including a 3,500-square-foot Presidential Suite complete with living room, fireplace, and baby grand piano. Some of these spacious accommodations have private balconies, fireplaces, wet bars, kitchenettes, Jacuzzis, and lanais overlooking Riverfront Park. Rates at Cavanaugh's Inn on the Park are $74 to $103 double.

MODERATELY PRICED HOTELS: Once again, moderate prices are more moderate here than in many cities of similar size—$40 to $60.

Holiday Inns are often too predictable to be noteworthy, but the **Holiday Inn–Downtown,** East 110 Fourth Ave., Spokane, WA 99202 (tel. 509/838-2711, or toll free 800/HOLIDAY), is an exception. In the lovely lobby here you'll be greeted by a brass-trimmed fireplace, wing chairs in delicate pink and brown flowers, and a cozy English library décor. In your room are more handsome furnishings in soft contemporary colors. Some of the 153 rooms in this six-story building even have a built-in steambath. For dining there's a bilevel dining room, and in the lounge there's entertainment nightly. Rates at this Holiday Inn, which has a sister property about two miles from the airport, are $43 to $75 double for a room with king-size bed and couch or chairs in a sitting area or for a suite. Singles pay about $6 less. Low weekend rates are available.

You'll find the **Ridpath Hotel,** West 515 Sprague Ave., Spokane, WA 99204 (tel. 206/838-2711, or toll free 800/426-0670, 800/522-7122 in Washington), smack in the middle of downtown Spokane. Ridpath's number-one claim to fame is Ankeny's Restaurant, a rooftop aerie offering elegant but quite reasonably priced dining and a panoramic view of this old city. Some rooms are large, some small, but all offer clean, contemporary quarters, particularly popular with families. An adjoining motor hotel, connected to the main hotel by a skywalk, wraps around a swimming pool that is often body-to-body on hot summer days. Motor-court rooms have large glass doors opening onto private balconies with a view of the pool below. Rates at the hotel are $55 to $65. Suites are $90 to $100, and in all rooms there is no charge for children under 17.

Quality Inn Oakwood, North 7711 Division St., Spokane, WA 99208 (tel. 509/467-3838, or toll free 800/228-5151), was completed in 1984, which means you'll find a very contemporary building and furnishings throughout. Narrow windows frame the lobby, where comfortable beige armchairs invite you to a seat by the fireplace. Contemporary colors and patterns decorate the 82 spacious rooms, some with kitchenettes or Jacuzzis. Other inn amenities include an indoor sauna, whirlpool, outdoor swimming pool, video-game room, complimentary continental breakfast, and evening snacks. Although the Quality Inn is some distance from the downtown area, it's quite convenient to many outlying shops, theaters, golf courses, ski areas, parks, and tennis courts. Rates are $46 to $52 double, $5 to $6 less for singles, including continental breakfast.

The **Red Lion Motor Inn,** North 1100 Sullivan Rd., Spokane, WA 99220 (tel. 509/924-9000, or toll free 800/547-8010, 800/452-0733 in Oregon), is a show spot about eight miles east of town on I-90, exit 291. Here you'll find a contemporary wood-trimmed building with lots of brick detail and welcoming fireplaces in wood-paneled public rooms. Sleeping quarters are spacious, with wide expanses of glass opening onto balconies or terraces. In this rural setting you have all the comforts of urbanity: king- or queen-size beds, big bathrooms, a heated pool and wading pool, a very handsome coffeeshop and brick-trimmed dining room (dinner prices in the $12 to $17 range), and entertainment in a lively lounge. Rates are $70 to $80 double, about $8 less single.

At the airport, the **Ramada Inn,** International Airport, Spokane, WA 99219 (tel. 509/838-5211, or toll free 800/228-2828), is a contemporary spot with 167 spacious and beautifully furnished rooms in a building trimmed in dark wood and stone. Four suites even have private swimming pools! Those who don't splash in private have both indoor and outdoor pools to play in, however. You'll find a top-quality restaurant called the Red Baron Room here. Evenings there's entertainment in the Flight Deck Lounge. Rates at the recently remodeled Ramada Inn are $53 to $59 for a room with a king-size or queen-size bed or two doubles.

Best Western has two representatives in the downtown Spokane area: **Best Western Thunderbird Motor Lodge,** West 120 Third Ave., Spokane, WA 99204 (tel. 509/747-2011), and **Best Western Tradewinds Downtown,** West 907 Third Ave., Spokane, WA 99204 (tel. 509/838-2091, or toll free 800/528-1234, 800/268-8993 in Canada). Best Western Thunderbird is a basic two-story motel with a small but pretty lobby with attractive wall hangings. Medium-size rooms here are fitted out with Naugahyde chairs and double beds. In all 60 rooms you'll find movies, cable television, and in-room coffee. When hunger strikes, you can head next door to the Elegant Egg coffeeshop. Rates are $46 to $52 in winter and spring, about $5 more in other seasons. Best Western Tradewinds Downtown is a big four-story curving building with 59 units. Rooms with sliding glass doors open onto small balconies. There's a heated pool enclosed in winter, plus a sauna, whirlpool, and steambaths. Rates are $44 to $48 double with continental breakfast.

Ski Condos Near the Slopes

If you're here in winter and want to stay out near the ski slopes on Mount Spokane, get in touch with **Mount Spokane Condominium Rentals** or **Snowblaze Condominium Rentals,** Mount Spokane Mead, Spokane, WA 99220 (tel. 509/238-4630). They'll help you find a condominium apartment of any size to accommodate you in winter—or for that matter in summer. Rates for apartments begin at $55 for two for a studio, increasing to $70 for a two-bedroom apartment.

BUDGET HOTELS: Spokane has quite a long list of budget hotels, many of them conveniently located right in the middle of this city's downtown shopping and sightseeing area.

The **Towne Centre Motel,** West 901 First Ave., Spokane, WA 99204 (tel. 509/747-1041), is a conveniently located, L-shaped hotel in the middle of the downtown area. A basic two-story motor inn with parking beneath the building, Town Centre is just a short walk to shops in the downtown area and to Riverfront

Park. Rooms here are rather small but are decorated in bright colors. Some offer larger queen-size beds and refrigerators. Ask for a room in the back wing to avoid street noise. Town Centre treats you to a complimentary self-service continental breakfast each morning in the lobby. Rates are $35 to $38 double.

The **Lincoln Center Inn,** West 827 First Ave., Spokane, WA 99204 (tel. 509/456-8040), is another small motel in downtown Spokane. Here you'll find 82 rooms of varying interest, the prettiest of which feature wall-size murals of forest or mountain scenes; one even has a moonscape! Other rooms are less interesting, with quite standard motel furnishings and a tiny alcove closet. One of the motel's rooms has been turned into a whirlpool center, featuring a small pool, while another houses a sauna. Outside, on an elevated platform that stretches between two wings of this U-shaped building is a small swimming pool. The Lincoln Center offers free airport service too. Rooms here are $37 to $40 double.

Jefferson House, West 1203 Fifth Ave., Spokane, WA 99204 (tel. 509/624-4142), occupies one of the loveliest locations in downtown Spokane. Perched on a bluff in a shady residential section, the 55-room Jefferson House is a four-story building with four wings that form a courtyard enclosing a small swimming pool and a tiny garden. Suites have a bedroom in a room separate from the kitchen, while standard rooms have a kitchen in a small entry alcove just off the main room. Quarters are simply decorated, often with Naugahyde chairs, shag carpets, and matching bedspreads and drapes, adding up to a look that's a bit dated but clean and well maintained. Just a few minutes' ride or walk from the center of the city, this attractive budget motel's best points are its quite large rooms and its serene location overlooking downtown Spokane. Rates at the Jefferson House are $30 double, $35 for a kitchenette suite.

Scots are known for their penuriousness so you can expect to find some budgetwise quarters at the **Royal Scot Motel,** West 20 Thurston St., Spokane, WA 99208 (tel. 509/467-6672). While this is not an elaborately appointed motel (really quite ordinary-looking from the outside), it's kept scrupulously clean. New furnishings were added in some rooms recently, so you'll find the latest colors and patterns in those quarters, but even older rooms are attractively decorated. The Royal Scot is set well back from the highway so you won't be bothered by noise. Rates are $32 to $35 for a room with one double or queen-size bed, two queen-size beds, or queen and twin.

The **Liberty Motel,** North 6801 Division St., Spokane, WA 99208 (tel. 509/467-6000), is a tiny 18-room motel painted a vivid pink with sparkling white trim. Owners Len and Janet Pederson will be glad to show you around and they'll even welcome Rover. Rooms are decorated in citrus colors, which contrast brightly with the dark-wood paneling. The Pedersons keep up with the times, so all units have new queen-size beds. Some also have kitchens in the rooms and all have attractive modern baths with a separate dressing area. Rates are $35 to $40. The Pedersons also have three two-bedroom cottages at higher rates.

On Sunset Boulevard you'll find a cluster of small budget motels. One of those is **El Rancho Motel,** 3000 Sunset Blvd., Spokane, WA 99204 (tel. 509/455-9400). Within a cluster of gold, wood-sided, two-story buildings, you'll find spacious, if potpourri-ly decorated, quarters. Rooms are large, helping to compensate for the profusion of colors. Prices also compensate: rooms with two doubles or queen-size beds are $28.50 to $34 double. Suites with kitchens begin at $32. There's a rec vehicle park here too.

CAMPING: Spokane KOA, North 3025 Barker Rd., Otis, WA 99027 (tel. 509/924-4722), ten miles east of Spokane, sports a swimming pool, playground, full hookups, gasoline, propane, and a souvenir shop. Rates are $15 double. To get to the campground, take I-90 to the Barker Road exit no. 293. You'll find it 1½ miles north of the highway on Barker Road.

4. WHERE TO DINE

Spokane is meat and potatoes country for the most part, but it serves those specialties up in some very interesting surroundings. Prices are quite moderate at even the poshest spots. Spokane restaurants have, in fact, the most reasonable prices we've ever encountered in a city this size.

DINING WITH A ZILLIONAIRE: Tiffany glass, huge house, the best of everything, don't you deserve it? Our vote for most interesting—and elegant—of all Spokane restaurants goes to **Patsy Clark's,** West 2208 Second Ave. (tel. 509/838-8300), a 27-room mansion built in 1898. Kirkland K. Cutter, the man who built most of the most imposing structures in Spokane at the turn of the century, had a hand in the construction of this huge house, now so beautifully renovated you feel as if you ought to drop your card on a little silver tray held by a butler. Don't be intimidated, though, it's not overpowering, just old-world beautiful—a lovely place to while away an evening amid Tiffany chandeliers, nine fireplaces including one in onyx, gold-leafed columns, salmon-pink walls, ornate ceiling moldings, a delicate pastel ceiling mural, petitpoint chairs, arched windows, a banquet table for ten that makes you wish you could fly in some friends. When dinner's over you can roam around this beautiful home, peeking into upstairs bedrooms furnished in antiques and a hall dominated by a peacock outlined in stained glass.

As for the food, well, terrific. Meditate on veal Matteo with mushrooms, green peppers, onions, spinach, ham, and creamy mozzarella cheese rolled inside veal scallops and topped with marsala sauce. Or fettuccine topped with scallops, prawns, and crab legs.

Patsy came to Washington, so the story goes, penniless and in search of gold, as are many of the penniless. The difference is, he found it. First, at Montana's Anaconda Mine, then more here and there until his mines extended from British Columbia to Mexico and included the famous Republic mine after which Republic, Washington, was named.

Prices here are in the $10 to $15 range for entrees, which include a vegetable, but beyond that are à la carte. Open from 11 a.m. to 2 p.m. and 5 to 10 p.m. weekdays from 5 to 11 p.m. on Friday and Saturday, and from 4 to 10 p.m. on Sunday. Sunday brunch is from 10 a.m. to 2 p.m.

OTHER TOP SPOTS: Patsy's outclasses everything, but here are some of the others vying for first place. **Ankeny's,** atop the Ridpath Hotel, West 515 Sprague Ave. (tel. 509/838-2711), is one of the city's best-loved spots. A rooftop restaurant with a beautiful view of the city, Ankeny's specializes in table-top cooking and such continental favorites as steak Diane and chicken financière for prices in the $10 to $15 range for entrees à la carte. Hours at this formal dining room are 11 a.m. to 11 p.m. weekdays, from 5:30 to 11 p.m. on Saturday, and from 10 a.m. to 2 p.m. for brunch only on Sunday.

Moreland's, North 216 Howard St., at the skywalk level (tel. 509/747-9830), is a study in brick, oak, and marble characteristic of the historic Bennett Block. Interesting soups are the stars of the buffet lunch, while dinner features rich sauces atop carefully cooked meats, chicken, and seafood poached, sautéed, or otherwise prepared with care and concern. All of this is natural perhaps for a restaurant operated by a lady with a doctoral degree in food science. Prices are in the $12 to $15 range or less. Hours are 11 a.m. to 4:30 p.m. for lunch and pastry weekdays and Saturday, and 5:30 to 10 p.m. Tuesday through Saturday for dinner.

STEAK AND SEAFOOD: Steak is Spokane's favorite food so you'll find a slab of beef on nearly every menu in town. Here, however, are the best places to seek steer.

Stuart Anderson is one smart cookie who knew a good thing when he saw it. That good thing was a slab of top-quality beef served with a hunk of baked potato, a crispy salad, and *voilà!*—an empire. **Anderson's Black Angus Restaurant,** 510 N. Lincoln (tel. 509/328-8120), is one of many such restaurants up this way, its popularity oft-proved. At this one you get some rib-sticking good food and a lovely view of Spokane Falls as well. If there's a cut of beef they don't offer . . . well, impossible. Prices are in the $7 to $16 range and there's a children's menu. Black Angus is open from 11 a.m. to 10 p.m. weekdays and from 3 to 10 p.m. on Saturday and Sunday. A cocktail lounge adjoins.

Anyone with nerve enough to call a restaurant **Chapter Eleven,** East 105 Mission St. (tel. 509/326-0466), deserves a try. Once you get there you'll discover a lively spot dedicated, they say, to all those who have become all too familiar with that grim section of the Bankruptcy Act or those who wish they could. On the back of the menu at this beef specialist you'll discover some amusing facts about bankruptcy laws in various states, including a California law that lets a bankrupt actor keep his wardrobe and an actress her fur coat, whether or not she has anything left to wear under it. Prime rib is the specialty here, and it comes in small to huge cuts. Steaks of all kinds, chicken, corned beef and cabbage, beef and seafood combinations, and of course, salmon are on the menu here for prices in the $8 to $12 range. Chapter Eleven is open weekdays for lunch from 11:30 a.m. to 2 p.m., and daily for dinner from 5 to 10 p.m., to 11 p.m. on Saturday, and from 4 to 10 p.m. on Sunday. Entertainment in the lounge too.

Milford's Fish House, North 719 Monroe St. (tel. 509/326-7251), adjusts well to circumstances. First it was a tavern, then during Prohibition it turned into a cigar store. When Prohibition dried up, it lost no time becoming a tavern again —you can still see the massive old bar and mahogany cooler installed in the '30s.

Built in 1911, the tavern is now a seafood center. You can down some Quilcene oysters on the half shell, try crab Louis, or get serious with steamed butter clams, broiled salmon, Pacific prawns Créole, halibut, snapper, or Alaskan king crab. Steak and seafood combos here too. Entrees, which average about $10 to $13, include clam chowder. Milford's is open from 4 to 10 p.m. daily (later on weekends).

Much loved among Spokane's trendier crowd is **Clinkerdagger, Bickerstaff and Pett's Public House,** in the Flour Mill at 621 Mallon St. (tel. 509/328-5965). Specialties here are baked prime rib in rock salt and grilled lamb with fresh herb crust. You can also sample many fresh fish prepared in a variety of ways. The surroundings are stained glass, lots of wood, and a pubby atmosphere with entree prices in a very reasonable $11 to $17 range. CBP is open from 11:30 a.m. to 2 p.m. weekdays and Saturday for lunch, 5:30 to 9 p.m. for dinner Monday through Thursday, and to 10 p.m. on Friday and Saturday, from 5 to 9 p.m. on Sunday. Later hours in the pub, which is open to 1 a.m. weekends.

TRENDY: Spokane may not be first to jump on the trend wagon, but it clambers aboard eventually. Here's a look at some of the contenders.

C.I. Shenanigan's, North 332 Spokane Falls Court (tel. 509/455-5072), is a trendy spot in town featuring lots of glass, brass, and greenery. Aged beef in various cuts is supplemented by some good seafood selections, and on Sunday a champagne brunch from 10 a.m. to 2 p.m. is popular. At cocktail hour the oyster bar's packed. Prices are in the $10 to $15 range, and hours are 10 a.m. to 11 p.m. daily, opening an hour earlier on Sunday.

Casa Blanca, West 200 Spokane Falls Blvd. (tel. 509/456-0350), is an attractive Mexican place with a plant-bedecked, skylit dining room filled with airy wicker furniture. Housed in a white Spanish-style building from which it takes its name, Casa Blanca offers all the favorites of Mexican cooking plus a few American adaptations like steak picado with chunks of beef sautéed in burgundy wine, tomatoes, onions, bell peppers, mushrooms, and spices, and served with Spanish rice and refried beans. Huachinango à la Veracruzano is another departure: snapper filet grilled with onions, tomatoes, green olives, and capers. So even those who spurn chimichangas, tacos, tostados, and the like should be happy here. Prices for most anything are less than $5 and always less than $10. Casa Blanca is open from 11 a.m. to 10 p.m. weekdays, to 11 p.m. on Friday and Saturday, later in the lounge where there's entertainment and dancing.

BUDGET: Spokane's low prices are even lower at several quite inexpensive restaurants.

The **Old Spaghetti Factory** is in a picturesque old brick building at South 152 Monroe St. (tel. 509/624-8916), and is packed with pasta lovers every evening. It is not only the endless array of pasta and sauces that they're here for; it's also the prices: $5 to $8 for dinner. Open from 5 to 9:30 p.m. weekdays, to 11 p.m. on Friday and Saturday, and from 4 to 9 p.m. on Sunday. Cocktails here too.

There are a number of interesting restaurants in the Flour Mill, West 621 Mallon St. **Pizza Haven** (tel. 509/922-5555) is a do-it-yourself spot in the Flour Mill, where you can choose your toppings for pizza and combine any ingredients to get just what you want. Prices are in the $7 range—or less—for practically any of the soups, salads, sandwiches, and pizzas. Dining is self-service and quite casual, with lots of wood on several levels and youngsters crowding around several video games. Pizza Haven is open from 11 a.m. to 11 p.m. Sunday through Thursday, closing at 1 a.m. on Friday and Saturday.

Hoyt's (tel. 509/327-1604) encourages you to "eat your Hoyt out," at this tiny eatery tucked away inside the Flour Mill. Featured creations are sandwiches on homemade bread served in a pleasant, subdued atmosphere of brick walls and polished wood floors. Perhaps a good place for parents to munch while the youngsters race down to Pizza Haven. Prices are in the $2 to $6 range and the restaurant is open from 11:30 a.m. to 6 p.m. daily except Sunday.

If it's pizza time, try **Europa Pizzaria and Restaurant,** South 125 Wall St. (tel. 509/455-4051), a sleek contemporary spot in which to dine amid plenty of greenery on your own pizza or calzone creation, gourmet calzones, or Europa pasta dishes. Depending on how hungry you are, prices amid the green are $4 to $10. Open every day from 11 a.m. to 2 p.m. and from 4:30 to 9 p.m., a little later on weekends.

5. AFTER DARK

Spokane is not a rollicking town filled with roisterous nightlife, but it does have a few lively spots.

Tops on the list of rip-roaring nightspots is the Sheraton Hotel's **J.J.'s Lounge** (tel. 509/455-9600). Rocking bands play here every night and dancing bodies are packed wall to wall from dusk to 2 a.m. For quieter environs in the same place, go upstairs to the 15th-floor **Inner Circle** hideout. You can settle into a wing chair and look out at a pretty view of Spokane's twinkling lights. Open from 4:30 p.m. to midnight.

Among restaurants already mentioned, one with an attractive lounge well suited to quiet conversations is **Patsy Clark's,** where you can imbibe on the veranda or in the wood-paneled bar where intriguing carved faces stare down at you from beamed ceilings.

More restaurants with active lounges: Check out **Casa Blanca,** which packs in a young crowd for rock bands; **C.I. Shenanigan's,** which lures a slightly older group to its action; and **Clinkerdagger, Bickerstaff and Pett's,** where a pub atmosphere is cozy.

Ahab's Whale, North 1221 Stevens St. (tel. 509/327-9778), has a changing round of entertainment, as do the **Flame Restaurant,** West 2401 Sprague Ave. (tel. 509/535-5500), and the **Swinging Door Tavern,** West 1018 Francis (tel. 509/326-6794).

6. WHAT TO SEE AND DO

Spokane is quite a quiet town in which you won't find any Disneylands or spangled dancing girls, but you will find friendly, welcoming folks proud of this year-round sun-and-fun sports-loving capital and pleased to help you discover why they're so enthusiastic. Here's a look at some of the things to see and do in Spokane.

DOWN BY THE RIVER . . . FRONT PARK: Riverfront Park, North 507 Howard St. (tel. 509/456-5512), is Spokane's peninsular pride and joy, its landmark and lounging spot. In 1974 the park was the center of the Expo '74 World's Fair and became a lovely legacy of that event. Here 100 acres of lawns, called meadows, are dotted with entertainment facilities, stretched out alongside the Spokane River.

In summer you will find artists showing their work, youngsters chasing Frisbees, toddlers acquiring grass stains, musicians tuning up, and weary parents stretched happily out beneath a tree. Free open-air concerts and folk festivals are frequent happenings in the park, which also is the site of a wing-ding Fourth of July celebration attended by what seems to be every mobile person in Spokane.

An **IMAX theater** here features a screen more than five stories tall, 69 feet wide, and with six-track stereo sound. Among recent films was an aerial acrobatics performance. Tickets are $3.75 for adults, $2.75 for youngsters under 18.

Don't miss the **Looff Carrousel,** a lovingly restored, hand-carved, antique piece that's still operating (rides are 60¢ for adults or children), and consider, at least, the **Gondola Ride** that lets you soar over the falls in a capsule (rides are $2.50 for adults, $1.50 for children), and the **Dragon Roller Coaster** (90¢).

The landmark of the park is a rakishly tilted Pavilion, in which you will find Eastern Washington University's **Science Center,** a miniature golf course ($1.75 for adults, $1.25 for children), ice skating from mid-October to mid-March ($3 for adults, $2.50 for youngsters under 17), and a couple of kiddie rides. A money-saving day pass is $8.50 for adults, $8 for children 6 to 17; under 6, $6.

There is no admission charge to the park, which has several entrances, most of them off Spokane Falls Boulevard, which runs alongside the park. Other entrances are across pedestrian bridges stretching over the river near the Flour Mill. Riverfront Park is open from 11 a.m. to 10 p.m. daily from Memorial Day to Labor Day. Tickets are available at the central ticket office in the Pavilion in the center of the park. Hours change in spring, fall, and winter. For schedule information, call 509/456-5511 or 456-5512.

ARCHITECTURAL HISTORY LESSONS: Those early settlers were no dummies. They took one look at the sparkling Spokane River and its cascading falls and built this city right around them. That's why you'll find an interesting array of early architecture along **Riverside Avenue** from Lincoln to Walnut Streets. The visitors bureau can supply you with a self-guided tour map.

Along this handsome street, ogle the imposing stone columns of the **Masonic Lodge**, next door to the gleaming white-columned brick façade of the **Spokane Club**, built by Spokane architect Kirkland Cutter at West 1002 Riverside Dr. Note the **Spokesman-Review Building**, West 927 Riverside Dr., built in the French Renaissance style in 1909 and still sporting its original revolving doors and brass railings; also, the chubby gray **post office**, the ornate **Carnegie Library** at First and Jefferson, the **Spokane Chamber of Commerce** at West 1020 Riverside, and an insurance building at no. 1116.

Grandiose architecture and frothy Victorian homes are everywhere you look in this city built by mining millionaires, some of whom spent $1 million on their homes—and think what $1 million bought in those days! Homes in the neighborhood of **Boone Street** are huge and sprawling homesteads—one of them, now called the Music Building, has 14 bedrooms and four fireplaces!

At Jefferson and Broadway Streets, that towering structure that looks like Sleeping Beauty's palace is really the **Spokane County Courthouse**, a French Renaissance–style structure built in 1894 by a man who had no formal architectural training, just a correspondence course in drawing!

For contrast, just two blocks away, that domed structure you see from all over the city is the **Spokane Health Center** at College Avenue and Madison Street. In its sleek domes equipment measures the quality of the air—and after Mount St. Helen's exploded, measured the amount of sulfuric acid in the air.

To see some of the city's most beautiful neighborhoods, head for **Maple and Poplar Streets** and all the cross streets thereabouts, First and Second Avenues, for instance. Then drive or walk the boulevards here for a look at imposing architecture, such as a three-story house with widow's walk or a Tudor-style manse.

You can also visit several beautifully restored Victorian mansions. One of those is the **Grace Campbell House**, West 2316 First Ave. (tel. 509/456-3931). Built in 1898 by a mining tycoon, this was one of the gracious dwellings that earned Spokane's Victorian period the monicker "Age of Elegance." Hours are 10 a.m. to 4:30 p.m. Tuesday through Saturday, from 2 to 4:30 p.m. on Sunday. Admission is $2.

In the same complex you'll find the **Cheney Cowles Museum**. Exhibits here relate to the Indian cultures and historical development of Spokane and eastern Washington, and the visual arts. Admission is free and hours are 10 a.m. to 5 p.m. Tuesday through Saturday, from 2 to 5 p.m. on Sunday.

Corbin House, West 507 7th St., was built for another tycoon, D. C. Corbin, in 1898, in a neocolonial style. It now houses an arts and crafts center open daily from 10 a.m. to 5 p.m. Free.

Back downtown, stop in at **Elk's Drugs**, 1931 W. Pacific St., a 1928 drugstore that still makes its own root beer and retains the original soda fountain.

The old **Davenport Hotel**, West 807 Sprague Ave., is no longer functioning, but take a look at this hotel around which a city grew. Louis M. Davenport was the brain—and the money—behind this building, which he ordered constructed in 1889 just after fire destroyed much of the city. Operating a one-man waffle factory, Davenport got rich, and by 1908 his restaurant was proclaimed the best in America by critics of the time. By 1917 his hotel had followed suit. Its massive lobby is something to see.

Everything about the hotel was done on a grand scale, as were most things of that era. The lobby is a massive two-story room with a fountain at center stage and tall columns rise to the ceiling of the second floor where hefty, ornately

carved wood beams stretch across a mezzanine creating a giant interior courtyard. Ornate wrought-iron railings trim the second-floor gallery, while on the
main floor wing chairs nuzzle up to an impressive fireplace. Crystal wall sconces
glitter and carved cherubs beam down at you from wooden columns.

So grand is this huge hostelry that people here say the city of Spokane grew
up around the hotel! A National Historic Landmark, the Davenport was completed in 1914 and when Will Rogers once visited here, he is said to have called it
the best place to stay outside his Oklahoma home.

Plans are afoot to restore this grande dame of the hotel business and we certainly hope that those plans are successful. Check to see what's happening.

MORE SPOKANE SIGHTS: The **Spokane House Interpretive Center,**
Aubrey White Parkway in Riverside (not to be confused with Riverfront) Park,
12 miles northwest of Spokane in the town of Nine Mile Falls (tel. 509/325-
4692), occupies the site of the first structure built by the settlers. That structure,
built in 1810, was a fur-trading post. Here you can learn some of the early history
of this fur-trading region and its developers, the feisty Hudson's Bay Company.
Admission is free.

Indian rock paintings still in good condition can be seen at Rutter Bridge.

Spokane certainly is proud of its **St. John's Cathedral,** East 127 12th St.
(tel. 509/838-4277), a towering sandstone Gothic-style Episcopal cathedral
completed in 1927. You'll see a window depicting the landing of the Pilgrims in
New England, a baptismal font made of Tennessee and Italian marble, a blue ceiling with cast aluminum and gold-leaf stars and fleurs-de-lis, and a mosaic depicting the travails of St. George and the dragon. Beautiful stained glass includes a
rose window 23 feet in diameter. You can visit the cathedral with its 49-bell carillon from 8 a.m. to 4 p.m. Monday through Friday, or on a free guided tour on
Tuesday, Thursday, Friday, and Saturday from noon to 4 p.m., and on Sunday
from 12:30 to 2 p.m.

AREA WINERIES: Spokane is home to three wineries, any of which will be
happy to show you around, explain the wine-making process, and let you sample
their product.

You can take a look at **Worden's Washington Winery,** West 7217 45th St.
(tel. 509/455-7835); **Arbor Crest,** West 4506 Buckeye (tel. 509/927-WINE);
and **Latah Creek Winery,** East 13030 Indiana Ave. (tel. 509/926-0164).

Worden's is a small, family-owned winery with a log cabin tasting room to
sample some of the vineyard's creations. It is open Monday through Friday from
10 a.m. to 4 p.m., to 5 p.m. on Saturday, and from noon to 5 p.m. on Sunday.

Arbor Crest, named after its grape arbors and berry fields, like both other
vintners, has won many awards for its creations. It's open daily from noon to 5
p.m.

Latah Creek, with its Mediterranean architecture, is one of the most picturesque wineries in the state. You'll sip samples in an oak-trimmed tasting room
after touring the fermenting and processing areas. Latah Creek is open from 10
a.m. to 4 p.m. weekdays, to 5 p.m. on Saturday, and from noon to 5 p.m. on
Sunday.

Worden's Johannisberg riesling, gewürztraminer, and fumé blanc are award
winners; Arbor Crest is proud of its premium "Cameo" label chardonnay,
sauvignon blanc, white riesling, gewürztraminer, and merlot; Latah Creek wins
awards for its light, fruity wines.

As all the wineries are on the outskirts of the city, they have produced a wine
tour map to help you find your way. Get your copy of the **wine tour map** at the

Spokane Regional Convention and Visitors Bureau, West 926 Sprague Ave. (tel. 509/747-3230).

GARDEN SPOTS: Gardeners and flower-lovers will want to take a look at Spokane's **Nishinomiya Garden,** a sedate and soothing collection of greenery and rock designed and built by artists from Spokane's Japanese sister city of Nishinomiya. Begun in 1967, the garden was finally completed in 1973. At its opening in 1974 the waters of Nishinomiya were blended with those of Spokane. Several Japanese architects contributed much of their time, and one dishwasher, Wasaburo Kiri, donated his life savings. Among the more unusual sights are metal temple entrance lanterns cast in 1914, a zigzag bridge designed to frustrate evil spirits, stone lanterns, a vermilion ceremonial bridge, a waterfall, and a lantern designed to catch falling snow. You'll find the garden at Bernard and 21st Streets (tel. 509/456-4311). It is open from 8 a.m. to dusk daily from May through November. Admission is free; donations are welcome.

Next door, **Manito Park,** South Grand Boulevard between 17th and 25th Avenues, is a haven of formal gardens, rose gardens, greenhouse gardens, and perennial gardens—with many a delightful bower. Tropical plants are displayed in the Conservatory, which is free and open daily from 8 a.m. to dusk in summer, 8 a.m. to 3:30 p.m. in other seasons. There are tennis courts here too.

Still more gardens: **Finch Arboretum,** West 3404 Woodland Blvd. (tel. 509/747-2894), a botanical and tree garden complete with identification plaques. Admission is free and the gardens are open in daylight.

You can roam 240 acres on which North American wildlife live at **Walk in the Wild,** East 12600 Euclid Rd. (tel. 509/924-7220). Take the Pines Road exit from I-90 one mile north to Euclid. It is open every day from 9 a.m. to 6 p.m. (to dark in winter). Admission is $2.50 for adults, $1.50 for seniors and for children 3 to 12.

The best view of the **Spokane Falls** is from the Monroe Street Bridge; best time for viewing is spring when mountain runoff sends the river rushing through the city and over falls. You can reach that bridge from Main Street or Trent Avenue.

AN OFFBEAT BUT ON-KEY STOP: If you've ever warbled a few nostalgic bars of "White Christmas," you won't want to miss this next one: the **Crosby Library,** East 502 Boone St. at Gonzaga University (tel. 509/328-4220). A raft of Bing Crosby memorabilia from gold records to pictures, artwork, even one of those famous hats, is on display. Why is all that here? Because Crosby, although born in Tacoma, spent much of his early life in Spokane. Hours are 8 a.m. to midnight Monday through Thursday, 8 a.m. to 5 p.m. on Friday, 9 a.m. to 5 p.m. on Saturday, and 1 p.m. to midnight on Sunday. Admission is free.

SPECIAL EVENTS: In the first week of May, a throng of running, jogging, walking, and exhausted bodies participate in the **Lilac Bloomsday Run** for the right to call themselves "Bloomies." More than 100,000 spectators cheer the 30,000 runners to speed along the 7½-mile route. That run is followed a week later by a **Lilac Festival and Torchlight Parade.**

In June musicians tune up at noon weekdays for free concerts at various downtown locations. You can find out where the tunes are by checking the *Spokesman-Review* and *Spokane Chronicle* newspapers or inquiring at the Visitor Information Office.

Spokane celebrates Independence Day with a huge outdoor party called **Neighbor Day.** It's a day-long sale of ethnic foods and art at Riverfront Park, plus concerts and, the finale, fireworks over the river and classical music under the stars.

In September the **Spokane Interstate Fair** lures the biggest and/or the best of everything grown, sown, or stirred in three states to the fairgrounds at North 602 Havana St. (tel. 509/535-1766). October 6 is the **Harvest Festival and Grape Stomp** at Worden's Winery: special tours, wine-tasting, and a real grape stomp.

ART AND CULTURAL ACTIVITIES: In the Northwest you'll find plenty of interest in Indian art and craft work. A good place to get a look at some of that talent is at the **Museum of Native American Cultures,** East 200 Cataldo, off Division Street behind Cavanaugh's River Inn (tel. 509/326-4550). Here is one of the finest and largest collections of Native American art and artifacts in the Western Hemisphere. The four-story facility houses nearly 30,000 such items and more than 30,000 photographs. Hours are 10 a.m. to 5 p.m. Tuesday through Saturday. Admission is $3 for adults, $2 for seniors and students, and $7 for a family.

The **Spokane Opera House and Convention Center,** West 334 Spokane Falls Blvd. (tel. 509/456-6000), is a slick modern building that's home to the city's symphony and performing arts companies. It also hosts concerts, exhibits, and trade shows.

The **Spokane Civic Theater,** North 1020 Howard St. (tel. 509/325-2507), is a cultural exchange center for the area. The $2-million facility offers a variety of musicals, classic drama, modern comedy, and experimental showcases throughout the year. Curtain time is 8 p.m.; ticket prices vary from $6 to $10.

In the last two weeks of July the city sponsors a Shakespearean festival at Boeing Amphitheatre in Riverfront Park (tel. 509/456-5511).

SHOPPING: Would that every downtown shopping area mimicked Spokane's system, which lets you shop hundreds of downtown stores without ever dodging traffic! You do that via the city's futuristic **skywalk system,** the second such system in the nation (Minneapolis/St. Paul was first). Here's how it works: from the street or from inside a shop, you walk up to an upper level, enter a glassy tunnel called a skywalk, and stroll right over top of the traffic huffing and puffing below. Skywalks connect hundreds of shops across 14 blocks so you can stroll in comfort for hours through intriguing boutiques and restaurants.

Bon Marché, with its sweeping double staircase at West Main and North Wall Streets, **Nordstorm's,** at West 724 Main St., and **The Crescent,** a Marshall Field's store at West 710 Riverside St., are among the major department stores.

The **Flour Mill,** 607 Flour Mill, built in 1893 on the north bank of the river, is a landmark, meeting spot, dining haven, and boutique heaven. A conglomeration of 25 shops and restaurants are tucked away in corners and up and downstairs. You'll find books and games, cards and gifts, leathers, lotions, jewelry, candy, potions, pottery, and needlecraft.

Sherwood Mall, West 510 Riverside Ave., at Riverside and Stevens, is a compact shopping mall with interesting clothing and gift shops, among others. **University City,** Sprague Avenue at University Street, can point to almost 15 years as a shopping center in the Spokane Valley. Anchored by J.C. Penney, The Crescent, and Newberry's, the enclosed mall offers more than 60 shops and restaurants.

Spokane's small Asian population concentrates around a place called the **Import Market,** 922 Division St. (tel. 509/327-9529). You can't miss it: there's a flashy gold eagle on top. Here you'll find bok choy and soy beans, wicker and rattan, kimonos and coolie hats.

If you like **public markets** at which treasure and, . . . um, nontreasure, is sold, you'll find one here at Riverfront Park at the Flour Mill entrance. It's open Saturday from 8 a.m. to 5 p.m.

7. SPORTS

As you would expect, sports play a big part in the lives of the inhabitants of this big sky country.

Horseflesh is an important topic of conversation, and the place to hear that talk is **Playfair Race Course,** Altamont and Main Streets (tel. 509/534-0505), the region's thoroughbred racing grounds. From April to October post time is 6:15 p.m. on Wednesday, Friday, and Saturday; at 1:30 p.m. on Sunday and holidays. Admission is $2, $4.50 in the Turf Club.

To do the riding yourself, call **Last Chance Riding Stable,** West 4812 Canyon Dr. (tel. 509/624-4646), about four minutes from downtown Spokane. You can trot over 1,000 acres of city parkland for various views of the city. Hourly rates are $7 and the stable is open from 9 a.m. to dark every day, but phone for an appointment first.

Bingo a sport? Maybe not, but you can still play three days a week: on Friday from 12:30 to 11:30 p.m., on Saturday from 9:30 a.m. to 11:30 p.m., and on Sunday from 9:30 a.m. to 10 p.m. Games are at **Big Brothers Sisters Bingo,** Boone and Monroe Streets (tel. 509/328-5673 or 326-2993), across the Monroe Street Bridge about a mile and a half north of town. You must be 18 to play the games, which are sponsored by Big Brothers and Big Sisters, a charity organization that befriends the children of broken homes.

For a day of swimming, boating, fishing, and picnicking, head north of Spokane 26 miles on U.S. 395 to **Granite Point Park** at Loon Lake (tel. 509/233-2100). On the shores of spring-fed Loon Lake you can gaze at surrounding mountains as you sit beneath towering cedar trees and nibble a Washington apple. Sandy shores make a great spot for the youngsters to dabble, while deeper waters offer fodder for fishing, swimming, and photography. A small grocery store stocks basic snacks that might, with a little luck, be supplemented by the lake's stock of rainbow, mackinaw, or silver trout, perch, or bass. Rowboats, small outboard motorboats, pedal boats, and canoes are available for rent. Daily admission to the park is $2 per car plus $2 per adult and $1 per child under 10.

You can rent bicycles at **Spoke's Sport,** North 212 Division St. (tel. 509/838-8842), for $8 a day. **Eagles Ice-A-Rena,** North 6321 Addison St. (tel. 509/489-9295), has ice 365 days a year, complete with lessons, skate rentals, and a pro shop.

Three scenic courses lure golfers: **Indian Canyon Golf Course,** an 18-hole championship course deemed one of the top ten in the U.S. by **Golf Digest,** at South Assembly and West Drives at the top of Sunset Highway (tel. 509/747-5353); **Downriver,** an 18-hole gently rolling course lined with pines, at North 3225 Columbia Circle; and **Esmeralda,** an 18-hole, par-70 course with flat open fairways and 2,000 young trees, at East 3933 Courtland St. in northeast Spokane (tel. 509/487-6291). Greens fees at any of the courses are a moderate $10.

You'll find **tennis courts** at Manito Park, South Grand Boulevard between 17th and 25th Avenues; in Franklin Park at Division Street and Queen Avenue; and at Mission Park at Mission Avenue and Perry Street. To find the courts nearest you, call the Spokane Parks and Recreation Department at 509/456-2020.

Spokane has a fleet of **swimming pools** open in summer from 1 to 4:45 p.m. and 6 to 8:30 p.m. daily. Two of the seven pools available are Cannon Pool at Mission and Elm Streets and Hillyard at Market and Columbia Streets.

We talked to one Spokane enthusiast who left town only to return because he loves to be able to drive 30 minutes or so out of town, put on his skis, and schuss down a mountainside. Spokane does offer that lure at **Mount Spokane,** 31 miles north on Wash. 206 (tel. 509/238-6281). From Thanksgiving to the end of March lifts are open from 9 a.m. to 10 p.m. daily. Lift prices are $20 for adults, $14 for children under 12. However, from 1 to 5 p.m. rates drop to $15 for adults and $10 for children, but rise again at 5 p.m. to match morning prices.

A little farther north, 48 miles on U.S. 395 to be exact, **49 Degrees North,** P.O. Box 166, Chewelah, WA 99109 (tel. 509/935-6649), has ski runs much loved by beginners and well-attended by more experienced skiers as well. Ski instruction and rentals are available, as are a restaurant, lounge, cafeteria, and nursery. Lift prices are $20 for adults and $14 for children under 12.

Farther east, **Schweitzer Ski Area** (write West 216 Park Pl., Spokane, WA 99220, or call 509/328-5632) is in Sandpoint, Idaho (tel. 509/263-9555, but call 509/328-5632 in Spokane for a ski report). You'll pay lift prices comparable to those at Mount Spokane.

At **Silverhorn Ski Area** in Kellogg, Idaho (tel. 208/786-9521), there's a mile-long chair and a 1,900-foot vertical drop plus fondue haus, ski rentals, a café, cocktail lounge, and ski school. For a ski report at Silverhorn call 509/327-7926 in Spokane. Lift prices, here too, are comparable to Mount Spokane's daily rate.

That indoor skiing we mentioned earlier takes place at **Magic Mountain,** East 428 Pacific St. (tel. 509/624-9994), where you step onto a simulator machine that moves beneath so you feel as though you're moving. An instructor helps you solve skiing problems. Price for the simulator is $68 for adults and $48 for children for six lessons.

Runners converge on the city in the first week of May when the **Bloomsday Run** draws more than 30,000 running fans known hereabouts as Bloomies! Call 509/456-5511 for registration information.

The **Spokane Indians** are a professional baseball team and part of the Pacific Coast League.

If rpm and mph are more your speed, get in gear and drag on over to **Spokane Raceway Park,** North 101 Hayford Rd. (tel. 509/244-3663 or 327-7353), where stock and drag racers rev up their engines every Saturday night from April through September. Gates usually open at 4 p.m. on Saturday, with time trials at 4:30 and racing at 7:30 p.m., closing at 11 p.m. If you call 509/244-3663, a recorded message will give you details on racing hours. Admission is $6 for adults, free for children under 12.

If you're looking for spectator sports, look to the **Spokane Coliseum,** North 1101 Howard St. (tel. 509/456-3204), where Spokane Chief hockey games, high school and college basketball games, concerts, even rodeos take place.

8. DAY TRIPS FROM SPOKANE

Spokane makes a good base for explorations around eastern Washington and into Idaho.

A NATIONAL WILDLIFE REFUGE: If you'd like to explore a natural environment, head for **Turnbull National Wildlife Refuge,** about 25 miles southwest of Spokane. Once a garden spot for the Indians after whom Spokane was named, the refuge still grows the roots and herbs, wild onion, and bitterroot the Indians came here to gather. In 1937 local residents and conservationists managed to get the region designated a national wildlife refuge, naming it after Cyrus Turnbull, an early pioneer. Restoration of lakes and marshes followed, and today the refuge is once again home to countless numbers of nesting and migrating water birds, including migrating Canadian geese. You may also see any of 200 kinds of birds and plenty of other wildlife from white-tailed deer to beaver, raccoons, coyotes, mink, muskrats, and squirrels. A Visitor Use Area has been designated for observation of wildlife and includes wetlands inhabited by geese, ducks, and trumpeter swans. For a map outlining an auto tour through the refuge, stop in the Information Center at refuge headquarters or write to the manager, Turnbull National Wildlife Refuge, Rte. 3, Box 385, Cheney, WA 99004 (tel. 509/235-4723).

To get to the refuge, take I-90 west from Spokane to Wash. 904, which goes to the refuge, and follow signs to the headquarters building and display pool. Admission is free.

MOUNTAIN VIEWS: You want panoramas? Spokane gives you panoramas. From the top of **Mount Spokane** you can see three states, two countries, two mountain ranges, and eight lakes! What are you looking at? Well, Washington, Idaho, and Montana; the U.S. and Canada; the Cascades and the Rockies; Lakes Coeur d'Alene and Pend Orielle in Idaho, and Liberty, Newman, Aloika, and some smaller waters in Washington.

There's plenty to do in the 16,000 acres of wilderness here too: skiing, picnicking, camping, photography, riding, hiking, wildlife-watching from deer to porcupines and coyotes, fishing for pike, trout, perch, sunfish, and bass, clamming in lakes and streams, snowmobiling, cross-country skiing, sledding, and bird-watching.

To get to Mount Spokane Park, take U.S. 2 north from Spokane to Wash. 206 (Mount Spokane Park Drive), which swoops and curves its way up to a rock lodge called **Vista House** (tel. 509/238-6282), about 30 miles downtown Spokane. Admission is free.

BREADBASKET LAND: For a lovely drive through some beautiful breadbasket scenery, you might try a drive to **Pullman,** 75 miles south of Spokane off Wash. 195. Centered in the rolling grainlands known as Palouse country, Pullman is home to **Washington State University,** which opened here nearly 100 years ago and still provides much of the sports and cultural life the city enjoys.

Among the amusements offered by the university are the Cougar football team (tel. 509/335-9626), the University Theater, Museums of Zoology and Art and Anthropology, a herbarium, a planetarium, and observatory. WSU even has the best view in town from the 13th floor of the Physical Sciences Center.

You'll find the campus by taking Wash. 270 east out of Pullman, for about a mile to Stadium Way, which turns north and leads to the heart of the campus. Parking stickers and a map of the campus are available at the Safety Building. One-hour guided tours leave at 1 p.m. daily, except during school holidays, from the Office of University Relations, French Administration Bldg. (tel. 509/335-4527).

Pullman also has a **Summer Palace theater** at Daggy-Jones Theatre (tel. 509/335-7236), eight parks, swimming, tennis, and a nine-hole golf course.

Stop by or write the **Pullman Chamber of Commerce,** North 415 Grand Ave., Pullman, WA 99163 (tel. 509/334-3565), for maps and information on the region.

COULEE DAM AND ENVIRONS: Dams have their opponents and proponents, but neither would deny the flat-out-awesomeness of **Grand Coulee Dam,** where the world's largest hydrogenerators produce 700,000 kilowatts of electricity. Enough to run your blow dryer for the next 80 years or so? To get this massive slab of concrete up and operating took 40 years of effort. When it was complete, its architects looked proudly upon what is said to be the biggest con-

crete structure in the world. Here come the numbers: the slab of concrete you see before you is almost a mile long, 500 feet wide at the base, and 550 feet high. It holds back the waters of the Columbia River, creating 151-mile-long Lake Roosevelt.

Begin your visit at the **Visitor Arrival Center** on the west bank below the dam. It's open daily from 8:30 a.m. to 10 p.m. Memorial Day to Labor Day, and closes at 5 p.m. the rest of the year. Here guides will answer the dozens of questions that will be popping into your head and arm you with maps so you can meander through a self-guided tour of the dam and hydroelectric plant. Part of that tour will take you on a glass-enclosed incline elevator, which travels up 330 feet to an intermediate stop, where you walk out onto a balcony and can look down on an awesome scene: the vast spillway and tailwaters.

Reboard the elevator and continue on for a tour deep inside a power plant, where massive whirling shafts on hydrogenerators produce huge quantities of electricity year round. In summer hundreds of thousands of gallons of water are released across the concrete face of the dam. From 1:30 to 2 p.m. daily June through early September water thunders down to the Columbia River. At night from 9:30 to 10 p.m. the waters shimmer with color from lights that play over the surface of the foaming water.

In 1989 the Grand Coulee Dam will begin showing a state-of-the-art laser-light show, replacing the present spillway light show.

Built for flood control, irrigation, and power in 1933, Grand Coulee Dam raised the level of the Columbia River high enough to form the 151 miles of **Lake Roosevelt.** Along the lake's 600-mile shoreland is the **Coulee Dam National Recreation Area,** where you can see bizarre geological creations wrought by the volcanos, glaciers, and water erosion that formed the Columbia River Basin eons ago.

Hundreds of **campsites,** ranging from big camping resorts to tiny pull-up-a-piece-of-ground camping areas, dot the region. Along the shores of the lake swimmers splash, fishing fans wait patiently for their big moment, and families roll out the picnic basket.

In case you're wondering where this dam got its name, the word Coulee comes from a French word *couler,* meaning to flow. It refers to a deep ravine or gulch scooped out by heavy rains or snow but left dry in summer. When you look at a map or sketch of the area, you will see how ancient glacial action did indeed scoop out deep ravines in this region.

Grand Coulee, the huge ravine for which the dam was named, is dampened now by Banks Lake, which filled the sere, desert-like coulee floor in the 1950s, providing sunseekers with 60 miles of sand. Fishing and water sports of all kinds are popular here, and hunters come in fall to fill their larders with pheasant, geese, duck, quail, and grouse. A steamboat, the *Coulee Queen,* cruises around the lake on 90-minute tours and out to Steamboat Rock on a three-hour daily tour. Prices for the tours range from $7 for adults and $4.50 for children on the shorter trip, to $12 for adults and $7.50 for children for the longer cruise.

North of the dam in the village of **Nespelem** is the burial ground of Indian leader Chief Joseph of the Nez Percé tribe, the chief who undertook a heroic march in resistance to usurpation of tribal territories. Tribes united into the Colville Confederated Tribes (tel. 509/634-4711) still live here and manage 1.3 million unspoiled pine-covered acres. You can get a close look at tribal custom and clothing during the first week of July at the annual **American Indian Pow-Wow,** which features July Fourth dance presentations of the Drum and Feather Club, in which dancers compete in handmade costumes. Information on that festival and other special events, like the May Colorama Festival featuring a rodeo, beer tent, and carnival, are available from the **Grand Coulee Dam Area**

Chamber of Commerce, 306 Midway (P.O. Box 760), Grand Coulee, WA 99133 (tel. 509/633-3074), open from 8 a.m. to 5 p.m. Monday through Friday.

On explorations around the dam you will also see **Steamboat Rock,** a huge flat-topped, prow-shaped rock that's home to Steamboat Rock State Park, a massive rock indentation called the Devil's Punchbowl, Barker and Northrup Canyons, and a town called Electric City.

Rental boats, ranging from sleek live-aboard houseboats to small power-boats, are available for prices that vary widely by season and size of craft. Folks at the Roosevelt Recreational Enterprises Reservations Office, P.O. Box 587, Grand Coulee, WA 99133 (tel. 509/633-0201, or toll free 800/648-LAKE in Washington), can supply you with a brochure detailing the boats and their prices.

Places to Stay

If you'd like to stay over here to explore the dam and its environs, a pleasant stopping spot is the **Ponderosa Motel,** 10 Lincoln St., Coulee Dam, WA 99116 (tel. 509/633-2100). Here you are a half block from the dam. Among the amenities are morning coffee, cable TV, and "view rooms," should you like to take your scenic splendor from the comforts of an armchair. Rates are $27 to $43 double.

At the east end of the Columbia River Bridge on Wash. 155 is **Coulee House,** 110 Roosevelt Way, Coulee Dam, WA 99116 (tel. 509/633-1101). Rooms have balconies that overlook Grand Coulee Dam and the house has a heated swimming pool and spa. Rates are $37 to $48 double.

If you're camping, Coulee Dam National Recreation Area, P.O. Box 37, Coulee Dam, WA 99116, is a National Park Service Campground offering covered rec vehicle sites, tent space, and swimming in huge Lake Roosevelt. Visitor activities and services include waterskiing, boating, picnicking, fishing, and hunting.

EXPLORATIONS NEAR THE DAM: Just 14 miles north of the small town of Wilbur, on U.S. 2, you can ride on a free ferry that sails across the Franklin D. Roosevelt Lake from 6 a.m. to 11 p.m. daily. You can reach the ferry by turning north on Wash. 21, just west of Wilbur. You will then be in the **Colville Indian Reservation.** From there the road travels on to Republic, where you join Wash. 20, heading east across Lake Roosevelt to Colville and back to Spokane.

To take another ferry ride, stay on Wash. 21 to a point about 14 miles north of Keller, where you turn on a road coming in from the east called Bridge Creek Pass Road, which immediately crosses the Sanpoil River. Drive 23 miles east to the village of Inchelium. There you can catch another ferry, this time across Lake Roosevelt to Gifford. The Inchelium-Gifford ferry runs eastbound from 7 a.m. to 7 p.m. and westbound from 7 a.m. to 6:30 p.m.

On the east side of the lake, you can join Wash. 25 and return south to U.S. 2 for the return to Spokane, or travel south to Hunters, where Wash. 242 joins Wash. 25 and shoots off east to Loon Lake, where it joins U.S. 395 South for the return to Spokane.

Colville is a small town in the middle of a national forest about 70 miles from Spokane on U.S. 395. All around it is a region Washington likes to call **Panorama Land.** It's aptly named. Many a panorama stretches out before you as you travel north through mountains and valleys, riverbeds and forests. The Hudson's Bay Company settled here in the early 1800s and built Fort Colville near a crashing cascade called Kettle Falls. That fort became the company's chief inland post.

Colville stayed that way for 30 years, then was caught up in the gold and silver rush of 1855. As a way station for miners in search of silver after the Old

Dominion Silver Strike in the hills north of the city in 1885, Colville was inundated by hundreds of prospectors who turned the small town into quite a thriving metropolis. One shrewd character named John Young figured all those miners and all that equipment needed toting, so he set up a stage service and livery stable to do the toting. He made a fortune. He used that fortune to invest in real estate and to buy part of a mine, thus making another fortune. When Young died, his widow married Louis Keller, a very rich fellow indeed, and the two of them preserved what has come to be known as the **Keller House.**

On a visit to this seven-acre estate and three-story antique-furnished home, in which nothing but the wallpaper has changed over the decades, you can get a good look at some of the detailed architectural furbelows of that day: beautiful beveled and leaded glass, a brick fireplace, red birch beams, elaborate moldings, wood columns at the entrance to the music room, and an interesting dining room wall cover made of woven cloth painted with gilt, then hand-painted with a floral design.

Keller House is part of the city's **Keller Historical Park** that includes a log schoolhouse and museum of farm machinery, including a horse-drawn ice cutter used to remove blocks of ice from Loon Lake, a covered wagon, and a two-wheel cart driven across the U.S. by pioneer Leland Wilson, who hitched up to it a 2,000-pound creature called a "catalo"—half Holstein, half buffalo!

Operated by the Stevens County Historical Society, the historical park is at 700 N. Wynne St. (tel. 509/684-5968). The museum is open daily May to September from 10 a.m. to 4 p.m.; the house, Wednesday to Sunday from noon to 4 p.m.

You can still see a primitive log chapel, called **St. Paul's Mission** (tel. 509/738-6266), built by Indians in 1845 and run until the 1870s. You'll find St. Paul's 12 miles northwest of Colville on U.S. 395 at the river.

If you'd like to stay overnight in Colville, you might consider an interesting alternative to the usual stopping spots: bed-and-breakfast at a ranch beside a sparkling stream, in a home beside a river or in a resort that has become part of the Panorama Land Bed-and-Breakfast program. To reserve a spot at which you will be carefully matched with a host family, call or write to **Panorama Bed and Breakfast,** 251 N. Main St., Colville, WA 99114 (tel. 509/684-2910).

CHAPTER V

IDAHO'S SUN VALLEY

□ □ □

If there's something missing in Sun Valley, we have yet to discover it. First it's part of a little-known but ruggedly beautiful mountain state that likes to call itself the Gem State, which is not only lyrically descriptive but literally true: Idaho produces the only opals in the U.S. and once topped *that* with the glitter of gold.

Beyond those literal interpretations, as you will soon discover, Sun Valley is a gem indeed. In winter this valley becomes a whitewashed wonderland of craggy peaks and emerald evergreens, frozen lakes and blazing fires. In summer the sun blazes, casting ebony shadows on silvery-gray cliffs and golden gleams on sapphire lakes, then disappearing to leave behind delightfully cool temperatures.

Through this sprawling wilderness, created eons ago by volcanic cataclysm, run the Snake and Salmon Rivers, the size of the Salmon's 900 miles of riverbank so vast it's often called the River of No Return. Those waters cascade over cliffs in spectacular falls and provide summer sport for thousands who come here to fish for huge trout or salmon, splash in crystal-clear streams, or pit their rafting skills against the racing waters.

Getting here takes you through some of the most bizarrely contrasting geology you're likely to encounter anywhere. In one direction is barren desertland soaked by irrigation that forces production from this resistant ground. In another, 750,000 acres of mountain scenery at Sawtooth National Recreation Area, a region of remote alpine lakes and vast forests. In yet another the eerie otherworldliness of volcanic wasteland fittingly known as Craters of the Moon National Monument, the training ground for America's spacemen.

In this valley you will always find the sun, but there is much more. From silent villages in which only ghosts reside to après-ski havens jammed wall to wall with ski bunnies, you will find a land that has often been brutal but has never been boring.

1. HOW THE SUN CAME TO THE VALLEY

Hands down, the number-one resort in Sun Valley is Sun Valley Resort. In fact, were it not for Sun Valley Resort there would have been no Sun Valley. How all this came about is a classic rags-to-resort story that begins—as do many American settlement stories—with a railroad. Back in the '30s, Averell Harriman, then board chairman at Union Pacific Railroad, was looking for a marketing plan. How, he wondered, could the railroad get passengers to use its new westbound trains? Aha, came the train brainstorm, a ski resort! No sooner had the idea-bulb lighted than Harriman sent for skiing Austrian Count Felix Schaffgotsch and dispatched him to find a place perfect enough to lure the beautiful and the bigbucks.

Legend has it that the count traveled far and wide, looking and leaving, rejecting such spots as Jackson Hole, Wyoming, where state officials refused to commit themselves to keeping the pass open all winter. One by one, the count rejected sites from Mount Rainier to Lake Tahoe to Yosemite—too high, too windy, too close, too far. When Idaho's turn came, officials dutifully straggled around with the questing count. After he had gone, someone remembered a mountain-rimmed, going-on-ghost valley left over from gold-mining days. Cables heated up the wires and Count Felix returned for a look at a minuscule little enclave called Ketchum.

Into the valley of the 300 rode the count—behind a snowplow. He saw. And he skied. As Count Felix schussed, he marveled. He liked what he saw but the folks in Ketchum were singularly unimpressed with what they saw: when local sheep farmers heard about this foreign royalty scouting the slopes for a spot to build a multi-million-dollar hotel, one wary scoffer promptly warned his countrymen: "Don't cash his checks." Schaffgotsch apparently had enough pocket money to avoid dependence on the locals and soon made up his mind. Enthralled, he wrote to Harriman, rhapsodizing that the valley "contains more delightful features for a winter sports center than any other place I have seen in the U.S., Switzerland, or Austria." Harriman wasted no time. He ordered up his private railroad car and headed out to Idaho. Once he saw the valley, he plunked down a few million post-Depression dollars to buy a 4,300-acre ranch on the edge of the village and build a resort on it.

But how were they to publicize the new resort? In those days when it came to publicity, it was hard to beat the glamour of Miami Beach, whose reputation had been created and spread with consummate skill by publicist Steve Hannagan, whom Harriman invited to come to Sun Valley and promote the country's very first complete ski resort. Hannagan came in out of the sun, took a look at his new project, and promptly dubbed the place a "God-forsaken field of snow." First impressions, however, are not always lasting. One day as Hannagan stood shivering in a snowbank, a bright winter sun came out, temperatures shot up to 70— and the snow everyone came to play in stayed there, as ski-worthy as ever, not a melt in sight! Eureka! Hannagan cried. Let's call this place . . . Sun . . . and thus was born Sun Valley.

Hannagan promoted this kind of sunshine much as he had promoted Miami Beach: with skin. His first poster showed a fellow schussing down Mount Baldy stripped to the waist. As it always has, skin sold. Hannagan's hullaballoo sold the valley, but Hannagan was not yet satisfied. So he did what came naturally to a Miami Beach buff—he brought the beach to the backwoods. On Hannagan's urgings the resort gave its patrons the best of both beach and butte. Sun Valley got a toasty glass-enclosed swimming pool, a formal dining room serving gourmet goodies, an orchestra for dancing.

All that remained was for Sun Valley to figure out some way to get the royal and the renowned comfortably up to the top of the mountain so they could ski elegantly back down. And in that desire was born the world's first chair lift, an adaptation of a gimmick used in the tropics to haul bananas onto trains! Not so different really.

When Christmas 1936 rolled around, Sun Valley's new-fangled snowfield banana-hauler was in place. A "log" lodge built of poured concrete "logs" was in place. A heated swimming pool was humming, an ice rink beckoned, the orchestra was tuning up, and a ski school directed by a champion Austrian skier was poised on the edge of the slopes waiting for its first novices.

They came. In droves. Claudette Colbert came to star in *I Met Him in Paris,* featuring mountain scenes filmed in Sun Valley. Ice skating star Sonja Henie came to join Milton Berle and the Glenn Miller Orchestra as star of a 1941 film called *Sun Valley Serenade.* For that film America's most famous skater, who loved ice but had no truck with snow, called on America's first gold medal skier, Gretchen Fraser, to double for her on the slopes (and when Gretchen had to leave, a local skier donned a blonde wig and filled in for both women).

Over the years many, many others came: Lucille Ball, Desi Arnaz, Ann Sothern, John Wayne, Marilyn Monroe (who filmed parts of *Bus Stop* at nearby North Fork), Gary Cooper, Tyrone Power, the Kennedy family, and many more of their ilk. Wonderful photographs of the rich and/or famous still adorn the walls of the resort.

Then came the first thaw, and those railroad entrepreneurs discovered they had bought more than just 4,300 acres of snow mass. Indeed, their deal doubled in value as they discovered this alpine valley look-alike was as softly seductive in summer as it was ruggedly majestic in winter. In went another swimming pool, trap- and skeet-shooting facilities, a stable, an 18-hole golf course, tennis courts, croquet, archery, bicycling. Orchestra leaders and gourmet chefs added to their ranks. Sun Valley boomed.

But as the years passed, Union Pacific officials discovered that running a burgeoning resort complex was a bit different from running a railroad, so they sold the by-now huge resort to Janss Corporation, the land development company that created Snowmass and Squaw Valley, among others. Janss began to fill the valley with tastefully designed condominium settlements bearing such lovely names as Villagers, Dollar Meadows, Cottonwood, Wildflowers, and Snowcreek, later selling it all to Bill Janss, who formed the Sun Valley Corporation. Today the corporation is owned by R. Earl Holding, president of Little America Travel Centers and chief executive officer of an oil-refining company.

As the fame of Sun Valley spread, others eyed the valley's success. Slowly more condominium projects were born—and today continue to grow both in size and number. Meanwhile down the road, Ketchum lived up to its name: it caught on—and fast. Chic boutiques moved in, artists set up easels, mountain trekkers advertised their services, and smaller resorts opened. Packed now in winter, the region has begun extolling the virtues of its summers—and there are many—and many are getting the message.

Still, despite its renown, this valley in the sun has lost little of its unspoiled rustic charm, its welcoming hospitality, and its quite endearing simplicity. And that is how a railroad created a resort.

A BIT ABOUT BOISE: Although we have focused our attention here on famous Sun Valley, you should know that there is a great deal more to Idaho than this long-time ski resort. For openers, there is Boise, a quite sophisticated city which annually sponsors a fascinating Summer Shakespeare Festival that's a real treat for Shakespeare fans—or for those at least willing to give the bard a try. There's also an Idaho Youth Theater, an opera company, and a number of art galleries and museums. Hotels and restaurants in all price brackets abound, and there is river rafting, skiing, and all manner of outdoor sports available, both near Boise and throughout the state.

READER'S TRAVEL TIP: "Boise is a small city with a lot going for it—good restaurants, theater, etc. It's a perfect stopping-off place, either by car or Amtrak on the way to Seattle, Portland, or Vancouver, and the people are extraordinarily friendly" (Binni Ipcar, Brooklyn, N.Y.).

2. GETTING THERE AND GETTING AROUND

GETTING THERE: Gateway cities for Sun Valley are Boise to the west, Idaho Falls to the southeast, and Twin Falls to the southwest.

Horizon Air flies to Ketchum/Sun Valley's **Hailey Airport** from Boise International, San Francisco, Seattle, Spokane, Salt Lake City, Portland, and other points. Hailey Airport is 12 miles from the valley.

Sun Valley Stages (tel. 208/344-0159 or 622-4200, or toll free 800/821-9064 outside Idaho) has daily scheduled bus service connecting with flights from Boise and other area airports. The company also operates charter bus service (tel. 208/622-4200). Fares from Boise Airport to hotels in Sun Valley, a 170-mile, three-hour trip, are $30 one way for adults, $50 round trip; half price for children under 10.

Greyhound Bus Lines services the region.

Major **roads** bracketing Ketchum/Sun Valley are **I-90** on the north, **I-15** to the east, and **I-84** to the south and west. From Boise take I-84/U.S. 20 to Idaho 75, and turn north to Ketchum. I-15 travelers will also pick up U.S. 20, but head west to Idaho 75. Drivers from Seattle or Sioux Falls will turn south on U.S. 93 and transfer to Idaho 75 into Ketchum.

GETTING AROUND: Although driving your own car is preferable, you are not lost without it in the valley. A number of rental-car companies have outlets in or around Sun Valley, including **Hertz,** at Hailey Airport (tel. 208/788-4593) and Sun Valley (tel. 208/622-3322); **National,** at Hailey Airport (tel. 208/788-3841) and Sun Valley (tel. 208/622-8221); **Budget,** in Hailey (tel. 208/788-3660); and **Avis,** at Hailey Airport (tel. 208/788-2382).

A limousine service operates in the area: **Luxury Limousine** (tel. 208/726-3535).

Ketchum's bus system is called **KART** and operates a **free public transport** system between Elkhorn, Sun Valley, and Ketchum from 7:30 a.m. to 10:30 p.m. daily, stopping at each stop every 30 minutes. For information on routes, call 208/726-7140.

ORIENTATION: Idaho Hwy. 75, just a branching loop of north/south-running U.S. 93, leaves U.S. 93 at Shoshone on the south and rejoins it as Challis on the north. As Idaho 75 runs through the village of Ketchum, it becomes Main Street in town, as it does in Hailey 11 miles away. Right in the middle of town,

Sun Valley Road crosses Idaho 75. If you turn east, the road takes you to Sun Valley Resort and on to Trail Creek Summit. If you turn west, you'll end up at River Run ski lifts. Dollar Road branches off from Sun Valley Road and goes to Dollar Mountain Ski Lifts and to Elkhorn. You can also get to Elkhorn, which is off Idaho 75 just south of Ketchum. Keep to the left, heading west on Main Street, to get to Warm Springs ski lifts. Street names often are not marked, so look for landmarks and don't be shy about asking.

VISITOR INFORMATION: Visitors are important to the valley, so they make it easy for you to get the information you need to get the most pleasure from your time there. The **Sun Valley/Ketchum Chamber of Commerce** is at 400 Main St., Ketchum, ID 83353 (tel. 208/726-3423, or toll free 800/634-3347). Workers there will help you out with maps and information on the region. The chamber also offers a hotel/motel/condominium rental **reservation service** at those same telephone numbers.

USEFUL INFORMATION: For **police emergency,** call 911. . . . Local **radio** station KSKI, 1340 AM, features news, weather, and shopping tips. . . . If you're driving in the area and need a report on local **road conditions,** contact 208/886-2266; for statewide road reports call 208/336-6600. . . . **Château Drug** and **True Value Hardware** are teamed up in the same building in the Giaccobi Mall (tel. 208/726-5696) and seem to have everything, open to 8 p.m. daily. . . . **Magic Lantern Cinema** (tel. 208/720-4274) and **Sun Valley Opera House** (tel. 208/622-4111) show films. . . . Take dry cleaning to **Sun Valley Cleaners** at 220 Lewis St. (tel. 208/726-9432), which has a self-service **laundromat** called Suds Ur Duds (tel. 208/726-9820). . . . **Western Union** is at Super Sec, 260 First Ave. North (tel. 208/726-4565). . . . One-hour **film processing** at F-Stop Film and Camera, Helm Station, Sun Valley Road (tel. 208/726-3419). . . . Ketchum Texaco service station is open from 7 a.m. to 10 p.m. daily (8 a.m. to 9 p.m. on Sunday) for **gas, groceries, beer, and wine** at 491 Main St. North (tel. 208/726-4766).

3. WHERE TO STAY

Sun Valley Lodge and Inn are the cornerstones of the most famous resort in the valley. Here you will find really a miniature city offering everything you need for a vacation: ski lifts sometimes just steps away from your door; year-round ice skating; top restaurants, interesting shops, even a deli-bakery. Just a cursory exploration of the resort takes a day or so. It is important to your wallet to note that Christmas is the peakest of the peak seasons here and prices are highest then. In summer and the fall value season before skiing begins, prices can be as much as 30% lower.

RESORT OF RESORTS: The **Sun Valley Lodge,** Sun Valley Co., Sun Valley, ID 83353 (tel. 208/622-4111, or toll free 800/635-8261, 800/632-4104 in Idaho), is the center of things. Here you'll find a roaring fireplace in the lobby from which you can watch skaters whirling summer or winter. Upstairs on the second floor the two-story Sun Room offers another cozy sitting spot, this one with a wall of windows overlooking the skating rinks, plus puffy couches, copper floor lamps, and two tall marble hearths. And down the way there's a billiard room and bowling alley!

Rooms here are cozy and comfortable, outfitted in contemporary furnish-

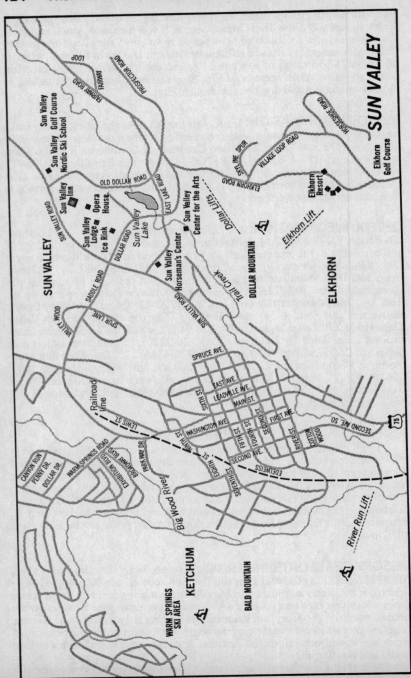

ings and lots of little extras. They are also convenient to the resort's posh Lodge Dining Room, where waiters garbed in tuxedos serve up a wide selection of continental treats. You'll find the inn tucked in among shops and restaurants along the edge of a rippling pond where swans splash in summer. Those rooms that overlook the pond are the loveliest, quite spacious with dark carpets, a beige-and-white décor, and comfortable chairs that offer an intriguing look at passing pedestrians.

If you're looking for some of those film-star photos we mentioned, begin your search at the Continental Cafeteria, open for all meals. It's just off the spacious lobby, where low couches offer intimate corners to meditate on the past and present of this sprawling resort. Facilities at the resort include tennis, swimming pools, saunas, skating, riding, and an 18-hole Robert Trent Jones–designed golf course. Restaurants range from the white-glove service of the Lodge Dining Room to Mexican food at Chez Pablo's, pastries and ice cream concoctions at the Konditorei, steak and seafood at the Ore House, and grilled steaks and cheese fondue at the Ram Dining Room. In winter horse-drawn sleigh rides to Trail Creek Cabin, a favorite haunt of author Ernest Hemingway, are a don't-miss. Reservations for restaurants can be made conveniently at a desk in the lobby of the lodge.

A free shuttle bus serves all parts of the resort, taking you from condominiums near the slopes to the cluster of boutiques and shops in the village shopping center. Films are shown in the chalet-like Opera House, and the resort even has its own semi-pro hockey team! Summer or winter there are organized playschool activities for children.

In winter rates at the lodge or the inn begin at $110 double for a standard room, rising to $156 for larger accommodations. A family unit offering space for four is $206 and a plush parlor suite for two runs $236. Condominium apartments range from $105 for a studio to $210 for a one-bedroom apartment, $260 for a two-bedroom, $310 for a three-bedroom.

Accommodations in the various enclaves—Atelier, Villager, Dollar Meadows, Cottonwoods, and Snowcreed—which are closer to the center of the resort, range from $110 for a studio accommodating two to $295 for a four-bedroom large enough for eight celebrants. An 11% state and local tax must be added to that, but two children under 12 are free. Money-saving four- and seven-night ski packages, including accommodations and lift tickets, are available.

Rates drop substantially—$49 to $78—in April and May and from October to mid-December, then rise $20 to $30 from June through September. Honeymoon, weekend, and tennis packages are available in summer.

LUXURY LEADER: The Elkhorn Resort at Sun Valley, Elkhorn Village (Box 1067), Sun Valley, ID 82353 (tel. 208/622-4511, or toll free 800/635-9356), is another massive Sun Valley resort property offering similar accoutrements to those proferred by Sun Valley Lodge. Here, too, you will find a self-sufficient community with a golf course, shopping mall, restaurants, a lodge, and many proud condominium owners who are happy to rent their homes when they're not using them. You can choose single or double rooms in a central lodge with all the services and conveniences of a hotel, or opt for larger, more private quarters in a variety of condominium accommodations. Among those latter accommodations are studio, one-, two-, and three-bedroom condominiums with or without a loft, and even four-bedroom quarters.

Whichever you choose, you will sooner or later stop by Elkhorn Lodge, a cozy spot with leather chairs and couches pulled up around a stone fireplace. Less than 100 paces from the lobby door is a ski lift. Inside the lodge are 144 attractively decorated rooms featuring wool hangings of Indian design. Everything you need for a vacation is right here, with no need to leave the property: an attractive mall with general store and plenty of boutiques; restaurants featuring everything from lobster to hot dogs to an 80-ounce margarita; and three nightspots with a variety of entertainment including a disco and an old-fashioned saloon. There's even a child-care center that offers a youth program and nightly babysitting service. If you're here in summer, you can golf on a Robert Trent Jones–designed 18-hole course, lob a few on one of 18 tennis courts, splash in two Olympic-size swimming pools, ease tired muscles in indoor or outdoor whirlpools, roast in a steamroom or sauna. There are trails for hiking and biking, and trout-stocked mountain streams. They'll even arrange a hot-air balloon ride or a glider flight! More? Of course: beauty salon, video-game room, sporting goods shop, even a real estate office.

For a room at Elkhorn Lodge you'll pay $65 to $105 year round, more on Christmas and President's Week holidays in February. Studios and apartments are $125 to $400 in winter months.

MODERATELY PRICED ACCOMMODATIONS: There's an alpine chalet look about the **Heidelberg Inn,** 1908 Warm Springs Rd. (P.O. Box 304), Sun Valley, ID 83353 (tel. 208/726-5361, or toll free 800/284-4863). Located about half a mile outside Ketchum on Warm Springs Road, this attractive blue-and-white two-story motel is done up in that cheery alpine style, flower boxes and all. Unlike most motels, the Heidelberg Inn has very spacious rooms, among the largest we've seen in this area. Those on the corners of the building—Rooms 101 and 102 for instance—are equipped with fireplaces. Décor here runs to citrus colors, golds, oranges, and the like, and rooms come in four configurations: a double room with two queen-size beds; a kitchenette room with queen-size bed and kitchen equipment; a fireplace room with king-size bed; and fireplace-kitchenette combination with queen-size bed. All rooms have cable color television, coffee makers, and a small refrigerator. If you're here in winter, you can warm up in a sauna and whirlpool hot tub, in summer you can swim in the motel's pool. In winter from Christmas to March rates vary from $60 to $75, with highest prices charged for the fireplace-kitchenette combo; in spring, summer, and fall rates drop about $10. In that money-saving off-season from spring through fall children under 18 are free. You can bring your pet here too for $3 a night.

In the little village of Ketchum just a mile from Sun Valley you'll find the **Christiana Lodge,** 651 Sun Valley Rd. (P.O. Box 439), Ketchum, ID 83353 (tel. 208/726-3351, or toll free 800/535-3241). A handsome two-story building of wood and stone, the Christiana has a variety of room layouts and prices, but our favorites are quarters with fireplaces. Those also have a clever wood-enclosed kitchen that looks just like a big dresser. Under the fold-back top you'll find a stove and sink and behind a door, a refrigerator. Spacious quarters here are attractively decorated in contemporary brown shades. Outside are the swimming pool and whirlpool. It's just a few blocks' walk to all the shops and restaurants in this small village, and a shuttle bus to the lifts stops on the corner. Prices range from $56 to $71 in summer, about 20% higher in winter. Figure about $80 in winter for one of those fireplace rooms at this Best Western member.

Another conveniently located motel in the Ketchum–Sun Valley area is **Tamarack Lodge,** 100 Sun Valley Rd. (P.O. Box 2000), Sun Valley, ID 83353 (tel. 208/726-3344, or toll free 800/521-5379, 800/622-6343 in Idaho). In its advertising Tamarack says, "Just imagine coming back from a great day on Mount Baldy, building a fire in your fireplace, and looking out on the ski runs you just conquered. In the summer soak up lots of sun in our garden courtyard or on your private balcony." Try Room 210, for instance, where you sit beneath a sloping ceiling and watch through a big window as skiers schuss their way down the mountainside. Quarters here are rather simply decorated but are comfortable and serviceable, what the resort likes to call "condo-style liveability." All have queen-size beds, remote-control cable color television, refrigerators, and coffee machines. Many have a private balcony and some open onto a pretty patio court-yard. After a long day on the slopes or the golf course you can relax in a whirlpool or redwood sauna or swim in a glassed-in swimming pool. To warm up muscles there's an exercise room. A few rooms have king-size beds and some quarters in-clude convertible studio beds good for families. Summer prices are $58 double for a basic room, $68 for a fireplace unit, and $70 to $78 for a family or executive suite with separate bedroom. In winter those rates rise to $76 to $99, and to both prices here, as in all hotels and motels in Sun Valley, you must add 11% tax. No pets at Tamarack Lodge. A shuttle bus stops at the front door to take you to sum-mer or winter sports activities in the region.

Another Best Western property in the area is **Best Western Tyrolean Lodge,** 308 S. Third Ave., Ketchum, ID 83353 (tel. 208/726-5336, or toll free 800/528-1234, 800/268-8993 in Canada). Carved-wood balconies, high-pitched roof, and a backdrop of lofty mountains give this spot a most Tyrolean look. Ideal for skiers, the 44-room lodge is steps away from the River Run Ski Lift at the base of the mountain. Two large indoor spas, a games room, sauna, and heated pool are busy year round, and in summer fisherpersons can play their fa-vorite games right here on the property. Rooms are spacious and attractively dec-orated and divided by the lodge into three categories: by size, location, and accoutrements (standard, and deluxe). The lodge is walking distance from town, about a mile from Sun Valley Resort, and rates range from $50 to $65 for a room with one double bed, from $60 to $75 for a room with two double beds.

BUDGET BESTS: A comparatively inexpensive stopping spot in this region is **River Run Motel,** 703 S. Main St., Ketchum, ID 83353 (tel. 208/726-9086), about a half mile south of town. Built on a small bluff overlooking Mount Baldy, River Run is an attractive, long, white building with cable color television, a heated pool, outside Jacuzzi, and a sauna, and charges $36 to $59 year round.

Another budget accommodation in this popular year-round resort is **Ketchum Korral Motor Lodge,** 310 S. Main St., Ketchum, ID 83353 (tel. 208/726-3510), a series of connected log cabins, some with fireplaces and some with kitchens. Furnishings are basic, and rooms are on the small side, but so are prices: $30 to $67 year round (higher at Christmas). You'll also find a large whirlpool here.

CAMPING: Campers should have little difficulty finding a place to pitch a tent or to park a recreation vehicle. Just eight miles north of Ketchum on I-75 is the southern entrance to the spectacular **Sawtooth National Recreation Area,** Star Rte., Ketchum, ID 83340 (tel. 208/726-8291). Rangers here will help you find a camping spot, but these are primitive campsites: no advance reservations are taken; no electrical or water hookups are provided. Camping fees range from $4 to $6.

One mile south of Ketchum on Idaho 75, campers will find **Sun Valley KOA,** P.O. Box 548, Ketchum, ID 83340 (tel. 208/726-3429). This camp-ground, which likes to call itself a "camping resort," has picnic facilities, hook-ups, water, laundry facilities, swimming, a store, games room, and hot tub. Rates are $11 to $16.

RENTING A CONDOMINIUM: There's practically no end to the numbers of individuals and groups marketing and renting condominiums in Sun Valley.

These condominium properties range from small apartments to huge, sleek contemporary houses. As with most things, price follows size. Price, however, can be one of the advantages of condominium rental. For about the same price you'd pay in a hotel, you get several bedrooms, a kitchen, living room, maybe even a private Jacuzzi. But you usually give up restaurants and the services offered by resorts. Here's a list of condominium agents offering daily *summer* rates from $55 to $160. Winter prices are about triple summer rates, all determined by size of accommodations.

Alpine Resort at Sun Valley, 271 Sun Valley Rd., Ketchum, ID 83353 (tel. 208/726-4340, or toll free 800/251-3037), has studio to three-bedroom accommodations. **Alpine Villa Town Houses,** 200 S. Third Ave., Ketchum, ID 83353 (tel. 208/726-8813), offers one-, two-, and three-bedroom condominiums about 500 yards from Mount Baldy's River Run chair lift. Trilevel units have balconies, wood-burning fireplaces, cable television, a laundry, and a heated pool. **Bitterroot Property Management,** 500 S. Main St., Ketchum, ID 83353 (tel. 208/726-5394), has condominium properties in Warm Springs near the River Run ski lift ranging from a studio apartment to a four-bedroom accommodation. **Ketchum Resort Reservations,** 407 Leadville Ave. North, Ketchum, ID 83353 (tel. 208/726-3003), is proud of the personalized service it offers in everything from a one-bedroom to a four-bedroom apartment. Weekly and monthly rates also are available at all of these spots.

In Warm Springs one interesting condo operation is **Lift Haven Inn,** 100 Lloyd Dr., Ketchum, ID 83353 (tel. 208/726-5601), located at the base of Warm Springs ski lift. Recently the inn did some redesigning, rebuilding, and redecorating, and has installed new lift-base facilities including a full-service ski shop, spa with steamroom, Jacuzzi, sun room, and massage. Rates at Lift Haven Inn, including breakfast, start in peak season at $125 double, one-bedroom suites at $185, and two-bedroom suites at $310 for four.

Still more? Of course. Other condominium apartment complexes offering summer rates of $55 to $150 and correspondingly higher ski-season rates include: **Mountain Resorts,** 470 Sun Valley Rd. (P.O. Box 1710), Sun Valley, ID 83353 (tel. 208/726-9344, or toll free 800/635-4444), featuring condominiums with fireplaces, heated pool, television, Jacuzzis, and saunas; **Resort Reservations,** 100 N. Main St. (P.O. Box 2387), Sun Valley, ID 83353 (tel. 208/726-3374, or toll free 800/635-8242 outside Idaho), with condominiums close to Ketchum and facilities that include swimming pool, saunas, or Jacuzzis; **River Run Lodge,** 300 Wood River Dr., Ketchum, ID 83353 (tel. 208/726-9086), near the River Run ski lift, with one- or two-bedroom condos with views of the mountains, balconies, color televisions, and access to a Jacuzzi; **Unlimited Condo Services,** 307 S. Main St., Sun Valley, ID 83353 (tel. 208/622-3094), with long- and short-term rentals in Elkhorn and Big Wood condominiums; and **Warm Springs Resort,** 119 Lloyd Dr., Ketchum, ID 83353 (tel. 208/726-8274), at the base of Mount Baldy (an easy walk to the Warm Springs lift), offering a swimming pool, saunas, Jacuzzis, bars, and a grocery/deli.

A NEW B&B: It would be hard to find nicer folks than those who operate the **River Street Inn,** 100 River St. West, Ketchum, ID 83340 (mailing address: P.O. Box 182, Sun Valley, ID 83353) (tel. 208/726-3611). Friendly and accommodating from the first phone call to the last farewell, the owners also are skilled decorators who have created a cozy nook with eight rooms, all with bath and queen-size beds. Some gaze out upon the mountains; others overlook meandering Trail Creek. Décor runs to antiques, country prints, and soft colors, and all rooms have color televisions, a small refrigerator, private telephones, and in the bathroom, showers and Japanese-style soaking tubs, a round soaker designed to ease the aches and pains acquired in skiing and hiking the valley. A full country breakfast is served each morning in the inn's dining room, but you can also have it sent up to your room, where there's a table large enough to accommodate dining. Rates at River Street are $85 to $140, depending on season and on room size, with money-saving deals in fall.

4. WHERE TO DINE

You can be sure you'll never starve in Sun Valley's Ketchum where there seem to be as many restaurants as skiers. Here's a look at some of the possibilities.

UPPER RANGE: The **Christiana Restaurant**, 303 Walnut Ave. North in Ketchum (tel. 208/726-3388), has long been one of the mainstays of valley dining and for good reasons: an attractive atmosphere, good food, good service. Could there be more? Housed in a massive A-frame building, Christiana has stone walls, candles, and all the cozily elegant atmosphere you'd expect in a ski resort. Chefs steam and roast in one corner of the room and in the bar there's entertainment. On the menu you'll find smoked trout served with tomato, marinated onions, and lemon, or tortellini in cream sauce for openers, followed perhaps by Caesar salad, rack of lamb, or tournedos with artichoke bottoms and béarnaise sauce—and for those who can never decide, a sampler plate that includes veal marinara, lamb with herb-spiced sauce, and filet with béarnaise sauce. Vegetables accompany dinner. For dessert try the pot de crème, a bittersweet chocolate treat. Prices are in the $12 to $17 range, and the restaurant is open from 6:30 to 10 p.m. daily.

Peter's Restaurant, 180 6th St., Ketchum (tel. 208/726-9515), is the culmination of a dream long harbored by Austrian Peter Weisz, who worked for others for many years before branching out on his own to create Peter's. A talented Bavarian artist as well as a skilled chef, Peter is now operating a cheerful restaurant in which seasonal treats are supplemented by year-round favorites like wienerschnitzel with Swedish lingonberries, Tiroler leber (liver) with roasted onions and bacon, roast saddle of lamb with tarragon sauce, and some pasta and Chinese dishes. Peter's is open for lunch from 11:30 a.m. to 2:30 p.m. Monday through Friday, and for dinner from 6 to 10 p.m. nightly, serving entrees in the $10 to $18 range. Peter's now has dining upstairs as well as down, and has enclosed with French doors a romantic patio known hereabouts as the Garden Room.

Down by the riverside you'll find **Evergreen,** 1st and River Streets in Ketchum (tel. 208/726-3888). Here you dine in a soothingly serene atmosphere decked out in navy blue and white with contemporary Breuer chairs. A wall of glass offers a view of evergreen mountain scenery as you dine on such as beef Wellington, veal au whisky sautéed in whisky and cream, grilled medallions of lamb loin served on artichoke bottoms with a madeira sauce, roast duckling with a Cumberland sauce, Idaho trout amandine, and scampi sautéed in garlic butter, shallots, wine, and cream. For openers try a spinach salad with hot bacon dressing or paper-thin carpaccio with a creamed caper sauce. Prices are in the $12 to $17 range for entrees, which include vegetable, potato, and home-baked bread. Open daily from 6 to 11 p.m.

Warm Springs Ranch Inn, 1801 Warm Springs Rd., Warm Springs (tel. 208/726-8238), is a bit more inn than ranch these days, but it's still a charming spot with just the right amount of rusticity. A big log cabin with a comfy country farmhouse look, Warm Springs Ranch in summer opens an outdoor platform beside a spring where trout fin around in search of a handout. American favorites are the order of the day: tender barbecued ribs, mountain trout baked in sherry, sourdough scones served with honey butter, crunchy salads, steaks, trout, vegetables, and sheepherder potatoes sautéed with onions. Prices are in the $10 to $15 range, and the restaurant is open from noon to 2:30 p.m. Monday through Saturday and from 6:30 to 10 p.m. daily.

EATING AT SUN VALLEY LODGE: Sun Valley Lodge is its own little village, which means, of course, that it has restaurants. Tops among those is the **Ore House** (tel. 208/622-4363), a refinedly rustic (how's *that* for a description!) spot that begins each dinner with a little pot of fondue. A big fireplace forms a focal point in a décor that runs to mooseheads and an attractive navy color scheme. With dinner come Idaho's interpretation of scones accompanied by honey butter. Corn-fed beef becomes such specialties as steak Ore House, featuring a filet wrapped in bacon and topped with crabmeat, béarnaise sauce, and mushrooms. Salmon filet basted with teriyaki sauce tops the seafood menu, which includes Idaho rainbow trout with sliced almonds and dill among other sea treats. All dinners, which range in price from $9 to $11, include soup or salad bar, steamed vegetables, and breads. Two wings here plus a sunken bar. Open daily from 5:30 to 10 p.m. for dinner.

The **Ram** (tel. 208/622-4111) is another handsome spot. This one creates specialty salads, thick steaks, wild game, trout, and other seafood for prices in the $8 to $17 range. For dessert a not-to-be-missed treat is hot fudge fondue with fresh fruit. Cheese fondue is also available at this restaurant which has live music on some evenings. The Ram bleats from 6 to 10 p.m. daily.

MODERATELY PRICED: Freddy's Taverne d'Alsace, 520 East Avenue North (corner of 5th Street), Ketchum (tel. 208/726-4660), is the place to go when you're Hungry, capital H. Here in a rustic, wood-beamed dining room you can feast on raclette valaisanne (melted cheese served with boiled potatoes and pickles and, here, with dried sliced beef). Other goodies include veal in a mushroom-cream sauce with spätzle, bratwurst, pork rib, knackwurst, white veal sausage, frankfurt sausage, and best of all, on really hungry days the Royal Alsatian Sauerkraut of lean pork, smoked bacon, sausage, boiled potatoes, and of course, sauerkraut. Prices are in the $6 to $10 range.

River Street Retreat, 120 River St. East, Ketchum (tel. 208/726-9502), is a very casual spot lauding the days of hops sheds. These days the hops are bottled, as is the wine, which lies aging in a most interesting cellar. Menu options include steaks, chicken avocado, shrimp Dijon, seafood Florentine, and mahi mahi. Prices are in the $10 to $15 range. Open daily from 5 to 10 p.m.

Jesse's, in the Elkhorn Village Mall, Sun Valley (tel. 208/622-4533), used to be the Charthouse and still features the fresh fish, steaks, prime rib, and seafood that has made the Charthouse chain popular across the country. Salad bar fans will find more than 60 items on the vast selection here. Jesse's is proud of its simple preparations and claims to create everything right down to salad dressings from scratch, eschewing fussy sauces. Big daiquiris are a favorite here and are consumed on an outdoor deck in summer. You'll pay about $12 to $17 for most entrees here, salad bar included. Open for dinner daily from 6:30 to 11 p.m.

BUDGET BETS: If you've acquired an adoration for tacos, tortillas, and margaritas, head straight for the **Bald Mountain Cantina,** 613 N. Main St., Ketchum (tel. 208/726-3353). Here for less than $10 you can gorge on all your favorites. Look for a small, gray, wood-sided house with piñatas in the windows.

On the way to the slopes, ski bunnies and friends stop in at the **Konditorei,** Sun Valley Mall in Ketchum (tel. 208/622-4111, ext. 2235), where freshly baked muffins, croissants, and pastries pour from the ovens. If morning is most decidedly not your time for chatter, you can read a newspaper thoughtfully provided on bamboo poles at the entrance. Lively Austrian décor adds an alpine flavor to such goodies as freshly squeezed orange juice, Swedish waffles topped with fresh strawberries and whipped cream, crêpes filled with blueberries, pancakes, and eggs any way you like them. Prices are in the $4 to $7 range and the Konditorei is open from 7 a.m. to 10 p.m. daily.

ATMOSPHERE AND . . . : Creekside at 317 Skyway Dr., Ketchum (tel. 208/726-8200), a cozy spot tucked in at the foot of Mount Baldy and overlooking Warm Springs Creek, draws après-skiers in winter, waterside revelers in summer. Entertainment here in the Cannon Bar and a menu long on seafood, steaks, lamb, and prime rib. Prices are in the $12 to $17 range and the restaurant is open from 6:30 p.m. to 11 p.m. daily; the bar opens at 9 p.m. A lovely spot for summertime mountain-contemplation.

Finally, if you're here in winter, you mustn't miss a trip to **Trail Creek Cabin,** Trail Creek, Sun Valley (tel. 208/622-4111). To set you up for the atmosphere that is to follow, horse-drawn sleighs convey you to this forest cabin as they have conveyed the likes of Gary Cooper and Papa Hemingway. In the center of the cabin is a bar dispensing warming libations under the watchful eye of a moosehead or two. Fires blaze in massive fireplaces and lanterns glow on huge beams. Trail Creek's menu is hearty: big cuts of prime rib, steak, chicken, pork ribs. Prices include soup, sheepherder spuds, vegetables, and squaw bread and honey butter. Sleighs leave from Sun Valley Inn on the half-hour ride. Entree prices at Trail Creek are in the $10 to $16 range and seatings are about every half hour from 6:30 p.m., but call for exact times.

PUB GRUB, PLUS: You need never fear you'll starve during your après-ski or après-summerday partying. Among the entertainment spots serving food (see addresses under "Nightlife") are **Louie's,** which produces some very good pizzas; brass- and fringed-lamp-trimmed **Slavey's,** which creates burgers, sandwiches, Mexican goodies, salads, potato skins, and the like; the **Yacht Club,** where you can dine rather more seriously on steak and seafood; and **Pioneer Tavern,** where the prime rib and Pioneer burgers are renowned among the ski set. Prices at those last two are in the $10 to $15 range, while the burger-pizza-taco spots charge prices in the $5 to $7 range.

5. NIGHTLIFE

In ski season—or come to think of it, any season—just walk up one side of Main Street and down the other and you'll have found 10 or 20 parties.

For more structured souls: in summer or winter try lounges at the **Christiana Restaurant and Lounge,** 303 N. Walnut Ave. (tel. 208/726-3388); **Louie's,** 331 N. Leadville Ave. (tel. 208/726-8325); **Pioneer Saloon,** 320 N. Main St. (tel. 208/726-3139); and the bilevel, backgammon-playing **Yacht Club,** 231 N. Main St. (tel. 208/726-5233)—all in Ketchum.

Whiskey Jacques, a stained-glass- and antler-trimmed spot at 209 N. Main St. (tel. 208/726-3200), and **Slavey's,** 280 N. Main St. (tel. 208/726-5083)—see what we mean about Main Street?—are the scene of much Ketchum entertainment, some of it musical (usually rock and roll) both summer and winter.

In Sun Valley try any of the lounges in the **Sun Valley Lodge** (tel. 208/622-4111) or on the grounds of the resort—the **Duchin Room** or the **Ore House.**

At Elkhorn the **Lobby Lounge** and the **Elkhorn Saloon** (tel. 208/622-4511) have—and are—entertainment.

Get a copy of the weekly *Wood River Journal* or the *Mountain Express* on

Thursday when it carries an entertainment section called **The Guide,** which outlines what's happening in Ketchum and environs.

6. EXPLORING

In this sports-oriented region, we couldn't find many sedentary activities, but we did manage to come up with a few things for you fence-sitters to do. Two drives offer a look at some awesome scenery: Sawtooth National Recreation Area and Craters of the Moon National Monument.

To visit Sawtooth, stop in at **Sawtooth National Recreation Area** headquarters, Ketchum (tel. 208/726-8291), where workers will help you plot a course through the recreation area. Idaho Hwy. 75, Ketchum's Main Street, runs right through the recreation area. Along the way marked side roads lead to Alturas, Pettit, Redfish, and Stanley Lakes. A stretch of Idaho 21 from just north of Stanley, a town about 60 miles from Sun Valley, to Boise is also heralded for its scenic beauty. When you see this region, named for the Sawtooth Mountains that loom over it, you will see what inspired all those mountain-scenery postcards you've been sending. Mountains 10,000 feet tall provide the backdrop to lakes deep blue and jade green with the reflected color of blue skies and giant pines. Ice Age architectural forces created crater lakes like Sawtooth Lake, cupped by clusters of massifs, and deep gorges filled by melting glaciers.

Next tour? **Craters of the Moon National Monument.** To get there, take Idaho 75. Just south of Bellevue turn east on U.S. 20 to its junction with U.S. 93. Craters of the Moon National Monument is about 30 miles north on U.S. 93. About halfway to Arco you will begin to see the strange formations stretching out before you on the south side of the road. What you see is only a small part of the volcanic area, which stretches across 83 miles of bleak, black, volcanic rocks. It really does look like the dark side of the moon, although just how much like it is known only by those moon-walking astronauts who trained here prior to their historic stroll!

Blaine County Historical Museum, at 221 N. Main St., in Hailey (tel. 208/788-2809 or 788-4491), offers a look at the rip-roaring days of the mining and sheep industries in the region. Admission is $1 for adults and 50¢ for students, and the museum is open from 10 a.m. to 5 p.m. daily except Tuesday.

To take a look at **Bald Mountain,** known to its few hundred thousand closest friends as Mount Baldy, drive about two miles out Warm Springs Road, or for an even lovelier view, ride out Trail Creek Road and look over your shoulder.

Soak in the **warm springs** of Warm Springs—they're at Frenchman's Bend.

Look up. **Meteor showers** are not uncommon in the region. A local newspaper, the *Mountain Express,* carries information about the starry showers.

To tour part of the region with a personal guide, stop by the **Ketchum Ranger District Office** in Sun Valley (tel. 208/622-5371), or the **Sawtooth National Recreation Area headquarters,** eight miles north of Ketchum (tel. 208/726-8291), and pick up a tape recorder and tour tape. Then you're set to take off on an escorted trip from Ketchum to Stanley through the beautiful Sawtooth National Recreation Area.

If you'd like to get a look at a **ghost town,** drive over to Custer (take Idaho 75 east from Stanley to the old Sunbeam Dam, turn left at Yankee Fork River Road, and follow it for 13 miles, 10 of which are hard dirt road). Custer and another ghost town called Bonanza are visible one mile past the gold dredge. Bonanza is on private land, but at Custer there's a small museum, the 1890 graves of three young girls killed in an avalanche, a processing mill, blacksmith shop, saloon, bawdy house, rooming house, carpenter shop, and one home. Deserted now, the town once boomed with a population of more than 3,000.

7. SPECIAL EVENTS

Nearby Hailey celebrates the Fourth of July with an event called **"Days of the Old West"** featuring a rodeo and fireworks.

The **Wood River Valley Music Festival**, starring string and brass performers, takes place in the first two weeks of July at various locations including the Sun Valley Opera House. Check the *Mountain Express* for information on times and places.

The **Sun Valley Ice Show** occurs at Sun Valley Lodge (tel. 208/622-4111) on Saturday evenings from mid-June through mid-September. Admission is $10 for adults, $8 for children, with a buffet dinner served from 7 to 8:30 p.m. before the show begins at 9 p.m.

Carey Pioneer Days take place in late July at the Blaine County Fairgrounds and come complete with rodeos, parade, and a "horse pull."

Tennis, golf, running, and riding competitions occur all summer long. Check with the chamber of commerce for information on your sport.

A big celebration locally occurs in the last week of August and is fittingly called **Ketchum Wagon Days.** On the schedule of events are a Big Hitch Parade, a bountiful breakfast, carnival, bike race, antique fair, chili cook-off, and ice show. Whew!

8. CULTURAL PURSUITS

While you're not likely to find Luciano Pavarotti singing *La Traviata* up here (although you might very well see him partying), there's still quite a lively art colony.

For its size Sun Valley seems to have more than its share of art galleries. Four, in fact, are clustered together at Fourth and Leadville Avenues: **Images Gallery** (tel. 208/726-5079), specializing in photography; **Sun Valley Center Gallery** (tel. 208/726-9491), featuring weaving, ceramics, sculpture, painting, and photography; **Trails West Gallery of Fine Art** (tel. 208/726-9261), specializing in western and wildlife art; and **Wood River Gallery** (tel. 208/726-5512), offering paintings by western artists, Pueblo pots, bronzes, and Navajo weavings.

Others include the **Kiva**, Sun Valley Mall (tel. 208/622-5451), featuring Indian art of the Southwest and Arctic Circle; **River Run Gallery,** First Avenue and Sun Valley Road (tel. 208/726-8878), showing art glass and watercolors; **Steven Mark Snyder Gallery,** Sun Valley Road and 1st Street (tel. 208/726-8100), specializing in photography; **Stonington Gallery,** Sun Valley Mall (tel. 208/726-3917), showing watercolors and photolithographic reproductions plus metal sculptures and prints.

9. SPORTS

Skiing is what put Sun Valley on the map. If you want to see what all the fuss is about, come here between November 22 and May 5, the resort's **ski season.** March has become more popular in recent years, but January and February remain the top months. One side of the mountain is always in sun, River Run and the bowls in the morning and Warm Springs after noon. Mayday Chair Lift at Lookout Restaurant on the Warm Springs side of the mountain takes you to a point at which you will have access to all sides of Baldy.

Lift tickets are $33 a day for adults, $19 for children, with a slightly cheaper rate for packages offering several days of skiing. The mountain is open from 8 a.m. to 4 p.m. daily and is carefully groomed by a squad of machines. Dollar Mountain is the beginner's slope, located at the edge of the Sun Valley Resort. Bald Mountain with 12 lifts is the spot for more experienced skiers. All lifts, which combined can carry more than 17,000 skiers an hour, open at 9 a.m. Lines are usually short.

Restaurants on the mountain include Lookout, Roundhouse, Northface Hut at Bald Mountain, and Dollar Cabin at the base of Dollar Mountain. All are cafeteria-style dining spots.

Sun Valley Nordic Ski School and Touring Center, Sun Valley Lodge (tel. 208/622-4111, ext. 2250), offers all kinds of lessons from beginner instruction at $45 an hour for private lessons to cross-country ski instruction at $20 for a half day. Moonlight ski tours, skiing on the tiki course to Trail Creek Cabin for dinner and dancing, bus ski tours and helicopter ski tours to remote country locations are available. Founder Leif Odmark, a former Olympic coach, oversees the operation.

If you have hunting or fishing plans, call or write the **Idaho Department of Fish and Game,** 600 S. Walnut St., Boise, ID 83707 (tel. 208/354-3700), for information on seasons and licenses. For a complete list of all guides, outfitters, river runners, equipment suppliers, and adventurers operating in the area, contact the **Idaho Outfitters and Guides Assn.,** P.O. Box 95, Boise, ID 83701 (tel. 208/342-1438), and ask for their current Idaho Outdoor Experiences publication.

Golfers have quite a selection of courses, including Bigwood Golf Course in the Bigwood development (tel. 208/726-4024), a nine-hole course charging $14 a day, $10 after 4 p.m.; Elkhorn Golf Course, a 7,158-yard, championship course in the Elkhorn condominium development (tel. 208/622-4511); and Sun Valley Golf course in the Sun Valley Resort and condominium property, charging $36 greens fees, $10.50 for a cart.

Equestrians should head for Sun Valley's Stables, where riding trips are $16 an hour. Dinner rides, hayrides, and pack trips are also available at the Elkhorn Village development (tel. 208/622-8503). More riding in the region at Trail Creek Cabin, two miles north of town on Sun Valley Road (tel. 208/622-4111, ext. 2263 or 2241). Rates are comparable, and the stables are open daily. Riders must be more than 8 years old. Instruction in riding and jumping is available too.

You can **rent bicycles,** five- or ten-speed and children's bikes, at the Elephant's Perch, 220 East Ave., Ketchum (tel. 208/726-3497), for $10 a half day, $15 a day, with weekly and monthly rates available. The Elephant can also outfit you with skis, camping equipment, tent, stove, the lot. They've got climbing gear and trail maps and information too.

Two-M River Outfitters, 201 Afton Dr., Ketchum (tel. 208/726-8844), zips off on **white-water raft trips** in the Sawtooth National Recreation Area daily at 9:30 or 10 a.m. A hearty lunch of ribs, chicken, or steak is included in the rafting expeditions. If there are four of you, you can go on a 4 p.m. evening float, which includes dinner. Trips run from mid-June or so through Labor Day. Prices are $52.50 for children, $63 for adults, 10% cheaper for groups of eight or more. Two-M can also arrange longer trips.

Another white-water-rafting outfit is the Triangle C Ranch in Stanley, about 60 miles from Ketchum. For a one-day float trip on the upper main Salmon River, you meet at the ranch for transport to the river, then float the white water of Shot Gun Rapids and through Sun Beam Dam on a 12-mile journey. About halfway you dine on a Dutch-oven-cooked meal, fish, swim, or hike, then continue your adventure. Cost is $60 per person and reservations are requested (tel. 208/774-2266).

Yet another white-water crowd: Middle Fork Co., 391 9th St., Sun Valley (tel. 208/726-8888), features three- or six-day trips on the Middle Fork of the Salmon River. Three-day trips are about $650; six-day sojourns, $995.

Tennis buffs can play at the Prospector Tennis & Swim Club, 319 Skyway

SUN VALLEY: SPORTS / SHOPPING □ 135

Dr. (tel. 208/726-9404), at the base of Bald Mountain. Court fee is $6 an hour, or longer if they're not busy. Guess what else you can do there? Another tennis spot: Fred Stolle's Warm Springs Tennis Club, 1801 Warm Springs Rd. (tel. 208/726-4040), where weekly memberships are available for $55 per person.

Glider rides over the cliffs? Sure, at Sun Valley Soaring at Hailey Airport (tel. 208/788-3054).

Swimming at Bald Mountain Hot Springs Swimming Pool, 151 S. Main St., in Ketchum, is $5 for adults, $4 for children under 12. Everybody's into the pool from noon to 4 p.m. on Monday, to 10 p.m. Tuesday through Friday, and from 10 a.m. to 10 p.m. on Saturday and Sunday.

Summer or winter you can go **ice skating** here at Sun Valley Lodge (tel. 208/622-3888 or 622-8030), which keeps its rink open all year long, all day long, and until 10 p.m. You pay $4.75 to skate ($3.75 for children) and skate rentals are $1.25. Lessons are $17 for 25 minutes.

10. SHOPPING

You'll find 16 shops at **Giacobbi Square,** which is enough of a landmark to be its own address. You'll find it right in the middle of town, between 5th and 4th Streets and Leadville and East Avenues. Wares include fashions, jewelry, candies, specialty coffee and kitchen items, groceries, and sports equipment.

Hand-knitted natural-fiber sweaters are sold at Sweaters Etc., Trail Creek Village, 220 S. Main St., Ketchum (tel. 208/726-3688). A number of other small shops operate in **Trail Creek Village,** including a French fabric purveyor, an antique dealer, a lingerie shop, and a mountain boot sales and repair operation that will help get you trekking.

Two new malls in the region include **Walnut Avenue Mall** and, across the street, **Colonade Center.** Both are on Sun Valley Road and offer plenty of places to spend your lucre. Walnut Avenue Mall's big on trendy boutiques.

CHAPTER VI

RIDING THE OREGON TRAIL

□ □ □

This is the land beyond, Oregon's vast outback, endless acres of home on the range for cowpuncher, sheepherder, and wheat farmer. So vast is this land and so rugged that even today much of it remains unexplored, its impassable terrain keeping out all but roaming elk and the most determined explorers.

Geology is at its showiest in eastern Oregon. Great mesas spread out across the landscape. Deep ravines create an awesome gorge known as Hell's Canyon. Rocky, towering mountains give no quarter to the feeble or the half-hearted.

That geological immensity has hidden—and perhaps still conceals—fortunes. Once from the depths of these forested hillsides cries of "Gold!" created a fever that lured thousands of miners who swept in here in the 1860s, only to sweep back out again when the take dwindled.

Eastern Oregon is rife with legend and riddled with the unusual: lava beds and towering buttes, the deepest gorge in the world, canyons and high passes, Indian reservations and cowhand bunkhouses, thriving market cities and eerily silent ghost towns, fossil beds that haven't changed for seven million years and wheatlands that are changing every day.

Those who live here can be pretty unusual too: rugged individualists, isolationists, dedicated environmentalists, Basque settlers who somehow made their way here from the north of Spain, and Chinese and Japanese workers who settled here in railroad-building days. Some of these hardy souls trace their roots back to those equally iconoclastic adventurers, the American pioneers, who saw just what you'll be seeing on the expressway that now traces the Oregon Trail they trod. Since those miles of wagons rolled along the Oregon Trail, leaving still-visible ruts in the earth, time hasn't stood still, but it certainly hasn't kept pace with the rest of the world.

If you're driving a vehicle that can take the tough terrain in remote sections of eastern Oregon, you will have access to some of the most spectacular backwoods and bywaters in the West—canyons in every color of the rainbow and brilliantly blue mountain lakes set in a backdrop of deep-green pines. Even if you're just throughway-ing past, you'll be rewarded with majestic scenery so immense, so timeless, that the memory of its impact will remain with you forever.

1. ORIENTATION

GETTING THERE: You can get to eastern Oregon by plane, train, or bus. **Horizon Airlines** flies into Pendleton from Portland. You can reach Ontario from flights that land at nearby Boise, Idaho. **Amtrak,** on its Portland to Salt Lake City run, stops at Ontario, Baker, La Grande, and Pendleton. **Greyhound** also serves the cities of Ontario, Baker, La Grande, and Pendleton, with stops at some smaller towns as well.

Ideally, you'll come here **by car.** From Portland and the Northwest, you'll find your way on **I-84,** which runs along the Oregon-Washington border—the Columbia Gorge—and then heads southerly across the eastern side of the state. **U.S. 395** is the main north-south artery in eastern Oregon. From Lakeview, just north of the California border, it runs north to Burns, on to John Day and then into Pendleton, where it joins I-84. Together they run east to near Hermiston, where U.S. 395 branches north and goes over the bridge from Umitilla into Washington. If you're coming from the state of Washington and points north, you can join I-84 on Ore. 11/125 from Walla Walla.

Those traveling from western Oregon have their choice of a number of roads heading east. The most direct route is **U.S. 20** from Newport through Corvallis and Albany to Bend, and on through Burns to Ontario. Alternatively a more northerly route will set you nearer to Baker and La Grande: from Bend take U.S. 97 to Redmond, then pick up Ore. 126 east to Princeville. Head east on U.S. 26 to the Ore. 7 junction, and follow this road into Baker.

From Klamath Falls on the south, Ore. 140 travels east to join U.S. 395 at Lakeview heading north. At Riley, U.S. 395 joins U.S. 20, the road west into Ontario.

2. ONTARIO

Ontario is the trading center of the Malheur Valley. This is cattle country, where weekly auctions of beef and dairy herds are attended by dusty-booted fellows who may look like paupers but are likely to be princes, both personally and financially. Ontario, largest city in Malheur County, is a quick punt across the Snake River from Idaho, main entry to Oregon from points east. As such it is ideally suited to some side trips that will lead you to lava beds and gold streams, thundereggs and the thundering hooves of wild horses, even to a colony of jai-alai–playing Basque settlers!

Although neighboring Baker was the center of the 1860s gold fever, plenty of panning was and still is done in this vicinity. If it's mystery you want, well, step right up. Seems that in 1912 a hallucinating sheepherder, suffering from spotted fever, stumbled into town, mumbling about a gold mine he'd found. A few hours later he was dead, and in his bedroll was some of the finest gold ever seen hereabouts, later sold by the county for a pretty penny. Where did it come from? Well. . . .

Another local mystery goes back to the days before the Civil War, when a troop of 93 U.S. soldiers came this way through the Owyhee Mountains and disappeared! No one ever saw them again, but a legend told for generations around Indian campfires has it that the soldiers were killed, their bodies—and presumably their strongbox—secreted in a cave. Where's the cave? Well. . . .

138 □ FROMMER'S DOLLARWISE NORTHWEST

GETTING THERE: I-84 from Boise and points southeast runs right through town, or you can pick it up in Portland, if you're coming in from the Northwest. Western Oregon travelers will note that U.S. 20 and U.S. 26 divide Oregon into thirds, with U.S. 20 giving access roughly to the southeastern and U.S. 26 serving the northeastern part of the state. So if you're Ontario bound, the most direct route from the west is U.S. 20. The nearest airport is in Boise, Idaho.

VISITOR INFORMATION: Folks with plenty of stories to tell, but sadly, no map to that mysterious gold field, can be found at the **Ontario Chamber of Commerce,** 125 S. Oregon St., Ontario, OR 97914 (tel. 503/889-8012).

WHERE TO STAY: Ontario has a few cozy places to rest your weary head. Best of those is the 100-room **Tapadera Motor Inn,** 725 Tapadera Ave., Ontario, OR 97914 (tel. 503/889-8621, or toll free 800/525-5333). Cedar shingles on mansard roof overhangs with lots of greenery around make this motel quite attractive. A moderately priced, 24-hour restaurant connects to the motel's lobby and rooms by covered walkway. Rooms are spacious and outfitted in comfortable modern furniture and bright colors. A few rooms even have waterbeds. For amusement there's a heated outdoor pool and a sauna. Rates are $33 to $38 double. You'll find the motel at the junction of U.S. 30 and I-84.

Next door, the **Colonial Motor Inn,** 761 Tapadera Ave., Ontario, OR 97914 (tel. 503/889-9615), offers prices in the $26 to $36 range for standard motel rooms with in-room movies. A heated indoor pool, whirlpool, and exercise room will help you keep, or get, in shape. There's a restaurant next door.

State campgrounds are 25 miles north of town off I-84 at **Farewell Bend State Park,** Farewell Bend Exit, Huntington, OR 97907 (no telephone reservations), where rates are $6 to $11. In town four spaces are available at **Idle Wheels Village Mobile Home Park,** 198 S.E. 5th St. (tel. 503/889-8433), at a $9 charge.

WHERE TO DINE: You can't go wrong sticking with steakhouses and beef specialists in this part of the state. The **Cheyenne Social Club and Midget Mary's Lounge,** 111 S.W. 1st St. (tel. 503/889-3777), has Victoriana overtones in its décor and basic good cooking in its kitchens, which produce plenty of good steaks from local beef, some simple seafood choices, very good prime rib, and a generous salad bar. Cooking is continental and prices are in the $10 to $15 range for dinner. Hours at Cheyenne are 11:30 a.m. to 2 p.m. weekdays, 6 to 10 p.m. Monday through Thursday, closing an hour later on weekends; closed Sunday.

Charolais Restaurant & Lounge, 125 E. Idaho Ave., at I-84 (tel. 503/889-8070), has longevity. Operating here under the same management for 25 years, the Charolais is a 24-hour spot featuring buffet meals from lunch through dinner and other steak, chicken, and seafood selections at reasonable prices in the $10 to $12 range.

Among the newer spots in town is **Sizzler,** 830 S.E. First Ave. (tel. 503/889-5005), where all-American beef is king. Open daily for lunch and dinner from 11 a.m. to 10 p.m. the Sizzler offers prices in the $10-or-less bracket.

If you're traveling with youngsters, **King's Table,** 2281 S.W. Fourth Ave. (tel. 503/889-3898), is a good choice here and in its many other locations in the Pacific Northwest. A buffet operation (that's the current euphemism for cafeteria), King's Table carves its roast beef right in front of you and features fresh ham as well each evening. Friday is "fisherama" night, and vegetarians can always manage here. Meals are unlikely to top $5. Hours are 11 a.m. to 8:30 p.m. daily except weekends, when closing hour is 30 minutes later, and on Sunday, when it closes at 8 p.m.

Casa Jaramillo, 157 S.E. 2nd St. (tel. 503/889-9258), goes south of the border to provide a Mexican atmosphere, a good bistek ranchero, enchiladas rancheras, and as a salute to Americana, sirloin slices sautéed with tomato and spices. Prices are in the $5 to $7 range, and tangy margaritas and other potables are available in the lounge. Hours are Tuesday through Sunday from 11:30 a.m. to 9 p.m.

AFTER DARK: The **Cheyenne Social Club** (see "Where to Dine") is the primary entertainment spot in town.

To see what may be cooking at other local lounges, check the city's *Daily Argus Observer* newspaper.

THUNDEREGGS, HOLD THE BACON: If you've ever had a niggling urge to try your hand at **prospecting,** this is the place to do it. Nearby Nyssa calls itself the Thunderegg Capital of the World, and it doesn't seem likely there will ever be many challengers. Thundereggs, for the uninitiated, are ancient egg-shaped volcanic formations that when broken open may prove to be a valuable hunk of agate. These ovoid gifts of nature are so beloved by Oregonians that they have made them the official state rock! Jasper and other semiprecious stones abound in quarries roundabout town, and everybody has a hunk of some kind of rock stuck up in a window or on a mantelpiece. Two agate-searching areas in the region are Wild Horse Picture Rock Mine and Graveyard Point for plume agate. To get started and learn what it's all about, stop at **Emil's Thunderegg Shop,** 707 Emison St. (tel. 503/889-4758). For the full scoop, try to be here at the beginning of August, when Nyssa sponsors a five-day **Thunderegg Days** celebration, complete with tours to rockhounding areas and displays of valuable agate, jasper, thundereggs, fossils, and petrified wood specimens. Nyssa is 13 miles from Ontario. To get there, take Ore. 201 west to its junction with U.S. 20/26 south. Follow 20/26 south to Nyssa.

WHAT TO SEE AND DO: To explore this scenically stimulating region:

A pleasant drive from Ontario takes you to **Owyhee Lake,** 40 miles south of town. Take Ore. 201 to Owyhee, then turn west on the secondary to Lake Owyhee State Park. Spectacular canyons accessible only by boat or Jeep are faced with sheer cliffs in rainbow hues of red, yellow, green, and brown. Red cliffs are a feature of the eastern shore of the lake. Farther south of Owyhee off Ore. 201, Succor Creek Canyon has yielded Indian artifacts that indicate long-time habitation of these rugged regions. To see these 1,000-foot canyons in all their glory, you might try to arrange for a guided tour in the region.

Marty Rust is a local outfitter who guides trips to Pinnacle Ranch, a remote fly-in guest ranch on the Owyhee River. You can personalize your arrangements by writing to him at 990 W. Main St., Vale, OR 97918.

Lute Jerstad Adventures, P.O. Box 19537, Portland, OR 97219 (tel. 503/244-4364), has been taking adventurers on white-water expeditions, horse pack trips, wildlife safaris, and the like for 20 years now. You can join one of those trips down the white waters of the Owyhee River through rarely visited desert canyon scenery. Trip dates and lengths vary, so contact the company for details.

Sundance Expeditions, 14894 Galice Rd., Merlin, OR 97532 (tel. 503/479-8508), is an outfit widely known for its hard-shell kayak school and raft trips on the Rogue River. It also features raft trips on the Illinois River and fishing trips out of its private lodge on the Rogue.

SPECIAL EVENTS: During World War II Ontario served as an internment camp for Japanese-Americans. After that conflict ended, many settled in here and remain here today, celebrating their heritage at the annual **July Obon Festival.** About the third week in July, out come the parasols and ornate kimonos as the residents invite one and all to visit the Buddhist Temple, learn Japanese story dancing, and dine on Japanese delicacies.

SIDE TRIPS TO THE OLD WEST: On a side trip from Ontario you can visit a town you've seen many times on the movie screen.

Burns

A happy hunting-ground for rockhounds and site of a Paiute Indian reservation, Burns has such an Old West look to its landscape that the countryside hereabouts has been used many times to film westerns. You'll find the city 130 miles west of Ontario on Ore. 20. Agate, obsidian, jasper, thundereggs, arrowheads, sunstones, petrified wood, and fossils are found in the region, and the **Harney County Chamber of Commerce,** 18 W. D St., Burns, OR 97720 (tel. 503/573-2636), will be happy to help you out with maps and information.

While you're here, you can take a look at **Harney County Historical Museum,** Broadway and D Streets (no phone), where memorabilia of Indians and rancher-pioneers are gathered. Hours are Tuesday through Friday from 9 a.m. to 5 p.m. and on Saturday from 9 a.m. to noon from June through September. Admission is $1 for adults, 50¢ for children.

Burns is also the nearest town to the **Malheur National Wildlife Refuge** (tel. 503/493-2323), 35 miles southeast of Burns on Ore. 205, open weekdays from 8 a.m. to 4:30 p.m. The 184,000-acre preserve is home to 301 species of birds. Admission is free, as is the wildlife museum at the refuge headquarters, which is open from 6 a.m. to 9 p.m. every day.

If you're staying over here, try the **Ponderosa Best Western,** 577 W. Monroe St., Burns, OR 97720 (tel. 503/573-2047, or toll free 800/528-1234). A simple, two-story motel with cheerful orange trim and a swimming pool, the Ponderosa charges $35 to $37 double.

Favorite restaurant in town is **Pine Room Café,** Ore. 20 and U.S. 395 (tel. 503/573-6631), famed locally for its German dumpling soup and butchered-here steaks served in an attractive dining room in which local history is accented. Prices range from $7.50 for light meals to $24 for lobster. Hours are 5 to 11 p.m. Tuesday through Saturday.

Frenchglen

Nearby Frenchglen was named by two ranchers, Peter French and Dr. Hugh Glen, who established a ranch here in 1872 and built it into a massive 132,000-acre empire called the **P Ranch.** In true Old West film style, Glen died when he was shot from his horse by a neighbor in 1897. You can still see a big round barn, once used to house wild horses later broken to the saddle for use by cowhands.

Frenchglen Hotel, Ore. 205, Frenchglen, OR 97736 (tel. 503/493-2825), a good center for driving tours of the Blitzen Valley, offers eight rooms with shared bathroom in a 1914 building constructed to house ranch guests. These are spartan accommodations, but the food cooked downstairs makes up for the lack of amenities. Rates at the hotel are $30 to $40 double. Family-style dinners of fresh local produce and meats are in the $8 to $14 range. They are served promptly at 6:30 p.m. and are open to the public by 24-hour advance reservation. Lunch prices top at $4.50 and it's served from 11 a.m. to 3 p.m. The hotel is closed from mid-December to March.

VISIT TO 7,000,000 YEARS OF HISTORY: Another Ontario side trip about 130 miles distant, this time heading northwest on U.S. 26, will take you to **John Day,** in the middle of cattle country.

John Day was, in its day, an important center in eastern Oregon: visited on the Oregon Trail, a stop on the Pony Express Trail, and part of a gold rush that racked up $25 million in nearby Canyon City.

These days John Day is best known as kick-off point for a visit to the **John Day Fossil Beds Monument,** which begins 40 miles west of town. This quite remarkable monument features striped hills called Painted Hills and ancient fossils that outline seven million years of history although their creation goes many millions of years beyond that.

Get oriented to what you will see in the monument region by stopping at the **headquarters office,** 420 W. Main St. (tel. 503/575-0721), where workers will arm you with maps and brochures. Fossil collecting is prohibited. Admission is free.

Park headquarters are in the town of John Day, named after the pioneer Virginian trapper and explorer, but the park itself really begins with rock formations just beyond Dayville on U.S. 26, about 70 miles west of John Day, with the Painted Hills located another 75 miles farther west.

In town, get a little historical perspective. Stop by the **Kam Wah Chung & Co. Museum,** two blocks north of U.S. 26 in John Day, at City Park (no telephone). The museum honors Chinese businessman Lung On and herbal doctor Ing "Doc" Hay, who treated the nearly 2,500 Chinese gold-mine workers and pioneers—including John Day. In 1887 the two young immigrants bought a trading post built 21 years before and turned it into their home, a general store, and the medical office of "Doc" Hay. As the fame and influence of "Doc" and Lung On spread, the building became the social and religious headquarters for the entire Chinese community in eastern Oregon. Among the hundreds of artifacts now on display are Chinese shrines, herbal medicines, and American store goods of the time. Hours are 9 a.m. to noon and 1 to 5 p.m. Monday through Thursday, and 1 to 5 p.m. on Saturday and Sunday from May to November. Admission is $2 for adults, $1 for children under 17.

If you're staying over here, **John Day Sunset Inn,** 390 W. Main St., John Day, OR 97845 (tel. 503/575-1462, or toll free 800/452-4899 in Oregon), can fix you up with room and meals. This 44-unit motel just off the highway is neat and clean and has an indoor pool and hot tub. Rates are $35 to $39 double. In the dining room, open from 5 a.m. to 11 p.m. daily, you can get a good steak and a trip to the salad bar for prices in the $8 to $12 range.

Information on what to see and do in the area is also available from the **Grant County Chamber of Commerce,** 281 W. Main St., John Day, OR 97845 (tel. 503/575-0547).

Special events here include the **Grant County Fair,** in late August, the oldest continuous county fair in Oregon complete with "Half-Fast" Marathon; the **Cinnabar Mountain Rendezvous,** at Mount Vernon, family fun on Memorial Day; **Kam Wah Chung Days,** in John Day, a mid-September weekend in honor of the Chinese who worked the gold mines; and the **'62 Day Celebration** in nearby Canyon City, which salutes the discovery of gold in 1862, with much fanfare including a medicine wagon show.

3. BAKER

Back in the 1800s people in Baker knew there were things more valuable than gold—but they couldn't for the life of them remember just *what* things. Baker was front and center of the eastern Oregon gold rush but has quieted down a bit. Just let the price of that shiny stuff rise, however, and the fever strikes all over again.

Those bedazzled by all that glitters continue to stake claims to land and a dream. In the 1860s miners occupying a nearby camp, called Sparta, turned up more than $2 million in gold—and in boom-to-bust Cornucopia, gold mining went on until the 1940s, producing at this one mine alone $16 million worth of nuggets!

You can snoop around the gold region and its ghost towns—using, we would suggest, some rudimentary safety precautions to protect yourself from both unstable mines and covetous claimants. Visits to old gold mines and the now-ghost towns among them offer a fascinating look at the way we were when riches lay hidden in the rocky rubble. Personally, we've never met a gold bar we didn't like, so we found this historic town on the Oregon Trail a fascinating place to let imagination run wild. Try it. You'll soon be seeing a golden gleam in every hunk of granite too!

GETTING THERE: Again, I-84 runs right through town, making it easy for travelers from the northwest or southeast. From the west U.S. 26 then Ore. 7 is your best bet. U.S. 86 runs east out of town into Idaho.

VISITOR INFORMATION: The **Baker County Chamber of Commerce,** 490 Campbell St., Baker, OR 97814 (tel. 503/523-5855), is right in the middle of this historic gold town on the Oregon Trail. You'll find the Visitor Information Center at exit 304 of I-84.

WHERE TO STAY: Baker's no land of high-rise hotels, so you'll have to be satisfied with standard but attractive motels.

After a long morning out in the gold fields, you'll welcome the cool waters of the stone-trimmed swimming pool at **Best Western Sunridge Inn,** 1 Sunridge Lane, Baker, OR 97814 (tel. 503/523-6444, or toll free 800/528-1234). The best quarters in this 124-room hostelry have private balconies or terraces overlooking that pool, but all are very attractively decorated and feature cable television, in-room movies, and telephones. The restaurant is open from early morn until the last revelers wind down in the cocktail lounge. Steak is big on the menu here in cattle country, and prices are in a reasonable $10 to $15 range. Rates at the resort, which you'll find at the City Center exit from I-84, are $48 to $58 double.

Campers can find a secluded spot at **Phillips Lake,** 17 miles south of the city on Ore. 7, Phillips Lake, OR 97814 (no telephone reservations).

WHERE TO DINE: Out here in eastern Oregon béarnaise sauce is a real rarity, but you can always count on a good steak dinner.

Long one of the mainstays in Baker, the **Fireside Inn,** 2000 Well St. (tel. 503/523-9280), was built of logs in 1913 and still has the original rock fireplace. There are plenty of juicy steaks here in a variety of preparations, and seafood too, all in the $6 to $14 range. The atmosphere is nice too—fireplace, pleasant views of the Blue Mountains from an outdoor dining deck, woodsy surroundings. Lunch is served from 11 a.m. to 2 p.m. weekdays; dinner, from 5 to 11 p.m. daily. Cocktail lounge here too. Fireside is just off I-80 at the middle exit to Baker.

If you're a lover of the simple life, the **Blue and White Café,** 1825 Main St. (tel. 503/523-6792), is your kind of place. You have to jump hard on the chow wagon to spend more than $5 at this little café specializing in good, simple home-cooking. Fruit pies baked here are not to be missed, but other productions of the bakery are top-notch too. Steaks and chops in the $5 and *under* bracket are featured at dinner, and there's always a daily special priced at $3—Swiss steak, for instance. And those prices include potatoes, vegetable, salad, homemade rolls, and coffee. Breakfasts are bounteous and reasonable. The Blue and White's open from 6 a.m. to 8 p.m. daily except Sunday.

WHAT TO SEE AND DO: From bullion to boxcars, Baker has some intriguing diversions. If you'd like to get a look at what gold looks like before it becomes a Rolex, stop by the **U.S. National Bank,** 2000 Main St. (tel. 503/523-7791), where an exhibit of native gold in all its forms from bar to banknote is on display. You can even see an 80.4-ounce nugget that would certainly be the perfect paperweight! Hours are 10 a.m. to 5 p.m. Monday through Friday. Staring in fascination is free.

Now for the boxcars: **Sumpter Valley Railroad** (tel. 503/894-2268) sends its steam choo-choo off on rides through Sumpter Valley each weekend from Memorial Day through September to give you an idea what life was like before four-wheel drive. They used to call this wilderness railroad the Stump Dodger!

Along the way you may spot beavers busily building, geese paddling about, or a deer bounding across the tracks. All aboard at 10 a.m., noon, 2 p.m., and 4 p.m. on Saturday, Sunday, and holidays. The conductor collects $4 for adults, $3 for children 6 to 16, and $10 for families. The depot is at Sumpter Valley. To get there, take Ore. 7, which heads south from Baker and then doubles back on itself to head east.

Excursions from Baker

One interesting side trip takes you through the gold fields, while another is a scenic journey to the edge of Hells Canyon National Recreation Area, at 5,500 feet the deepest river gorge in the world.

Exploring the gold fields around Baker gives you a chance to see some reconstructed ghost towns and some wonderful scenery as well. One trip, called the **Elkhorn Mountain Loop,** is a 100-mile drive that takes you through the ghost towns of Whitney and Bourne. Folks at the chamber of commerce will provide you with a map that will take you on Ore. 7 along the route of that Sumpter Valley Railroad, connecting with Ore. 220 up the Powder River. Along the way you'll pass Red Bridge Overlook, Sumpter Valley smelter, and the now-quiet village of Sumpter, where an 1899 vault in the Bank of Sumpter is about the only tangible evidence that the gold rush was once on here. Your route goes through the mining town of Bourne, up nearly 6,000 feet, then through a rather lively ghost town called Granite, past Anthony Lakes Recreation area, and back to U.S. 30.

Hells Canyon is such a mass of stupendous and dramatic scenery you'll soon be oohh-ed and ahhh-ed into exhaustion. Now a major sporting region on this eastern side of the state, Hells Canyon even has its own Hells Canyon Chamber of Commerce, P.O. Box 841, Halfway, OR 97834 (tel. 503/742-2726, 785-3393, or 742-7744). Others who can help you with maps and information in the region are Hells Canyon National Recreational Area, Wallowa-Whitman National Forest, Enterprise, OR 97828 (tel. 503/426-3151); the Oregon Department of Fish and Wildlife, Baker Office, 2995 Hughs Lane, Baker, OR 97814 (tel. 503/523-5831); and Pine Ranger District, General Delivery, Halfway, OR 97834 (tel. 503/742-7511).

To reach the region, take Ore. 86 east past Flagstaff Hill Summit. About 20 miles from town, a gravel road on the left heads north past that deserted mining camp at Sparta (when the road forks to the left, stay to the right). That road becomes paved again at New Bridge and goes on to Richaland, where you get back on Ore. 86 and head to Halfway, 11 miles north. From Halfway (nobody's quite sure what it's halfway to, or halfway from) you can take a part-paved, part-gravel road to the ghost gold town of **Cornucopia,** or follow a paved road for another 17 miles to Copperfield, right at the tip of the recreation area. From Copperfield a gravel road takes you another seven miles along the edge of the recreational area. In this region seven distinct life zones have been discovered in what is the earth's deepest gorge, from subarctic at the top of 10,000-foot He Devil mountain to the semitropical atmosphere of Granite Creek at 1,400 feet.

Kayaking and rafting are the most popular activities here, with thriller trips down Granite Creek Rapid and roaring Wild Sheep Rapid, two of the ten top rapids in the U.S. Naturally, **hunting, hiking, trail riding, river rafting, and fishing** are top lures. To arrange your kind of trip, write **Eastern Oregon Outfitters & Guides Association,** P.O. Box 266, Joseph, OR 97846. At last count 15 association members operated on three million acres of land offering a wide variety of travel and outfitting services to help you get the most out of your vacation time. Among the services members offer are guided hunts, white-water river trips by raft or jet boat, horse-packing, llama trekking, and scenic tours by vehicle.

Among the **river rafters** in the area are Wild West River Rovers, Rte. 1, Box 39-B, Elgin, OR 97827 (tel. 503/437-4491), specializing in two- to five-day rafting trips; and Don Merrell, Northwest Whitewater Expeditions, P.O. Box 3765, Portland, OR 97208 (tel. 503/236-9706). Beamer's Heller Bar Excursions, 23 miles south of Asotin, Wash., on Wash. 129 (tel. 509/243-4499), runs rafting trips on the Snake River right through the heart of Hells Canyon.

If you'd like to traverse a great, fascinating chunk of the Snake River as it pours out of Hells Canyon, contact **Snake Dancer Excursions,** 614 Lapway Rd., Lewiston, ID 83501 (tel. 208/743-0890). Gary Watson will take you from Clarkston at 7:15 a.m. on a 90-mile trip up the Snake River to Johnson Bar and back again. The day-long trip includes lunch, coffee breaks, and sightseeing at petroglyphs, lava flows, abandoned mining areas, and Indian crossings. Price for all this is $75 for adults, $40 for children under 10. Call to reserve.

SPORTS: In winter, skiers play here and in other seasons they turn over this playground to those who swim, raft, fish, hunt, and hike.

In Winter

This area's ski region is **Anthony Lakes Ski Area,** about 25 miles west of the village of North Powder (tel. 503/856-3277, 856-3387, or 963-8282). Here nine miles of varied terrain and a base elevation of 7,100 feet should be a challenge even for Olympian talents. A day lodge with cafeteria, lounge, and coffeeshop overlooks the slopes. Ten miles of trails welcome cross-country skiers and there are places for snowmobilers to play too.

A chair or poma lift takes you to the top from 10 a.m. to 5 p.m. on Saturday and Sunday only in winter, daily from May to October. Lift prices are $16 for adults, $12 for children under 13. Details on instruction and equipment rentals are available by writing Anthony Lakes Corp., P.O. Box 1370, La Grande, OR 97850. Ski season begins at the end of November and runs through April.

In Summer

Summer playground is **Phillips Lake and Union Creek Campground,** 17 miles southwest of Baker, where you can swim, hunt, fish, boat, and waterski. You'll find the lake on Ore. 7.

Bordered by the Wallow Mountain Range on the west and the Elkhorn Mountains on the south, Baker County is prime playground for hunters, who seek here for everything from pheasant and quail to the deer and elk that roam the sagebrush-covered flats.

High mountain lakes are paradise for fishermen. **Powder River** shelters rainbow trout, while the **Snake River** is home to bass, trout, steelhead, and salmon.

ARTS AND SHOPPING: Those two categories are united here at **Crossroads Creative and Performing Arts Center,** 2020 Auburn Ave. (tel. 503/523-3704), in the town's old Carnegie Library where art and craft work is on display and for sale. In late July arts and crafts play a big part in the **Miners' Jubilee.** Hours at the center are noon to 5 p.m. Tuesday through Saturday. The **McCord Corner Gallery,** 2080 Resort St. (tel. 503/523-7058), features western art in a historic building dating from 1872. Hours are 10 a.m. to 4 p.m. on Monday, Wednesday, and Friday. Finally, this is the place to get boots to go with the handcrafted saddle you buy in Pendleton. **Tom's Boot Shop,** 1668 Resort St. (tel. 503/523-5704), ships boots handmade by bootmaker George Ziermann to connoisseurs all over the world.

4. LA GRANDE

Those localites with Madison Avenue inclinations will tell you that La Grande got its name because, "well, folks, because it is Grande." The truth of the matter seems to lie a little closer to a story that the town took its name from the Grand Ronde Valley, dubbed such by a French-Canadian trapper who admired the valley's round contours.

Home of Eastern Oregon State College, the only four-year upper-level educational facility in eastern Oregon, La Grande is best known as a starting spot for excursions into the dramatic scenery of the Wallowa (rhymes with allow-a) Mountain Range.

Those mountains and the valleys surrounding them were the great frontier for courageous pioneers who slogged their way across the Oregon Trail to make homes and history here. They were also the site of a terrible battle between the Nez Percé Indians, who loved this place, and those newcomer pioneers.

Led by Chief Joseph, the legendary son of a legendary father, the Nez Percé tribe fought to remain in their "valley of the winding waters" against troops dispatched in 1877 to alter the balance of power. Although they fought valiantly and won many battles against hordes of troopers far outnumbering their own warriors, they were in the end pursued more than 1,000 miles northward and finally captured at the Canadian border, just a few miles short of sanctuary. Joseph, a small town about 70 miles east of La Grande, honors the memory of that courageous young chief and his father, who is buried beside the waters of a lake.

GETTING THERE: Roads crossing through town are I-84 from north and south; Ore. 244 comes in from the west and Ore. 82 skips in from the east.

VISITOR INFORMATION: The **La Grande–Union County Chamber of Commerce** at 101 Depot St., La Grande, OR 97850 (tel. 503/963-8588), can supply you with information on the region.

WHERE TO STAY: A small hotel roster here makes decision-making easy. The **Pony Soldier Motor Inn,** Rte. 4, Box 4009, La Grande, OR 97850 (tel. 503/963-7195, or toll free 800/528-1234, 800/268-8993 in Canada), with 151 well-kept units, is the largest stopping spot in the vicinity. Some rooms have balconies, most have refrigerators and radios, but all have air conditioning, cable color television, and in-room movies. Outside you'll find a heated swimming pool, a sauna, and two whirlpools. Next door is a restaurant serving reasonably priced meals. The rates at the Pony Soldier, which is part of the Best Western chain, are $51 to $56. You'll find the motel on Ore. 82, one block east of I-84 exit 261.

The **Royal Motor Inn,** 1510 Adams St., La Grande, OR 97850 (tel. 503/963-4154), is a much smaller place, with just 45 units, but is equally well maintained. Simple but adequate rooms are furnished in standard motel style and include cable color television. You can rent a refrigerator for a small extra charge. Rates are $31 double, and additional persons sharing a room are $3.

WHERE TO DINE: Fast-food spots dominate this dining scene, with a few exceptions. One of these is **Ten Depot,** 10 Depot St. (tel. 503/963-6305), a rustically attractive dining room where the sound of sizzling steaks can be heard. Steaks cooked just to your taste are the goal here, but a number of shellfish and seafood options are available too. Prices are in the $10 to $15 range for most things, and there's a menu for the youngsters. A cocktail lounge provides potables. Sunday brunch is a popular feature. Hours are 5 to 11 p.m. daily except Sunday, when the restaurant is open for brunch only from 9 a.m. to 3 p.m.

In deference to the many Oriental folk who settled in this area years ago, you might join many local diners who tie on their wontons and fried rice at **Fong's,** 1808 4th St. (tel. 503/963-5500). A favorite Chinese stop in La Grande, Fong's is open from 11 a.m. to 10 p.m. daily.

While we haven't tried this one, word has it that the krinkle pups at **Nell's-N-Out,** Ore. 82 and Adams Avenue (tel. 503/963-5733), are not to be missed. What is a krinkle pup? Hey, everybody knows that: it's a hot dog rolled in cornflakes and deep-fried. "Kurly" fries and steak and burgers are the mainstays cooked up in the kitchen. If you pay more than $5 for a meal, you'll be overstuffed. Hours are 11 a.m. to midnight daily.

WHAT TO SEE AND DO: La Grande makes a good base for explorations of the Grande Ronde Valley at the foot of the Blue Mountains and the Wallowa Mountains to the east.

One of those expeditions should take you to **Joseph,** about 70 miles east on Ore. 82. Along the way you'll drive through postcard-perfect high-country scenery that residents like to call "the Switzerland of America," arriving finally on the shores of Wallowa Lake, focus of local Indian folklore. Chief Joseph, leader of the Nez Percé Indian tribe, is buried at the north end of the lake, where a memorial to his memory has been placed. Once the scene of bloody fighting between Indians and U.S. troops, the four-mile lake is today one of eastern Oregon's best-loved boating, swimming, and fishing areas.

You can board a gondola here at **Wallowa Lake State Park** and ride to the top of 8,000-foot Mount Howard, where a world of craggy peaks stretches out before you. Rides are $8 for adults, $4.50 for children under 13, and the gondola operates from 10 a.m. to 4 p.m. June through September, same hours on Saturday and Sunday only the remainder of the year.

In town, look at the building at 1 Main St. It was the county's first bank, constructed in 1888. These days the building is really more interesting than its contents: pillars decorated in restored red-tin rosettes, ornately carved doors, and rooms decorated with ornamental multicolored handmade, plaster light fixtures, each color poured separately. No two in the building are alike.

Many people come here just to stay at **Wallowa Lake Lodge,** Ore. 82, Joseph, OR 97846 (tel. 503/432-9821), a rustic, 50-year-old, three-story lodge, where a fire blazes in a huge lobby fireplace. There are just 31 simply and rather eclectically furnished rooms in the lodge, most sharing a bath. A few of the eight cabins on the grounds are a touch less historic in feeling but better equipped, all with private baths, fireplaces, complete kitchens, and one or several separate bedrooms. Try for one of the lakeside cottages. Rates are $42 to $86 with a five-day minimum stay in peak summer months, somewhat lower prices for more spartan accommodations. Wallowa Lodge is open from mid-June to Labor Day and sometimes in late September for an Alpenfest Festival.

A dining room at the lodge turns its talents to local herbs, berries, and fruit, offering an imaginative presentation of meat and seafood unexpected in such rustic surroundings. Open Wednesday through Sunday for breakfast from 9 to 11 a.m. and for dinner from 5:30 to 8:30 p.m. The lodge's dining room charges dinner prices in the $6 to $10 range for such treats as clam fettuccine with tomato, basil, and garlic sauce; pan-fried Northwest snapper in hazelnut butter; and several Oriental selections including a vegetable stir-fry. It should be noted that the lodge is very, very strict about its no-smoking, no-alcohol policy and will evict you if you have either in your room. Beer and wine are served in the dining room, however.

5. PENDLETON

If there really is a Marlboro man, he is surely living in Pendleton, home on the range to many of his counterparts.

Pendleton put itself on the map with a rip-roaring annual Roundup Rodeo, complete with mule trains, tepees, and Indians in feathers. Pendleton Roundup and a similar spring celebration called Rendezvous are so popular that Pendleton bursts at the seams during those festivities—and is thrilled with all the attention.

Some of those who participate in this annual salute to cowpunching skills are rodeo circuit riders, but plenty are local fellows—and gals!—who tackle bawling calves and wield flaming branding irons for a living. Ten-gallon hats are required wear hereabouts, so plan on getting yourself outfitted at one of the nation's top western saddlemakers.

GETTING THERE: Horizon Air flies into the **Pendleton Municipal Airport,** 3½ miles west of town. Most of the area's motels provide free transportation from the airport. **Greyhound** has service to the city with a terminal at 320 S.W. Court St. (tel. 503/276-1551). **Amtrak** trains stop at South Main and Frazer (no telephone). **Hertz Rental Car** operates at the airport (tel. 503/376-3183). **Elite Taxi** (tel. 503/276-8294) operates service throughout the city for $1.75 at flag drop plus $1 a mile. **Pendleton Bus Company,** 100 Mission Hwy. (tel. 503/276-5621), operates buses in the region. Fares are 60¢. **Oregon Hwy. 37** crosses the city from the north and **Ore. 74** comes in from the south. **I-84** paves the way from the west to the southeast.

VISITOR INFORMATION: You'll discover everything you ever wanted to know about the Pendleton Rodeo and far more at the **Pendleton Chamber of Commerce,** 25 S.E. Dorion St., Pendleton, OR 97801 (tel. 503/276-7411, or toll free 800/547-8911, 800/452-9403 in Oregon).

USEFUL INFORMATION: For **police or emergency medical help,** call 503/276-4411. . . . You'll find a **24-hour grocery** at 7-11, 707 Southgate (tel. 503/276-4126). . . . You can eat a burger or breakfast any time of day or night at **Charburger,** I-84 at exit 216 (tel. 503/276-6154), open 24 hours.

WHERE TO STAY: Pendleton packs 'em in during its big annual rodeo, so if you're planning to be in town in September, make reservations well ahead of your arrival. The **Red Lion Indian Hills Motor Inn,** 304 S.E. Patawa Rd. (P.O. Box 1556), Pendleton, OR 97801 (tel. 503/276-6111, or toll free 800/547-8010), is the city's top hostelry. Biggest and best known of the city's hotels, the

168-room Red Lion is an impressive spot themed around those local cowboy activities. You're greeted in a large and comfortable lobby and shown to notably bright and spacious rooms with king- or queen-size beds. Many rooms have balconies and views through a wall of glass to hills that surround this round valley. Dark-wood furnishings are offset by colorful décor and attractive carpeting. Outside there's a heated swimming pool. A coffeeshop offers casual dining, while a more formal restaurant presents beef and seafood dishes in a glass-enclosed dining room with multihued sunset views. Evenings a woodsy lounge becomes a popular dancing and entertainment spot. Rates at Red Lion at Indian Hills are $59 to $72 double and free airport transportation is available.

It's not often a hotel brags more about its food than its rooms, but the first thing you'll hear about at **Tapadera Motor Inn,** 105 S.E. Court St., Pendleton, OR 97801 (tel. 503/276-3231, or toll free 800/722-8277), is the inn's great barbecued ribs. Dished up in a handsome woodsy restaurant, those ribs are backed up by spacious and well-equipped motel rooms, some of which feature waterbeds. Airport transportation is offered free at this 48-room motel in downtown Pendleton. Rates are $37 to $43 double, higher for suites, and restaurant prices are in the $10 to $15 range.

Pendleton Travel Lodge, 310 S.E. Dorion St., Pendleton, OR 97801 (tel. 503/276-6231, or toll free 800/255-3050), has just 40 spic-and-span units equipped with in-room movies. A coin laundry here is convenient after a dusty day at the rodeo, and a heated pool is a favorite gathering spot in summer. Rates are $37 to $45 double.

If all this riding and roping sounds like something you'd like to try, you can immerse yourself in atmosphere at the **Bar M Ranch,** Rte. 1, Adams, OR 97810 (tel. 503/566-3381), about 30 miles south of town, where the Baker family has been saddling up for experienced and novice riders since 1938. In their spare time they oversee a working 2,500-acre dude ranch nestled in pine forests and mountain scenery. The Bar M occupies a historic hand-hewn log ranch house built in 1864 and once used as a stage station on a toll road through the valley. The swimming pool is filled with heated water provided by natural warm springs. A stream trickles its way across the acreage, which comes complete with a small lake and waterfall. Evenings there's square dancing in a barn. In July and August one-week minimum rates of $450 to $495 a week per person apply. However, that rate includes meals of home-baked breads, vegetables, and berries raised right here, and trout from the stream. Use of the ranch's horses is also included. To get to the ranch, take I-84 south to exit 216, turn left, go two miles to a blinking light at Mission, turn right and go 1½ miles, then turn left at the Bar M signs to Milepost 28. From Walla Walla you can get to the ranch on Ore. 11, turning left at the third junction just west of Athena and following the signs.

Pendleton's Roundup has become such a popular event that it jams the city's few hotels and motels. To help accommodate the overflow, local townspeople open their homes to welcome revelers. To find a **room in a private home,** write or call the Pendleton Chamber of Commerce and ask about lodging alternatives, which also include special Roundup camping space. Placement activities begin after August 1 each year.

Several campgrounds in the region offer hookups for $10 to $15: **Brooke Trailer Court,** 5 N.E. 8th St., Pendleton, OR 97801 (tel. 503/276-5353); **Emigrant Trailer Court,** 300 S.W. 22nd St., Pendleton, OR 97801 (tel. 503/276-2482); and **Shadeview R.V. Park,** 1437 S.W. 37th St., Pendleton, OR 97801 (tel. 503/276-0688).

WHERE TO DINE: Once again stick with beef. With all those steaks-on-the-hoof roaming about, you can't go wrong.

Try them, for instance, at **Cimmiyotti's,** 137 S. Main St. (tel. 503/276-4314), which has been broiling up juicy steaks for more than a quarter of a century. Steaks and beef are the specialties here, but some seafood is on the menu too, and all of it arrives with home-baked bread, crispy salad, and a hefty baked potato. Prices are in the $10 to $15 range, and steaks even begin at $1 or so below that lower figure. Hours are 5 p.m. to 11 p.m. daily except Sunday, when hours are 5 to 10 p.m. A lounge in this western theme restaurant is open to 2:30 a.m. most nights, closing earlier on Sunday.

The **Tapadera Restaurant** (see "Where to Stay") serves up a slab of barbecued ribs that is popular with local diners. Lots of good steaks are available here too, of course, and fettuccine is a house specialty. The atmosphere is woodsy and attractive at the Tapadera, where prices are in the $10 to $15 range. Tapadera's open from 6 a.m. to 9 p.m. daily, opening an hour later on Saturday and Sunday. Cocktail lounge here too.

Sizzler Family Steak House, 1515 Southgate (tel. 503/278-2663), features fresh fruit on its bounteous salad bar, a nice accompaniment to moderately priced steaks and seafood selections. Sizzler's prices are in the $8 to $12 range, and hours are 11 a.m. to 9 p.m. daily, closing an hour later on weekends.

Chowder is the specialty at **Skipper's Seafood & Chowder House,** 709 Southgate (tel. 503/276-9484), a simple but satisfying spot featuring chicken strips and some fish 'n chips—variety seafood in the under-$10 bracket. Hours are 11 a.m. to 10 p.m. daily, closing an hour later on Friday and Saturday nights.

Riders coming through this way used to have to pay a toll, a historic tax honored at **Tollgate Mountain Chalet,** about 35 miles northwest of town on Ore. 204 (tel. 503/566-2123). Despite its remote location 16 miles west of Weston, Oregon (take Ore. 11 to Ore. 204), Tollgate does a brisk business, thanks to beautiful views and a country-kitchen atmosphere. Seafood is delicately grilled and the chili wins raves. An irresistible scent of baking pies wafts through the air so you'd be wise to pace your chowing to include a slice. You can begin local explorations with breakfasts here, stop by for lunch, or plan on a view-ful evening. Prices for dinner are in the $10 to $15 range or less, and hours are 10 a.m. to 9 p.m. daily, opening at 11 a.m. on Monday and closing at 8 p.m. on Sunday.

Pizza? Try **Grizzly Bear Pizza Parlor,** 828 Southgate (tel. 503/276-2776), where you can belly-up to the salad bar too. Pizzas are in the $5 to $7 bracket and up, according to appetite. The restaurant is open from 11 a.m. to 10:30 p.m. weekdays, to 1 a.m. on Friday and Saturday; closed Sunday.

NIGHTLIFE: Pendleton's cowboy atmosphere extends to its nightlife, which often features country music at local lounges. If you're looking for convivial companionship and some musical entertainment, here's where to begin your search: **Fireside Inn,** 1703 S.W. Emigrant St. (tel. 503/276-8454), which has bands for dancing until 1 or 2 a.m.; **Silver Saddle,** 430 S.E. Emigrant St. (tel. 503/276-5201), open daily to 2 a.m.; and the **Red Lion Indian Hills Motor Inn** (see "Where to Stay"). To see what entertainment might be passing through town, take a look at the *East Oregonian* newspaper.

WHAT TO SEE AND DO: Pendleton loves its cowboys-and-Indians atmosphere, but it's also proud of its history.

To get a look at the best of Pendleton's architectural landmarks, stop at the chamber of commerce for a copy of its *Guide to Pendleton's Historical Homes* brochure. Armed with that you can take a walking or driving tour through the city for a look at some interesting Victorian-era homes with "eyebrow" windows, beautiful wide verandas, round and hexagonal turrets, even a Dutch Colonial Revival—style home with seven gables.

If you're lucky enough to be here in July or September when **historical home tours** are available, don't miss a stroll through these homes whose interiors are outfitted with such decorative elements as ornate mahogany stairways, ballast bricks from clipper ships, huge fireplaces, ceiling friezes, and beveled window glass. These are private homes, so you'll have to be satisfied with a look at the outside, if you're not on a tour.

Pendleton Woolen Mills, 1307 S.E. Court Pl. (tel. 503/276-6911), have been producing world-famous woolens since they began making Indian-design blankets in 1909. Free tours are at 9 a.m., 11 a.m., 1:30 p.m., and 3 p.m. Monday through Saturday in summer, weekdays only in winter. Mills are closed for two weeks in July, so give them a call if you're visiting here in that month. At the plant a tour traces the creation of cloth from sheep to finished product. You can watch wool being dyed, carded, spun, and woven.

Harris Pine Mills, 2203 S.W. Court Pl. (tel. 503/267-1421), is a lumber and pine furniture company that will show you around its operation on free tours at 9:30 a.m. and 2:30 p.m. Monday through Thursday and at 9:30 a.m. on Friday.

McNary Dam produces 8.6 million megawatt-hours of electricity annually by harnessing the waters of the Columbia River. Here you can watch through an underwater viewing station as fish swim the ladder that helps them move upstream. Upstream a couple of miles you can see **Wallula Gap,** where more than 13,000 years ago huge Lake Missoula broke through an ice dam and thundered south, carrying 9½ cubic miles of water over the basalt columns of Wallula, more than ten times the combined volume of all the world's rivers! To get to the dam, take I-84 east 21 miles to Echo, and turn north on U.S. 395 to Ore. 207, which will take you to the dam.

In the nearby village of **Echo,** you can get a close look at everything from Indian beadwork on a squaw dress to the silk outfits of a local teacher who splurged two months' salary on her fancy duds. A brass bed, antique glass, and some old furnishings are also on display at the **Echo Historical Museum,** 230 W. Main St. (no phone). Admission is free and the museum is open from 1 to 5 p.m. on Saturday and Sunday from April to October.

RIDING THE OREGON TRAIL: As you've been driving along I-84, you've been paralleling the famed Oregon Trail, but near Pendleton you can take a detour to see ruts carved into the ground by the hundreds of covered wagons that passed this way. So deep are they cut into the earth that the passage of time has not been able to erase them. To see this stirring natural memorial to pioneer travelers, make your way to the nearby village of Rieth, and follow the signs to Echo, about 20 miles northwest. You will be riding beside Umatilla Creek, and along its banks those ruts are visible. Now designated a National Historic Trail, the 2,170-mile-long Oregon Trail begins at Independence, Missouri, and ends at Oregon City. Along it, 125 historic sights are commemorated by the National Park Service, and there are seven cross-country trail segments totaling 318 miles. Some of the historic sights are on private land and may not be visited without the owners' permission. For information about access to parts of the trail, contact: La Grande District, Wallowa-Whitman National Forest, Rte. 2, Box 2018, La Grande, OR 97805 (tel. 503/963-7186).

For general information about the Oregon National Historic Trail, contact the Pacific Northwest Regional Office, National Park Service, Westin Bldg., 2001 Sixth Ave., Seattle, WA 98121 (tel. 206/442-5565).

BUCKING BRONCS AND BUFFALO CHIPS: Walk through these streets some evening in the first weeks of September and you'll think you've stepped into a time warp! Indians in flowing feather headdresses tether paint ponies beside dozens of tepees. A stagecoach rumbles by as a 20-mule team clomps down main street.

For a week or so the town goes cowboy crazy at the annual **Pendleton Roundup,** a weird and wonderful event that begins with a two-hour parade you just won't believe you're seeing—pack trains and stagecoaches, Mormon carts and ox teams, beautiful Indian lasses and sixgun-toting cowboys. A week later the rootin'-tootin' roundup ends with tribal ceremonial dancing, a cowboy show, and the finals events of this famous rodeo. This celebrating has been going on for more than 75 years now, making this one of the best-known and most important rodeo events in the nation.

Rodeo participants walk away with some sore spots as they compete in the final events, after bronc-busting and roping at no fewer than four(!) rodeos in an event called the "Big-4," sponsored by rodeos in Walla Walla, Ellensburg, Lewiston, and Pendleton. Winner gets his just rewards at the Pendleton Roundup.

Tickets for this wild and wooly western weekend are sold out well in advance, so get your reservations in early to the Round-Up Association, P.O. Box 609, Pendleton, OR 97801 (tel. 503/276-2553, or toll free 800/524-2984, 800/824-1603 in Oregon). Prices range from $5 to $12 for seats at the rodeo, and from $5 to $10 for seats at the Happy Canyon Pageant and Dance, an evening show that traces the cowboy and Indian history of this brawling frontier town. If you're not going to be here in September for the big event, don't despair: there's a rodeo just about every month all summer long! Tickets are sold out well in advance for the five days of festivities that occur in the first full week of September, so make your reservations early.

SPORTS: Eastern Oregon's Wallowa Mountains are the region's sporting ground in both summer and winter.

In summer the gondolas take nature lovers up to the top of the peak for hikes across two miles of nature trails, offering spectacular views of nine peaks in the Wallowa Mountains and across Eagle Cap Wilderness, Seven Devil Mountains, and Wallowa Lake and Valley. Deer graze tamely in pastures along the way and rainbow-hued wildflowers speckle the landscape. You may even see an elk or bear roaming about atop Mount Howard. Trips are $8 for adults, $4 for children under 10. You will find the slopes just south of Joseph on Ore. 82.

For information on tram trips and other park activities, contact **Wallowa Lake Tramway,** Rte. 1, Box 349, Joseph, OR 97846 (tel. 503/432-5331).

Those of you who really get into the spirit of this bronco business can do a little riding of your own at **Bar M Ranch** (see "Where to Stay"), just east of Gibbon (tel. 503/566-3381).

The **Pendleton Parks and Recreation Department** operates 12 parks in the city and will be happy to help you find the swimming pool, tennis, and other recreational activities near you. Call them at 503/276-1811.

Golfers can play at the nine-hole Pendleton Country Club course, 100 Pilot Rock Hwy. (tel. 503/278-0355). You'll find the course seven miles south of town on Ore. 395.

At **McKay Reservoir,** six miles south on Ore. 395, there are facilities for boating, waterskiing, and swimming.

ARTS AND CULTURAL ACTIVITIES: The **Pendleton Civic Music Association** provides a concert series each year (check local newspaper for information) and often has theater productions. Each year the city sponsors an **Arts Festival** in mid-May. A number of artists show their work in many public build-

ings around town. A current list of what's showing where is available from the chamber of commerce.

SHOPPING: This is the place for you urban—or urbane—cowpokes to get yourself togged out in western duds and saddles. The place to do that is **Hamley's Western Store,** 30 E. Court Ave. (tel. 503/276-2321), one of the nation's top suppliers of saddles and tack. Hamley's creates its custom-made leathercraft right here and has been sending handmade saddles to riders around the world for more than 100 years. Hours are 9 a.m. to 5:30 p.m. daily except Sunday.

CHAPTER VII

WALLA WALLA AND THE TRI-CITIES

□ □ □

There's something about Walla Walla that tugs at your heartstrings, or perhaps it just tugs at *our* heartstrings for the family roots we have there.

Certainly as we explored the quiet streets of this still-small town, it wasn't difficult to imagine a young farmer washing off the dust of the fields, carefully donning Sunday-best, and riding off through miles of rolling, rippling wheat fields to meet his back-East bride-to-be who'd waited many a week for this summons. Nor was it difficult to imagine what that traveling bride was thinking as she stared out at the wilderness with nary a house in sight! That's our story, but there were many more like it here in this grain belt of southeastern Washington, where hardy pioneer men and women faced the wilderness with a hoe, a horse, a little hope, and a lot of trepidation.

Named after the Indian tribe that inhabited this rolling valley, Walla Walla means "many waters," the presence of which convinced missionary Marcus Whitman and his wife, Narcissa, to settle here in 1836, creating the first permanent white settlement in the Northwest. Would that the Whitmans had been a little less rigidly demanding in their attempts to convert the local Indians: in 1847 angry Cayuse tribesmen massacred them and 11 other settlers.

Through the once-barren basalt rock here ran a rugged and not very hospitable section of that famed Oregon Trail, by 1858 so traveled that the military had moved in to create Fort Walla Walla.

Today fewer than 30,000 people live here at the foot of the misty Blue

Mountains, in the center of rolling fields famous in Washington for their fat Walla Walla sweet onions as well as for the millions of bushels of wheat produced here each year.

So little has Walla Walla changed over the years that on a drive through its endless miles of wheatlands or through its shady streets you move effortlessly back in time to a day when architecture was grand but most bank accounts weren't, when life was hard but happy.

1. GETTING THERE AND GETTING AROUND

GETTING THERE: Airlines serving Walla Walla and the Tri-Cities from **Pasco's Tri-Cities Airport** are Horizon and United Airlines, which also serve Walla Walla's City-County Airport. **Amtrak** serves Walla Walla and the Tri-Cities through the Pasco station, located at Clark and Tacoma Streets (tel. 509/545-1554). **Greyhound Bus Lines** serves the Walla Walla area with a terminal at 3rd and Rose (tel. 509/525-9313). In Pasco, telephone Greyhound at 509/547-3151; in Richland, telephone 509/946-4504.

Automobile travelers coming from the east to Walla Walla and the Tri-Cities of Richland, Kennewick, and Pasco will get here on U.S. 12. Tourers from eastern Oregon's Pendleton can take Wash. 11 north to Walla Walla. From Yakima drivers will take U.S. 12 for 64 miles to arrive at Richland, westernmost of the Tri-Cities. Five miles farther west, stretched along the shores of the Columbia River, is Kennewick. A bit farther, four miles, is Pasco. Walla Walla is 45 miles from the Tri-Cities.

From the north Wash. 240 heads down to Richland, while U.S. 395 crosses U.S. 12 in Pasco. Travelers from points south can reach Kennewick and Pasco on Wash. 14, or can travel along the banks of the Columbia River to reach Pasco on U.S. 395. Washington Hwy. 124 comes here from the east to join U.S. 12/395 four miles east of Pasco.

GETTING AROUND: Local bus, rental car, and taxi will make sure you get around this area.

In Walla Walla **American International Rent A Car** (tel. 509/525-8811) and **Hertz** (tel. 509/529-5555) have offices at Walla Walla's City-County Airport. **Budget Rent-A-Car** (tel. 509/735-8481) and **Crystal Carriage Hertz Rent-A-Car** (tel. 509/547-0111) serve the Tri-Cities area.

The **Valley Transit** bus system operates from 6 a.m. to 7 p.m. and can give you information on its routes if you stop in at 8 W. Poplar or call them at 509/525-9140 or 529-2850. Fares are 25¢. In the Tri-Cities **Ben Franklin Transit** (tel. 509/545-5550) provides public transportation, for 50¢.

A-1 Cab (tel. 509/525-5000) and **ABC Taxi Service** (tel. 509/529-7726) are Walla Walla's two cab companies.

2. TOURIST AND USEFUL INFORMATION

TOURIST INFORMATION: The information you need to enjoy your trip will be happily provided by several greeting organizations. The **Walla Walla Area Chamber of Commerce** is at 29 E. Sumach, Walla Walla, WA 99362 (tel. 509/525-0850), and folks there will be happy to plan a tour of this historic area's most interesting spots. They're open from 8:30 a.m. to 5 p.m. weekdays, but also open on Saturday and from noon to 5 p.m. on Sunday in summer months. The

Tri-Cities Chamber of Commerce is at Center and Gage Boulevards (P.O. Box 2241), Tri-Cities, WA 99302 (tel. 509/586-4015).

USEFUL INFORMATION: For **police or emergency medical help,** call 911. . . . Walla Walla **area code** is 509, but nearby Oregon is in area code 503, and towns in Idaho are 208 . . . Send telegrams at **Western Union,** 1 S. 1st St. (tel. 509/525-7440) . . . Bill Singer's **Chevron Service,** 102 N. 2nd St., is open to 9 p.m. weekdays, to 8 p.m. on weekends . . . **Speedwash Self Service Laundry,** 2023 Isaacs St. (tel. 509/525-9856), is open daily from 7 a.m. to 10 p.m. . . . For quick photo processing try **One-Hour Photo Processing,** 40 S. Colville (tel. 509/525-3570). . . . For one-day cleaning service call **Holiday Cleaners,** 1500 Isaacs St. (tel. 509/525-3463) . . . If you're from Alaska, Delaware, Montana, Oregon, New Hampshire, Oklahoma, or Alberta, you can buy at the chamber of commerce a $5 nonresidents **tax permit** that excludes you from some sales tax in Washington . . . **Eastgate Drugs,** 1936 Isaacs St. (tel. 509/529-2171), is open from 9 a.m. to 9 p.m. daily.

ORIENTATION: Getting oriented to the area is painless. The Walla Walla exit from U.S. 12 brings you to 2nd Street in **Walla Walla.** Turn south and you're on a major east-west dividing street, Main Street, the major shopping street of the city. Rose Avenue makes the longest east-west traverse of the city as it joins Isaacs, which continues east to the edge of town.

Richland and **Kennewick** stretch out along the south and west side of the Columbia River, while **Pasco** occupies the north side. Downtown Richland is bounded by Swift and Lee Boulevards running east and west, and Thayer and George Washington Way running north and south. Kennewick Avenue and Tenth Avenue provide the north and south borders of downtown Kennewick, while Garfield and Washington Streets edge the area on the east and west. Pasco's downtown area is near the river, bounded by Lewis Street on the south but running the short length of Clark Street a block to the north.

3. WHERE TO STAY

Walla Walla is quite a small town, despite its grandiose architecture, so you won't find big, busy hotels here, just small motor inns that will make you both welcome and comfortable.

Whitman Motor Court, 107 N. Second Ave., Walla Walla, WA 99632 (tel. 509/525-2200, or toll free 800/237-4436, 800/237-1495 in Washington), is the best of Walla Walla's downtown hostelries and home to a popular restaurant with steaks at amazingly inexpensive prices. Spacious rooms at the 71-unit Whitman Motor Court occupy a three-story building atop an area of covered parking. Cool, contemporary colors are offset by warm wood furnishings that have to work hard to fill these very large quarters. Baths are large and modern too, and the rooms have large and convenient dressing areas. Some also have refrigerators and all have televisions, in-room movies, free telephone calls, and coffee makers. Downstairs you'll find a small swimming pool tucked away between a wall of glass and a high sheltering wood fence.

A few steps beyond is Whitman's, a woodsy-plantsy, contemporary and popular restaurant in which you can feast on a big, juicy steak or slab of prime rib for $7 to $14. Whitman's adjoins the antique Marcus Whitman Hotel, to which it connects. While you're here, poke around until you find, at the rear of the restaurant, a hallway that takes you into the hotel's ballroom, still used for special parties. Its columned magnificence is quite an insight to the grand old days of this imposing structure. Rates at the motor inn are $46 to $49 for two.

Next door the **Tapadera Budget Inn,** 211 N. Second Ave., Walla Walla, WA 99362 (tel. 509/529-2580, or toll free 800/722-8277), offers convenient, if basic, motel rooms just steps from downtown shops and restaurants. Rates are quite reasonable, however: $25 to $35 double for rooms with cable television and telephones.

The **Walla Walla TraveLodge,** 421 E. Main St., Walla Walla, WA 99362 (tel. 509/529-4940, or toll free 800/255-3050), is an attractive, white two-story building trimmed in brown. A small spot, the TraveLodge has just 38 units of rather standard décor and accoutrements plus a heated pool. Rates at the lodge are $45 to $49 for two.

Best Western Pony Soldier Motor Inn, 325 E. Main St., Walla Walla, WA 99362 (tel. 509/529-4360, or toll free 800/528-1234), sports an A-frame lobby trimmed with tall strips of glass. Quite an attractive spot, the motor inn has 82 units, many with lanais, some with refrigerators. A heated pool offers amusement on hot summer days, and there's a small adjacent restaurant open for all three meals at quite moderate prices, in the $10 to $12 range or less. Rates are $51.50 to $55.50 double.

Imperial 400 Motor Inn, 305 N. Second Ave., Walla Walla, WA 99362 (tel. 509/529-4410, or toll free 800/368-4400), is a small, two-story motor inn with two wings sporting bright-orange doors. Rooms are medium-sized, clean with nice carpeting, television, and colorful décor. Outside is an L-shaped swimming pool. Rates at this simple standard motel are $30 to $34 double year round.

Comfort Inn, 520 N. 2nd St., Walla Walla, WA 99362 (tel. 509/525-2522, or toll free 800/228-5151), is a newcomer to this town but a welcome one. Its 40 rooms opened in 1987 at the city's now-defunct railroad station, which also is getting a facelift and will soon house several boutiques. Comfort Inns are simply but adequately furnished and here in Walla Walla, the chain property echoes the look of its historic neighbor. Rates are $40 to $46 double.

READERS' HOTEL SELECTION: "We were glad to see you had included Walla Walla in your *Dollarwise Northwest.* We were there recently and were amazed at the unique history of the community and wondered why it wasn't more of a tourist attraction. It is a city older than Seattle, and at one time bigger, so it has some of the most historically important buildings in the state. We were also fortunate to discover a motel that was 'home grown' and a very special place to stay. The **City Center Motel,** Ninth and Main, Walla Walla, WA 99362 (tel. 509/529-2660) . . . is a jewel! It has a garden-like setting, only 17 units, and each has an additional dressing room and coffee in the room" (Beverly and Winfred Stocker, Anacortes, Wash.). [*Authors' Note:* Rates at the City Center are $32.50 to $34.50.]

4. WHERE TO DINE

Whitman's, at the Whitman, 107 N. 2nd St. (tel. 509/529-6000), has excellent steaks and prime ribs at great prices! Look back a few paragraphs to find a description of it under Whitman Motor Court in "Where to Stay." It's open from 6:30 a.m. to 9 p.m. daily.

Wong's Restaurant, 14 N. Columbia, Milton-Freewater (tel. 509/983-5525), is just a few miles from town and is much touted for its outstanding American and Chinese specialties. Fried fish is particularly good here, and the restaurant's fruit and meat selections are delightful. Entree prices are in the easily under-$10 range, and hours are 11 a.m. to 10 p.m. daily except Wednesday, when they're closed, and weekends, when closing time is an hour later.

The **Modern Restaurant and Lounge,** 2200 Melrose St. in Eastgate Plaza, Walla Walla (tel. 509/525-8662), is more of the same: good basic American cooking and some Chinese specialties produced in a simple but comfortable atmosphere. Prices are in the money-saving $8 bracket or less, and the restaurant is open from 11 a.m. to 10 p.m. daily except Saturday, when it closes at 11 p.m., and on Sunday, when quitting time is 9 p.m.

The **Red Apple,** 57 E. Main St. (tel. 509/525-5113), is good for a quick lunch downtown and attracts many families for its simple, good cooking and low prices, well under $10 for dinner. Hours are 7 a.m. to 9 p.m. daily.

Prime Cut Meat Market and Restaurant, 1780 Isaacs St. (tel. 509/522-0312), is cutting and selling its top-quality meats right there, so you can order up any cut you want. Sirloin's the favorite at this casual spot, which also features some basic seafood concoctions. Prices are in the $10 to $12 range, and the restaurant is open from 11 a.m. to 9 p.m. daily, an hour later on Friday and Saturday.

Merchant's Limited, 21 E. Main St. (tel. 509/525-0900), is packed wall-to-wall with more than 200 meats and cheeses plus every kind of gourmet treat available. In this casual indoor-outdoor trilevel deli you can sip a glass of local wine or a cup of espresso and ogle the architecture, both immobile and mobile. And now there's an upper-level buffet serving lunch only from 11 a.m. to 2 p.m. Tuesday through Saturday. Cool salads and hot foods with freshly baked breads and desserts are served in an airy restaurant atmosphere. Merchant's downstairs is open from 6 a.m. to 6 p.m. daily except Sunday, and prices are under $5 for most things.

A small spot in town is **Yogi's,** 2 S. 1st St. (tel. 509/525-1998), where the fare is light and thrifty, centered on pita pocket sandwiches and yogurt in yummy flavors. Yogi's is open from 11 a.m. to 5 p.m. daily.

5. WHAT TO SEE AND DO

Walla Walla calls itself the cradle of Northwest history, as well it should: Lewis and Clark stopped by in 1805, a fort was built by fur trappers in 1818, the Whitmans settled in with their frontier mission in 1836, only to be massacred in 1847, and in 1858 the military moved in with Fort Walla Walla.

To begin your exploration of this historic city, visit **Fort Walla Walla Museum Complex** on Myra Road near the junction of U.S. 12 and Wash. 125 (tel. 509/525-7703). Here imagine yourself armed with musket and plow as you roam 14 buildings in which the labor and laughter of those courageous early pioneers is chronicled. You'll see the original Ransom Clark log cabin, Union School, and the Babcock Railroad depot. You'll also get a look at the best collection in the Northwest of the primitive farming equipment pioneers used to carve homesteads out of this rugged land—including a 33-mule-team harvester hooked to life-size Fiberglas mules! Here, too, are the graves of both Nez Percé warriors and cavalrymen who died in the Battle of Boise and another fight at Whitebird Canyon in 1877. Open from May through October: in May and October, weekends only from 1 to 5 p.m.; June through August, daily except Monday from 10 a.m. to 5 p.m.; in September, 1 to 5 p.m. daily except Monday. Admission is $2 for adults, $1 for children 6 to 13.

Whitman National Historic Site, seven miles west of town on U.S. 12 (tel. 509/522-6360), commemorates the Indian mission set up by Marcus and Narcissa Whitman, who came here in 1836. Once called Waiilatpu, meaning "the place of the people of the rye grass," the site was among the first missions in the region. Things went well for 11 years until measles killed half the Cayuse Indian tribe. Difficulties compounded when Whitman's medicine helped the white children but not the Indian children, who had no resistance to the disease. The Indians, fearing they were being poisoned by the missionaries, massacred them and 11 other settlers. Cabins burned following the massacre have been excavated and their sites outlined. At the visitor center you can see demonstrations of the crafts that kept Whitman and his settlers going: wool spinning, churning, candlemaking, dyeing, and trail and Indian cookery, as well as the Indian crafts of corn-husk weaving and tule mat construction. Here, too, you can walk right on the Oregon Trail and visit the graves of those who died in the massacre. A mile-long self-guided walking tour, complete with audio stations, tells you the story of this land. Hours are 8 a.m. to 6 p.m. from June through August and 8 a.m. to 4:30 p.m. in other months. Admission is $1 for adults, $3 per family.

Many buildings in town are imposing turn-of-the-century structures. To get a look at them, stroll Main Street, noting the fanciful Tyrolean façade of **Liberty Theater;** the ornate elegance of the old **Whitman Hotel;** the massive colonnades of the **Baker Boyer Bank;** the **old clock** in front of Falkenberg Jewelers and the elaborately trimmed building next door; the pretty **brick courtyard** imprinted with tiny roses outside the Left Bank Restaurant, where an **antique water fountain** burbles; at 17 Main St. an **old time shoeshine parlor;** and at the corner of Main and North Second Avenue, the frothy window trim and the **ornate balcony railing** rimming the roof. To see some beautiful **old homes,** drive or stroll South Palouse, West Birch, and Catherine Streets, and don't miss the 1880 **Kirkman House** at Colville and Cherry Street, a magnificent old National Register home with an ornate iron widow's walk, columns, bay widows, white trim, under-the-eaves carvings, and rolling green lawns.

Green & Jackson Drugs at 10 W. Main St. is Washington's oldest drugstore. It opened here in 1872! Stop by the chamber of commerce (Colville Street and Sumach) for a self-guided tour map of the city.

SPECIAL EVENTS: If you're here in the fall, you can get an exciting look at pioneer days. At the Waitsburg oldtime **mule harvest** huge teams of 20 or so mules, four abreast, are driven by intrepid harvesters. Waitsburg is on U.S. 12 about 22 miles northeast of Walla Walla. Don Thomas, 201 W. 6th St. (tel. 509/337-6525), is the man who makes this festival move, literally and figuratively— he drives the huge mule team.

On the first weekend in May Walla Walla's **Annual Hot Air Balloon Stampede** is a colorful display and a photographer's delight as dozens of brightly colored ballons take to the air.

WINE TOURS: Lots of volcanic soil and water are what it takes to make fat grapes that will one day find their way into a wine bottle. Those bottles will, in turn, find their way to local tables and to the boards of many a gourmet, anxious to try the wines of this comparatively new wine-making region of the nation. Exploring the large and small wineries of southeast Washington makes an enjoyable way to spend a day or two. Here's a look at some of them, working west from Walla Walla in a loop.

Château Ste. Michelle, a well-known winery in Seattle and environs, has a large and beautifully designed cellar in Patterson called River Ridge (tel. 509/875-2061). You can try some of the wines in the wine-tasting room, then learn a little about the wine-making process from workers who will show you around the cellars. Château Ste. Michelle has a wine shop with picnic supplies too. You'll find the vineyard a couple of miles east of the junction of Wash. 221 and Wash. 14, on the north side of Wash. 14. It's open daily from 10 a.m. to 4:30 p.m.

Hinzerling Vineyards, 1520 Sheridan Ave., in Prosser (tel. 509/786-2163), is open from 10 a.m. to noon and 1 to 5 p.m. daily except Sunday, when hours are noon to 4 p.m. In the winter months between mid-December and April the vineyards are closed on Sunday. You'll find the vineyards off the Prosser exit of I-82; just follow U.S. 12 into town.

The Hogue Cellars has a staff ready and waiting to greet you on Wine Country Road in Prosser (tel. 509/786-4557). In summer the winery offers complimentary wine tasting from 10 a.m. to 5 p.m. daily (from noon to 5 p.m. on Sunday); in winter, weekends only. To get there, take the Prosser exit off I-82 and follow U.S. 12 to the Prosser Industrial Park.

Tucker Cellars, in Sunnyside (tel. 509/837-8701), has a fruit stand next door so you can try some of the region's wonderful produce with your wine. Chenin blanc is a specialty of this cellar, which is open daily in summer from 10 a.m. to 5 p.m. To get there, take exit 69 to U.S. 12 and turn right. The winery is next to the Sunnyside Golf Course.

Quail Run Winery is on Morris Road in the village of Zillah (tel. 509/829-6235) and will welcome you from 10 a.m. to 5 p.m. Monday through Saturday and noon to 5 p.m. on Sunday. To get there, take the Zillah exit off I-82 and drive north on the Old Inland Empire Hwy. to Roza Drive. Turn right on Roza and right on Highland Drive, left on Morris Road.

Langguth Winery, 2340 S.W. Road F-5, Vernita Bridge (tel. 509/932-4934), opens its tasting room at 10 a.m. on Friday, Saturday, and Sunday, closing at 5 p.m. To get there, take Wash. 240 north to Vernita Bridge, then Wash. 24 to the junction of Wash. 243.

At **Kiona Vineyard,** Benton City (tel. 509/588-6716), you're invited to set up a picnic at a table overlooking the vines, and treat yourself to a little glass of wine, of course. Hours are noon to 5 p.m. daily, May through September. To get there, take Wash. 224 from West Richland to Sunset Road and turn right.

Preston Wine Cellars, 502 E. Vineyard Dr., five miles north of Pasco on U.S. 395 (tel. 509/545-1990), has a self-guided tour and plenty of samples of its product, plus picnic tables if you want to make an afternoon of it. Preston is open from 10 a.m. to 5:30 p.m. daily.

Within just a few miles of Walla Walla are several new wineries, one in an interesting location—an old schoolhouse. Among them are:

Leonetti Cellars, 1321 School Ave. (tel. 509/525-1428), is operated by Gary and Nancy Figgins who specialize in cabernet sauvignon and merlot wines.

L'École No. 41, at 41 Lowden School Rd., in Lowden (tel. 509/525-0940), the one in the old schoolhouse, is the creation of Jean and Baker Ferguson, who produced their first merlot wine in 1983 and their first semillon in 1984.

Woodward Canyon Winery, on Wash. 12 in Lowden (tel. 509/525-4129), is yet another Walla Walla winery, this one specializing in chardonnay, cabernet sauvignon, and white rieslings.

6. SPORTS

When it's time to play, head for **Pioneer Park,** Division and Alder Streets (tel. 509/527-4403), where you can splash in a swimming pool, lob a couple on the tennis courts, feed the ducks, romp in a playground, or watch exotic birds tweet and chatter. No admission to the park, which is open daily, all hours.

Wallula Lake, a stretch of water 64 miles long, was created when McNary Lock and Dam was constructed in the 1940s. A link in the seaway from the Pacific to Idaho, Lake Wallula fills a bluff-lined gorge. Fishermen seek in its depths for trout, bass, and salmon; hunters come in search of migrating birds; and along the shoreline sunseekers swim and camp among the wildflowers. To get there, take U.S. 12, which joins U.S. 395 at the lake, then heads north or south to follow its course.

Golfers should head over to Kennewick, where **Canyon Lakes Golf Course,** at 3700 W. Canyon Lakes Dr. (tel. 509/582-3736), or **Tri-Cities Country Club**

and Golf Course, 314 N. Underwood (tel. 509/783-6014), both 18-hole, par-72 courses, await. Greens fees are $10 to $15; carts, $15.

7. DAY TRIPS IN THE TRI-CITIES

Three cities have teamed up to present themselves to the world as the Tri-Cities: Richland, Pasco, and Kennewick.

This part of Washington's claim to rather controversial fame came when the region was selected as one of three sites in the nation for development of the atomic bomb. Over the years the cities became the home of many technological facilities, including Boeing Computer Services, Exxon, Rockwell, and United Nuclear Industries.

This, too, is the land of a modern bomb: Washington Public Power Supply, all too well known among stockbrokers as WHOOPS, a project that disappointed many investors.

RICHLAND: In Richland, science lovers will want to take a look at the **Fast Flux Test Facility Visitor Center,** 11 miles north of the city on Stevens Drive (tel. 509/376-5101 or 376-3026). Here workers, aided by photographs, a model, and an audio-visual presentation, will explain the operations of a sodium-cooled nuclear reactor. It's open from 10 a.m. to 4 p.m. Wednesday through Sunday and is free.

At **Hanford Science Center** you can play computerized games and toy with some exhibits that will teach you something about the mysteries of energy and its production. Operated by the U.S. Department of Energy, the facility is at 825 Jadwin St. (tel. 509/376-6374) and is open from 8 a.m. to 5 p.m. weekdays, opening an hour later on Saturday, and from noon to 5 p.m. on Sunday.

PASCO: Pasco's location at the junction of the Snake and Columbia Rivers means you'll see plenty of river traffic chugging along here, just as it has done for decades. Eons ago blocked ice and floods carved the bizarre basalt outcroppings you will see in the region. Those geologic eras past are honored at **Ice Harbor Dam and Visitor Center,** 12 miles east of Pasco. This dam is one of several that enable barges to be towed up from Portland to Idaho. You can look over the dam, its fish ladders, hydroelectric plant, and locks on a self-guided tour with information provided by the Visitor Center at the dam (tel. 509/547-7781). It's open every day.

Nearby is **Sacajawea State Park and Interpretive Center** (tel. 509/545-2361). The park and the center were named for the 16-year-old Shoshoni Indian woman who was a member of the Lewis and Clark expedition. Exhibits in the Interpretive Center tell the story of the expedition, of the "interpretess," and of their three-day stay at the park site, October 16–18, 1805. Artifacts of stone and bone tools tell the story of Sahaptin- and Cayuse-speaking Indians' culture in the area. Many of these artifacts date back 10,000 years. The park is open year round. The Interpretive Center is open Wednesday through Sunday from 10 a.m. to 6 p.m., mid-April through mid-September. Free.

McNary National Wildlife Refuge is motel for thousands of migrating water birds, which stop by here on their way to and from points north and south. Headquarters for the refuge is about a quarter of a mile north of U.S. 12 near Burbank. Fishing and hunting are permitted here, although not at the same time. For regulations and licensing information, call 509/545-1990.

KENNEWICK: Kennewick is the breadbasket of the region, its arid lands fertile now, thanks to a massive irrigation project. Grapes that grow here produce the best wines in the state as well as some top-quality alfalfa, beans, and corn. From here you can catch a four-day Sunshine Charters **cruise down the Columbia River** to Vancouver, Washington, in September and October (tel. 509/547-4076 for information).

STAYING IN THE TRI-CITIES AREA: Sports fans and others who think they'd like to stay over in the Tri-Cities area should head for Pasco's **Red Lion Inn,** 2525 N. 20th St., Pasco, WA 99301 (tel. 509/547-0701, or toll free 800/547-8010), an oasis in a sometimes-severe landscape. You'll be greeted at the Red Lion in a sprawling lobby with a high beamed ceiling. On the walls hang massive mural-like woodcarvings. Someone with a green thumb keeps feathery trees and plants growing, and fresh flowers trim an open lobby coffeeshop furnished in rattan. Spacious rooms feature tasteful wall murals, comfortable furnishings, dark-wood headboards, and bright contemporary colors and prints on queen- or king-size beds. Rooms have balconies or lanais plus all the amenities, from radio to television, large bath, telephone. Evenings you can dine in Misty's, the Red Lion's sleek and chic dining room, in which continental favorites are the specialty. Later you can dance in the inn's Misty's Lounge. Outside, two swimming pools are gathering spots for eastern Washingtonians who come here in search of the sun and fun in which the Tri-Cities region specializes. Rates for a pair at the Red Lion Motor Inn are $64 to $87 for a room with a queen-size, king-size, or two queen-size sleepers. Singles pay $8 less.

In Kennewick, **Cavanaugh's Motor Inn,** 1101 Columbia Center Blvd., Kennewick, WA 99336 (tel. 509/783-0611, or toll free 800/THE-INNS), is another very attractive hotel with beautiful cedar woodwork. A bilevel dining room is packed with plants and trimmed with wood, a very serene place indeed. You'll find 164 rooms here, a pretty restaurant, and some very showy surroundings. Some rooms have refrigerators, and all have cable television, radio, and attractive furnishings. You can splash in a heated pool or relax in a whirlpool. Rates at Cavanaugh's are $55 to $61 double, including free airport transfers.

If you're **camping** in the Tri-Cities region, you have many options at the multitude of parks and recreational centers here. To find out more about those recreation areas you can contact the Washington State Parks and Recreation Commission, 7250 Cleanwater Lane, KY-11, Olympia, WA 98504 (tel. 206/753-2027, or toll free from Memorial Day to Labor Day 800/562-0990). For complete campground and other information, contact the **Tri-Cities Visitor and Convention Bureau,** P.O. Box 2241, Tri-Cities, WA 99302 (tel. 509/735-8486). It's open weekdays from 8:30 a.m. to 5 p.m.

TRI-CITIES EVENTS: Special events in the region include the **Winter Wine Fair** in March, which comes complete with wine tastings amid a Mardi Gras atmosphere; the **Tri-Cities Water Follies Grand Parade and Carnival** capped by the best known of the region's events, the annual **Hydroplane Competition,** all of it in late July; in mid-August the **Prosser Wine and Food Fair,** followed by a rodeo in late August; a **chili blast-off** at the end of October; and a **Christmas Lights Boat Parade** in December.

CHAPTER VIII

VISITING THE COLUMBIA GORGE

□ □ □

Waterfalls crash over the side of a golden cliff. Snow-capped peaks float in the distance. A sternwheeler steams down a wide waterway that curves and coils on itself like a sea serpent undulating through this great crevice in the earth.

Past mountains and through valleys, the mighty Columbia rolls along on its 1,200-mile journey to the Pacific, but here at the Oregon-Washington border it is at its most geologically dramatic. In 30 million years it has carved its way through cliffs to create the Columbia River Gorge in a land tossed up by cataclysmic volcanic action through which the shimmering river flows toward the Pacific. On its long journey to the sea, the Columbia drains nearly 260,000 square miles of the Northwest, carrying twice as much water to the Pacific Ocean as the Nile sends to the Mediterranean. It flows at ten times the strength of the Colorado River, falling two to five feet every mile of its length.

It didn't take awed onlookers long to realize that this rapidly falling water could be harnessed to create electricity. Now the Columbia River, which has 40% of the nation's potential for hydropower generation, produces 80% of the region's electric power. Dams created to accomplish those massive hydroelectric projects have also made the Columbia navigable, creating a 470-mile waterway from the Pacific to Lewiston, Idaho, and irrigating seven million acres of land. Four dams are at work on the river west of Walla Walla: McNary Dam at Umatilla, John Day Dam just east of Biggs, Dalles Dam at The Dalles, and Bonneville Dam just west of Cascade Locks. You can cross this border river on five spans connecting Oregon and Washington at Biggs, The Dalles, Hood River, Cascade Locks, and just west of Troutdale. Along its course the river provides water to fruitful valleys, both literally and figuratively: the gorge produces some of the state's most coveted apples, pears, and cherries.

To these shores came the foot-sore wanderers of the Oregon Trail, and here they ended their overland trip, journeying the rest of the way by water. Those early visitors were seeking a better, more expansive way of life, while latter-day travelers search only for the serenity of this scenery. Both were—and are—equally rewarded at the Columbia Gorge, Grand Canyon of the Pacific Northwest.

1. GETTING THERE AND GETTING AROUND

Air service is available to Portland on the west end of the gorge and to Pendleton on the east end. **Portland International Airport** is served by both major commercial air carriers and regional airlines including Alaska Airlines, American, Continental, Delta, Eastern, Northwest, TWA, United, and USAir.

The **Amtrak** *Pioneer* train makes a spectacular run right along the banks of the Columbia straight through the gorge. So thoughtful is the Amtrak service to the area that you can board the *Pioneer* in Portland and get off at Cascade Locks, where you will have time to take a sternwheeler down the river before catching the westbound train back to Portland.

Greyhound buses serve most towns on both sides of the gorge, a pleasant way to leave the driving to them.

Still, if you want to explore this glorious scenery and discover the fascinating history that has so profoundly affected the lives of all Americans, we'd suggest an **automobile tour.** To do that, you can come in from the west on I-84; or from Spokane and Pasco, Washington, on U.S. 395, which joins I-84 just south of Umatilla, itself a historic town built practically overnight—11 buildings in four days!—to accommodate frantic gold miners headed for the Idaho gold fields.

If you're headed this way from Portland, just take I-84 out of the city and you'll be on your way to the gorge.

2. THE DALLES

It was a very long walk from points east, but once those pioneers reached this settlement, they set foot on the official end of the overland Oregon Trail. Here they piled belongings on barges and floated downriver to Portland or Astoria. Eight hundred of them arrived here in 1843 with a group called Oregon Trail Wagons. Some went on to California to open an overland route through the Willamette (say "Wil-dam-it") Valley—and a toll road across it. Parts of the road can still be seen.

Explorer Kit Carson came by in that same year and his logbook reckoned all mileage from a starting point at The Dalles. Lewis and Clark had passed by here 38 years earlier in 1805. On the banks of the river they visited Nixluidix, a Wishram Indian village that had been here for more than a thousand years.

Years before those travelers arrived, early French explorers had dubbed the place The Dalles (pronounced "Dolls"), naming it, some say, after the resemblance of rugged cliffs to *les dalles,* or flagstones, in France. Others say the name salutes *le grande dalle,* or great trough, of the river.

That those early visitors didn't like the place much no one would dispute: dangerous rapids made this the most terrifying navigational point on the river and, for many, the last waterfalls they saw—ever. Long, long before any of those latter-day travelers stopped here, Indians left their mark on the land with still-mysterious petroglyphs drawn on cliffs near what is now Horse Thief State Park. In the gorge, created when massive eruptions caused 400 cubic miles of water to flood over the region, archeologists have uncovered bones of mastodons, horses, and even camels!

Once salmon leaped Celilo Falls just upstream from The Dalles to jump into the waiting nets of Indian fishermen, but today those cascades are gone, running silently now beneath waters restrained by the Dalles Dam.

Marcus Whitman, Walla Walla's earliest settler, came through here with his wife, the first white woman to cross North America. When Indians massacred those two missionaries and their fellow settlers near Walla Walla in 1847, fear spread and volunteers built an armed camp here, expanding it to a full-fledged fort a few years later.

In the early 1860s Idaho's gold strike ignited gold fever throughout the Pacific Northwest and The Dalles boomed. At one point this small town provided for the needs of the miners with provision stores—and 25 saloons!

VISITOR INFORMATION: On weekdays in summer **The Dalles Area Chamber of Commerce** operates from a small building at 404 W. 2nd St. (P.O. Box 460), The Dalles, OR 97058 (tel. 503/296-2231). On weekends workers move into the town's tiny original courthouse next door. Delicious dark Bing cherries grown hereabouts are often on sale at the chamber for 50¢ a pound!

WHERE TO STAY: Along the gorge, view is a top consideration. Once you see the fabulous views from the lobby windows of the **Execu-Lodge**, P.O. Box 211, The Dalles, OR 97058 (tel. 503/298-5502), they're going to have to tear you away from here. A large and serviceable motel, the Execu-Lodge is perched on the bluff beside the river, overlooking one of the loveliest views of any hotel along the gorge. Before the construction of the Dalles Dam destroyed Celilo Falls, this was a natural portage point for river travelers, including Lewis and Clark. While it's not architecturally showy, the Execu-Lodge is pleasant and homey, attractive and functional. In the lobby a two-story glass entrance wall fills the reception area with light. Beyond a lobby souvenir shop, a spacious living room-like seating area is positioned to take full advantage of that dramatic river view below. More views greet you in a large and tranquil dining room serving all three meals, and in the lounge that offers dancing and entertainment nightly.

There are historic elements here too. Wind Rock, an ancient stone once used by Indians to influence the god of the wind, now occupies a place of honor in front of the picture windows in the lobby. Buildings nearby were once part of the Indian Shaker church, which turned out to be quite a union of Indian gods and Shaker beliefs. Back of the hotel bar, two impressive carved-wood ladies known as the "Twin Virgins" reign. Brought here by ship from Italy all the way around Cape Horn in 1879, this elaborate back bar was once part of an elegant hotel called Umatilla House. When the hotel closed, the ladies moved around some, landing finally here at the Execu-Lodge.

Rates at the lodge are quite reasonable: $48 for a room with a queen-size or king-size bed.

Camping

Those in search of a campground should cross the river to the Washington side, where **Horsethief Lake State Park,** just west of the intersection of Wash. 14 and U.S. 97 (Rte. 677, Box 27-A), Goldendale, WA 98620 (no telephone reservations), has 50 fully equipped campsites. Rates are $10 to $12 for full hookups. The 98-acre **Maryhill State Park,** 12 miles south of Goldendale on U.S. 97 (Rte. 677, Box 27-A), Goldendale, WA 98620 (no telephone reservations), has 50 campsites. Rates are $10.50 for full hookups.

WHERE TO DINE: Most restaurants in the region are fast-food spots and by now you need no guide to those. For something a bit more elaborate, try the dining room of the **Execu-Lodge** (tel. 503/298-5502), where that fabulous view is supplemented by simply cooked but good food. At lunch on a sidewalk table, try the cheese steak, a pile of sliced roast beef topped with mushrooms, peppers, and onions, and set atop a French roll, then topped with Swiss cheese and popped into the oven to melt the cheese. The Execu-Lodge also features a "spud bar" at lunch: you pick your baked potato toppings yourself from a lineup of cheese, bacon, sour cream, onions, tomatoes, and more. At dinner steaks and fresh local fish are featured, and there's often after-dinner entertainment in the lounge. Prices are in the $5 to $7 bracket for lunch, $12 to $17 for dinner. Hours are 6 a.m. to 11 p.m.

If you're driving the scenic route from here, stop in at **Dobre Deli,** 308 E. 4th St. (tel. 503/298-8239), and ask them to pack you a picnic lunch. Then dine on picnic tables here or take sandwiches, nachos, homemade soups, croissants, desserts, and espresso or a bottle of Oregon wine with you to some scenic spot. Hours are 8 a.m. to 7 p.m. daily, to 8 p.m. in June, July, and August.

For Mexican food try **Casa Del Rio,** 1240 W. 6th St. (tel. 503/298-4661), for all the tacos and salsa you can consume. Hours are 11:30 a.m. to 9 p.m. weekdays, closing an hour later on weekends and open 1 to 9 p.m. on Sunday. Prices are in the $5 to $10 bracket.

Good rib-sticking German flavors at **Zum Engel,** 728 E. 3rd St. (tel. 503/296-1606), where they'll cook up German dumplings, if you'll call in advance, but at any time provide homemade sausages and good German desserts for prices in the $10 bracket or less.

NIGHTLIFE: In two words: not much. However, you'll find music at the **Execu-Lodge's Lounge** (see "Where to Stay") and usually some activity on weekends down the road apiece at the **Cascade Inn,** Wa-na-pa Street, Cascade Locks (tel. 503/374-8340), open to 2:30 a.m. daily, with live music weekends.

Several taverns in town are popular, including **Chug's Tavern,** 113 3rd St., Hood River (tel. 503/386-4121), a watering hole for windsurfers, and **Spillway Tavern,** 1416 W. 6th St. (tel. 503/296-9267), where deep-fried pressure-cooker-cooked chicken is a specialty.

WHAT TO SEE AND DO: From the serene beauty of an eccentric's mansion to a do-it-yourself children's museum, The Dalles area offers something for every age.

Maryhill Museum of Art, an elegant country mansion that looks like a displaced English manor house, occupies a lonely, windswept bluff-top site 100 miles from the nearest major city, but alongside some of the most stupendous scenery along the gorge. No accident that, but just the way eccentric millionaire Sam Hill planned it when he ordered construction of this eerily magnificent home in 1914. Not only did he build a mansion so handsome the architecture and site alone are worth traveling many miles to see, but it's now filled with an outstanding collection of work by French sculptor Auguste Rodin, art glass by Galle, icons, Indian artifacts, and an extensive collection of chess sets. One room is named in tribute to Queen Marie of Romania, granddaughter of England's Queen Victoria and the Tsar of Russia, who dedicated the museum in 1926. Maryhill Museum is also home to an amazing collection of miniature fashion design called Théâtre de la Mode, created by top French couturiers of the 1940s. To add to the bizarre unreality of things, nearby is a full-size replica of Stonehenge! It's a memorial to the soldiers of World War I.

Recently, Maryhill added the Maryhill Museum Café where you can break from your touring to snack on specialty coffees, pastries, and sandwiches in the $5 range. Hours are 10 a.m. to 4:30 p.m. daily.

Maryhill, 35 Maryhill Museum Dr., at Wash. 14, 2¾ miles west of the U.S.

97 junction in Goldendale (tel. 509/773-3733), is open from 9 a.m. to 5 p.m. from mid-March to mid-November. Admission is $3 for adults, $1.50 for children. Stonehenge, a mile east of the U.S. 97 and Wash. 14 junction and three-quarters of a mile south, is open during daylight hours and is free. To get to both sites you can cross the river from the Oregon side at Biggs, just east of The Dalles, and at The Dalles. Maryhill Museum is on Wash. 14 between White Salmon and Goldendale.

Nearby, at **Horsethief Lake State Park,** just west of the intersection of Wash. 14 and U.S. 97, you can see Indian rock paintings thousands of years old. They're just west of the park entrance.

Give the youngsters a break at a museum designed just for them: **Wonder Works, A Children's Museum,** 505 W. 9th St., The Dalles (tel. 503/296-4864). Here there's no one telling them not to touch things, quite the opposite in fact. This is a hands-on spot where youngsters can see a little mathematics in action, try out computers, and take a trip back in time to grandma's attic. Wonder Works is open from 10 a.m. to 4:30 p.m. Tuesday through Saturday, and admission is $1.25 per person. Youngsters under 10 must be accompanied by an adult or another youngster at least 12 years old.

Twelve miles west of The Dalles, you'll spot a shining white tower. That's the **Victor Trevitt Memorial,** a pillar honoring a pioneer and friend to the Warm Springs Indians, many of whom were buried here in ancient tribal burial grounds called Memaloose Island.

St. Peter's Landmark Church, West 3rd and Lincoln Streets, is a local landmark built in 1897. Leering gargoyles stare down at you from the walls of this red-brick Gothic cathedral, which features a madonna carved from a wooden ship's keep, six rose windows, and many other glowing stained-glass creations. St. Peter's called the faithful on a sonorous old bell, and a rare tigerwood pipe organ filled the resonant old building with music. You can visit the church from 11 a.m. to 3 p.m. Tuesday through Friday and 1 to 3 p.m. on Saturday and Sunday; closed Monday. Free.

The Dalles Art Center, 220 E. 4th St. (tel. 503/296-4759), is both historic sight and shopping spot. Housed in one of Andrew Carnegie's libraries, the art center, features both exhibit and sale of artwork and a free look at this historic library. Operated by the Dalles Art Association, the gallery is actually two galleries, one for sales and one for exhibits which change each month. Those changing exhibits often include some fascinating work by local craft workers and artists, many of them portraying Columbia Gorge scenery. A September Festival of the Arts is planned for 1989 with music, dance, drama, and a street art fair. Hours are 10 a.m. to 4 p.m. Tuesday through Saturday.

If you'd come here as a pioneer in 1850, you would have camped at **Fort Dalles,** 15th and Garrison Streets (tel. 503/296-4547). In those days it was known as Camp Drum and was the only post between Fort Vancouver and Fort Laramie. A few years later it became a full-fledged fort, although never a stockaded one, and was renamed. A captain with a taste for the good life built himself a $100,000 house at the fort and some other snappy quarters as well. Those have fallen to the ravages of time and fire, but one building remains, the Gothic-inspired house of the surgeon. It's now a museum housing some interesting pioneer exhibits, including a good-looking clock dating from the 1850s, some early guns, furnishings, and saddles. In summer from May to October, hours are 10:30 a.m. to 5 p.m. Tuesday through Friday, opening a half hour earlier on Saturday and Sunday; closed Monday. In other months hours are noon to 4 p.m. Wednesday through Friday, 10 a.m. to 4 p.m. on Saturday and Sunday; closed Monday and Tuesday. No admission charge.

To visit more of the historic district of The Dalles, stop at the chamber of commerce for a **self-guided walking tour** map outlining an hour-long stroll past some handsome old architecture and historic sites.

A looping **scenic drive** here (get on it at West 14th and Trevitt Streets) takes you past Sorosis Park, named after a women's organization that established it. Millions of years ago this park was underwater, part of an ancient lake created when Lake Missoula spread 400 cubic miles of water across the land. Bones of camels, horses, and mastodons have been found here. Today the park offers pretty picnic grounds amid a beautiful panorama of the valley and city below. A bit farther along the short drive is a pioneer cemetery in which some of the first emigrants were buried.

At **The Dalles Dam,** you can tour on a little red train that scoots about the dam and powerhouse. During the salmon run in late fall, salmon leap up the fish ladders to return to their spawning grounds. At the visitor center (tel. 503/298-8732) displays outline the Lewis and Clark Expedition and tell you a little about the ancient history of this region. Hours at the center, just east of The Dalles Bridge, are 10 a.m. to 4:30 p.m. daily from Labor Day to Memorial Day, guided tours by appointment only the remainder of the year. It's free.

SPECIAL EVENTS: On the fourth weekend in April, The Dalles celebrates its best-known product at the **Northwest Cherry Festival,** following that in May with an **All-Indian Rodeo** at Tygh Valley, and then the **Fort Dalles Rodeo** on the third weekend in July.

SPORTS: Here, as all along the gorge, the wide waters created by the dam provide for every kind of recreational activity from picnicking to swimming, fishing, hunting, and an unexpected sport, windsurfing, in breezes that blow constantly down this massive natural open tunnel. See more about windsurfing a little further on under Hood River sports.

SHOPPING: You'll see plenty of T-shirts and souvenir ashtrays here in this now very popular Oregon resort area, but if you look closely you may also find some treasures. Some of those can be found at **Dobre Deli,** 308 E. 4th St., which in addition to purveying a wide variety of culinary treasures also sells handmade silver jewelry depicting ancient rock art of the region, the 10,000-year-old petroglyphs that still can be seen here. Dobre Deli's owner sells the jewelry in another shop, Columbia Legends, which does indeed have some interesting legends to tell you about life here a few millennia ago.

3. HOOD RIVER

In April the gleaming Columbia River becomes the second-best sight in the Hood River Valley. In that month an undulating froth of apple blossoms fills this rolling valley with a floral cloud as ethereal as the flakes that cover the peaks of Mount Hood hovering on the horizon. Early settlers took one look at this fertile valley, watered by the Hood and Columbia Rivers, and knew they had struck gold, albeit nonmetallic. They planted and cultivated pear and apple trees that have been growing here for generations, their fruit shipped east for more than a century.

The most prolific apple orchards in the state, these Hood River providers are supplemented by pear and cherry trees that provide the main ingredient in many a crusty pastry creation here. People date their days here from Blossom Day to Blossom Day the way the rest of us remember Christmas. On that Blossom Day, the last Sunday in April, all Hood River turns out to tour orchards, celebrate the upcoming crop, and exchange a toast or two in cider that's been steeping since last fall's crop was harvested.

To see what all the fuss is about, take a 40-mile drive up Ore. 35 from Hood River to Panorama Point. There you'll be apple royalty for a day, monarch of an orchard kingdom stretching to the slopes of snow-clad Mount Hood. If you're here in autumn, you can buy Hood River's most famous product right off the tree or drink it squeezed into cider and purveyed at roadside stands.

When Oregon began building roads for those fellows in the new-fangled horseless carriages, the state showed some of that famed Oregon reverence for nature: this spectacularly scenic byway was one of the first highways in the state. When traffic clogged the old road, not one Oregonian entertained a blasphemous thought of giving up this revered view: they just built a new and straighter roadway a little closer to the view!

VISITOR INFORMATION: The Hood River County Chamber of Commerce, Port Marina Park, Hood River, OR 97031 (tel. 503/386-2000), can lead you to sporting and recreational activities in the region and works closely with the **Mount Hood Recreation Association,** Zig Zag, OR 97073 (tel. 503/622-3101).

WHERE TO STAY: Here in the valley is a hotel that's both a beautiful stopping spot and one of the region's most famous historic sights. The **Columbia Gorge Hotel,** 4000 W. Cliff Dr., Hood River, OR 97031 (tel. 503/386-5566), has occupied what may be the most beautiful site along the gorge for more than 65 years. Built in 1921, the hotel perches serenely atop a bluff high over the river and under a stand of towering pines. On a quiet evening you'll hear the sound of crashing waters as a nearby cascade pours 200 feet to the river below. A tiny stone bridge nips over a creek that winds its way across lawns that sweep to the hotel door. A red-tile roof tops the simple, unornamented building that has mellowed to a golden yellow.

Built by lumber jillionaire Simon Benson, who also created the elegant Benson Hotel in Portland, the Columbia Gorge Hotel was once the playground of the jazz age's jet set—Clara Bow, Rudolph Valentino, and the like. From the minute you sweep down a drive shaded by giant pines to the wide, flower-trimmed entrance doors, you know this hotel is something special. To confirm your suspicions, the hotel's limousine (an aged, finny, white Cadillac) sits superciliously at the front door.

Inside you'll find no showy atriums or slick flash. Instead polished woods glow, a fireplace blazes, wide windows spread the gorge out before you like a mural. Here is a courtly old country inn-hotel to which contemporary comforts have been added to retain the cozy ambience that has been luring serenity-seekers for decades. Step into the lobby and you step into an era of massive pillars, glittering chandeliers, and ornate moldings. A broad corridor leads to a wide parlor where expansive windows overlook the gorge. A piano plays; a lounge beckons.

In your room you may find a canopy bed, antique chest, fireplace, a dramatic view of garden or river, lacy country elegance. Big modern bathrooms await with fluffy towels, perfumed soaps, contemporary plumbing. When the morning sun peeks through the pines, waitresses in long dresses serve locally famed six-course farm breakfasts: a platter of fresh fruit for openers, followed by the inn's own oatmeal–brown sugar combination, then bacon, eggs, buttermilk pancakes, and hash browns. The finale is a showy presentation of "apple blossom honey from the sky"—a stream of golden liquid poured from shoulder height onto a fluffy fresh biscuit. Lunch and dinner are equally satisfying, with dinner entree prices in the $20 to $25 range.

For all this countrified elegance, you pay $95 to $125 for queen-size, king-size, or double beds on the garden side of the hotel; while rooms on the river side range from $135 to $145 for queen-size or king-size bed and $175 for a room with fireplace. Extra persons pay $25 each.

There's yet another lovely place to settle in this enchanting valley. Across the river in Washington, the picturesque village of White Salmon winds its way up a cliff beside the river. From the alpine architecture to the massive brass bed in the honeymoon suite, you're going to love the **Inn of the White Salmon**, 172 Jewett Blvd., White Salmon, WA 98672 (tel. 509/493-2335). Built in 1937, the brick inn with Tyrolean touches occupies a beautiful hill looking out over the Columbia Gorge. Owners Bill and Loretta Hopper have operated the White Salmon Inn for more than ten years and turned it into a study in tasteful décor and concerned service.

You enter a tiny lobby outfitted with striped wing chairs flanking a counter on which reposes a big antique brass cash register. Workers in floor-length denim aprons and ruffled blouses show you to your room, one of 19 antique-filled quarters, each more charming than the last. Antique brass headboards, polished mahogany desks, heavy quilted bedspreads in handsome colors, lace curtains, velvets—these are the ingredients that have spelled success here. At breakfast each day you'll meet still more ingredients: 35 to 40(!) kinds of ethnic pastries are created here, six different egg dishes, and all kinds of surprise treats served on antique china and lace tablecloths! Rates are $68 double, $25 for additional persons, $138 for honeymoon quarters, and $108 for quite large suites.

The **Hood River Inn and Village Resort,** Hood River Village, Hood River, OR 97031 (tel. 503/386-2200, or toll free 800/828-7873), has plenty of its own diversions and many others nearby in this valley of 4,000 residents. For openers there's a swimming pool, lively cocktail lounge, coffeeshop, and plenty of entertainment evenings. Set right alongside the river, the inn has never-ending views of the action on this busy waterway and rooms that take full advantage of the view through big glass doors leading to a patio or balcony overlook. In the resort's dining room you can keep the view in sight while dining on prime beef, seafood from the Pacific, or a platter of the region's fresh fruit. Slake your thirst in the wine cellar or Riverview lounge. Rates are $55 to $89 double.

Across the river, Bingen, Washington, plays up its scenic similarities to a town of the same name in Germany. Here, two enterprising souls have taken a big old Victorian home and turned it into a bed-and-breakfast inn. This one's called **The Grand Old House**, 120 Wash. 14 (P.O. Box 667), Bingen, WA 98605 (tel. 509/493-2838), which describes the place quite well indeed. Built in 1860, the house has two big bay-windowed turrets behind which you'll find a spacious parlor turned into a cozy sitting room. You can sit here to peruse the inn's menu before proceeding into the lace-curtained dining room for dinner.

The rooms are large and sunny, trimmed in lace and pretty pastel shades, each different and many with antique touches. Such attention to detail is there here that a hall linen closet is carefully stacked with alternating pink and blue towels. Baths are shared in most quarters, but breakfast is included in rates that range from $48 to $68 double. If you're a windsurfer, the inn offers wetsuits, dry suits, sailboards, and a hot tub too.

Rippling River, 68010 E. Fairway Ave., Welches, OR 97067 (tel. 503/622-3101, or toll free 800/547-8054 in the western states, 800/452-4612 in Oregon), likes to call itself Portland's Alpine Resort and that alpine connection certainly does exist. Nestled in the foothills of Mount Hood, Rippling River has all the requirements of a modern resort from golf course to tennis courts, indoor and outdoor pools, restaurant and imbibing spots. Accommodations are in hotel rooms or in condominium apartments with a fireplace, king-size bed, kitchenette, and wet bar. One-, two-, and three-bedroom condominiums are available, all with quite breathtaking mountain or valley views. Rates are $60 to $97 for a hotel room and $85 to $110 for a one-bedroom condominium, higher for larger units.

WHERE TO DINE: By popular acclaim the **Columbia Gorge Hotel** (see "Where to Stay") has the lock on Hood River dining, but there are a few other possibilities as well.

The **Hood River Inn** (see "Where to Stay") is a country-inn restaurant with both decorative style and good taste. Good uncomplicated cooking is the style here, with top-quality steaks and beef and fresh seafood heading the list, closely followed by delicately cooked lamb selections and very good pasta. Desserts are bountiful and will always feature some of the wonderful local apples, pears, and cherries. Prices are around $10 for most selections and hours are 6 a.m. to 10 p.m. daily. Reservations are wise at this popular dining room.

The **Stonehedge Inn,** 3405 Cascade Dr. (tel. 503/386-3940), is a beautifully restored turn-of-the-century house with several dining rooms. Our favorite is a cozy corner lined with dark-wood paneling, but the library is also charming, while the porch room garden view is tempting. French flavors predominate here, so begin with a homemade pâté or creamy soup, then move on to one of a dozen entrees from steak Diane to chicken featuring the flavors of Dijon mustard, lamb, veal sauced with champagne and cream, coquilles touched with cognac, delicately cooked salmon, even duck. Finish with imaginative desserts or fruit right off the tree. Light meals are available, but prices are in the $13 to $18 range generally, and hours are 5 to 9 p.m. Wednesday through Sunday; closed Monday and Tuesday. Reservations appreciated.

Across the Hood River bridge in the village of Bingen, you can try some local delicacies and some very good cooking in the home of Greg and Cindy Debruler, who operate **The Grand Old House** (see "Where to Stay") and also a restaurant in its charming dining room. Among the treats on the menu here are sole sautéed in butter and flamed in bourbon, then sprinkled with walnuts and almonds; fresh whole trout or salmon; puff pastry filled with shrimp, scallops, and clams; and steak flamed with champagne cognac. Wood-smoked local trout makes a good starter, as does a pie layered with avocado, onions, and herbs. Soups and Greek and Caesar salads are also on the menu, which ranges in price from $8 to $15, including soup or salad and vegetable. Hours are 6 to 9 p.m. daily except Monday.

If you're looking for light snacks, try **The Coffee Spot,** 12 Oak St., Hood River (tel. 503/386-1772), where bagels, croissants, English muffins, yogurt, granola, and whole-grain buttermilk waffles topped with fresh local fruit are available for breakfast. Fancy coffees and teas are always on the menu, but the Coffee Spot doesn't limit itself to coffee: it also has imported and local beers, regional and international wines. This dining spot likes to describe its desserts as decadent, and few would quarrel with that description. Sandwiches range from cheese with a savory pesto spread to a three-cheese offering topped with avocado. Prices are in the under-$5 range, and you can even order just half a sandwich on Russian rye, sourdough, and several other kinds of breads. And surely a first— "The Java Hour," 3 to 5 p.m. daily, when coffee drinks are half price.

WHAT TO SEE AND DO: Hood River's right in the center of the most dramatic part of the gorge, so "jest lookin' " is what most people come here to do.

To get a look at the early days of the area, however, **Port Marina Park,** on I-84 just beyond the bridge, is the home of **Hood River Visitor's Center** and the **Hood River County Historical Museum** (tel. 503/386-6772). The museum has compiled exhibits outlining pioneer development of the area. From April to November the museum is open from 10 a.m. to 4 p.m. Wednesday through Sunday.

In other months it's open Monday and Tuesday by appointment only. No admission charge.

SPORTS: If you're the active type, this is the place to find yourself a board and a sail and launch them out there on the river. It's **windsurfing** we're talking about, a sport that's becoming extremely popular here where the breezes blow ceaselessly down a kind of natural tunnel created by the high walls of the gorge. Better really than the ocean for learners, the Hood River area is now also home to annual windsurfing championship competitions.

Get in on the fun yourself at **Gorge Windsurfing,** 319 E. 2nd St., The Dalles (tel. 503/298-8796), which will rent you a sailboard and teach you how to get it working. Rental rates are $35 to $40 a day for board and sail, and they'll teach you how to get it moving for about $85 a couple for nine hours. The site of most of the action is **Port Marina Park,** I-84 just beyond the bridge.

Some people think of nothing but **fishing** when they come here, and indeed it's difficult not to think about it when there are so many swimming around right in front of your eyes at river dam viewing points. If you're one of those who wants to forget looking and get hooking, stop in to see **Luhr Jensen & Sons,** 400 Portway (tel. 503/386-3811), a company that has won quite a reputation for the excellence of its fishing lures, rods, reels, and good wishes. You can tour the company to see what they're offering Tuesday through Thursday at 11 a.m. and 1:30 p.m.

4. CASCADE LOCKS

When Meriwether Lewis, William Clark, and, later, weary pioneers reached this place, they were less than thrilled: massive cascades blocked river passage, forcing passersby to carry their belongings, lock, stock, and barrel, across the river at a portage above the falls. Today those grueling portages are honored at mid-September Portage Days complete with an Indian salmon bake.

Legend and fact mix easily in these ancient lands. Indian legends tell of a crossing built by the gods, a natural rock bridge across the river here. No one in recorded history has seen that bridge, but there's every likelihood the river did indeed carve its way through rock, leaving some of it behind as a natural crossing. Although that stone passage no longer exists, its memory is recalled by a modern Washington-bound span called Bridge of the Gods.

Over the centuries things have changed here, but not a great deal: you may still see Indians plunging long-handled nets into the river and scooping out their catch, fishing in a style used on these banks for 10,000 years by countless generations of their ancestors.

Today, although the Cascade Locks are submerged by the backwaters of Bonneville Dam and no longer operating, a lock tender's 1905 museum/home in Cascade Locks Marine Park is a National Historic Site. In the museum, memories of Indian tribes' long and bountiful residence are outlined, while outside the *Oregon Pony,* the first steam locomotive in the Pacific Northwest, offers a look at more contemporary activities.

In romantic days gone by, sternwheelers took fluttering maidens and handsome escorts on chugging river journeys. Eyewitness accounts from those who took these trips—pretty heady stuff in those days—are chronicled at Sternwheel Museum, in the Cascade Locks Visitor Center at the east end of Marine Park (tel. 503/374-8619). No admission charge.

VISITOR INFORMATION: Cascade Locks City Hall, 140 S.E. Wa-na-pa St. (tel. 503/374-8448), can help with information on the region. More help is available in the Troutdale/Sandy River area at **Sandy Area Chamber of Com-**

merce, 39261 Proctor Blvd. (P.O. Box 536), Sandy, OR 97055 (tel. 503/668-4006), where workers can fill you in on activities in and around this part of the gorge.

WHERE TO STAY: With a few exceptions, most of the accommodations in the region are small, standard properties offering cozy simplicity rather than showy luxury.

The **Scandian Motor Lodge,** on U.S. 30 (P.O. Box 398), Cascade Locks, OR 97014 (tel. 503/374-8417), is one of those cozily simple spots, one that lives up to the suggestion of its Scandinavian name. From rooms on the upper story here, you even get a bit of a fjord feeling as you look out over the gorge. Inside, décor features Scandinavian wall hangings, bright colors and prints, handsome wood furnishings, and even bathrooms tiled in Scandinavian style with those European hand-held showers. One room even has its own sauna!

For dining there's a small restaurant next door. You'll find the Scandian on U.S. 30, just off I-84 at the Cascade Locks exit. Rates are as irresistible as the rest of this well-kept 30-room motel: in summer, $32 to $40 single and $34 to $44 double, less the rest of the year.

Camping

For camping, try **Cascade Locks K.O.A.,** Star Rte, Box 660, Cascade Locks, OR 97014 (tel. 503/374-8668). To get to these wooded sites along the gorge, take I-84 to Cascade Locks exit 44. The camp is two miles east of town on Forest Lane. Cascade Locks K.O.A. is 35 miles east of Portland. Rates are $15 for RVs and $12 for tents. Extra persons are $2 each.

WHERE TO DINE: Pickings are pretty small in this village, so you might plan a little drive before dinner over to the Troutdale/Welches area where you'll find a wider selection.

You'll have to allot even more driving time to have dinner at Welches (sometimes also called Wemme), but you couldn't ask for a more scenic route or more delightful atmosphere when you arrive. Here in this tiny town—named for the inordinate number of people named Welche who live here—**Chalet Swiss,** Ore. 26 and Welches Road, Welches (tel. 503/622-3600), is a much sought-after place packed in summer with lovers of hearty Swiss cooking. Up here in the shadow of this towering peak, it even *feels* like Switzerland, as you dine on tender veal and irresistible fondues set off with those often difficult-to-find, light and delicate Swiss wines. Don't gamble: call for reservations. Hours are 5 to 10 p.m. Wednesday through Sunday. You'll find the restaurant on Ore. 26 about 14 miles east of Sandy.

Rippling Rivers Resort, 68010 E. Fairway Ave., Welches (tel. 503/622-3101, 503/224-7158 in Portland), is both pleasant resort and good dining room. Here you can tuck into sizzling steaks and an array of seafood in an attractive setting created by someone who loves blue no matter what color it is. Wide windows offer a view over the resort's pool. Prices for dinner are in the $12 to $17 range and the dining room is open from 11 a.m. to 10 p.m. daily.

WHAT TO SEE AND DO: A delightfully old-fashioned way to explore the gorge is aboard the **Columbia Gorge Sternwheeler,** a 599-passenger reproduction of river steamers that cruised the Snake, Columbia, and Willamette Rivers more than 100 years ago.

Two-hour trips on the river depart from Cascade Locks Marine Park, I-84 exit 44 (tel. 503/374-8427), at 10 a.m., 12:30 p.m., and 3 p.m.; from Bonneville Dam at 10:30 a.m. and 1 p.m.; and from Stevenson, Washington, at 11:15 a.m. and 1:45 p.m. daily from mid-June through September. Fare is $9 for adults, $5 for children 4 to 12, and free for children under 3.

Dinner cruises under the stars depart at 7, return at 9 p.m., on Thursday, Friday, and Saturday and include a barbecued salmon dinner aboard at $27 or $28 for adults, $24 or $25 for children 4 to 12.

In fall and spring the boats occasionally cruise downriver from Portland on the Willamette River. Tickets to summer cruises are also available in Portland at the company's ticket outlet (tel. 503/223-3928), with fall and spring schedules available by writing Columbia Gorge Sternwheeler, P.O. Box 307, Cascade Locks, OR 97014.

First-born of the federal dams that now dot the river, **Bonneville Dam** was built in the late 1930s and named for Capt. Benjamin de Bonneville, one of the region's early explorers. An ancient Indian burial ground on Bradford Island lies between the two sections of the dam, which form barriers in the two branches of the river here.

Bonneville Dam holds back waters that form 48-mile-long Bonneville Lake. At the visitor center on Bradford Island, you can get a good look at this man-made wonder through glass walls. From July 4 to Labor Day, naturalists guide tours explaining how the dam works. You'll also get a look through underwater windows at fish navigating fish ladders, which help them make their way upstream. A nearby hatchery shows how millions of tiny salmon are raised and released to return years later.

Bonneville now has three sections: at the Second Powerhouse Visitor Complex you can see an operating powerhouse, fish viewing, and an orientation presentation. That facility is accessible from Wash. 14 in Washington. Hours and interpretive activities are the same at both the Bradford Island visitor center and the Second Powerhouse Visitor Complex.

Bonneville Lock and Dam Visitor Center, Bradford Island, Cascade Locks, OR 97014 (tel. 503/374-8820), is at exit 40 from I-84, about 23 miles west of Hood River. Folks there will be happy to outline recreational facilities in the region. Visitor center hours are 10 a.m. to 6 p.m. daily from Memorial Day to Labor Day, from 9 a.m. to 5 p.m. in other months. There's no admission charge. Admission to the adjacent fish hatchery is also free, and hours are 7:30 a.m. to 5 p.m. daily.

SPORTS:
High in the glaciers of Mount Hood, rivulets form and merge to create the Sandy River, which flows through foothills and joins the Columbia about 28 miles downriver from Cascade Locks near Troutdale.

In spring you'll find Troutdale inhabited by an eager, if somewhat strangely dressed crowd, carrying long-handled nets and wearing hip boots. While they may look like butterfly catchers out for a swim, they're really fishing fans in search of smelt, which they scoop up in great clumps from the lower end of the Sandy River. When Lewis and Clark passed by here in 1805, they dubbed this river the Quicksand River but, quicksand being rather a hard sell, in recent times that name's been trimmed to Sandy River.

Those two explorers are honored at the **Lewis and Clark State Park,** 16 miles east of Portland near the mouth of the river. The flowers you still see here today were noted in the explorers' journals.

A fine fishing river, the Sandy is fishing ground for shad in late May and June and for steelhead in autumn. For nature lovers a five- to nine-mile section of it is pure paradise: expert rafters or kayakers can tackle the isolated six-mile stretch from Dodge Park downriver to Oxbow County Park. There, novice floaters can launch a raft or canoe for a serene journey five miles downriver to Dabney State Park or nine miles to Lewis and Clark State Park.

If that sounds like fun—and in spring speedy waters can make it quite exciting—you can rent a raft or canoe for the trip at **River Trails**, 336 E. Columbia St., Troutdale (tel. 503/667-1964). Rental rates vary according to size and kind of craft you rent, so give the company a call.

Hikers head for Cascade Locks, where they join the famed **Pacific Crest Trail**, which passes just east of Cascade Locks, continues south through Mount Hood National Forest, through Willamette National Forest to the southern border of Oregon. That trail continues north on the Washington side of the river through Washington to the Canadian border.

SCENIC GORGE DRIVES: Two scenic drives, one following the old highway through the region, the other snaking up the side of a mountain, offer postcard-pretty scenery on this lower end of the river. A third drive visits the dramatic alpine scenery of towering Mount Hood.

Troutdale is the end—or the beginning—of a drive along the old highway that served the area before I-84 was constructed. You may join the highway, now called the **Columbia River Scenic Highway**, at I-84 about five miles west of Bonneville Dam. There the scenic highway scoots off to the south a short distance and runs parallel to I-84 through deep forests, past cascades shooting over the cliffs to the river. Short trails lead you to views of waterfalls in pine forests, lovely picnic spots. The waterfalls have lovely names, intriguingly descriptive of what you will see: **Bridal Veil Falls, Mist Falls, Horsetail Falls,** and the very beautiful **Oneonta Falls,** which course down mossy gorge walls up a streambed about 1,000 feet from the road.

Most famous of the falls along this highway are those at Multnomah Creek, where **Multnomah Waterfall**, at 620 feet, is the highest in Oregon. A photogenic bridge across the falls connects with a trail to a viewing platform above the falls. At the visitor center you can hear more about the history and legends of this age-old geological wonder. (Hours are 1 to 5 p.m. Tuesday through Friday, 10 a.m. to 6 p.m. on Saturday and Sunday.)

Back on the scenic highway, you ascend to **Crown Point**, a beautiful view from a point 700 feet over the river. Just beyond Crown Point, **Larch Mountain Road** turns off to the south, then winds back east on a wiggly route to Larch Mountain. In summer this is a popular road for berry pickers, who come to fill pails—and mouths—with huckleberries.

If you remain on the scenic highway, you will find the road winding down to the Sandy River, which it follows past Lewis and Clark State Park, finally rejoining I-84 at Troutdale. Briefly, then, those drives are the Old Scenic Highway from Ainsworth Park past Multnomah Falls, Bridal Falls, Latourell Falls, Corbett, Springdale, and on to Troutdale; and the Larch Mountain Drive heading east from just beyond Corbin to Larch Mountain. On the Larch Mountain Drive you must return the same way you came, while the scenic drive loops around to rejoin I-84.

One other drive, often called the **Mount Hood Loop** highway, will take you from Hood River on Ore. 35 past Timberline Drive to the road's junction with U.S. 26 just east of Government Camp. Stay on U.S. 26 and you'll wind through the delightful little alpine-like villages of Welches (also called Wemme), Alder Creek, Cherryville, Sandy, and on to connect with I-84 or, farther on, to join I-205 into Portland and Vancouver.

5. ALONG THE WASHINGTON SIDE OF THE COLUMBIA GORGE

Washington's side of the gorge is much more sparsley populated than the Oregon side of the river, but beauty abounds no matter which side you drive.

On the Washington side, Wash. 14, called the Lewis and Clark Hwy., follows the course of the river, offering you a delightful look at waterfalls, villages, a few hotels on the Oregon side of the Columbia Gorge, and rising high over all, the lofty snow-topped Mount Hood.

Highlights of the Washington side of the gorge are: across the river from The Dalles, Maryhill Museum and Horsethief Lake, which we've already outlined for you; **Klickitat Gorge,** a dramatic spot with terrifying rope bridges and Indian dip-net fishing (just north of Wash. 14 on Wash. 142 along the Klickitat River); and **Ice House Bird Sanctuary,** an old gas ice plant now doing duty as a home for birds (just off Wash. 142 west of Klickitat).

Across the Columbia from Hood River: **White Salmon River** is first a pretty little highland village and second a favorite fishing ground and white-water-rafting spot. At the mouth of the White Salmon River, the nine-mile **Broughton Log Flume** is the last of its kind still operating in the U.S. **Bingen,** a tiny town nearby on Wash. 14, has made itself over to resemble its German namesake, complete with winery.

North on Wash. 141 from White Salmon, at **Trout Lake,** you'll find a viewpoint that was a sacred place for Indian tribes for thousands of years. Today it offers a stunning view of Mount Adams and from mid-August to mid-September is frequented by huckleberry pickers. Here, too, you can visit **ice caves** formed by volcanic action. You'll find the caves ten miles west of Trout Lake, but there are no guides; you're on your own.

West of Bingen and just past the village of Cook, the historic Carson Hotel still invites you to splash in **mineral baths** fed by natural springs. About 28 miles north on the Carson Road, a **Mount St. Helens Viewpoint** offers a very good look at the devastation wrought by that erupting volcano. Binoculars help.

Across from Cascade Locks and Bonneville Dam: Along the Lewis and Clark Hwy. (Wash. 14) you'll find the Washington half of the **Bonneville Dam** at North Bonneville.

Head west about three miles from North Bonneville for a look at **Beacon Rock,** an 800-foot, straight-walled monolith, the largest such formation in the nation. A state park with a mountain trail is a favorite with youngsters. Cape Horn Viewpoint, 15 miles west, is a favorite spot for views of the west entrance to the gorge.

CHAPTER IX

PORTLAND

□ □ □

Portland began with a historic swap: a two-bit land claim in exchange for a couple of pickaxes. A century later, this city is still firmly in the swapping business. Deals, capital D, are made here, and there's no greater praise in town than the assertion that a fellow's a good horse trader.

This bustle for the buck can trace its roots clear back to the embryonic days of the city. In 1844 Francis Pettygrove made the first of many deals that were to be transacted on this land: he traded some clothes and gold-mining equipment to Bill Overton, who figured he'd struck a pretty canny deal when he unloaded a claim to 640 acres of dirt he'd bought for all of 25¢. Just 30 years later Overton's penny-ante trade had become a full-fledged Pacific Northwest trading center called Stumptown, in salute to its land-clearing leftovers, and our boy Pettygrove was in the bucks. He won a historic coin toss too, thereby acquiring the right to ax a suggested Boston monicker and name the city Portland after his Portland, Maine, origins.

Building bucks continues to be the major pursuit of those who live and visit here, but these days building blocks have been added to the activities. If there's one city in the Pacific Northwest in which you will not only see progress but feel it, that city is Portland.

For this city is growing like the proverbial Topsy. On its skyline, construction cranes seem to outnumber buildings. Everywhere you look, multistory edifices are rising in a boggling maze of smoked glass and brushed steel. And beneath your feet the ground rumbles with the passing of cement mixers and bulldozers.

Yet in the midst of it all, Portland's historic beginnings are being carefully preserved. Old Town, the second-largest collection of cast-iron-fronted buildings on the West Coast, is returning to the splendor of its former days when these streets were the heart and soul of Portland commerce.

Portland is called the City of Roses, a name that derives from an era when a flower-fancying mayor set up a now-famous rose garden experiment called Rose Test Gardens, a scent-ful delight still in business. Enthusiastic gardeners took up the cudgel—well, the spade—to plant roses all over town and to create an annual citywide party called the **Rose Festival.**

Such oddities amid the haste are not uncommon in this quite uncommon city. On a walk through Portland's surprisingly compact downtown, you will pass dozens of drinking fountains, the gift of Prohibition-era lumber millionaire Simon Benson, who donated them as his own kind of Joe-sent-me contribution to what he called the "frustrated thirst" of Portlanders.

While Portland can't seem to get new buildings up fast enough, the city hasn't been allowed to forget that people live here. That's why you will find, amid the high-rises and the hustle, dozens of parks of all sizes. Playing in them are throngs of people, many of them lunchbreak workers, happily dipping toes—or whole bodies—into a cascading waterfall with nary a frown from local gendarmes. There are, in fact, more than 160 parks and gardens inside city limits rimmed by virgin forest, bounded on one side by a wilderness forest park and on the other by a sports-oriented greenery belt. At the Willamette River waterfront, more than a mile of land has been turned into shady, scenic strolling grounds.

Unlike many cities in which progress seems to control people, in Portland people give every appearance of controlling the city's progress. When a historic building is threatened, alarmed preservationists rally awesome forces to fight back.

Once dubbed the biggest small town in the West, Portland is a little like Chicago: urbanization sans sophistication. Yet there are growing signs of change. Provinciality is being ousted by increasing internationality, meat and potatoes supplemented with béarnaise sauce, plain talk upstaged by second languages.

Amid the growth and growing pains, Portland has retained its welcoming western hospitality to present to you a refreshingly frank and open countenance. People here speak their minds and even have historic speakers' corners, Lownsdale and Chapman Squares, on which to do that. They are quick to spot pretensions and hollow promises, just as quick to embrace cards-on-the-table candor.

That western simplicity and warmth fly in the face of the cold calculation and steely determination so many regions have come to believe necessary for progress, but for this city it's working. Portland's rivers are running clean, its air is smog-free—and even ozone-free, following a ban on sale of aerosol products —and business is booming.

A city with a rosy future indeed.

1. GETTING THERE AND GETTING AROUND

Portland is one of the major hubs of the Northwest, so you won't have any trouble getting here. As for getting around, the city is a delight to drive in, but navigating downtown, as in most cities, will test your patience and skill.

GETTING THERE: Home to most of the action is **Portland International Airport,** nine miles east of town off I-84, which welcomes every major domestic airline and a number of smaller local commuter aircraft. Among the airlines flying in here are Air Canada, Alaska, American Airlines, Canadian Coastal, Continental, Delta, Eastern, Hawaiian Air, Horizon, Mexicana, Northwest, TWA, United, USAir, and Western.

178 □ FROMMER'S DOLLARWISE NORTHWEST

To get from the airport to downtown hotels, board the **Portland Airporter** (tel. 503/246-4676), which keeps to an every-20-minutes schedule Monday through Friday from 5:30 a.m. to midnight and has 30-minute trips on Saturday, Sunday, and holidays from 5:30 a.m. to 1 a.m. Fare is $5 for adults, $1 for children.

Cab fare from the airport to downtown hotels is about $15.

Two dozen of the city's hotels have free airport transportation services, so once you've decided on a hotel, ask if they have a **courtesy car** from the airport terminal.

Tri-Met, the city's public bus service, has buses from the airport on a regular schedule, but you'll have to transfer to get to downtown hotels. Fare is 85¢. Give them a call at 503/233-3511 for schedule information.

Amtrak trains pull into town at 800 N.W. Sixth Ave. (tel. 503/241-4290 or 248-1146).

Greyhound serves the city from everywhere with a terminal at 550 N.W. Sixth Ave. (tel. 503/243-2357).

By car you'll get to the city on **I-5** from Seattle and other points north of Portland or from all points south of the city; on **I-84,** which comes in from the Columbia Gorge on the east side of the city; or on **U.S. 26** from Astoria and other points west.

GETTING AROUND: Portland's many rental-car companies, taxi cabs, and public transportation system, together with a straightforward city plan, make this an easy city in which to move around.

Many **rental-car companies** operate in Portland, but once again we're saluting Budget, which offers free parking at associated Diamond Parking lots throughout the city. That can mean a lot when a parking lot space may cost you $2 or more an hour. As in any big city, on-street parking places are such a rarity in Portland as to be an endangered—if not extinct—species.

You can rent a **Budget Rent-A-Car** at five locations in the city, including the airport (tel. 503/249-4556), downtown at 2033 S.W. Fourth Ave. (tel. 503/222-9123), on the east side at 2332 N.E. Columbia Blvd. (tel. 503/228-2969), in nearby Beaverton at 10835 S.W. Canyon Rd. (tel. 503/626-3040), and in Clackamas at 10176 S.E. 82nd St. (tel. 503/775-8580). Other car-rental companies in the region include **National,** 620 W. Burnside (tel. 503/228-6637); **Avis,** 400 W. Burnside (tel. 503/249-4954) and at the airport (tel. 503/249-4950); and **Hertz,** at the airport (tel. 503/249-4080) and downtown at 1009 S.W. Sixth Ave. (tel. 503/224-7700).

Taxis operating in the city include **New Rose City Cab Co.** and an associated company, **Radio Cab** (tel. 503/227-1212), and 50-year-old **Broadway Cab Co.** (tel. 503/227-1234). You can flag cabs if you see an empty one, but it's often easier and quicker to call. Taxis park in front of major hotels downtown, so they're easy to find anytime except rush hours, from 7 to 9 a.m. and 5 to 7 p.m. Fares are $1.30 when the flag drops and $1.40 a mile.

Portland has a new rapid-transit system. **Tri-Met LightRail** tracks run on Yamhill and Morrison Streets from 1st Street to 11th Street and along 1st Street north.

Portland's **Tri-Met bus service,** named in honor of the three counties it serves, generously provides downtown travelers with free bus service in a district called **Fareless Square.** Boundaries of the district are Hoyt Street on the north, I-405 on the south, the Willamette River on the east, and I-405 again on the west. In that area are major shopping malls, car-less Portland Mall, and Old Town.

So thoughtful are they at Tri-Met buses that they've built sleek passenger shelters that come complete with computer video screens on which you punch in some information and the computer tells you what bus to take and when! It's wonderful. Maps help you figure out where you are and where you want to be; then you just hop on the bus and ride anywhere in that district day or night for free.

If you travel beyond the free zone, you pay by zone: 85¢ for the first two zones, $1.10 for suburbs, and $1.35 for points farthest away from downtown. Exact change is required. Buses run from about 5:30 a.m. to 9 p.m. and some until later, about midnight, a few all night long. For **route information,** stop by the Tri-Met office, at 522 S.W. Yamhill St., or call them at 503/233-3511.

In recent years Portland has created a new way of getting from here to there: **MAX.** MAX is an acronym for Metropolitan Area Express, one- or two-car electric trains running a 15-mile route between downtown Portland and Gresham. Cost of the ride is 85¢ to $1.35, depending on how far you ride; free in the downtown district.

For trips farther afield (for example, to Hood River, Vancouver, Washington, and other similarly distant points), call the **Airporter** (tel. 503/249-1837), which offers regular service for prices that range from $9 to $14.50 for the Hood River journey.

ORIENTATION: We wish we could say it's easy to get around town, and in a way it is. On foot it's easy; in a car . . .

For openers, the city's delightful Portland Mall, a mass-transit center, is a pleasure for pedestrians, who can stroll around the tree-lined streets without worrying about traffic, but it plays the devil with drivers, who must skirt those streets on one-way thoroughfares in every direction. You can get muddled easily, and we're predicting you will. That's why we'd advise selecting a downtown hotel, parking the car, and letting your feet do the driving. On the brighter side, the most popular parts of the downtown area are comparatively compact, so you can learn your way around in a short time—and even if you're lost, you're never too far off the path.

Outside of that downtown bustle, Portland is a driver's city trimmed with wonderfully rapid expressways that will take you out of downtown and in any direction quickly and efficiently. Once again, it may take you a little while to familiarize yourself with all the options, but once you do, you can be in and out of town in a flash.

So let's get started. First the expressways and river crossings.

I-5 runs north and south through the city while **I-84,** called the **Banfield Freeway** here, runs east from the Willamette River to the Columbia River Gorge. Got that? Okay, let's move right along to downtown streets.

You'll find the city divided into quadrants, with the **Willamette River** dividing east from west and **Burnside Street** dividing north from south.

Portland Center, once a section of town known euphemistically as a "blighted center," is now a garden spot of shops and cafés. It is closed to traffic, so you will have to go around its boundaries, which are S.W. First and Fourth Avenues and Lincoln and Market Streets.

Bridges span the river at more than half a dozen locations. Major crossings are, from south to north: **Marquam Bridge** (I-5), connecting to the southwest section of town; **Hawthorne Bridge,** joining S.E. Hawthorne and S.W. Madison Streets; **Morrison Bridge,** connecting S.E. Morrison and S.W. 1st Streets; **Burnside Bridge,** joining East Burnside and West Burnside Streets; **Steel Bridge,** linking the Coliseum area and North Interstate Street to N.W. Flanders and N.W. Glisan Streets; **Broadway Bridge,** spanning the river to join N.W. Lovejoy and N.W. Broadway Streets and the northeast side of town in the vicinity of

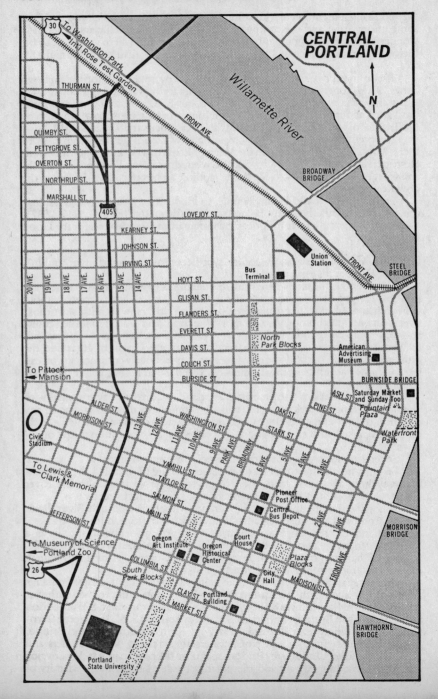

CENTRAL PORTLAND

North Interstate Street; and the **Fremont Bridge,** linking U.S. 405 and U.S. 30 to I-5.

2. TOURIST AND USEFUL INFORMATION

TOURIST INFORMATION: Portland dwellers love their town with a fervor rare in this day of cynic-chic.

So, stop by the **Portland Oregon Visitors Association,** 26 S.W. Salmon St., Portland, OR 97204 (tel. 503/222-2223), and give them a chance to exhibit a little city-love. A very pleasant and accommodating staff will help you find your way to anything from the nearest tennis court to the best huckleberry ice cream.

Other helpful types in town can be found at the **Portland Chamber of Commerce,** 824 S.W. Fifth Ave., Portland, OR (tel. 503/228-9411).

USEFUL INFORMATION: For **emergency police or medical help,** dial 911 . . . For the correct **time,** call 503/282-2202. . . . **Weather** information is available at 503/281-1911 and **road conditions** info at 503/222-6721 . . . For reports on **mountain road conditions,** call 503/238-8400 . . . **Portland Dental Society** (tel. 503/223-4731) can help you find a dentist . . . **The Multnomah County Medical Society** lists doctors and will help you find one, if you call them at 503/222-0156. . . . Portland's daily **newspaper** is *The Oregonian* . . . If you want a tan and the weather's not cooperating, stop in at **Tan Your Hide,** 401 Fourth Ave. at Washington Street (tel. 503/241-SUNN), and seek help . . . One-hour film processing at **Quick Stop Photo,** 323 S.W. Morrison St. (tel. 503/223-5016) . . . **Shoe Repair** at Cobbler's Corner, 110 S.W. Yamhill (tel. 503/224-5511), in Yamhill Center . . . For emergency veterinary help, call **Dove Lewis Emergency Animal Clinic** at 503/228-7281. . . . For quick cleaning, try **Cox's One Hour Martinizing,** 14th Avenue and N.E. Fremont Street (tel. 503/221-6133); free pickup and delivery to hotels too. . . . For 24-hour **car repair** help, call 503/285-6643. . . . You'll find a **grocery** open to 1 a.m. at 1101 S.W. 23rd Ave. (tel. 503/228-5682). . . . You'll find a coin-operated laundry at **Coin Laun-dry,** 1329 S.E. 39th Ave. (tel. 503/236-2669). . . . For a 24-hour grocery store, try **Steenson's AM PM Market,** 3917 N.E. Tillamook St. (tel. 503/282-7411).

3. WHERE TO STAY

From elegant and old to sleek and new, Portland offers a wide range of hotels. Parking is difficult in this busy city, so we've selected a range of downtown hotels that will make it easy for you to park and explore on foot or public transport. Our best-of-the-rest choices are listed in descending price order.

LUXURY HOTELS: From a wonderful old beauty to a chic modern hostelry, Portland's luxury hotels are as interesting as the city itself.

Grand dame and outstanding beauty of Portland hotels is an antique lady built over 70 years ago by millionaire lumber king Simon Benson, who also created a charming country hotel along the Columbia River Gorge. These days, hotel builders seem to equate flash and glitter with elegance but often succeed only in creating flashpaper trendiness in which impact dissipates at second glance. Not so at the glamorous **Westin Benson,** 309 S.W. Broadway (at Oak), Portland, OR 97205 (tel. 503/228-2000, or toll free 800/228-3000), where time seems to have stood still for generations, thanks to true architectural elegance that will never go out of style. Enter the magnificently paneled lobby and a faint hush reigns: no clamor of sound reverberating off the walls, no hard surfaces on which the clatter of a dropping pencil sounds like a platoon on maneuvers. Instead crystal chandeliers gleam overhead, their glow echoed in dark woods polished for so many years they glisten with a patina only age and loving care can confer. Enormous, ceiling-high windows are curtained by heavy drapes with voluminous folds that create the look of an English manor house library. Off to one side a uniformed concierge occupies an antique desk. Across the way, high-backed wing chairs are mixed with low seating in an open lobby lounge where Northwest movers and shakers gather at day's end. Benson is said to have taken a damn-the-expense attitude toward construction costs. While that may be legend, it's not difficult to believe.

For openers, all that lobby paneling is rare Circassian walnut, delicately carved and now offset by furnishings reminiscent of an elegant age. Yet there's nothing overpowering about this hotel—no 20-story atriums, no waterfalls running through the lobby, no acres of seating space—just old-world refinement at its finest. A 13-story brick hotel trimmed in marble, the Benson is now operated by Westin hotels, which has seen to the modernization of sleeping quarters here. A new section of the hotel added in 1959 has quite grand accommodations, very spacious with a king-size bed, enormous bathroom, desk, and large seating area with couch, coffee table, and chairs. In 1984 many more rooms were renovated, so you can expect very attractive quarters here. Rooms in the original section of the hotel are smaller but also attractively furnished. The Westin Benson offers two dining spots, Trader Vic's and an elegant English grill basement dining room called the London Grill. Begin perhaps with cocktails and the specialty hors d'oeuvres that Trader Vic's offers, then move on to the clubby intimacy of the London Grill, where fine continental cooking prevails. Rates at the Westin Benson are $125 to $144 double, higher for suites.

The **Portland Hilton,** 921 S.W. Sixth Ave., Portland, OR 97204 (tel. 503/226-1611, or toll free 800/445-8667), is a bright new hotel with an open staircase that curves up to a sunny upper-level dining room outfitted in deep burgundy, hung with crystal chandeliers, and lined with a wall of glass overlooking a landscaped roof garden. In the lobby plush furnishings grouped into intimate seating areas are set off by fresh flowers and potted palms. A little stream in part of the lobby supports a garden of greenery under a skylight overhead. Dining spots in this hotel are particularly attractive. On the 23rd floor is a plush restaurant famous for its city views and continental selections, focusing on good beef and seafood preparations in the $20 to $25 price range. A rather glamorous coffeeshop, rattan and etched-glass Twigs, is tucked unobtrusively away about halfway down the very large reception area. Prices are in the $10 to $15 range for dinner.

The rooms are typically Hilton, spacious and thoughtfully equipped. Muted shades predominate throughout, accented by attractive paintings and chic accessories. All have color TVs, in-room movies for a small charge, radios, and telephones. Very attractive views from your room. In the bath you'll find a kit filled with everything you might conceivably forget. For entertainment the hotel has a heated indoor swimming pool and at night a disco rocks. Rates at this centrally located hotel, surrounded by offices and shopping mall, are $92 to $112 double, about $20 less single. If you're here on a weekend, special money-saving rates are in effect.

The **Marriott Hotel,** 1401 S.W. Front Ave., Portland, OR 97201 (tel. 503/226-7600, or toll free 800/228-9290), runs a flash operation in Portland, as you'll see when you roll up the winding drive to enter the two-story lobby where planter boxes glitter with lights. A 15-story building, the Marriott has 504 spacious rooms, designed to appeal to those in search of plenty of action from sauna to whirlpool, indoor pool, full gymnasium, even a video-game parlor. You'll find all the usual amenities in your room, from shampoo and special soaps to televisions with in-room movies. Although bright and splashy, the Marriott has an attractive library-ish lounge for quiet conversations. Two restaurants fill the void at dining times. Rates at the Marriott are $101 single and $111 double, with rooms high and overlooking the river your best choice. Special rates some weekends.

Among the newest hotels in Portland is a creation of Seattle's Alexis Hotel people. Dubbed the **Alexis Hotel RiverPlace,** 1510 S.W. Harbor Way, Portland, OR 97201 (tel. 503/228-3233, or toll free 800/227-1333 outside Oregon), this sleek, contemporary, 74-room hostelry is set right at the city's Willamette River harbor overlooking the edge of downtown Portland. A rotunda roof and turrets quickly made this a new city landmark. Within stepping distance is a two-mile-long waterfront park. French doors, an inviting courtyard, a light and airy lobby sporting handmade rugs and comfy chairs are abetted by oak winscoting, marble fireplaces, antique pieces, and plenty of softening greenery.

In your room you'll find a terrycloth robe in the bathroom, all the usual extra amenities from special soaps to shampoos, even a welcome-to-Portland glass of sherry. Wing-back chairs and teak tables, writing desks, and remote-control televisions all work together to pamper you. About a third of the rooms are suites with wet bars, wood-burning fireplaces with valets to tend them, and whirlpool baths. A group of adjacent condominum apartments are also available if you're seeking lots of space. Room service is on duty around the clock here, and a concierge stands ready to help you find what you seek in Portland. A welcome no-tipping policy adds to the allure.

When hunger strikes, the hotel's Esplanade Restaurant is a chic, contemporary spot focusing on regional culinary triumphs. Soft jazz pours from a piano in the hotel's lounge, and on sunny summer days you can head outdoors for al fresco dining and sipping. Outside the hotel, the view of the city is stunning and a nearby esplanade will tempt you with boutiques and restaurants housed in pretty quarters. If you're intent on keeping in shape, you can jog on a trail that starts practically at the door or sit it out in the RiverPlace Athletic Club which sports three pools, racquetball courts, and aerobics, as well as a spa and whirlpool.

Rates at the resort are $135 to $150 double for rooms with two double beds and junior suites with combined bedroom and sitting room; higher for two-room suites or quarters with fireplaces. Included in the rates are continental breakfast, a morning paper, whirlpool and sauna, and evening turn-down service complete with the ubiquitous chocolate on your pillow.

Portland's newest old hotel is the historic **Heathman Hotel,** S.W. Broadway at Salmon, Portland, OR 97205 (tel. 503/241-4100, or toll free 800/551-0011). Built in 1927, this luxurious downtown hotel reopened in 1984 after a $16-million restoration. Here, polished woods glow in firelight and candlelight, brass shines, a piano tinkles. Elegance reigns here from the handsome lobby to 160 rooms decorated in earthy colors teamed with English country-garden chintzes. Baths are mirrored and marbled and come equipped with fluffy bathrobes and European soap. Midnight snackers will find a chocolate on their pillow and 24-hour room service, and there's a 250-film library of movies you can watch in your room. Heathman's handsome restaurant is fast becoming a local "in" spot for consumption of Northwest specialties prepared with classic culinary flourishes. If you're inclined toward the elegant, you can take tea each afternoon by the fire in the Tea Court. Rates for pampering at the Heathman are $115 double, $135 for a junior suite. Larger suites also are available.

Jantzen Beach

On the north side of town, Portland has its version of a beach, a favored local getaway spot called Jantzen Beach. Here the Columbia provides the water and a couple of large and well-equipped hotels provide the resort atmosphere.

Tops among those is the **Red Lion Motor Inn/Jantzen Beach,** 909 N. Hayden Island Dr., Portland, OR 97217 (tel. 503/283-4466, or toll free 800/547-8010). Unlike Portland hotels that focus on the needs of business travelers, who play so vital a part in this busy city's economy, this Jantzen Beach hotel is designed for fun. A big, lighted, riverside swimming pool, set off with light-trimmed beach umbrellas, sets the pace and is backed by lighted tennis courts right on the grounds, plus an ice rink, golf, fishing, and boating nearby. At night the hotel is quite a showpiece, with strips of light glowing across its rooflines.

The rooms at the Red Lion take full advantage of its unobstructed river views. Set in a cluster of three-story buildings that stretch out around the central swimming pool, these spacious accommodations have a wall of glass and most have balconies aimed straight at the view. All are kept up-to-date in décor and comfort, some featuring mirrored walls, and suites are equipped with sectional couches, wet bar, and whirlpool. Naturally televisions, radios, air-conditioning everywhere. Rates at the Red Lion Jantzen Beach are $94 to $106 double, higher for suites and two-bedroom units. Airport transportation is complimentary.

MODERATELY PRICED HOTELS: Portland has a number of hotels in the medium-priced bracket.

The **Red Lion Inn/Lloyd Center,** 1000 N.E. Multnomah St., Portland, OR 97232 (tel. 503/281-6111, or toll free 800/547-8010), offers both a convenient location on the east side of town and comfortable quarters near Lloyd Center, one of the city's top shopping malls. A most contemporary spot, glittering with metallic chandeliers and plush furnishings, Red Lion is Today, with a capital T. Outside, three bubble elevators, enclosed in glass, rise showily up the outside of this 15-story building. An outdoor pool and garden provide a view for many rooms and a gathering spot when the sun's shining. And if swimming's out, you can exercise off the pounds at the hotel's well-equipped gymnasium, fitted out with professional weight-training equipment, bikes, everything you need to muscle up and slim down.

For dining Eduardo's Mexican Restaurant and Cantina sports Spanish tiles and arches. More formal dining is at the hotel's flower-trimmed Maxi's Restaurant, sleek with metallic trim that shines in the glow of tableside preparations. Later, stop by Maxi's Lounge, where the dancing goes on as long as the crowd does, or for quieter moments try the soft, curving banquettes of the aptly named Quiet Bar.

A large hotel, the Red Lion has 520 rooms and lays claim to the title of largest hotel in the state. Those rooms are every bit as modern in design and décor as the rest of the hotel. Wood furnishings, soft muted colors, metallic accents, a wall of glass beyond which a balcony beckons, large and fully equipped bathrooms—all add up to one of the city's most attractive contemporary hotels. Rates, including a courtesy van from the airport, are $96 to $127 double.

Another Red Lion in Portland, this one called **Red Lion Motor Inn at Portland Center,** 310 S.W. Lincoln St., Portland, OR 97201 (tel. 503/221-0450, or toll free 800/547-8010), is smaller but every bit as sleek. Here you'll find soaring architecture. At the front of the hotel a long hallway with a wall of glass meets yet more glass at roof level, all of it shining with small klieg lights and trimmed in cedar. A small lobby is cozy with overstuffed furniture that is both contemporary and comfortable. In the intimate dining room a harpist plays as you dine on flamed tableside preparations, while in the Tiffany Lounge the crowds set a faster pace long into the night. An outdoor swimming pool provides amusement in daylight hours.

This conveniently located downtown hotel is on a sedate street, lined with quiet offices and apartment buildings set among trees and fountains. With 237 newly remodeled rooms, it enjoys an atmosphere enhanced by the surrounding stroll-around neighborhood. Accommodations are attractive, with king- or queen-size beds and decorated in muted modern colors. All rooms here have cable color televisions, direct-dial telephones, and an in-house movie system, and there's a coin laundry on the premises. Here, too, complimentary airport transportation is included in rates of $79 to $90 double.

The Rose Manor Motel, 4546 S.E. McLoughlin Blvd., Portland, OR 97202 (tel. 503/236-4175), is a couple of miles south of town on Ore. 99E at Holgate Boulevard. You can really spread out here on the acres of grounds across which this cluster of buildings spreads. Flowers are everywhere, a blooming profusion of color you can see from many rooms. Some of those accommodations are in one-story buildings, some in two-story frame constructions, and some are full houses large enough for a family or several couples. A number of accommodations have kitchens, as do the two- and three-bedroom units, but if you're not cooking on this vacation, there's a restaurant next door. Furnishings tend toward the eclectic, but colors are bright, and upkeep is to be praised. Prices here range from $30 to $34; higher, naturally, for very large accommodations.

The Mallory Motor Hotel, 729 S.W. 15th Ave. (at Yamhill Street), Portland, OR 97205 (tel. 503/223-6311, or toll free 800/228-8657, 800/824-4919 in Oregon), is a moderately priced favorite that has won the loyalty of many, including the late chef James Beard. Rooms are very spacious in this older hotel, and they're pleasantly furnished. Tucked away in a quiet neighborhood close to the Civic Auditorium, the Mallory has the advantage of easy parking outside crowded downtown streets. Many rooms have an attractive view of the west hills and the city farther away. As an extra lure, checkout time isn't until 2 p.m. Rates at the hotel are downright wonderful: $42 to $70. Really, really large suites are a very modest $65 to $70.

An outstanding choice both for price and location the **Riverside West Motel,** 50 S.W. Morrison St., Portland, OR 97204 (tel. 503/221-0711, or toll free 800/648-6440), is, as its name suggests, located right alongside the river. It's kept spiffily up-to-date, with good-looking furnishings in paneled rooms. Wide windows overlook the river and park across the way or city views, with those on the river side offering by far the best vistas. Rooms begin one level above the ground and extend up four floors, thus helping to alleviate traffic noises. Good soundproofing aids too. The Riverside's lobby has recently been decorated and is togged out in pleasant contemporary colors and fabrics. Its bilevel dining room is cozily intimate with attractive dark woods and shutters, strategically placed greenery, low lighting, and nice views. Even better, its kitchen has garnered good reviews for its preparation of shrimp scampi and prime rib in a reasonable $10 to $13 price range. A cozy bar features big banquettes in rose shades, intimate lighting, and a living-room atmosphere. The location could hardly be more convenient, near the city's historic section, restaurants, and office buildings, yet off by itself in one of the less congested sections of town. Free parking here too. Rates are $59 for rooms with queen-size beds, $63 for rooms with two double or king-size beds and balcony rooms.

A sister property, the **Portland Motor Hotel,** 1414 S.W. Sixth Ave., Portland, OR 97201 (tel. 503/221-1611, or toll free 800/648-6440), is a moderately priced downtown hotel with all the amenities plus the convenience of free parking. A small flower-rimmed swimming pool and sundeck, raised a story up from the street, are popular on sunny days. A cleverly executed wall mural backdrop gives you the feeling you're down on the Oregon coast swimming within view of pines. That attractive pool area also provides a garden view from wide windows in the hotel's 144 rooms. Built in an L-shape overlooking the pool, the Portland Motor Hotel has a particularly attractive coffeeshop that, unlike many similar facilities, offers diners private corners in an attractively decorated atmosphere including a bank of windows and fresh flowers. Dinner prices are in the $10 to $13 range. Free parking beneath and behind the hotel too. Service is courteous, prompt, and efficient, as befits a hotel frequented by business travelers. Rates at the Portland Motor Hotel are $65 to $70 double for rooms with queen- or king-size beds or two doubles. An additional person sharing a room is $8.

A cocktail lounge and coffeeshop are particularly attractive at the **Imperial Hotel**, 400 S.W. Broadway (at Stark), Portland, OR 97205 (tel. 503/228-7221, or toll free 800/547-8282, 800/452-2323 in Oregon). Dark-wood paneling, brass trim, and low lighting create an intimate atmosphere conducive to quiet conversation and out-of-the-office business meetings. While this is not a fancy hotel, it is well maintained and features extra-long beds and wood furnishings in small rooms. Paneled walls add a homey warmth enhanced by bright color schemes. All rooms have color televisions, air conditioning, alarm clocks, radios, and free parking. Rates at the Imperial, which is within easy walking distance of downtown shops and offices, are a reasonable $40 to $55 double, with the higher of those prices buying a queen- or king-size sleeper. Single rates are about $5 to $6 less.

Outside town near the airport, the **Chumaree Comfortel**, 8247 N.E. Sandy Blvd., Portland, OR 97220 (tel. 503/256-4111, or toll free 800/248-6273), is a stand-out among a cluster of moderately priced motels. The Chumaree has 120 units, some with balconies, and all with movies, radios, telephones. There's also a heated pool, sauna, and free airport transportation. Some suites here have fireplaces and a whirlpool. A pleasant restaurant, open from early morning to late evening, and a disco that takes over from there keep you filled and busy. Rates at the Chumaree are $55 to $61 double, including breakfast.

Small hotels are always pleasant, and a pleasant one here in Portland is the **Mark Spencer Hotel**, 409 S.W. 11th Ave., Portland, OR 97205 (tel. 503/224-3293). A bright and airy hotel with lots of nice little touches, the Mark Spencer features kitchens in every room, good-looking furnishings, and a friendly staff that's ready and willing to help you find your way around this city. This hotel is right downtown so it's easy to get from here to almost anywhere. Popular with traveling executives, the hotel has arrangements for its guests at a nearby athletic club. You'll find 104 studios or one-bedroom apartments here, and there are guest laundry facilities on the grounds. A sleek and contemporary spot, the Mark Spencer charges $49 to $69 a day for its quarters.

BUDGET-PRICED MOTELS: Dollarwise travelers will find motels here in the $30 to $40 range.

The **Jade Tree Motel**, 3939 N.E. Hancock St., Portland, OR 97212 (tel. 503/288-6891), is a simple three-story motel with parking beneath two stories of rooms. Some rooms are quite spacious and all are well maintained, with color television, radio, and free in-room movies. Located a bit out of town, the Jade Tree is on a main road that makes it easy to get into the center of the city. Colorful décor, one-day valet service, direct-dial phones, and courtesy coffee 18 hours a day all add to the allure of this modestly priced motel, which charges just $34 to $45 double.

If you happen to be arriving by helicopter, you can land at the **Best Western Flamingo Motel**, 9727 N.E. Sandy Blvd., Portland, OR 97220 (tel. 503/255-1400, or toll free 800/621-4358, 800/556-0006 in Oregon). This 200-unit motel near the airport offers some other amenities as well. Suites or deluxe rooms are all quite attractively decorated in light modern colors. The Flamingo has a coffeeshop and a more formal dining room plus a lounge with frequent evening entertainment. When outdoor entertainment's the goal, there's a swimming pool supplemented by a whirlpool and steamroom. The Best Western Flamingo charges $53 to $86 double.

Near the Portland Airport at the 82nd Avenue exit from I-84 at Ore. 213 are several inexpensive choices: The **Best Western Capri Motel,** Portland, OR 97220 (tel. 503/253-1151, or toll free 800/528-1234), has 42 rooms with color TV, movies, combination or shower baths, and phones in most rooms for $28 to $31. The **Cameo Motel,** 4111 N.E. 82nd Ave., Portland, OR 97220 (tel. 503/288-5981), has 41 units, most with refrigerators, air conditioning, color TVs, and some with radios, for $35 double.

The Bed-and-Breakfast Option

Pacific Bed & Breakfast, 701 N.W. 60th St., Seattle, WA 98107 (tel. 206/ 784-0539), can guide you to a network of private homes whose owners will welcome you into their homes and to their breakfast table. Rates at bed-and-breakfast stops are in the $30 to $50 range.

You may never see a lacier Victorian home than the **John Palmer House,** 4314 N. Mississippi Ave., Portland, OR 97217 (tel. 503/284-5893). One look at this wonder of spindles and rosettes, knobs and stained glass, columns and rooftop icing, and you'll wonder how on earth we turned to such mundane edifices as the all-American ranch house. A National Historic Landmark, this fabulous house is the work of two dedicated preservationists who spent more than 18 years sanding and painting, plastering and wallpapering. Here you will see the works, à la Victoriana: wainscoting, ceiling fans, borders, friezes, dados—and 37 different wallpaper patterns in keeping with the Victorians' love of mixing several different but complimentary wallpapers in the same room.

You can tour the house, have high tea there (see "What to Do"), or settle in here for a night of "Victorian Romance" during which you'll do some very elegant sleeping, complete with gardenias on your pillow, chilled champagne in silver coolers, baskets of fruit or flowers, chocolate, a private maid or butler, a five-to seven-course dinner, a massage, a carriage ride, even Victorian sleepwear! One of those memory-makers is $400 but wait—there are lower fewer-frills prices.

Rooms named for famous composers (Debussy, Schuman, Beethoven) or flowers (Wildflower and Chrysanthemum) are in the main house or the separate Grandma's Cottage. Some share a bath and some have private baths. Rates for a room with private bath are $65 to $95; those with shared bath are $40 to $65. If you'd like to learn more about Victorian homes, owners Mary and Richard Sauter will tell you how to get a copy of a new book, *Daughters of Painted Ladies,* which features Victorian homes all over the nation. Naturally, the John Palmer House is in it.

Camping and Hosteling

Campers can find a berth at the **Trailer Park of Portland,** 6645 S.W. Nyberg Rd., Portland, OR 97225 (tel. 503/692-0225), which has full hookups, showers, and a store nearby. Rates are $15.

Hostel fans—well, *female* hostel fans—have an option here: the **YWCA Youth Hostel,** 1111 S.W. Tenth Ave., Portland, OR 97205 (tel. 503/223-6281), which offers accommodations for $8.75 in a shared room, $17.50 single. Recent renovations have made this Y spiffier and now there's a small lounge with television, a laundromat, and a microwave oven and refrigerator for light meal preparation.

4. WHERE TO DINE

Old Town is Portland's most historic district, its original riverfront business center. Restored in recent years, the region now offers some of the best dining spots in the city. But historic or flashy, Portland does not lack for restaurants in every price range. We've picked out some of the most popular restaurants and arranged them for you by specialty and in roughly descending price order.

SEAFOOD: With water, water everywhere, seafood is always a good choice. Crayfish, a cult hereabouts, are featured on many a menu and some people even go out digging in the rivers for their own supply. A restaurant called **Jake's Famous Crawfish,** 401 S.W. 12th Ave. (tel. 503/226-1419), has made itself famous hereabouts serving those and other fishy fare. You will chow into a stupor here on quantities of food, blithely served up with good sauces and plenty of accompaniments. Salmon is on the menu, of course, as are Oregon oysters, crab, snapper, whatever's up out of the blue today. Stop by even if you've already eaten to cozy up to a fireplace and fancy bar. You're not likely to pay more than $10 to $15 for dinner, although you might add a bit for a bottle of Northwest wine. Jake's is open from 11 a.m. to 3 p.m. weekdays for lunch, from 5 to 11 p.m. daily for dinner.

Up in these cold waters, oysters are downright wonderful. If you'd like to try them in several different forms, head for **Dan & Louis Oyster Bar,** 208 S.W. Ankeny (tel. 503/227-5906), where Yaquina Bay oysters turn up on the half shell and in a fabulous oyster stew, among other preparations, including steamed seafood. Very lively nautical atmosphere here to get you in the mood. Prices are in the $10 or less range for dinner, and hours are 11 a.m. to midnight daily.

You'll find those finny creations in almost every Portland restaurant, but the most unusual surely must be **Digger O'Dell's,** 532 S.E. Grand Ave. (tel. 503/238-6996). Digger's, you see, is in an old funeral home turned restaurant. While that may seem a bit on the funereal side, it manages to be just the opposite, thanks to some good cooking. Gumbo and filé, spiced crayfish, all those Créole flavors that are sweeping the country these days, are on the menu. Served as they are in Digger's oldtime Cajun atmosphere, these vittles draw lively crowds. You'll pay $12 to $17 or so for dinner, served from 5 to 10 p.m. daily. Lunch weekdays is from 11 a.m. to 4 p.m.

Opus Too, 33 N.W. Second Ave. (tel. 503/222-6077), is widely known for its recorded jazz music and noted as well for good steaks, chops, and seafood broiled over mesquite wood. Mesquite broiling has become the rage in recent years, so if you've never tried it, this is the place to sample it. Prices are in the $12 to $15 range. Opus Too has a lounge called Jazz de Opus where entertainment is often featured. Hours at Opus Too are 11 a.m. to 3 p.m. weekdays and Saturday, 5 p.m. to midnight daily, closing at 11 p.m. on Sunday.

The **Couch Street Fish House,** 105 N.W. Third Ave. (tel. 503/223-6173), is a showy spot with a bilevel dining room outfitted in velvet. On the menu are some excellent seafood dishes, ranging from lobster that you can pick out of the tank yourself to scallops, sole, snapper, and tuna. Prices are in the $12 to $17 range, and hours are 5 to 10 p.m. (later on weekends) for dinner daily, closing half an hour earlier on Sunday.

Who can resist a seafood restaurant that says it's "approved by the Sturgeon General"? Certainly we can't, and we were glad we didn't after we tried the **Newport Bay Restaurant,** 0425 S.W. Montgomery (tel. 503/227-3474). A two-story spot with a stunning full-circle view, the Newport Bay features fish and chips on the floating deck and an excellent, light seafood menu. Prices for dinner fall in the $12 to $15 bracket and the restaurant is open from 11 a.m. to 11 p.m. daily, later on weekends.

CONTINENTAL/STEAKS: Continental preparations of beef and seafood couldn't be better than in this cattle land by the sea.

The Westin Benson Hotel is quite a beauty, so it won't come as any surprise that the hotel's **London Grill,** 309 S.W. Broadway (tel. 503/228-2000), is a serene sanctuary too. Unlike many restaurants, it is as much the service as the food that sets this place apart. Efficient, refreshingly frank in suggestions both for and against certain menu items, these formally dressed workers are what service ought to be everywhere, neither arrogant nor fawning. Meanwhile, the surroundings are as beautiful as the workers are efficient. That beautiful wood paneling that makes the rest of the hotel such a showpiece turns up here too, lining the walls and rising to a vaulted ceiling where chandeliers glow. Fresh flowers everywhere add the final touch to perfection. All this creates an atmosphere that suits the name of this restaurant quite well indeed. A London Grill it is, and a London Grill it remains, in menu as well. Top selections here are steaks and beef in various continental preparations, chops, and seafood. You'll pay prices in the $15 to $25 range for dinner, but you will delight in every minute of the serenity, sophistication, and good food. The London Grill is open from 6:30 a.m. to 2 p.m. and 5:30 to 11 p.m. daily (remaining open two hours later at Saturday and Sunday lunch).

Ringside, 2165 W. Burnside (tel. 503/223-1513), is everyone's answer to a request for a good steakhouse. It turns out that the ephemeral "everybody" is right this time, so when you're in the mood for a great steak cooked exactly the way you want it, head over here. Onion rings are as famous as the steak, so you might as well indulge in some of those as well. Salads are salads, their crisp greens just what you've come to expect—no funny-looking surprises, no odd flavors. Service is steakhouse efficient, no-nonsense that gets the job done and right—great place. Good prices in the $12 to $17 range. Hours are 11 a.m. to 2:30 p.m. weekdays and 5 p.m. to midnight daily, opening and closing an hour earlier on Sunday. Ringside East is at 14021 N.E. Glisan (tel. 503/255-0750).

The view is quite spectacular at Hilton's **Panorama Room,** 921 S.W. Sixth Ave. (tel. 503/226-1611), high atop the Hilton, overlooking this glittering waterside city. Continental preparations including plenty of steak and beef selections, interspersed with good local seafood, are featured for prices in the $20 range. Hours at the top are 5:30 to 10 p.m. daily.

Atwater's, 111 S.W. 5th St., in the U.S. Bancorp Tower (tel. 503/220-3600), is perhaps the poshest place in town, or at least well in the running. Occupying a lofty aerie on the 30th floor of the tallest building in the city, Atwater's is a toney spot in which to see and be seen by the city's power brokers. An elegant eaterie in the grand style, Atwater's has often been named the most atmospheric and the best all-around restaurant in Portland. Steaks, poultry, and the freshest of seafood presented imaginatively and with flair are the mainstays of this classic, where the prices can soar as high as the floor if you indulge in grand style but will probably average out about $15 to $20 for entrees. Hours here are 5:30 to 10 p.m. daily, plus 10 a.m. to 2:30 for Sunday brunch, with extended hours in the lounge where light meals also are served.

Thirty One Northwest, 31 N.W. 23rd Pl. (tel. 503/223-0106), is another award-winning spot that has been wowing Portland's gourmets for many a moon now. You can never predict just what will be on the menu here, which is one of the restaurant's charms. By design the options are altered every two months, not so difficult a task up here in the Northwest where the seasonal specialties are many and varied and oft-changing. Northwestern touches—unusual combinations of food, a nouvelle approach—appear here, but European touches are more evident. A very, very good restaurant, Thirty One Northwest is open from 11:30 a.m. to 2:30 p.m. weekdays and 5:30 to 10 p.m. daily except Sunday. Prices are in the $12 to $17 range for entrees. If you like wine, Thirty One has a most impressive wine list that has garnered many plaudits in the Northwest.

TRENDY SPOTS: Here are a few of the places where the up-and-coming get up and go.

You can always count on **McCormick & Schmick's,** 235 S.W. First Ave. (tel. 503/224-7522), to be wall-to-wall with the up-and-coming, who up and come here to dine in a slickly moderne spot that prepares salmon smoked over alderwood. In a décor of wood floors, paddle fans, brass, and glass, M & S produces a menu of fresh seafood offerings, each day supplemented by fettuccine, salads, steaks, duck, veal—in short, something for everybody. For dinner at this very popular place you'll pay $9 to $25. Hours at McCormick & Schmick's are 11:30 a.m. to 2 p.m. weekdays, 5 to 11 p.m. daily, closing an hour earlier on Sunday.

Sweet Tibbie Dunbar's, 718 N.E. 12th Ave. (tel. 503/232-1801), is filled with antiques and plants that give a cozy, pubby atmosphere. That pubbiness is why most people come here, although the food is good too, focusing on steaks and seafood served by helpers in 18th-century costumes and waiters in tuxes. Open daily from 11 a.m. to 11 p.m., with prices in the $10 to $15 range.

Metro on Broadway, 911 S.W. Broadway (tel. 503/227-2746), is a local gathering-spot of note. An eclectic mélange of chic and trendy—the restaurant has six separate establishments serving everything from breakfast to pizza, pasta, Chinese, Mexican—it's a very, very favorite with the region's fashionable and artsy crowd who come here to meet a friend or to make one. Espresso, specialty coffees, imported and local beer, and wine join crêpes, sandwiches, salads, and even waffles. Penultimate place to see and be seen in Portland, the Metro on Broadway, also happens to be quite convenient to the city's Schnitzer Concert Hall, movie houses, and Pioneer Square. Hours are 7 a.m. to 11 p.m., later on weekends, and 11 a.m. to 7 p.m. on Sunday.

B. Moloch, 901 S.W. Salmon St. (tel. 503/227-5700), is named after the artist whose large paintings grace the walls of this large hotel just off the Park Blocks. A spin-off of the Heathman Hotel, the restaurant is perhaps better known locally for its bakery and pub. Breads and innovative pizzas—say, topped with smoked salmon, roast peppers, feta cheese, and shrimp—pour from a huge wood-burning oven. Salads and made-today specialties chalked on a blackboard are all part of this deli-like spot that also specializes in a game pâté. Open from 7 a.m. to 11 p.m. on weekdays and 8 a.m. to midnight Saturday and Sunday, the restaurant manages to keep its prices low: $2 to $4 for breakfast, $2.50 to $6 for lunch, and $4.95 to $8.95 for dinner.

Modern Times, 53 N.W. First Ave. (tel. 503/223-0743), is subtle and understated in both interior design and cuisine. You'll find some unusual Northwest concoctions on the menu here: smoked fish ravioli; cucumber soup; lamb sirloin with juniperberry glaze; a veal, pork, and range-fed chicken pâté. As for the décor: brick walls, wood floors, some artwork, simply designed tables, and outside, a handsome and tranquil brick patio. Lunch, Tuesday through Friday from 11:30 a.m. to 2 p.m., will run from $4.50 to $7.50. Dinner, available Wednesday through Saturday (Tuesday in summer only) from 5:30 to 10:30 p.m., ranges from $6.95 to $14.

FRENCH: At **L'Auberge,** 2601 N.W. Vaughn St. (tel. 503/223-3302), your evening may begin with a homemade country pâté and some crusty bread and move along with creamy, herbed soups. Whatever looks best in the market will be featured in main courses that are likely to range from chicken to lamb to trout. Beef lovers will always find flavorful tournedos topped with a perfect béarnaise sauce, while fans of unusual flavors should seek out one out-of-the-ordinary choice: lamb marinated in pomegranate juice. Vegetables are as fresh as other foods and are treated with a light touch in this kitchen, which also produces flaky pastries and fruit-filled desserts. If you're looking for a light dinner, it can be had in a cozy bar here. Otherwise, prices are likely to run in the $24 to $35 range. Hours are 5 p.m. to midnight Monday through Thursday, to 1 a.m. on Friday and Saturday, and 5:30 p.m. to midnight on Sunday.

Le Cuisinier, 1308 W. Burnside (tel. 503/224-4260), may be small in size but is huge in reputation. You'll find fewer than a dozen tables in this enormously popular restaurant presided over by a former chef at Chicago's famed La Perroquet. In these tiny but tastefully decorated environs you will dine on six or seven courses that begin with an elegant apéritif, move on to an array of tiny appetizers, then to a creamy soup. With it comes French bread, incorporating whole grains, hot from the oven. Each night chef Karl Schaefer produces four or five selections that range widely from a delicately roasted breast of duck lightly touched with herbs (from a garden here) to the best of fresh salmon or beef in elegant, carefully orchestrated preparations. On then to salad, light soufflé desserts, or pastries. For a wonderful dinner in cozy surroundings, for which reservations are mandatory, you should figure $25 to $35 per person plus wines. Hours at Le Cuisinier are 6 to 10 p.m. Thursday through Saturday.

Café des Amis is in a cozy location at 1987 N.W. Kearney (tel. 503/295-6487), formerly the home of another French restaurant. Café des Amis applies its French flavors to an interesting range of fresh-from-the-market basics teamed with unexpected ingredients. Highlights of this small but very popular restaurant are filet of beef with port-garlic sauce, duck with lime and green pepper sauce, and a seafood selection that may include salmon Troisgrois or marlin grenoblois. We, however, are partial to a selection called Chicken in Hell's Fire! Salads are wondrous and include, as do many entree selections, a sprinkling of nuts and/or cheese. Flavors of mustard, saffron, walnuts, or champagne are accompanied by fresh breads baked right here. Wonderful, as are prices: figure $10 to $15 for dinner and trimmings. Café des Amis is open from 5:30 to 10 p.m. Monday through Thursday, to 11 p.m. on Friday and Saturday; closed Sunday.

ITALIAN: Buon appetito! Easily at the top of the Italian dining list in Portland is **Genoa,** 2832 S.E. Belmont St. (tel. 503/238-1464), where you feast your way through seven courses. For an opener at this tiny restaurant you may find a not-often-seen Italian treat called bagna cauda, a hot vegetable dip redolent with the flavors of garlic, herbs, and cream. On to soups with market-fresh ingredients, then to pastas topped, perhaps, with vegetables, then to main courses treated with those ingredients only the Italians seem able to use successfully: pine nuts, prosciutto, cheeses. As for dessert, well, throw caution to the wind and tuck into a layer cake and ice cream combo that does indeed border on indescribable. Because it's very small, Genoa is very crowded, so reservations are a must. For a dinner to remember here, you will pay a fixed price of $35 but you won't regret a penny of it. Genoa is open from 6 to 10:30 p.m. daily except Sunday.

On a cool, rainy day—and there are occasionally such things here—we'd head for the warmth and goodwill at Delphina's, not even to mention the hot pizzas rolling out of the ovens. A very cozy spot, **Delphina's,** 2111 N.W. Kearny (tel. 503/221-1195), is a study in bricks, arches, high ceilings, and a packed bar. If pizza's not your pie, pastas are first-rate too. Beyond that, try one of the special preparations of chicken or veal in robust sauces. Prices are in the $10 to $15 range, and hours are 11:30 a.m. to 2 p.m. weekdays and 5 to 11 p.m. daily. Weather permitting, you can dine al fresco.

You'll find the **Old Spaghetti Factory,** 6715 S.W. Bancroft (tel. 503/222-5375), playing its historic connections to the hilt to create a restaurant that's cozy, charming, brash, eclectic, lively, and very modestly priced. On the wood floors are some lovely carpets, including a smashing royal-blue one at the front. Antiques abound. You'll see old plug-in switchboards, 19th-century barber chairs, heavy antique tables and buffets, even a massive old black safe. An antique Wurlitzer is featured at the entrance. On the menu are fresh pastas, made right here from semolina flour and served in many shapes and with many kinds of sauces. An unusual option is spaghetti with browned butter and Mizithra cheese. Even the bill will make you smile here. For a pasta dinner accompanied by fresh sourdough bread, garlic butter, salad, beverage, and spumoni, you won't pay more than $6 or $7, and kids eat for less than that. Inexpensive California wines and beers are available too. Hours here are 11 a.m. to 2 p.m. and 5 to 10 p.m. weekdays, closing at 11 p.m. on weekends, and from 4 to 10 p.m. on Sunday.

A POTPOURRI OF FLAVORS: Internationality is characteristic of Portland and its restaurants are no exception.

Alexis, 215 W. Burnside (tel. 503/224-8577), fancies Greek flavors and does them so well the crowds throng here to partake. Greek salads are, of course, among the bestsellers, but moussaka and dolmadakia are close rivals. The décor's not showy, and in fact there's not much to look at beyond white walls and bustling waiters, but it's just that simplicity that makes it so like a part of Greece removed to foreign shores. Great Greek olives, of course, and some interesting preparations of seafood, á la grecque, naturally. Prices are in the $7 to $12 range for dinner, served from 5 to 11 p.m. daily. Lunch is served from 11:30 a.m. to 2 p.m. weekdays.

Uncle Chen, 529 S.W. Third Ave. (tel. 503/248-1199), offers every kind of Chinese culinary style imaginable to audiences that have been pouring in here for ages. Szechuan, Peking, Canton, Hunan—could you ask for more? Local seafood in one of these distinctive styles, in the $10 to $12 range, is a good way to make the best use of Northwest products and those deliciously fresh Chinese flavors. Uncle Chen is open from 11 a.m. to 10 p.m. Monday through Saturday and 5 to 9 p.m. on Sunday.

The biggest crowds in town are at **Casa de Rios,** 4343 S.E. Hawthorn (tel. 503/234-0137), the local favorite of taco and tamale fanciers. Prices are in the $10-or-less bracket, and hours are 11 a.m. to 11 p.m. daily.

Polynesian flavors and those showy drink concoctions are featured at **Trader Vic's,** in the Westin Benson Hotel, 309 S.W. Broadway (tel. 503/295-4130), here and everywhere. Despite its many clones in Westin hotels, Trader Vic's still does a great job turning good basic ingredients into interesting dishes featuring the best of Chinese and Polynesian ingredients. Take a look at the Chinese ovens, if you haven't seen them before—quite impressive. Service is wonderfully efficient and the atmosphere is always exotic, if predictable. Hors d'oeuvres are particularly outstanding at this Trader Vic's. Prices are high, in the $15 to $20 range, and hours are 11:30 a.m. to 2:30 p.m. weekdays for lunch, daily except Sunday from 5 to 11 p.m. for dinner, until 2 a.m. or so in the lounge.

Once you've discovered the subtleties and exotic flavors of Indian cooking, you'll be hooked. Now's as good a time as any, so why not stop by **Indigine,** 3725 S.E. Division St. (tel. 503/238-1470), where you can sample all the flavors, and then some, at weekend banquets specializing in Indian treats. You will also find some good vegetable and seafood simply cooked. And the price is right—$10 to $15 or less for a three-course dinner, served from 5:30 to 10 p.m. Tuesday through Saturday; closed Sunday and Monday.

Chinese flavors are irresistible, and one always feels so, well, saintly, when dining on bamboo sprouts and the like. Take a chance at sainthood, however temporary, at **Chang's Yangtze,** 921 S.W. Morrison (tel. 503/241-0218). All the Chinese favorites are here as well as some of the spicier, red-hot cooking, if you like. On really flush days, order a feast for the whole party and try a little of everything. Prices are typically Chinese-reasonable, with dinner unlikely to top $10 to $15, perhaps less. Hours at the restaurant are 11:30 a.m. to 11 p.m. Monday through Saturday and on Sunday from 5 to 10:30 p.m.

Koji Osakaya, 7007 S.W. Macadam St. (tel. 503/293-1066), is as Japanese as you probably would want to get this side of the Pacific. A lively, chattery, busy spot, Koji Osakaya has a big sushi bar and, for those with a yen for the unusual, there's sumo wrestling on video—beat that! Prices are in the $12 to $15 range or less, depending on the size of your appetite, and hours are 11:30 a.m. to 2 p.m. weekdays and 5:30 to 10 p.m. daily.

You'll find four **Macheesmo Mouse** havens in Portland, the primary one at 811 N.W. 23rd Ave. (tel. 503/274-0500) and others at 3553 S.W. Hawthorne (tel. 503/232-6588), 715 S.W. Salmon (tel. 503/228-3491), and 1200 N.E. Broadway (tel. 503/249-0002). All feature trendy, contemporary-even-unto-the-21st-century décor with hi-tech overtones and lots of glitz. This mouse has skyrocketed to popularity in Portland, thanks in part to its good, inexpensive ($2 to $4), and very quick Mexican cooking. A beer-and-wine-only spot, the mouse roars from 11 a.m. to 10 p.m. daily, opening at noon on Sunday.

LIGHT DINING:

Portland has plenty of interesting spots offering light meals and lunches.

Molly Bloom's, 50 S.W. Pine St. (tel. 503/224-2270), is one of those places you hate to categorize because they could fit so many places. We've put Molly's here only because it's so refreshing in its offerings and atmosphere that it seems to us the kind of place you select when you're seeking a restaurant that's casual in dress but careful in cooking.

At Molly's high-backed booths line an open, airy storefront restaurant adorned with lamps hanging from high ceilings. Each day whatever's cooking in the kitchen is chalked onto a blackboard at the front, while always-available offerings appear on a small paper menu. Among those always-available choices are a bouillabaisse filled with steamer clams, snapper, prawns, and saffron; and fettucine topped with fresh scallops or a salmon-cream sauce. Creamy chocolate cheesecake is always on hand, as are shrimp salad and sandwiches, including a vegetarian selection of cheddar, havarti, and cream cheese with avocado, tomato, and almonds. Top it off with an imported brew or one of the Northwest's beers or wine. You needn't fear a terrifying check either: nothing on the menu tops $10! Hours are 11:30 a.m. to 2 p.m. for lunch Monday through Friday, and 5 to 9 p.m. for dinner Monday through Saturday; closed Sunday.

Breakfasts are the lure at the **Bijou Café,** 132 S.W. 3rd St. (tel. 503/222-3187). A simple spot with wood floors and plain furnishings, the Bijou produces eggs in any style you can dream up, good waffles and pancakes, fresh muffins, roast beef hash, and something different: a breakfast of bacon and tomatoes on toast. Hamburgers predominate at lunch, vying with salads, and that's it for the day—the restaurant closes at 3 p.m. Prices are very reasonable, in the $5 bracket, give or take a little, and opening hour is 7 a.m. daily.

Crêpes star at **Crêpe Faire,** 133 S.W. Second Ave. (tel. 503/227-3365), a really lovely place with tall columns, enormously high ceilings, and banquettes outfitted in soft rosy shades. Rich quiches with interesting ingredients are on the menu, as are quite innovative salad combinations. Evenings the list expands a bit to include beef, veal, and chicken entrees, but even those are kept light in accordance with the culinary philosophy here. A small espresso/wine bar is Crêpe Faire owner Hank Hazen's latest and very popular innovation; the espresso has been specially blended for Crêpe Faire and complements the extensive Northwest wine list Hazen has developed over the last 15 years. Dinner entree prices are in the $10 to $15 range. Crêpe Faire is open from 7:30 to 10:30 a.m. for breakfast, from 11:30 a.m. to 2:30 p.m. for lunch, and from 5:30 to 11 p.m. for dinner; closed Sunday.

Another popular breakfast spot is the **Original Pancake House,** 8600 S.W. Barbur Blvd. (tel. 503/246-9007), out of town a bit but not far enough to discourage the crowds that pour in here, particularly on weekends. As you might guess, pancakes are the lure, and at this spot they're created with every kind of ingredient and topping as yet invented. Pancakes are light and huge, so be hungry when you head for this spot. The Original Pancake House has been around since forever, so they must be doing something right. Hours are 7 a.m. to 3 p.m. daily except Monday and Tuesday, and prices are in the $5 to $7 range.

5. AFTER DARK

From theater performances to a few orchestrated yuks, Portland can fill your evenings. We hasten to add, however, that lounge entertainment fads wax and wane here, just as they do in any big city. What's hot today is not tomorrow, so check around before you go.

Portland likes its laughs, so you'll find several clubs catering to comics. Among them is **Last Laugh,** 426 N.W. Sixth Ave. (tel. 503/29-LAUGH).

Among the hotel lounges at which you can expect to find entertainment designed to match the prevalent fancy are several in hotels we've already mentioned, including the lobby lounge and Trader Vic's at the Westin Benson Hotel, and lounges at the Portland Motor Hotel, the Hilton Hotel, and the Riverside West Motor Hotel.

Some other very popular trendy lounges with entertainment are **Sweet Tibbie Dunbar,** N.E. 12th Ave. and Irving Street (tel. 503/232-1801); **Wilf's,** 800 N.W. Sixth Ave. (tel. 503/223-0070); and **Remo's,** 14th Avenue and Gleason Street (tel. 503/221-1150), which also serves up priced-right Italian cuisine in the $10 to $15 bracket. Music begins at 9 p.m. nightly and goes on to the wee hours, but dinner is served from 5:30 to 11 p.m. only, a bit later on weekends.

For country and western folks, a 24-hour (!) twanger called **The Rimrock,** 240 N.E. Columbia Blvd. (tel. 503/289-1723), is the place, with entertainment and dancing nightly.

Jazz buffs can be found at **Key Largo,** 31 N.W. First Ave. (tel. 503/223-9919); **Jazz de Opus and Opus Too** (see "Where to Dine"), which features jazz musicians too at its restaurant and lounge at 33 N.W. Second Ave. (tel. 503/222-6077); at **The Hobbitt,** 4420 S.E. 39th St. (tel. 503/771-0742), where jazz musicians pour out the sounds every night and the dining emporium here is open from 11 a.m. to 2 a.m.; and in a dozen or more other clubs in the city. The Greater Portland Convention and Visitors Association can provide you with a list of local jazz clubs.

6. WHAT TO SEE AND DO

Parks are big in Portland, and if the natural world piques your imagination, you'll find a wide range of flora and fauna from lotus blossoms to penguins, from stunning rose gardens to acclaimed Japanese gardens.

BONSAI, BLOOMS, BEAVERS, AND BIG TREES: Washington Park is one place where you can visit all of these in one spot. Begin with the **Washington Park Zoo,** which you'll find west of town on U.S. 26, at 4001 S.W. Canyon Rd. (tel. 503/226-1561). A large herd of Asian elephants lives here, its adorably pudgy babies carefully protected by proud mamas and papas. You can watch the otters paddle around underwater and see beavers cuddling up in their watery homes or get a closeup look at an orangutan which may bear a surprising resemblance to your boss. Hours at the zoo are 9 a.m. to 7 p.m. May to September, to 5:30 p.m. in other months (closing at 4 p.m. in October), and admission is $3 for adults, $1.50 for children 3 to 11. Open daily. A new restaurant here is called Africafé and serves a variety of sandwiches, salads, fancy desserts, and even dinners.

At the zoo you can climb aboard a convenient little train that toots off through the forest and drops you off near the **Japanese Gardens,** on S.W. Kingston Street (tel. 503/223-1321). Surely there is no serenity created by man that can surpass that of a Japanese garden. Portland has one of the most beautiful Japanese gardens in the world according to people who rate these things. Here you can wander through the five traditional garden types: Sand and Stone Garden, Flat Garden, Strolling Pond Garden, Tea Garden, and Natural Garden. One of the most authentic such gardens outside Japan, this retreat covers more than five acres and features a new pavilion where Ikebana and Bonsai exhibits are often staged. Hours at the garden, which is just as lovely in summer as in winter, are 10 a.m. to 6 p.m. from mid-April to mid-September, closing at 4 p.m. in other months and closed Thanksgiving, Christmas, and New Year's Days. Admission is $3.50 for adults, $2 for seniors and students.

Washington Park is also home to the **International Rose Test Gardens** (tel. 503/796-5193), where thousands of blooms in every color of the rainbow fill the air with rose perfume. A section of the garden at 400 S.W. Kingston Street is called the **Shakespeare Garden** and features all the flowers mentioned by the bard.

The **Oregon Museum of Science and Industry,** 4015 S.W. Canyon Rd. (tel. 503/222-2828), is adjacent to Washington Park Zoo and is a highly praised museum, featuring everything from a walk-through human heart to a planetarium, stereoscopic vision display, sugar-makes-electricity exhibit, a ship's bridge, a DC-3 aircraft, and a visit with Dr. Know, a computer psychologist. Hours are 9 a.m. to 5 p.m. Saturday through Thursday, to 8 p.m. on Friday. Admission is $5 for adults and $3 for children 3 to 17.

Forestry was—and is—an industry vital to Oregon's economy. To learn more about how that industry operates and what effect it has had on growth here, stop by the **World Forestry Center,** 4033 S.W. Canyon Rd. (tel. 503/228-1367). Located about three miles out of town at the Zoo-OMSI-Forestry Center exit, the center is open from 10 a.m. to 5 p.m. daily. A 1909 Shay steam locomotive used to haul logs is on display.

To complete your education, you can drive to **Magness Memorial Tree Farm,** 30 minutes south on I-5, and see forestry refurbishment in action (open daily during daylight hours). Admission to the Forestry Center is $2 for adults, $1 for youngsters 7 to 18. A gift shop offers some interesting Oregon wood products.

Still more in or near Washington Park: **Hoyt Arboretum,** a tree-lovers' paradise and home to 650 kinds of trees and shrubs you can see on a self-guided tour of the grounds. Hours are dawn to dusk daily and the visitor center is open from 10 a.m. to 4 p.m. daily. On Saturday and Sunday at 2 p.m. from April to November guides conduct tours through the arboretum. Admission is free.

To get to Washington Park, take I-405 to U.S. 26 west. Zoo, OMSI, and garden entrances can all be reached from S.W. Canyon Road. You can telephone the park bureau at 503/796-5193 or 228-8732.

MORE PARKS AND GARDENS: Portland is a pretty city, one very aware that human eyes need sky views as well as skyscrapers. Among the most beautiful open spaces in town is **Forest Park,** 2960 N.W. Upshur (tel. 503/796-5193). Here you'll find a huge 4,800-acre park that is still a natural wilderness. Hiking the 40 miles of trails may give you a look at a deer or one of the many other animals that live deep in this forest acreage. Information on the park and its facilities are available at the park from the Visitors Association.

    Peninsula Park's Sunken Rose Garden, at North Ainsworth and North Albina Street (tel. 503/796-5193), is home to more than 700 different kinds of roses that begin blooming in May and just bloom their colorful little hearts out all summer and well into the fall. Admission is free and the park is open from dawn to dusk daily.

    Rhododendrons are tough to spell but they're beautiful to look at here in the **Crystal Springs Rhododendron Gardens,** Crystal Springs Island, East-moreland Golf Course, 6149 S.E. 28th Ave. (tel. 503/775-2900). Thousands of the frothy blossoms bloom on command in April and May each year, and the display is free, open daily from 8 a.m. to dark.

    Grotto, Sanctuary of Our Sorrowful Mother, at N.E. 85th Street and Sandy Boulevard (tel. 503/254-7371), is a grotto garden operated by the Friar Servants of Mary (Servites) who keep 60 acres of tranquility abloom. The sanctuary includes a replica of Michaelangelo's *Pietà* set into a grotto and some handsome woodcarvings as well as a monastery rose garden. Panoramic views are pretty, too, in this very peaceful clifftop garden. Mass is celebrated outdoors here May through September at noon each Sunday. The lower grounds are open from 9 a.m. to 6 p.m. daily and the upper gardens are on view from 9 a.m. to 5 p.m. An elevator whizzes you up the ten-story cliff at $2 for adults and $1 for students 6 to 18 and seniors. To get to the grotto, take U.S. 205 to Sandy Boulevard.

TOURING RIVERS AND ROSES: By land or by river there's plenty to see. Portland's proximity to water, as its name suggests, put it on pioneer maps. Although today the city seems to take less advantage of its waterways than it could, you can explore them on **riverboat cruises** down the Columbia or Willamette Rivers. Operated by Yachts-O-Fun, 5215 N. Emerson Dr. (tel. 503/289-6665), the cruises depart from docks on the Willamette just off I-5.

    From May through October twilight dinner cruises from downtown Portland to Oswego are a pleasant way to spend an evening. Departures are Wednesday through Sunday at 6:30 p.m. downtown at the I-205 bridge over the Willamette for the Oswego cruise; the highlight of the trip is a look at the waterfront homes. You're served dinner on board and return about three hours later. Price for that cruise is $29.50 per person including dinner.

    On Sunday a 90-minute brunch cruise leaves at 10 a.m. and 12:30 p.m. from Riverplace Marina and cruises the Willamette River for $19.50. On Wednesday, Thursday, and Friday harbor cruises leave at 1 and 3 p.m. and are $9 for adults, $5 for children. On Saturday, four-hour cruises depart at 10 a.m. for a trip up the Willamette to spectacular Willamette Falls. Price is $24.50 for adults, $17.50 for children under 12.

    The cruise season begins in May and runs through October aboard the *Cruis Ader Princess,* a 57-foot vessel. Some special cruises during the Rose Festival in June and at Christmas also are scheduled, but you'll need to call for exact dates and times.

    Grey Line Tours, Imperial Hotel, 400 S.W. Broadway (tel. 503/226-6755), offers an interesting variety of tours ranging from popular visits to snow-clad Mount Hood to Oregon coastal tours and Mount St. Helens expeditions. You might start with a tour of the city's plush west side, where you'll visit, among other stops, the Rose Gardens of which Portland is so proud. That tour departs daily from May through mid-October at 9 a.m. and lasts three hours. Price is $12 for adults, $6 for children under 12. Grey Line also has a three-hour tour to the delightful Japanese Gardens and Pittock Mansion, departing daily at 1 a.m. costing $11 for adults, $5.50 for children under 12. A city tour combining Rose and Japanese Gardens is $19 for adults, $9.50 for children under 12, and lasts seven hours. Visits to the Columbia Gorge and the Mount St. Helens volcano are $20 to $25 for adults, $10 to $12.50 for children under 12.

Portland Walking Tours (tel. 503/223-1017) will take you on two-hour walking tours of this city's intriguing downtown region with an accent on history and architecture for $3 per person with a minimum of $30 per tour. Advance scheduling is necessary. You can telephone, or write them at P.O. Box 4322, Portland, OR 97208.

Portland on Foot, 1611 S.E. Nehalem (tel. 503/235-4742), concentrates on the historic district on its Saturday tours. Tour groups meet at 10 a.m. at the Skidmore Fountain at S.W. First Avenue and Ankeny Street for a look at Old Town, and at 2 p.m. at S.W. First Avenue and Morrison Street for a tour of Yamhill Historic District. Prices are $2.50 for adults and $1 for children 6 to 17.

Broadway and Radio Cab Companies (see "Getting Around") both offer individual tours for flat fees to be negotiated.

VISITING PORTLAND'S PAST: As a vital part of the Old West, Portland is proud of its historic past and tries hard to preserve it. To begin your exploration of that past, stop in at the **Oregon Historical Society,** 1230 S.W. Park Ave. (tel. 503/222-1741), where ship models, a miniature wagon trail, and archeological discoveries will help put things into perspective. A free research and exhibit facility, the historical society has permanent exhibitions featuring Northwest explorers, Indians, and pioneers of the Oregon Trail. Admission is free and hours are 10 a.m. to 4:45 p.m. Monday through Saturday.

There or at the Portland Police Historical Museum (see below) you can pick up a map for a self-guided tour of the city's historic district called **Old Town.** Boundaries of this restored section of town are N.W. Tenth Avenue, S.W. Ankeney and N.W. Glisan Streets, and the Willamette River. Interesting restaurants and shops have moved into the old buildings, so you have a chance to examine some intriguing architecture while you're dining and shopping. In the Old Town be sure to take a look at **Ira's Fountain,** S.W. Third Avenue and Clay Street; here is a whole blockfull of watery resting places, complete with waterfalls, streams, and pools shaded by trees. Stylized concrete "trees" are splashed by 13,000 gallons of water a minute from 8:30 a.m. to 11 p.m. daily except Wednesday, the fountain's day of rest. Portland's most "people" place, Ira's Fountain lures laughing splashers, and toe-dipping is not discouraged.

Pittock Mansion, 3229 N.W. Pittock Dr. (tel. 503/248-4469), is a huge and glamorous old home built in 1914 by Henry Pittock, founder of Portland's daily newspaper, *The Oregonian.* Writing must once have been a profitable career, for this turreted mansion has no fewer than 22 rooms. Its delightful French Renaissance architecture features many gables popping out of the roofline and a bevy of fireplaces. The mansion takes full advantage of its lofty 1,000-foot-high position with a spectacular view across two states, the Willamette and Columbia Rivers, and five snow-clad mountains in the Cascades. Now owned and operated by the Portland Bureau of Parks, the mansion is furnished with antiques and European artwork as well as some American furnishings. Delicate plasterwork, stunning marbles, and beautiful hardwood floors and paneling add to the glamour. Admission is $3 for adults, $2.50 for seniors, and $1 for students 6 to 18. Mansion hours are 1 to 5 p.m. daily; closed on major holidays and the first half of January.

A short walk down the Wildwood Trail from the Pittock Mansion is the

Portland Audubon Society, 5151 N.W. Cornell Rd. (tel. 503/292-6855). The sanctuary features over 110 species of birds fluttering about in a natural habitat that is open for hikes and picnics—the birds won't mind. The Audubon complex includes a wildlife rehabilitation center which is surrounded by a 160-acre sanctuary. Trails are open from dawn to dusk. There is no admission charge.

Another restored antique home in the area is the **John Palmer House,** a National Historic Landmark at 4314 N. Mississippi Ave., Swan Island exit from I-5 (tel. 503/284-5893). A good example of furbelowed Victorian architecture, the home was built in 1890 and sits up high off the ground, its gingerbread trim demanding attention. It's been featured in many national magazines for its delightful architecture and antique furnishings. Hours are 12:30 to 5 p.m. Thursday through Sunday, and admission is $3, free to youngsters under 8. A very refined spot, the John Palmer House also offers high tea and a tour by advance reservation only at 2 p.m. and 3:30 p.m. Thursday through Sunday for $10.

Old Church, 1422 S.W. 11th Ave. (tel. 503/222-2031), has outlasted all the other churches in the city—it's been a Portland landmark since 1883. Its architecture, known as carpenter Gothic, is as great a treat to the eye as its organ concerts are to the ear. Concerts are at noon Wednesday, and you're encouraged to avoid a rumbling tummy by bringing lunch. You can tour on your own with the help of information available at the church. Hours are 11 a.m. to 3 p.m. Tuesday through Saturday, and there is no admission charge.

It's difficult to separate Portland's history from lumber, for logs have always been vital to the city's growth and prosperity. You can get a look at the history of the logging industry in the state at the **Georgia Pacific Historical Museum,** 900 S.W. Fifth Ave. (tel. 503/248-7500). A diorama, photographs, and actual logging equipment are on display here, and a film in the museum theater helps you get the picture. Hours are Tuesday through Friday from 10 a.m. to 3 p.m., and there is no admission charge.

Police have a history too, albeit a rather frightening one at times. Here in Portland, however, the police force has put together its own **Portland Police Historical Museum,** 1111 S.W. Second Ave. (tel. 503/796-3019), where you can see some of the uniforms the officers used to wear and get as close a look as anyone would want at handcuffs and police guns. Officers here can also arm you with maps and a brochure that will guide you through a walking tour of the city's historic Old Town. The Police Museum is open from 10 a.m. to 3 p.m. Tuesday through Friday and is free.

KID STUFF: Portland has some places especially designed to unfetter the imaginations—and the energy—of children. Parks welcome children too, and have plenty of intriguing places for them to play.

At the **Children's Museum,** 3037 S.W. Second Ave. (tel. 503/248-4587), youngsters clamber about in a tree house, burrow in a tunnel, and participate in role-playing environments like a grocery store, a medical center, and a Zulu village. They can even investigate the Clayshop, a ceramic studio for the young. There's a playground here too. Hours are 9 a.m. to 5 p.m. Tuesday through Saturday and 11 a.m. to 5 p.m. on Sunday. Donations are requested: $2 for adults and $1.50 for children.

James F. Bybee House, in the 100-acre Howell Territorial Park, 13901 N.W. Howell Park Rd., over Sauvie Island Bridge, Sauvie Island (tel. 503/222-1741), was built in 1856 and focuses on pioneer life. Youngsters love the agricultural museum created with them in mind and its accent on farm life. Pioneers planted appleseeds here to create an orchard, now featuring many kinds of apples. Hours are noon to 5 p.m. daily from June through Labor Day, and while there's no admission charge, a donation is a nice gesture. While you're here, take a look at Sauvie Island itself, a wilderness island formed at the union of the Willamette and Columbia Rivers.

Some of the other attractions we've already mentioned—Washington Park Zoo, Oregon Museum of Science and Industry, the Western Forestry Center—are also favorites with the kids.

If it's rides they're demanding, head for **Oaks Amusement Park,** at the foot of S.E. Spokane Street (tel. 503/236-5722), where those tummy-turners operate from late May to September.

ARTS AND CULTURAL ACTIVITIES: Portland itself occupies a beautiful setting at the confluence of two rivers and in the shadow of Mount Hood and the Cascades, lovely scenery conducive to beautiful music and art.

The **Portland Art Museum,** 1219 S.W. Park Ave. at Jefferson (tel. 503/ 226-2811), covers quite a gamut in artwork from Renaissance paintings to current artists, from Pacific Northwest Indians' work to Greek art. That Indian work is among the finest in the Northwest and well worth a visit. A collection of English silver is fascinating too. Films and lectures occur regularly. Museum hours are 11 a.m. to 7 p.m. on Wednesday and Friday; 11 a.m. to 9:30 p.m. on Thursday, and noon to 5 p.m. on Saturday and Sunday. Admission is $3 for adults, $1.50 for seniors and students, and 50¢ for children 6 to 12.

Portland's Civic Auditorium and Arlene Schnitzer Concert Hall are now part of the **Portland Center for the Performing Arts,** 1111 S.W. Broadway (tel. 503/248-4335). It is home to the Ballet Oregon, the Choral Arts Ensemble, the Oregon Repertory Singers, the New Rose Theater troupe, the Pacific Ballet Theater, the Portland Civic Theater, the Portland Gay Men's Chorus, the Portland Symphonic Choir, the Storefront Theater group, and the West Coast Chamber Orchestra. Whew! To make this an even more intriguing place, the center is built around an antique structure, an ornate movie and vaudeville place opened in 1928 as the Paramount Theater. Some $20 million later, this is one of the city's top showplaces.

There's something going on here nearly every night of the year. You can find out what's happening when by calling the center or by looking in the entertainment sections of the daily *Portland Oregonian* newspaper, the *Portland Guide,* or the *Willamette Weekly.*

Portland's Repertory Theatre, Willamette Center, Skybridge Level, Salmon and S.W. Front Streets (tel. 503/224-4491), operates year round, producing a series of six plays in a compact and well-designed theater. Recent productions ranged from *Foxfire* to *Tartuffe.* Each of the plays in production in a season run for about a month. Willamette Rep is quite popular in Portland, so pre-opening previews and Saturday-night performances are often sold out well in advance. Individual tickets are $15 to $20. You can write for tickets to 25 S.W. Salmon St., Portland, OR 97204, or call and charge them by phone at 503/224-4491.

In summer months, primarily July and August, the city sponsors **free plays, recitals,** and **concerts** in the Washington Park amphitheater (tel. 503/ 226-1561).

To get a look at some **local art and craft work,** stop by the Lawrence Gallery, 842 S.W. First Ave. (tel. 503/224-9442), where changing exhibits feature the work of hundreds of artists. Hours are 10 a.m. to 6 p.m. weekdays and noon to 5 p.m. on Saturday and Sunday, and admission is free.

SPECIAL EVENTS: Portland celebrates its own version of the Rose Parade each spring and amuses itself in other seasons with everything from top jazz musicians to a lively shake-up of the art world called ArtQuake.

If you're here in early June you'll be treated to the city's favorite party, the lavish annual **Rose Festival.** This celebration of the city's symbol goes on for ten days, during which Portlandites participate in pageants and parades, races and running events, culminating in a deluge of roses called the Grand Floral Parade. All this takes place in early June, but information on what will be happening when is available long before that at festival headquarters at 503/227-2681.

If you love a block party, Portland throws one on the third Sunday in July. It's called **Neighborfair** and features lots of ethnic goodies, plenty of folkloric entertainment, and finale fireworks.

The county fair hereabouts is called the **Multnomah County Fair,** an annual event that occurs in late July, lapping over into early August. Site of the blue ribbon pies and piglets is Multnomah County Expo Center, 2060 N. Marine Dr., just off I-5 near Jantzen Beach (tel. 503/285-7756).

Don't look for a musician in town in early August: they're all out at Mt. Hood Community College at 26000 S.E. Stark St. in nearby Gresham (tel. 503/665-1131 or 666-3810), where they're jamming at the annual **Mount Hood Jazz Festival.** Top musicians from all over the nation come here to entertain themselves and everyone else at this event. General admission is $18.

Artwork, some of it wonderful and some of it, well, different, fills downtown streets early each September when the city sponsors its **ArtQuake Festival.**

If you can never get enough of beautiful and talented horses, plus ropin', ridin' cowboys, and fat, sassy livestock, you get a second chance to see and hear it at the **Pacific International Livestock Show** each October at the County **Expo Center.**

In September farmers from the vicinity come to the James F. Bybee House on Sauvie Island (tel. 503/621-3344) loaded down with harvest goodies that will get you in the mood for Thanksgiving. This even is called **"Wintering-in"** and it occurs at the end of September.

In July and August each year the city features evenings of music, dance, theater, and opera under the stars at **Washington Park.** Productions are free, begin at 8:30 p.m., and are for many an excuse for a picnic in the park, in case an excuse is needed. Check at the Visitor's Association to see what's on the schedule when.

7. SPORTS

In Portland you can ski your way down a slope some July morning wearing a bikini and a jacket, then shed the jacket and take the plunge. As you can see, this very versatile city plays in a most versatile way too.

Golfers have plenty of choices, among them 18-hole courses at **Eastmoreland Golf Course,** 2425 S.E. Bybee St. (tel. 503/775-2900); **Delta Park Golf Course,** 10901 N. Denver Ave., West Park (tel. 503/289-1818); and **Rose City,** 2200 N.E. 71st Ave. (tel. 503/253-4744). Greens fees are in the $9 to $12 range or less for most 18-hole public courses, about half that for nine holes.

Tennis players have their pick of courts, indoors or out, free at many city parks, and $1 to $5 or so an hour at indoor or private facilities including the indoor **Portland Tennis Center,** 324 N.E. 12th St. (tel. 503/233-5959).

Folks at the **Portland Parks Bureau** (tel. 503/796-5193) oversee an enormous empire of parks and sporting facilities. They will be happy to help you locate golf, tennis, and swimming facilities near you.

You'll find **horseback riding** in Forest Park, at 2960 N.W. Upshur St. (tel. 503/248-4492 or 796-5193), where rides are $12 an hour. The park is a favorite for **hiking** too, and folks at the information center there will help you pick a trail. For other hiking trails in the region, give the U.S. Forest Service a call at 503/221-2877.

Portland's hilly, which makes it both easy and difficult for bikers—

depending whether you're headed up or down. If you want to get out there and wheel in both directions, you can rent a bike from the **Bike Gallery,** which has three locations eastside, westside, and downtown at 1201 S.W. Morrison St. (tel. 503/222-3821). Pick up a bike route map there too. Rental rates are in the $10-a-day range, depending on how elaborate a bike you choose.

Boaters can rent a craft at the **Sailing Center,** at the foot of S.E. Marion Street (tel. 503/233-1218), or **Freedom Sailing Charters,** 250 N. Tomahawk Island Dr. (tel. 503/283-3493), or **River Trails Canoe and Raft Rentals,** 336 E. Columbia, Troutdale (tel. 503/667-1964). Rates vary widely according to the size and type of boat you want, so give them a call.

You can walk right down to the Willamette River and drop in a hook or head for some of the beautiful parks in the city to try your luck at **fishing.** Chinook salmon mill around in the Willamette in March and April; steelhead trout paddle around in the Clackamas River December through February. Folks at the **Oregon Department of Fish and Wildlife,** 500 S.W. Mill St. (tel. 503/229-5403), can fill you in on licensing details and perhaps suggest some good fishing spots. They have information on hunting seasons and locales too.

Steve Smith's Pisces Expeditions, 2603 S.E. 170th St. (tel. 503/761-3031), has floated across 12,000 miles of fishing grounds and can guide you to fishing holes to fly-fish or drift-fish for steelhead, salmon, or trout.

White-water rafting is very, very popular in Oregon, although you won't find much white water in Portland. Just a short distance away, however, the waters foam and spill over rapids and several Portland companies can arrange expeditions for you. Among those are **Lute Jerstad Adventures,** P.O. Box 19537, Portland, OR 97219 (tel. 503/244-4364); **Don Merrell's Northwest Whitewater Expeditions,** P.O. Box 3765, Portland, OR 97208 (tel. 503/236-9706); and **Cascade Waterways,** 1096 N. Rainmont Rd., Portland, OR 97229 (tel. 503/643-2897). Trips range in price from about $35 to $50 for a day-long floating adventure. Also available are two-, three-, and four-day white-water and scenic float trips including fishing and camping.

Those who would rather leave the playing to them can watch favorite sports at **Memorial Coliseum,** a riverside sporting ground at 1401 N. Wheeler St. (tel. 503/235-8771 or 239-4422). Here the city's popular Portland Trail Blazers play winning basketball and the Winterhawks play semi-pro hockey.

If baseball's your favorite, the Portland Beavers, the Pittsburgh Pirates' farm team, tries to smack 'em out of the park at **Civic Stadium,** 1844 S.W. Morrison St. (tel. 503/235-8771 or 248-4345).

Thoroughbred and harness racing fans should take their money and their opinions to Portland Meadows, 1001 N. Schmeer Rd. (tel. 503/285-9144), where the equine tests begin in late October and continue through late April. Admission is $2 to $5 and post time is 7:30 p.m. on Wednesday and Friday, 1:30 p.m. on Saturday and Sunday. You'll find the track off I-5 at the Delta Park exit.

It's chase-the-bunny time Monday through Saturday from May through August at **Multnomah Kennel Club,** Murray Kemp Greyhound Park, N.E. 223rd Ave. between Halsey and Glisan Streets, which you'll find 15 miles east in the town of Fairview, near Gresham, Oregon (tel. 503/667-7700). Admission is $1 for general admission to $3.50 for a table in Club Skyview, where you can dine while watching the puppies. Post time is 7:30 p.m. Tuesday through Saturday, with a 1 p.m. matinee on Saturday; no racing Sunday or Monday. Children under 12 may attend matinees but must be over 12 to attend night racing. To find the track, take I-84 to the Wood Village exit and head south to the Kennel Club.

Those who love the roar of a good engine should head for **Portland Speedway,** 9727 N. Union St. (tel. 503/285-2883), or **Portland International Raceway,** 1940 N. Victory Blvd., West Delta Park (tel. 503/285-6635), where racing on a 1.95-mile track goes on year round. Admission varies, but begins at $5 for adults, $3 for children 6 to 15.

8. SHOPPING

Portland is a big bustling city lined with shops downtown and shopping centers in the suburbs. Shopping malls are generally open to 9 p.m. weekdays, to 5 or 6 p.m. on Saturday and Sunday, while many downtown shops close at 5 or 6 p.m. most days, but are sometimes open to 9 p.m. on Thursday or Friday nights.

Shopping is a delight in downtown Portland, where a number of streets have been cordoned off for use only by pedestrians and buses. Boundaries of that section of town are S.W. Yamhill and Washington Streets and S.W. Fourth and Tenth Avenues. In that vicinity you will find major department stores and more than enough specialty shops and restaurants.

As a shipping center, Portland is a natural for imports, and you'll find a bundle of them at **Import Plaza,** 1 Couch St. (tel. 503/227-4040), a huge warehouse full of, well . . . things.

Yamhill Marketplace, 110 S.W. Yamhill St., at S.W. First Avenue (tel. 503/224-6705), is a good shopping spot to combine with a historic tour of the city. A couple of dozen shops, cafés, and produce stores are tucked away in a five-level maze here.

On a summer weekend the only place to be in town is **Portland Saturday Market,** Burnside Bridge at 108 W. Burnside St. Despite its name, the market is also open on Sunday from 11 a.m. to 4:30 p.m. (on Saturday from 10 a.m. to 5 p.m.). Opening day occurs in early March and continues to Christmas. Saturday Market is an open-air event, particularly pleasant in warm spring and summer months. This is the place everyone goes for locally made crafts, artwork, gorgeous produce, and ethnic creations from Greek pastries to Roman pastas. Lots of impromptu performers making their way in the world here too. You'll find the market between Front Street and N.W. First Avenue, under the shelter of the Burnside Bridge. From I-5 take the Coliseum/Broadway Bridge exit or City Center/Morrison Bridge exit. Parking is $2 for all day at One Pacific Square, a parking lot at 220 N.W. Second Ave., between N.W. First and Second Avenues on Davis Street, and at the Broadway Cab Co. parking lot, 234 N.W. First Ave. at the foot of N.W. Everett Street. Parking on the street is free on Sunday. A call to 503/222-6072 will fill you in on scheduled entertainment.

Historic as it is, Portland makes a good hunting ground for antique enthusiasts. If you'd like to see some of the treasures of ages past, hie on over to **Old Sellwood Antique Row,** at the east end of the Sellwood Bridge, S.E. 13th Avenue between Bybee and Clatsop Streets. You'll find more than two dozen antique shops offering art, furniture, and collectibles there.

Galleria Downtown is both shopping spot and historic site in Portland, a shopping area since 1905. Once home to the Olds & King department store, the buildings that house this delightful open colonnaded indoor marketplace have been extensively renovated with the best of its architectural elements retained. Seven restaurants and 40 shops can be found under a 75-foot atrium, and there's even free purchase-validation parking across the street in a lot accessible by skybridge from the Galleria's third floor. You'll find the Galleria at S.W. Tenth Avenue and Morrison Street (tel. 503/228-2748).

Johns Landing, Water Tower, 5331 S.W. Macadam (tel. 503/228-9431), is an unusual shopping spot in an old mattress factory. Lots of crafts and some clothing here.

If you'd like to pack up some of the wonderful local seafood and take it with you, get in touch with **Troy's Seafood Market,** which has a downtown place at 816 N.E. Grand Ave. (tel. 503/231-1477), and five other locations around town. They'll pack up a long list of goodies from salmon and crab to oysters, scallops, sturgeon, even ling cod, and send the package with you or ship for next-day arrival.

9. SKIING AND SEEING MOUNT HOOD

Summer or winter this towering peak is a lure for skiers. It's quite amazing to be able to take off for this 11,235-foot mountain some summer day, ski away the morning, then come back into town and go swimming or work on a tan.

IN SUMMER: In summer you can drive up here via a delightful loop drive that climbs up from Portland on U.S. 26 or from points east on Ore. 35. The timber-line is six miles off the road at Government Camp and not to be missed. Oregon Hwy. 35 joins up with I-84 at Hood River and brings you back to town, having completed a 175-mile round trip brimming with unforgettable scenery.

Summer brings out the climbers so you'll often see someone scaling this peak to stand more than 5,000 feet above the tree line overlooking Cascade peaks with names like Three-Fingered Jack, Mount Washington, North and Middle Sister. Climbing is possible in winter too, of course, but demands more climbing experience. Summer or winter the folks to call upon to guide you up this moun-tain or other nearby slopes are **Timberline Mountain Guides,** P.O. Box 464, Terrebonne, OR 97760 (tel. 503/548-1888). Rock-climbing courses can be ar-ranged in summer or winter. Rental equipment is available at varying prices from Timberline (tel. 503/226-7979).

Hikers come here to walk the **Pacific Crest Trail** which runs through Mount Hood National Forest.

If you'd like to go up to the top of the mountain in summer for a look around, the lift charge is $3 for adults, $1.50 for children.

SKIING MOUNT HOOD: Mount Hood has three major skiing areas—Timberline, Mount Hood Meadows, and Mirror Mountain, the latter the closest to Portland—with 16 chair lifts, 7 of them open at night in winter.

Timberline Lodge, a marvelous place we're coming to in a minute, offers private or group **skiing lessons** daily. You'll find instructors at Wy-East Day Lodge at Timberline (tel. 503/231-5402, or 503/295-1827 in Portland). If you're looking to save a little, you can book lesson packages that include lessons, lift tickets, and equipment, or any combination of those.

If you're a speedy skier you can participate in races Friday through Monday from 10 a.m. to 2:30 p.m. daily from December 23 through the winter season.

If you didn't bring your skis, you can **rent equipment** by calling Timber-line at 503/226-7979. If you're planning to ski every day for several days, you'll save money by renting your equipment for those several days all at one time rath-er than each day.

Lift rates on the mountain are $19 a day, a sum that entitles you to schuss from 9 a.m. to 10 p.m. in winter, $12 for a night only. In summer the fee is $16 for skiing from 9 a.m. to 4 p.m. In summer a Summerski season pass is $265. Lifts operate in summer from 7:30 a.m. to 1:30 p.m. during the week and from 8 a.m. to 1:30 p.m. on weekends. Rental equipment is a few dollars cheaper in summer too.

Getting There

Let's deal first with the matter of getting to the mountain. To do that, take the **AES Snow Coach,** 8383 N.E. Sandy St. (tel. 503/285-4040), which charges $10 one way from Portland Airport or a variety of hotels and even a few restau-rants to the slopes. Operating daily in the prime winter months (from about November through April), the bus departs from the airport and stops at major hotels including the Marriott Hotel, the Hilton Hotel, the Westin Benson, the Red Lion Lloyd Center, and Rippling River Resort in Welches. Return is by the same route at 5:30 p.m. The bus also offers trips to the mountain and back on Friday nights and has extra runs on weekends. You must make reservations on any of those buses.

Ski Areas

Slopes are open at **Mirror Mountain** from early December through mid-April daily except Monday with skiing to 3 p.m. on all four lifts. You can reach them at P.O. Box 400, Government Camp, OR 97028 (tel. 503/272-3522 or 243-1963). Mirror Mountain is 53 miles east of Portland, the closest slopes to the city. Season runs from early December through mid-April with both day and night skiing daily except Monday. Its longest run is a 1½-mile drop.

Mount Hood Meadows, P.O. Box 470, Mount Hood, OR 97041 (tel. 503/337-2222, or 503/227-SNOW for a snow report), is open mid-November to mid-May. The longest run is three miles, dropping 2,777 vertical feet. Six lighted chair lifts open up 142 acres for night skiing. Hours of operation are 9 a.m. to 4:30 p.m. on Monday and Tuesday, to 10 p.m. Wednesday through Saturday, to 7 p.m. on Sunday. The Meadows is 67 miles from Portland, 38 miles south of Hood River.

Timberline, Timberline Lodge, Timberline, OR 97028 (tel. 503/272-3311), is open November through mid-September with a 2½-mile run among its 23 ski runs. Night skiing daily and cross-country trails too. The slopes are 60 miles east of Portland.

Where to Stay

If you're planning a stay up here among this beautiful mountain scenery, the most impressive stopping spot on the mountain is historic **Timberline Lodge,** Government Camp, OR 97028 (tel. 503/226-7979, or toll free 800/452-1335 in Oregon outside Portland, 800/547-1406 in Washington, Idaho, Utah, Nevada, and northern California). A national historic monument, Timberline Lodge is six miles and 6,000 feet up in these mountains and traces its history back to the Depression when its construction was accomplished by the Works Progress Administration and the Civilian Conservation Corps. Both those organizations were set up in the wake of the Depression to create jobs for thousands of unemployed workers.

To do the job right, the government imported European stonemasons to teach Americans how to use the natural stone so abundant in these parts. You'll see the soaring results of their training in a massive central fireplace that has a chimney 100 feet high. Top carpenters were brought in to teach wood construction and their efforts resulted in massive Ponderosa pine pillars cut in forests near here and erected inside to support the roof. Skilled blacksmiths taught workers how to make the hand-wrought iron gates, huge lighting fixtures, and the lacy trim you'll see throughout this beautiful old lodge. Iron became part of heavy wood furnishings and rawhide became chair seats. Slabs of hardwood were turned into plank tables.

Enter the lobby here and if you don't gasp at the sheer size of it, well, you must have been born in a barn (there are churches smaller than this lobby). But despite the awesome size of everything it's the small details we like best: carved bird and animal heads on the stairways, delicate iron ornamentation wrapping a beam, hooked rugs, appliquéd draperies.

There must be something about the mountain air that inspires people to work hard to create something special. You can imagine the hard work done by the unskilled—but trying-hard—laborer who must have struggled to learn the careful craftsmanship required to build this lodge in the first place. Now you can also see that stick-to-it-iveness in the painstaking restoration efforts carried out by a dedicated restoration group called the Friends of Timberline. Their work and study has produced hangings, furnishings, and rugs that follow the original patterns and re-create the art deco style here.

In the lodge's 50 rooms you'll still find those art deco touches and get a look at original massive wood furnishings now supplemented by bright, strong colors that are a perfect complement to the acres of wood around you. Blue Gentian Room is an especially smashing choice, its beamed ceiling set off by royal-blue décor. All rooms have private bath except bunkrooms called chalet rooms, and it's well worth the splurge for a room with a fireplace so you can enjoy the romantic, cozy surroundings a lodge like this one offers.

For a room and a welcome from one of the picturesque St. Bernard dogs that adorn the place, you pay $47 double for chalet rooms with bunkbeds and a bath down the hall, $64 to $127 double for rooms with private bath, a large corner room, or a really spiffy, spacious room with a fireplace. An additional person sharing a room is charged $8.

After a long day on the slopes, walking or skiing, you'll be served big hearty meals of bouillabaisse, fettuccine, paella, steaks, or interesting ethnic specialties for prices in the $10 to $15 range. All three meals are served here: breakfast is from 8 to 10 a.m.; lunch, from noon to 2 p.m.; and dinner, from 6 to 10 p.m. Before or after, stop by the Blue Ox deli or the rustic Ram's Head lounge to see who's who and what's happening.

Another resort up here in the mountains is **Rippling River,** 68010 E. Fairway Ave., Welches, OR 97067 (tel. 503/622-3101, 503/224-7158 in Portland, or toll free 800/547-8054). A very complete modern resort, Rippling River has extensive recreational facilities including 27 holes of golf, tennis courts, indoor and outdoor pools and whirlpools, exercise room and sauna, bicycles, and rental sports equipment. Nearby is an Alpine Slide, and skiing at Mount Hood is 20 minutes away. Two restaurants stave off starvation and two lounges amuse in the evening.

Spacious and well-kept rooms are in rustic wood-sided balconied buildings set amid mountain scenery. Dark-wood furniture and walls of glass offer comfort, luxury, and views. One- to three-bedroom condominiums and town houses are available, as well as hotel rooms with double, queen-, or king-size beds—and all are equipped with color television. Year-round room rates for two at the resort range from $60 to $97; a one-bedroom condominium goes for $85 to $125. Money-saving ski-season packages, including champagne to celebrate your arrival, and transportation to the slopes and lift tickets, are available.

10. OREGON'S WINE COUNTRY

On interesting excursions from Portland you can sip your way through Oregon's wine country, attend a historic pageant re-creating the life and times of pioneers who settled this region, get a look at the homes of those early settlers, and even see the results of Einstein's Theory of Relativity!

A WINE TOUR: Let's start with a wine tour. To get a close look at the grapes that made the wines you've been drinking here in the Northwest—and of course, to sample a few varieties you might have missed—stop by, call, or write the **Oregon Winegrowers Association,** 644 S.E. 20th Ave., Portland, OR 97214 (tel. 503/233-2377), which will arm you with a booklet outlining several different tours of wine-making regions near Portland and throughout the state. On one of those tours, you will visit nearby vineyards located on and around

Ore. 99W, which you can reach from I-5. Among the wineries you can visit (and this isn't all of them by a long shot) are **Ponzi Vineyards** in Beaverton (tel. 503/628-1227), producing chardonnay and riesling; **Adelsheim Vineyard** in Newberg (tel. 503/538-3652; open by appointment only), featuring chardonnay and pinot noir; **Knudsen Erath Winery** in Dundee (tel. 503/538-3318), specializing in pinot noir; **Sokol Blosser Winery** in Dundee (tel. 503/864-3342), featuring white riesling, merlot, and gewürztraminer, among others; **Château Benoit Winery** in Carlton (tel. 503/864-2991 or 864-3666), producing blanc de blanc and pinot noir nouveau; **Eyrie Vineyards** in McMinnville (tel. 503/472-6351 or 864-2410), featuring pinot gris, muscat ottonel, and pinot noir; **Arterberry Winery** in McMinnville (tel. 503/472-1587), with white riesling, cider, and apple-berry blends; **Amity Vineyards,** also in McMinnville (tel. 503/835-2362), producing solstice blanc and merlot; and **Hidden Springs Winery** in Amity (tel. 503/835-2782), featuring cabernet sauvignon and pinot noir blanc.

Oregon actually sports more than 30 wineries, most located west and southwest of Portland or along the Hood River and in the Willamette Valley along the Cascades near Salem, Eugene, Roseburg, and Medford. Most of the wineries are open every day or on weekends in summer months (with shorter hours in winter) for visits and tasting in tasting rooms that are often elegant and quite picturesque.

SEEING THE SIGHTS: While you're visiting wineries or on a separate trip, take some time to look around you. As some of the first settlements in the state, small villages along the Columbia west of Portland have often changed very little over the decades.

Among the interesting stops is **Clatskanie,** where a fellow named Thomas Flippin got a job in the logging camps when he was 17, borrowed enough money to repair a run-down old saw mill on Roaring Creek, and proceeded to become a "gypo," or contract, logger. Little by little, he and his wife saved up lumber from the mill and built a home he liked to call his castle. It's still called **Flippin Castle** today, and looks much as it did then, a quite grandiose spot complete with verandas and turrets. You can tour the house at 620 Tichenor St. (tel. 503/728-2026) from 10 a.m. to 4 p.m. daily at $1 for adults, 50¢ for children under 12.

A little farther along the river, in the town of **Rainier,** the past is home to something quite futuristic—the **Trojan Nuclear Power Plant,** on U.S. 30 (tel. 503/226-8510). Here you can get a closeup look at a nuclear plant and its landmark cooling tower and/or picnic on 75 acres of recreation area as well. Visits to this physical manifestation of $E = mc^2$ are possible Wednesday through Sunday from 9:30 a.m. to 5 p.m. all year; closed holidays. There's no admission charge and tours of the power plant, turbine generators, and controls take about an hour. You'll find the information center, which houses fascinating displays of various kinds of energy generation methods, on U.S. 30 about 42 miles west of Portland and five miles south of **Rainier.**

St. Helens, a small settlement about 28 miles west of Portland on U.S. 30, has managed to retain many **turn-of-the-century homes** which are now restored and on display or still in use. Among these are the Cox House, the Columbia County Courthouse, and the Orcadia and St. Helens Hotels, the latter now called Klondike Tavern.

In nearby historic **Columbia City,** two miles north of St. Helens on U.S. 30, is a complex of restored buildings including the **Caples House Museum,** 1915 1st St. A carriage house, the children's quarters in an attic, a pioneer tool shed, and a country store are all owned and operated by the Daughters of the American

Revolution who open them from 11 a.m. to 5 p.m. Wednesday through Saturday and from 1 to 6 p.m. on Sunday. Admission is $1 for adults and 50¢ for children.

This is also strawberry and blueberry country, as you'll see in the roadside stands at which those and other tempting local fruit and vegetables, well . . . tempt.

To get the complete scoop on what to see and do in this historic part of northwestern Oregon, stop by the **St. Helens Chamber of Commerce,** 174 S. Columbia River Hwy., St. Helens, OR 97501 (tel. 503/397-0685).

If you're visiting northwest Oregon in July, there's an interesting way to absorb some history and a little drama at the same time. In the town of **Newberg,** the Champoeg State Park Amphitheater, 8239 Champoeg Rd. NE (tel. 503/538-1800), is for four weeks site of an annual **outdoor drama** conceived and executed by Denis Hagen, music professor at a local college. At this outdoor production you are treated to a look at the lives of rough mountain men, brave but unprepared pioneers, and not-very-pleased Indians, all trying to work it out together here in the wilderness. Each season the players focus on a particular historical incident and design costumes, props, and sets to bring those dramatic early days to life. Music joins muskets and muslins to produce a dramatization you will long remember.

Champoeg (pronounced "sham-*poo*-ee") **State Park** is itself a historic site, a one-time Calapooya Indian camp at which French-Canadian and American settlers met in 1843 to set up a provisional government. While you're here, you can visit historic Newell House and Pioneer Cabin, both offering a look at early pioneer life and dwelling places.

Champoeg is 26 miles southwest of Portland just off I-5 at U.S. 99W. Tickets are $8 for adults, $5 for students 5 through 16. Performances are every Thursday, Friday, Saturday, and Sunday in July at 7 p.m. You can reserve tickets in advance by writing to Champoeg Historical Pageant, P.O. Box 707, Newberg, OR 97132, or reserve by phone (tel. 503/538-1800) with credit cards.

Oregon City, about 13 miles south of Portland on I-295, is quite a historic place settled early on by pioneer travelers who made it the first capital of this state. A lovely town, Oregon City is on the east bank of the Willamette River at a scenic point where the river drops over a ridge to create **Willamette Falls.** You can get a good look at the falls by taking the Municipal Free Elevator up the face of the cliff at 7th Street and Railroad Avenue to an observation deck.

Here, too, you can get a look at one of the state's most important historic sites, the **John McLoughlin House National Historic Site,** a pioneer home operated by the U.S. National Park Service. One of the nation's few remaining pioneer structures, the house was built in 1845–1846 by Dr. John McLoughlin, a doctor and honcho of the Hudson's Bay Co. as well as a local mill owner, a powerful fellow indeed. He is said to have been quite a friend to pioneers in need. He sent food to starving immigrants at The Dalles, loaned seed grains and provisions to newcomers at Fort Vancouver, and helped some of the early arrivals get through a very rough winter in the Oregon country.

Things got a little tough when McLoughlin sided with the new provisional government of the region instead of the Hudson's Bay Co., which didn't much care for opposition. McLoughlin finally resigned in 1845 and began building this house.

You'll find the result of his efforts in McLoughlin Park on Center Street between 7th and 8th Streets in Oregon City (tel. 503/656-5146), about four blocks east of Ore. 99, which is also known as the Pacific Hwy. It's open Tuesday through Saturday from 10 a.m. to 5 p.m. in summer, closing an hour earlier in winter, and on Sunday from 1 to 4 p.m. year round. Admission is $2.50 for adults $2 for seniors, and $1 for children under 18. Next door is another historic home, **Barclay House.**

A VISIT TO OLD VANCOUVER: Hudson's Bay Co. settled here in Vancouver in the 1820s and stayed around for two decades collecting furs and fame. Now the oldest continuous settlement in the Pacific Northwest, Vancouver was chosen by that shrewd company for its proximity to deep-water navigation on the Columbia River. Built in 1824, it is the oldest city in Washington and an apple tree at Wash. 14 and I-5 is believed to have been planted in 1892 by traders who trekked overland with the seeds.

Many early pioneers sailed down the Columbia here from The Dalles and then went on to the Willamette River, a final destination for most. Later a gentleman who was to go on to considerable wartime fame spent some time here learning how armies work. His name? Gen. Ulysses S. Grant.

So well preserved is this antique city that you can walk by its historic sites on a self-guided walk that is now five miles long, and plans are to make it 20 miles long! To find out where to walk, ask folks at the **Greater Vancouver Chamber of Commerce,** 404 E. 15th St., Suite 4, Vancouver, WA 98660 (tel. 206/694-2588), for a walking map of the city.

Just across the bridge from Portland, Vancouver's chief lure is **Fort Vancouver,** where a museum and reconstructed stockade and buildings give you an idea what life must have been like for those fellows who sat it out here chalking up income for that powerful Hudson's Bay Co. You'll find the fort covering 165 acres off East Evergreen Boulevard (tel. 206/696-7655), just off I-5 at the Mill Plain Boulevard exit. The visitor center is open from 9 a.m. to 5 p.m. daily April to September, closing at 4 p.m. in other months; closed holidays. No admission charge.

One square in town is an interesting place: **Esther Short Park,** at the corner of Columbia and West 8th Streets, a public meeting place since 1857. You'll see an 1867 home there, the Slocum House, built in Rhode Island style and now home to a community theater. There's also a huge carved wooden Indian, a monument to pioneer women, and a restored steam **locomotive.**

Museums in the city include the **Clark County Historical Museum,** 1511 Main St. (tel. 206/695-4681), which features some early medical tools, a print shop, and country store, and recently acquired a collection of Gen. Ulysses S. Grant's furniture and books. It's open Tuesday through Sunday from 1 to 5 p.m. No admission is charged but donations are encouraged.

Another is **Covington House,** 4201 Main St. (tel. 206/693-9571), a log cabin that can trace its history back to 1846. Once a schoolhouse, the cabin is now open on Tuesday and Thursday from 10 a.m. to 4 p.m. June to September and is free.

Food and Lodging

If you're staying over, Vancouver has a nice hotel, the **Thunderbird Inn at the Quay,** on the dock at the foot of Columbia Street, Vancouver, WA 98660 (tel. 206/694-8341 or toll free 800/547-8010). Overlooking the Columbia River, the Thunderbird has many rooms with a pretty view of the river through lots of glass. All have color televisions, radios, and phones. A heated pool provides amusement and there's free airport transportation too. A dining room here is open from 6:30 a.m. to 11 p.m., a bit later on weekends, and offers steaks and seafood in the $12 to $15 range, plus cocktails and entertainment in a lounge. Rates at the inn are $68 to $79 double.

For casual dining, head for a Mexican place called **Who-Song and Larry's Cantina,** 111 E. Columbia Way (tel. 206/695-1198). Who-Song and Larry's is as unusual as its name suggests, but has good Mexican specialties, good views, and good prices in the under-$10 bracket. Hours are 11 a.m. to 11 p.m. daily.

When hunger strikes, head for the **Hidden House Restaurant,** 100 W. 13th St. (tel. 206/696-2847). One of the city's historic homes, Hidden House often turns its culinary talents on Northwest produce to come up with intriguing specialties. You'll pay about $15 for prime rib and most steaks with all the trimmings. Hours here are 11 a.m. to 2 p.m. for lunch weekdays and 5 to 10 p.m. for dinner daily except Monday. Sunday brunch is from 10 a.m. to 2 p.m.

At **The Crossing,** 900 W. 7th St. (tel. 206/695-3374), you'll dine in a collection of antique railroad cars. From the kitchens here come lots of steaks and seafood for dinner, and the usual selections for lunch and Sunday brunch. Prices are in the $10 to $15 range for entrees, and hours run from 11 a.m. to 2:30 p.m. weekdays and 4:30 to 9:30 p.m. daily, closing later on weekends, earlier on Sunday. If Sunday brunch is your delight, you can find it in full steam here from 10 a.m. to 2 p.m.

CHAPTER X

OREGON'S WILLAMETTE VALLEY

□ □ □

1. SALEM
2. EUGENE

Rest easy, world, all those Woodstock attendees are alive, well, and living in Oregon. You'll find many of them in the university town of Eugene, where the natural beauties of mountains and valley added to an anything-goes attitude have proven quite a lure for those seeking an alternative lifestyle.

In local publications you'll read a lot about zen and rolfing, bean sprouts and peace, vitamins and vitality in a city that is downright nuts about jogging! Eugene's jogging tracks were, in fact, the practice grounds for several Olympic teams.

History is important in this land of pioneers. Old Victorian homes and covered bridges, those delightful leftovers from days of Mason jars and oak sideboards, abound. There are 21 covered bridges and countless numbers of old Victorian homes dotting the countryside around both Eugene and Salem.

This was gold-mining country once upon a time, and you can still visit abandoned mines. Just don't go too far afield, for there are those who still work claims here, and they don't take too kindly to city folks out nosing around.

Despite jokes that claim Eugene's 42 inches of rain a year means bike-riding residents drown if they fall off their bicycles, the region has a blissfully mild climate, rarely reaching temperatures higher than 60° to 80° in summer or lower than 30° to 45° degrees in winter.

Meanwhile, 60 miles up the road, the small town of Salem experiences a similar change of population each year when legislators and their groupies flock here from every corner of the state to debate the wisdom of changing anything about their much-loved homeland—and once to hear a governor say there oughtta be a law against tourists and new residents cluttering up all this Oregonian perfection!

1. SALEM

To tell you the truth there's not much to be said about Salem. First, good accommodations and good restaurants are few and far between, as often seems to be true, strangely, of capital cities. Perhaps the periodic population bulge that occurs when legislators pour into town just doesn't encourage construction of luxurious places to stay and play.

And we cannot resist telling you this one small snippet of local lore, which may indeed be the single most singular event to have occurred in any U.S. state capital city and legislative center: *One Flew Over the Cuckoo's Nest* was filmed here. Are they telling us something?

Beyond those basics, Salem offers few diversions, and even its state buildings are not particularly noteworthy. There is one exception to that lack of diversions: a very attractive cluster of buildings that once was an old mill and a couple of historic homes and is now the city's Visitor Information Center, and a very nice center it is too. You'll also find in Salem the oldest university in the West, the state capitol, and the Oregon State Fair.

VISITOR INFORMATION: Salem has one of the most interesting Visitor Information Centers we've come across, certainly the most intriguing in the Pacific Northwest. Part of that is due to its location in the city's **Mission Mill Village,** 1313 Mill St. SE, Salem, OR 97301 (tel. 503/585-7012), a 4.5-acre park with a collection of beautifully restored historic buildings. In one of them you will find the Visitors Center, its racks of books, maps, and brochures artfully displayed among antique shops, craft shops selling handmade items like potpourri stuffed into calico cats, and a wool shop purveying thick, fluffy locally grown wools and other fabrics.

Folks at the **Salem Area Chamber of Commerce,** which occupies a lovely old building at 220 Cottage St. NE, Salem, OR 97301 (tel. 503/581-1466), can provide you with a map that will help you find your way around a walking or driving tour of the city.

These tourist information centers, or the **Salem Historic Preservation Office,** 525 Trade St. (tel. 503/588-6173), can provide you with a good enlarged map of the most historic parts of town, with dozens of historic homes and businesses marked and described.

GETTING THERE: Salem is not the easiest place to reach.

Airlines including American, Horizon, and United fly into Eugene, 60 miles away, or to Portland.

Greyhound travels to the city. You can get here **by car** on **I-5,** which travels here south from Portland and north from Eugene and points south.

GETTING AROUND: Getting around, let us be the first to tell you, is no fun. Downtown Salem is a maze of poorly marked, one-way streets very difficult for the uninitiated tourist to negotiate. As we discovered, it's important to know that if a street has only white lines on it, it's a one-way street. If it has yellow lines, traffic goes both directions.

You'll need to know that I-5 runs along the eastern edge of town, the Willamette River along the western edge. Market Street, an east-west artery, on the north side of town has a cluster of fast-food eateries, shopping spots, and motels. Capitol Street, which runs north and south with an exit from Ore. 99, leads to the state capitol buildings, situated between Court Street and State Street, adjacent to Willamette University. Downtown Salem is roughly bounded by Market and Mission Streets north and south, the river and 17th Street east and west. Oregon Hwy. 99, which runs southwest-northeast through town and is also known as Pacific Hwy., takes you near the Fairgrounds at 17th and Silverton. Streets in town have a NE, NW, or SE appended to their names to identify the section of town in which they are located. Center Street is the dividing line between northeast and southeast, the river the dividing line between northwest and northeast.

Three small six-car ferrys, last of a dying breed, make an interesting way to cross the Willamette River—for free. To catch one, take River Road North to McNary Golf Course; take the left fork of the road and continue to the signs for Wheatland Ferry, about ten miles north of town. Buena Vista Ferry, operating since 1853, moors about 15 miles southwest of Salem; to get there take Commercial Street SE to Liberty Road South, then take the right-hand fork at the major intersection and continue on to Buena Vista Road. Third of the three floaters is three miles north of Canby, west of Ore. 99E.

WHERE TO STAY: Despite its status as the capital of this state, Salem has a small-town feeling and is not given to lovely resorts. The best of what you'll find here are hotels and motels designed to lure government workers or legislators who fill the town when the legislature is in session.

The **Executive Inn,** 200 Commercial St. SE, Salem, OR 97301 (tel. 503/363-4123, or toll free 800/452-7879, 800/547-8733 in Oregon), is modern, with clean, sleek lines inside and out. Aimed, as many hotels in Salem, at the commercial traveler, the Executive Inn offers all the accoutrements from swimming pool to spa, sauna, in-room movie and sports channels, free local phone calls, even free use of racquetball and fitness equipment at a nearby facility. Each morning you're treated to a free breakfast in the inn's VIP room. Next door to the inn is a wood-lined Black Angus steakhouse with live entertainment and dancing. Rates, including tax, are $52 single, $57 to $64 double.

Rodeway Capitol Motor Inn, 745 Commercial St. SE, Salem, OR 97301 (tel. 503/363-2451, or toll free 800/228-2000), is an attractive spot featuring king- and queen-size beds in rooms, a cocktail lounge with entertainment, and a restaurant. Rooms, while not elaborately decorated, have big panels of glass and doors opening onto a common balcony or terrace overlooking a swimming pool. Its location makes it quite convenient if you're planning to spend some time in downtown Salem. Rates are $39 to $40 double.

The **Best Western Pacific Highway Inn,** 4526 Portland Rd. NE, Salem, OR 97303 (tel. 503/390-3200, or toll free 800/528-1234), is another attractive spot in Salem. Here you'll find an outdoor swimming pool tucked between two buildings, one a little farther back from the highway and quieter. Large and attractively landscaped grounds, plus a small children's playground, make this a good spot to let the youngsters romp after a long day in the car. Just off I-5, the motel is easily identified by its orange roof tiles and matching trim. Medium-size rooms with one or two double beds are attractively decorated in brilliant colors and furnishings with the look of dark wood. Stone trim and wood siding add a cheerful touch to a standard two-story motel. Next door is a Pancake House restaurant open from 6 a.m. to 8 p.m. daily (to 2 p.m. on Sunday). Rates at the Pacific Highway Inn are $49 to $52 double.

Just Outside Town

At exit 256, the Market Street exit from I-5, you'll find a cluster of 24-hour restaurants and fast-food places offering everything from burgers to pizza. There's a shopping plaza here too, and a cluster of motels.

Top choice here is **Chumaree Hotel and Convention Center,** 3301 Market St. NE, Salem, OR 97301 (tel. 503/370-7888, or toll free 800/CHUMARE). Located just at the edge of Salem, the Chumaree is a four-story building difficult to miss, perched as it is on the top of a rise. You can hardly miss the antique engine on the front lawn either. Chumaree and its adjoining Steamer's Restaurant greets you with wide copper doors, stained glass, and a sunning area tucked away behind dark stone walls. In 1988 Chumaree remodeled from top to bottom and now sports a dramatic color scheme in soft contemporary colors. There's an indoor pool here, a Jacuzzi, saunas, free cable television, videocassette recorders and movies for rent, a guest laundry, and free parking and airport shuttle. Antiques are popular here, as you will see on the front lawn and in the pretty wing chairs and couch in the lobby. Some of the medium-size rooms have balconies, and all have queen-size beds, a couple of chairs, dresser, and a color scheme that runs to soft pastels. Steamer's Restaurant, which got its unusual name from the nickname of Chumaree's owner, is bright with lots of plants and attractive décor and open daily from 6 a.m. to 11 p.m. with quite reasonable $8 to $12 prices for dinner entrees. At Chumaree you pay $59 for a room with queen-size bed, $69 to $71 for a king-size or two double beds. There's no charge for children under 16 in their parents' room.

Best Western New King's Inn, 3658 Market St. NE, Salem, OR 97301 (tel. 503/581-1559, or toll free 800/528-1234), is a pleasant strip of two-story buildings trimmed in stone and bright-orange doors. Among the amusements are a whirlpool, a big indoor swimming pool set under a vaulted ceiling hung with brightly colored flags, a slide and playpool area for the youngsters. You'll find rather standard décor, leaning to oranges and reds in the guest rooms, all of which are set far back from the highway but convenient to it. Rates are $49 to $52 double.

WHERE TO DINE: You'd think that the presence of legislators and big-buck lobbyists would have led to rafts of good restaurants, but such is not the case. Here's a look at the best of the lot.

The **Union Street Oyster Bar,** 445 State St. (tel. 503/362-7219), is much like its namesake in Eugene, purveying good Oregon oysters and scads of other seafood, as well as a few steaks for the immovable steak-and-potatoes eaters. Most of the 84 menu items are in a very reasonable $5 to $11 bracket and hours are 11 a.m. to midnight; closed Sunday.

Speaking of those I-want-a-good-steak types, here's one for them: **Stuart Anderson's Black Angus,** 220 Commercial St. (tel. 503/585-1011), that popular western chain, here taking the form of a woodsy-plantsy place lined with dark, secluded booths perfect for the kinds of smoky-room conversations that go on in a legislative town. The Black Angus cooks up prime rib daily and carves it to order, grills top sirloin, New York cut, filet mignon, and T-bones. Seafood like prawns or shrimp is served alone or teamed, and prices range from just $8 for London broil to $16 for combinations of steak and lobster. Hours are 11 a.m. to 10 p.m. daily (from 4 p.m. on Saturday).

Gepetto's, 616 Lancaster Dr. NE (tel. 503/378-1271), is a good place for families intent on a simple and inexpensive meal as palatable for youngsters as for parents. All kinds of pizzas here for $4 to $10, plus sandwiches, ribs, and chicken in the same low price range. Hours are 11:30 a.m. to 11 p.m. weekdays, to 11 p.m. weekends, with delivery to your door from 5 p.m.

The **Terrarium,** 156 Church St. (tel. 503/363-1611), is another seafood specialist with something special each day—prawns, perhaps, or oysters or clams. Prices are in the $8 to $12 range, and the restaurant is open Monday through Friday from 11 a.m. to 2:30 p.m. and 5 to 10 p.m., on Saturday from 5 to 10:30 p.m., and on Sunday from 5 to 10 p.m. Continental specialties are also on the menu here. Accolades have been heaped on the Terrarium's special battered perch and prawns. A number of lighter meals are also offered, including a mushroom casserole joining mushrooms, vegetables, and cheeses.

Boon's Treasury, 888 Liberty St. NE (tel. 503/399-9062), which really was the state treasury once, has been restored to become the home of this eatery, where sandwiches, salads, and soups are the popular fare. Brick walls, newspapers on wall racks, and a pubby atmosphere make this a popular gathering spot, as does the abundance of imported and domestic beers. Prices are in the under-$10 range. Hours are 9 a.m. to 1 a.m. daily, opening at 10 a.m. on Sunday. There's often entertainment here evenings.

Aviation fans can watch airplanes swoop down and land as they dine at **Flight Deck,** McNary Field, 2680 Aerial Way SE (tel. 503/581-5721), two blocks south of the tower. Here since 1967, the Flight Deck's owner has spiffed the place up in soft, earthy colors. The specialty here is steak Diane cooked tableside, supplemented by steak and seafood preparations in the $10 to $15 price bracket, including salad bar or soup, and vegetable; at lunch, burgers and seafood baskets. Hours are 7 a.m. to 11 p.m. daily except Monday, later in the lounge.

Remodeled old houses are quite the rage in Salem so you'll often find their owners making the mortgage payments with profits from a restaurant they operate at home, so to speak:

The Inn at Orchard Heights, 695 Orchard Heights Rd. NW (tel. 503/378-1780), offers a wide variety of steaks, seafood, and veal for prices in a very reasonable $10 to $15 range. Salads are on the menu here too. Hours at the inn are 11:30 a.m. to 1:30 p.m. and 5 to 9:30 p.m. weekdays, dinner only on Saturday; closed Sunday.

Heritage Tree Restaurant, 574 Cottage St. NE (tel. 503/377-7075), a charming restaurant with oldtime touches specializes in pasta, quiches, sandwiches, and homemade soups and the like for prices in the $4 range. Hours are Monday through Friday from 9 a.m. to 3:30 p.m. You can dine here downstairs, upstairs, or outside.

McGrath's Publick Fish House, 350 Chemeketa NE (tel. 503/362-0736), is a trendy spot featuring equally trendy cooking—alder-baked salmon and halibut, plus mesquite-broiled treats. Prices are in the $10 to $15 range at this lively spot which is open from 6:30 a.m. until 10 p.m. daily.

Many are the diners who troop over to **Night Deposit,** 195 Commercial St. NE (tel. 503/585-5588), where there are nightly dinner specials, a big salad bar, wines by the glass, and plenty of fresh seafood, poultry, and beef creations, sizzling and steaming. Prices are in the $10 to $15 range and hours are 11 a.m. to 2 p.m. for lunch weekdays, 5 to 10 p.m. for dinner daily, closing an hour later on weekends.

NIGHTLIFE: Salem's nightlife occurs at lounges with entertainment and at lounges where you provide the entertainment.

Among the lounges are **Night Deposit** and the **Union Street Oyster Bar,** which we've already mentioned as restaurants; likewise **Stuart Anderson's Black Angus,** a dancing spot.

You'll get pizza and rock music at the **Stone Lion,** 114 S. Main, in Independence (tel. 503/838-3838), and sandwiches and western music at the **Wooden Nickel,** 1610 Pine St. in Silverton (tel. 503/873-9979), both a 30-minute drive away.

There's music Friday and Saturday nights at **Boon's Treasury,** 888 Liberty St. (tel. 503/399-9062), served with bouillabaisse every first and third Friday.

The Ranch, 3260 Portland Rd. NE (tel. 503/362-9887), has two-for-one drinks after 9 p.m. many evenings and live entertainment.

There's more music at **Battle Creek Lounge,** 616 Commercial St. SE (tel. 503/362-7964), and **Busick Court,** 250 Court St. SE (tel. 503/370-8107).

WHAT TO SEE AND DO: If you don't want to look at politicians at work, there's not a great deal to do in this small city. It is, however, a historic town, one in which you can get a good look at a few lovely old homes.

Perhaps we should begin, however, with what put this town on the map, the **State Capitol Building** on Court Street (tel. 503/378-4423). Made of marble in a contemporary design, the Capitol is adorned with a golden statue of a pioneer. You'll also see some interesting murals here of historic events in the state and nation. Hours are 8 a.m. to 5 p.m. weekdays from Memorial Day through Labor Day, and tours are available every 30 minutes from 9 a.m. to 3:30 p.m., but no tour at noon. No charge for admission or tour.

Across from the Capitol is **Willamette University,** 900 State St. (tel. 503/370-6303), the oldest university in the West, founded in 1842 by Methodist missionaries.

Now on to the old homes, most of them located on streets quite near the Capitol, close enough to walk once you've found a parking spot.

Historic Deepwood Estate, 1116 Mission St. SE at 12th Street (tel. 503/363-1825), is one of those. Located at the east end of Bush's Pasture Park, this elegant Queen Anne–style house has stained-glass windows of Tiffany quality, complemented by golden oak woodwork. The 1894 mansion and the nearly six acres of formal, informal, and natural wildflower gardens are open to the public May to September from noon to 4 p.m. daily except Tuesday and Saturday. In winter, hours are 1 to 4 p.m. on Sunday, Monday, and Friday. The gardens are open from dawn to dusk unless a wedding is in progress. Admission is $2 for adults, $1.50 for seniors and students, and 75¢ for children under 12.

Mission Mill Village, 1313 Mill St. SE (tel. 503/585-7012), is a 4.5-acre park with a collection of beautifully restored historic buildings. Take time to roam through the pristine white **Parsonage** and **Jason Lee Home,** built in 1841, and the **John D. Boon Home,** both restored and outfitted in period furnishings. Historic houses guided tours are available Tuesday through Saturday at 10 a.m., noon, and 2 p.m. Entry fees are $2 for adults, $1.50 for seniors and students, and $1 for schoolchildren.

Also part of the Mission Mill Village is the **Thomas Kay Woolen Mill Museum.** Built in 1889, the woolen mill is so well restored that its waterpower operating system is still working. Supporting the floor here are 48 beams, each 12 by 16 inches and 60 feet long, unspliced. Woolen Mill Museum guided tours are Tuesday through Saturday at 11 a.m., 1 p.m., and 3 p.m. Admission fees are identical to historic houses guided tours. Woolen mill self-guided tours are free and ongoing from 10 a.m. to 4 p.m.

Tours of all three historic homes and the Thomas Kay Woolen Mill Museum are available at a combined admission of $3, $2.50, and $2 respectively.

Allow extra time for this stop, as it just might be among the most interesting places you'll see in Salem. Mission Mill Village is open Tuesday through Saturday from 10 a.m. to 4:30 p.m., and summer Sundays (June through September) from 1 to 4:30 p.m.

Bush's Pasture Park, 600 Mission St. (tel. 503/363-4714), is the setting for another old home, the Bush House Museum, built in 1877 as home for pioneer banker and newspaper publisher Asahel Bush. You'll see original wallpaper and some of the original furnishings here, even marble fireplaces. Open Tuesday through Sunday from noon to 5 p.m. June through August. In other months the home is open Tuesday through Sunday from 2 to 5 p.m. only. Admission is $1.50 for adults, $1 for seniors, 75¢ for students, and 50¢ for youngsters 6 to 12.

While you're here take a look at **Bush Barn Art Center,** 600 Mission St. (tel. 503/581-2228), next door, where the Salem Art Association features exhibits of

Pacific Northwest artists' work from 10 a.m. to 5 p.m. Tuesday through Friday and 1 to 5 p.m. on Saturday and Sunday year round; closed Monday. It's free. The **Bush Conservatory,** built in 1882, also has been restored and is open weekdays from 9 a.m. to 4 p.m. and weekends from 2 to 5 p.m. Also free. In the park you'll also find tennis courts and tables for picnics.

If you're here when the Oregon State Fair is roaring in late August and September, you can see an old one-room schoolhouse called the **Criterion School,** built in 1912. Moved here to the fairgrounds from Maupin, Oregon, in 1975, the schoolhouse is open during the fair.

Wine lovers can sample fruit wines at the **Honeywood Winery,** 501 14th St. SE (tel. 503/362-4111), built in 1934 and one of the state's longest-running wineries. A bit offbeat, this winery offers loganberry, apricot, blackberry, strawberry, raspberry, even rhubarb wine! Tours are scheduled Monday through Saturday at 10 a.m. and 2 p.m. and on Sunday at 2 p.m., complete with tasting of the product. Admission is free.

Quite a number of other wineries are within an easy drive of Salem. Among those are **Glen Creek Winery,** 6057 Orchard Heights Rd. NW (tel. 503/371-9463); **Amity Vineyards,** 18150 Amity Vineyards Road, Amity (tel. 503/835-2362); **Bethel Heights Vineyard,** 6060 Bethel Heights Rd. NW (tel. 503/581-2262); **Ellendale Vineyards,** 300 Reuben Boise Rd., Dallas (tel. 503/623-5617); and **Serendipity Cellars Winery,** 15275 Dunn Forest Rd., Monmount (tel. 503/838-4284). All are open for tastings and tours by appointment, at least from May to December and sometimes longer, but it would be wise to give them a call first.

Silver Falls State Park occupies more than 8,500 acres of ground 26 miles east of the city on Ore. 214. Largest in the state's park system, Silver Falls lives up to its name with 14 waterfalls, some of them cascading more than 100 feet.

Here's one for the youngsters: the **Enchanted Forest,** 8462 Enchanted Way in Turner, six miles south on I-5, exit 248 (tel. 503/363-3060), offers a couple of hours of amusement in a natural forest setting where storybook characters live among the trees. A re-created mining town, an old-world village, a haunted house, ice mountain bobsleds, and summer comedy theater are fun. Hours are 9:30 a.m. to 6 p.m. daily from March 15 to October 1. Admission is $3.50 for adults, $3 for children 3 to 12. To get there, take I-5 to Sunnyside-Turner exit to Enchanted Way.

You'll see lots of lambs romping about Oregon and you can see what happens to some of their wool at **Mt. Jefferson Woolens,** 1827 Talbot Rd. SE, Jefferson (tel. 503/327-2203). Located just outside Salem, the mills are open from 9 a.m. to 4 p.m. weekdays for tours that will show you all the processes from washing to carding, spinning, and weaving into cloth. Give them a call first to be sure there's someone available to show you around.

SPORTS: If you haven't had a chance to try **rafting,** now is your chance. **Leierer's Outdoors,** 934 Hylo Rd. SE (tel. 503/581-2803), offers trips on the North Santiam River, about an hour's drive from Salem. Guides, rafts, and lunch are part of the deal, which costs $45 per person for a party of four. A two-hour trip on weekends is $20 per person, with an additional $5 if you want lunch (which stretches the trip out to about three hours). Children must be 7 to participate and reservations are required 24 hours in advance.

Tennis courts can be found at many places around town including lighted ones at **Bush Park** at Mission, High, and Lefelle Streets South; **Highland Park,** Highland and Columbia NE; and **Orchard Heights Park,** Parkway and Orchard Heights Roads NW.

Outdoor swimming pools at **Leslie Swimming Pool,** Cottage and Howard

Streets SE (tel. 503/588-6339), and **Walker Swimming Pool,** 8th and Gerth Streets NW (tel. 503/588-6334). Indoor pool is **Olinger,** 1310 A St. NE (tel. 503/588-6332).

Salem Regional Parks and Recreation Agency (tel. 503/588-6261) sponsors many activities for children and adults and can help you find the recreational facilities nearest you.

SHOPPING: The **Reed Opera House,** Liberty and Court Streets, was built in the late 1800s and is now a good way to combine shopping and history; it's been restored and is filled with small shops.

Lancaster Mall, at 831 Lancaster Dr. NE, just off I-5 between Center and D Streets NE (tel. 503/585-1338), an enclosed mall, has four major shopping stores, including the Bon and Montgomery Ward, plus more than 100 small shops and restaurants.

You'll find Salem's major department stores and smaller downtown shops in the vicinity of **Chemetka and Liberty Streets.**

ART AND CULTURAL ACTIVITIES: In winter and fall the **Mid-Valley Arts Council,** 208 Reed Opera House, 189 Liberty St., Salem OR 97301 (tel. 503/364-7474), sponsors operatic productions. At last check season tickets to three performances were just $30, so if you're planning to be in the area, call to see what's playing.

The **Pentacle Theatre,** 324 52nd Ave. NW (tel. 503/364-7121 or 364-7200), about five miles west of Salem, presents plays ranging from serious drama to comedy and ghost stories. The season runs from May through November. Tickets cost $4.50 to $8.50.

In late July the Salem Art Association sponsors an annual **Salem Art Fair and Festival,** with everything from arts and crafts to hot-air balloon rides and samples of Oregon wines and cheeses. It's at Bush Park, 600 Mission St. SE (tel. 503/581-2228).

Salem Theatre of the Performing Arts, 1071 Commercial St. SE (tel. 503/588-7002), performs a changing round of plays with tickets at about $5 each.

2. EUGENE

Set in a lovely mountain valley beside the Willamette River, Eugene is surrounded by serene scenery. Perhaps all that pastoral tranquility is what has lured the many artists and writers who have come to call this place home.

Once here, art lovers exhibited strong support for art and cultural activities. Witness the city's annual Bach Festival and masses of money spent to build Hult Center, a much-ballyhooed showcase for the performing arts and one of the top such facilities in the West.

Art galleries abound and you'll find that many artists who live here, like most people in Eugene, do something unusual. One, for example, creates beautiful kaleidoscopes made from fine hand-turned woods.

Each fall Eugene's 103,000 population burgeons by 15,000 as students return to classes at the lovely historic buildings of the University of Oregon.

That's the way it is here, nothing quite what you would expect and never what it seems at first glance. All of which adds up to a most intriguing town with many a surprise.

GETTING THERE: Airlines flying into Mahlon Sweet Airport include American, Horizon, and United. Some hotels and motels in the region offer free shuttle service from the airport. **Mahlon Sweet Airport** is off Ore. 99, about nine miles northwest of town.

Amtrak brings passengers here daily, stopping at a red-brick station at East Fourth Avenue and Willamette (tel. 503/687-1383).

Greyhound, 987 Pearl St. (tel. 503/344-6265), brings passengers in here from points east and west.

If you're driving into town, you can get here off I-5. Other major highways leading to the city include U.S. 126, Ore. 58, and Ore. 36. From Eugene, Ore. 126 offers a scenic route to the coast and to central Oregon year round.

GETTING AROUND: Eugene is quite prepared for visitors, despite its small size and pastoral surroundings.

If you decide to rent a car, you can do so at a number of rental-car companies. Heading the list in Oregon for our money is **Budget,** at Mahlon Sweet Airport (tel. 503/689-1421), which always has rates at the most competitive levels and offers free parking in many parking lots throughout the Northwest. Others operating in this area include **Avis,** at Mahlon Sweet Airport (tel. 503/688-9053); **Hertz,** Mahlon Sweet Airport (tel. 503/688-9233); and **National,** Mahlon Sweet Airport (tel. 503/688-8161).

Lane Transit Co. (tel. 503/687-5555) runs **bus service** throughout the region. Fares are 60¢ for adults, 30¢ for children 5 to 11, and on weekends from Friday at 6 p.m. through Sunday fares are just 30¢ for adults, 25¢ for children.

ORIENTATION: Eugene and Springfield share billing here in the Willamette Valley. Springfield is on the northeast side of the Willamette River, Eugene on the southwest side. To cross the river you will find bridges at I-5 and on Washington Avenue, which becomes Delta Hwy. on the north side of the river.

In downtown Eugene east-west streets are numbered, with the lowest numbers near the river. North-south streets have names. Willamette Street runs through the middle of town in an east-west direction; Broadway and 11th Avenue also run east-west, with 11th Avenue connecting to Franklin Boulevard, where you'll find the University of Oregon.

Fern Ridge Lake is off Ore. 99 or Ore. 126. To get to Spencer Butte Park, drive south on Willamette Street about five miles to signs at the base of the butte.

To get to the McKenzie River white-water area, take Franklin Boulevard east and follow the signs through Springfield, or take Ore. 105 exit on Coburg Road east past Springfield to Ore. 126. Above McKenzie Bridge on Ore. 126, the old highway, open only in summer, heads off for some fabulous views of the Cascade Mountains, while an all-seasons road weaves through the mountains to join Ore. 20 leading to Sisters and Bend.

VISITOR INFORMATION: At the **Eugene-Springfield Convention and Visitors Bureau,** 305 W. Seventh Ave., Eugene, OR 97401 (tel. 503/484-5307, or toll free 800/547-5445, 800/452-3670 in Oregon), the very helpful staff can lead you to everything from a campground to a gourmet dinner. With 15,000 students pouring into the town each fall, they're accustomed to answering questions and solving problems here, so if you've got one or more of either, stop by and make a friend.

The **Eugene Chamber of Commerce,** 1401 Willamette St. (P.O. Box 1107), Eugene, OR 97440 (tel. 503/484-1314), can also help you out with maps and information on the region.

USEFUL INFORMATION: For **police or medical emergency,** call 911. . . . For same-day **photofinishing,** try Dot Dotson's, 430 E. 11th Ave. (tel.

503/485-1771). . . . One-hour **cleaning** can be done at 77 W. 11th St. (tel. 503/484-2453), open Monday through Saturday from 8:30 a.m. to 5 p.m. . . . **Downtown Mall** has an information booth that will help you find your way around the shops. It's open from 10 a.m. to 5 p.m. and is stocked with maps and monster cookies. . . . You can call for the time at 503/345-8911 or the weather at 503/689-1321.

WHERE TO STAY: Eugene has a wide range of hotel choices.

Top of the Crop

Valley River Inn, 1000 Valley River Way, Eugene, OR 97401 (tel. 503/ 687-0123, or toll free 800/547-8810, 800/452-8960 in Oregon), tops the list of stopping spots, just close enough to town, just far enough away, and a beautiful place to boot. Set among trees, the Valley River Inn is right alongside a tranquil section of the Willamette River. In the lobby comfortable chairs cluster about a massive copper-clad stone fireplace adorned with huge tools of the logging trade. Massive ceiling beams, hewn from woods of a forest down the way, make it seem a little like coming home to a cozy, albeit very large, Northwest home after a long day exploring the wilderness. Rooms are in several buildings that wind about the grounds, and many have balconies overlooking the river or the resort's big outdoor swimming pool. All sport the most contemporary of furnishings, light woods, and smart, muted color schemes; some even have sleek modern versions of four-posters! If you're in the mood for a real treat, try one of the inn's suites. They're nothing short of full apartments, with a big bedroom (king-size bed), a full kitchen outfitted with the latest in appliances, and a pretty living room with a view through glass doors to the private balcony beyond. The colors are soothing modern tones that are a delight to behold.

When it's playtime you can splash in the resort's swimming pool, take rafting trips on the river from the docks, rent a bicycle and ride the bike and go jogging on a trail that whips right past the resort alongside the river, relax in a whirlpool, or bake in a sauna.

In the lounge a fire crackles summer and winter, and in the adjacent woodsy, multilevel dining room, treats like roast duckling or prime ribs are served amid pots of flowers that trim the cozy, candlelit tables and intimate banquette seating. Rates at the inn are $72 to $97, depending on location and size of your room. Suites begin at $100.

To find your way there, take I-5 to exit 194 and continue west along I-105, following the Valley River center exits. If you're downtown, head for the Washington Street Bridge to Delta Hwy., and you will find the inn tucked along the perimeter of Valley River Shopping Center. If you pass the mall, you've gone too far.

In downtown Eugene, the **Eugene Hilton,** 66 E. Sixth Ave., Eugene, OR 97401 (tel. 503/342-2000, or toll-free numbers varying by state), is a soaring high-rise steps away from the city's Downtown Mall and its 5th Street Public Market. Hilton always does things with style, as it has here: a plant-strewn lobby, a tropically pretty coffeeshop decked out in photographic soft sculpture tributes to movie personalities, the plush rooftop nightclub where the view through walls of glass goes on forever, and the Encore Lounge for more view while you dance. In 1988 the hotel completed a $1-million redecoration of all its rooms, adding new televisions, phones, bedspreads, carpeting, and landscaping. In spacious rooms live plants fill empty corners, slick modern décor is soothing, and wide windows offer still more beautiful views across a balcony to the lights of Eugene. Suites add a wet bar to the accoutrements and a separate sitting room. To keep you in shape there's a health club with an exercise room, indoor swimming pool, and whirlpool spa. Rates at the Hilton are $68 to $88 double, about $10 less single.

Moderate Price Range

Thunderbird-Eugene Inn, 205 Coburg Rd., Eugene, OR 97401 (tel. 503/342-5201, or toll free 800/547-8010, 800/452-0733 in Oregon), features the cedar-shingle mansard roof that characterizes so many of the Thunderbird chain. Inside it offers just what you can always expect from this popular and extensive chain: bright and spacious rooms with a wall of glass and comfortable, fashionable furnishings, a bright, glass-enclosed coffeeshop, an intimate dining room specializing in continental cookery, and a lively lounge with entertainment. Rooms at the inn have private balconies or terraces too, many of them overlooking the outdoor swimming pool and attractively landscaped grounds. Rates at the Thunderbird are $46 to $49 double, and airport transportation is available.

The **Holiday Inn,** 225 Coburg Rd., Eugene, OR 97401 (tel. 503/342-5181, or toll free 800/HOLIDAY), has a very good-looking representative of its chain in Eugene. The center of attention here is an enclosed, two-story play place with everything from a swimming pool to miniature golf and table tennis. Spacious and attractively decorated rooms open onto and overlook this "Holidome" entertainment center, so you always have a view of activities. Holiday Inn has a café, and a lounge with entertainment and dancing too. You'll find it about two miles out of town. Rates are $46 to $53 double.

If you'd like a country setting not far from town, try the **Village Green Motor Hotel,** P.O. Box 277, Cottage Grove, OR 97424 (tel. 503/942-2491, or toll free 800/343-ROOM), a really cozy spot with lots of wood and greenery and 16 acres of grounds on which to amuse yourself. Little touches here are the most memorable: antique gas lanterns imported from Denmark, French doors, paned-glass windows, imported Belgian linen draperies, woodcarvings, and a weather vane atop a cupola. A cozy country air prevails in the handsome décor of comfortable rooms, and one- or two-bedroom suites have fireplaces to boot. For dining, two delightful restaurants: a bright coffeeshop called the Copper Rooster; and an intimate brick-walled spot dubbed the Cascadia, complete with blazing fireplace and American cuisine for prices in the $8 to $15 range. For sporting moments this woodsy spot offers a heated swimming pool, a playground, whirlpool, jogging trail, and tennis courts. You can even fly in here, landing on an adjacent paved lighted runway. Rates are $40 to $77 for rooms, with price depending on view, from $75 for suites.

Two other moderately priced hostelries in the Eugene-Springfield area are **Nandels,** Beltline and Gateway Road, Springfield, OR 97477 (tel. 503/726-1212, or toll free 800/547-0106), which offers a family dining room, a heated swimming pool, cable TV, a coin laundry, and airport transportation for $46 to $48 double; and the **Shilo Inn,** 3350 Gateway Blvd., Springfield, OR 97477 (tel. 503/747-0332, or toll free 800/222-2244), where you'll find an outdoor swimming pool, laundry, limo service to the airport, a restaurant, lounge, and a number of efficiency apartments with kitchens. Double rates are $48 to $60.

If golfing's your goal, the **Emerald Valley Sports Center,** 83293 N. Dale Kuni Rd., Creswell, OR 97426 (tel. 503/895-2147, or 503/485-6796 in Eugene), is the place for you. Located right on the golf course, the golf club is a study in natural woods, jewel-toned fiber wall hangings, handsome furnishings, and contemporary dining spots offering favorite American entrees. Among the amenities available to you are a complete health club/exercise room, the 18-hole championship golf course, a swimming pool, sauna, and whirlpool. You can stay here in a 72-room motel a mile away from the main lodge for prices that range from $27 to $32 for a room to $47 for a suite.

Best Western New Oregon Motel, 1655 Franklin Blvd., Eugene, OR 97440 (tel. 503/683-3669 or toll free 800/528-1234), is convenient to the University of Oregon and just a few minutes from the center of the city. Rooms are simply decorated and many have a balcony overlooking a stream that runs through the woods here. If you'd like a workout, you can swim in an indoor heated pool or play on the motel's free racquetball courts, then ease tired muscles in a whirlpool or roast in a sauna. Laundry facilities on the grounds are convenient, and local telephone calls are free. The Oregon Motel, part of the Best Western chain, even offers you complimentary coffee. Rates are $50 to $54 double.

TraveLodge, 540 E. Broadway St., Eugene, OR 97401 (tel. 503/342-1109, or toll free 800/255-3050), is a two-story motel with a heated, outdoor swimming pool and free in-room movies and coffee. Another conveniently located spot, the TraveLodge has medium-sized rooms basically furnished. Rates here are $35 to $40 double.

Budget Bets

Some folks who got their start operating a hostel, the Mill Street Hostel, have shuttered that operation and opened **Schnelli's Bed and Breakfast,** 542 Mill St., Springfield, OR 97477 (tel. 503/741-2735). While we haven't seen this one, we hear good reports. Each of the two units here has its own entrance, kitchen, bath, television, and microwave. Breakfast is optional and can be served in your room. Rates are $30 to $49 a night, and weekly rates are available without breakfast. Schnelli's is seven minutes from the university and ten minutes from downtown Eugene.

Two other bed-and-breakfast operations in the Eugene/Springfield area, neither of which we've seen: **Campus Cottage,** 1136 E. 19th Ave., Eugene, OR 97403 (tel. 503/342-5346), is a 1922 cottage renovated expressly for use as a bed-and-breakfast hostelry. Its three rooms are outfitted in queen-size brass bed with sitting room and bath or queen-size oak bed with private bath. Rates are $68 to $78. **The House in the Woods,** 814 Lorane Hwy., Eugene OR 97405 (tel. 503/343-3234), is a turn-of-the-century house tucked away in a quiet wooded glen and features three rooms, two sharing a bath and one with private bath and sitting room on the main floor. The House in the Woods also has a comfortable parlor and there is jogging nearby on an old country road. Rates with complete breakfast are $50 double with shared bath or $55 with queen-size bed and private bath.

WHERE TO DINE: Eugene is a college town so you can expect to find more than the average number of taco spots. It's also a health-conscious region so you'll find scads of sprouts-and-soyburgers restaurants. You'll also find some top-quality restaurants featuring wonderful local produce bought and sold in this historic market town—at very low prices. Here's a look at some of the favorites in Eugene, arranged more or less by cuisine.

Continental

Valley River Inn's **Sweetwater Restaurant** (tel. 503/687-0123) is an intimate spot with pretty scenic views across the McKenzie River. A fire blazes in the lounge as you dine amid flowers on such treats as prime rib with Yorkshire pudding, Caesar salads, French onion soups, and bouillabaisse, for prices in the $10 to $15 range. Sweetwater Restaurant is open every day of the week, serving breakfast from 6:30 to 11 a.m., lunch from 11 a.m. to 2 p.m., and dinner from 5:30 to 9:30 p.m. Monday through Saturday. On Sunday breakfast goes from 7:30 a.m. to noon, brunch from 10 a.m. to 2 p.m., and dinner at the regular hours.

At **Scampi's,** 388 W. Seventh Ave. (tel. 503/485-0601), two chefs have teamed up to produce such goodies as salmon Wellington; breast of chicken Bombay, blending béchamel sauce and curry; steak piquante topped with salsa de vega, mozzarella, and romano cheeses; and tournedos with béarnaise sauce. Specialty of the house is scampi à la grigilla, featuring prawns cooked with garlic, lemon, wine, shallots, and herbs, then topped off with pasta. A rack of lamb can be produced on 24-hour notice. You'll pay $12 to $16 for entrees, including Anna potatoes or pasta and vegetables. Hours at this attractive restaurant in a big veranda-rimmed home are 5:30 to 10 p.m. Monday through Saturday, to 1 a.m. in the jazz lounge; closed Sunday.

At the **Central Café,** 384 W. 13th Ave. (tel. 503/343-9510), a much-touted dining spot, you can stoke up on such delicacies as light and flaky French bread, goat cheese and walnuts on salad greens, and a changing array of lunch and dinner items incorporating whatever's fresh into such treats as smoked salmon terrine and lamb in port wine sauce. Prices are in the $10 to $15 range. The Central Café now has a garden courtyard that makes for a pleasant summer retreat. Pastries, breads, and even chocolates are made right here at the restaurant, which is open from 11 a.m. to 11 p.m. daily, except Saturday when it opens at 5 p.m. and Sunday when it's closed.

At the University of Oregon campus, the **Excelsior Café,** 754 E. 13th St. (tel. 503/342-6963), occupies a pretty Victorian home with greenhouse dining on sunny days. The Excelsior has a European flavor in both atmosphere and taste with a lauded French onion soup, yummy cassoulet, French steaks, and fresh fish in various preparations. Entree prices are in the $6 to $14 range. For a light lunch try the beggars banquet of fruit, cheese, and soup. Sunday brunch is a big business here too. Recipient of many accolades from Northwest cooking experts, the Excelsior also features a full bar of Oregon wines by the glass. Hours are 11:30 a.m. to midnight Monday through Friday, from 5:30 p.m. on Saturday. Sunday hours are 10 a.m. to 2 p.m. and 5:30 to 11 p.m. The Excelsior Café also operates a Charcuterie about ten blocks away at 901 Pearl St. (tel. 503/342-3110), open similar days and hours.

Café Zenon, 898 Pearl St. (tel. 503/343-3005), features a long menu that includes some wonderfully innovative, not to mention fresh, salads, ceviche, pâtés, and many more serious dining choices featuring gingery spices, fruit flavors, and delicate and unusual twists. Prices are in the $10 to $15 range for dinner entrees, and hours are 8 a.m. to 11 p.m. Monday through Thursday, closing at midnight on Friday and Saturday. Zenon, by the way, changes its menus every day, but can always be counted on for such unusual breakfast treats as hazelnut waffles topped with crème fraîche. At dinner such tempters as grilled goat cheese with vinaigrette dressing or pesto-filled ravioli in gorgonzola cream sauce appear.

French

If—make that *when*—you're perishing for some wonderful French flavors, try **La Auberge,** 770 W. Sixth Ave. (tel. 503/485-8000), but reserve for dinner as far in advance as possible. It's very small and very popular. It's also very elegant in a beautifully restored old home. The menu features lots of fresh fish entrees and some traditional continental selections like steak Diane and rack of lamb. Hours are 5:30 to 10 p.m. Tuesday through Saturday, and $12 to $20 six-course dinners include soup, salad, appetizer tray, entree, and vegetables, topped off by a platter of fruit and cheese.

American

The **Union Oyster Bar,** 870 Pearl St. (tel. 503/686-2873), has a bountiful supply of fresh oysters, crab, prawns, clams, and the like supplemented by a long list of complete seafood dinners ranging from Louisiana catfish to Idaho stuffed trout, sand dabs, razor clams, Australian lobster tail, and sautéed Dungeness crab legs. For landlubbers, there's a range of sandwiches, pasta, steak, chicken, pork, fish and chips, of course, plus chips with oysters, scallops, prawns, or clams. No shortage of chips here. Prices are quite reasonable, averaging about $7 to $11 including salad or chowder and potato or rice. Open from 11 a.m. to 9 p.m. Monday through Thursday, an hour later on Friday and Saturday nights, 4 to 9 p.m. on Sunday.

Wild Plum Restaurant and Pie Shop, 1081 Valley River Plaza, 1081 Valley River Way (tel. 503/484-2666), is a handsome wood-sided building along the river. Specialties here are Belgian waffles, homemade soups and chili, vegetable plates, old-fashioned chicken dumplings, and a sumptuous salad bar. Very reasonable prices well under $10 for most selections. Hours are 7 a.m. to 11 p.m. daily.

Sooner or later you're going to have a rib attack. When that happens, head to **Perry's on Pearl,** 959 Pearl St. (tel. 503/683-2360), where you can gorge on extra-large beef short ribs, barbecued pork back ribs, ribs basted in a spicy sauce, all kinds of ribs, for prices in the $10 range. Hours are 10 a.m. to 10 p.m. daily.

Terry's Diner, 296 E. 5th, in the 5th Street Public Market near the fountain courtyard (tel. 503/683-8196), is lauded for its top-quality burgers. Proof of that: The restaurant was winner of a local taste-off competition. When nothing but a burger will do, Terry's will provide an awesome array of pocket burgers, burger sausagola, avocado burger, Terry-aki burger, barbecued burgers, and bacon buster burger! At breakfast there's a list of 24 kinds of omelets, including one called What a Gas! with chili and lots of other stuff, another called A You've Got To Be Kidding Omelet with more than 40 ingredients! Sandwiches, soups, salads, muffins, stuffed baked potatoes—all that and more for prices in the $5 range or less. Terry's is open weekdays from 7 a.m. to 8 p.m., an hour later opening on Saturday, and 9 a.m. to 6 p.m. on Sunday.

If you'd like a little history with dinner, head for the **Log Cabin Inn,** 56483 McKenzie Hwy., McKenzie Bridge (tel. 503/822-3432), a genuine log structure originally built as a coach stop. These days it's a restaurant serving up crispy fried chicken, tender lamb chops, charcoal-broiled steaks, and fresh trout for prices in the $8 to $15 range.

The **Mill Camp Steakhouse and Saloon,** 215 Q St., Springfield (tel. 503/747-0577), adds historic flavors to its culinary ones. You'll dine in what was once an ice-skating rink but is now rigged out with rustic hand-cut beams and walls, on which are displayed a collection of old photographs and antique logging tools. Feast on such logger's rib-stickers as homemade bread served hot from the oven and hearty homemade soups as well as a collection of steaks and chops. Prices are in the $10 to $15 range and the restaurant is open from 11:30 a.m. to 9:30 p.m. weekdays and 5 to 10 p.m. on Saturday.

The **Terrace Café,** 490 Valley River Center (tel. 503/344-8369), is a simple and elegant spot featuring some wonderful soups, salads, and sandwiches, and a very good $8 Sunday brunch. Open from 11 a.m. to 8 p.m. weekdays, closing at 4 p.m. on Saturday, and open only from 10 a.m. to 2 p.m. on Sunday.

Ethnic Spots

Pasta fans flock to **Jo Federigo's,** 259 E. Fifth Ave. (tel. 503/343-8488), where a spaghetti bar has been the rage for ages. News here is some nouvelle culinary activity featuring Northwest treats like Oregon scallops and fresh mushrooms and seasonal greens. Prices are in the $10 to $15 range, cheaper for pastas, and hours are 11:30 a.m. to 3 p.m. for lunch weekdays and 5:30 to 10 p.m. for dinner daily, an hour later on weekends.

Poppi's was for a decade a popular stop for Eugene's Greek food enthusiasts. Although that restaurant is no more, Poppi and her enthusiastic crew are back in the kitchen, this time operating **Anatolia,** 992 Willamette St. (tel. 503/343-9661). You'll find it downtown in the heart of the Eugene Mall. To the menu of Greek favorites like chicken in lemon sauce have been added some exotic Indian treats like vegetable thali, one of several vegetable concoctions produced here. Hours are 11:30 a.m. to 10:30 p.m. weekdays and 5:30 to 10:30 p.m. weekends. Sunday is Greek Night with a special Greek menu.

Tabletop theatrics are a way of life at **Shoji's,** 2645 Willamette St. (tel. 503/343-8483), where nimble-fingered waiters chop, slice, stir-fry, and flip from grill to plate at 75 rpm. Chicken, stir-fry oysters, filet mignon, sukiyaki steam, shrimp, and scallops are the basics here, accompanied by Japanese salad and vegetables, ginger and mustard sauces. You pull a chair right up to the grill and wait to be flipped something. Prices are in the $11 to $17 range and hours are 5 to 9:30 p.m. weekdays, an hour later on weekends, and from 4 to 9 p.m. on Sunday.

Chinese food enthusiasts should head on over to the **Genghis Khan Restaurant,** 900 W. Seventh Ave. (tel. 503/687-2130). In keeping with GK's formidable reputation, you'll find spicy Szechuan cooking as well as wok cooking and Hunan cuisine. For a real Genghis event try the Mongolian barbecue. Dinners are in the $8 to $15 range, and Genghis Khan is open every day from 5:30 to 9:30 p.m., an hour later on Friday and Saturday nights.

For some good Mexican food in a lovely and historic old home, try **Moreno's,** 433 E. Broadway (tel. 503/343-5612). Great margaritas and traditional Mexican dishes served from 5 to 9 p.m. daily except Monday. Bills may very well be under $10.

Trendy Spots

If you're looking for lunch, try the 81¢ bagel sandwiches at **Oak Way Wine and Deli,** 305 Oakway Mall (tel. 503/343-3088), open from 10 a.m. to 7 p.m. daily except Sunday; or **Deb's the Original,** 1290 W. Seventh Avenue, Eugene (tel. 503/343-8307), and **Deb's Family Restaurant,** 4229 Main St., Springfield (tel. 503/726-6271), for curlicue french fries and burgers in baskets. Hours: 6:30 a.m. to 10 p.m. Monday through Saturday and 6 a.m. to 8 p.m. on Sunday.

Natural-food fans can find some of their favorites at **Genesis Juice Bar,** 296 E. Fifth Ave. (tel. 503/344-0967).

De Frisco's, 99 W. Tenth Ave. (tel. 503/484-2263), is a pleasantly trendy spot with a library look heavy on wainscoting, with intimate little booths, books, and backgammon. Primarily a cozy watering hole, this pubby spot also manages to produce some quite creditable offerings for all three meals, served on a terrace in the Atrium Building: eggs steamed over an espresso maker at breakfast, pâtés at lunch, crêpes, quiches, soups, and sandwiches. Prices are in the $5 range, give or take a dollar or two, and hours are 11 a.m. to 1 a.m. daily.

Finally, two bakeries in town are oft-frequented spots and rightly so: the **Metropole Bakery,** 296 E. Fifth Ave., in the 5th Street Public Market (tel. 503/687-9370), which features yummy cinnamon rolls, cream puffs that are to die for, tortes, and fresh local berries topping creamy pastries; and **Fall Creek Bakery,** 881 E. 13th Ave. (tel. 503/484-1662), next to the University Bookstore, beat all the competition in a recent bake-off.

NIGHTLIFE: Nightlife in Eugene is not what you'd call scintillating, but what you do find can be very pleasant indeed.

The **Valley River Inn,** 1000 Valley River Way (tel. 503/687-0123), has an intimate little bar and dancing to live music most nights of the week, as does the **Holiday Inn,** 225 Coburg Rd. (tel. 503/342-5181), and the **Eugene Hilton,** 66 E. Sixth Ave. (tel. 503/342-2000), which at last check was about to open a snazzy new restaurant and cocktail lounge with dancing on the 12th floor of the hotel.

The **Red Lion Motor Inn,** 3280 Gateway (tel. 503/726-8181), has a lounge with good live music, but it's a very popular place, so expect to compete for space.

You'll find the college crowd amusing each other at **G. Willacker's,** 440 Coburg Rd. (tel. 503/343-1221).

Perry's on Pearl, 959 Pearl St. (tel. 503/683-2360), is a basement disco frequented by a fair number of very free-thinkers but well attended by more traditional partiers as well.

For western sounds, try the **Driftwood,** 5094 Main St., Springfield (tel. 503/746-0169).

Eugene doesn't lack for happy hours: **North Bank Restaurant,** 22 Club Rd. (tel. 503/343-5622), with an outside patio on the river, is a favorite, as is **Oregon Electric Station,** 27 E. Fifth Ave. (tel. 503/485-4444), which features jazz on weekends.

WHAT TO SEE AND DO: From historic covered bridges to fanatical adoration for jogging tracks and bike paths, Eugene offers you plenty of ways to spend your days. Here's a look at some of them.

For openers, you might stop at the Visitors Bureau and ask for a copy of a quite informative pamphlet called "Exciting Adventures." Outlined in it are many **loop drives** you can take to see some of the wonderful valley scenery.

One of the loveliest ways to spend a few hours in Eugene is just looking at the place! Quite an old town—it dates back to the 1850s—Eugene has some glamorous old Victorian homes that have been carefully restored and look as beautiful today as they did in their heyday. At the Visitors Bureau you can get a map that will guide you past **historic homes** and tell you a little about the people who lived there. The pamphlet is called "Historical Eugene" and is a product of the Junior League of Eugene.

Many of the homes are in the Third Avenue and Pearl Street section and on Eleventh Avenue. Another similar pamphlet guides you around the historic landmark area of East Skinner Butte. That one's called "East Skinner Butte Historic Landmark Area" and is produced by the Eugene Planning Department (tel. 503/687-4581). You can pick it up at the Visitors Bureau too.

There's something so nostalgically Currier & Ives about a covered bridge, isn't there? This section of Oregon is rife with **covered bridges,** many of them lovingly preserved by residents who treasure this wooden remembrance of days past. You can see three in a row on Mosby Creek (take I-5 south 18 miles to the Village Green exit and go east on Dorena Road, taking the right fork to Mosby Creek), and a very pretty one 31 miles up the McKenzie River on Ore. 126 east out of Springfield. There are 21 covered bridges in the region and the Visitors Bureau can help you find your way to others.

The **Albany Area Chamber of Commerce,** 435 1st St. West (P.O. Box 548), Albany, OR 97321 (tel. 503/926-1517), has a self-guided driving tour map called "Covered Bridges of Linn County" that points the way to ten covered bridges in a variety of styles.

There's more history at the **Lane County Historical Museum,** 740 W. 13th Ave. (tel. 503/687-4239), adjacent to the Lane County Fairgrounds, where you can see textiles and tools and some of the things the early pioneers packed lovingly and brought with them over the plains. Hours Tuesday through Friday are 10 a.m. to 4 p.m., on Saturday from noon to 4 p.m., and admission is $1 for adults, 50¢ for children.

The **University of Oregon** has a beautiful 250-acre campus with 82 buildings, many of them historic structures, set amid fir and cedar trees. You can take a free tour of the campus Monday through Friday at 10:30 a.m. or 2:30 p.m. Meeting spot is Oregon Hall, East 13th Avenue and Agate Street (tel. 503/686-3014). There's convenient parking in a lot at 13th Avenue and Agate Street.

Naturalists can see some interesting anthropological exhibits relating the history of Oregon's native cultures at the university's **Museum of Natural History,** University of Oregon (tel. 503/686-3024). It's open from noon to 5 p.m. Wednesday through Sunday. Admission is free.

There's a whole world up there. Up where? Up there in the sky, where things are happening even as you read. You can discover what some of those things are at **Willamette Science and Technology Center,** 2300 Centennial Blvd. (tel. 503/484-9027 or 689-6500). That kid in all of us can talk to a friend on a fiber optics telephone, play with sound and light, and watch the stars and planets in the comfort of an easy chair here. Hours at the center are noon to 5 p.m. Tuesday through Sunday, with planetarium shows at 1 and 3 p.m. weekends. Admission is $2 for adults, 75¢ for children 3 to 18.

Local vineyards of note include **Forgeron Vineyard,** 89697 Sheffler Rd., Elmira (tel. 503/935-1117), a family-run winery planted in 1972 that now produces 10,000 gallons of varietal wine annually. Tucked into a stand of pines at the bottom of a hill bearing the vines, the winery has a pretty garden and a loft, both picturesque spots for a picnic accompanied, of course, by a sip of wine practically right off the vine. After lunch, walk up the hill for a view of the snow-capped Cascades.

To get there, take Ore. 126 to Elmira or I-5 to West 11th Avenue or Belt Line exits. Just north of Elmira turn left on Warthen Road, then right on Sheffler Road. Admission is free, and the winery is open from noon to 5 p.m. daily from May through September. In other months Forgeron is open only on Saturday and Sunday from noon to 5 p.m. On the third weekend in July the vineyard sponsors a weekend Bluegrass Festival with music, tours, and a barbecue.

Hinman Vineyards, established in 1979, sports a brick building with Bavarian touches. Recently the vineyard added a new tasting room and tank room, and rescuptured the landscaping with such skill the grounds are now popular for bridal celebrations. Hinman has introduced a new wine called Tior (pronounced "Tee-or"), an Old High German word for deer, to its line which also includes pinot noir, riesling, and cabernet sauvignon. In summer the winery features concerts in its amphitheater. To get there, take the West 11th Avenue exit from I-5 (or the Beltline exit), then go south on Bailey Hill Road, east at Spencer Creek Road, and south on Briggs Hill Road. The winery is about 15 miles from Eugene. Open daily from noon to 5 p.m.

Nearby **Cottage Grove** has been a gold-seeker's heaven for many a year, as it is still. At the Cottage Grove Chamber of Commerce, 710 Row River Rd. (tel. 503/942-2411), or the Ranger station, McKenzie Bridge, east of I-5 (tel. 503/822-3381) you can get a map and guide describing historic features of the mining district so you can make your own tour around this historic **gold-mining region.** One note of caution: More than 2,000 gold bugs have laid claims to land in the area, and some of them don't take kindly to sightseers, so stick to the map.

SPECIAL EVENTS: Nearby Junction City, about 12 miles away on Ore. 99, has been celebrating its Scandinavian ancestry for a quarter of a century now at an annual celebration called **Scandinavian Days (Forbindelsestad).** About the second weekend in August the city dusts off its yodels, begins cooking Swedish meatballs, and whittling out woodcarvings to amuse the crowds, who throng in here for four days of Scandinavian dance, costumes, food, crafts, and naturally, a brew or two. Streets are closed off for the festival, and townsfolk in Scandinavian costumes turn the whole place into a little touch of Baltic heaven. Festivities, all of them free, go on from morning to well into the night. Good spot to begin your Christmas shopping.

Cultural pursuits are well-attended in Eugene, so you can expect to see crowds at the **Oregon Bach Festival** in late June. An annual event for two decades, the two-week festival features an international array of artists specializing in everything from classical guitar to organ music. Most days begin with free concerts at noon on the University of Oregon campus, where jazz is as likely to be on the program as chamber music.

In mid-July the town of Cottage Grove sponsors an event called **Bohemia Mining Days,** with fashion shows of pioneer costumes, an excursion to the mining district, and tours of historic homes. Folks are still laying claim to mines in the region so you can get a look at real mining operations.

SPORTS: Rafting tops the list of sporting activities in Eugene, where the paddling and pounding takes place on the McKenzie River. Largest river-rafting outfitter in the Eugene area is **Oregon River Experiences,** 1935 Hayes St., Eugene, OR 97405 (tel. 503/689-6198), which also is the second-largest outfitter in all of the Northwest. Oregon River Experiences offers trips on the McKenzie and North Umpqua Rivers close to Eugene, but if you'd like to venture a bit farther out they'll arrange trips on Oregon's Rogue, Deschutes, Grande Ronde, John Day, and Owyhee Rivers. This company also rafts on Idaho's Salmon River and on the Klamath River in northern California. Trips on the McKenzie and North Umpqua Rivers depart from Hellford's Landing in Eugene and are $35 per person. Prices for longer trips vary according to length and number of participants.

Wild Water Adventures, P.O. Box 249, Creswell, OR 97426 (tel. 503/ 895-4465), will pick you up at your hotel and spirit you off to the river for a day on the bouncy, but not terrifying, rapids for $30 a person. Wild Water operates other tours too, most of them day or overnight trips on the waters of the Deschutes River and longer trips to Owyhee, Oregon's answer to the Grand Canyon, or to John Day River for three to eight days by arrangement.

Ouzel Outfitters, P.O. Box 11217, Eugene, OR 97440 (tel. 503/747-2236), borrowed its name from the ouzel bird, which, they say, is the only chirper with nerve enough to brave the white waters—a fitting name for a group that makes a living shepherding thrill-seekers through rafting trips on Oregon's rivers. Ouzel operates one- to five-day trips on the McKenzie, Rogue, Umpqua, Deschutes, Klamath, and Owyhee Rivers, where rapids range from kid stuff to eek! Billing their trips as "adventure with a splash of class," Ouzel does not ask you to forgo the best of civilized life just because you're out there communing with nature: at evening camp you dine on such as caviar on wafers, a cameron salad with Greek feta cheese topping, chicken coq au vin or snapper Huachinango poached in a Créole sauce, chocolate fondue, and Oregon wines. Sounds like our kind of roughing it. You can also learn how to paddle your own inflatable kayak at a school operated by this company or go on a trekking trip. One-day rafting trips are $40 to $60 depending on the river, with two- to five-day trips $178 to $450.

One more outfit, **Outdoor Adventures Plus,** 4030 W. Amazon Dr., Eugene, OR 97405 (tel. 503/485-6419), has an interesting variety of trips ranging from white-water river trips to hunting, fishing, cross-country skiing, horseback riding and pack trips, mountain climbing, backpacking, and any combination thereof! Prices vary according to the length and distance of the trip, so call or write the company for detailed information.

Many guides lead fishing or rafting expeditions in the region, so many, in fact, that they've formed an association which publishes a list of members. That list is available at the Eugene-Spring Visitor and Convention Bureau or from the **McKenzie River Guides Association** or president Greg White, 1041 N. Park St., Eugene OR 97401 (tel. 503/689-2144).

Hikers can warm up their boots on the 26.5-mile **McKenzie River Trail** in the Willamette National Forest. The route begins 1.2 miles east of McKenzie Bridge on Ore. 126. A shorter but hardier trail along the McKenzie wends its way to Scott Mountain from an old quarry on the Scott Lake access road 6½ miles away. Views of the Three Sisters Mountains are terrific, and the lake makes a good cooling-off spot. Rangers at McKenzie Station, McKenzie Bridge (tel. 503/822-3381), will help you find the way.

For many, if not all, of your recreational plans, call on folks at the **Eugene Parks and Recreation Dept.**, 301 N. Adams St. (tel. 503/687-5329).

Swimmers can splash in **swimming pools** operated by the department. Among those are Amazon, an outdoor pool at 26th Avenue and Hilyard Street, and Sheldon, an indoor pool at 2445 Willakenzie Rd.

Tennis players will find courts throughout the city in parks, including Skinner Butte and Hendricks Parks on the south bank of the river and Spencer Butte Park at the south edge of the city. Rec department workers can help you find the courts closest to you.

Bicyclists have plenty of in-town bicycle paths to choose among as well as longer trips. Once again, call on the recreation department, which can help you plan an exploration. You can rent a bike at **Pedal Power,** Sixth Avenue and High Street (tel. 503/687-1775), for $10 a day, $30 a week. Pedal Power's open from 10 a.m. to 6 p.m. Monday through Saturday, and 11 a.m. to 5 p.m. on Sunday.

Those who'd rather ride on hooves than bikes can do so at **Pruitt's Equestrian Center,** 27705 Lorane Orchard Rd., Lorane, OR 97451 (tel. 503/942-7428). You can trot about on 75 green acres for $12 an hour on a two-hour trail ride.

For those to whom a cast has nothing to do with theater, all the fishing action is at Clear Lake, where rainbow and brook trout swim through submerged tree stumps. Cougar and Blue River reservoirs on the Upper McKenzie River are stocked with trout. So is the McKenzie River's main branch from Armitage Park near Eugene to Trail Bridge Reservoir, which is stocked with 120,000 rainbow trout each spring. Steelhead and salmon are caught here too. Check with the local rangers at McKenzie Ranger Station (tel. 503/822-3317).

In summer months workout fans can use the swimming pool, weight room, and tennis and racquetball courts at the University of Oregon's Esslinger Hall, 15th and University Street (tel. 503/686-4113).

Golfers have plenty of options too: **Oakway Golf Course,** 2000 Cal Young Rd. (tel. 503/485-7033), an 18-hole course; or **Springfield Country Club,** 90545 Marcola Rd., Springfield (tel. 503/747-2517), open dawn to dusk. Both have greens fees in the $10 to $15 range and have all equipment and lessons available.

ART AND CULTURAL ACTIVITIES: Many of Eugene's musical and theatrical events occur at the city's new **Hult Center,** One Eugene Center (tel. 503/687-5087), a sleek contemporary theater with a cream-colored curtain woven of undyed velour delicately depicting Oregon blackberry bushes. Opened in 1982, Hult Center has been lauded for the acoustic excellence of its two theaters: the **Silva Concert Hall,** which seats 2,500 in curving ground-floor and balcony seats so cleverly designed that no seat is more than 112 feet from the edge of the pit; and the **Soreng Theater,** a 500-seat asymmetrical open-ended room with a proscenium arch that can be moved to vary effects.

Thousands of visitors stop by each year to see what's showing at the **Univer-**

sity of Oregon's Museum of Art (tel. 503/686-3027), open from noon to 5 p.m. Wednesday through Sunday October to July (on Tuesday only in July).

You'll have no trouble finding theater productions in Eugene and environs. Among the theaters operating here are the **University of Oregon Carnival Theater,** performing at Robinson Theatre on campus; **Lane Community College Theatre,** also performing on its campus at 1509 Willamette St. (tel. 503/726-2202 or 484-2278); **Mainstage Theatre Company,** performing in summer at the downtown mall (tel. 503/683-4368); **Very Little Theatre** and the **Eugene Festival of Musical Theater,** and **Oregon Repertory Theater,** 1231 Olive St. (tel. 503/485-1946), performing at Hult Center's Silva Hall. Tickets vary widely in price from $2 to about $20, averaging perhaps $5 to $10.

The **Eugene Symphony Orchestra,** 1231 Olive St. (tel. 503/687-0344), and the **Eugene Opera** share quarters and perform here frequently, the opera company featuring productions in English. To find out what's playing when, check the Eugene *Register Guard*.

SHOPPING: It's amazing what you can do with an old chicken-processing plant. You'll see what we mean when you visit **Fifth Street Public Market** shops. Local entrepreneurs in 1976 turned it into a many-splendored thing that's now a meeting place, a landmark, a shopping spot, and a place to just stroll about enjoying the beauties—and the temptations—of this lovely urban space. On a sunny summer day you can collapse on a bench under a tree and be serenaded by public conerts that occur here. Craft purveyors, coffee sellers, cafés, and boutiques offer a fabulous collection of national and international treasures.

Two levels of mezzanines overlook a ground-floor fountain at the market. The Fifth Street Public Market occupies the area between Pearl and High Streets from Fifth to Sixth Avenues. Here you'll also find a mélange of eating places like **Agadir Deli** (tel. 503/344-0908), a simple sandwich shop open from 9 a.m. to 6 p.m. daily, an hour earlier on Sunday; **El Patio** (tel. 503/686-9819), a Mexican restaurant with prices in the $5 to $7 range, open from 10 a.m. to 6 p.m. Monday through Saturday and 9 a.m. to 5 p.m. on Sunday; **French Horn** (tel. 503/343-7473), for française flavors and continental cuisine, open from 7 a.m. to 6 p.m. six days and 9 a.m. to 5 p.m. on Sunday; and **Greek Isle** (tel. 503/683-6500), which dishes up those Greek classics in the $5 to $10 range, open from 11 a.m. to 6 p.m. Monday through Saturday, to 5 p.m. on Sunday.

From there you can move right up a couple of blocks to Eugene's **Downtown Mall,** from Eighth to Eleventh Avenues between Pearl and Charnelton Streets. Bon Marché and Sears department stores are the biggies here, backed by dozens of small boutiques. Several streets in the area are pedestrian malls, closed to traffic. There's free parking at Over Park North and South at Oak Street and Tenth Avenue.

Right here is where you'll also find one event in Eugene that you don't want to miss; it's the **Saturday Market.** Now a 20-year tradition in town, the market is a gathering place for an intriguing cross-section of Eugene residents and visitors. You'll see mimes mixing with matrons, strummers and drummers, weavers and weirdities at the market, which also manages to feature some wonderful craftwork. You can buy everything from a string of garlic buds to a strand of gold beads here every Saturday around the fountain at 8th and Oak Streets (tel. 503/686-8885).

If you're in the market for arts or crafts—or just want to take back some souvenirs better than ashtrays with Oregon written on them—ask at the Visitors Bureau for a directory of art dealers in the region. Among those selling work of local arts and crafts workers are **Made in Oregon,** 295 E. Fifth Ave. (tel. 503/344-5051), which features some of the best of Oregon craftwork, porcelain, stoneware, jewelry, weaving, wood, and stained glass, and is open Monday through Saturday from 10:30 a.m. to 5:30 p.m.; **Opus 5 Gallery of Crafts,** 136 E. Broadway (tel. 503/484-1710), showing textiles, jewelry, glass, and woodwork, open daily except Sunday from 11 a.m. to 5:30 p.m.; and **Soaring Wings,** 760 Willamette St. (tel. 503/683-8474), showing wildlife art, open from 10 a.m. to 5:30 p.m.

If you'd rather have chocolate than anything, stop by **Euphoria Chocolates,** 6 W. 17th Ave. (tel. 503/343-9223), a chocoholic's downfall proud of its "world-class" truffles.

Delta Village is a collection of shops featuring everything from Oregon sheepskin to microwaves. You'll find the village near Valley River Inn.

Valley River Center, on Delta Hwy. (tel. 503/683-5511), has more than 100 stores in an air-conditioned mall, and **Springfield Mall,** also known as Mohawk Mall, at 2303 Olympic St., in Springfield, is a popular shopping spot.

If we intrigued you with the fancy kaleidoscopes at the beginning of this section, write **Dorothy Marshall** at 705 W. 23rd St. Eugene, OR 97401 (no phone).

BEND AND CENTRAL OREGON

□ □ □

Snow-capped Mount Bachelor is Bend's raison d'être in winter, while in summer the lure is the region's warm weather. Those tempting temperatures have made the city the sporting capital of Oregon, a place many coastal dwellers head when they want to dry out after many days of moisture.

Skiing is king in winter, but in summer dozens of lakes and the white waters of the Deschutes River lure swimmers, anglers, rafters, and surfboarders.

Despite year-round skiing on the mountain, Bend's advantageous geographical position means you'll find temperatures in the 80s and 90s in summer, rarely below zero in winter. It doesn't rain much either: the city gets only 12 inches of precipitation a year, and much of that is winter snow, which averages about three feet annually.

In this desert-to-mountain city you'll find 25 parks to explore along the river and plenty of interesting places to stay while you play.

Nearby Deschutes National Forest is home to a lava river cave and a spooky lava tube a mile long. A desert museum offers you a peek behind arid scenery. On the other end of the spectrum, a dozen waterfalls crash over rugged bluffs into rivers where white waters and blue swimming holes merge.

Many, many parts of this craggy, pine-strewn land are a photographer's delight. Scenery rises in splendiferous grandeur, white-topped peaks peeking from behind a screen of pines or towering over a golden field.

Holidays like Memorial Day and Labor Day are busy times here. That's when the traffic streams from Eugene, Portland, Klamath Falls, and points west, pouring into this sleepy town in search of the first spring sunshine or a final fling before fall. In winter you'll see similar streams of traffic, this time skiers headed back to lodging spots at 4 p.m. when the lifts to the ski slopes close. A very versatile—and vigorous—place, this Bend in the road.

1. GETTING THERE AND GETTING AROUND

GETTING THERE: Horizon flies to the **Redmond-Bend Airport,** about 16 miles north of Bend, with connecting flights from Portland and Eugene from such airlines as Alaska, American, Continental, Delta, Eastern, Northwest, and United.

Amtrak trains carry their share of visitors. Amtrak's regular run from Seattle to San Diego includes a stop 65 miles south of Bend at Chemult Station, at 2nd Street and Santiam **Hwy. (U.S. 97).**

To get to lodgings in Redmond or Bend, an airport limousine service and taxis stand ready. If you've arrived at Portland International Airport, you can climb aboard the **Central Oregon Shuttle** (tel. 503/382-9371), a service that has daily direct connections between Portland International and Bend. The one-way fare is $29 for adults and $21 for children under 12; round-trip fares are $49 for adults, $41 for children.

Transportation from Portland to Bend is also available on **Greyhound** (tel. 503/382-2151), which has a local stop.

Bend comes close to being the geographic center of Oregon and is a crossroads for travelers from all compass points. **U.S. 97** bridges the Columbia River on the north from Marysville, Washington, skirts the Warm Springs Indian Reservation, divides Bend east from west, and cuts through the eastern reaches of the Cascades as it heads south to Klamath Falls and the California border.

Travelers from the northwest and southwest will approach Bend on **U.S. 20.** U.S. 26 channels Bend-bound drivers from the east onto Ore. 126 into Redmond, where it joins U.S. 97 for the short run south. From Eugene, due west of Bend, you might want to cross the Cascades on Ore. 126, transferring to U.S. 20 east at the junction for your final leg into town.

GETTING AROUND: In winter there's a shuttle-bus service operated by **Resort Bus Lines,** from Bend and other nearby cities to Mount Bachelor ski lifts. Call them at 503/389-7755 for time and fare information.

Occasionally, during the highly competitive winter season, rental-car companies will offer special rates to skiers. At Redmond Airport check with **National Car Rental** (tel. 503/548-8166, or toll free 800/328-4157) or **Hertz Rent A Car** (tel. 503/923-1411, or toll free 800/654-3131). At Portland International call **Budget Rent A Car** (tel. 503/249-4559, or toll free 800/527-0770).

Whether you rent one or bring your own, this is a region in which a car is most welcome, if not downright vital. A car gives you quick access to ski slopes in winter and in summer freedom to visit beautiful villages that surround Bend—like Sisters and Sunriver—and to take some spectacular mountain drives you'll never forget.

You shouldn't have much trouble finding your way around Bend. Its main street from north to south is **U.S. 97,** which becomes **3rd Street** as it passes through town. A short way from the city limits the street splits to become one-way Division Street heading south and one-way 3rd Street heading north. Turn west off Division or 3rd Streets at Greenwood Avenue, and you'll shortly find yourself in the downtown shopping area overlooking Mirror Pond on the

Deschutes River. If you miss Greenwood Avenue, Franklin Avenue will get you there too. It becomes Riverside Boulevard as it follows the curve of the river.

You won't be long in town before you hear a lot about two beautiful villages —Sisters and Sunriver. When curiosity surges, you'll find **Sisters** just 21 miles north on U.S. 20, set in the Cascades, while **Sunriver** flourishes as an Eden about 15 miles south of Bend just off U.S. 97. Both of these communities provide idyllic mountain-forest settings for resorts known throughout the West. You'll learn more about them below.

2. TOURIST AND USEFUL INFORMATION

TOURIST INFORMATION: At 164 N.W. Hawthorne Ave., Bend, OR 97701, you'll find a lovely little house that will, until the summer of 1989, be home to the **Bend Chamber of Commerce** (tel. 503/382-3221). Thereafter, look for the chamber's friendly workers at the Central Oregon Welcome Center on North U.S. 97 in Bend. No address had yet been assigned to the chamber when this book went to press, but they'll be forwarding their mail from the old address. In that same new building you will also find a Visitor's Information Center, the Central Oregon Recreation Association, and the Regional Arts Council of Central Oregon. That new Visitor's Center will be dispensing information and brochures on all of central Oregon as well as on Bend. Hours here are 9 a.m. to 5 p.m. Monday through Friday.

Information about neighboring Sisters is available at the **Sisters Chamber of Commerce,** 339 Cascade, Sisters, OR 97759 (tel. 503/549-6122), and you can seek still more information on recreational activities in the region by writing the **Central Oregon Recreation Association,** P.O. Box 230, Bend, OR 97709 (tel. 503/389-8799 or 382-8334).

The sales office at **Mount Bachelor Ski Resort** (tel. 503/382-8334, or toll free 800/547-6858 outside Oregon) can also help you out with hotel and motel reservations. Staffers at the sales office operate a Central Reservation Office which lists rates and room availability at 14 area resorts, led by the two largest local properties, Sun River Resort and Inn of the Seventh Mountain, and moving down to budget motels.

USEFUL INFORMATION: For **police or medical help,** dial 503/388-5555 in Bend, 503/549-2333 in Sisters . . . For information about **Mount Bachelor,** write to P.O. Box 1031, Bend, OR 97709 (tel. 503/382-8334) . . . For a **snow report,** call 503/382-7888 . . . Check the *Bend Bulletin,* daily except Saturday, for information on **special events** in the area . . . Bend's population is about 18,000 . . . You can get your car washed after the drive across the mountains at **Red Carpet Car Wash,** 1144 N.E. 3rd St., where both automatic and self-service facilities are available . . . Gardiner Goodyear Tire Center, 61335 S. U.S. 97 (tel. 503/382-7911), offers complete **auto and rec vehicle maintenance services.** . . . For a **24-hour restaurant,** try Shari's Family Restaurant, 3098 N. U.S. 97 at Bend River Mall (tel. 503/382-0674) . . . You'll find a **24-hour supermarket** called Wagner's Thriftway at N.E. 3rd and Revere Streets.

3. WHERE TO STAY

Thanks to its lure as a ski resort and as a summertime playground, Bend has an interesting variety of places in which to settle for a while.

One of the loveliest of those is a resort with an intriguing name: **Inn of the Seventh Mountain,** P.O. Box 1207, Bend Branch, OR 97709 (tel. 503/382-8711, or toll free 800/547-5668 in the western states, 800/452-6810 in Oregon). Closest quarters to Mount Bachelor, Inn of the Seventh Mountain features plush lodge rooms, suites really, in a cluster of buildings overlooking Lava Butte. A very well-known spot, the Inn of the Seventh Mountain is jammed with skiers and ice skaters in winter, with sunseekers and hikers in summer. To accommodate them the inn has two swimming pools, a sauna, three heated whirlpools, a recreation building, tennis courts, trail riding nearby, bikes, river rafting, and fishing. You'll stay in one of the resort's 320 rooms, many of them contemporary apartments with a flip-up Murphy bed, kitchen, fireplace, and private deck with a view you won't want to leave even to sleep. Larger quarters are available for families. At hunger time the Poppy Seed Café will start your day, pack you a box lunch, and serve you an early dinner. Party-minded types from this and many another resort congregate in the bar downstairs, where a fireplace roars as merrily as the entertainment. Rates at the Inn of the Seventh Mountain range from a low of $48 double daily for studio apartments to a high of $215 for the plushest places. To get to the inn, head south out of Bend on the Cascades Lakes Hwy. (Century Drive) for about seven miles.

Another large resort in the area is **Sunriver Lodge and Resort,** P.O. Box 3589, Sunriver, OR 97707 (tel. 503/593-1221, or toll free 800/547-3922 in the western states, 800/452-6874 in Oregon). A condominium resort, Sunriver has more than 350 apartments and homes, all with kitchens, which it rents for owners, so it's almost like visiting a friend. You'll find quarters attractively decorated, in the most contemporary styles, all with fireplaces, television, and telephone, so location is your only decision. You can choose from views of the national forest, Mount Bachelor, or the championship golf course, which is also operated by the resort. Developed by the man who created the famous coastal resort of Salishan, Sunriver Lodge is nothing short of a city: shopping mall, stores, homes, post office, two golf courses, 29 tennis courts, jogging courses, boating and rafting trips, stables, bikes, two swimming pools, and so many hot tubs you could go to one a day for a week without repeating the experience. In winter ice skaters whirl and cross-country skiers push off on treks across the acres of grounds. When all that exercise leaves you starving, you can fill up at an elegant restaurant called the Meadows (open from 6 to 10 p.m. for dinner and from 9 a.m. to 2 p.m. for Sunday brunch), which specializes in a crunchy Caesar salad. For more casual dining there's the Provision Company, Hook Wine and Cheddar, and the Deschutes River Trout House. You'll find the resort off U.S. 97 about 15 miles south of Bend. Rates range from $87 to $115, higher for larger condominium accommodations or homes, about $20 less in winter.

Another serenely lovely spot in this region is **Lake Creek Lodge,** Sisters, OR 97759 (tel. 503/595-6331), nestled in an enormous stand of Ponderosa pine that filters the sun's rays into a green glow. If there's a more peaceful mountain setting than Lake Creek Lodge, we haven't found it. This delightful, off-the-beaten-track resort is a cluster of small and large cabins circled about a central lodge and dining room, where a fire blazes in a stone hearth. In front of the fire guests gather to discuss quiet days spent slumbering in the sun beside a small natural pool, playing tennis in nearby courts, fishing in a stream, riding, cycling, climbing or hiking on snow-capped peaks nearby, playing horseshoes or shuffleboard. Youngsters get special sports treatment: they're the only ones permitted to fish in the stocked trout pond, and they get to be first in line at the dinner buffet. In winter the lodge becomes a ski resort—you can schuss off into the sunrise right from the steps of the cabin. Not a slick or fancy place, Lake Creek's cottages blend into the forest—no discos here, just the sound of wind rustling through the pines and a view that goes on forever.

For dining, you can drive to Sisters or Bend, or eat right here in a rustic wood-lined dining room on a country buffet of basic American preparations of lamb, fresh salmon, thick steaks, and fried chicken. Children have their own separate dining room. In summer dinner is often outside. As for accommodations, some cottages are small, with just a double bed, small chair and table, and a refrigerator out on the porch. Larger accommodations, paneled in knotty pine, accommodate two to eight with a living room, two or three bedrooms with single or double beds, kitchen, and screened porch. Some have fireplaces and dressing rooms. In summer, cottages are $90 double. If there are three or four of you renting a cottage, you'll pay $120 to $150. Note that those prices *include* dinner daily. Houses, which are the larger accommodations, are $110 double a day, rising to $156 for three and $200 for four. Those rates are in effect from mid-June to mid-September. Off-season rates are 20% to 30% lower. If you want to stop by for dinner, you'll pay $14 for the buffet, $5 for a rib-sticking wrangler breakfast. This is a BYOB spot but they'll be happy to chill your wine.

You'll find the resort by following U.S. 20 or Ore. 126 to Sisters, then heading north on U.S. 20 to the turnoff to Camp Sherman at Metolius Junction. If you fly to this area, a staffer will come to pick you up in Bend or Sisters.

Riverhouse Motor Inn, 3075 N. U.S. 97, Bend, OR 97701 (tel. 503/389-3111, or toll free 800/452-6878 in Oregon, 800/547-3928 elsewhere in the Northwest). At this sprawling and attractive riverside hostelry you'll find all the amenities from swimming pool to sauna, whirlpool, air conditioning, phones, laundry facilities, and color televisions, but you needn't do anything strenuous: just strolling about the green lawns here is a refreshing experience. You'll find some rooms at street level, some a few steps down overlooking the river and near the swimming pool tucked way between the two wings. All rooms have private patios or terraces; the best rooms, of course, overlook the river. If you've forgotten something you can walk across the street to the shops of Bend River Mall. Rates are $42 to $52 double. The Riverhouse dining room here is a local favorite for its lovely view of the Deschutes River and its showy tableside cookery. It's open daily from 7 a.m. (for sumptuous breakfasts) to 10 p.m. (for dinners and homemade pastries), a half hour later on weekends, with prices in the $10 to $15 range. Entertainment in the lounge here too.

Mount Bachelor Village, 19717 Mount Bachelor Dr. (off Century Drive), Bend, OR 97702 (tel. 503/389-5900, or toll free 800/547-5204, 800/452-9846 in Oregon), is a group of 96 condominiums in cedar-sided buildings at Deschutes River Canyon. You can curl up before the fireplace in your apartment on a cold winter evening while a fondue bubbles on the stove in the kitchen. In active moments you can stroke through a swimming pool, bubble in a whirlpool, lob on six tennis courts, or head for the slopes just minutes away. Rates are $65 to $110 for a one-bedroom apartment or a two-bedroom loft apartment for four to six. In winter prices rise $5 to $10.

Best Western Entrada Lodge, 19221 Century Dr. (P.O. Box 975), Bend, OR 97702 (tel. 503/382-4080, or toll free 800/528-1234), occupies a secluded spot bordering the Deschutes National Forest about 20 minutes from the lifts at Mount Bachelor. Skiers flock here in winter to chatter over après-ski snacks served around a roaring fireplace. Mornings they're all at breakfast, a $3.50 ribsticker that will get you off to the good start your mother was always warning you not to miss. The 80 contemporary rooms are spacious and clean, the owners are friendly, the grounds are lush and spacious—25 acres—what more could there be? Rates at Entrada are $40 to $45 double.

The **Thunderbird Motel,** 1415 N.E. 3rd St., Bend, OR 97701 (tel. 503/382-7011, or toll free 800/547-8010, 800/452-0733 in Oregon), has 76 rooms housed in a contemporary cedar-trimmed building with shingled mansard roof with room doors a soft shade of blue. A lovely purple lobby here sports a tall stone fireplace and warm wood furnishings. Outside, a swimming pool is in the center of things and gets plenty of use in those hot summer months. Inside, your room has big windows, attractive furnishings, soft colors, and all the amenities, from telephones to televisions and air conditioning. There's a sauna for winter baking. Year-round rates at this handsome entrant in the Thunderbird chain are $48 double for a room with queen-size bed, $57 for accommodations with two double beds. The Kopper Kitchen Restaurant and Lounge on the premises provides for hunger and thirst 24 hours.

The **Red Lion Motel,** 849 N.E. 3rd St., Bend, OR 97701 (tel. 503/382-8384, or toll free 800/547-8010, 800/452-0733 in Oregon), is a sister property to the Thunderbird Motor Inn and just as attractive. Its location is particularly good for downtown visitors: just seven blocks east of the main business district at U.S. 97 just south of its junction with U.S. 20. You'll find 75 large air-conditioned rooms. You'll also find a cooling swimming pool and next door a 24-hour restaurant, so you can snack anytime. Room prices range from $47 to $56 for two. Pets are accepted here too.

CONDOMINIUMS: Condominiums are very popular in ski areas, both for the extra space they offer and for the privacy and price. Among the condominium rental agents operating locally are: **Mirror Pond Management,** 849 N.W. Wall St., Bend, OR 97701 (tel. 503/382-6766); **Mountain View Properties,** P.O. Box 4337, Sunriver, OR 97702 (tel. 503/593-1671, or toll free 800/522-2311 in the western states, 800/452-6820 in Oregon); and **Resort Realty,** P.O. Box 4306, Sunriver, OR 97702 (tel. 503/593-1234, or toll free 800/452-6870).

4. WHERE TO DINE

You'll find all kinds of rib-sticking treats in Bend, ranging from buffalo steaks to Indian fry bread, all of it at reasonable prices. Here's a look at some of the top spots.

Frieda's Restaurant and Stein Room, 1955 N.E. Division St. (tel. 503/382-3790), is much loved by many who come here to ski or to enjoy the region's sunny summer weather. The prices are very reasonable—ranging from $10 to $12 for dinner, including homemade soup, salad, homemade bread and butter, potatoes or homemade buttered noodles, and a dessert of apple fritters. Story has it that the owner of this restaurant worked here for 16 years to earn the money to buy it. She fills empty spaces with such German classics as hasenpfeffer (rabbit cooked in red wine), sauerbraten pot roast, smoked German sausage served with tangy sauerkraut, bratwurst, wienerschnitzel, and Bavarian sausages. For dessert a Black Forest torte, of course. There's plenty of seafood and cheese fondue here too. Open from 11:30 a.m. to 10 p.m. Monday through Friday and 4:30 to 11 p.m. on Saturday; closed Sunday.

Another Bend restaurant with Bavarian connections is the **Black Forest Inn,** 25 S.W. 14th St., at Century Drive (tel. 503/389-3138), where the walls are lined with photographs and copper. Veal fans have six choices here, served with that German noodley creation called spaetzle. The décor, inside and out, gives you a feeling of the Black Forest, not a very different place, after all, from this mountain-rimmed city. Open from 5 to 11 p.m. daily, with prices in the $7.50 to $11.50 range for entrees.

If you're in the mood for a big, tender steak or some fresh seafood, try **McKenzie's Ore House Bar and Grill,** 1033 N.W. Bond St. (tel. 503/388-3891). If you notice a resemblance to the Ore House in Idaho's Sun Valley, you notice correctly; the two are relations. Always a lively crowd at the bar here, some good seafood, and top steaks, all of it produced in a chic atmosphere. Hours are 5:30 to 10 p.m. daily. Prices are in the $12 to $17 range.

You can have your caloric sins satisfied, if not forgiven, at **Le Bistro,** 1203 N.E. 3rd St. (tel. 503/489-7274), a whimsical restaurant operating inside a former church! All the French favorites are here, from lamb to some intriguing sea-food dishes, including seafood Wellington, fish baked in almonds, shrimp, and french-fried steaks, in the $11 to $18 range. Owned and operated by a European chef, the restaurant has been whipping up things like duckling with wild plum sauce and grilled veal steak with béarnaise sauce. Open now for more than a decade, the restaurant was recently named the best French restaurant outside Portland by a regional magazine. Le Bistro is open Tuesday through Saturday from 5:30 to 10 p.m.

You'll have to search for **Cyrano's**, 828 N.W. Wall St. (tel. 503/389-6276), which is hidden away in an alley, but you'll be rewarded with five-course dinners from a menu that changes weekly. Judi and Mark Chambers dish up a wide variety of nouvelle fare featuring regional products with fine wines. Thick steaks grilled slowly over red oak are, they promise, a never-to-be-equalled taste. Other options on the menu are such creative culinary triumphs as pesto- and spinach-stuffed veal roll. Cyrano's also has a sidewalk café. Prices are in the $10 to $14 range or less, and hours are 5 to 10 p.m. weekdays and Saturday, and serving Saturday lunch from 11 a.m. to 3 p.m. and Sunday brunch from 10 a.m. to 2 p.m.

The **Pine Tavern**, 967 N.W. Brooks St., at the foot of Oregon Street (tel. 503/382-5581), is a dramatic spot with trees growing in the dining room. Serving travelers for nearly 50 years, the Pine Tavern specializes in foods Americans love best: prime rib, hefty New York strip steaks, lamb chops, and mountain trout. You can dine among the pines in the Garden Room or pick a table overlooking a pond called Mirror on the Deschutes River. Sunday brunchers make a beeline for this place. Prices run from $8 to $12 for petite dinners designed for nongourmands, while regular trencherman feasts are $10 to $15, including soup, salad, an interesting "sheepherder potato" pan-fried with onions and garlic, vegetable, and sourdough scones with honey butter. Hours here are 11:30 a.m. to 2:30 p.m. for lunch Monday through Saturday, 5:30 to 10 p.m. daily for dinner, and Sunday brunch from 10:30 a.m. to 1:30 p.m. We'd advise reservations as this is a very popular place in all seasons.

Another steak specialist is **Beef and Brew**, 3194 N. U.S. 97, in Bend River Mall (tel. 503/388-4646), which is open daily from 5 to 10 p.m., an hour later on weekends, and 4:30 to 9:30 p.m. on Sunday, lounge open a little later daily except Sunday. Complete dinners here include salad and bread, homemade dressings, rice pilaf or potatoes, and choice of wine or beer. Seafood Newburg is the most interesting of a list of seafood options. Prices are in the $10 to $15 range.

Tumalo Emporium and Bonanza Saloon Restaurant, 64619 U.S. 20 West, six miles west of Bend (tel. 503/382-2202), is an antique store turned restaurant. The accent is on good home-cooking with fresh ingredients, served amid antique furnishings. On Sunday champagne brunch is popular here, but at any time you'll find such goodies as chicken breasts with artichoke hearts, beef Stroganoff, baked scallops, and cannelloni. At lunch sandwiches are served on homemade bread baked here daily. Open Tuesday through Saturday from 11:30 a.m. to 10 p.m., on Sunday from 10:30 a.m. to 2 p.m. Figure $20 to $30 for dinner for two.

When it's pizza time, try **Izzy's**, 2490 N. U.S. 97 (tel. 503/382-2135), one of a chain of restaurants in Oregon with some hush-hush recipes for three-eighths-inch thin crust and fat Sicilian pies. You can have a mild tomato sauce or a lively spicy one, and choose among ingredients ranging from black olives to Canadian bacon, pineapple, sausages, and jalapeños. A double pizza with three toppings is about $11; a family-size pizza, a little over $12. Saturday the restaurant has a buffet luncheon with a big salad bar, salmon rolls, chicken, mojos, barbecued chicken, pasta, garlic rolls, baked beans, cornbread, and fresh fruit for under $7. On Sunday and some other days a buffet is $8. Even those who don't regularly salivate over pizza can find something here—there are a couple of Mexican selections, a salad bar, sandwiches, even some vegetarian dishes. Open daily from 11 a.m. to 10 p.m.

Once upon a time drive-in restaurants were the rage. If you remember those days, you'll want to stop in at **Pilot Butte Drive-In,** 917 N.E. Greenwood, which is U.S. 20 east (tel. 503/382-2972). You can eat in the dining room, but it's much more fun to be served by a carhop—remember those? Nothing fancy here, just the usual hamburgers, steak sandwiches, hot dogs, and cheeseburgers with fries served in a basket, with choice of salad, for $2 or $3, and at dinner you can try fried shrimp or fish, hamburger, or chicken-fried steak with gravy for a few cents over $4!

Rolaine's Cantina and Lounge, 785 S.E. 3rd St. (tel. 503/382-4944), is one of several Mexican places in town. This one has an attractive Mexican-style fireplace and features gold margaritas made with gold tequila. Free appetizers at fiesta hour from 5 to 7 p.m. daily. House specialty: burrito Rolaine. Prices are in the under-$10 range, and the cantina is open from 11 a.m. to 10 p.m. Monday through Friday, from noon to 10 p.m. on Saturday and Sunday. Latest additions to the menu here: enchiladas, burritos, and chimichangas stuffed with seafood. No reservations here, you'll just have to wait your turn.

Soy sauce fans can find some of their specialties at **Hong Kong Restaurant,** 530 S.E. 3rd St. (tel. 503/389-8880). Dine on ginger beef or duckling stewed with spices, pressed with water chestnut flour and deep-fried with a sweet-and-sour sauce. Dinner is not likely to cost you more than $8. If you can't make up your mind, try one of the family dinners for two or more at $8 to $10, which offer you a wide range of goodies to sample. Open seven days from 11 a.m. weekdays, from noon on Saturday and Sunday; closing is midnight on Friday and Saturday, 11 p.m. other days.

The **Riverhouse Motor Inn Restaurant,** 3075 N. U.S. 97 (tel. 503/389-3111), occupies an enviable position alongside the Deschutes River, so you're guaranteed a serene view as you dine on roast pork aux poivres rosé with pink peppercorns, scallops sautéed with bacon and onions in a cream and brandy sauce, fowl à la grecque, or a chicken breast combined with spinach, bacon, shallots, lemon, and seasoned tomatoes. Prices are quite reasonable for such an elegant spot: figure $10 to $15 for complete dinners, including soup, salad, vegetable, rissolé potatoes, and home-baked bread, about a dollar or so less for à la carte selections, including entree, vegetable, and bread. The Riverhouse is open at 7 a.m. daily for breakfast and from 11 a.m. to 2 p.m. for lunch; dinner hours are 5:30 to 10 p.m. Sunday through Thursday, to 11 p.m. on Friday and Saturday.

Fat and sassy trout that fail to keep their mouths shut on important occasions often end up at the **Deschutes River Trout House,** 1 Marina Dr., Sunriver (tel. 503/593-8880). Here you can try some very fresh trout stuffed with crab, a variety of other seafood, and steaks for prices in the $10 to $16 range. A Sunday brunch served from 8 a.m. to 2 p.m. with champagne is $6.25. Trout House is open from 8 a.m. to 10 p.m. daily.

Oddity seekers should head for **Dan'l Boone's Tom Tom Restaurant,** 3650 N. U.S. 97 (tel. 503/382-1391), a 24-hour spot specializing in buffalo steaks and burgers! If those treats buffalo you, settle for the beef, veal, chicken, pork, and seafood dishes, or just gorge on homemade desserts. Prices are in the $8 to $10 range for dinner. Owned, by the way, by a real Dan Boone and his wife, Claudette, Dan'l is open 24 hours.

Finally, if you've always wanted to find out how the Indians lived, you can chow down on Indian fry bread, birds in clay, rainbow trout, and broiled salmon at the **Juniper Dining Room,** at Kah-Nee-Ta Vacation Resort in Warm Springs (tel. 503/553-1112). As you dine you'll overlook a 200-year-old juniper tree and Kah-Nee-Ta village. Hours vary, so you'll have to give them a call to find out when they're open. Prices are in the $15 to $20 range. You'll find the restaurant and the resort off U.S. 26 in Warm Springs.

5. AFTER DARK

You won't find a bevy of leggy, sequined dancers here, but you will find some lively lounges and quiet spots for a nightcap. Most of Bend's entertainment is teamed with its top restaurants.

Brandy's, 197 N.E. 3rd St. (tel. 503/382-2687), is a contemporary woodsy-plantsy restaurant with a lounge that's popular with local up-and-comers.

McKenzies Ore House Bar & Grill has a changing entertainment scene, as do the **Riverhouse Restaurant, Tumalo Emporium,** and a rustic burger spot called **Deschutes Station Tavern,** 61219 U.S. 97 (tel. 503/389-7574).

In nearby Redmond the **86 Corral Club,** 250 N. 6th St. (tel. 503/548-6105), is good for a diversion.

6. WHAT TO SEE AND DO

SIGHTS IN AND AROUND BEND: To get the low-down on everything that you can see and do in this region, contact the **Bend Chamber of Commerce** (tel. 503/382-3221), which publishes a comprehensive brochure on what to do that ranges from backpacking to balloon flights, birdwatching, riding, jogging, llama trekking, rockhounding, spelunking, and more.

For a tour of the region, call the **Inn of the Seventh Mountain** (tel. 503/382-8711). Mountain-loving folks there will take you on a two-hour guided bike or moped tour including all the geological attributes of this area—mountains, river, desert, and volcanic formations—and toss in a little history of Bend as well. Tours cost $10 to $15.

Woodcarver Bill Goldman, who whittled wood creations owned by Sen. Mark Hatfield and President Lyndon Johnson, opened a museum, at which you can see some of his carved characters. Goldman, who likes to call himself the Old West Whittler, has carved dozens of cowhands and riverboat gamblers and placed them in humorous Old West settings. His **Oxbow Studio** homestead is at 19760 Cannarn Rd., Bend, OR 97701 (tel. 503/382-1205), just west of Bend on Ore. 20. Go a mile past Tumulo to Gerking Market Road, then follow the signs to the museum. Admission is $1 for adults, 50¢ for children, and it's open Monday through Saturday from 9 a.m. to 5 p.m., on Sunday from 1 to 5 p.m.

Deschutes Historical Center, 129 N.W. Idaho St. (tel. 503/389-1813), highlights regional history with, among other exhibits, a room full of prehistoric and pioneer artifacts. Museum hours are Wednesday through Saturday from 1 to 4:30 p.m. Admission is free.

Lava Lands Visitor Center, 11 miles south of Bend on U.S. 97 (tel. 503/388-5664), has some interesting exhibits describing the violence and devastation of the Mount St. Helens eruption. From mid-March to late October the center has guided geological tours. You can also visit the Lava River Cave, a mile-long lava tube created by the cooling of the volcanic rock. Call them for tour hours, which vary.

Newberry Crater, about 40 miles southeast of Bend, is the caldera of an ancient volcano that collapsed upon itself. Good trout fishing in nearby Paulina and East Lakes. Take U.S. 97 south to Newberry Crater Road and turn east.

The **High Desert Museum,** six miles south of Bend at 59800 S. U.S. 97 (tel. 503/382-4754), has historic and prehistoric exhibits to give you an idea what life is and has always been like in the Pacific Northwest. Nature trails, forestry exhibits, and lots of live animal exhibits here. The museum's open from 9 a.m. to 5 p.m. daily in summer, to 4 p.m. in winter. Admission is $3 for adults, $2.50 for seniors, and $1.50 for children 6 to 12.

If you like looking at deserts in the sky, you can do so at **Pine Mountain Observatory** (tel. 503/382-8331), 30 miles southeast of Bend on Ore. 20 to Millican. Three telescopes here are the largest in the Northwest. This free facility is open daily from 9 a.m. to 5 p.m. and sometimes at night.

Art lovers should stop in at the **Blue Sky Gallery,** 147 N.W. Minnesota (tel. 503/388-1877), for a look at some attractive western creations.

SPECIAL EVENTS: If you come here in August, you can't miss a **county fair** —there are three of them in this region each August.

Sisters Rodeo, which includes a parade, foot races, dances, a big Buckeroo Breakfast, and of course those rodeo competitions, occurs in early June, followed in mid-June by an All-Indian rodeo and in August by the Deschutes County Rodeo.

Horse shows occur in most summer months, as do get-togethers for rockhounds, who congregate in nearby Nyssa in early August to celebrate **Thunderegg Days** honoring agate rocks spewn out by volcanic action. Nyssa even calls itself the thunderegg capital of the world.

SHOPPING: An interesting purchase here is a newly issued poster of Mount Bachelor at its snow-white best, available in art galleries and ski shops in the region.

Among the most popular of area shopping spots is **Mountain View Mall,** where you will find all kinds of boutiques, theaters, an ice cream shop, even a shop that will tog you out in western duds.

Mountain Country Sporting Goods, 1225 N.E. 3rd St. (tel. 503/388-2366), has sleeping bags, hip boots, used rifles, and even softball bats.

Randy Barna's Ski Shop, 345 S.W. Century Dr. (tel. 503/389-0890), will pick you up at your motel so you can come over and have a look at their wide range of ski equipment. They'll arrange lessons and rentals, and outfit you with a surfboard too.

SCENIC DRIVES: One of the most gorgeous scenic drives in the eastern Cascades is a 100-mile looping drive into the Deschutes National Forest over the **Cascades Lakes Hwy.** You can reach the Cascades Lakes Hwy. by heading south out of Bend center on Division Street and turning west on Colorado Avenue to the Cascades Lakes Hwy. A south turn puts you on the highway and headed in the right direction.

You'll shortly swing west, and the full splendor of **Mount Bachelor,** looming about 15 miles away, engulfs you. Farther to the north as you drive you'll be able to pick out Broken Top mountain followed by the South, Middle, and North Sister mountains, known locally, of course, as the Three Sisters. As the road approaches its sweep southward, broad, blue mountain lakes begin to mirror mountains, sky, and the bitter-blue green of the forest. There are more than ten of these named mountain lakes for you to enjoy on this 35-mile stretch of the drive.

One of the few osprey nesting grounds in the nation is at **Crane Prairie Reservoir,** just at the corner where your road heads east on its southernmost leg. You'll see the signs to guide you to the best viewpoint.

Before you reach U.S. 97, 19 miles away, you'll go through the **La Pine Recreation Area,** be able to stop at a fish hatchery, and cross the Deschutes River at Pringle Falls. Take your camera.

In nearby Madras **Lake Billy Chinook** is a spectacular sight, its deep-blue waters nestled into mesa-like cliffs. To get there from Bend, take U.S. 97 north to Madras, then U.S. 26 west to the lake, which is just south of Kah-Nee-Ta.

In Deschutes National Forest you will find Lava Lands, a volcanic region of short trails through **lava flows,** along the crater of a quiescent volcano, past one of the world's largest flows of obsidian, which is also known as **volcanic glass,** and through lava formations. You'll find the **Lava Lands Visitor Information** at 211 N.E. Revere St., 11 miles south of Bend (tel. 503/382-5668).

Another "don't miss" drive is to **Tumalo Falls,** a lovely 97-foot waterfall deep in a pine forest. To get there, follow Franklin Avenue west via Drake Park and on out Galveston Avenue. Drive 11 miles to the end of the surfaced road, then 3½ miles farther on unsurfaced forest road.

About 37 miles northwest of Bend on Ore. 242, the **McKenzie Pass,** at an elevation of 5,324 feet and right in the heart of Mount Washington Wilderness, will give you a drop-jaw view of the Cascades and lava flows. The route is closed in winter, and trailer traffic is not advised. To get there from Bend, take U.S. 20 to Sisters, then turn west on Ore. 242 about 16 miles to the pass. To complete a round-trip loop, follow Ore. 242 another 22 miles to Proxy Falls and the McKenzie River. Turn north at the Ore. 126 junction for 19 miles to where Ore. 126 joins U.S. 20 heading east. Within 10 miles you'll top out at Santiam Pass at 4,817 feet, near Lost Lake, where you'll see other waterfalls. It's all downhill from there into Sisters, 19 miles to the southeast.

A brochure available from the Bend Chamber of Commerce called "Points of Interest" leads you through other drives to the **Metolius River Recreation Area** and the **Deschutes River** white waters.

7. SPORTS

Equestrians can trot off along the Deschutes River on rides that begin and end at the Inn of the Seventh Mountain stables. Rides of an hour, 90 minutes, or two hours are available from 9 a.m. to 6:30 p.m. year round. Rates are $12 to $22, depending on the length of the ride. Children under 9 must be accompanied by an adult, and children under 5 can ride double with parents for $2 more. Contact **Nova Stables,** Inn of the Seventh Mountain, P.O. Box 908, Bend, OR 97709 (tel. 503/389-9458).

Nova will also take you on half-day, 12-mile rides along the river for $40 per person, minimum four people; call for reservations. You don't have to be an experienced rider here. Nova pays special attention to children and first-time riders, so if you've always wanted to try, now's the time. You'll never ride through more beautiful scenery.

And if you're here in the winter, call and ask Nova about their prime-rib dinner sleigh ride, a two-hour outing with dinner in a tent warmed by a roaring fire. Adults pay $30, $18 for children under 11, for this winter cheer.

If you're looking for a rafting trip, get in touch with **Hunter Expeditions,** P.O. Box 346, Downtown Station, Bend, OR 97701 (tel. 503/389-8370), which will take you on a three-mile mini-expedition on the upper Deschutes River for $21 per person. The more adventurous will want to try the 12-mile journey down the lower Deschutes for $58 per person, including lunch.

Cascade Adventures, Town Square Bldg., Suite 201, Cascade Street (P.O. Box 873), Sisters, OR 97759 (tel. 503/549-1047 or 548-1562), also offers a wide variety of fishing trips, airplane rides, trail trips, river floats, nature tours, and hunting trips here and elsewhere around the United States.

The **Central Oregon Athletic Center,** 1569 N.E. Second Ave. at Penn Street, Bend (tel. 503/389-2009), has seven racquetball/handball courts, saunas, Jacuzzis, weight rooms, a swimming pool, big-screen television in a lounge, aerobics classes in and out of the water, massage rooms, sun rooms, a weight-loss clinic, deli, pro shop, and nursery. It's open from 6 a.m. to 10 p.m. daily except Sunday.

For information on all the many recreational activities available through the **Bend Metro Park and Recreation District,** call 503/389-PARK. That office offers information on bike paths, basketball, jogging trails, and racquetball, among others. You'll find **tennis courts** at Juniper Park (tel. 503/389-PARK); Sunriver Resort, Sunriver (tel. 503/593-1221); and Tennis Village at Mount Bachelor Village, 19717 Mount Bachelor Dr. (tel. 503/389-0270). For **golf,** try Black Butte Ranch, Black Butte, Sisters (tel. 503/595-6689); Orion Greens Golf Course, 61525 Fargo Lane, Bend (tel. 503/388-3999); and Sunriver Resort, Sunriver (tel. 503/593-1221), among others.

Practically everything hereabouts is part of the **Deschutes National Forest,** which covers more than 1.85 million acres with dramatic scenery. A camper's paradise, the forest has more than 125 campgrounds, 13 resorts, marinas, stores, 301 lakes, and 617 miles of streams. Winter sports occur at Bachelor Butte Ski Area, 20 miles west of Bend (see below). Animal-watching is comparatively easy in the park, which is home to everything from antelopes to black bears, elk, and mountain lions. As if that's not enough, five wildernesses, including the Three Sisters Wilderness, border the Deschutes.

There is much to see and do in the park. If you like caves, you can go on a self-guided tour of **Lava River Cave,** one of the first lava tubes discovered by early settlers in the region. All the cave requirements are here: stalactites, stalagmites, an echo hall, a two-tube tunnel, and a sand garden created over centuries from volcanic sand.

Guided walks depart from the **Lava Lands Visitor Center,** 58210 S. U.S. 97 (tel. 503/593-2421).

If you never met a desert you didn't love, you'll adore the **High Desert Museum,** which is yet another part of this vast park. You'll find it quite near the Lava Lands Visitor Center at 59800 S. U.S. 97 (tel. 503/382-4754). Displays include a wildlife observation pavilion, reconstructions of historic and prehistoric dwellings, a slide show, and daily presentation of river otters, porcupines, and birds-of-prey.

Guided fishing trips can be made through most motels and resorts in the area including Riverhouse Motor Inn (tel. 503/389-3111) and Inn of the Seventh Mountain (tel. 503/382-8711, ext. 595).

Top **backpacking** areas in the region are Diamond Peak, Mount Jefferson, Mount Washington, and the Three Sisters Wildernesses. Maps are available at the Deschutes National Forest Office, 1645 U.S. 20 East, Bend, OR 97701 (tel. 503/388-2715).

That same office can help put your feet on the right **hiking trails and nature walks,** of which there are many in the Bend area. One of the more interesting walks is the Newberry Crater **Obsidian Trail of Glass,** about 22 miles south of Bend on U.S. 97. It's one of the largest volcanic glass flows in the world and takes about 15 minutes.

Rockhounding? Sure. Call **Cascade Lapidary** at 503/548-6769 for the latest word on where to find thundereggs, petrified wood, jasper, crystal, agate, and the like.

Cave exploration, otherwise known as spelunking? Call the Deschutes National Forest Office for maps and information. Ask for a copy of "Spelunking Guide to Central Oregon."

SKIING AND EXPLORING MOUNT BACHELOR: Bend's Chamber of Commerce can provide you with a Mount Bachelor **trail map,** which shows ski lifts and runs with degree of difficulty indicated. Skiing hours at the mountain, which has snow from early November to late spring, are 9 a.m. to 4 p.m.

You can schuss Mount Bachelor on daily **lift tickets** that cost $23 for adults, $15 for children. Half-day prices are also available from 12:30 p.m. and are $18 for adults, $11 for children 7 to 12. If you live in Oregon or nearby and frequent the slopes, you can buy an individual season ticket for about $500. Ski lift tickets for use on consecutive days are money savers. If you need equipment, you can rent it here or learn ski racing or just plain skiing in private or group lessons for adults and children.

The **central information number** for the mountain is 503/382-8334, 503/382-7888 for ski information. Accommodations and dining spots are about 20 minutes from the lift. Packages including accommodations and reductions on ski lessons also are available. If you just want to go up and look around, **sightseeing** tickets, available May to September, are $6 for adults, $4 for children. On the mountain you'll find Main Lodge, Blue Lodge, Sunrise Lodge, and Egan Lodge waiting to provide for your needs. In Main Lodge a cafeteria serves breakfast and lunch and a lounge serves lunch and cocktails. To get to the mountain, which is 22 miles from Bend, take Century Drive, also called 14th Street. At the fork keep right onto Cascade Lakes Hwy., which heads west to the mountain.

8. AN EXCURSION TO KAH-NEE-TA

For a memorable day trip just 69 miles from Bend, hidden away in a deep valley beside a sparkling mountain river nestles a most unusual vacation resort. Not just luxurious, though it is that too, **Kah-Nee-Ta** sets another kind of pace, another kind of style, in another kind of culture. A resort owned and operated by the Confederated Tribes of the Warm Springs Reservation, Kah-Nee-Ta is the centerpiece of a half-million-acre Indian reservation.

We don't guarantee you'll learn to live as the Indians did during your stay here, but you'll at least get a feel for the traditions and way of life of this ancient people—and all without leaving comfort behind. Not only does Kah-Nee-Ta offer luxurious accommodations at Kah-Nee-Ta Lodge and the Nee-Sha Cottages, but you can even elect to spend your days here in a tepee! To add to your understanding of the Indian way of life, in summer you can attend performances of Indian ceremonies, festivals, and rodeos with all the attendant colorful pageantry. A real must is a taste of Indian history, a salmon bake where an open fire and preparation of salmon filets is presided over by Indian chefs in colorful, authentic dress.

To get into the spirit of the thing, saddle-up an Indian pony, or do as the Indians have always done—jump in the mineral-rich waters of natural hot springs. Here, at Kah-Nee-Ta, these famous waters fill an enormous pool, a children's pool, and a special wading pool for toddlers, as well as a Jacuzzi.

Nee-Sha Cottages offer bedrooms, living and dining rooms, baths, and kitchens. Rooms at Kah-Nee-Ta Lodge come with contemporary décors, some with balconies, and all with Indian motifs and spectacular views. Kah-Nee-Ta Lodge rises unexpectedly from the side of a bluff, its sweeping contemporary design blending with the rugged landscape. A multilevel lobby is bathed in natural light that spreads across wooden beams and an imposing, hexagonally based, white stone fireplace that soars through the ceiling: Indian design amplified and translated into modern luxury.

Kah-Nee-Ta claims that to stay here is to be transported to a different time, and certainly the Indian specialties served in the elegant dining room offer a departure from just another steak. Dining room hours here vary and prices are in the $15 to $20 range for dinner entrees. The flip side of ancient is modern, and Kah-Nee-Ta isn't caught short in modernity, from tennis courts to jogging trails, bicycling paths, and an 18-hole, par-70 golf course, winding along Warm Springs River.

Rates at the lodge from May to October are $69 for two. At the Nee-Sha Cottages rates are $49 for two. You can hook up your rec vehicle for just $12. Contact **Kah-Nee-Ta Resort** at P.O. Box K, Warm Springs, OR 97761 (tel. 503/553-1112, or toll free 800/831-0100 in Oregon).

Although it's a bit off the beaten path, Kah-Nee-Ta is easy to find. From Bend take U.S. 97 north for 42 miles to Madras. There, take U.S. 26 and continue north for another 16 miles to Warm Springs. The road to Kah-Nee-Ta out of Warm Springs is clearly marked as you head north for another 11 miles to the Kah-Nee-Ta Village. Pilots of small planes can fly into Madras Airport.

CHAPTER XII

SOUTHWESTERN OREGON, CRATER LAKE, AND THE OREGON CAVES

□ □ □

1. ORIENTATION
2. JACKSONVILLE
3. ASHLAND
4. WHAT TO SEE
5. AFTER DARK IN SOUTHWESTERN OREGON
6. DAYTIME ACTIVITIES
7. SHOPPING
8. CRATER LAKE
9. OREGON CAVES
10. REDWOOD NATIONAL PARK

Yes, America, there is good news tonight: the Bard is alive and well and living in southwestern Oregon.

Behind a timbered Tudor façade in the smallest of small towns is the Oregon Shakespearean Festival, a regional theater that has been winning acclaim for more than 50 years—and more recently a Tony Award for best regional theater in the nation!

Here you will find a stage patterned after London's 1599 Fortune Theatre and resembling as closely as possible the boards on which the Bard's players romped. Here on a starry night or a sunny afternoon, you will sit in a breezy amphitheater glorying in colorful and elaborate costumes, beautiful sets, and the always witty, often wise, interchange of weird and wonderful Shakespearean characters.

That's Ashland, a backwater town that applied a little Oregonian pioneer spirit to make itself one of the most visited valleys in the state. Down the road is another little town that made itself known by using just what it has plenty of—

history. Once a booming gold-mining town with its own mine and a bevy of miners scurrying to get their piece of the action, tiny Jacksonville rode the boom and faded with it. For years this village was just short of a ghost town, never more than a pass-through on the way to somewhere else.

Then one day, as seems to have happened so many times in this innovative —and determined—part of the nation, villagers got together and decided to build their fascinating past into a promising future. Because history's about the only thing they had plenty of in Jacksonville, people here decided to peg their future on the nation's interest in its past. Soon historic houses boasted carefully lettered plaques telling the world when they were built and by whom. A general store became a delightfully modern anachronistic hotel. Old West false fronts were painted and polished, and antiques came out of hiding.

Walk the shady streets of Jacksonville on a quiet summer evening and you'll be transported to another era, when only the creak of buckboard wheels and the swish of a petticoat broke the summer silence. All the accoutrements are here to put your imagination to work. There really is an old barrel lying casually beside a false-fronted store. A weathered farmwagon waits on a corner; a gleaming set of assayer's scales await that gold-laden prospector, who will move on with his money to the antique teller's cages of the bank next door.

Not content to be a star of film and television westerns, Jacksonville went head-to-head with neighboring Ashland's drama brainstorm, dreaming up its own cultural coup: an annual music festival, featuring some of the nation's top musicians performing before an audience seated on the rolling lawns of a beautiful old home.

As if top drama, music, and history aren't enough, there's an endless array of sports opportunities from rafting rapids to hiking with a llama! Close as they all are to each other, both in geography and genealogy, the Rogue Valley towns of Ashland, Jacksonville, Medford, Grants Pass, Talent, and other even-smaller smaller villages team up to give you a close look at a slice of rural America that encompasses the best of modern country life, both sophisticated and refreshingly innocent.

They also offer a convenient central location from which to visit two of nature's most intriguing contributions to Oregon: sparkling, mile-high Crater Lake and, on the opposite end of the earth, the state's underground Oregon Caves National Monument.

Among them, these small towns and the somnolent Rogue and Applegate River Valley villages that surround them offer you a chance to spend some lovely summer days blending history, music, and drama—both man-made and natural —into an experience you will long remember and perhaps soon repeat.

1. ORIENTATION

GETTING THERE: United and Horizon fly into the **Medford-Jackson County Municipal Airport,** about 20 miles from Ashland.

From the airport you can take a **Rogue Valley Transportation bus** for about $1 to Ashland, Medford, or Jacksonville.

Nearest stop for **Amtrak** trains is Klamath Falls, 70 miles from Ashland.

Greyhound serves the region with a terminal at 91 Oak St., Ashland (tel. 503/482-2516).

GETTING AROUND: You can rent a car, by far the best way to see this beautiful valley, or use local buses for transportation.

Budget Rent-A-Car, Medford-Jackson Airport in Medford (tel. 503/

773-7023), offers free pickup at Medford and from Ashland for a small fee, with special weekly and weekend rates available. Also operating in the region is **Executive Rent-a-Car**, 1977 Ore. 99 North, Ashland (tel. 503/482-8310).

Rogue Valley Transportation operates local buses serving Ashland, Medford, White City, and Jacksonville. Fares are by zones, 50¢ for the first zone, 10¢ for each additional zone; children pay 25¢ for the first zone, 10¢ thereafter. For schedule information, stop in at 3200 Crater Lake Ave., Medford (tel. 503/779-BUSS).

VISITOR INFORMATION: You'll find plenty of smiling faces waiting to help you in the region. In Ashland those helpful folks are at the **Ashland Visitors and Convention Bureau**, 110 E. Main St. (P.O. Box 606), Ashland, OR 97520 (tel. 503/482-3486). In historic Jacksonville you can get maps and information on the region at the **Jacksonville Chamber of Commerce**, Rogue River Valley Railway Depot, Oregon and C Streets, Jacksonville, OR 97530 (tel. 503/899-8118). **Grants Pass Visitors and Convention Bureau**, 1439 N.E. 6th St., Grants Pass, OR 97526 (tel. 503/476-7717, or toll free 800/547-5927), can help with rafting plans on the Rogue River and trips throughout the region. **Medford Visitors and Convention Bureau**, 304 S. Central St., Medford, OR 97501 (tel. 503/772-5194), has the latest news on what's going on in that city.

USEFUL INFORMATION: For **police or medical emergency,** call 911. . . . You can do your own laundry or drop it off and let them do it at the **Laundry Room**, 66th Street and Siskiyou Boulevard (tel. 503/488-1756), in Ashland. . . . Varney's Clothing Care Center, 1662 Siskiyou Blvd., Ashland (tel. 503/482-4515), will pick up and deliver laundry and **dry cleaning** and offers one-day service. . . . If you'd like to make all your theater, hotel, and touring reservations at the same time, call on **Southern Oregon Reservation Center**, 521 E. Main St., Ashland, OR 97520 (tel. 503/488-1011), which also has money-saving vacation and theater packages. . . . For one-hour **photo finishing,** try Frodsham, Ashland Shopping Center (tel. 503/488-2313). . . . For an after-hours drugstore, try **Rexall,** 275 E. Main St. (tel. 503/482-3366). . . . For **late-night groceries,** try Minute Market, open from 7 a.m. to midnight daily at 1690 Siskiyou Blvd. (tel. 503/482-8834), and in nine other locations in the area. . . . **Talent Truck Stop,** Valley View West and I-5 (tel. 503/535-4257), has gasoline and restaurant service 24 hours.

2. JACKSONVILLE

Jacksonville plays history to the hilt, and in late July and August plays music too! That's when the annual Peter Britt Festival of Music comes to town featuring a bluegrass festival followed by a classical festival followed by a jazz festival followed by a dance festival!

A grand total of 1,950 people occupy Jacksonville, and all of them, it seems, are enthralled with the history of their small town. You'll see plaques on houses identifying their original owners and the date of construction. You'll see white picket fences and enough calico to clothe all the original pioneers. So well has it all been put together, in fact, that the whole town is a national historic site.

All this history got started back in 1852 when gold was discovered just outside town. Miners poured in here in search of more glitter. Jacksonville boomed. In its wildest days Jacksonville packed more than 10,000 people into the city, and its muddy streets became southern Oregon's stagecoach and pack train hub. In those days the United States Hotel, which still stands but is now the most interesting bank you'll ever see, was home to many a man away from home. From the

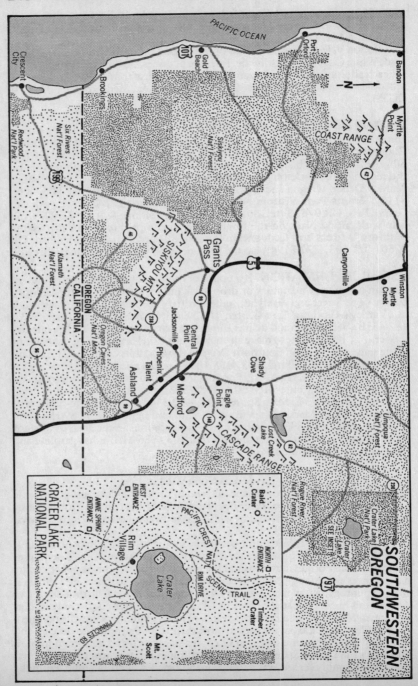

doors of dozens of saloons came the sound of high C and hilarity. At Beckman Bank, built in 1854 and still containing its original equipment, more than $23 million in gold dust was weighed and shipped. But when the railroad bypassed Jacksonville and the mine played out, so did Jacksonville, which in its later years came close to ghosthood.

Then villagers with an interest in their history and a determination to put their town back on the map began restoring the century-old buildings. Today you will see Jacksonville in all its reconstructed glory, an Old West town whose modern residents have all the spunk and vivacity of their pioneer ancestors.

WHERE TO STAY: From a general-store-turned-hotel to a cluster of lovely old homes converted to intriguing bed-and-breakfast inns, there's a small but fascinating choice of stopping spots in Jacksonville.

A Historic Lodging

There can be no place to stay more evocative of pioneer days than the **Jacksonville Inn Hotel,** 175 E. California St. (P.O. Box 359), Jacksonville, OR 97530 (tel. 503/899-1900), which seems not to have changed one whit in a hundred years or so. Right in the middle of this delightful village, the hotel occupies the quarters of what was once a sort of general store. Built in 1863, the four-story structure is brick on the original first two floors, wood on the upper two, which are newer but still historic. Everything here has been lovingly restored, with every attempt made to use original materials. Original brick flooring was pulled up and relaid to even it out. Paneling in the front dining room and foyers was matched with wood taken from a pioneer hotel. Massive beams were transported from an early sawmill on the upper Umpqua River, and an outside staircase was salvaged from an 1800s-era structure. Handmade puffy comforters, ruffly shams, lots of calico touches in delightful colors, marble-topped and oak furnishings, beveled mirrors, and high wood bedsteads combine to give you the feeling you really ought to be hanging your six-gun on the bed post, or dressing for dinner in voluminous petticoats or a ten-gallon hat. Dinner can be had downstairs in one of the best restaurants in southwestern Oregon (see "Where to Dine"). For a room—and a step back in time—at the Jacksonville Inn, you'll pay $58 to $66 double.

Bed-and-Breakfast Inns

Like neighboring Ashland, Jacksonville has some wonderful houses turned into antique-furnished bed-and-breakfast inns. There could not be a more delightful alternative to standard hotel and motel accommodations.

Among the bed-and-breakfast homes in Jacksonville are: the classic white, lace-curtained **McCully House,** 240 California St., Jacksonville, OR 97530 (tel. 503/899-1942), its stately columns dating to 1860; the Craftsman-style **Judge Touvelle House,** 455 N. Oregon St., Jacksonville, OR 97530 (tel. 503/899-8223), where two high-ceilinged rooms feature fireplaces, a canopied bed, antique clocks and lamps, baths down the hall, and a swimming pool and a hot tub outside; the **Livingston Mansion,** 4132 Livingston Rd. (P.O. Box 1476), Jacksonville, OR 97530 (tel. 503/899-7101), where the owners scraped away years of neglect to find beautiful wood floors in this inn which now features soft colors, private baths, a newly created library, a swimming pool and duck pond, and beautiful views over the valley; **Reames House** 540 E. California St., Jacksonville, OR 97530 (tel. 503/899-8963), a Victorian home listed on the National Register of Historic Places; and **Under the Greenwood Tree,** 3045 Bellinger Lane, Medford, OR 97529 (tel. 503/776-0000), yet another charming home, this one a few miles outside Jacksonville in the town of Medford. All charge prices in the $60 to $80 range.

WHERE TO DINE: Certainly you need never fear starvation here in southwestern Oregon, where breakfast is liable to be enough food to keep a logger going until dinner.

The **Jacksonville Inn and Dinner House,** 175 E. California St. (tel. 503/899-1900), has one of the best restaurants in the area, with good American cooking served in historic surroundings. Brick walls, heavy beams, and a brick fireplace are background to a sumptuous dinner that begins with a tray-full of relishes and vegetables and ends with a tray of irresistible desserts. In between you dine on juicy prime rib, thick steaks, fresh salmon or razor clams, succulent Oregon scallops, and tender veal in a variety of presentations. Your seven-course repast includes complimentary wine, fabulous pies, fruit, and an irresistible selection of elaborate pastries. An extensive wine list of more than 500 wines is another plus. Later, wander into the tiny lounge next door for a postprandial libation. Prices are in the $10 to $20 range, and hours are 5 to 10 p.m. Monday through Saturday and 5 to 9 p.m. on Sunday.

Trombino's Italian, 605 N. 5th St. (tel. 503/899-1340), puts together some wonderful Italian flavors in rich sauces that top homemade manicotti, lasagne, calzone, and veal dishes in the $10 bracket or less. Open daily for lunch from 11:30 a.m. and for dinner from 5 p.m.

Bella Union, 170 W. California St. (tel. 503/899-1770), is a pretty place right on the main street through town. During a recent remodeling, brick walls that were part of the three buildings built in 1856 were uncovered. In recent years the restaurant has added outdoor dining under a huge canopy of wisteria. A popular après–Britt Festival spot, Bella Union recently played host to Chuck Mangione and his band. In the kitchen the accent is Italian, with all the standard Italian treats on hand from ravioli and lasagne to antipasti, garlic bread, and plenty of pizza. Top it all with this Oregon treat: raspberry-hazelnut cheesecake. Prices are in the $6 to $10 range and hours are 11 a.m. to 3 p.m. weekdays, 4 to 10 p.m. daily, and 9 a.m. to 3 p.m. for Sunday brunch. A lounge is open daily until midnight. One more note for Britt-goers: Bella Union will make up box lunches for you.

MUSIC UNDER THE STARS: Mention Jacksonville anywhere in the Northwest and someone will sigh rapturously, "Ahh, the Britt Festival." Music-lovers throng here from all over the Northwest—and the nation—to hear this famous festival that's been going on for a quarter of a century. The oldest outdoor festival in the West, the **Peter Britt Festivals,** run from July through August and sometimes longer. The sights are as interesting as the sounds: everything from elegant picnics complete with the family silver to beans and hot dogs, as transported music fans spread out across the grass. Over it all, through the cool, pine-scented air float the sounds of chamber music, bluegrass or country music, or jazz. Some of the most famous names in music have appeared here, including jazz stars Dave Brubeck, Count Basie, and Stan Getz. In 1984 the festival produced its first dance program, featuring ballet and folk dances, the English Ballet ensemble, and the Royal Ballet dancers of Covent Garden.

The site for the festival is the sloping garden of the Peter Britt House, Britt Pavilion, Ore. 238, built by a fellow who came here to find a fortune in gold but ended up a photographer. Tickets to the festival are $7 to $8.50 for adults, $3 to $7.50 for children 8 to 12, and can be obtained by contacting the Peter Britt Festivals, 46 N. Front St. (P.O. Box 1124), Medford, OR 97501 (tel. 503/779-0847, or toll free 800/88-BRITT in the western states).

3. ASHLAND

Ashland has boomed, busted, boomed and busted again several times in its history, but these days things could hardly be going better.

It all started back in 1852, when three adventurers crossed the mountains, saw this valley, and decided it ought to be home. When you take a look at it, you'll understand why they liked what they saw: a broad sheltered bowl stretching across miles of pine-strewn land to misty blue mountains that spawn cascading rivers hiding—perhaps still hiding—gold.

A gold strike in nearby Jacksonville had already lured thousands of get-rich-quick hopefuls to that town when Abel Helman and Eber and Jacob Emery set about building Ashland into a town that would supply miners. They named it Ashland after the Ohio city from which they had come. Helman returned across the mountains to Ohio to bring back wives and children. Together the little colony opened flour and sawmills and grew steadily. Then the gold played out, along with Ashland's hope for metropolis status.

In the late 1800s, however, the railroad selected Ashland as its southern terminus, and the boom began again, leaving Jacksonville on the wrong track, and Ashland the main stop between San Francisco and Portland. The population doubled to all of 2,634, almost as big as Eugene was, with settlers operating lumber, flour, and woolen mills and expanding a burgeoning trade in apples, pears, cherries, and peaches that are still grown here.

Ashland's next boom came when the city discovered sulfur-rich, lithium-laden waters—the same waters that had made Saratoga famous. Springs were tapped, and the city enjoyed a little flurry of spa activity. You can still taste some of that water today in Ashland Plaza. Next came a spurt of interest in the town's granite quarry, whose stone is said to equal the quality of Vermont's famous granite.

But the railroad that had proven so beneficial to Ashland soon turned its back on the town, diverting most of its traffic away from the Rogue Valley. That proved a killing blow, worsened by the arrival of the Depression. After World War II Ashland boomed again, this time providing for the nation's increasing need for lumber. During its heyday Ashland welcomed the Chautauqua, a national entertainment and education network that was housed in a domed building with canvas windows. That project thrived for years, then died in 1925, leaving behind a sagging, leaky building ready for the junkman.

Then into the valley rode a young English professor who put together a play. That one play became another play and another, and soon Angus Bowmer was presiding over a laughing group of actors who called their creation the Teensy-Weensy Theater. A man of boundless energy and matching enthusiasm, Bowmer talked local entrepreneurs into a revival of Fourth of July activities—supplemented by two Shakespearean plays. In 1935 the First Annual Shakespearean Festival opened at the by-now-domeless remains of the Chautauqua structure.

In just its second year the plays profited to the tune of $84.23, a grand sum intended to form the economic base of the following year's plays—but promptly spent by Bowmer's school to support the football team! That settled it. Bowmer set up a nonprofit corporation to run the theater, which operated for a few years, was dark for a few, then revived and went on to even greater success. In recent years young actors have clamored for even bit parts, in hopes of using the theater as a stepping stone to a career in professional theater. Playing to sell-out crowds, Ashland's theater nearly outgrew itself but has added over the years two additional theaters designed to showcase modern and experimental plays. Now the players have expanded the season and won their greatest honor—a Tony Award for the Best Regional Theater, beating out Yale and Harvard theaters, among others. And the play goes on.

WHERE TO STAY: Turned magically into a kind of latter-day Stratford-upon-Avon, Ashland has some very attractive hotels and in recent years has added a renovated historic hotel and some lovely bed-and-breakfast inns. If you've ever wanted to try one of those, this is the time.

A Historic Hostelry

Let's begin with that renovated hotel. It's the **Mark Antony Hotel,** 212 E. Main St., Ashland, OR 97520 (tel. 503/482-1721), a beautiful old hostelry into which several entrepreneurs have sunk what is certainly by *our* standards a fortune. Now a national historic landmark, the Gothic-looking eight-story hotel, glowing with stained glass, looms over downtown Ashland like a doting dowager. You enter into a sunny, high-ceilinged, wide, and airy lobby with elegant white furniture upholstered in burgundy.

In the hotel's bright rooms you will find comforters as soft as a cloud, perhaps an antique armoire, Austrian drapes, and leaded-glass windows. Baths are comfortably modern, with fluffy towels, tiles, and good lighting. Up a few steps from the lobby is an elegant restaurant outfitted with a massive crystal chandelier. Just a few steps from the Shakespearean Theater, the Mark Antony also has a swimming pool and lounge and charges $55 to $70 double. From November through May prices drop 20%.

Two Contemporary Choices

From antique to moderne: enter the **Ashland Hills Inn,** 2525 Ashland St., Ashland, OR 97520 (tel. 503/482-8310, or toll free 800/547-4747, 800/452-5315 in Oregon). In the subdued Olde England atmosphere of Ashland, this large Best Western hotel-motel is just the opposite: slick, sleek, and contemporary. Attractively togged out in wood siding, the Ashland Inn is located a bit outside of town, so it offers beautiful views from most rooms across the rolling land of this valley. Beyond the big showy lobby adorned with heavy beams, you'll find spacious rooms decorated in chic modern style and outfitted with comfortable furniture. Many rooms have glass doors opening onto private balconies. You can play on lighted tennis courts, dance in a lovely lounge with entertainment, putt around a green, and dine on continental cuisine. A free shuttle takes you to plays. Rates for two at the inn are $50 to $80 for rooms with one or two queen-size beds or a king-size bed.

The **Stratford Inn,** 555 Siskiyou Blvd., Ashland, OR 97520 (tel. 503/488-2151, or toll free 800/547-4741, 800/452-5319 in Oregon), is a spiffy, wood-sided motel trimmed in bright blue with blue roof tiles. Here you'll find 53 spacious, attractively decorated rooms, some of them connecting to a second room containing a complete kitchen and hideaway bed. Opened in 1981, the motel has a clean new look and comes complete with an indoor swimming pool surrounded by windows, plus a whirlpool; many rooms have queen-size beds. Rates are $62 double. Kitchenettes are $77 to $82.

Traditional Inns

Along a shady, quiet street, just a short walk from town and theater, you'll find the **Winchester Inn,** 35 S. 2nd St., Ashford, OR 97520 (tel. 503/488-1113), a house that traces its history back to 1886. All the best of those old days —spacious rooms, blooming gardens—remain. To them has been added some of the light and luxury more in keeping with the modern world. In this cream-colored Queen Anne–style Victorian home you'll still see leaded-glass windows and a gazebo in the flowering gardens. Seven charming guest rooms feature queen-size beds set on antique bedsteads reformed to fit today's larger beds. Color schemes in burgundy, peach, and light blue highlight the rooms' beautiful antique pieces, marble-topped tables, and oak armoires. Unlike some bed-and-breakfast hostelries, each room here has a private bath, all with showers, some with clawfoot tubs. Guests find homemade chocolate truffles or chocolate-covered strawberries, sherry, and a vase of flowers awaiting them in their rooms. Mornings, you dine in the pretty dining room overlooking sloping gardens. The fare includes such treats as freshly made scones or fruit-nut breads, fresh fruit, and such treats as eggs Benedict and strawberry pancakes. The Winchester Inn also opens its dining room to the public for dinner (see "Where to Dine"). Rates at the inn are $84 single, $89 double, in summer; $54 single and $59 double in winter months. Additional persons are $15, and money-saving winter packages are available.

At **Ashland's Main Street Inn,** 142 N. Main St., Ashland, OR 97520 (tel. 503/488-0969), talented restorers have created three spacious guest rooms in a renovated Victorian home, each named after its predominating color. In all quarters you'll find pretty lace curtains or Austrian drapes, TV, and beautiful décor. In the Red Room are three single beds and, down the hall a few steps, a bath specifically for that room also decorated in red. The Blue Room, which seems largest of all, has deep-blue décor, a double bed, and its own bathroom in the room. You can step out onto the Blue Room's balcony and look down on the world. The owners thoughtfully keep a book stocked with menus from local restaurants and guests' comments on them. Located just three blocks from the theater and main city plaza, the three-floor house is surrounded by a profusion of flowers. Rates are $60 double, about $10 less from November through February.

On another quiet Ashland street you'll find the **Romeo Inn,** 295 Idaho St., Ashland, OR 97520 (tel. 503/488-0884). Here you will dwell in a house built in Cape Cod style on a rise overlooking the valley, a curving driveway, and gardens. The large rooms are outfitted with an eclectic mix of antique and traditional furnishings in attractive, subdued colors, and all have private baths. All also have king-size beds, and one has a fireplace. In a recent remodeling the inn opened a new suite sporting hand-stitched Amish quilts and relandscaped the yard, adding garden paths, benches, and a fountain. At the back of one wing is a swimming pool and Jacuzzi shaded by pine trees. At 5 in the afternoon the Halversons serve tea. Rates at the inn, which does not accept small children or pets and is open year round, are $86 to $110 double.

The **Chanticleer Inn,** 120 Gresham St., Ashland, OR 97520 (tel. 503/482-1919), is the creation of Jim and Nancy Beaver, who have done a marvelous job of creating a home-away-from-home filled with ruffled eyelet shams, airy comforters, delicate floral wallpaper, brass beds, and French windows. Named after that fabled Chanticleer rooster, the inn has six rooms with French names: Aerie, with queen-size bed, twin bed, and view over the valley; Fleur, an attic room with view, queen-size, and twin beds; Maître, on the main floor with queen-size brass bed and French windows; Rosette, Jardin, and Pertelote, rooms with antique wrought-iron beds and private patio entrances. The Chanticleer Suite has two bedrooms with queen-size beds, full kitchen, and private garden. Nancy turns out breakfasts that include, among other goodies, fresh juices and fruit, hot blueberry muffins, and cheese-baked eggs. Each room has a private bath and rates, including those hearty breakfasts, are $90 to $105 in peak summer season.

More B&B Choices

Ashland has beautifully restored old homes open for sleeping and dining as glamorous bed-and-breakfast inns.

The **McCall House,** 153 Oak St., Ashland, OR 97520 (tel. 503/482-9296), an Italianate Victorian home, was built in 1883 and now features queen-size beds.

Edinburgh Lodge, 586 E. Main St., Ashland, OR 97520 (tel. 503/488-1050), features six rooms named for Scottish castles and all with private bath, for $62 double.

The Woods House, 333 N. Main St., Ashland, OR 97520 (tel. 503/488-1598), is a bungalow with a carriage house across a courtyard and queen-size beds.

Morical House, 668 N. Main St., Ashland, OR 97520 (tel. 503/482-2254), is an 1880s house with five bedrooms, all with private bath, plus stained-glass windows, ornate woodwork, antique furnishings, homemade comforters, beautiful gardens, and mountain views, for $70 to $80 double.

The **RoyAl Carter House,** 514 Siskiyou Blvd., Ashland, OR 97520 (tel. 503/482-5623), features a two-room Victorian suite with two double beds, a 1920s-style oak two-room suite with king-size bed and sitting room, a sewing room converted to canopied queen-size bedroom, and a billiard room turned into a bedroom of wicker furnishings and separate entrance.

Prices at these B&Bs range from $45 to $65, including breakfast.

Budget Bet
If you're here on the strictest of budgets, a youth hostel may be the answer. The **Ashland Hostel,** 150 N. Main St., Ashland, OR 97520 (tel. 503/482-9217), occupies a pretty Victorian home on Main Street. Travelers share the dining room, living room, kitchen, and laundry. There are separate showers for men and women, and families must make reservations if they want to share a bedroom. Rates are $6.50 for hostel members and $9.50 for nonmembers; children pay half price. Reservations are wise during the Shakespearean Festival. Check-in is from 5 p.m. to midnight, to 11 p.m. in winter.

If you're camping, try **Glenyan KOA,** 5310 Ore. 66, Ashland, OR 97520 (tel. 503/482-4138). Glenyan offers full hookups, playground, swimming pool, and games room. Rates are $12 for no hookup to $15 double for full hookups.

WHERE TO DINE: Despite its aura of rural Americana and Olde England, Ashland is becoming quite a cosmopolitan place with many nationalities represented in its kitchens.

A Potpourri of Choices
Chateaulin, 50 E. Main St. (tel. 503/482-2264), is a pleasant spot draped with ivy where you'll have to fight the crowds before play performances, but it's worth it. French flavors are the order of the day here, from excellent pâtés to delicately cooked veal and beef selections. If you'd like to see the Shakespearean performers winding down after the play, this is the place. Prices are in the $12 to $17 bracket, and the restaurant has seating from 5 to 9:30 p.m. daily, and the bar is open to 2 a.m. with lighter snacks.

Jazmin, 180 C St. (tel. 503/488-0883), got its name from its jazz-producer owner who runs this restaurant and still swings enough jazz clout to get some jazz greats like Ahmad Jamal to stop in and say hello. Greek salads are a specialty here, supplemented by traditional steak and seafood selections. Prices are in a quite reasonable $10 to $13 range for dinners and the restaurant is open from 4 p.m. to 2:30 a.m. daily.

On a cold winter day you can't beat a rib-sticking piroshka or golabki cabbage rolls stuffed with beef, olives, and onions and topped with a creamy tomato sauce. For that matter it tastes pretty good on a summer day too! You can try some of those treats or such things as lamb chops or rich hazelnut torte at **Chata,** 1212 S. Pacific Hwy. (tel. 503/535-2575), in the village of Talent. If you can't make up your mind, try one of the restaurant's platters, which give you a taste of many tastes. Then back those up with a variety of vodkas. Prices are in the $8 to $10 range for dinner, and hours are 5 to 9:30 p.m. daily in summer; closed Monday through Wednesday in winter.

Those Créole flavors that have captured the American culinary imagination in recent years have found their way west, all the way to tiny Ashland where they turned up at the **Bayou Grill,** 139 E. Main St. (tel. 503/488-0235). Everything you ever wanted in the way of blackened fish, shrimp Créole, Cajun barbecued shrimp—the entire Cajun drill is whipped up in the kitchen here. They've even managed to get a Northwest twist to the whole thing: bayou grilled salmon. Bayou Grill occupies very attractive quarters on the second floor of a building overlooking the hills that surround this pretty town and even a view of the comings and goings at the Shakespearean theater nearby. Prices are in the $8 to $15 range, with that top price buying you a whopping seafood platter. Bayou Grill is open from 5 to 9 p.m. daily except Monday.

Winchester Inn, 35 S. 2nd St. (tel. 503/488-1115), is a lovely old home turned bed-and-breakfast inn and restaurant. In its sunny dining room overlooking a garden full of bright blooms, you can dine on some skillfully blended flavors. For openers, try a Dungeness crab fondue with artichokes or Sonoma goat cheese marinated in olive oil and fresh herbs. Then move on to duck with a seasonal fruit sauce, filet of beef with lemon zest and cracked pepper, or loin of lamb served with a different sauce each night. Dinner prices are in the $11 to $18 range. Sunday brunch is also served and features everything from scallops Benedict to stuffed French toast. Hours are 5:30 to 9 p.m. for dinner daily except Monday. Sunday brunch is from 10 a.m. to 2 p.m.

You can fill corners you didn't even know you had at **Callahan's,** 7100 Old Ore. 99-S (tel. 503/482-1299), where they think you're not eating enough if you consume only a trencherman's portion of everything. You do your consuming accompanied by a gorgeous view of forests and mountain scenery. Don't miss the minestrone, the veal selections, or the very good fried chicken. Prices are $8 to $16 for a complete dinner, and the restaurant is open Tuesday through Friday from 5 to 10 p.m., opening an hour earlier on Saturday and from 2 to 9 p.m. on Sunday; closed Monday. Callahan's is up in the hills, so if you're planning a winter visit, call first to ask about road conditions. To get here, take the Mount Ashland exit from I-5, six miles south of Ashland.

Look up to find **Alex's Plaza,** 35 N. Main St. (tel. 503/482-8818), which occupies a balcony overlooking the main downtown square. It's a subtly elegant spot with brick walls, shining wood floors, some chic architectural touches like arched windows and French doors, lots of wood antiques, and mirrors. One of the favorites of the house is a thick steak topped with a béarnaise sauce spiked with a local horseradish—zappy! Recently the restaurant experimented with another, lighter café menu stocked with pastas and individual pizzas and some very good appetizers, best of which is a mushroom pâté in red-pepper sauce. Dinner entree prices are in the $10 to $15 range, and Alex's is open for lunch from 11:30 a.m. to 2 p.m. Tuesday through Sunday and 5 to 9 p.m. daily for dinner. Hours are extended on weekends in the restaurant and are always later in the popular lounge.

Light Dining

If you're looking for a light snack, say a salad, some flaky pastries, and espresso, try the **Beanery,** 1604 Ore. 66, Ashland (tel. 503/488-0700), open daily from 7 a.m. to 10 p.m., an hour later on Friday and Saturday.

Omar's, 1380 Siskiyou Blvd. (tel. 503/482-1281), has been around for 40 years or so, making its own soups, sauces, dressings, and desserts and pleasing lots of people with them. Such things as calamari piccata in a caper-butter sauce, pan-fried fresh Pacific oysters, many seafood options, Dijon chicken with mushrooms, and vegetables teriyaki are served with a salad tray and hot whole-grain breads. Seasonal specials might include petrale sole amandine or calamari tempura, while regular features are "grubhouse" fries sprinkled with parmesan, fried zucchini or onion rings, and a whole hot or cold artichoke. Prices are in the $9 to $13 range and hours are 11 a.m. to 2 p.m. weekdays for lunch, 5 to 10 p.m. daily for dinner, closing a half hour later on weekends.

What they may lack in an elaborate menu at **Cuppa Joe,** 60 E. Main St., they certainly make up in enthusiasm. You'll have fun talking to the two owners of this standup espresso bar that purveys cappuccino and hot or iced espresso, Italian sodas called cremosas—they like to call them "West Coast egg creams"—in 23 fruit flavors, and homemade ice creams that won three gold medals at a recent Los Angeles County Fair. Cuppa's open from 9 a.m. to 5:30 p.m. weekdays, closing at 5 p.m. weekends. A great pre- or post-theater stop.

Brothers' Restaurant and Delicatessen, 95 N. Main St. (tel. 503/482-9671), features lots of deli goodies, including some vegetarian specialties like farmer chop suey, featuring raw vegetables on a bed of lettuce with sour cream or yogurt topping, or a burrito stuffed with refried beans, cheese, avocado, sprouts, onions, tomatoes, and green chili. A few Mexican flavors are even available for breakfast, when Brothers' turns out eggs with that peppy Mexican sausage called chorizo, plus huevos rancheros served on a corn tortilla with hot sauce. Nothing on the dinner menu tops $9, and most selections are about $6. Hours are 7 a.m. to 8 p.m. Tuesday through Sunday.

And finally, something for burger babies: **Goodtimes,** 1951 Ore. 66 (tel. 503/482-4424), where you can chow down on 13 different kinds of burgers and top those juicy slabs of beef with all kinds of different toppings. Prices don't rise above $3.25 for a half-pound burger. Hours are 11 a.m. to 11 p.m. daily, closing at 9 p.m. on Sunday.

Dining in Medford

Nearby Medford has its fair share of hospitable restaurants as well. For a family dinner that won't cost you a penny over $5 each, stop in to see Nanette and Joel Brown, two nice people who operate **King's Table,** 266 Jacksonville Hwy., Medford (tel. 503/779-8287). King's Table has many branches of its buffet operation in the Northwest, but this is a very special one that likes to be the first to try something new and different. Wait until you hear the prices: a lunch buffet is $4.25, dinner runs $6, and children pay 40¢ for each year of their age through 10. You just might find a taco bar here on Saturday to keep the youngsters—and the not-so-youngsters—happy, and if you're very good boys and girls, the Browns will tell you a little of the history of this area in which they have lived all their lives. Hours are 11 a.m. to 8:30 p.m. weekdays, to 9 p.m. on Saturday, and from 8 a.m. to 8 p.m. on Sunday. The King's Table also caters parties, and recently the Browns won the company's most-sales award, so they must be doing something right!

SPENDING A NIGHT WITH SHAKESPEARE: Need we tell you that the numero uno event in Ashland is the summer **Oregon Shakespearean Festival?** That tribute to the Bard opens in February and continues through October, showing at least ten plays on a rotating basis. Real theater buffs have been known to attend six plays in three days, suffering nothing worse than terminal theater-seat-bottom!

Those plays are shown at one of three theaters, queen of which is the 1,194-seat outdoor **Elizabethan Stagehouse,** a glamorous Tudor lookalike stage facing an audience seated in an amphitheater-like slope so every seat is a good seat. The **Angus Bowmer Theater** is a 600-seat indoor theater, as is the **Black Swan,** smallest of the three with 140 seats. Although many of the theatrical productions are Shakespearean plays, with all the elaborate costumes and stage sets those plays require, the list of offerings may range from Dracula to Noel Coward to Tennessee Williams.

Wonderful plays in a glamorous setting and performances by a professional company are what put Ashland on the map, so the festival is very well attended. If you're planning to be one of those attendees, make hotel and ticket reservations early.

Tickets

Tickets are $10, $14, and $18 for plays at the Angus Bowmer Theater (which features a wide range of drama) or the Elizabethan Stage (which is the setting for Shakespearean plays), and $14 at the Black Swan Theatre (which often showcases the work of contemporary playwrights). You can buy tickets at the box office when you get here, but you risk a sell-out, particularly in prime-time summer months. All three theaters and box office are at 15 S. Pioneer St. (tel. 503/ 482-4331). The box office is closed from November through mid-February. From mid-February to October, hours are 10 a.m. to curtain time on performance days, closing at 5 p.m. on days when there is no evening show.

If you don't mind risking a sell-out, you can wait until 11 a.m. daily to see if the theater has decided to "rush" tickets. That means they'll sell unfilled seats at a lower price, usually about half price. You're likely to find rush performances in spring and fall, in summer at simultaneous performances, and on Sunday and Tuesday evening performances.

If you're planning to see several of the shows, you might consider buying a membership in the **Festival Association.** A $35 membership ($25 for students and senior citizens) gives you an opportunity to order tickets before sales are opened to the general public, saves you half the price of a ticket to preview performances, and offers discounts on tickets to plays from February to June and after Labor Day, plus two tickets at half-price to rush performances. You also get a 10% discount in the Tudor Guild Shop. To order tickets in advance or to ask questions about performances and donations, get in touch with the Oregon Shakespearean Festival, P.O. Box 158, Ashland, OR 97520 (tel. 503/482-4331).

Renaissance Celebrations

Plays are not all they do here. In mid-June the players celebrate a tradition dating back 30 years. It's called the **Feast of Will** and honors the opening days of the outdoor Elizabethan stage. Costumed players romp among the guests at this $12 park event, which includes festival musicians and dancers, plenty of food, and a general good time.

In late June, Southern Oregon State College sometimes sponsors a **Renaissance Feast** of foods prepared from Elizabethan recipes and dance and music presentations from that period.

At the beginning of each performance on the outdoor stage, festival musicians and dancers perform **songs and dances** of the Renaissance court and countryside at 7 p.m.

Many things happen at noon during the festival. At 12:15 p.m. on many summer days from mid-June to September, you can **talk with the actors** free at a picnic lunch in the Herb Garden outside the Elizabethan Theatre. Actors, directors, and scholars often lecture on Wednesday or Friday in summer months (admission is $2 for adults, $1 for children). Musicians and dancers present special concert performances on Wednesday or Saturday (admission is $2 for adults).

You can even take classes—one called Wake Up with Shakespeare, the other Festival Round Table—at the **Festival Institute,** Education Office, P.O. Box 158, Ashland, OR 97520 (tel. 503/482-2111). That wake-up session ($135) is a five-day event Tuesday through Saturday mornings and features discussions of the plays with company members, while the Round Table gives you a chance for in-depth discussion with a drama scholar ($190). Fees include reserved tickets to eight plays, backstage tours, and noon events.

In March and October you can talk with the cast after Sunday matinees and Tuesday-evening performances.

There's a big cast party to which all ticketholders are invited on opening night of the company in February.

Youngsters can get a close look at the costumes of Shakespeare's kings and crazies at the **Exhibit Center,** which lets the kids sit on a Shakespearean royal throne, prance across the stage, and try on some of the costumes. Miniature stage sets are on display along with many photographs of players in action. Admission is $1 for adults, 50¢ for children under 12.

Hardly anything could be more fascinating than a look at what goes on backstage at Shakespearean plays in which someone is always disappearing, leaping up out of the floor, or sailing off through the air. You can find out how they do all those tricks on a **Backstage Tour** that takes you through the maze of backstages at both the Angus Bowmer and Elizabethan Theatres. You visit the Green Room where the company relaxes, and the costume Exhibit Center the theater calls its "touchy-feely" room. You even meet some of the backstage wizards who make things appear and disappear and create swords that kill but don't kill. This tour, which includes the Exhibit Center visit, departs at 10 a.m. on performance days, lasts about two hours, and costs $6 for adults, $3 for children under 12.

4. WHAT TO SEE

From huge caves to hot-air balloons, from moustachioed villains to covered wagons, you'll find plenty of things to amaze and amuse you here in southwestern Oregon.

EXPLORING JACKSONVILLE: To imagine what life was like in those sometimes-bleak days, take a walk about this Old West small town so perfectly reconstructed you expect a posse to come racing down Main Street and the sheriff to step out of his office for a stroll over to the livery stable. Stop by the **Jacksonville Chamber of Commerce Information Center,** in the railroad depot at Oregon and C Streets (tel. 503/899-8118), to pick up a walking map that directs you past the many historical buildings in this old town and tells you a little about each of them. Some of the best of those include: the **Armstrong House** at 6th and California Streets, built in 1856, now the Southern Oregon Historical Society Headquarters; the **Beekman Bank,** built in 1863 at 4th and California Streets and unchanged since 1912 (open from 1 to 5 p.m.; donations requested); the **Beekman House,** 470 E. California St., where the banker lived in considerable style, as you will see (open from 1 to 5 p.m. daily May to September, free); the **Children's Museum,** 206 5th St., in the old jail that now houses exhibits on Indians and settlers in the 1850s (open from 10 a.m. to 5 p.m. daily June to September; closed Monday the rest of the year; free).

If you can come on over for a look some evening, you really will think you've stepped into a "Gunsmoke" remake. On silent streets you walk by a bank still sporting oldtimey teller's cages, an assay office with shining scales, and a weathered, wooden buckboard just begging you to pick up the reins. As the crickets chirp in the background, you wander among old homes and false-fronted stores that in a century or so have changed only owners and products. Jacksonville is the Old West at its un-hokey, non-tourist-trap best.

In the **Jacksonville Museum of Southern Oregon History,** 205 5th St. (tel. 503/899-1847), you can see some of the things the pioneers brought with them when they settled the area and some of the things they built after they got here. Peter Britt's photographs are on display, as are, oddly enough, some memorabilia of another local fellow, Pinto Colvig, who left here to become Bozo the Clown! Admission is free, and hours from June to September are 10 a.m. to 5 p.m. daily; in winter closed Monday.

For those who have never quite gotten over dolls, the **Jacksonville Doll Museum,** 5th and California Streets (tel. 503/779-6536), is an important stop. Here you'll see an amazing collection, from a 1640 Italian crèche doll with ivory hands to Dutch and French dolls. Dolls are on display Monday through Saturday from 11 a.m. to 4:30 p.m. and on Sunday from 1 to 4 p.m. Admission is $1 for adults, 50¢ for children 6 to 12; others, free.

ASHLAND'S ATTRACTIONS: Like Jacksonville, Ashland itself is the best thing to see. To take a look at Ashland, make your first stop the **Ashland Visitors and Convention Bureau,** 110 E. Main St., where enthusiastic workers will arm you with a map so you can walk or drive through town and see the beautifully restored collection of old homes.

Among the loveliest and most interesting structures in town are the **Orlando Collidge House,** 137 N. Main St., built in 1875 and reminiscent of the owner's Maine background; the **Domingo Perozzi House,** 88 Granite St., built in 1902 in a blend of Italianate and Queen Anne styles; the arched windows and ornate roof line of the **International Order of Oddfellows,** 57 N. Main St., the first brick structure to be built on the plaza after the fire that destroyed it in 1879; the **Lithia Springs Hotel,** built in 1925 when it was the tallest building between Portland and San Francisco, now operating again as a hotel called the Mark Antony; the imposing 1888 **H. B. Carter House,** 91 Gresham St., an elaborate Victorian structure built for one of the founders of the Bank of Ashland; the fancy **E. V. Carter House,** 505 Siskiyou Blvd., built in 1886 for another Carter banker; and the big, but simple, white frame ranch home built in 1860 at 4224 Ore. 66 for Irishman Dunn, who made the ranch a smoke-filled playground for the politicians of Oregon's early days. All these homes are now private residences, so be content with a look at the outside.

In Talent, a small town seven miles north of Ashland, stop by the **Cole Rivers Fish Hatchery,** Ore. 99 (tel. 503/878-2236), a hatchery built to compensate for spawning areas lost by dams. Here you can visit six holding ponds, two brook trout ponds, a fish ladder, and an incubation center where more than five million fish from spring Chinook salmon to rainbow trout are raised. You can see handling and spawning activities from September to mid-April, free.

Farther afield in Winston, a small town near Roseburg, you can visit a little bit of Africa in Oregon at **Wildlife Safari,** Winston-Coos Bay exit 119 from I-5 (tel. 503/679-6761). More than 600 animals, representing nearly 100 species, roam free on a 600-acre reserve. You drive among them. Admission is $6.50 for adults, $4.50 for children 4 to 12, and $1 per vehicle; hours are 8:30 a.m. to 8 p.m. from mid-June to September, 9 a.m. to 5 p.m. in other months. Open daily. A new addition to the park are some massive North American animals including elk, bison, moose, and musk ox.

If you'd like to try your tastebuds on some wine from the region, several wineries invite you to come on over and see what they've got. Included among those are **Bjelland Vineyards,** Bjelland Vineyards Lane, Roseburg (tel. 503/679-6950); **Henry Winery,** Ore. 9, Upmqua (tel. 503/459-5120); **Hillcrest Vineyard,** 240 Vineyard Lane, Roseburg (tel. 503/673-3709); **Siskiyou Vineyards,** 6220 Caves Hwy., Cave Junction (tel. 503/592-3727); and **Valley View Vineyard,** 1000 Applegate Rd., in Ruch, eight miles south of Jacksonville (tel. 503/899-8468). All are free and open from 11 a.m. to 5 p.m. most days, but call first.

5. AFTER DARK IN SOUTHWESTERN OREGON

No razzle-dazzle here, no casinos or dancing girls, but some wonderful evenings with Shakespeare or out under the stars at a music festival. Here's a look at some of the other entertainment in the region.

Southern Oregon State College offers summer **dinner theater** with a buffet dinner at 7 p.m., curtain at 8 p.m. daily in July and August. You'll find the Theatre Arts Center on Palm Avenue, on the campus, which is located just off Siskiyou Boulevard. Tickets are $13 to $15 for dinner and show (tel. 503/482-6348 Thursday through Sunday for reservations).

"You must pay the rent!" (Hiss). "But I can't pay the rent!" (Ooh). "I'll pay the rent!" (Whew! Sigh!). Another close one between Evil Villain and Fair Maiden rescued by Brave and Handsome Hero at a whoop-de-doo, merrily melodramatic evening put together by the **Gilded Cage Players.** Here you don't have to sit still and be good. You can squirm around, hiss, boo, cry, laugh, and have a rip-roaring good time. Everything goes at this lively evening, now celebrating its 20th year of evil vs. curls. There's also a Gay '90s revue, can-can dancing, popcorn, and sarsaparilla. Showtime is 8 p.m. on Friday and Saturday from June to September at the Minshall Theatre, 101 Talent Ave., in the nearby village of Talent (tel. 503/535-5250), and tickets are $6 for adults and $3.50 for children 12 and under. To find Talent, take I-5 north to the Talent exit.

To find out what's happening at local lounges, consult Ashford's newspaper the *Daily Tidings,* Jacksonville's the *Jacksonville Nugget,* or Medford's *Mail Tribune.*

6. DAYTIME ACTIVITIES

You'll find a wide range of activities here in this valley that's close to both the beaches of the coast and the slopes of the Cascades.

SKIING: If you're here from November to May, head straight for **Mount Ashland,** nine miles west of I-5 (tel. 503/482-2897); take the Mount Ashland exit at the Siskiyou Summit and follow the signs. Shakespeare himself wouldn't believe the lengths to which Ashland has taken this slavish adoration for the Bard: here you even ski Shakespeare on slopes dubbed Tempest, Ariel, Juliet, Romeo—well, you should have guessed. You have 23 runs to challenge your skills, two chair lifts, a T-bar, rope tow, and Poma lift to get you up and schussing. Lift rates are $16 per day, $12 for a half day beginning at 12:30 p.m. Rope tows are $4, and children 7 to 12 pay $12; under 6, free. Mount Ashland now has night skiing from the Windsor chair lift on Thursday, Friday, and Saturday nights until 10 p.m., when lift tickets are $12. For a snow report in Ashland/Medford, call 503/482-2754. From Ashland you can get to the mountain on the Ski Bus, which stops at area motels and costs $3.

AIR VIEWS: See it all from the great beyond aboard a hot-air balloon, operated by **Rogue Valley Balloon Flights,** 474 N. Main (tel. 503/482-4310 or 482-2210). Flights last about four hours and cost $225 for two, including the traditional champagne and picnic.

THE SPORTING LIFE: You can go boating, waterskiing, swimming, and fishing at **Emigrant Lake,** six miles south of the city on Ore. 66 (tel. 503/482-4657).

In summer the region is rife with sports opportunities ranging from golf to tennis and swimming.

Golfers can putt about at nine-hole **Oak Knoll Golf Course,** 3070 Ore. 66, Ashland Airport Road (tel. 503/482-4311), where greens fees for 18 holes are $10 weekdays, $11 weekends; carts are $14. To get there, take I-5 to exit 14, and go east on Ore. 66. You'll find the course one mile southeast of Ashland Hills Inn, across from Ashland City Airport. Two other nine-hole courses in the area are **Bear Creek,** 2355 S. Pacific Hwy., Medford (tel. 503/773-1822), and **Cedar Links,** 3155 Cedar Links Dr., Medford (tel. 503/773-4373).

Hikers can walk part of the **Pacific Crest Trail,** one of the nation's most famous trails, stretching from Canada to Mexico. You can join the trail ten miles south or east of Ashland and get information on the trip from the Visitor and Convention Bureau.

River Trips

Rafting trips on the Rogue and Klamath Rivers are the specialty of **Rogue-Klamath Whitewater Co.,** 1202 E. Main St., Medford (tel. 503/772-8467). Most popular of the company's offerings is a white-water run on the upper Rogue River, about a 20-minute drive from Medford. You spend about four hours on the river, where salmon paddle about beneath you. Small to medium rapids make this a good spot for beginners and for inflatable kayaks, while wilder waters are lures for more experienced rafters. Trips leave at 9 a.m., returning about 4 p.m. Cost is $35 per person. Two-day trips are also available for $150 per person; half-day trips begin at $20.

Wild River Adventures, 5759 Crater Lake Hwy., Medford (tel. 503/826-WILD), says you can stay home and do nothing or spend a wild weekend with them, tooling around in a 12-passenger van over the mountains into the Siskiyou National Forest where waterfalls, pine forests, and wildlife await. There you board a Rogue River jet boat for a 30-minute trip to a lodge on the Rogue, stay overnight, dine on feasts prepared by an open fireplace, hike, fish, swim, take photographs, study wildlife. Next day you take another jet-boat journey back through the mountains to Medford. Trips leave at 8 a.m. on Saturday, return Sunday, and are $150 per person.

Paul Brooks Raft Trips, P.O. Box 638, Merlin, OR 97532 (tel. 503/476-8051), has long been operating rafting trips on the Rogue, these leaving from Galice, about a 90-minute drive from Ashland. You can rent a raft for $30 to $55; join a guided trip at $40 for adults, $30 for children under 12; or try a dinner float trip. The trip begins at 8:15 a.m. and returns at 3 p.m., lunch included.

And in Ashland, **Four Seasons Adventures,** 1746 Ashland St. (tel. 503/482-8352), runs river trips on the nearby Applegate River as well as expeditions on the Klamath, upper Rogue, and Sacramento Rivers. Day trips are $45 to $60, depending on the river you select; overnight camping trips are $140 to $160; longer trips are higher in price. Children pay 10% less.

SPECIAL EVENTS: Several events in the valley take place at Jackson County Expo Park in nearby Central Point (tel. 503/776-7237), including the **Rogue Valley Rodeo** in May, the **Oregon Expo** in June, and the **Jackson County Fair** in July.

ART AND CULTURAL ACTIVITIES: The **Rogue Valley Symphony,** 1250 Siskiyou Blvd., Ashland (tel. 503/482-6353), performs from October through May at various locations in Medford, Grant's Pass, and Ashland. Season tickets are $30 to $50, and individual performances run about $10 to $20.

You'll also find several art museums and galleries in Ashland: the **Shakespeare Art Museum,** 460 B. St. (tel. 503/481-3865), has changing exhibits of 20th-century paintings, prints, and art miscellany on Shakespeare's plays, and is open daily except Tuesday, April to October, from 10 a.m. to 5 p.m. for a $2 admission charge. **Hanson Howard Galleries,** 505 Siskiyou Blvd. (tel. 503/488-2562), features the works of Oregon and West Coast artists.

7. SHOPPING

You can find some really unusual treasures here, ranging from antiques and calico fabrics to brass rubbings.

Brass rubbings, in case you haven't seen them, are done by placing paper over ornate old tomb markers and rubbing over the raised design with soft black or colored pencils, transferring the design to paper. You'll find one of the best collections of brass rubbings outside England at the **Tudor Guild Shop** at the Elizabethan Theatre in Ashland. Lots of other unusual gifts here too.

An enclave for historians and artists, southwestern Oregon is a good spot to search for antiques and craftwork. To see some attractive fiber craftwork, stop by the **Web-sters,** 10 Guanajuato Way, Ashland (tel. 503/482-9801), which features hand-spun yarns you can use for your own weaving or knitting plus finished garments, rugs, and wall hangings.

The **Ponycart Peddler,** 1960 W. Main St., in Medford (tel. 503/772-1872), is one of many antique dealers, and **Grandma's Cards & Gifts,** 322 E. Main St., Medford (tel. 503/773-3339), has unusual domestic and imported cards and gifts.

8. CRATER LAKE

Discovered in 1853 by a wandering prospector, this breathtakingly blue lake is one of the deepest in the world. High atop Mount Mazama, Crater Lake makes a fascinating day trip from the southwestern corner of Oregon. Ashland and environs are about 70 miles away.

On your way up the mountain, you may pass intrepid, helmet-clad bicyclers pedaling along the roads that are often steep enough for a very good workout. You'll see snow any month of the year as you ascend the mountain—and you'll often see youngsters out frolicking in it, parents having fun too, albeit a tad less thrilled by the icy white stuff.

When you are about 7,000 feet above sea level, you will see the lake, now about a thousand feet below you, glittering just like that sapphire jewel to which it so often is compared. If it hadn't been for a wandering prospector named John Wesley Hillman, you might not be up here. In 1853 as he prowled through the mountains in search of gold, he discovered the lake, aptly naming it Deep Blue Lake.

Why is it so blue? Light rays striking clear water are absorbed color by color, with red the first color to be absorbed, followed by orange, then yellow and green. Blue is the last color to be absorbed, so in this deep water, only the deepest blue color is reflected back to the surface.

Some more facts about this cold and silent lake hidden away in mile-high snowfields: At its deepest point Crater Lake is 1,932 feet deep, the deepest lake in the U.S., sixth deepest in the world, about one-third the depth of Siberia's Lake Baikal, the world's deepest lake. Emptied by evaporation about as fast as it's filled by water from rain and melting snow, the lake varies little in depth from year to year. It has frozen over only once since people have been recording such things, and that was in 1949.

At its greatest width the lake is six miles across. On a trip around the rim you will drive 35 miles. Its total area is 21.3 square miles. In the lake are rainbow trout, brown trout, and kokanee salmon. You can go after one, if you like, and you don't need a fishing license to do it. In summer Crater Lake warms up to a not-very-toasty 50° to 55°, 38° at the bottom.

So what is this lake doing way up here? Well, picture a huge volcanic mountain sleeping quietly in a range of many such mountains, its sides covered with pine in summer, snow in winter. That mountain you've just pictured is the one you're traveling on, quiescent Mount Mazama, a towering peak, once more than two miles high. One day 6,800 years ago the earth shuddered with earthquakes and Mazama blew its top—quite literally. Gas and steam exploded into the sky, red-hot pumice stone filled the valleys for miles in every direction, and the mountain's cone collapsed into itself.

Just as Mount St. Helens blew its top off, so did Mazama, leaving in its place a huge caldera, or bowl, 4,000 feet deep. Inside that bowl smaller eruptions continued to explode, one of them forming a 764-foot cone you now see sticking up in the lake. It's called Wizard Island. Invisible beneath the surface of the lake are many more such cones, witness to many smaller eruptions following the major explosion.

As the years passed, rainwater and melting snow filled the caldera. As you travel around the rim of Crater Lake, you are 900 feet above the water. The highest point along the rim is Hillman Peak, located 8,156 feet above sea level.

From the top of a hill known as the Watchman at an elevation of 8,025 feet, you can see 14,000-foot Mount Shasta more than 100 miles away. The mountain you see on the horizon above the lake is Mount Thielsen, 9,182 feet tall.

You will see snow in the park every month of the year—about 50 feet of it falls here annually—but in summer you don't have to worry about impassable roads. In late fall and winter, however, you'll need to ask before you go. Snow usually closes the Rim Road about October. Winter temperatures are 10° or 20° below zero, and summer temperatures rarely get above 85°.

From the Cleetwood parking area, 11 miles from the lodge and Rim Village, the Rim Road is one way on the west side of the lake, two way on the east side. Crater Lake National Park remains open all year, and there's cross-country skiing up here in winter.

Crater Lake is, by the way, the only national park in this state, but other park service areas in Oregon are the Oregon Caves National Monument (more on that below), John Day Fossil Beds National Monument near John Day, and Fort Clatsop National Historical Memorial near Astoria.

SEEING THE LAKE: To learn more about the lake and the creatures that live in the forests here, stop by the **Visitors Information Center in Rim Village,** at the entrance to the lodge. Rangers here conduct hourly tours in summer. You'll also find some interesting books of photographs of the lake, and you can see some of the animals that live in these mountain forests. Each evening there are lectures by park rangers and naturalists. Park hours are 8 a.m. to 7 p.m.

If you want to go down to the surface of the lake, be prepared for a hike. You must go to **Cleetwood Cove,** directly across the lake from Crater Lake Lodge. In the parking lot there are steps descending a winding 1.1 miles to the surface, where you will find tour boats. These steps are the only access to the lake. It takes about an hour to drive to the cove and walk the trail.

From park opening day sometime in May, depending on the weather, until June 30, **lake cruises** are at 9 and 11 a.m., and 1 and 3 p.m. From July to the beginning of September the boat leaves every hour from 9 a.m. to 3 p.m. and stops at Wizard Island. After that date, cruises return to that spring schedule. Fare is $10 for adults, $5.50 for children under 12. On the trip a naturalist points out interesting geological formations, lava flows, underwater tumeroles, and cones created by volcanic eruptions.

In winter you drive up here through massive snowbanks, a world covered in glittering white. Fifty miles of marked **cross-country ski trails** traverse the park, and rangers lead snowshoe walks at 1 p.m. daily from the Rim Center Building at Rim Village. Skis can be rented here every day for $8 a day. The cafeteria's open daily from 10 a.m. to 4 p.m. For help in the park, summer or winter, stop in or call ranger headquarters at 503/594-2211, or write the **Visitor Information Center** at P.O. Box 7, Crater Lake National Park, Crater Lake, OR 97604.

WHERE TO STAY: If you want to stay here overnight, you will find, at the top of your drive, **Crater Lake Lodge,** Crater Lake National Park, Crater Lake, OR 97604 (tel. 503/594-2511), which despite its glamorous setting is badly in need of a mentor. Built in 1911 and opened in 1914, with an addition in 1924, Crater Lake Lodge is a large and aging chalet that houses a massive lobby where the view through picture windows is breathtaking.

As you stand in the massive central hall here it's not difficult to imagine early adventurers—many of them women wearing long dresses and carrying parasols —stepping daintily into boats for an afternoon on the lake. In the lodge you can see some photographs of those early parasol-ed travelers.

These days most of the lodge's earlier elegance is gone, and rooms are sparsely furnished, halls narrow and lined with visible waterpipes. Cottages across the road have little more to offer and, sadly, there is talk of closing this lovely antique.

If you want to stay up here, the least expensive quarters are twin-bedded lodge rooms without bath for $40; full-bath rooms are $50 to $60.

New cabins equipped with electric heat, lights, and blankets are $60 to $70. Cottages are open from about May to October.

The lodge, open from early June to early September, serves meals in its rustic dining room. While you're at the lodge, stop at the gift shop to buy a "mountain egg," an egg-shaped hunk of lava rock which, if you're lucky, may contain a beautiful piece of agate.

9. OREGON CAVES

Oregon's vast underground caves make a fascinating day trip from southwestern Oregon. You'll find them about 90 miles from Ashland and Jacksonville.

There is quite a story behind the creation of the National Park Service's Oregon pride, the **Oregon Caves National Monument.** Eons ago—actually 200 million years—deep in the sea, compressed layers of lava, mud, and lime solidified into a rock that was to become known as limestone. Pressure and heat worked on that limestone rock, eventually destroying all traces of seashells in it and forcing it to recrystallize, creating a much harder rock that would come to be known as marble.

More millions of years passed during which erosion of the land stripped away the rock layers covering these caves, and water seeped down into the marble, dissolving it along the cracks and creating huge spaces that look like corridors and rooms.

Next, water trickled into the caves, by now drained of water, and deposited coatings of calcite on the roofs of the caves. Those on top became known as stalactites, while those rising from the floor were called stalagmites. Some drips fused together creating columns. Some seeped over walls and floors creating formations that look like stone waterfalls or rippling sheets of stone. Whatever they formed, these geologic creations are today an eerie series of underground caverns of spectacular beauty and awesome mystery.

Often known as the Marble Halls of Oregon, the caves are a fascinating conglomeration of rooms and corridors with such interesting names as the Ghost Room; Paradise Lost, where draped stone formations look like parachutes; the Grand Column, where stalactites and stalagmites have united into a huge column; Neptune's Grotto, which looks a little like an underwater scene; Niagara Falls, a huge cascade of calcite "flows" (marked with early explorers' graffiti); Banana Grove, where formations look like bunches of bananas; the Passageway of the Whale, which makes you feel like Jonah walking through one as you look up at a whale's "spine" above you; the River Styx, where a flowing stream evokes that mythological river between Life and Death; the Imagination Room, where you can see most any creature your imagination can cook up; and the Petrified Garden, where you'll see a variety of formations.

If you're planning a visit to the caves, wear good walking shoes with nonslip soles, take a jacket, and don't go if you have physical disabilities that preclude your walking up 550 stairs and about half a mile. Children under 6 are not permitted in the cave, but a babysitting service can take care of the little ones at the entrance.

Tours are scheduled from 9 a.m. to 5 p.m. in May, from 8 a.m. to 7 p.m. June to mid-September, and from 9 a.m. to 5 p.m. mid-September to May. In those winter months tours leave at 10:30 a.m. and 12:30, 2, and 3:30 p.m., or whenever groups of 16 or more are formed. Admission is $4.75 for adults and $2.50 for children under 12.

To get to Oregon Caves, take U.S. 199 south from Grant's Pass to Cave Junction, turning east there on Ore. 46. The park is about 50 miles south of Grant's Pass and about 20 miles east of Cave Junction. You'll get more thrills on the last 13 miles of Ore. 46, which is narrow and winding. Forget it if you're towing a trailer and don't plan on turning back—there are next to no turning spaces.

That winding road does have this saving grace: it runs through a dense forest where Douglas firs are often six feet thick. If you're passing through in early morning or evening, you're likely to see black-tail deer, squirrels, chipmunks, and plenty of birds.

If you are looking for a campground in the area, head for **Grayback Campground,** eight miles down Ore. 46, where trailers are permitted, or **Cave Creek Campground,** four miles from the park on Ore. 46, where no trailers are permitted. Neither has showers or utility connections. Fees are $2.

For information contact Oregon Caves Co., Oregon Caves, OR 97523 (tel. 503/592-3400).

10. REDWOOD NATIONAL PARK

Only one road goes from the southern Oregon coast to southwest Oregon, U.S. 199, and to get to it you must drive into California and across the northern tip of the Redwood National Park.

What a trip! As you drive through this park the sunlight is dimmed to a green glow by massive 600-year-old trees that line your route. These coastal redwoods, officially known as *Sequoia sempervirens,* are taller than any other trees in the world. One discovered in 1963 on the banks of Redwood Creek is 367.8 feet high, the tallest known tree.

The volume of living material in redwood forests is greater than any other forest, so the scientists say, even greater than their cousins, the giant sequoias, which grow larger in girth but not as tall.

If we could figure out how they manage to age so gracefully, there would be many a happy matron around: redwoods usually live 500 to 700 years, but can survive to be 2,000 years old. No insects can damage them and nothing can kill them except man or fire. Wind is also a threat—despite their enormous girth, these tall trees have a shallow root system and can be toppled by high winds.

What helps them grow so tall and so huge—8 to 20 feet in diameter!—is what makes life a little weird for folks around here: fog.

Mists caused by warm air over cold Pacific waters stir up those fogs nearly every summer morning, burn off at noon, and often return at sunset. While it may be a hazard for boaters and drivers, it's a delight to the redwoods. That fog adds constant moisture to the soil and decreases the rate at which water evaporates from the tree. Add to that a rainfall of 25 to 125 inches a year, and you have the makings of a very big and happy tree.

It looked for a while there as if these redwoods would end up as fence posts. Once so dense it took an early explorer ten days to cover just a few miles, the forests in the mid-1800s became the target of logging interests that had already depleted eastern forests. When it looked as if these forests might fall to the ax and the nation's insatiable thirst for wood, environmentalists arose.

You may think the preservation forces you hear so much about these days began only yesterday, but the campaign to save *these* trees from destruction began as long ago as 1902. Six years later, President Theodore Roosevelt set up the Muir Woods National Monument, and in 1918 the Save-the-Redwoods League was organized. During the years of its existence the league has set up more than 280 memorial groves, and in 1968 the Redwood National Park became an official part of the national park system that now covers 106,000 acres.

In the forests live 300 species of birds, huge Roosevelt elk, mountain lions, blacktail deer, bald eagles, peregrine falcons, and the Aleutian Canada goose. Along the rivers and streams, river otter, mink, and beaver splash.

You'll drive through these awesome trees on your way to southwestern Oregon, but you can take a detour onto U.S. 101 and follow it south to Crescent City, where you will find **Redwood National Park Headquarters,** 1111 2nd St., Crescent City, CA 95521 (tel. 707/464-6101). If you're planning on camping in the park, they can help you with reservations and fill you in with information on the park's five major regions stretching from north to south and known as Hiouchi/Jededia Smith, Del Norte Coast, Klamath, Prairie Creek, and Orick Areas.

You'll find a ranger station on U.S. 199 ten miles east of Crescent City open daily from 8 a.m. to 7 p.m.

CHAPTER XIII

OREGON'S COAST

□ □ □

Whether you're in search of bikini-clad beauties or scenic beauties, dunes or drama, Oregon's coast cooperates.

Nature has divided the fascinatingly varied geography of this coastline up quite conveniently. On the south coast you get an eyeful of monolithic rocks that suddenly disappear, to be replaced by towering sand dunes. The dunes, in turn, give way to rocky headlands that relinquish their hold on your wondering eyes to enormous stretches of wide, sandy beaches that line the north coast.

In this scenically dramatic region you'll find 31 chambers of commerce teamed up as the Oregon Coast Association, whose staff will be happy to provide you with an indispensable, magazine-size publication called *Pacific Coast Travel Guides & Maps,* outlining points of interest, hotels, motels, and restaurants operating in the region. Most useful of all in the booklet are the maps that will help you find your way up and around this popular coastline.

To travel here, head for U.S. 101, and point your car north following this good and scenic highway all the way from the California border to historic Astoria at the Washington border. The biggest lure along the coastline are the sandy beaches of the north coast at Seaview, Cannon Beach, Lincoln City, and a little farther south at Newport. Here you'll join thousands of pail-toting toddlers, fishing and boating fans, swimmers, windsurfers, hikers, bikers, and bikinis, all seeking a place in the sun.

Along the central coast near Florence, rocky headlands begin, offering you smashing views across the waters with dunes stretching out behind you. Between Florence and Coos Bay, the world's busiest lumber harbor, the scenery changes dramatically. Rocks disappear to become high sand dunes washed by gentler waters lapping on beaches that snuggle into a rolling landscape.

Farther south at Gold Beach, the landscape changes once again to giant monolithic rocks rising from the ocean along miles of highway within sight of the Pacific. Waves crash over these landmark stones, spraying rainbows in the air. Traveling north from the California border, you'll pass giant rocks plunked down in the sea like dragon's teeth. To some, this is the most dramatic section of Oregon's chameleon coast. Huge monolithic rocks are scattered in the sea, as if cast there by Atlas hurling part of the globe around for exercise. These massive boulders open welcoming arms to the Pacific, which rolls into tiny caves and inlets frothing and roaring, sending fountains of spray high into the air.

In many places the giant rocks stand like sentinels between rolling waters and sandy shore, creating shallow lagoons where the sea undulates softly onto the sands. Deposited here millions of years ago by the volcanic action that created much of this part of the world, these boulders take many shapes, sometimes rising tall and narrow, sometimes hunkering down to form jagged peaks, loafs, and granite haystacks. Immobile and implacable as palace guards, these craggy, shadowy surfaces over which light plays like a butterfly are hauntingly beautiful and soberingly ancient.

It's quite a place, this coast, not a spot for the frivolous in search of ruffled frippery, but a place for thinkers and dreamers, a place for those in search of nature's majesty and its meaning to all of us—perhaps a place for you.

1. ORIENTATION

GETTING THERE AND GETTING AROUND: There are several ways to reach Oregon's coast, the most popular of which is **U.S. 101,** a highway that runs the entire length of the coast from the California border to Astoria at the Washington border.

Major east-west roadways to the beaches are, from south to north: **U.S. 199,** which dips down from Grant's Pass to northern California, where it joins U.S. 101; **Ore. 99/38,** which departs from I-5 at a point 12 miles south of Cottage Grove and ends at the coastal town of Reedsport; **Ore. 126,** which heads west to the beaches from I-5 at Eugene to reach Florence in the central section of the coast; **U.S. 20,** which leaves I-5 at Albany to take you to Newport; **Ore. 18,** which goes from I-5 at Salem to just north of Lincoln City; and **U.S. 26,** which goes west from Portland to beaches between Cannon Beach and Seaside or branches off at Ore. 6 to take you to Tillamook.

As for getting around, well, it's not easy without a car. Transportation from town to town is not simple here, so unless you're prepared to settle in one place or spend too much of your time organizing your transportation, we'd suggest renting a car. It is really the only practical way to explore this coast.

In keeping with our plans for your Grand Tour of the Northwest, we'll give you a look at the coast moving from south to north.

VISITOR INFORMATION: Very helpful folks at the **Oregon Coast Association,** P.O. Box 670, Oregon Coast, OR 97365 (tel. 503/265-2611, or toll free

800/98-COAST in Washington, Idaho, Utah, Nevada, and California), will be happy to help you find your way around their dramatic coastline. For $3 to cover postage and handling, they'll send you their "Coast Travel Pack" which includes a guide, events calendar, brochures, maps, and tidebooks.

2. GOLD BEACH

These days Gold Beach is famous throughout the Northwest for the dozens of hydro-jet boats that offer swift trips up the Rogue River into the wilderness that surrounds these roiling waters.

People have been sailing up this river since 1895, when Elijah Price and his son, Nobel, became the area's river mailmen, ferrying letters to isolated villages on three-day journeys up the river. Mail expanded to include freight, and soon everyone wanted to ride along.

So villagers did what comes naturally in the U.S. They capitalized. These days dozens of fleet hydro-jets take you on trips through deep canyons and spectacular scenery and across shallows called riffles on 64- or 104-mile round trips.

GETTING THERE: U.S. 101 crosses the Rogue River north of town then cuts through the middle of the action. Main east-west streets in town are numbered, beginning at 1st Street and rising in number southward. Streets on the north end of town have names, as do north-south streets.

VISITOR INFORMATION: You'll find the **Gold Beach Chamber of Commerce** at City Hall, 510 S. Ellenburg, Gold Beach, OR 97444 (tel. 503/247-7526, or toll free 800/452-2334).

WHERE TO STAY: Tops among local hostelries is **Tu Tu Tun Lodge,** 96550 North Bank Rogue, Gold Beach, OR 97444 (tel. 503/247-6664). Dan'l Boone might have had trouble finding this place, tucked alongside the waters of the famous Rogue River. Seven miles inland, it occupies such a tranquil spot beside the Rogue River that we even saw a deer happily grazing in an apple orchard near the lodge. Operated by Dirk and Laurie Van Zante, the lodge is Oregon coastal living at its coziest and best. Under a high beamed ceiling, guests gather around a massive stone fireplace. On either side of it, tall floor-to-ceiling windows offer views across the heated outdoor pool, and glass doors open onto a cedar deck that runs alongside the river. In summer guests often meet here for cocktails before moving on to dinner in the cozy gold and light-wood dining room. Dinner may be fresh salmon, steaks, or prime rib, but whatever it is, it will include homemade starters and breads baked right in these kitchens.

Travelers come here to fish on this river, renowned for its steelhead and Chinook salmon. Some come to hike the hills that shelter this resort. Others climb aboard the jet boats that race up the river after a stop here, while still others do nothing more ambitious than paddle about the swimming pool or putter around the four holes of golf here. You'll find your room in a two-story building connected to the lodge by a covered walkway. All rooms have a view over the river and glass doors that open onto a private balcony. Extra-long double beds are supplemented by attractive contemporary furnishings. Several suites including bedroom, living room, dining room, and kitchen are available. Open only May through October, the lodge charges $93 double for its spacious rooms, $120 to $130 for suites. Pets are welcome here too, for a $3 extra charge. Tu Tu Tun opens its dining room for all three meals and charges $6 to $8 for breakfast or lunch, and $18.25 for dinner.

To get there, take the marked turnoff from U.S. 101 north of Gold Beach. If you come to a tall tree stump with a roof, you've come too far. When you come to

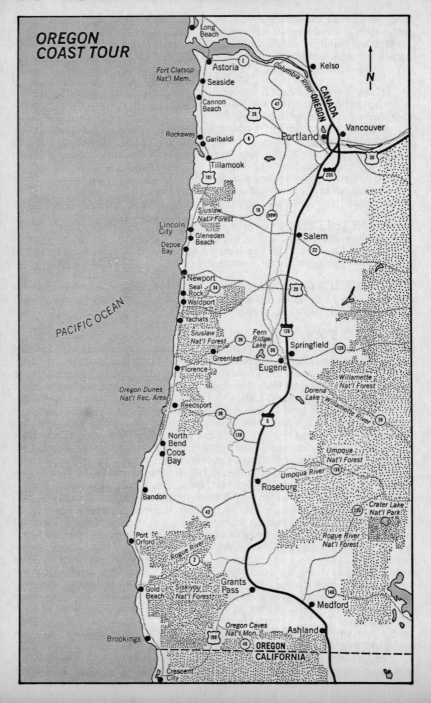

OREGON COAST TOUR

a fork in the road, take the fork that goes downhill. You will follow the river for seven miles.

Ireland's Rustic Lodges, 1120 Ellensburg (P.O. Box 774), Gold Beach, OR 97444 (tel. 503/247-7718), are tucked away under pines at the ocean. Someone with a very green thumb has been at work here creating a wonderland of blooming things bordering green lawns and highlighted against the dark wood of the cottages. Inside these log cottages you'll find a stone fireplace and rustic but comfortable furnishings. Some newer units have a fireplace and spectacular ocean view. Rates are $39 to $51 double.

Jot's Rod-n-Reel, 94360 Waterfront Loop (P.O. Box J), Gold Beach, OR 97444 (tel. 503/247-6676), a two-story, wood-sided motel stretches out alongside the Rogue River. Accommodations range in size from rooms to two-bedroom suites and have queen-size beds, color televisions, telephones, and fully equipped kitchens. Sliding glass doors and long balcony decks overlook the water, and the resort's docks are a lovely spot to watch activities on the river. For amusement the motel offers a heated swimming pool with swooping slide and those jet-boat rides up the river. You can also rent boats and canoes here and take your own upriver journey. For dining Jot's has a river-view restaurant and lounge serving all three meals, at prices in the $8 to $12 range for dinners of fresh seafood or steaks. Rates are $75 to $125 double from July to October, dropping $10 to $20 in spring and fall months.

If you're considering a camping trip to Gold Beach, you can hook up at **Kimball Creek Bend RV Resort,** 97136 N. Bank Road, Gold Beach, OR 97444 (tel. 503/247-7580). Kimball Creek is located on the Rogue River at a spot trimmed with plenty of berry vines. Deer often cross the lawn of a rustic new timber lodge on the grounds. Less hardy souls can watch them gambol from the comforts of one of the lodge's three comfortable motel rooms. That handsome new lodge also serves as store, recreation hall, and tackle shop for the many fishing expeditions that begin here. There's also space for volleyball, horseshoes, badminton, and tether ball. Sites have patios, and many are under shady trees, but there's a camping area for rough-it fans. Recreation center, laundry, showers, and reading room here too. To find the campground, which charges $9 to $10, turn off U.S. 101 at the north end of the Gold Beach bridge and head upriver, following the Rogue River Road for 3½ miles. Turn right onto North Bank Road and follow the river for 4½ more miles, turning right on the access road.

If you're driving up the coast from California, the first small coastal town you'll find along the way is Brookings, about 30 miles south of Gold Beach. There, Sheldon and Gro Lent operate an attractive bed-and-breakfast inn called the **Ward House** 516 Redwood St. (P.O. Box 86), Brookings, OR 97415 (tel. 503/469-5557). Built in 1917, the inn was for many years the home of the president of a local lumber mill. You'll find the ocean a few blocks away and tiny downtown Brookings right outside your door. All the typical Oregon pursuits are available in the region, from fishing to boating, beachcombing, hiking, swimming, and storm watching. Handsomely decorated bedrooms share a bath but have a queen-size bed, sitting area, and television or radio. Guests gather in the living room or out on the sundeck where a hot tub bubbles and a sauna awaits. Rates in peak summer season are $40 to $55 for two, including a full breakfast that might include eggs Benedict, Norwegian waffles, or homemade jams. Evenings the Ward House serves refreshments in the living room, and dinner is available upon request.

WHERE TO DINE: Watery views are a specialty in Gold Beach.

Tu Tu Tun Lodge (see "Where to Stay") is open to the public for dinner, but give them a call in advance at 503/247-6664.

Nor'wester Seafood Restaurant, Port of Gold Beach, a block west of U.S. 101 (tel. 503/247-2333), occupies a pretty waterfront spot overlooking the harbor. Naturally enough, seafood offerings fill most of the spaces on the menu, but you'll also find a fair number of steaks for the beef fan in your crowd. Among the more involved preparations are coquilles St-Jacques, crêpes Madagascar (filled with lightly curried crabmeat and topped with mornay sauce), and snapper Florentine (stuffed with creamed spinach, baked, and topped with a cream sauce and shrimp). For a dinner that begins with clam chowder and includes a green or spinach salad, fresh fruit, potatoes or rice, and hot French bread, you pay $10 to $15 for most selections. The Nor'wester is open for dinner from 5 to 10 p.m. daily year round. The lounge closes after dinner.

Views are pretty inside and out at the **Captain's Table,** 1225 U.S. 101 (tel. 503/247-6308). Outside are the glories of rolling waves, inside, antiques in a cozy dining room. Fresh seafood is, of course, on the menu, dominates it, in fact, with plenty of abalone, sole, snapper, cod, clams, and scallops available. The steaks are good too: they bring them in from Kansas City. Prices are in the $10 to $15 range for most selections, and hours are 11 a.m. to 2 p.m. for lunch, 5 to 11 p.m. for dinner.

The **Chowderhead Restaurant,** 910 S. Ellensburg St. (tel. 503/247-7174), offers casual dining on a long list of seafood, chowder of course, and a few beef offerings. Hours at the Chowderhead are 11 a.m. to 9 p.m. daily, with a Sunday brunch from 10 a.m. to 2 p.m. Prices range from $3 to $6 for lunch, $9 to $12 for most dinners, and $3 to $9 for brunch. Closed the last two weeks in December.

Rod 'N Reel, U.S. 101 on the west side of the bridge in Wedderburn (tel. 503/247-6823), is quite a pretty bridge-side dining room, specializing in Italian flavors at dinner but serving all three meals. Prices are in the $10 to $15 range, and hours are 6 a.m. to 2:30 p.m. and 5 to 11 p.m. daily.

NIGHTLIFE: Jot's Rod-n-Reel (see "Where to Stay") has dancing and entertainment.

WHAT TO SEE AND DO: Doing—specifically jet boat doing—is the draw here. Best known of the jet-boat operators on the river is **Rogue River Mail Boat Trips,** which still actually delivers the mail upriver. Boats leave from the company's docks a quarter of a mile upstream on the north side of the river, east of U.S. 101 on Rogue River Road (tel. 503/247-7033). From May to November, Mail morning trips depart at 8:30 a.m., returning at 2:30 p.m. From July 1 to Labor Day additional afternoon trips begin at 2:30 p.m. and return at 8 p.m. Either trip includes two hours for lunch or dinner at any of three restaurants in Agness, your choice. Fares, which do not include meals, are $25 for adults, $10 for children 4 to 12; under 4, free. Mail Boat Trips also operates a "Wild Water" trip that takes you on a 104-mile round trip through white-water rapids, quiet canyons, and the Devil's Staircase Rapid. Trips depart from mid-May to mid-October at 8 a.m., returning at 3:30 p.m. with a two-hour lunch at remote Wilderness Lodge. Fares are $50 for adults, $20 for children 4 to 12. Mail Boat Trips can also arrange two-day trips that include a stay at Wilderness Lodge and have dinner cruises.

Court's Rogue River White Water Trips, at the north end of Rogue River Bridge, on U.S. 101 (tel. 503/247-6504), charges the same fare for similar trips up the river. Court's 104-mile trip includes a rest stop at Agness, then goes on to Paradise Bar Lodge for lunch or overnight. All trips operate April through October.

Jerry's Rogue River Jet Boat Trips run daily May to November from the docks at Port of Gold Beach Small Boat Basin (tel. 503/247-7601). You'll find the docks just south of the Rogue River bridge at U.S. 101. Trips operate from May to November, with a 64-mile round trip at 8:30 a.m. and an additional run at 2:30 p.m. from July 1 to Labor Day. Fares are $22.50 for adults, $10 for children 4 to 12. Jerry's also stops at Paradise Bar Lodge on the long trips that depart at 8 a.m., return at 4 p.m., and are $45 for adults, $20 for children.

3. PORT ORFORD

Port Orford lays claim to the title of oldest town site on the coast. You can be through this little town almost before you notice it, but you'll certainly notice the rugged scenery in which it thrives.

These cliffs were first sighted by Capt. George Vancouver, who sailed past in 1792 and named them after Britain's Earl of Orford. When gold fever struck the coastline in the 1850s, Capt. William Tichenor dropped anchor here and sent two search parties out, one north and one south, to cut a road to the gold fields. Legend has it that one group didn't follow the captain's outlined route across a nearby mountain and spent days wandering about in some pretty inhospitable country. When they finally got back, they dubbed that mountain Tichenor's Humbug and the name stuck. Today it's still called Humbug Mountain.

Five years later when the gold rush petered out and the wars with Rogue River Indians ended, just about everyone left town. Three families remained, and in 1868 even they had their problems—most of the town burned down in a fire that also destroyed many of the region's cedar. Little by little the lumber industry returned, however, and today the port remains a cedar-logging center.

GETTING THERE: U.S. 101 cuts right through the middle of Port Orford, becoming Oregon Street as it goes through town. Oregon Street also heads off to the west, where it circles around past a scenic overlook and into 5th Street, which has access to the small, rustic port. From the vista point you can get an idea how early logging was done here: logs were rolled to the edge of the cliff and lowered over it to ships below.

VISITOR INFORMATION: The **Port Orford Chamber of Commerce**, U.S. 101 South (P.O. Box 637), Port Orford, OR 97465 (tel. 503/332-3923), will be happy to tell you about their bailiwick.

WHERE TO STAY: Your options are limited, but no less interesting. **The Sea Crest Motel,** 1 U.S. 101 South (P.O. Box C), Port Orford, OR 97465 (tel. 503/332-3040), one of several very small motels in town, offers 18 units about half a mile south of town. The units are medium-sized, clean, and set in attractively landscaped grounds. You'll have a pretty view of ocean and bay at Sea Crest, where you pay $37 to $52 from June to October, about $10 to $15 less in other months.

WHERE TO DINE: The **Wheelhouse Restaurant,** U.S. 101 at Battle Rock State Park (tel. 503/332-1605), will serve you juicy hamburgers and seafood chowder as you watch the sea roll across the rocks. Nice view here and just a couple of bucks for meals. Big breakfasts here, too. It's open daily from 7 a.m. to 8 p.m.

Next door, the **Truculent Oyster/Peg Leg Saloon,** 236 6th St. (tel. 503/332-9461), is a favored local watering spot and quite a good restaurant too. They do everything themselves here, from cutting their own meats to sautéing seafood fresh from the seas just inches away. You'll actually find a few oysters at the Truculent one, but the main fare is other seafood and steaks, plus some Mexican specialties. Prices for dinner are in the $10 range, about half that for lunch. This bivalve pries open at 11 a.m., shuts at 11 p.m. daily.

WHAT TO SEE AND DO: Seeing is the important part of a visit here.

Cape Blanco, about 11 miles north of town and six miles west of U.S. 101, is a cliff made of seashell fossils that look white from a distance—thus the Blanco name given it by Spanish explorers. A lighthouse here has been working since 1870, and down below on some rocks you can see a large and happy collection of sea lions.

In a park at the cape you will also find the **Hughes House,** built in 1898. In the house are some interesting photographs depicting the early days in Port Orford and some antique furnishings. It's open Wednesday through Sunday from 9 a.m. to 5 p.m. June to September only.

South of town about 12 miles, dinosaurs come back to life, re-created by **Prehistoric Gardens,** U.S. 101 (tel. 503/332-4463), which has set *Tyrannosaurus rex* in a rain-forest setting. The gardens are open from 8 a.m. to dusk daily and admission is $3.50 for adults, $3 for children 12 to 18, $2 for visitors 5 to 11.

4. BANDON

If you never met a cranberry you didn't like, you'll love Bandon. Cranberry bogs just about surround this town and provide a tangy side dish to most anything most any time of year. Plenty of them end up on your Thanksgiving table too, raised here and exported everywhere.

On the beaches here rockhounds assume the posture, bent double in this case, and gaze intently at what looks to the rest of us like the gravel in our driveways. What they see, however, are valuable nuggets of agates, jasper, and their semiprecious relatives. Old buildings damaged in a fire here have been restored and renovated and dubbed Oldtown Harbor. Art galleries, weavers, potters, cafés, even a candy shop and wine-tasting store occupy these spaces now.

One of the coastline's quieter hideaways, this small town often seems to have been discovered only by artists and other creative types who display considerable enthusiasm for their village. There's also a small but active harbor and odd rock formations along the wide white beach.

GETTING THERE: U.S. 101 goes straight through town, where it is joined by Ore. 42S coming in from Roseburg. If you turn west at that junction, you will find Oldtown Bandon and Jetty Road. U.S. 101 is crossed by 9th and 12th Streets, among others, both of which lead to Beach Loop Road.

WHERE TO STAY: From an inn with an Indian legend to some small scenic places, Bandon has several interesting stopping spots.

The **Inn at Face Rock,** 3225 Beach Rd., Bandon, OR 97441 (tel. 503/347-9441), fits right into the rugged coastal feeling of this part of Oregon. Built just four years ago, it's a condominium resort whose white buildings rise up off the ground on brick pillars. Before you stretch miles of ocean and around you are pines rustling in the breezes. A nine-hole golf course awaits duffers in search of tee with a view. In a bright and airy restaurant home-baked breads, fresh seafoods, juicy steaks, and good wines await. A stone's toss across the street is the beach. This is a condominium, so accommodations are spacious suites, outfitted in nubby fabrics, light-wood furnishings, fireplace inset into a wall, and televisions tucked away in cabinetry. Each is large enough for four, with queen-size beds, cable color television, two baths, telephone, and full kitchen. All have ocean views through glass doors and from wood-railed balconies.

That name Face Rock is derived from an Indian legend that tells of the willful daughter of Chief Siskiyou, who was cautioned against wading too far into the water but didn't listen. Instead she went right out there in the surf, accompanied by her dog and two kittens that watched from the beach. Meanwhile the evil spirit Seatka lurked in the waves, willing her to look at him so he could capture her with his power. Willful she may have been but evil-spirit-tempted she was not. Instead of looking at the evil prince, she gazed steadfastly at the moon and is still doing so today. You can see the whole group—princess, evil-spirit Seatka, the pusses, and girl's best friend still standing there in the water, stonily determined to best each other. Rates at the inn are $85 to $95 for two-room suites on weekends, $10 less on weekdays; in winter rates are lower.

Windermere Motel, 3250 Beach Loop Rd., Bandon, OR 97411 (tel. 503/ 347-3710), is a moderately priced group of cottages set high on a cliff overlooking the beach. They're sometimes a little too rustic for some tastes, but they do sport interesting loft bedrooms with living room on the ground floor. Small cottages are indeed small, but a cozy atmosphere and really stupendous views help make up for minuses. You'll have to be the judge on how well they make up for minuses. Rates are $52 to $68, dropping in winter to $37 to $53.

If you're here on a really strict budget, try the **Sea Star Hostel,** 375 2nd St., Bandon, OR 97411 (tel. 503/347-9533), a restored lodge on the riverfront in the historic district of town. Sea Star, a hostel that has acquired a superior rating from the hostel association, boasts an open-beam ceiling with skylights, a complete kitchen, small carpeted dorms, and rooms for couples. Outside a courtyard is surrounded on three sides by decking. Pretty nifty at prices of $6 to $9. Sea Star also operates a guesthouse where rates are $25 to $49 double for private rooms with baths or small apartments with living rooms and kitchens. A new addition to the facility is the Sea Star International Coffeehouse (see "Where to Dine"). You won't find a lot of razzle-dazzle activity in this region, but you will find some spectacular scenery that easily makes up for the loss.

WHERE TO DINE: Rustic, atmospheric dining spots are Bandon's specialties. **Bandon Boatworks,** South Jetty Road (tel. 503/347-2111), is a bit of a challenge to find, but once you get there you have a great view and food to match. Prawns baked in a mustard sauce or sautéed with mushrooms, shallots, brandy, and cream top the list of dinner entrees, followed by a long list of fresh local seafood, a couple of veal and steak dishes, and chicken sautéed with ham, mushrooms, and artichokes, and topped with a brandy cream sauce. For openers—or as a complete meal—the choices are Mexican, ranging from guacamole to chile verde, burritos, and flautas. At lunch the menu specializes in any-seafood-and-chips. Prices for dinner, including the salad bar and clam chowder, are in the $10 to $15 range. Boatworks is open Tuesday through Saturday from 11:30 a.m. to 2:30 p.m. for lunch, 5 to 9 p.m. for dinner, and Sunday for brunch from 10 a.m. to 8 p.m.; closed Monday.

You never know what you'll find at **Andrea's Oldtown Café,** 160 Baltimore St., between 1st and 2nd Streets (tel. 503/347-3022), but you always know it will be good. Each night the cuisine of a different region of the world is highlighted and one night's offerings might feature Cordon Bleu touches or Thai tastes. Less exotic choices are always on the menu too, so if you're not a fan of any foreign flavors, you can always order lamb raised right here, salmon encased in pastry, roast beef with unusual touches, or oysters spiked with herbs. You can also be sure you'll have wonderful breads on your table: Andrea and her husband run an adjoining bakery. What was once the restaurant, before it moved and expanded, is now a deli, where you can pack up a beach picnic of considerable style. Pastas are wonderful at Andrea's, and breakfast features a nifty list of crêpes and omelets guaranteed to stuff. Prices are in the $10 to $15 range for dinner, and hours are 10 a.m. to 9 p.m. daily, 10 a.m. to 2:30 p.m. for Sunday brunch, and 5:30 to 9 p.m. for dinner. No credit cards here.

Sea Star International Coffeehouse, 375 2nd St. (tel. 503/347-9632), whips up a tempting array of specialty coffees, plus imported and herbal teas, and has a light menu of sandwiches, salads, baked potatoes, soups, snacks, and desserts for prices that don't top $3. This budgetwise spot is in the Sea Star Hostel (see "Where to Stay").

WHAT TO SEE AND DO: A weird but wonderful collection of wild animals that are real pussycats awaits you at the **West Coast Game Park Safari,** on U.S. 101 about seven miles south of Bandon (tel. 503/347-3106). All the animals you will meet here, from camel to buffalo to bear and leopard, have been raised by hand so they're pleased to get a pat. You can walk and talk with hand-raised wild creatures ranging from snow leopards to tigers, lions, chimps, and bears. Many animals, more than 70 species, roam free in the park and will follow you around in search of a little attention. Price of a visit to this animal kingdom is $4.75 for adults, $3.50 for children 7 to 13. Hours are 9 a.m. to dusk daily from March to November, but vary in other months.

At the spot where the waters of the Coquille River meet the sea, there have been some terrifying boating experiences leading to the locals' name for the place: navigator's nightmare. Leading also to the Coquille River Lighthouse, a handsome and oft-photographed sentinel. You'll find it at the south end of the spit at **Bullard's Beach State Park,** one mile north of town on U.S. 101. Admission to the park is free.

Occult fanciers and other holistically inclined types may find the **Continuum Center,** 175 2nd St. (tel. 503/347-4111), interesting. All kinds of books on the occult and its offshoots are here, as well as exhibits of holograms, Kirlian machines, out-of-body research, and the like. Hours are 9 a.m. to 5 p.m. daily except Sunday.

Philatelists have one chance here (and two farther up the coast in Florence and Yachats) to put their stamp on the Oregon coast. Here the stamp-seekers' haven is the **Pacific Stamp Gallery,** housed in an interesting old building that looks a little like a church. It's across from the cheese factory at 680 U.S. 101 (tel. 503/347-3087), and is open from 11 a.m. to 7 p.m. Tuesday through Friday or by appointment. In Florence, **Brower's Stamp Shop** is at 493 U.S. 101 (tel. 503/997-9202), and in Yachats, **Seashore Stamps** is at 430 N. U.S. 101 (tel. 503/547-3998).

Tangy cheddar and jack cheese are made right here in town at a **cheese shop** equipped with a big window, through which you can watch the cheese-making process in action. You'll find onion, garlic, jalapeño, and smoked cheeses here too. Hours are 8 a.m. to 5 p.m. daily in summer; closed Sunday September through May. Free.

SPECIAL EVENTS: Each year the city sponsors its **Fall Cranberry Festival** in September, when the cranberry is picked, praised, cooked, and consumed.

In spring the **Phoenix Festival** celebrates the city's recovery from two disastrous fires.

WHERE TO SHOP: River's End Gallery, north of town at the junction of U.S. 101 and Ore. 42S (tel. 503/347-4451), offers crafts and artwork by local creators. Hours are 9 a.m. to 5 p.m. from June to October, 10 a.m. to 4 p.m. in other months.

Myrtlewood factories abound in the area, offering everything from clocks to goblets in the caramel-colored wood.

REEDSPORT/WINCHESTER BAY: There are many small towns along the Oregon coast so, sad to say, we can't mention each one of them. However, boating enthusiasts should take a look at the Winchester Bay/Reedsport area, which has long been a lure to small-boat captains. **Salmon Harbor Moorage** in Winchester Bay (tel. 503/271-3495) harbors more than 900 slips for small boats and has 900 campsites for self-contained rigs only. Salmon Harbor is a department of Douglas County and the Port of Umpqua, to which you can write for information at P.O. Box 7, Winchester Bay, OR 97467.

Dune country to the core, this handsome stretch of beach also has some other wonderful scenery. To see some of it, contact the **Lower Umpqua Chamber of Commerce,** P.O. Box 11, Reedsport, OR 97467 (tel. 503/271-3495), for a map that will help you traverse a scenic loop through forests, lakes, and recreation areas.

Reedsport also is home to the **Oregon Dunes National Recreation Area** headquarters, 855 Highway Ave. (tel. 503/271-3611). Dune-buggy rides are the big attraction here, but there is much more to do, ranging from hiking to backpacking, swimming or fishing in lakes, birdwatching, and a campground with horse corrals.

5. COOS BAY

One look at Coos Bay's miles of sheltered waterfront and you won't have any trouble figuring out what has made this the largest city on the Oregon coast.

That forest of tall pines you see at the outskirts will give you another clue. They're part of the forests that keep Coos Bay in business. Logs, lumber, wood chips, and every conceivable wood product are loaded onto huge lumber ships that sail in here daily to load up for yet another run. This port is, in fact, one of the world's largest wood-shipping ports.

Those forests grow green and tall thanks to the 60 inches of rain that fall here each year. Temperatures in Coos Bay, as all along the coast, are mild, very rarely toasty-hot or ice-cold.

A major lure in Coos Bay is the annual Oregon Coast Music Festival, an event that takes place each July and features symphony, chamber music, jazz, folk music, and concert band melodies presented in a pretty park. Coos Bay is closely allied to the nearby small towns of North Bend and Charleston, the latter providing docks for the region's lively charter fishing business.

Here the dunes end and the land reverts to a dramatic series of rocky headlands on which waves crash furiously, a photographer's—and a nature watcher's —paradise.

GETTING THERE: U.S. 101 runs right through town and Ore. 42 from Roseburg joins it here.

VISITOR INFORMATION: You'll find the **Bay Area Chamber of Commerce** at 50 E. Central St., Coos Bay, OR 97420 (tel. 503/269-0215, or toll free 800/824-8461, 800/762-6278 in Oregon).

WHERE TO STAY: Your options are limited in this historic bay town.

Top of the line is the **Thunderbird Motor Inn,** 1313 N. Bayshore Dr., Coos Bay, OR 97420 (tel. 503/267-4141, or toll free 800/547-8010, 800/

452-0733 in Oregon). Thunderbird Motels can be counted on for spacious, serviceable rooms that are sometimes outstanding. At this Thunderbird you are greeted by a long lobby with dark-wood paneling and deep comfortable chairs, a bit of traditional look. The spacious rooms are decorated in bright colors and feature paintings of sea scenes. You can swim in a heated pool, dine in a good restaurant focusing on fresh seafood, then dance later in an intimate lounge. Thunderbird's rooms have queen-size beds, and if you want to stay in yours for breakfast, they'll deliver. Rates are $58 to $65.

Coos Bay's Best Western Holiday Motel, 411 N. Bayshore Dr., Coos Bay, OR 97420 (tel. 503/269-5111 or toll free 800/528-1234), is part of the Best Western chain and features king- or queen-size beds, cable color television, and serviceable furniture in quite large rooms or individual spa units. Two thoughtful touches are blackout drapes and soundproofing, effective in this centrally located motel stretched out between the two one-way sections of U.S. 101. Best of all, the Best Western is quite conveniently located to shopping, fishing, and restaurants. At a small coffeeshop next door you will be treated to pleasant, concerned service and good simple cooking at reasonable prices in the $10 range. Rates at this Best Western are $41 to $95 double.

Timber Lodge Motel, 1001 N. Bayshore Dr., Coos Bay, OR 97420 (tel. 503/267-7066), does indeed sport plenty of timber. Clean and serviceable rooms come with cable and satellite television channels. A restaurant next door offers all three meals. Dinner specialties include Qualman oysters, gulf prawns, razor clams, and a generous seafood platter for prices in the $8 to $11 range. You can have coffee free in your room or come on down to the restaurant for a logger's breakfast of, say, a pork chop or steak, three eggs, hash browns, toast, and coffee. Rates are $38 to $39.

The **Sea Gull Summer Hostel,** 438 Elrod St., Coos Bay, OR 97420 (tel. 503/267-6114), is located a few miles inland from the dunes and beaches in the First Presbyterian Church, just six blocks from the bus station. The rate of $10 per person per night includes a home-cooked dinner of generous proportions, with vegetarian specialties, and breakfast. The Sea Gull opens at 4 p.m., and dinner is from 6:30 to 8:30 p.m. The hostel is open from mid-June to mid-September.

Campers can find space at **Sunset Bay State Park,** U.S. 100 (P.O. Box 102), Coos Bay, OR 97420 (tel. 503/888-4902), 12 miles southwest of North Bend. Fees are $5 to $7. The park is open mid-April to November. It's wise—and often imperative—to have reservations in summer.

WHERE TO DINE: Gourmet restaurants do not line the streets of Coos Bay, but there are several good cooks in town, providing meals in pleasant atmospheres. Tops among those is **Hurry Back Café,** 100 W. Commercial St. (tel. 503/267-3933), a charming little café with paddle fans, murals, and posters. Hurry Back thinks big. They bake their own sourdough rye bread, whip up unusual sauces and pastas, and even some vegetarian selections that, unlike most of those creations, actually taste good. Whatever is fresh in the markets will turn up on tables here, be it fish, fruit, or vegetables. Service is rapid and hospitable. You can even order an express lunch and if it takes longer than ten minutes to get to you, it's free. Among the dinner selections are homemade fettuccine with chicken and mushrooms, blackened snapper, five kinds of ravioli, and baked oysters. Earlier in the day Belgian waffles topped with fresh berries is the lure. You will pay less than $12 for dinner entrees. Hurry Back is open from 7 a.m. to 9 p.m. six days, from 9 a.m. to 3 p.m. on Sunday. Hearty breakfasts include whole-grain pancakes topped by real maple syrup or freshly baked croissants.

The **Thunderbird Motel** (see "Where to Stay") has a dark and intimate dining room in which flaming tableside creations play a dramatic role. Continental specialties appear on the menu with plenty of seafood balanced by a suitable selection of red meats and poultry. Fresh, hot breads and good wines plus skillful service will add up to a very pleasant evening. Hours are 6 a.m. to 10 p.m., closing an hour earlier on Sunday, and prices are in the $10 to $15 range for most entrees. Cocktails and entertainment in the lounge.

Mo's, that popular coastal chowder house, has a restaurant at 700 S. Broadway (tel. 503/269-1323). Like its sister restaurants in Newport and Florence, this Mo's offers low prices in the $5 range for a selection of sandwiches, salads, burgers, and best of all, that steaming chowder. Hours are 11 a.m. to 9 p.m. daily, an hour later on weekends.

Portside, Small Boat Basin, Charleston (tel. 503/888-5544), is a pleasant waterside dining spot specializing in local seafoods. You dine here in a room outfitted with a couple of couches, some trees, and tables that take full advantage of the restaurant's waterside location. On the menu are deep-fried crab legs and scallops, grilled empire clams, sautéed halibut, scampi, and for landlubbers, prime rib and steaks, for prices in the $10 to $15 range. Hours are 11:30 a.m. to 11 p.m. daily.

NIGHTLIFE: The **Thunderbird Motel** (see "Where to Stay") has entertainment and dancing many nights, as does **Gussie's,** 1088 Newmark (tel. 503/888-5213), which has a band playing all kinds of music from country rock to top-40s.

What's hot in nightlife this week will be outlined in the local newspapers, the *Coos Bay World* or the weekly *Coos Bay Empire Builder.*

DIG IT! In this neck of the woods, necks are very important parts of the anatomy—of a clam. **Clamming** is one of the best-loved pursuits in these tidal flats, where some clams grow as big as sunflowers, some as tiny as rosebuds. Many of them get dug up out of those tidal waters too, to appear on platters in just about every restaurant in the Pacific Northwest. In the interests of increasing your education and perhaps filling your chowder bowl, here's a brief lesson in the fine art of clamming. You'll need a shovel, obtainable at bait and tackle shops everywhere along the coast. In Coos Bay the most common clams are called gaper (sometimes empire) and razor clams. These are big fellows, at least five inches long. Small clams found on this shoreline are called cockle, softshell, butter or Quahog, and littleneck clams. In Coos Bay you'll find gaper and cockle clams down about 15 inches along the tidelands across the bay from the town of Empire to Charleston, and on an island that appears only at low tide due west of Empire. In nearby Bandon softshell clams can be found on a mud flat about three-quarters of a mile from the mouth of the Coquille River up the bay to about three miles from the harbor's entrance.

Digging is done on falling tides; the lower the tide, the better. At extreme low tides you find the biggest clams, because that's the only time those really big fellows can be seen. Minus tides of 0.4 or more are called clam tides. To find out what the tide will be wherever you are, you must consult tide tables, available here in many shops, restaurants, chambers of commerce, even banks!

To locate a clam in the sand and mud, watch for a hole or a slight indentation in bottom grass indicating a hole. If you see one, scrape across it with your shovel to remove about a half inch of dirt. If there's a clam there, it will squirt water up in the air, sometimes as high as two feet in the air, as it retracts its neck. Now dig down about a foot, digging close to the hole but not directly over it. Lift off the dirt to leave the hole intact. Your clam should be just a couple of inches below your shovel, at about 14 to 16 inches beneath the surface.

There is a daily limit on the number of clams you may take: 20 bay clams a day, including only 12 gaper or empire clams; 24 razor clams, and you must take the first 24 you dig regardless of size; 36 softshell clams. You can dig at any time, without a license. Many of the best low tides occur on weekdays, more's the pity for the nine-to-fiver, but good for you. You won't have to fight crowds out digging. In Coos Bay, by the way, you need to subtract about an hour and 25 minutes from most tide books to get the right time for the Coos Bay Bar.

Great, you've got a bucketful of fat clams! Now what? Well, now you have to clean them. To do this, immerse them in fresh water for about 24 hours until the neck lengthens and the outer skin slips off easily. Then, with a knife, peel off the outer skin from the neck, run the knife through the neck, and slit it open lengthwise. Then split open the stomach and remove all the dark material and the gelatinous rod. Don't try this with a cockle clam—there's no neck on a cockle.

Now to cooking: First grind the whole clam and add both meat and nectar to a chowder base you like. Many people sauté chopped onions and bacon together, pour off the fat, and add water and diced potatoes. Cook the potatoes until they're soft, mash them and add milk, clams, and nectar, and simmer for five minutes.

For fried clams, pound the neck meat to tenderize it, dip into flour, beaten egg, and milk, roll in bread or cracker crumbs, and fry. For fritters, find a fritter recipe and substitute clams. You can even can clams, using a pressure cooker, and freeze them by putting them in a bowl, covering them with water and sticking them in the freezer. And you thought this was *just* a guidebook!

WHAT ELSE TO SEE AND DO: The most scenic spot in this bayside city is **Shore Acres State Park,** a park retrieved from the ruins of a lumber magnate's estate. Formal botanical gardens bloom with thousands of flowers. Located 4½ miles west of Charleston, the gardens, a delight for strollers, have sandstone bluffs and a rugged shoreline. A glass-enclosed observation shelter offers some good views of the wildest wave action along the Pacific coast, particularly in winter.

We've often wished all the world's antiques and artifacts could be catalogued by computer so collections could be coordinated, thus avoiding the eclectic conglomerations you often see in small museums. Coos Bay's **Coos County Historical Museum,** Simpson Park in North Bend, U.S. 101 (tel. 503/756-6320), works hard to avoid that small-museum syndrome. Permanent and temporary exhibits focus on local history and culture: Indians and early settlements and the development of the logging, coal-mining, and shipbuilding industries. The museum is open Tuesday through Saturday from 10 a.m. to 4 p.m., and from June to September it's also open on Sunday from noon to 4 p.m. Admission is 50¢ for adults and 25¢ for children.

Another historic sight is the **Marshfield Sun Printing Museum,** 1049 N. Front St., U.S. 101 North, home of the *Sun* newspaper, which began publishing in 1891. You can see the original printing presses, type cases, and big layout tables. Tour dates vary, so call the chamber of commerce for information.

Lumbermen made and make fortunes here and some of those early millionaires built beautiful homes with the profits. You can see some of those homes on a **walking tour** past the town's historic homes. A brochure and map are available from the chamber of commerce.

Another guide available from the chamber will lead you through some of the interesting historical sites of the region, including **Cape Arago,** a prominent headland thought to be the bay where English buccaneer Francis Drake dropped anchor in 1579; **Brandon Lighthouse,** built in 1896; an old and still harrowing

wagon road traveled by the pioneers; and the imposing **Andrew J. Sherwood House,** a 1901 Queen Anne structure that's one of the loveliest you'll see anywhere in the state.

To see what happens to some of the logs collected here, take a tour of the **Weyerhaeuser Sawmill,** on U.S. 101 (tel. 503/756-5121). Tours are available free from mid-June through August, at 1:15 p.m. weekdays. In winter tours are only on Friday. Tours depart from the front steps of the company's headquarters on U.S. 101 in North Bend.

If you wonder what on earth they're doing with all that myrtlewood you've seen advertised all along the coastline, you can watch the myrtlewood artists in action at **House of Myrtlewood,** 1125 S. 1st St. (tel. 503/267-7804), open daily with tours from 9 a.m. to 5 p.m.

South Slough National Estuarine Reserve was established in 1974, the first estuarine reserve in the nation. Marshes cover much of this 4,400-acre sanctuary, which shelters many species of plants and animals. Hiking trails and a canoe launch area are available. In summer organized activities are sponsored by the headquarters. To reach the Interpretive Center, turn off Cape Arago Hwy. on Seven Devil's Road and go four miles to Hinch Road, then turn left immediately to the headquarters (tel. 503/888-5558). Hours are 8:30 a.m. to 4:30 p.m. daily from June through August, Monday through Friday only from September through May. Admission is free.

If you've never seen an oyster bed, you can remedy your loss at **Qualman Oyster Farms,** 4898 Crown Point Rd. (tel. 503/888-3145), a company that's been springing open the bivalves for over 50 years. The oysters you see under Joe Ney Bridge are seeded by attaching tiny oysters to empty shells and wiring the shells to stakes, which are set out during low spring tides. Results can be seen at low tide any time of year. They are harvested by boats. When pulled out, each stake will yield a quart of shucked oysters. Although Qualman doesn't give formal tours, they'll be happy to answer your questions. Here's one answer for you: Yes, you can safely eat oysters in months without an "R" in them.

SPORTS: Family Four Stables, 255 Transit Hill Rd., seven miles south of Coos Bay on U.S. 101 (tel. 503/756-7466), can provide you with a horse for guided trail or beach rides for $10 to $15 an hour.

Charter fishing boats include Charleston Charters in Charleston (tel. 503/888-4846); Betty Kay Charters (tel. 503/888-9021), and B & B Charters (tel. 503/888-4139), all at nearby Charleston Docks (U.S. 101).

Golfers can putt around at **Coos Country Club,** 900 Coos City–Sumner Rd. (tel. 503/267-6313). Greens are open daily except Wednesday and Thursday to non-members. Greens fees are $12 to $14.

Five miles north of North Bend you can rent three- or four-wheel **motorcycles** to race over the dunes. Far West Rentals, 320 Sandy Way, in Hauser (tel. 503/756-2322 or 756-4274), is located on the edge of the dune park. Rates are $20 per hour, $32 for two hours.

SPECIAL EVENTS: Coos Bay and environs kick off the summer season in May with a **Charley Town Seafood Festival** in nearby Charleston, following that with the **Oregon Coast Music Festival** in July. Performances at the Music Festival are often in outdoor settings. Tickets are $4 to $9.

If you never met a blackberry you didn't like, you can gorge at the August **Blackberry Arts Festival** to which all kinds of yummy contributions are made by local gourmets with food for thought by local artists.

Things wind up in September when the city sponsors its **Charley Tuna Festival,** a celebration of the albacore arrivals.

6. FLORENCE

Here the land formations change from rocky cliffs and dramatic promontories to mile after mile of high, rolling, windswept sand dunes, the delight of dune-bike riders, strollers, and scenery-watchers.

These 42 miles called the **Oregon Dunes National Recreation Area** are bounded on the north by the Siuslaw (pronounced "See-*oos*-law") River, on the south by Coos Bay.

Who is the Florence that gave the town its name? Well, there wasn't one. What happened, legend has it, is that beachcombing Indians stumbled on the remains of a shipwreck and found a board proclaiming the ship's name: *Florence*. They kept the board, the story goes, and it ended up on the front door of the first hotel in town, and *voilà!* the city of Florence was born.

Whales sometimes find their way into the Siuslaw River here, so townspeople in this village of 5,000 are wont to boast that their town is so friendly even whales swim up the river to visit them!

GETTING THERE: U.S. 101 cuts right through the middle of town crossing Ore. 126, connecting Florence to Eugene. Florence's historic district is just east of the road and on the south side of the bridge over the Siuslaw River.

VISITOR INFORMATION: You can meet some of those friendly people at the **Florence Area Chamber of Commerce**, 201 U.S. 101, Florence, OR 97439 (tel. 503/997-3128).

WHERE TO STAY: A number of small motels inhabit these shores.

The largest resort in town is **Driftwood Shores Surfside Inn,** 88416 First Ave., Florence, OR 97439 (tel. 503/997-8263, or toll free 800/824-8774, 800/432-5091 in Oregon), a sprawling complex of four-story buildings high on a dune overlooking the sea. Attractive quarters are decorated in bright colors and come in a variety of sizes, up to and including rooms big enough for six or more. The Driftwood Inn has 136 units, some of which have fireplaces and kitchens. All are attractively decorated and spacious, and these very large quarters have three bedrooms. All have radios, telephones, and balconies facing the ocean. You'll find a heated indoor swimming pool plus saunas and a whirlpool. A restaurant is open from breakfast through dinner with prices in the $8 to $12 range. Rates in summer are $53 to $65 double; more, of course, for those very large units, about $10 less in winter.

Le Château Motel, U.S. 101 and Ore. 126 (P.O. Box 98), Florence, OR 97439 (tel. 503/997-3481), is a two-story motel of medium size, going on small. A wood-sided motel trimmed in brown, Le Château has simple but attractive quarters that offer cable televisions, movies, radios, a heated pool, saunas, and whirlpool. A restaurant nearby will stave off starvation. Rates here are $32 to $38 double.

The **Park Motel,** 85034 U.S. 101, Florence, OR 97439 (tel. 503/997-2634), is nestled under some pine trees close to the dunes. The Park has just 15 units, four of them two-bedroom quarters and two with unequipped kitchenettes. Don't expect anything fancy, just the basics at a very reasonable price: $32 to $36 double, $3 for an extra person.

There's no better way to get a feeling for the history of a place than living there. You can do that at the **Johnson House,** 216 Maple St., Florence, OR 97439 (tel. 503/997-8000), a welcoming old home built in 1892 now serving as a bed-and-breakfast inn. In a big two-story house with a wide porch you occupy one of four antique-filled rooms, one with private bath, for $55 to $65. The price tag includes a breakfast of fruit, breads, eggs, ham, cheese, coffee, tea, and a surprise treat served in a charming dining room. For $3 you can also have a sumptuous afternoon tea with homemade jam and pastries.

Campers can find a haven at the **Florence Dunes Campground,** 87115 Rhododendron Dr., Florence, OR 97439 (tel. 503/977-6431). The campground has full hookups, tent space, and secluded campsites close to the sea three miles north of Florence. Turn west off U.S. 101 on 35th Street, then go one mile to Rhododendron Drive. Rates are under $12.

WHERE TO DINE: Florence has an array of diverse dining spots.

The **Windward Inn Restaurant,** 3757 U.S. 101 (tel. 503/997-8243), is a contemporary spot trimmed in cedar and sparked with beveled glass, lots of plants, and a charming atmosphere that's neither hokey California-camp nor fernsy-woodsy-cutesy. Instead they've concentrated on producing a serene dining room that's sunny by day, sophisticated and intimate by night. You will dine in candle glow at this award-winning restaurant on good seafood simply cooked. Operated by Van and Kathie Heeter since 1968, the Windward Inn had very humble beginnings as a service station, then as a forgettable café. What the Heeters have done is all the more remarkable when you see pictures of what it used to be. On the evening menu, served to a background of grand piano notes, are such selections as grilled local razor clams, baked yearling oysters, and in winter, sea mussels steamed in white wine and garlic. Seafood appetizers are supplemented by a homemade liver pâté, a whole steamed artichoke, and frenchfried zucchini or mushrooms. At lunch try tabbouleh, that Middle Eastern dish of cracked wheat and spices, teamed with hummus, a garbanzo paste with sesame sauce with dilled cucumber in yogurt. Home-baked breads and pastries are a highlight. Oregon shrimp with avocado served on an English muffin and topped by mornay sauce is another unusual selection. Dinner prices are in the $10 to $17 range. Hours are 8 a.m. to 9 p.m. daily except Monday.

Oyster fans chowing their way along this oyster-rich coastline will want to stop at the **Bridgewater Restaurant,** 1297 Bay St. (tel. 503/997-9405), where oysters are available one by one, as oysters Rockefeller, oysters baked, and in a couple of other ways. Those are supplemented by steamed clams, a seafood platter, and a comparatively long list of fresh fish, simply prepared. Recent renovations resulted in a new interior, a patio service area, and a now-broader menu including a fruit and salad bar. Clam chowder created by these talented cooks recently won first place in a state cook-off competition. Steaks are offered here too—all of it for prices in the $10 to $15 range. Hours are 9 a.m. to 10 p.m. daily.

Ice cream? **BJ's Ice Cream,** 2930 U.S. 101 North (tel. 503/997-7286), has 48 flavors from apple pie to root beer marble.

DOING THE DUNES: Top of the list of things to see—and to do—are the miles of rolling dunes. To see them close up take a ride aboard a **Sand Dunes Frontier Dune Buggy.** On that ride you'll sometimes feel like Lawrence of Arabia as you zip down the side of one sandy dune only to find yourself face-to-face with another. These shifting sands are sometimes low, sometimes nearly 400 feet high. They're created, geologists say, by river quartz washed out to sea, then washed back ashore again and tossed about by winds that blow ceaselessly along this coast. These dunes are moving inexorably inland and have already buried what was once a dense pine forest! Sand Dunes Frontier operates the only dunebuggy rides in this national recreation area and charges just $5 for adults for a ride, $2.50 for children under 10, free for youngsters under 5 if you hold them in your lap. Rides take about 30 minutes. You'll find the dune-buggy headquarters at 83960 U.S. 101 South (tel. 503/997-3544). Rides begin at 9 a.m. and cease at dusk.

Displays explaining the dunes can be seen at the **Oregon Dunes National Recreation Area Headquarters,** 855 Highway Ave., Reedsport (tel. 503/271-3611), open mid-May to September from 8 a.m. to 4:30 weekdays and 9 a.m. to 5 p.m. on weekends, from 8 a.m. to 4:30 weekdays only in other months. You can drive the dunes yourself by following U.S. 101 south across the Siuslaw River bridge and up the hill to the intersection of South Jetty Road, turn right and watch out for the dune buggies!

Some people want to do everything themselves. For them **Dunes Odyssey Rentals,** on U.S. 101 in Winchester Bay (tel. 503/271-4011), provides rental dune buggies for $25 an hour, $15 for each additional hour. You must also leave a $50 deposit, which will be returned. Stay away from the water or they'll charge you $25 to clean off the salt. Hours are 8 a.m. to 5 p.m. daily in summer; closed on Wednesday the rest of the year.

If you're on the south end of the dunes near North Bend, you can rent a three-wheel dune bike to roar over the sands from **Oregon Dunes,** U.S. 101, North Bend (tel. 503/756-2322). Rates are $17 to $20 an hour. Hours are 8 a.m. to 8 p.m. daily.

If you'd rather ride the dunes on four feet, you can gallop down the sands on a steed provided by **C & M Coastal Mountains Stables,** 90241 U.S. 101 North (tel. 503/997-7540 or 997-3021). Ninety-minute beach rides are $16 to $18; a two-hour ride, $23. C & M can also arrange sunset and mountain rides or, for the youngsters, a pony ride ($3 for ten minutes). You'll find the stables eight miles north of Florence on U.S. 101.

Catherine Stephenson, the area's public affairs officer, says she's anxious to correct the "misconception that the dunes are strictly a playground for dune buggies. Half of the national recreation area is closed to off-road vehicles. We have 30 miles of hiking trails, backpacking opportunities, 32 freshwater lakes for fishing, birdwatching par excellence featuring 247 species of birds, and even a campground (Wild Mare Horse Camp near Coos Bay) with horse corrals. In the summer we offer guided nature hikes and evening campfire programs for visitors."

OTHER SIGHTS AND ACTIVITIES: Indian Forest, four miles north of town on U.S. 101 (tel. 503/997-3677), will show you what the dwellings of many North American Indians looked like through full-size re-creations of everything from a hupa to a birchbark dome, a hogan or a tipi. This enclave is also home to roaming buffalos and a few deer too. Shoppers can find some interesting Indian arts and crafts in the shop, things like Navajo rugs, Hopi pottery, and Zuñi beadwork. Indian Forest is open daily mid-May to October from 9 a.m. to 6 p.m. Admission is $3 for adults, $2 for children 12 to 18, and $1.50 for youngsters 5 to 11.

Darlingtonia Botanical Wayside, six miles north on U.S. 101, specializes in rare carnivorous cobra lilies that eat flies and other bugs.

More flowers: If you're here mid-May through June you can follow a scenic nine-mile drive that takes you past **wild rhododendrons** in bloom. Take Rhododendron Drive west and continue north to Heceta Beach Road.

Holiday Charters (tel. 503/271-3702 or 271-3175) or **Shamrock Charters** (tel. 503/271-3232), both south of Florence in Winchester Bay, will take you out fishing. You pay about $35 to $40 for a fishing trip.

About 12 miles north of town is one of nature's own amusements, the honking, splashing, rolling, clowning sea lions that bask and blather about at **Sea Lion Caves,** 91560 U.S. 101 (tel. 503/547-3111). You descend in an elevator to look at these hams of the sea, dwelling happily in their year-round homes, the only one like it on the mainland.

The sea lions were not captured and put here in this huge grotto. They are wild and choose to live here, the pups clowning around for your amusement, the great whoofing bulls watching over their women. Those bulls, by the way, leave each fall to paddle their 2,000-pound hulks into cold water as far north as the Bering Sea. But when spring arrives in Florence, so do those peripatetic bulls— or perhaps it's the other way around! Sea Lion Caves are open from sun-up to dusk daily, and admission is $4 for adults, $2.50 for children 6 to 12.

SHOPPING: Florence's earliest roots were dug down by the river in an area bounded by U.S. 101 and Harbor Street between Bay and 2nd Streets. For years it was run-down and grubby; then in 1970 ambitious restorers moved into old stores and warehouses, lived there, and repaired them. Today it's called **Old Town Florence** and is a spiffed-up group of historic buildings and shops.

Shops are on Bay Street, and historic buildings include the Kyle Building, a 1901 general store at Bay and Laurel Streets, the Florence Telephone Company at Bay and Maple, Johnson House at Maple and 1st, and Florence Rooms, a one-time boarding house still a boarding house.

The **Toy Factory, 88878 U.S. 101** (tel. 503/997-8604), five miles south of Sea Lion Cave, has toys, toys, and more toys, and they aren't all for the kids either! Folk toys like a whimmydiddle or a flipperdinger, kites to fly on the dunes, games, and hobby kits are for sale daily from noon to 5 p.m. in winter and 10 a.m. to 5 p.m. in summer; closed some winter days.

The **Siuslaw Gallery of Local Arts** is on U.S. 101, a mile south of town on the lower level of the Siuslaw Pioneer Museum (tel. 503/997-3037).

7. YACHATS

On your way south, look quickly and you will see Yachats, a small town almost as difficult to pronounce as it is easy to miss. First the pronunciation: *"Yah-hots."* That's quite a pretty name in the Chinook Indian dialect, which translates it as "dark waters at the foot of the mountain."

This is a good place to settle to take a look at the sea lions gathered at Sea Lion Cave nearby, to visit Cape Perpetua, the highest point on the Oregon coast, to watch some spectacular winter storms crash and rumble across the rocky promontories, and between April and October to dine on silvery sardine-like smelt that come into shore here, one of the few places in the world where they come so close to shore. The smelt catch is so important in Yachats that in July there's an annual **Smelt Fry.**

WHERE TO STAY: If you're staying over, you have a couple of attractive options: Shamrock Lodgettes and the Fireside Motel.

Rustic, wood-floored log cabins on a beach of the Yachats River, the **Shamrock Lodgettes,** 105 U.S. 101 South (P.O. Box 364) Yachats, OR 97498 (tel. 503/547-3312), are surrounded by lawns and flowers. Inside, a stone fireplace and simple, hewn-wood furnishings welcome you, as cedar paneling trims everything including the ceiling. While they're simple and rustic, these lodges are also quite comfortable, with big picture windows looking out onto the lawns and river. You forgo maid service here (unless you pay an additional charge), but you get fresh towels daily and new firewood plus some other services, including a morning newspaper delivered daily. Shamrock has a health spa with a sauna and spa tub and can arrange massages. A wide variety of cabins, some accommodating up to nine, and motel rooms at the resort's motel are available. Log cabins are the more interesting and are reserved months ahead of the summer season, so take heed.

Rates are $47 to $65 double for motel units, $65 to $77 double for cabins. Discounts are available for stays of a week or more.

The **Fireside Motel,** 1881 U.S. 101 North (P.O. Box 313), Yachats, OR 97498 (tel. 503/547-3636), lies in a pine forest at the edge of the sea with some beautiful views across the Pacific. It's well back from the highway, so the only noise you'll hear will be waves rolling onto shore. Accommodations at the Fireside are clean, light, and airy. Some have fireplaces, many have refrigerators, and all have color television. Rates are $36 to $56 double.

The **Yachats Inn,** 331 U.S. 101 South (P.O. Box 307), Yachats, OR 97498 (tel. 503/547-3456), is yet another choice. Here you can splash in an indoor pool or stroll the beach to see a waterspout splutter. Just 20 units are spread over three acres of ground, so you have lots of space to roam. Rooms have kitchens and fireplaces and are $35 to $70 for two.

WHERE TO DINE: You have an octet of restaurants to choose among, the best of which are La Serre and the Adobe.

La Serre, 2nd and Beach Streets (tel. 503/547-3420), specializes in fresh seafood prepared in interesting ways, including a crab-filled pastry topped with sour cream and avocados. Other choices are equally imaginative, whether the main ingredient is clam, shrimp, or snapper. Salads are fresh and crunchy, fruits play a big role on the menu, and homemade breads are scrumptious. Prices are in the $10 to $15 range for dinner, and the restaurant is open from 9 a.m. to 10 p.m. daily except Tuesday.

At the **Adobe,** 1555 U.S. 101 North (tel. 503/547-3141), which also is an attractive seaside hotel featuring handmade bricks and beamed ceilings, you can dine on continental specialties ranging from scallops au beurre blanc sautéed in a tarragon butter to sautéed razor clams and an adobe-baked crab pot of local Dungeness crab blended with mushrooms and cheddar cheese and baked in a cream sauce. Prices are in the $10 to $15 category including soup, a toppings-laden baked potato, and cheese bread baked here. The Adobe is open from 8 to 11 a.m. and 6 to 9 p.m. daily.

WHAT TO SEE AND DO: Amusements here are about the same as those in most cities along the coast with a couple of exceptions. One of those is a scenic side trip to **Cape Perpetua** (pronounced "Per-peh-*tua*"), a rocky promontory that is the highest spot on the Oregon coast. You'll find signs guiding you to the visitor center (tel. 503/547-3289) about 2½ miles south of Yachats, where you can learn how this cliff was formed and how it was named by British seafarer Capt. James Cook in 1788. He dubbed it in honor of a saint's day celebrated when he spotted the cape. He said the incessant winter storms here kept him perpetually in sight of the rock. You can take a dramatic drive across 22 miles of hauntingly beautiful scenery (begin an eighth of a mile north of the visitor center at Klickitat Ridge Road at FS55) or walk trails through a forest, mounds of shells, spooky rocks, to watery places called Devil's Churn and Restless Waters.

About 13 miles south of the city on U.S. 101, a landmark called **Heceta Head** (pronounced "Heh-*seat*-ah") rises from the sea. Named by a Spanish captain who sighted it in 1775, the promontory proved a good spot for a lighthouse, so one was built in 1889 and remains there still, an often-photographed red-and-white tower accompanied by a keeper's white-columned home, built among the pines in 1893.

8. SEAL ROCK

This tiny village is lined with shops in which some quite lovely crafts, jewelry, ceramics, and wood sculptures, and some less interesting items as well, can be found. One place to look for good local crafts is the **Seal Rock Art Gallery**, on U.S. 101 ten miles south of Newport (tel. 503/563-2016 or 563-2576), which has an interesting selection of local artists' works. Summer hours are 11 a.m. to 5 p.m. daily.

An amusement here is **Sea Gulch**, U.S. 101 (tel. 503/563-2727), where you—and especially the youngsters—will giggle over 400 wood sculptures displayed along a quarter-mile trail. Western and hillbilly characters predominate in the humorous scenes, open from 9 a.m. to 5 p.m. daily. Admission is free, and you can buy the chain-saw carvings.

9. NEWPORT

Newport Beach is a little like a very small San Francisco—you do have to use your imagination a bit—with a long bridge sweeping into town and plenty of rusticity. Alongside the bridge, a picturesque waterfront is lined with small shops selling freshly steamed crab and shrimp cocktail amid colorful fishing boats and heaps of colorful nets.

Over in Tillamook creameries make prize-winning cheeses popular all over the West, and roundabout they produce some fine wines to go with them.

VISITOR INFORMATION: If you need a map or some information on the area, stop by the **Greater Newport Chamber of Commerce**, 555 S.W. Coast Hwy., Newport, OR 97365 (tel. 503/265-8801), where smiling helpers and some very nice volunteer workers will struggle to make you happy. In summer the chamber is open Monday through Friday from 8:30 a.m. to 6 p.m. and on Saturday and Sunday from 10 a.m. to 4 p.m. Winter hours are Monday through Friday from 8:30 a.m. to 5 p.m.; closed weekends.

WHERE TO STAY: Newport's rustic bayside harbor is its best feature. No hotel takes better advantage of that than the **Embarcadero Resort Hotel & Marina**, 1000 S.E. Bay Blvd., Newport, OR 97365 (tel. 503/265-8521, or toll free 800/452-8567 in Oregon). To find it you must make your way to Bay Boulevard, then traverse the sweeping curve of the harbor to its end. There the Embarcadero climbs up and down the sloping ground and out over the water. Clever design and construction have blended the weathered gray buildings into the rising hillside so unobtrusively that from a distance they seem to be part of the cliff and water. On closer observation, you discover there are some very chicly decorated apartments under those sloping roofs. Inside, high ceilings angle down to a wall of glass leading to balconies with views of this active harbor. Quarters are one- or two-bedroom suites, each with a living room outfitted in sleek contemporary furnishings, light woods, a dining area, fireplace, kitchen, and bath. For entertainment you can paddle about an indoor pool walled in glass. A heated whirlpool warms you up on chilly days, and a sauna relaxes you in any weather. A few steps up from the airy lobby, a flower-filled restaurant offers all three meals at prices in the $10 to $15 range. Fresh seafood bought right off the docks here is, of course, the specialty. Pretty views over glittering yachts in the hotel's marina add to the allure. Embarcadero charges $78 for a patio room with queen-size bed, sitting area, and convertible couch, $110 for a one-bedroom suite with fireplace and kitchen, and $159 for a town-house suite with two bedrooms and two baths, a fireplace, living room, and kitchen. Children under 18 are free.

The **Hotel Newport**, 3019 N. Coast Hwy., Newport, OR 97365 (tel. 503/265-9411), is set high on a dune. All rooms have a big glass wall and balconies, many overlooking the sea. Spacious rooms are outfitted in snappy contemporary colors and chic accessory pieces. For exercise there's a heated swimming pool, hot tub, and whirlpool, and a game room. A showy restaurant called Casey's is a trilevel spot adorned with greenery and flowers, not to mention some gorgeous sunset views. Specialties here are hot breads and pastries, good salads, homemade soups, and at dinner, continental preparations priced from $10 to $16. In the lounge a fire blazes, an antique wood bar welcomes, and wainscoting is trimmed with yet more flowers. Rates for two at the Newport are $50 to $78.

At **Windjammer**, 744 S.W. Elizabeth St., Newport, OR 97365 (tel. 503/265-8853, or toll free 800/528-1234), you can play on a wide, wide beach, search for agates that wash up here, or try clamming or crabbing, maybe even surf fishing. Rooms are in long three-story buildings with tall windows offering a view of rocky cliffs. Some have kitchenettes and some have fireplaces; all have ocean views. Queen-size beds are a nice addition. Part of the Best Western chain, the Windjammer charges from $65 to $75.

For slim wallets the **Newport Hostel**, 212 N.W. Brook St., Newport, OR 97365 (tel. 503/265-9816), offers ocean views of sandy beaches just two blocks away. Advice on hiking, swimming, fishing, clamming, crabbing, and museums is available. Rates are $9, or $6 if you belong to the hosteling organization. Clam chowder's always on a back burner here.

Surfview Resort Motel, 1400 S. Hemlock, Cannon Beach, OR 97110 (tel. 503/436-2623, or toll free 800/345-5676), occupies a dune top hard by Haystack Rock, one of the local things to see and do. When the tides are low, you can see an amazing variety of sea life in the tidal pools around the distinctive rock. This shake-shingle motel has much to offer: rooms with whirlpools, ceiling mirrors, picture windows, big beds, and attractive décor, not to mention a spiffy view over dune, beach, and sea. You'll find a newspaper at your door each morning. Some suites have Jacuzzis, kitchens, fireplaces, and lanais. Rooms with full ocean views are the best at this hostelry which also sports an indoor pool, spa, sauna and weight room, and stairs to the beach. A restaurant called Cade's comes up with hearty meals. Newport is popular in summer when the thundering herds head for this beach, and in recent years has managed to promote itself even in winter as a cozy place to watch wild weather. Rates are $55 to $154 double.

A zany, funky spot designed to appeal to the literary buffs among us is the **Sylvia Beach Hotel**, 267 N.W. Cliff St., Newport, OR 97365 (tel. 503/265-5428). For openers, it's named after the publisher who produced James Joyce's *Ulysses* — see what we mean? An owner of this hotel also runs a Portland coffeehouse called Rimsky-Korsakoffee. Here she's created an Agatha Christie Room, with clues to 80 murders scattered about the room; the Edgar Allan Poe Room, in which you sleep under a pendulum; and the Oscar Wilde Room, which sports the worst wallpaper you've ever seen in tribute to Wilde's deathbed threat: "Either that wallpaper goes or I do." Don't say we don't ferret out the unusual for you. Rates at this small hostelry are $50 to $90.

If you're driving a rec vehicle or camping, try **Whalers Rest** at Lost Creek, U.S. 101 and Passmore Road, Newport, OR 97366 (tel. 503/867-3100), five miles south of the Yaquina Bay Bridge. A new campground, Whaler's Rest is set in 26 acres of forest with a heated indoor pool, tennis court, big-screen movies, and miles of beach. Sounds like un-roughing it to us! Rates are $12 to $14.

WHERE TO DINE: On this coastline with its big razor clams, sample some rich and buttery clam chowder. When you're looking for a filling bowl in Newport, try **Mo's** and **Mo's Annex**, 622 S.W. Bay Blvd. (tel. 503/265-2979), a rustic spot that has acquired considerable local fame for its top-notch, creamy chowder, jam-packed with fresh local clams. Prices at this no-frills, good-food spot are in the under-$10 range, and hours are 11 a.m. to 9 p.m. daily. Complete dinners, including the chowder or salad, and home-baked bread, are about $6!

Slumgullion's on the menu here along with calamari, salmon, halibut, even a few hot dogs and chili burgers for what Mo calls "flatlanders."

If Mo's is packed, as it very well may be, try the **Chowder Bowl** at Nye Beach, 728 N.W. Beach Dr. (tel. 503/265-7820). The Chowder Bowl lays claim to the finest clam chowder on the coast, and while that may be just a tad on the Madison Avenue side, it's close enough to the truth to send you away content. You can also dine on a dozen different kinds of juicy hamburgers and some interesting sandwich combinations—an oyster-wich, perhaps?—or put together a salad at the restaurant's salad bar. Prices are in the $5 to $7 range, and hours are 11 a.m. to 8 p.m. six days, noon to 8 p.m. on Sunday.

The **Whales Tale,** 452 S.W. Bay Blvd. (tel. 503/265-8660), is an eclectic spot decked out in local artwork and some stained glass, plants, and rustic wood tables. Diners saunter in to try local recipes they've loaned to national gourmet magazines, including seafood selections and some good ethnic specialties like cioppino or a German plate of sausage, meat, sauerkraut, German potato salad, and black bread. Plenty of foreign brews are available. Dinner entrees are in the $7 to $14 range, and the restaurant is open from 7 a.m. to 10 p.m. daily except Wednesday, when they're closed, and weekends, when they stay open to 11 p.m. for dinner. On Sunday try eggs Newport, topped with shrimp, one of the items the restaurant serves from 9 a.m. to 1 p.m. Entertainment some days.

Port Dock One, 325 S.W. Bay Blvd. (tel. 503/265-2911), looks like a big gray warehouse, but step inside and you find a chic second-floor lounge and dining room of walled-in glass and fireplaces. There's no better view of fishing boats and sailing craft than from the windows of this contemporary spot. Those views enhance the seafood selections, which range widely from broiled fish to fresh local clams and oysters, and steaks. A big bowl of crab and shrimp Louie topped by cheesecake makes a first-class lunch or dinner. Prices are in the $10 to $15 range for dinner, well worth it for this fine combination of view and good food. Hours are 11 a.m. to 10 p.m. daily.

If fish and chips is your special treat, try **McIvar's Landing,** 1226 N. Coast Hwy., at 12th Street (tel. 503/265-9233), where dozens of those paper-wrapped crunchies pour into hungry mouths from 11 a.m. to 10 p.m. daily. Light on atmosphere, but well endowed with one of the coast's favorite treats. Prices are in the $3 to $6 bracket.

Hard to think of pizza with all those fish and clams around, but if that's where your thoughts are wending, try **Abbey's Pizza Inn,** 932 N. Coast Hwy. (tel. 503/265-9336), a pleasant spot with pizzas from $5 to $17, depending on how carried away you get with toppings. Hours are 4 to 11 p.m. Monday through Thursday, from 2 p.m. to 1 a.m. on Friday and Saturday, and 1 to 10 p.m. on Sunday.

WHAT TO SEE AND DO: Newport has an eclectic conglomeration of attractions. Seatauqua is an Oregon State University program of lectures, films, and field trips that takes place all summer at **Hatfield Marine Science Center,** Marine Science Drive, Newport, across the bridge (tel. 503/867-3011). The Marine Science Center also features aquaria and museum displays, and a pool with sea creatures you can touch is a popular spot here. Hours are 10 a.m. to 6 p.m. from mid-June to September, closing at 4 p.m. in other months. Open every day except Christmas. Admission is free, but donations would be rewarded with a happy smile.

Several attractions are grouped together in a historic section of town called Mariner Square, 250 S.W. Blvd. First is the **Wax Works** (tel. 503/265-2206), a living museum that's a new concept in wax museums. You will see some of the latest in special effects and animation, as well as some of your favorite characters, immortalized in wax. Open daily except Thanksgiving and Christmas. June through August, hours are 9 a.m. to 8 p.m.; in other months they are 10 a.m. to 5 p.m. Admission is $4.50 for adults, $3 for children 12 to 17, and $2 for youngsters 5 to 11.

Next comes **Oregon Undersea Gardens** (tel. 503/265-2206), which lets you walk under the ocean without getting wet. You watch through windows as sea creatures that may look just like your boss are fed by a diver. Hours are 9 a.m. to 8 p.m. June to September, 10 a.m. to 5 p.m. in other months. Open daily except Thanksgiving and Christmas. Admission is $4 for adults, $3 for children 12 to 17, $2 for youngsters 5 to 11.

You'll also find **Ripley's Believe It or Not,** an eclectic collection of the weird and wonderful. Wanna see a shrunken head? Or a four-eyed Chinese emperor? Or a ghost? This is the place. Hours are the same as the other attractions in Mariner Center, and so are the admission prices.

Devil's Punch Bowl State Park, eight miles north of Newport, is a big rock bowl that looks every bit like something from which a devil might sup, particularly when high tides fill the bowl with a ferocious roar.

Yaquina Visual Art Center, 239 N.W. Beach Dr., Newport (tel. 503/265-5133), has interesting exhibits of local art and is open daily from 11 a.m. to 4 p.m. May through September, from noon other months.

Lives there a soul who doesn't love a lighthouse? To get a look at one on this coast where, goodness knows, it's really needed, stop at **Yaquina Bay Lighthouse,** Yaquina Bay State Park, Newport. Admission is 50¢ for adults (under 6, free), and the lighthouse, built in 1871 and one of the oldest on the coast, is open from noon to 5 p.m. daily May to September, weekends only in other months.

The **Lincoln County Historical Society,** 545 S.W. 9th St. (tel. 503/265-7509), occupies an old Victorian home built in 1895 for all of $1,400! Many new exhibits of period furnishings and clothing are on display here, while the adjacent **Log Cabin Museum,** 579 S.W. 9th St. (tel. 503/265-2013), houses artifacts that will help you understand a bit better the relationship between Indians and pioneers of the day. Hours are 10 a.m. to 5 p.m. June through September, 11 a.m. to 4 p.m. October through May.

Either can supply you with a map that will guide you to historic sites including: an 1837 campsite occupied by two missionaries and their brides of one month; Coyote Rock, where salmon gather before ascending to upriver spawning beds; and the homesite of Daniel Boone's great-grandson, who settled here in 1852.

SPORTS: Once again, fishing tops the list of activities here with steelhead running in winter, salmon and bottom fish waiting to jump on your hook, hungry trout swimming in rivers and streams.

Sea Gull Charters, 343 S.W. Bay Blvd., Newport (tel. 503/265-7441), goes after the big ones with six boats including a new 51-foot craft, carrying six to ten passengers on five-hour or all-day trips. Salmon fishing is June to September, and a license is available at the office here. Departure times are 6 to 8 a.m., varying by month.

You can call **Depot Bay Tradewinds,** 653 S.W. Bay Blvd. (tel. 503/265-2101), 24 hours a day, whenever the fishing bug strikes, and arrange a fishing or whale-watching trip. From August through October the tuna are running. When whales are in town, boats depart four times a day for a close look at them.

South Beach Charters, South Beach Marina (tel. 503/867-7200), takes you fishing or on scuba-diving trips.

Figure about $30 to $50 for these four- to eight-hour adventures.

Clamming in Yaquina Bay is a popular pursuit, one best carried out at extremely low tides. Tide tables are available at the chamber of commerce and at many area hotels and motels.

Yaquina Bay calls itself the Dungeness Crab Capital of the World, so if you'd like some fresh crabs, try capturing them yourself. Local tackle shops can help with information on good searching areas and the equipment necessary for success.

For racquetball courts, try **Newport Bay Club,** 111 S.W. 10th St. (tel. 503/265-9225), open from 6 a.m. to 10 p.m. daily, and for **tennis** call the city's Parks and Recreation Department (tel. 503/265-7783) or lob over to **Surftides Beach Tennis Club,** 2945 N.W. Jetty Ave., Lincoln City (tel. 503/994-9667), where indoor courts are open to 10 p.m. and are $7 an hour.

Nearest golf courses are Salishan (see Lincoln City), 17 miles north on U.S. 101, and **Agate Beach Golf Course,** 4100 N.E. Golf Course Dr., a nine-hole course just north of town on U.S. 101 (tel. 503/265-7331). Greens fees at Agate are $10 for nine holes.

HUNTING GEMS FROM THE SEA: Newport and Agate Beach are well known for the quantities of agates that are found here. Agates are the gemstone for those born in June and are actually quartz formed in rock cavities. Oxides and metals in the rock give it color. Moonstone agates are brilliant and clear, carnelian are bright red and transparent, ribbon agate has stripes of color, and cloud agates are transparent stones with dark formations in them. Other agates come in apple green, a seven-color stone called rainbow agate, plus tiger eye, onyx, azure, sardonyx, and agatized honeycomb coral. Jasper is a related stone, and some forms of it are called bloodstone or heliotrope.

Best finds of all are rare water agates which contain a bubble of water and air. You can buy them in local shops or search for them yourself on Otter Rock beaches, at Agate Beach, and at Newport Beach. Other good-looking spots in the region are south of Yachats, at Bob Creek, Ten-Mile, and Heceta Head.

Hunting is best done in winter and spring on an outgoing tide when tides help uncover gravel in which you may find the transparent stones. Look for piles of gravel atop the sand. If the sun is shining, all the better—you can see them sparkling. Most common agates in the Newport and Agate Beach area are jaspers, agatized wood, coral, clear agate, ribbon agate, and bloodstones.

SHOPPING: Many shops line the main coastal highway here and quite a few are clustered together in a salt-box style enclave called **Sea Towne Shops,** 1600 N. Coast Hwy., on U.S. 101 just north of Ore. 20. A woodcarving and scads of blossoms make this a pretty place to spend some time.

10. DEPOE BAY

Depoe Bay is famous as the best spot on the coast to watch massive gray whales blowing and sputtering by on their way to the Bering Sea for a cool summer. Later they whizz by on their way 6,000 miles south to the lagoons of Mexico, where they breed and bring up their babies. Those migrations take place as the whales head south from Arctic waters in November, and last until February.

HOW TO WATCH A WHALE: Now for a little lesson on whales. These gray whales are not really gray, but barnacles and healed wounds seen in the water make them look gray. They trudge along at about five miles an hour on their way to Mexico, about half that speed on their way north. Adult males lead the parade, followed more slowly by females with calves, who usually pass by this coastline in early May. The best sighting time is early morning in calm weather, when waves won't obscure your view. To spot a whale, look first for the vapor they blow as high as 12 feet into the air when exhaling. Once you've spotted that, keep your eye on it. Other whales are likely to appear in the same vicinity. Short, shallow dives, which are common before a deep dive, cause eddies which help you spot the passage of a whale and follow its progress. If you see a whale's tail flukes raised high, the whale will dive deeply. That's called sounding. A whale with its head partly out of the water and its eye above the surface is said to be "spy-hopping." It may be doing that to orient itself visually. A whale is said to be breaching when it rises vertically out of the water showing much of its body, then falls on its side or back with a resounding whack. Best viewing points in Depoe Bay are the seawall just across from the harbor on the west side of U.S. 101 and at Depoe Bay State Park just up the road.

GETTING THERE: Once again, that ubiquitous U.S. 101 runs right through town.

VISITOR INFORMATION: At the **Depoe Bay Chamber of Commerce,** U.S. 101 (P.O. Box 21), Depoe Bay, OR 97341 (tel. 503/765-2889), workers can help you find your way around this maze of coves and cliffs.

WHERE TO STAY: Depoe Bay's popularity at whale-watching time—and anytime—has encouraged some attractive resorts.

The **Inn at Otter Crest,** Otter Rock (P.O. Box 50), Depoe Bay, OR 97369 (tel. 503/765-2111, or toll free 800/547-2181, 800/452-2101 in Oregon), is not the easiest place to find, but it's worth the search. Occupying the point at a cape named Foulweather by an unhappy Capt. James Cook, who sailed by here in 1778, the inn is a cluster of buildings on several levels, each blending beautifully into this rocky headland. Accommodations are in long buildings that curve about a cliff overlooking the sea. Far beneath, waves crash against the rocks, and around you the wind whistles through the pines.

If you're a golfer, you can putt around what surely must be one of the most dramatic settings in the world—high atop the cliff right at the edge of the sea. Other amusements on these tranquil grounds include swimming in a pool overlooking the sea, indoor or outdoor tennis, and roaming about the pine forest and nature trails on 40 acres here. No cars impede your progress across the grounds: you park your car near the main lodge and walk or take one of the shuttles that scurry about with luggage and passengers. Evenings, you can pull up to a place beside the fire in your apartment or watch the sun set over the Pacific from your balcony. A sprawling resort, the Inn at Otter Crest offers studio and larger apartments, quite comfortably furnished and containing refrigerators. Amenities include saunas, whirlpool, a playground, and a recreational program. A dining room, open from 8 a.m. to 9 p.m., offers continental cuisine in the $12 to $15 range. Rates at Otter Crest are $65 for bedrooms with a queen-size bed or Murphy bed plus sitting room; $95 to $110 for loft suites with two double or queen-size beds, an upstairs loft, two-story living room, convertible sofa, fireplace, kitchen dining area, and deck; up to $165 for even larger quarters. Package plans for honeymoons or tennis holidays, among others, can save you money.

An interesting alternative to a large resort or one of the standard small motels in Depoe Bay is **Channel House,** P.O. Box 56, Depoe Bay, OR 97341 (tel. 503/765-2140). Finding this aerie on a cliff over the sea is a real trick, but you will be rewarded by an enchanting spot filled with puffy comforters and lace curtains, flowery touches, and canopied beds. Each of the 11 rooms here has a bath, almost every one has an ocean view, and each is a jewel. On the top floor a glamorous suite (no. 5) has a full kitchen, a fireplace in the living room, and a fireplace in the bedroom, where a queen-size bed beckons. In the bathroom is a whirlpool and out front a deck. Large enough for four, the suite is $140 a day. A similar suite (no. 3) is one floor down. Downstairs in an equally charming breakfast room are more beautiful views, some of them from an oceanfront deck. Rates at the Channel House are $40 to $120 for rooms, $100 to $140 for those suites, including breakfast. You'll find Channel House at the top of a hill west of U.S. 101, just south of the bridge in Depoe Bay.

WHERE TO DINE: Where else can you watch a whale swimming by while you dine? **Channel House** (see "Where to Stay") is one of the town's top dining spots, certainly one of the most scenic ones. Food is good too, with a wide range of seafood and steaks interestingly prepared, priced in the $10 to $15 range. Hours are 6 to 10 p.m. daily; closed Wednesday.

    Sea Hag, 5858 E. U.S. 101 (tel. 503/765-7901), sometimes open in the wee hours of the morning to send fishing fans off to sea with its acclaimed blackberry tarts, the rest of the day produces simply prepared seafood they say is "so fresh the ocean hasn't missed it yet." Believe it. A salad bar is included in dinners that fall in the $10 to $15 range. Hours are 4 a.m. to 1 a.m. with live music in the bar every night.

    Spouting Horn Restaurant, Depoe Bay Harbor, Depoe Bay (tel. 503/765-2261), has been in business for nearly 50 years with a coffeeshop downstairs and a dining room and lounge upstairs. Steaks and very fresh seafood in the $10 to $15 range are the fare; hours are 8 a.m. (4 a.m. June to September) to 10 p.m. daily except Tuesday. A spouting horn, by the way, is a shooting spray of water that rises into the sky as waves hit rocks.

WHAT TO SEE AND DO: The **Depoe Bay Aquarium and Shell Shop,** U.S. 101 at Bay Drive (tel. 503/765-2259), amuses you with a herd of squawking seals and an aquarium with an octopus and other sea creatures.

    Cape Foulweather is one of the oldest historical spots along the coast. It was sighted and named in 1778 by Britain's Capt. James Cook, who took a dim view of the weather that nearly scuttled his ship here. At Cape Foulweather two miles south of town on U.S. 101 (tel. 503/765-2270), you can watch seagulls wheeling over cliffs 500 feet high and sea lions flapping about in the sun. A shop here offers a fine selection of local craftwork and glass fishing floats up to 24 inches in diameter, set afloat from Japanese nets. To get there, take Otter Crest Loop about two miles south of town.

SPECIAL EVENTS: Each Memorial Day the city honors those who have lost their lives at sea at the annual **Fleet of Flowers Ceremony,** during which a blanket of flowers is cast upon the water.

SPORTS: Fishing is the sport in town. If you're interested in taking a trip, make your way to the harbor, where you'll find many **charter boats** ready to take you fishing or whale watching.

    Two of the many charter operations in the area are **Deep Sea Trollers,** at the Spouting Horn Restaurant (tel. 503/765-2705 or 765-2248), and **Tradewinds Trollers** (tel. 503/765-2345). Expect to pay about $35 to $50 for a trip. Bargaining is in order, particularly if you have a group.

11. LINCOLN CITY / GLENEDEN BEACH

    Although this coast has been here a long, long time, Lincoln City was just incorporated in 1965 when a cluster of local communities united to become this small metropolis. Now the city occupies 7½ miles of beachfront, bounded on the east by the Coastal Range Mountains. Through the city runs what locals call the world's shortest river, the D River—pretty short name too—which connects to a large freshwater lake. Life is simple and rustic here, pretty chilly much of the year, but sunny and serene in summer, when walking the driftwood-laden beach is a breezy, balmy experience.

GETTING THERE / GETTING AROUND: U.S. 101, the main highway along the Oregon coast, runs right through the middle of town, and most shops and restaurants are located on it or very, very near it. **Oregon Hwy. 18/22** also comes in here from Salem.

Greyhound Bus Lines makes a stop here at 1011 S. U.S. 101 (tel. 503/994-8418).

To get around, try **Dolly the Trolley,** a clanging trolley that perambulates up and down U.S. 101 at 50¢ for adults, 25¢ for children.

Security Cab (tel. 503/996-2772) operates in the city, charging $1.75 for the first mile, $1.25 for each additional mile.

VISITOR INFORMATION: The **Lincoln City Convention and Visitor's Bureau,** U.S. 101 and 40th Street (tel. 503/994-3070, 994-3078, or 994-8378, or toll free 800/452-2151 in Oregon), awaits.

USEFUL INFORMATION: For **police or emergency medical help,** dial 503/994-3636. . . . For **weather** information, call 503/994-5851. . . . You'll find a coin laundry at **Oceanlake Coin Laundry,** 2100 N.W. U.S. 101 (no telephone).

WHERE TO STAY: Lincoln City's most luxurious resort is not actually in Lincoln City but in adjoining Gleneden Beach. Oregon's wild and rugged coast could not be more beautifully complimented than it is by **Salishan Lodge,** U.S. 101, Gleneden Beach, OR 97388 (tel. 503/764-2371), a large—and very complete—resort development that blends so well into the rock and pine it seems to have been planted here. That feeling of outdoors indoors continues as you enter a room to find a brick fireplace blazing, deep-green or gold color schemes that evoke the forest, and original artwork by Oregon artists saluting the rugged land in which they live. Very large rooms (especially Chieftain units) are tucked away in a series of lodges faced in cedar and connected to the main lodge by covered walkways. They spare nothing in modern comfort. Big bathrooms are stocked with fluffy towels and special soaps. Balconies offer beautiful views of deep forests. At the main lodge the elegance grows yet more grandiose. Behind imposing wood doors is a large but cozy lobby, its chic furnishings clustered about a massive gray stone fireplace. Beyond lie the lodge's three outstanding restaurants, each a study in contemporary décor and fine cooking.

Most impressive of those is the Dining Room, a trilevel room where tall windows offer a view of pines and the ocean. A huge wine list, with something like 20,000 bottles, one of the state's most extensive, is supplemented by continental cuisine with plenty of fresh broiled local seafood and a variety of steaks and roasts. Pacific brioche is a combination of Oregon shrimp, Dungeness crab, and scallops sautéed with mushrooms and cognac and topped with a lobster sauce, the lot presented in pastry; potlatch salmon is lashed to alderwood planks and broiled over charcoal; beef tenderloin filets are sautéed tableside with morel sauce and brandy. Prices are in the $17 to $25 range. Cedar Tree, a light, airy dining room, is open for brunch. The Sun Room is the hotel's breakfast and light-meals spot, serving Brie in brioche, steak tips in a wine sauce with mushrooms and onions, Pacific crab cakes, good salads, and buttery clam chowder for prices in the $5 to $10 range.

You will never lack for something to do here, dawn to dusk and well beyond. A huge recreational facility offers indoor tennis courts and you'll also find an indoor swimming pool, whirlpool, 18-hole golf course, gymnasiums, sauna, and children's playground. So extensive is the property, which recently added 48 rooms, that you would do well to specify the sport you plan to play, so workers can set you up in quarters that cut down the walk. Salishan is not right on the ocean but has three miles of beach on a secluded, driftwood-trimmed peninsula half a mile away. Hikers will be happy here too, with plenty of walking space across a 750-acre nature preserve and 1,000 adjoining acres! Even shoppers will be pleased: a small lobby gift shop is supplemented by a large cluster of shops called the Marketplace at Salishan. Marketplace Restaurant, a comparatively new addition to this plush resort, has a lovely view of the bay through acres of windows and a menu that focuses on light foods, taco salads, fish and chips, seafood chowder, and the like, for prices in the $7 to $10 range. There is entertainment in the cozy Attic Lounge, where a fireglow illuminates beamed ceilings. You can even participate in a wine-tasting of some of those thousands of wines at the resort's Wine Cellar, a candlelit underground hideaway with an oak refectory table. They'll take you on a guided tour of it for the asking. In summer at Salishan you pay $115 a day for rooms, $152 for chieftain rooms with bay or gulf view, king-size bed, sitting room, and refrigerator in addition to the fireplace, television, and balconies of all rooms. Packages include golf or tennis fees, and some save you money on winter getaways. Rates drop $15 to $25 in winter months from November through April.

The **Inn at Spanish Head,** 4009 S.W. U.S. 101, Lincoln City, OR 97367 (tel. 503/996-2161, or toll free 800/547-5235 in the Northwest, 800/452-8127 in Oregon), is a cliffside resort that occupies an enviable position on rugged rocks overlooking the Pacific. Step through the glass sliding doors that cover one wall of your room out onto a balcony and you can see all the way to . . . well, Hawaii, maybe. That Spanish influence is carried out architecturally at this tile-roofed building with arches that curve across the front of the building. A ten-story hotel, the Inn at Spanish Head has accommodations in 146 quarters ranging from a spacious bedroom to apartments with one or two bedrooms. The inn, a condominium resort, specializes in large apartments, many of them decked out in furnishings reminiscent of Spain.

On the tenth floor you'll find a lounge and restaurant specializing in fresh seafood that seems all the fresher with all that water right outside the wide windows. Beachcombers head *down* ten floors to the sand, while sunseekers may just stretch out by the hotel's pool. A sauna offers solace from cold winter days.

Rates at the inn from July to October are $66 to $74 for a room with twin or queen-size beds; $100 for one-bedroom apartments with a kitchen, living room with a convertible couch, and bedroom; $167 for a two-bedroom large enough for four or six.

D-Sands, 171 S.W. U.S. 101, Lincoln City, OR 97367 (tel. 503/994-5244), is indeed right on de sands and has quite nice rooms and spacious efficiency apartments, many with balconies and some with fireplaces. You'll find a heated indoor pool here and a sauna. The rates are $60 to $69 double.

The **Nordic Motel,** 2133 N.W. Inlet, Lincoln City, OR 97367 (tel. 503/994-8145, or toll free 800/452-3558), is another ocean-overlook spot with Nordically clean rooms and housekeeping apartments, some suites with fireplaces. The Nordic also has a heated indoor swimming pool, saunas, and a strip of beach out front. Rates are $46 to $64 double.

If you're camping in the region, try **Lincoln City KOA,** 5298 N.E. Park Lane, Otis, OR 97367 (tel. 503/994-2961), a recreational vehicle campground charging $9 to $12 for hookups.

WHERE TO DINE: Most restaurants in town are strictly quickies, but a few offer pleasant atmosphere and good food.

The restaurants at **Salishan Lodge** (see "Where to Stay") are quite chic and elegant places to dine. The Dining Room (tel. 503/764-3635) is open from 6 to 10 p.m. daily; the Marketplace (tel. 503/764-3681), from 11:30 a.m. to 10 p.m. daily; Cedar Tree (tel. 503/764-3644), for Sunday brunch from 10 a.m. to 2 p.m.; and the Sun Room (tel. 503/764-3644), open from 7 a.m. to 9 p.m. daily.

Bay House, 5911 S.W. U.S. 101 (tel. 503/996-3222), provides a dramatic setting in jewel tones of burgundy and forest green with two rock fireplaces adding a glow to artwork adorning this view-some spot. As you look out over Siletz Bay, you dine on continental preparations of fresh local seafood with some interesting touches like toppings of sesame seeds or Dijon mustard. Homemade chutneys are not to be missed. Prices are in the $11 to $15 range, and hours are 6 to 10 p.m. daily, changing occasionally in winter, so give them a call.

The décor at **Pier 101,** 415 S.W. U.S. 101 (no phone), centers on stained-glass windows abetted by plenty of plants and wood trim. A contemporary spot, Pier 101 is a local favorite for its spicy chowder, simple preparations of fresh seafood, fish stew, burgers, and fish and chips. Prices are in the $4 to $12 range, and the restaurant is open from 11:30 a.m. to 10 p.m. Monday through Saturday and from noon to 10 p.m. on Sunday.

Clam chowder is the specialty of the **Road's End Dory Cove Restaurant,** on Logan Road in Road's End (tel. 503/994-5180), and it draws crowds of folks who love to tuck into this thick, rich soup on a cool or busy day. We hear they stand in line for a gargantuan hamburger—the 2¼-pounder!—and judging from the good grilled fish and homemade desserts, they know what they're doing. Many prices are in the under-$10 range, and the hours are 11:30 to 9 p.m. six days, noon to 8 p.m. on Sunday.

The **Inn at Spanish Head** (see "Where to Stay"; tel. 503/996-2161) also has quite good continental fare and seafood in the $10 to $17 range from 8 a.m. to 10 p.m. daily.

To sample some Oregon wines, try **Oak Knoll Winery / Shipwreck Cellars,** 3521 S.W. U.S. 101 (tel. 503/996-3221); **Wine and Cheese Restaurant,** 4095B N.W. Logan Rd. (tel. 503/994-3736); or **Honeywood's Winery,** 30 S.E. U.S. 101 (tel. 503/994-2755).

WHAT TO SEE AND DO: Most of what you will want to see and do here is connected with the sea, but there are a few other points of interest you may find amusing.

One of those is **Lacey's Doll and Antique Museum,** 3400 N. U.S. 101 (tel. 503/994-2392), where you can spend hours looking at more than 4,000 dolls, some weird, some wonderful, and some quite old. Admission is 50¢.

A similarly amusing way to spend a rainy day is at the **Christmas Cottage,** 3305 S.W. U.S. 101, Lincoln City (tel. 503/996-2230), where Barbara Jenkins, decked out in Bavarian lederhosen, reigns over a magic kingdom of Christmas decorations. Not just another Christmas shop, this store specializes in hard-to-get, handmade Austrian and German decorations ranging from wooden-soldier nutcrackers to delicate glass ornaments made in the Bavarian mountains. Many of the enchanting items she buys and sells go on to become collector's items, their precision crafting a rarity in a world of mass production.

The **Sitka Center for Art and Ecology,** 2225 N.W. U.S. 101 (tel.

503/994-5485), has classes, concerts, lectures, and exhibits in summer. Check to see what's going on when you're here.

SPORTS: With all that beach and water around, it stands to reason that most of the sports activities in the area would be involved with one or the other. There are, however, a few other things to do along these sandy shores. To find a **charter boat** to take you out after the big ones, head for nearby Depoe Bay, about 15 miles south on U.S. 101.

Neskowin Riding Stables, 48490 Hawk Ave., Neskowin (tel. 503/392-3277), will find a horse for you to ride for $15 an hour. **Windsurfing Oregon,** 4933 S.W. U.S. 101 (tel. 503/996-3957), can provide boards and instruction to get you sailing. The region's number-one resort, **Salishan,** has an 18-hole **golf course** that charges $22 greens fees; **tennis** fees on indoor or outdoor courts are $14 indoor, $8 outdoor, with a $7 early-morning or late-night special. You can also go hiking across the grounds (see information on Salishan in "Where to Stay").

SPECIAL EVENTS: In May the city sponsors a **kite festival** that's a rip-roaring event, usually literally. On Memorial Day in late May the **Fleet of Flowers** is a colorful event. A **Sandcastle Building Contest** in August draws some sand artists with a great sense of humor as well as a winning way with a pail. On the third Saturday in September, nearby Depoe Bay celebrates with a **salmon bake** that's a favorite with local seafood fans. Finally, in October Lincoln City has a **Driftwood Derby** race with horses galloping down the beach and tops that in the same month with the **Clam Chowder Cook-Off.**

SHOPPING: Art and antique shops abound in this small town with more than a dozen history-sellers present. Most of those are along U.S. 101. Among these are **Birds Nest,** 1542 N.E. U.S. 101 (tel. 503/994-5551); **Herself Antiques,** 1439 S.W. U.S. 101 (tel. 503/994-9566); and **Panache Antiques,** 3536 S.E. U.S. 101 (tel. 503/996-2268).

A long list of art and craft galleries offers you a choice ranging from Indian art to fabrics, candles, and leather. Most of those also are right along U.S. 101. **Nelscott Neighborhood,** on U.S. 101 two miles south of the D River, has about 20 shops between 32nd and 35th Streets. **Mossy Creek Pottery** at Mossy Creek, on Immonen Road in nearby Gleneden Beach (tel. 503/996–2415), offers some fine handmade porcelain and stoneware. Finally **Hawk Creek Gallery,** U.S. 101, Neskowin (tel. 503/392-3879), about 200 yards on the right just outside Neskowin, features jewelry, portraiture, paintings, and pottery by local artisans.

Barnacle Bill's, 2174 N. U.S. 101 (tel. 503/994-3022), has acquired quite a reputation for its smoked salmon, albacore tuna, and other local sea treats.

12. TILLAMOOK

Tillamook County and its namesake center, the town of Tillamook, produce Oregon's famed Tillamook cheeses. You could make up quite a picnic from local food products that include sausages, jerky, smoked meats, and pepper bacon, French cheese, fresh shrimp and crab, good breads, and pastries and, in Nehalem, wines.

An inland town, Tillamook has several tiny oceanside neighbors including **Netarts,** a community popular for beachcombing and for digging up fat, succulent razor clams, and **Oceanside,** where beaches are popular with sea lions that live here year round in a refuge officially known as Three Arch Rocks National Bird and Sea Lion Refuge. May and June are the best months to see the tiny new sea lion pups playing in the surf.

At **Cape Meares,** a pretty, but inactive lighthouse lording over the rugged coastline below is the focus of many a photograph. You can explore caves in the cliffs here, try your hand at surf fishing and collect a houseful of silvery gray driftwood, Japanese net floats, and perhaps agates.

GETTING THERE: U.S. 101, the coastal road, runs through Tillamook on its way north. If you turn west on 3rd Street, that road becomes Bay Ocean Road and takes you to Cape Meares. If you turn right on 3rd Street when the road splits, you can visit Netarts, Oceanside, and Agate Beach.

VISITOR INFORMATION: Stop by the big, wooden barn-like structure that is home to the **Tillamook County Chamber of Commerce,** 3705 U.S. 101 North, Tillamook, OR 97141 (tel. 503/842-7525). You'll find it, fittingly enough, right next to the factory that produces the area's most famous product: cheese.

WHERE TO STAY: There is a limited selection of hostelries here. **Mar-Claire Motel,** 11 Main Ave., Tillamook, OR 97141 (tel. 503/842-7571, or toll free 800/528-1234), is a pleasant place with 47 units, some of them motel rooms, some one- or two-bedroom apartments. Mar-Claire, which is part of the Best Western chain, has a heated swimming pool, a whirlpool, and a restaurant and cocktail lounge. Rates are $42 to $46.

If you're traveling in a recreational vehicle, you can park at **Old Mill Marina and RV Park,** 100 3rd St., Garibaldi, OR 97118 (tel. 503/322-3242). You can launch and moor a boat right here too. Full hookups are $11 a day in summer months, $8 in winter.

In Tillamook the **Tillamook KOA,** 11880 U.S. 101 South, Tillamook, OR 97141 (tel. 503/842-4779), has a store, laundry, campfire program, and a play area for the youngsters. Hookups are $10 to $20.

WHERE TO DINE: In the rustic little villages here you will find some atmospheric dining places. An old country store has been converted to a tiny café called **Roseanna's Café,** Ore. 131, Oceanside (tel. 503/842-7351). Fresh oysters in a variety of presentations are the chief lure. They're served on a tiny outside deck in summer or inside in an equally tiny, rustic spot with paddle fans and plants. Just plain oysters are supplemented by oyster quiche—even an oyster burger! Prices are in the $9 to $12 bracket, and Roseanna's homemade desserts and fruit pies are not to be missed. Hours are 8 a.m. to 9 p.m. weekdays, to 10 p.m. on Saturday and Sunday.

In nearby Wheeler the **River Sea Inn,** 380 Marine Dr., two miles south of Nehalem (tel. 503/368-5789), occupies a riverside setting and echoes its surrounding gardens inside with dangling plants. A tranquil spot, River Sea Inn features simple cooking of chicken, veal, prime rib, seafood stew, and salmon. Mexico's cuisine is saluted here with some of the popular south-of-the-border options. River Sea Inn is open daily May to September from 11:30 a.m. to 10 p.m., opening at 9 a.m. on Sunday. In winter months the inn may close on Monday and Wednesday. You'll find dinner prices here in the $6 to $11 range.

WHAT TO SEE AND DO: This city is the only one on the Oregon coast in which you can eat your way through a tour! Stop in at the Tillamook Chamber of Commerce and ask for a "Cheese, Food, and Wine Tour" brochure. That map will show you the way to a winery, some seafood shops, a bakery, and a sausage and smoked-meats shop.

While you're here, you'll also want to get a look at how they make this popular Tillamook cheese at the **Tillamook County Creamery,** U.S. 101 about two miles north of Tillamook (tel. 503/842-4484), open from 8 a.m. to 6 p.m. daily. Another cheese factory here is the **Blue Heron French Cheese Factory,** 2001 Blue Heron Dr., off U.S. 101 north of town (tel. 503/842-8281), open daily from 9 a.m. to 6 p.m. in summer, 10 a.m. to 5 p.m. in winter.

Three rocky headlands have a connecting road that takes you on a **scenic drive** through 40 miles of some of the most dramatic scenery on this coastline. To take the 20-mile drive, which stretches between Cape Meares on the north to Cape Lookout in the center and Cape Kiwanda on the south, take 3rd Street west in Tillamook to Cape Meares, then head south to the other two capes, returning to U.S. 101 at Pacific City.

If you're headed north, leave U.S. 101 at Cloverdale and head west, following the signs to Cape Kiwanda State Park. At Cape Meares you can also see a tree that once had the dubious honor of appearing in Ripley's "Believe It or Not": the Octopus Tree, actually seven trees in one!

In Tillamook the **County Pioneer Museum,** 2106 Second Ave., at the junction of U.S. 101 and Ore. 6 (tel. 503/842-4553), offers an interesting look at early pioneer furnishings in a replica of a pioneer home. It's housed in a 1905 building that served as the county courthouse for many years. The museum is open from 8:30 a.m. to 5 p.m. Monday through Saturday and noon to 5 p.m. on Sunday from May to October; closed Monday other months. Admission is $1 for adults and 50¢ for students 12 to 17.

If you turn east onto a gravel road about five miles south of Tillamook, you'll find yourself at **Munson Creek Falls,** where a cascade drops 319 feet, the highest drop in the Coastal Range. You'll have to walk a short trail to the viewpoints, but even toddlers can manage it.

HAVE A CRABBY DAY: You may think Peanuts' Lucy has cornered the market on crabbing, but hereabouts crabbing has an entirely different meaning. If you want to try your hand at this tasty sport, you will need to buy a crab ring or pot, which is actually a trap for crabs. You put bait in the trap and let it sink to the bottom, where curious crabs will enter it in search of the food inside. About 20 minutes later up comes the pot and, with any luck, your dinner. Bayside boat-rental companies can provide you with all the equipment, and some even cook the live crabs for you by plunging them into boiling salt water for 15 minutes or so. Maps showing the best crabbing and clamming grounds around are available from the chamber of commerce. You are permitted to take 12 Dungeness crabs a day. The best clamming grounds are at Netarts Bay, where very low tides let you get in there and dig easily.

13. CANNON BEACH

Cannon Beach is a tiny oceanfront community off the beaten path, so it's as quiet as it is beautiful. Certainly Clark of Lewis and Clark fame found it so when he climbed Tillamook Head hill with an Indian guide to hunt for a whale that had been sighted near the beach. Struck, as many are, by the view, Clark said he "beheld the grandest and most pleasing prospect which my eyes ever surveyed." People in this beach community couldn't agree more—and their admittedly biased opinion is echoed by thousands of families and beach lovers who come each summer to take yet another look at the sand and sea views that abound here.

Surprisingly, these communities are popular in winter too, when romantic souls come to watch spectacular storms send the waters of the Pacific crashing across the sands. Those storms can be so ferocious, in fact, that Tillamook Rock lighthouse keepers have reported winds vicious enough to throw large rocks through their warning lights and toss fish 100 feet in the air onto the decks of the lighthouse! But in most seasons the waters here are lullingly quiet, tiny wavelets lapping against the shoreline. You can play on no less than seven miles of beach and get a look at Haystack Rock, one of the world's largest free-standing monoliths, formed by volcanic action eons ago. More than 200 feet high, the rock welcomes puffins and sea gulls to its tops and shelters mussels, starfish, and other sea creatures at its feet.

"Downtown" Cannon Beach is about three blocks long, a warren of gaily painted shops and restaurants. Cannon Beach was named, by the way, for a cannon that dropped off a shipwrecked schooner called *Shark* in 1846 and washed up on the beach.

GETTING THERE: U.S. 101 joins Ore. 26 just north of the first of four westbound roads that will take you to Cannon Beach. That first road becomes **Hemlock Street,** the town's one main street. If you miss the first turn, you'll come to a second entrance called Sunset Boulevard, which runs west to Hemlock Street. The third and fourth entrances are at Tolovana Park, which goes west to Old Oregon Coast Hwy., Tolovana Park's only main street. That Old Oregon Coast Hwy. becomes Hemlock Street in Cannon Beach, the more northerly of these two side-by-side villages.

VISITOR INFORMATION: You'll find a helpful group of workers at the **Cannon Beach Chamber of Commerce,** 201 E. 2nd St., Cannon Beach, OR 97110 (tel. 503/436-2623).

WHERE TO STAY: A couple of large resorts are supplemented by many tiny, rustic beach havens.

The **Surfview Resort Motel,** 1400 S. Hemlock St., Cannon Beach, OR 97110 (tel. 503/436-1566, or 503/222-5432 in Portland, or toll free 800/547-6423, 800/452-7132 in Oregon), occupies an enviable spot high on a dune overlooking the beach. This handsome cluster of gray-shingled buildings is as up-to-date as it can be, with glass doors opening onto balconies overlooking the ocean. A very large condominium-style development with rooms and apartments, the Surfview lies in the shadow of a great monolithic outcropping called Haystack Rock. In your room you will find the most contemporary furnishings in subtle but cheerful colors. Some accommodations have wood-burning fireplaces, and some are luxurious spa suites with a big whirlpool bath surrounded by mirrors. All rooms have refrigerators; some have complete kitchens with dishwashers. Logs for your fireplace and morning newspapers are delivered to your door. There's even a complete indoor recreation complex featuring everything from a heated swimming pool with an aqua slide and pool for the youngsters to a heated whirlpool, a sauna, and exercise room. Rates at the Surfview, which has a cozy restaurant serving all three meals, are $55 to $86 with a less thrilling view; $99 double for an oceanfront room with king- or queen-size bed, fireplace, and refrigerator; $139 for a room with a private whirlpool. Larger accommodations for three to six people are available.

The **Tolovana Inn,** two miles south of town on U.S. 101 (P.O. Box 165), Tolovana Park, OR 97145 (tel. 503/436-2211, or toll free 800/333-8890), has similar contemporary, gray-shingled architecture and 170 spacious accommodations. Some units have kitchens and fireplaces and many have a smashing view of the ocean. One- and two-bedroom apartments are ideal for families. Among the amenities at this resort are a heated indoor pool, a sauna and whirlpool, playground, and billiard room. Tolovana charges $40 to $90 for most quarters, up to $155 for larger apartments.

Other accommodations in Cannon Beach are much smaller but every bit as nice. Try, for instance, **Argonauta Motel,** 188 W. 2nd St. (P.O. Box 3), Cannon Beach, OR 97110 (tel. 503/436-2601), which has just five units for rent. Some of these are in a small two-story weathered-wood building adjoining the owner's matching oceanfront home surrounded by a profusion of rainbow-colored flowers. For small but pretty quarters with a kitchen, fireplace, double beds, and television you pay $46 to $89, depending on size of the quarters.

Across the street, **Lands End Motel,** 263 W. 2nd St., Cannon Beach, OR 97110 (tel. 503/436-2264), is also a silvery gray building with balconied apartments, some with bay windows. It's just a few feet from Ecola Creek where Lewis and Clark found that whale we mentioned earlier (they named the creek Ecola, a word meaning big fish). All units have fireplaces and fully equipped kitchens, and some have queen-size beds. You can't miss ocean views, either: every room has either a 90° or 180° outlook. Lands End charges $65 to $86 double.

The **Sea Sprite Motel,** Nebesna Street and Ocean Front, Cannon Beach, OR 97110 (tel. 503/436-2266), has six units, some featuring kitchen and fireplace, right at the oceanfront. Large rooms are decorated with homey touches like plants, books, rocking chair, or Franklin fireplace. The Sea Sprite provides the firewood for you and even has some picnic tables where you can sit outside and enjoy the sunshine. Four more units, owned by the same people, are tucked in a cluster of little cottages called the **Hearthstone Inn** at Hemlock and Jackson Streets (same address and phone as Sea Sprite), one block from the sea. Here one spacious studio has a blue tile kitchen counter in one corner, a convertible couch near the fireplace, and plants growing in a loft. Pretty stone fireplaces add a glow to the day or evening. Rates are $49 to $65 for quarters at the Sea Sprite, $104 for a two-bedroom cottage for four on the oceanfront, and $60 a day double at the Hearthstone Inn. November through March the inns offer a three-night "Storm Watcher / Whale Watcher Special" Sunday through Thursday at a 20% to 40% reduction.

For camping, the **Sea Ranch Trailer Village,** U.S. 101A (tel. 503/436-2815), has hookups and tent sites, and rents horses for riding on the beach. Fees are $10 to $12.

WHERE TO DINE: Several small but interesting restaurants operate in Cannon Beach and nearby Tolovana. One of those is **Daggatt's at Tolovana,** Tolovana Inn, Tolovana Park (tel. 503/436-2211). Here chrome and wicker furnishings attractively upholstered are drawn up to linen-clad tables under tall windows overlooking Haystack Rock. You dine on seafood that comes right out of the sea you're looking at, or steaks that are aged and tender. Fresh flowers often adorn tables of this attractive restaurant, which features prices in the $10 to $15 range. Hours are 7 a.m. to 9 p.m. daily, closing an hour earlier in winter months.

Café de la Mer, 1287 S. Hemlock St., Cannon Beach (tel. 503/436-1179), is another tiny spot in this equally tiny town that has acquired local—and occasionally statewide—renown. First, it's a pretty place with a bright greenhouse-patio filled with plants. Second, its seafood is skillfully cooked and topped with delicate sauces and fresh herbs. Café de la Mer goes all-out: mint leaf in your water glass, homemade pâtés, and sinfully wonderful desserts. In between you dine on fresh salmon accented with a touch of Dijon mustard. Marvelous Oregon scallops appear in a coquilles St-Jacques. You'll pay $12.50 to $18.50 for dinner here, including fresh homemade hot or cold soups, a shrimp-topped salad sprinkled with bleu cheese, and crunchy breads.

Mideast flavors spice the cooking of the **Brass Lantern,** 1020 Hemlock St., about ten blocks south (tel. 503/436-2412), where the whole family gets in on the production of evening meals. Dilled yogurt tops salads; pita bread's on the menu; hummus is a starter. Seafood like snapper, scallops, and halibut is treated to a variety of subtle spicing and is often served with unexpected vegetable accompaniments. The Brass Lantern gets raves for a Sunday brunch laced with seafood specialties, perhaps crab in an omelet. Prices are in the $10 to $15 range for dinner, and the restaurant is open from 5:30 to 9 p.m. Friday through Tuesday; closed Wednesday and Thursday in winter.

The **Lazy Susan Café,** 126 Hemlock St., in Coaster Square (tel. 503/436-2816), a bright and woodsy small restaurant, serves hearty breakfasts that are welcome in this often-breezy seaside town. Lunches focus on interesting sandwiches served on fresh whole-grain bread and accompanied by minty tabbouleh salad. Quiche, salad niçoise, a good poached chicken with curry mayonnaise, plus lots of homemade desserts are on the menu too. Hours are 7 a.m. to 2 p.m. daily, and prices are in the $5 range.

The **Lemon Tree Inn,** 140 N. Hemlock St. (tel. 503/436-2918), is a casual and appealing spot that turns out omelets all day long. Homemade clam chowder is always bubbling on the back burner, and fresh seafood is wonderful. Fat, juicy hamburgers are a big draw here too. In summer you can dine outside. Prices are in the $6 to $11 range for most things. To show you how casual things are in this town, the Lemon Tree Inn cites its "usual" hours as 7 a.m. to 9 p.m.

You never know what will be on the menu at an eclectic spot called the **Bistro Restaurant and Lounge,** 263 N. Hemlock St. (tel. 503/436-2661). Read the blackboard to see what's being dished up, then count on walking out of this candlelit restaurant stuffed. They don't do things in a small way here. What looks like pounds of pasta may be accompanied by fat slabs of garlic bread topped with tomato and cheese. Other choices are likely to include Italian flavors—lasagne, for instance, and plenty of seafood or shellfish, perhaps with a touch of garlic. You'll pay about $10 to $15 for dinner here, or less, including openers of marinated vegetables. Hours are 11:30 a.m. to 2:30 p.m. for lunch, from 5 to 10 p.m. for dinner, and much later in the bar, which keeps serving until the wee hours. Open daily except Tuesday and Wednesday.

You can learn a little about whaling and tuck into a whale of a good dinner at the same time at **The Whaler,** 200 N. Hemlock St. (tel. 503/436-2821). Inspired by the huge creatures that splutter and splash practically past their doorstep, the Whaler salutes those intrepid whaler-sailors with cuisine that would have been pretty sophisticated for a whaler's palate: crab rarebit, chicken Kiev, big steaks, "Greenie" salads that salute greenhorn whalers, and "lobcouse," a bouillabaisse concoction that won the crab-cooking Olympics recently and is a sealubber's fantasy of salmon, shellfish, Dungeness crab, and white fish simmered gently in seafood stock and served in a tureen. Prices are in the $10 to $15 range for dinner entrees, which include soup or salad, vegetable, relishes, and garlic or cheese bread. The Whaler opens at 7 a.m. for bountiful breakfasts of homemade cinnamon buns; ham, egg, and cheese breakfast sandwiches on an English muffin; fried eggs in grilled sourdough bread—even clams and eggs! Lunch and dinner are also served at the restaurant, which features entertainment nightly in summer, on weekends in winter, closing when the last die-hard heads home.

On warm summer days a picnic along this pretty beach may be just what is in order. If that's your plan, stock up at **Osburn's Grocery Store and Delicatessen,** 240 N. Hemlock St. (tel. 503/436-2234), where the railed front porch of this turn-of-the-century building is a favorite and always-occupied sittin' spot in town. Hours are 9 a.m. to 7 p.m. daily.

NIGHTLIFE: Bill's Tavern, 100 Main St. (tel. 503/436-2202), is a favored local watering spot that dishes up hamburgers, jumbo hot dogs, and homemade chili along with the potables. You'll pay just a few dollars for food, beer, and wine at the tavern, which is open from 11 a.m. to whenever things slow down.

The **Coaster Theater,** 108 N. Hemlock St. (tel. 503/436-1242), has a year-round schedule of dance, concerts, chamber orchestras, jazz, and ballet. Call them to see what's playing when you're here.

Daggatt's at Tolovana, 3400 S. Hemlock St. (tel. 503/436-1111), often has entertainment in its cocktail lounge. Likewise the **Driftwood Inn,** 179 N. Hemlock (tel. 503/436-2439); the **Bistro Restaurant and Lounge,** 263 N. Hemlock (tel. 503/436-2261); the **Wayfarer Restaurant,** 1190 Pacific Dr. (tel. 503/436-1108); and the **Whaler Restaurant,** 200 N. Hemlock (tel. 503/436-2821).

WHAT TO DO AND SEE: Naturally the beach and its rock formations are the primary lure here, but there are a few other diversions. Among those is **Ecola State Park and Indian Beach,** a lovely place to hike, fish, picnic, surf, or just sit and watch the scenery. It was here Clark is said to have come with an Indian friend who told of a whale that had come ashore. When he got there, Clark did indeed find a beached whale and bought many pounds of meat and oil from Indians who were some of the first grocers out this way. You'll find the park a mile north of the city. In it are six miles of beachfront.

Oswald State Park, three miles south of town (tel. 503/238-7488), has a primitive but very pretty campground set deep in the trees, about a quarter-mile walk from the parking lot and a short distance from a sea cove and tidal pool. It's a pleasant place to while away some time, whether or not you're camping there.

Haystack Rock is one of the largest monoliths in the world and is lovely to look at but forbidden to hold: climbing it is prohibited, but you can poke around the tidal pools beneath it.

SPORTS: Seaside and Cannon Beach are just a short distance apart so they share major sporting facilities. Look in the Seaside section to see more sporting possibilities. Right here in Cannon Beach you can go riding on the sands with horses supplied by **Sea Ranch Stables,** on the north end of town at Ecola Creek (tel. 503/436-2815). Rides are $15 an hour. You can rent a bike at **Mike's Bike Shop,** 248 Spruce St. (tel. 503/436-1266). Rates are in the $10- to $12-a-day range, depending on the size of bike you seek. In Seaside you can **rent a moped** at Seaside Arco, 231 S. Holladay Dr. (tel. 503/738-7015).

SPECIAL EVENTS: In mid-June Cannon Beach welcomes hordes of sand lovers who come here to create—or cheer others on—at the annual **Sandcastle/Children's Parade.** Sandcastles may have started out as something for the kids, but in Cannon Beach the youngsters take a back seat to imaginative souls who create some of the darnedest things out of huge piles of sand. A miniature Notre-Dame, for instance!

SHOPPING: Cannon Beach and its spectacular scenery have attracted quite an artists' colony, so you will find a number of interesting craft shops here. Among those are **Once upon a Breeze,** 241 N. Hemlock St. (tel. 503/436-1112), a kite shop; **Hannen Glass Studio,** 987 S. Hemlock (tel. 503/436-2761), specializing in stained glass; **All This and Heaven Too,** Cannon Beach Mall (tel. 503/436-2504), featuring pottery and other crafts; and **Tis the Season,** 182 N. Hemlock (tel. 503/436-1400), a year-round Christmas shop. **Bruce's Candy Kitchen,** 265 N. Hemlock (tel. 503/436-2641), cooks up saltwater taffy and its own chocolate.

14. SEASIDE

Thanks to its miles of wide beach and its proximity to Portland, Seaside is among the most popular beach resorts on the Oregon coast. On a visit here you can stretch out on the beach beside a campfire and watch the stars glowing overhead. The wide beaches become even wider in the summer months, when low tides leave hundreds of feet of beach uncovered and available for tentative toes and toddlers. So wide is it, in fact, that between neighboring Gearhart and Fort Stevens Park, ten miles away, you can actually drive right on the sand. Just be sure the tide is out—and staying that way!

While this lively town has some undeniable touches of honky-tonk seaside schmaltz, the taffy-pull atmosphere is so innocently appealing you'll forgive it those touches of commerciality. It has its historic side too: Lewis and Clark came here, making this the end of their Lewis and Clark Trail, no matter what other claims to that fame there may be. Those two early travelers built something here called a "salt cairn," a walled-in fire over which buckets of salt water were boiled to extract the salt. They boiled hundreds of gallons of water to collect 20 pounds of salt for their long journey home, back the way they had come.

Today Seaside's pride and joy is its Promenade, a wide strip of concrete built above the sands and stretching for two miles of beautiful views. Busy all day, "the Prom," as it's called hereabouts, slows up a bit at night, when it's given over to strolling young lovers and wave watchers. As darkness falls, some bonfires dot the beach, lighting the night for groups of laughing partiers roasting hot dogs and for youngsters rolling out sleeping bags on the sand.

GETTING THERE / GETTING AROUND: On its long way down the coast, **U.S. 101** runs right through the middle of Gearhart and moves on to adjacent Seaside, where the road is called **Roosevelt Drive.** U.S. 26 from Portland joins U.S. 101 here just south of town.

Broadway, the main east-west artery is all decked out in greenery following a million-dollar renewal project. It is also the main route across the Necanicum River to the Promenade and the beach. There are four other crossings: from north to south they are 12th Avenue, 1st Avenue, Avenue B, and Avenue G. Broadway is also the street that divides north and south in Seaside. East-west streets north of Broadway are numbered; those south of Broadway are lettered.

Seaside's Promenade has south and north ends and many addresses refer to one end or the other. So you'll know which is which, the dividing point is the turnaround at the seaside end of Broadway. North of that, or to the right as you face the sea, is North Promenade and left is South Promenade.

Seaside Transit (tel. 503/738-7083 or 325-4274) operates the only bus service in town and offers trips to Gearhart, Warrenton, and Astoria, with a number of local stops in Seaside. Fares range from 50¢ to $2.

VISITOR INFORMATION: The **Seaside Chamber of Commerce** is at 7 Roosevelt Dr. (which is U.S. 101) and Broadway, Seaside, OR 97318 (tel. 503/738-6391).

USEFUL INFORMATION: For **police or medical emergency,** dial 911. . . . Minor medical needs are handled by **Seaside Minor Emergency Center,** 580 Ave. U (tel. 503/738-5571), open from 8:30 a.m. to 7 p.m. weekdays, closing at 4 p.m. on Saturday and on call Sunday. . . . For **24-hour car repair** needs, call Ralph's, U.S. 101 at Main Gearhart Junction (tel. 503/738-5702). . . . **Seaside Stop and Go grocery,** 860 S. Roosevelt Dr. (U.S. 101) (tel. 503/738-7300), is open 24 hours. . . . If you're here with youngsters, ask at the chamber for a copy of **"A Kid's Guide to Seaside"** prepared by some pretty savvy sixth-graders at Seaside Heights School.

WHERE TO STAY: Seaside has dozens of small motels at the beach or near it. Tops among those is **Ebb Tide Motel,** 300 N. Prom, Seaside, OR 97138 (tel. 503/738-8371), which has a terrific view out across miles of sand. Alongside the city's oceanfront Promenade, the motel has really attractive rooms outfitted in blues and complete with small gaslog-burning fireplaces. Wide windows overlook the Promenade and the sea. Some rooms have kitchenettes tucked into one corner. All are attractively decorated with tall wall units that hide televisions. You'll find a heated swimming pool, color television, and sauna here too. **Hi Tide,** 30 Ave. G, Seaside, OR 97138 (tel. 503/738-8414), is a sister property, smaller but of similar quality. Also on the oceanfront, Hi Tide has 64 attractive units with gas-burning fireplaces, refrigerators, cable color television, movies, and many efficiency accommodations. There's a heated indoor pool and whirlpool. Rates at both motels are $69 to $78 double, and rooms for as many as four people are available.

The **Hallmark Seaside,** 441 Second Ave., Seaside, OR 97138 (tel. 503/738-9581), is a new and quite lovely motel. Although it isn't on the beach, it's just two blocks away. A 47-unit motel, it is scrupulously maintained and comes with all the comforts from heated indoor swimming pool to saunas, whirlpool, and color television. Ten of the rooms are efficiencies, and there are two- and three-bedroom units. Rates are $54 to $57 double, $80 to $125 for larger units.

The **Riverside Inn,** 430 S. Holladay, Seaside, OR 97138 (tel. 503/738-8254), is a cozy little bed-and-breakfast inn on the Necanicum River, just a few blocks from the beach. Greenery grows up trellises here and frames frilly drapes and shutters. Three of the inn's seven rooms are in cottages with beamed ceilings and skylights, four in the main house. All have private bath and color television, and each has its own entrance. Puffy comforters cover ruffled flounces here in this comfortable riverside home where quiet gardens beckon and a dinghy is moored at a dock. Guests gather mornings in the main house for a complimentary continental breakfast of baked muffins and breads, juices and fresh fruit, and specially blended coffees and teas. Rates at the inn are $35 to $65 year round.

Bed-and-breakfast fans should head for **Gaston's Beachside Bed and Breakfast,** 921 S. Promenade, Seaside, OR 97138 (tel. 503/738-8320), where they will find an oceanfront home now welcoming guests. Just four blocks from downtown Seaside, the house has beautiful views of the Pacific and of breakers cascading over a long sand beach. There are only two rooms here and they share a bathroom.

WHERE TO DINE: Seaside has an interesting variety of restaurants, from quickie eateries to some lovely tranquil dining rooms. One of the most appealing of those is a locally famous restaurant called the **Crab Broiler,** at the junction of U.S. 26 and U.S. 101, four miles south of Seaside (tel. 503/738-5313), long the area favorite. Way back in 1946 owner Bill Daggatt and his wife, June, moved to Seaside, bought the Crab Broiler, and turned it into a phenomenal success. Today the Daggatt family is still operating the restaurant, which has multiplied in size several times and is now a warren of rooms, each lovely. Among the additions is a pond and serene Japanese garden where the restaurant's resident kittens romp on a small island. Start an evening here in the cozy—and often packed—cocktail lounge, then move in to dinner in the handsome dining rooms lined with walls of glass and decked out in fresh flowers and candles and highlighted with handsome polished antiques. In the series of dining rooms, young and eager helpers work hard to make your evening a success. They get plenty of aid from a good kitchen that prepares the best of fresh local seafood, naturally focusing on crab, from crab au gratin topped with Oregon Tillamook cheddar to barbecued crab to cracked crab and Dungeness crab legs. Lots of other seafood, including some terrific razor clams, are on the menu, plus thick, aged steaks. Breads are a specialty: select from a choice of French, garlic, or bleu-cheese-topped. Don't leave without at least one piece of the best blackberry pie that will ever cross your lips! Prices are in the $10 to $15 range for entree, breads, salad, potatoes. The Crab Broiler is open from 11:30 a.m. to 9 p.m. daily, and from 9:30 a.m. to 1:30 p.m. for Sunday champagne brunch.

Norma's, 20 N. Columbia St. (tel. 503/738-6170), offers nautically atmospheric surroundings, fresh seafood simply prepared, hearty chowder, and, the topper, peanut butter pie, for prices in the $10 to $15 range. Hours are 11 a.m. to 10 p.m. daily from May to September, to 7 p.m. in other open months; closed November through February.

When Mexico's on your mind, **El Toucan,** 311 Broadway (tel. 503/738-8417), should be. Top of the list here is a tostada grande packed with beef, beans, lettuce, shredded cheddar cheese, olives, and tomatoes. Add tacos, a rich chili burrito topped with green salsa and melted cheddar, and finish off with a buñuelo with ice cream. Only a trencherman could leave here with a $10 check, and the rest of us should get away for under $5. Hours are noon to 2:30 a.m. daily.

Kan's Chop Suey Inn, 402 Broadway (tel. 503/738-8781), has been cooking up Chinese specialties for three generations. Delicately fried shrimp is a treat, both for the light hand at the fry table and for the fresh shrimp that goes into it. An interesting option is beef chow yuk, strips of sliced top sirloin sautéed with wine, stir-fried with bok choy, onions, green peppers, and mushrooms, and topped with a special sauce. Also on the list: ginger beef, steaks and seafood, chow meins, chop suey, sweet-and-sour selections, and of course, eggrolls. No price tops $10, and most are in the $5 to $7 bracket. Hours are 5 to 10 p.m. daily.

If you're looking for quick meals near the beach, **Geri's,** 1101 S. Holladay (tel. 503/738-9701), offers a dozen different fruit-filled breakfast crêpes, broasted chicken, and home-cooked dinners, luncheon salads, and sandwiches. The atmosphere is bright and attractive, with three walls of glass, a brown and bright-green décor. Geri's prices are in the $6 to $12 range for dinner. Open from 6 a.m. to 9 p.m. Sunday through Thursday, closing an hour later on weekends.

In Gearhart the **Fish House,** 4340 U.S. 101 North (tel. 503/738-5468), is a very casual spot that will feed a family of four for less than $15! Included in that are 12 pieces of fish, a platter of potato wedges, and salad or chowder for each person. If you want a selection of fish, prawns, and oysters, four people can eat for $16 and six for just under $25. If there are just two of you, you can dine on oysters, salmon, prawns, scallops, razor clams, cod, steamed clams, and fish and chips for $6 to $10. Hours are 11:30 a.m. to 10 p.m. daily.

Seaside Stop and Go, 860 S. Roosevelt Dr. (U.S. 101) (tel. 503/738-7300), will fix up sandwiches and salads for a beach picnic or feed you right from a list of overstuffed sandwiches. Prices are in the $3 to $5 bracket. Stop and Go is open 24 hours every day.

NIGHTLIFE: After-dark activities in Seaside center on the region's cocktail lounges. For pop music, try the **Bounty Bar & Grill,** 504 Broadway (tel. 503/738-7342), and for a variety of music, stop in at the **Frontier Club,** 405 Broadway (tel. 503/738-9466).

El Toucan, the Mexican restaurant at 311 Broadway (tel. 503/738-8417), has top-40s rock music Wednesday through Sunday in summer months, and in

Gearhart, **Captain Morgan's,** U.S. 101 at Gearhart Junction (tel. 503/738-6782), usually has some musical entertainment.

WHAT TO SEE AND DO: Most of the amusements here are nature's beauties, but a few are also historical.

The official **end of the Lewis and Clark Trail** is at the oceanside end of Broadway and is called the Turnaround. At Lewis and Clark Drive on the South Promenade, you'll find a reconstruction of the **Salt Cairn,** at which Lewis and Clark and their helpers boiled hundreds of gallons of water to extract 20 pounds of salt, 12 of which they packed to take with them on the long trek back home.

More history at the **Seaside Historical Museum,** 570 Necanicum Dr. (no phone), where the pioneer history of this region is outlined.

At the **Seaside Aquarium,** Second Avenue at the Prom (tel. 503/738-6211), you can have a tête-à-tête with an octopus and giggle over the antics of the seals. Hours are 9 a.m. to 8 p.m. daily June through August, 9 a.m. to 5 p.m. Wednesday through Sunday in other months. Admission is $4 for adults, $1.50 for children 6 to 12.

SPECIAL EVENTS: In April the city salutes the beach that has earned the city its place in the sun since Lewis and Clark stopped here a century ago. The citywide party is called the **Beach Festival.** In July Seaside plays host to the **Miss Oregon Pageant** and in August draws crowds to an **Arts and Crafts Festival.**

SPORTS: You won't lack for some energetic way to spend your time here. You'll find a **public swimming pool** and other sports facilities in **Broadway Park,** 1140 Broadway.

Trail's End, a half mile east of Seaside on U.S. 101 at Lewis and Clark Road (tel. 503/738-5690), will saddle up a bronc and show you where to ride the beaches. Riding is by appointment only and the fee is $14 an hour.

You can play **Bingo,** if that can be considered a sport, at **Old Spa,** 80 Ave. A (tel. 503/738-9632), on the north end of Beach Drive. Games are at 7:30 p.m. on Monday, Wednesday, Thursday, and Friday.

If it's tee time, **Seaside Golf Course,** 451 Ave. U (tel. 503/738-5261), can accommodate you. Greens on this nine-hole course are open dawn to dark and fees are $6. In Gearhart the **Gearhart Golf Links,** 1000 N.W. Marion St. at Gearhart-by-the-Sea (tel. 503/738-5248), is one of the oldest in the Northwest, with huge old trees shading its 18 holes. Greens fees are $15 for 18 holes, $11 for nine.

RED FLAG AT MORNING, SWIMMER'S WARNING: Glittering and tempting as they are, these waters are often pretty chilly. If you're planning a surfing trip, winter is the best time for surfing, but you'll need a wet suit. Any time you swim on these beaches you should be accompanied by another swimmer and keep an eye on the lifeguards, who are generally on duty from 10 a.m. to 5 p.m. Areas protected by lifeguards have flags posted at either end of the covered region. Riptides and other dangerous tidal conditions are not uncommon on these beaches. If there are dangers, lifeguards will hoist a red flag. That means get out immediately and stay out until further notice. If lifeguards hoist a yellow flag, it means swim with caution.

Don't swim or play around drifting logs. Logs move. Their tremendous waterlogged weight can crush you.

If you are caught in a rip tide, which moves swiftly out to sea, don't fight against it. Instead, raise one arm straight up as a signal for help. While you're waiting for help or if there isn't any, assume a horizontal position in the water and swim parallel to the shoreline. Don't try to fight against the tide. If you swim parallel to the riptide, you will move out of it into incoming top water that will help bring you into shore. Above all, keep your wits about you and don't panic.

In some shallow water you may encounter sudden drop-offs where water currents have washed out the sand, leaving a deep hole called a crab hole. Again, keep your head and keep swimming parallel to the shore and you will shortly encounter a sand bar and shallow water.

Even if you are just exploring near the water or on the rocks, keep a wary eye on the sea. Waves called "sneakers" are high waves that come in suddenly without warning, just as their name suggests. Be wary of incoming tides too, and don't let yourself be trapped on rocks and headlands.

15. ASTORIA

Astoria and environs call themselves the Sunset Empire, Oregon being full of empire builders of one kind or another.

GETTING THERE: Portland is the transportation hub for the area, so check the "Getting There" section in Chapter IX on Portland to learn how to get here. If you're driving, U.S. 101 runs up the Oregon coast and through Astoria. From Portland, take U.S. 30 along the river or U.S. 26, which joins U.S. 101 just south of Seaside.

VISITOR INFORMATION: There are a lot of details you'll want to know about this beautiful land, so be sure to stop at the visitor centers and chambers of commerce along the way.

The **Astoria Area Chamber of Commerce** occupies interesting quarters in the city's historic Port Docks Building, just off U.S. 101 at the Astoria Bridge to Washington. It's official address is Port Dock Building (P.O. Box 176), Astoria, OR 97103 (tel. 503/325-6311). Another office of the chamber is easy to find too: just look for the huge Astoria Column looming over the city from the top of Coxcomb Hill, and you'll find a branch office at the base of it.

USEFUL INFORMATION: For **police or medical emergency,** call 911; for non-emergencies, call the Oregon State Police at 503/325-2231. . . . You'll find a **drive-through car wash** at Wild Willy's, 75 W. Marine Dr. (tel. 503/325-4142). . . . OK Tire Stores, 65 U.S. 101A (tel. 503/325-2861 or 325-0233), has **24-hour road service** for emergency car repair. . . . Johnson's 469 One Stop, 469 W. Marine Dr. (tel. 503/325-4365), is open from 6 a.m. to midnight daily for **gasoline, beer, wine, snacks, and camping needs.** . . . The **Compleat Photographer,** 457 14th St. (tel. 503/325-0759), can process film overnight.

WHERE TO STAY: Pickin's are a bit sparse in this small town, but we've turned up four for your selection.

The **Crest Motel,** 53 Leif Ericson Dr., Astoria, OR 97103 (tel. 503/325-3141), occupies an enviable top-of-the-hill perch with beautiful views way down to the Columbia River and across to Washington. Set in a stand of pines, the Crest is a simple spot with three separate buildings housing simply furnished rooms, most of which have glass doors, leading to balconies overlooking that mighty river. In-room coffee-making equipment lets you get your morning caffeine down quickly. You can also order a continental breakfast at the motel office that will be delivered between 8 and 10 a.m. for $2 each. The Crest charges $38.50 to $62.50 for a room with one or two queen-size beds.

The **Thunderbird Motor Inn,** 400 Industry St., Astoria, OR 97103 (tel.

503/325-7373, or toll free 800/547-8010), has one of its clean and attractive chain motels here. Rates are $62 to $73 for two.

The **Rosebriar Inn,** 635 14th St., Astoria, OR 97103 (tel. 503/325-7427), occupies an 1895 house built by a local banker and lovingly restored by its three hostess/owners. Leaded glass sparkles, woodwork glows, and lace curtains cover the windows. Under a carved plaster ceiling are antiques, wood floors, and wing chairs. Rosebriar has eight rooms, all with wash basins but most sharing a bath. Mornings you are treated to a buffet in the wainscoted dining room. Rates are $38 to $50, including breakfast. No children under 12 are accepted.

If you're **camping** in the region, try **Fort Stevens,** U.S. 101, Hammond, OR 97121 (tel. 503/861-1671, or toll free 800/452-5687), where you'll find full hookups for $10 a night. Plan time to explore the Fort Stevens Military Reservation with seven concrete gun batteries that date back to the Civil War.

WHERE TO DINE: Astoria is rather short on top dining spots but there are a few restaurants featuring basic home-cooking. One of those is the **Ship Inn,** 1 2nd St. (tel. 503/325-0033). Beer batter on the fish is made with dusky Guinness stout, and seafood is fresh from the waters practically outside the door. British touches abound, from the Cornish pastries to the pubby look of the place. Prices are in the $10 to $15 range, and hours are 11:30 a.m. to 9:30 p.m. weekdays, to 10:30 p.m. weekends.

At the foot of 10th Street is an interesting conglomeration of shops and home of the **Pier 11 Feedstore Restaurant and Lounge,** 77 11th St. (tel. 503/325-0279). You can watch the busy river traffic as you dine among baskets of ferns on good homemade soups, salads, and sandwiches. Service is from 11 a.m. to 10 p.m. and prices are in the $10 to $15 range.

Café Uniontown, 218 W. Marine Dr. (tel. 503/325-3005), is nestled down under the Astoria Bridge and produces some good down-home cooking in the $10 to $15 range or less. A special feature of the restaurant is the 1907 logback bar in the lounge. Hours are 11 a.m. to 9 p.m. daily.

Columbian Café, 1114 Marine Dr. (tel. 503/325-2233), is a favorite with locals who come here to down crêpes, vegetarian selections, and plenty of the region's abundant seafood. A deli next door is a good spot for snacks and has an espresso bar too. Hours at the Columbia are 11 a.m. to 10 p.m. daily.

NIGHTLIFE: Astoria is a quiet town in which most of the nightlife is a gathering of friends in a lounge or piano bar. Here's a look at some of the more convivial spots.

Café Uniontown, 218 W. Marine Dr. (tel. 503/325-3005), offers piano music on weekend evenings, while **Hazel's Tavern,** 1313 Marine Dr., has Sunday jam sessions.

You'll find bluegrass and jazz at **Ship Inn,** 1 2nd St. (tel. 503/325-0033). Top-40s fans head for the **Thunderbird Seafare,** 400 Industry St. (tel. 503/325-7373).

More information on the lounge scene is in the *Daily Astorian.*

WHAT TO SEE AND DO: As you might suspect from Astoria's location at the mouth of the Columbia River, pioneer adventurers and travelers figure in its early history.

Fort Clatsop National Memorial, about six miles south of Astoria off U.S. 101 (tel. 503/861-2471), commemorates those two famous Northwest travelers, Meriwether Lewis and William Clark, who spent the winter of 1805–1806 here. During that winter the two men labored over their journals to fashion an organized account of their long journey from St. Louis—over 4,000 miles. Here

Clark prepared maps of what he and Lewis had seen, maps that would contribute to the settlement of the Pacific Northwest. Routes described by Indians they had met along the way or who came to the fort to trade caused the team to change their return route in hopes of finding an easier way home.

At the visitor center you can learn something of the hardships of the 106 days Lewis and Clark spent here. Among other difficulties it rained every day for 94 of those days! Clothing rotted, everyone suffered from aches, pains, and rheumatism, and fleas in the bedding were so bad Lewis complained he was unable to get a full night's sleep!

As part of the park's Living History program, park personnel dress in period costumes so authentic you expect Lewis and Clark to step out to greet you. They demonstrate some of the frontier skills necessary to survive the winter of 1805–1806 and show you how dugout canoes were built, fires started by hand, hides tanned, and maps and clothing made. Begin your tour with a stop at the reconstruction of Fort Clatsop, a log stockade 50 feet square with two rows of cabins separated by a parade ground. Lewis and Clark occupied the Captains' Quarters, while Toussaint Charbonneau and his wife, Sacajawea, and their baby lived in the Charbonneau quarters nearby. The reconstruction follows the floor plan and dimensions drawn by Clark on the elkhide cover of his fieldbook. You can also see the canoe landing at which Lewis and Clark and their little band pulled up their canoes and marked the end of their long journey that began at the Mississippi River and ended at the Pacific Ocean. You can walk the trail they did to the camp spring. Fort Clatsop's rangers-in-costume presentations are from mid-June to September only; the park is open from 8 a.m. to 5 p.m. daily through mid-June, to 6 p.m. June 15 to September. Admission is free.

With its sheltered harbor just off the Pacific, Astoria has had a long and historic association with the sea. You can learn something about that union at the **Columbia River Maritime Museum,** 1729 Marine Dr. (tel. 503/325-2323). A fine display here includes ship models, a restored Columbia River lightship, scrimshaw, charts, whaling equipment, and the reconstructed bridge of a navy destroyer. Hours are 9:30 a.m. to 5 p.m. daily from April to October; closed Monday October through March. Admission is $3 for adults and $2 for children.

In 1942 the quiet of this riverside city was shattered by the blast of a Japanese submarine, which fired on Battery Russell in **Fort Stevens,** nine miles southwest of Astoria off U.S. 101. You can hear all about that shelling, the first time the mainland had been attacked by a foreign power since the War of 1812. Take a look at the concrete gun emplacements and explore the underground tunnels daily from 9 a.m. to 5 p.m. The shattered hulk of a four-masted ship that went aground here in 1906 can also be seen. A park has a nice beach and trails, a lake, and an interpretive center open from 10 a.m. to 6 p.m. mid-June through September and noon to 4 p.m. in other months. Admission is $1 a car on weekends and holidays in summer.

Fort Astoria is what put Astoria on early maps. Built by John Jacob Astor's Pacific Fur Company in 1811, the fort was handed over to the British during the War of 1812 and returned in 1818. In recent years it has been partially restored, so you can get a look at it on Exchange Street between 14th and 15th Streets. Open daily 24 hours, and admission is free.

High atop Coscomb Hill you'll see a strange monolithic column towering over the city. It was put there by descendants of John Jacob Astor and his Great Northern Railroad workers who constructed the 125-foot **Astoria Column** in 1926 to outline in friezes the history of this city. Up 166 steps you can get a spectacular view of the Columbia River. It's open from 8 a.m. to dusk daily.

This city was, after all, once the stomping grounds of J. J. Astor, who did not do things in a small way. That's why you will see many **Victorian homes** here, their fancy fretwork and towering cupolas reminding you that this was one of the nation's major ports in the mid-1800s. You can see many of them on a walk or drive down Franklin Avenue from 7th to 17th Streets.

At 8th and Exchange Streets, you'll find a glamorous Victorian mansion built in 1885 by Columbia River bar pilot Capt. George Flavel and now the region's **Clatsop County Historical Museum** (tel. 503/325-2203). **Flavel House** is home to an intriguing collection of period art and artifacts. You can also get more information on other Victorian homes here. Hours are 10 a.m. to 5 p.m. daily May to October, 11 a.m. to 4 p.m. November through April. Admission is $3 for adults, $1 for children under 12.

The **Clatsop County Historical Society's Heritage Center** is in Astoria's old city hall at 16th and Exchange Streets. Built in 1905, the museum features audio-visual programs on the area's history. Hours and admission fees are the same as at the Flavel House. **Jewell Wildlife Management Area** may be 27 miles east of Astoria (on Ore. 202), but it's worth the drive to see huge elks munching away as contentedly as cows right along the road.

SPECIAL EVENTS: Each June Astoria sponsors a two-day **Scandinavian Festival** featuring typical foods, music, and dance of the city's Scandinavian ancestors. Hydroplanes race and salmon bake at the four-day **Astoria Regatta** each August. In the same month you can attend the **Clatsop County Rodeo.**

Most special activities in this region occur from mid-July to mid-August when the weather's the most predictable and school's out for the youngsters. One of those activities is the Astor Street Opry Company's presentation (see "Art and Cultural Activities") which performs on weekends and often on Thursday. Another is the **Lewis and Clark Outdoor Drama,** a stage production with professional actors. Called *Journey to the Pacific,* the drama first took to the boards in the summer of 1988 and was expected to continue in ensuing years. Lewis and Clark go on stage at Broadway Park in the nearby town of Seaside at 8 p.m. on Thursday, Friday, and Saturday. Admission is $6.50 for adults, $5.50 for students.

SPORTS: Water sports predominate in coastal Oregon, and Astoria is no exception, although we did manage to dig out a few terra firma sports.

Salmon fishing is king of the sports in this region, so if you've ever thought it might be fun to pull one of those hungry creatures out of the sea, now is the time to have a go at it. Call **Thunderbird Charters,** 352 Industry St. (tel. 503/325-7990), to arrange a fishing trip. Salmon fishing trips are $30 to $50 per person.

If golf is your passion, you can play at **Gearhart Golf Links,** at Gearhart-by-the-Sea Resort, 10 N. Marion St. in Gearhart (tel. 503/738-8331 or 738-5248), a public course charging $15 for 18 holes of golf—one of the oldest courses in the state.

You'll find free public **tennis courts** at Columbia Court, 37th and Leif Erikson Drive, and lighted courts at Niagara Park, corner of 6th Street and Niagara Avenue.

Hikers can walk the **Oregon Coast Trail,** a 62-mile hike south to Tillamook from Fort Stevens, nine miles west of Astoria. Some of the trail takes you along the beach, while other parts explore the hills.

ART AND CULTURAL ACTIVITIES: Westerners are enthusiastic about the arts. Here are a few selections to be enjoyed in this small town.

Astor Street Opry Company presents oldtime live theater fun with an original historical musical melodrama *Shanghaied in Astoria.* The show, complete with cabaret-style vaudeville acts, is presented weekends July to mid-August in a historical landmark, the John Jacob Astor Hotel, 14th and Commercial Streets, Astoria. Admission is $7 for adults, $5 for children. For information about performances, call the Astoria Chamber of Commerce at 503/325-6311.

In nearby Oysterville the **Shoalwater Storytellers** perform Saturday afternoons at 4 p.m. in the Oysterville Church, 100 Main St.

The **Northwest Oregon Symphonic Band** has free Sunday-afternoon concerts at Tapiola Park and other locations. The Astoria Parks and Recreation Department (tel. 503/325-7275) will know where and when.

The **Fourteenth Street Gallery**, 14th and Duane Streets (tel. 503/325-0759), offers works by local artists, as does the **Port Shop**, 1 Portway St. on Pier 1 (tel. 503/325-3175).

SHOPPING: Among other things, here's another chance to buy some of that salmon you've been hearing so much about.

Josephson's Smoked Salmon, 106 Marine Dr., Astoria, OR 97103 (tel. 503/325-2190), will mail smoked Chinook salmon, Nova-style lox, smoked sockeye salmon, and kippered products, including sturgeon, cod, and tuna, to you or to friends. Quite well known, the company has been featured in several national gourmet magazines.

Pier II, 77 11th St., has 50 shops.

MOUNT ST. HELENS AND SOUTHWEST WASHINGTON

□ □ □

Washington's window on the Pacific is a lonelier, less-visited place than Oregon's rugged and popular coastline. In many sections windswept strips of rock, deserted stretches of sand, and dramatic promontories combine to create a hauntingly lovely land better adapted to meditation than to merriment.

Surf rolls in to little fanfare here, and sands are trampled only by an occasional clammer. Settlements are little more than villages in most places, hopping-off spots for fishing trips or crabbing expeditions.

Nature smiles upon this coastline, according it a bounteous array of salmon, oysters, crabs, and clams. But what Nature giveth, Nature can—and does—take away.

In the aftermath of El Niño, the warm wind that swept incessantly across the western coastline of the Americas, this Pacific coast has suffered a dramatic decline in the salmon for which it became famous. As if that weren't enough, a parasite attacked the razor clams, diminishing that population, which now, however, is rebounding rapidly.

Finally, national economics dealt a blow to the southwest sector of the state. Tough economic times, past and present, have slowed and at times halted the progress of its lifeblood industry, logging.

All those adversities have left these lonely beaches even lonelier, but what Nature takes, Nature may, on a whim, give back. Little by little salmon seem to be returning, and the razor clams are increasing, while oysters are still plucked from the waters by the thousands.

And Nature may have bestowed even a greater gift, albeit a backhanded offering. On May 18, 1980, a pleasant symmetrical mountain named Mount St. Helens rumbled ominously, puffed and smoked, and seconds later blew its top off, creating a massive volcanic explosion that destroyed everything in its path.

That top-blowing volcano became a maimed mountain, but in the process also became one of southwestern Washington's most important tourist attractions. This eerie ash-covered land of silence is a must-see sight, a theater of the bizarre in which nature's bone-chilling power has produced a scene of devastation and destruction you will never forget. If the truth of that one-time television commercial chuckle "Don't mess with Mother Nature" is ever to come home to you with a vengeance, it will do so on the slopes of Mount St. Helens.

Cataclysmic eruptions of that magnitude are rare anywhere in the world and were heard only in legends here, but less violent natural forces have long been at work in southwestern Washington. Its waters can be treacherous, its inland territory rugged enough to discourage all but the hardiest adventurers. Even Lewis and Clark, who certainly classified as hardy, found this coastline more than a little discomfiting. On their 1805–1806 winter visit, they encountered cold, fierce gales. Tremendous winds, the explorers wrote, picked up drifting logs "five or six feet thick" and tossed them across their camp with the ease of a child playing pick-up-sticks. Violent salt sprays drenched them, leaving them chilled and miserable "and drenched with rain during the rest of the day."

So terrifyingly treacherous have the offshore waters near the Columbia River been, in fact, that a jutting promontory lighthouse was long ago dubbed Cape Disappointment. In the waters surrounding it, more than 200 ships have foundered in evil seas once called the "graveyard of the Pacific."

Southwestern Washington and its coastline have dangerous waters to one side—and frequent waters from above. Yes, it does rain often here, but not quite as much as it does farther north along the Olympic Peninsula—although that's little consolation to drubbed dwellers hereabouts. Rain in measurable quantities falls about one day of every two, but nature compensates a little by narrowing the temperature extremes: Washington's southern coast registers just a few 90° days in summer and never, or practically never, gets a 0° reading.

Westport is the fishing center, where seas filled with salmon and tuna are a sirens' call to many a hopeful angler. Other dedicated nature-lovers—who also think highly of their palates—come to these rich waters to search for fat, sassy, and ever-so-speedy razor clams. Those clams find these silty-sandy waters a delightful homeland and are quite determined to stay in it—so determined that when chased by clamdiggers they can burrow in at a speed of nine inches a minute!

Other visitors, eyeing a still-different dinner menu, come here lugging crab rings to lure those claw-ful creatures into a starring appearance in their private dinner theater.

Waters are cool here and home to thousands, maybe millions of oysters that are unkind to unshod toes, so only a few open strips of sand lure swimmers. That means, of course, that the rugged beauty of cliff and coastal village has not been desecrated by golden arches. Here, as in few places along the Pacific coast, you will see time, if not standing still, at least moving only at oyster speed. To visit these unspoiled coastal lands is to understand why those who live here often view the absence of change as progress.

1. ORIENTATION

GETTING THERE AND GETTING AROUND: Washington's coastline is so refreshingly remote that driving around by car is virtually the only way to explore it. To do that you can fly into Portland and rent a car, as outlined in our discussion of that city in Chapter IX.

If you're already in possession of a car, you can begin your explorations on the south coast and work your way north or vice versa. In keeping with the general see-the-Northwest plan we've outlined in the Introduction to this guide, we've opted for the vice versa here—south to north.

To get to the coast from Vancouver and points south, take I-5 to Longview-Kelso, where Wash. 4 branches off to the west, meeting Wash. 401, which heads south to the Columbia River, where it winds along the river to join U.S. 101. You will see a turnoff to Wash. 103 and Ilwaco. You must branch off on Wash. 103, which heads north to Long Beach, Ocean Park, Nahcotta, Oysterville, and the end of the peninsula.

There is no bridge across Willapa Bay, so to get to Grayland and Westport you must return on Wash. 103, back the way you came, to U.S. 101, and head north toward South Bend. Just north of Raymond, Wash. 105 heads west to Grayland and Westport, looping around to rejoin U.S. 101, which goes on north to the Olympic Peninsula.

You can also get to the Washington coast beaches from Astoria on U.S. 101, which crosses the Columbia River there on its northward journey to the Olympic Peninsula.

From Seattle or other points on the north coast, I-5 will get you to Chehalis, where you pick up Wash. 6 headed west toward South Bend. From there stick with U.S. 101 along the coastline to its junction with Wash. 103, which is the only road up the long beachy peninsula that creates Willapa Bay.

Amtrak trains also run through on their way to Portland and Seattle and points beyond. Stops include Centralia, Kelso-Longview, and Vancouver.

Pacific Transit System operates buses around the peninsula beach area and into Astoria. Fares are 35¢ to 50¢. For route information, give them a call at 206/642-4475.

2. LONGVIEW / KELSO

Deep in the pine forest that covers many thousands of acres in Washington and neighboring Oregon, Kelso was the boom town, a village that welcomed raucous loggers to lusty Allen Street where barbershops provided backroom bathtubs and upstairs alcoves offered other pleasures. Longview proceeded at a somewhat more sedate pace. It was, in fact, one of the nation's first planned communities, carefully plotted in 1918 by Kansas City planners intent on constructing attractive residential neighborhoods well away from the mainstream of mill life.

Both these communities were hard hit when the Depression slowed the nation's demand for wood. World War II, however, turned many of the mills operating along the Columbia River into defense plants, and prosperity continued for many years. In the late 1970s a worsening national economy led to strikes and lay-offs that closed many mills forever and, at one point, raised the jobless rate to a whopping 20%. Recovery remains very slow; the local economy is tied to the lumber industry, on the apron strings of the massive Weyerhaeuser Company or to Reynolds Metals Company, the region's two major employers.

Longview has other, even less controllable, worries. When Mount St. Helens exploded in 1980, it created a natural phenomenon that is both worth and worry for these small communities. Now tourists come here to travel the slopes of the mountain for a look at what nature has wrought, and their money is providing an unexpected bounty.

Beneath their delight with increased tourism, however, lies the dread that should the mountain explode again, as one Longview resident put it, a grim

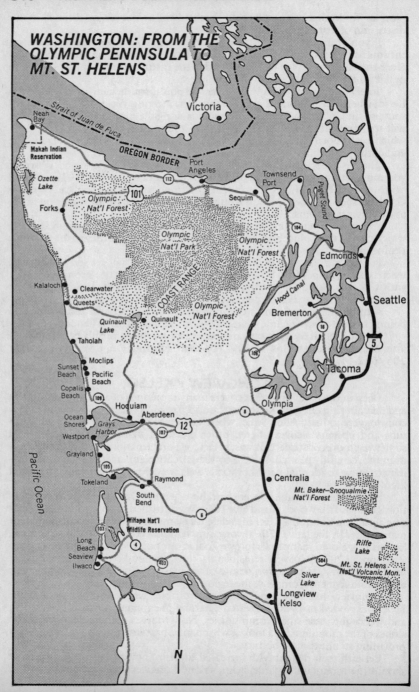

WASHINGTON: FROM THE OLYMPIC PENINSULA TO MT. ST. HELENS

frown creasing an otherwise sunny countenance, "We may be an American Pompeii."

There is every reason for concern. Only hastily constructed dams hold back a mountain of muck that continues even now to pour down the Toutle Valley aimed straight at Longview and Kelso. Other engineering devices help drain clogged mountain lakes, but that engineering was not designed to stop the great rush of water, mud, and debris that could engulf this region if the mountain were to repeat its fiery act. In fact, residents fear, if the mountain erupts again, the land you will be seeing on a drive through here will be a river of mud flowing from mountain to sea, engulfing these small towns. In short, Longview, Kelso, and environs face annihilation.

In the meantime they provide a stopping spot for an expedition up the side of Mount St. Helens to see just the power of nature here. There are few more awesome experiences in the world.

GETTING THERE AND GETTING AROUND: Longview-Kelso

Airporter (tel. toll free 800/247-2272) has a daily shuttle service from Portland International Airport at 9 a.m., noon, and 4 p.m. The fare is $13.50 each way.

You can also get here on **Amtrak** (tel. toll free 800/872-7245), which pulls into the station at 501 S. First Ave. in Kelso. Three trains, the morning *Mount Rainier,* the afternoon *Coast Starlight,* and the early-evening *Pioneer,* depart daily on north- and southbound schedules.

Owl Taxi (tel. 206/577-6777) operates in the region, charging $2 at the flagdrop, $1.50 a mile.

Greyhound (tel. 206/423-7330) operates from a terminal at the Broadway Hotel, 1150 Broadway.

Community Urban Bus Service (tel. 206/577-3399) operates daily except Sunday throughout the region, charging 50¢ for adults.

VISITOR INFORMATION: Folks at the **Longview Chamber of Commerce,** 1563 Olympia Way, Longview, WA 98632 (tel. 206/423-8400), can help you find the best things to see and do. The **Kelso Chamber of Commerce,** exit 39 from I-5 (P.O. Box 58), Kelso, WA 98626 (tel. 206/577-8058), will be happy to see you too.

You'll also find a visitor center called the **Skamania County Chamber of Commerce,** P.O. Box 86, Raymond, WA 98577 (tel. 509/427-8456), operating an information center at Skamania County Parks and Recreation Fair Grounds. In Raymond, the **Raymond Chamber of Commerce,** 625 Heath St. (P.O. Box 86), Raymond, WA 98577 (tel. 206/942-5419), operates a visitor information center one block from the junction of U.S. 101 and Wash. 6.

The **Tourist Regional Information Program,** P.O. Box 128, Longview, WA 98632 (tel. 206/577-3321), is a helpful organization with promotional activities for several cities. The staff can provide you with a 48-page guide to the region detailing what to see and do and how to get there to see and do it.

WHERE TO STAY: There's a decided dearth of anything approaching a resort, but there are one or two places to settle in reasonable comfort. Tops among those is in nearby Cathlamet (pronounced "Cath-*lam*-ette"). A quiet, small town, Cathlamet is a market center for an island dairy farming region called Puget Island and a fishermen's village called Skamokawa (pronounced "Ska-*mawk*-away") that occupies a picturesque slough riddled with waterways. At nearby Grays River is the state's last remaining usable covered bridge.

As to accommodations here, well, first the bad news. Loveliest spot in town, the **Cathlamet Hotel,** 67 Main St., Cathlamet, WA 98612 (tel. 206/795-8751), was at last check suffering serious reverses and had closed. Hope springs eternal, of course, so it would be a good idea to check its current status if you're headed this way. A dozen or so rooms had been delightfully updated, some but not all with baths, and were renting for all of $25. Next door Pierre's, 69 Main St. (tel. 206/795-3997), a renovated 1886 home served as a pretty restaurant but may also be closed. We mention this only because exciting accommodations are so few and far between up this way that it's worth checking in the hope that they may have regenerated.

In the Longview/Kelso area the **Thunderbird Motor Inn,** 510 Kelso Dr., Kelso, WA 98626 (tel. 206/636-4400, or toll free 800/547-8010), is the showiest spot, a 163-unit motor inn just off I-5 at exit 39. Rooms are comfortably appointed and all have cable color televisions, radios, and telephones. A heated pool plus a wading pool for the youngsters await, as does a pleasant dining room featuring quite moderate prices in the $10 to $15 range and a coffeeshop. Rates at the Thunderbird Motor Inn are $64 to $67 double, about $8 less single.

WHERE TO DINE: Once again, there are not multitudinous choices but some interesting ones. Steaks are the main lure at **Henri's,** 4545 Ocean Beach Hwy., Longview (tel. 206/425-7970), supplemented by good salads, oft-praised seafood soups, and some good wines. You'll pay $12 to $17 for the continental cooking and French atmosphere here from 11 a.m. to 10 p.m. Monday through Friday, and 4:30 to 10 p.m. on Saturday; closed Sunday.

To dine amid 1920s atmosphere, stop in at the **Monticello Hotel,** 1405 17th Ave., Longview (tel. 206/425-9900). Located downtown right across from Civic Center Park, the Monticello has rooms as well as food—29 of them, two with fireplaces—in a motel unit attached to this 1923 hotel. In the hotel's dining room you'll find a wide variety of selections ranging from Mexican specialties to seafood and beef. Atmosphere is chic, prices are in the $10 to $14 range for dinner, and hours are 6:30 a.m. to 2 p.m. for breakfast and lunch, 5 to 10 p.m. for dinner, opening and closing a bit later on weekends. There's frequently entertainment in the adjoining lounge too.

WHAT TO SEE AND DO: The chief lure, of course, is Mount St. Helens, the fiery volcano whose explosive display was viewed with awe by all the nation a few years back. Such a long story is the mountain that we've accorded it a section of its own immediately following this one. In the meantime there are a couple of interesting things to do right here in these flatlands.

Port of Longview, 10 Port Way (tel. 206/425-3305), is a busy place with lots of marine activity. You can take a look at the port on free tours that operate daily at 10:30 a.m. and 1:30 p.m. daily in summer months from June to September. In other months the port can arrange a tour, but you'll need to call them in advance to make arrangements.

Reynolds Metals Co., 4029 Industrial Way (tel. 206/425-2800), will take you on a ride around their facility and show you some slides that explain how everything operates. Tours are on the last Tuesday of the month at 1 p.m. and they're free.

Lake Sacajawea Park honors that Indian maiden with a park that stretches for more than a mile of water and rolling lawns trimmed with rhododendrons that bloom in spectacular pink magnificence each May.

For sports fans there are **tennis courts** at John Null Park, Pacific Way and Corman Road (no phone). There's a challenging 18-hole golf course, **Mint Valley Municipal Golf Course,** par 71, at Ocean Beach Hwy. and 38th Street, just north of Wash. 4 (tel. 206/577-3395). Greens fees are $9 to $16.

The **Lewis River,** which ambles, and sometimes races, down from the mountains to meet the Columbia, offers playing spaces for fishing and white-water enthusiasts, while dammed waters along its flow provide ponds for sailing. You can trace the course of the river and visit **Merwin Lake** on Wash. 203, which loops around from I-5. Merwin is a favored swimming hole in the area and has picnic sites and boat-launching areas. Two other lakes in the area, **Yale Lake** and **Swift Lake,** like much of the terrain around Mount St. Helens, are operated by Pacific Power as recreational lands.

At **Cedar Creek** you can see a pioneer grist mill built in 1876. To find it, go nine miles east of Woodland on Rte. 16 and left on Grist Mill Road.

Ferry rides are fun, and there are so few of them left in the nation that riding when you can is almost obligatory. If you'd like to chug around a bit here, you can take a ferry across the Columbia River from Cathlamet by first crossing to Puget Island. Westport, Oregon, is the ferry's destination, and the fare is $2. Puget Island, by the way, is known as "Little Norway" for its many Scandinavian inhabitants.

Cathlamet is home to the **Columbia White-Tailed Deer National Wildlife Refuge,** which shelters those animals on nearly 5,000 acres. You'll find the visitor center, which will help you find your way to sighting spots, just off Wash. 4 at Cathlamet (tel. 206/795-3915). The best time to see deer is early morning and dusk.

Kelso likes to call itself the "Smelt Capital of the World," and they don't mean the past tense of "smell." The reference, of course, is to the little fish that run up the Cowlitz River into the clutches of smelt lovers. You can watch or participate with nothing more complicated than a pair of hip boots and a net.

Finally, that **covered bridge:** it's on a small marked local road near the town of Grays River, which is just west of Skamokawa. You'll find the bridge 1¾ miles south of Grays River off Wash. 4. Built in 1905, it is said to be the oldest covered span in the Northwest and the only one left in Washington.

3. VISITING MOUNT ST. HELENS

It was a sunny Sunday morning in May. In Portland, comic strips were being read over breakfast, clothes laid out for churchgoers, picnics and rafting trips being planned, while late sleepers were just rolling over to shut off the alarm. It was 8:25 a.m., and in minutes there would be no more sleep in Portland this Sunday morning.

With a great roar, a mountain that had been a somnolent southwest sentinel for more than a century awoke, the blast of its explosion and earthquakes shaking the streets of Portland 50 miles away. There would be no picnics on that terrible Sunday. Instead, families and friends in Portland would sit on slopes behind their houses or in front of television sets watching, waiting for word on the effects of the most awesome natural spectacle anyone in the Northwest had ever seen. And sometimes waiting for word of relatives and friends who were up there on that mountain.

Mount St. Helens, a lovely pine-clad snow-capped peak of perfect conical symmetry, had come back to life with a bang. Atop this 9,677-foot slope, lightning flashed, thunderous booms rocked the earth, and huge billows of smoke spread from the peak like atomic clouds. Day became night. A massive cloud of ash and kiln-hot pumice rock, some of the pieces as big as snowballs, rose from the cone of the mountain into the skies, and a northeast wind pushed the cloud away from Portland straight toward the vineyards of sunny Yakima, 80 miles away. There frightened families watched a foot of ash pile up atop their cars, in the streets, on their porches and roofs—covering everything with a gray blanket that would take weeks to clear. The cloud that wreaked such havoc in Yakima carried ash onward, its 63,000 feet of gray mass crossing the nation to the East

Coast in four days, circling the globe before it dissipated. Miraculously, the nearby areas across which that ash-laden, gaseous cloud passed are sparsely inhabited, so many were spared. But there were those who were not spared.

Like hurricanes, tornadoes, and other natural forces, the mountain had rumbled its warnings for months. On March 27 a noon eruption had blasted a crater in the glacial ice that covers this peak all year long. Smaller eruptions that night provided a fiery display for watchers, enlarged the crater, and created a second crater near the first. Subsequent small eruptions enlarged both craters until they were joined into one. About a week later on April 3, scientists, who had been monitoring the activities of the mountain night and day and had been warning the Northwest of the potential for a massive eruption, heard the first of a new kind of seismic activity. Like a dull hum the tremors came, not in staccato bursts but in a continual vibration, indicating that deep inside the mountain, fiery liquid rock called magma was moving. As they watched, amazed, scientists saw the north side of the mountain begin to swell, puffing out four to five feet a day, its rock sides actually burgeoning under the incredible pressure from within.

Little puffs of steam and ash billowed from the snow-capped peak, creating a scene as lovely as it was lethal. At first the earth shook occasionally, but soon those death rattles increased in frequency, totaling in two months nearly 3,000 earthquakes registering 3.0 or greater on the Richter Scale. By the end of March, scientists could barely tell when one quake ended and another began. Mount St. Helens trembled incessantly.

Then at 8:30 a.m. May 18 all the watching, waiting, and trepidation ended. Mount St. Helens exploded with a giant boom that shot a cubic mile of pulverized rock and ash 14 miles into the sky. A huge blast, as powerful as 500 of the bombs dropped on Hiroshima, hurled hot gases, ash, and huge pieces of rock across a fan-shaped area 8 miles long and 15 miles wide. In its path trees six feet in diameter were ripped out of the ground, snapped off at their trunks, stripped of foliage and limbs, and flattened against the now-gray earth.

Temperatures of 1,600° accompanied the eruption, incinerating every living thing in the immediate vicinity, touching off forest fires, and melting the mountain's glaciers in seconds. In minutes waters from the melting ice picked up a huge wall of mud and debris and tore down the North Fork of the Toutle River at 60 miles an hour, ripping through this pristine, pastoral valley and racing to the Columbia River, 50 miles away, halting shipping there.

An earthquake measured at 5 on the Richter Scale rocked the ground for 90 seconds. That massive explosion created a wind that blew 400 miles an hour. Within three minutes slopes in every direction were leveled. Mount St. Helens' conical top was gone, replaced by a deep U-shaped bowl. Touched off by the earthquake, an avalanche of rock, massive fallen trees, and mud roared down the side of the mountain at speeds up to 100 miles an hour. Sparkling Spirit Lake was blue no more as hundreds of thousands of pounds of debris caused a tidal wave 800 feet high. If you had been standing that day on Windy Ridge, where you will stand today, looking down on that lake so small below you, the tidal wave would have reached almost to your toes. In minutes the surface level of the lake, packed with mud and debris, rose 600 feet.

Meanwhile the avalanche, moving with such power it was able to rise up and over a 3,000-foot ridge, continued on to destroy a creek and create a new lake, now called Coldwater. Trees carried by the avalanche filled the water, engulfing hundreds of acres.

Although they had been warned repeatedly of the threat of eruption, 57 people were on Mount St. Helens' slopes that fateful day. Some, like a couple mining a claim on the mountain, lived there and wanted to stay with their homes. Their cabin was demolished, and they died instantly, with no chance for even a thought of escape. Their car, hurled hundreds of feet by the force of the explosion, remains where it landed, crushed and crumpled. A photographer camping on the slopes of the mountain tore down the hill to escape the blast but managed to snap some photographs now on display at the visitor center. A child died lying on the back of his father's truck, his father and brother dead nearby. Many of those who died were killed by inhaling the fine particles of ash that saturated the air. A few who made it out of the devastation did so by holding damp clothing over their faces to filter out the ash.

All this happened in less time than it takes for us to tell the story.

The closest point to the crater is Windy Ridge, overlooking Spirit Lake (we've described various ways of getting to this point below, under "Getting There"). That lake, its natural outlet blocked by rubble, has been fitted with a barge-mounted pumping facility that removes about 81,000 gallons of water a minute from the lake through 3,400 feet of buried steel pipe 60 inches in diameter.

Water is pumped into the North Fork of the Toutle River. That water removal is necessary to keep the lake from eroding the rubble barrier and flooding the downstream towns of Longview and Kelso. Without the pumps, the lake would be 45 feet higher. Present pumping efforts are only a temporary solution to the problem, which is expected to be solved permanently by a 8,200-foot tunnel that will drain excess water produced by glacial run-off streams.

Unlike Hawaiian volcanoes, Mount St. Helens had no molten lava flows. Instead its explosion was in a burst of hot pumice rock called a pyroclastic flow. You will see the rock all around you at Windy Ridge and on the way up the mountain. Pick it up and you will discover that although it looks like any light-colored rock, it is very light and will actually float in water.

As you approach and leave Windy Ridge, you will see amid the devastation several green areas that look exactly as if they were never touched by the effects of the eruption. They weren't. Called islands of survival, these green pockets and their small animal inhabitants were miraculously spared and have gone on to aid in the biological recovery of the landscape.

That recovery is occurring apace. Small pocket gophers surprisingly survived the Mount St. Helens blast, even on the most severely damaged slopes above Spirit Lake. Gophers may be a nasty nuisance in many parts of the country, but here they are lifesavers, pushing fertile underground soil, seeds, fungi, and organic material up to the surface where it takes root, the first small step in the rejuvenation of the forests. Reforestation has begun with trees planted deep beneath the ashy covering on more than 8,000 acres.

In the years since the volcano burst its seams, small eruptions have continued building up a cone inside the huge crater that now exists atop this once-sugarloaf-shaped peak. No one can predict what, if anything, will happen next or if the mountain will explode again. Mount St. Helens erupted once before in written history, about 1800, with small eruptions continuing for more than 50 years.

Long before that, Indian legend recorded by early explorers tells of this mountain, called Louwala-Clough, or smoking mountain. Indians attributed the mountain to the Great Spirit Sahale, who was said to have turned his two sons and a beautiful maiden over whom they were feuding into three neighboring mountains: lovely symmetrical Mount St. Helens (the maiden) and the two other peaks, Wy'East (Mount Hood), a warrior raising his head in pride, and Klickitat (Mount Adams), the other warrior bending his head, weeping, as he gazes on his mountain maiden.

St. Helens got its English name from British explorer Capt. George Vancouver, who honored Baron St. Helens, British ambassador to Spain. Vancouver saw the mountain from his ship in 1792 when he anchored at the mouth of the Columbia River.

GETTING THERE: You won't have any trouble finding your way to Mount St. Helens: just follow the rosy pink cloud that encircles the still-steaming mountain. Visitor information facilities for Mount St. Helens are about 100 miles from Seattle, about 70 miles from Portland. There are several ways to reach the mountain, your choice depending largely on where you have settled. We drove up from Portland on a day-long trip. We'd recommend you leave after breakfast and plan to return for or after dinner. Although the distance is not great, about 60 to 90 miles to the turnoff to the mountain (depending on which one you take), the drive up the side of the mountain is on narrow gravel roads that are a downright terrifying series of sharp turns, certainly no place you'd even dream of speeds greater than 20 miles an hour or so.

To get there **from Portland,** take I-5 to Woodland exit 21 (Wash. 503), where you will find a tourist information center. Another similar facility, called the Yale Information Center, is about 25 miles farther on, just west of the village of Cougar. At Cougar, a tiny settlement with a gas station and grocery store, they'll show you the pumice that pelted down on them a month after the eruption, when the wind changed, blowing pumice rock over Cougar. Attempts to leave the region were thwarted by rain, which turned roads into slick runways, and pumice rock that fell so heavily on cars that windshield wipers were unable to remove it.

If you are staying in **Longview or Kelso** or coming in **from Seattle,** or other points north, you can take exit 60 or 68 from I-5. From exit 68 turn south toward Toledo at Mary's Corner; from exit 60 turn north at Toledo. Between Toledo and Mary's Corner you will find **Mount St. Helens National Volcanic Monument Visitor Center,** Jackson Highway, Toledo, WA 98591 (tel. 206/864-6699).

Another interesting way to get there—and to get your first look at the devastation wrought by the eruption—is to leave I-5 at Castle Rock, exit 49, turning west on Wash. 504 to the intersection of Wash. 505. Just before you reach that intersection, you will see the river of mud and debris that destroyed this once-clear river, turning it into a silt-laden stream. Turn off to Toledo on Wash. 505 and find your way to the visitor center as indicated above.

This visitor center, part of the Gifford Pinchot National Forest, makes a good beginning for a visit to the volcano. Exhibits, murals, and a 22-minute film shown every 30 minutes explains a little about what happened and shows you how scientists are monitoring the mountain. You can even see the seismograph that measures the continuing tremors inside this hill.

From the visitor center return to Mary's Corner and take Wash. 12 east to Randle, a 50-mile trip. At Randle you turn south on Forest Road 25, which meets an even less impressive roadway, called Road 99, about 20 miles from Randle. At Bear Meadow, about four miles from the junction of the two roads, you will get your first look at the volcano. A photographer, camping out here on that fateful day, took some of the most memorable pictures of the explosion.

At this point let us add that no matter which of the roads you take to the mountain, only Forest Roads 99 and 26 actually climb the sides of the mountain. Some parts of this roadway, including at least six miles of it up to Windy Ridge overlooking Spirit Lake, are gravel road and terrifying.

Once you are on the road, there are only a few turnoffs at which you can turn back, so consider yourself committed. A gravel road, it is just wide enough for two cars, so don't plan on any hotrodding and don't try it unless you are sure you have plenty of daylight hours ahead of you to get up and back down again—

don't forget that it gets dark earlier in the shadow of the mountain. This is not one of the most wonderful driving experiences you will ever have, but even an acrophobe is likely to admit the trip is worth the terror.

At one of the few wide spots in the road, you will see the remains of a car that belonged to a couple who lived up here on the mountain. They were among the 57 who could not or would not leave the mountain and were killed. Their car was picked up by the force of the blast and hurled across the road where it remains, mute testimony to the forces at work here.

All around you are huge trees, cracked off at the trunk and lain on their sides as if the proverbial wolf had huffed and puffed and blown them all down. Meta Lake, once a sparkling blue lake a few hundred yards from the roadway, is now a gray, dead pool in a matching landscape.

OTHER THINGS TO SEE: The best time to visit the mountain is May to October. In other months snow may close the roads.

You can **fly over the mountain,** a fantastic sight on helicopter or small-plane tours. On your way up the mountains you will pass the small airstrips of several companies operating flights. One of those companies, based in Kelso, is **AeroWest Aviation,** 2222 S. Pacific Rd., Kelso (tel. 206/423-4902). Flights are $75 for the pilot and the plane, which can accommodate up to three passengers.

Near Cougar, you can visit **Ape Cave,** at 12,810 feet the longest continuous lava tube in North America. Rangers give guided walks through the tube, which was created by cooling lava that hardened around an inner core of hot lava. When the eruption ended and hot lava drained out, this long cave remained. Ape Cave was not, however, formed by this eruption of Mount St. Helens but by former volcanic action: it's nearly 2,000 years old. Tours, guided by rangers carrying a lantern, are free. You should also bring a flashlight for a close look at formations and wear sturdy shoes and warm clothes. Temperatures in the cave are about 42° year round, and a wind blows through, often as fast as seven miles an hour.

You can get a good **view into the crater** from Strawberry Mountain off Forest Road 25, about 30 miles south of Randle on Forest Road 2516. A sign notes the turnoff. You can also see into the crater from the edge of Riffle Lake. To get there, take Wash. 12 east from I-5 to about five miles east of Mossyrock at Hopkins Hill viewpoint. Signs show the way to viewing points at both sites.

WARNING: Mount St. Helens has been comparatively quiescent for several years since the eruption but is still sending up steam and still erupting, although the eruptions are small and occur inside the crater. Some zones once dubbed danger zones no longer bear that designation.

If you are driving up here, you have nothing to fear (except the incredible almost 90° bends in the road). No one will be permitted in the area if there is danger. You would do well to stop by one of the several visitor centers mentioned above, however, before venturing into the park. Not only will you learn a great deal about the mountain, but rangers also keep close tabs on road conditions and will give you wise advice. Your last chance for food and gasoline are at Cougar, if you are coming up from the south, and at Randal, if you are coming in from the north.

If you are considering camping or hiking in the region, a stop at a visitor center or a ranger station at Packwood (tel. 206/494-5515) or Randle (tel. 206/497-7565) is vital. There are dangers in hiking the region and rangers will be able to outline those for you. For information on the mountain, contact the Gifford Pinchot National Forest Supervisor's Office, 500 W. 12th St., Vancouver, WA 98660 (tel. 206/696-7500). A very good topographical map of the mountain is available from them for $1.

4. LONG BEACH, SEAVIEW, AND ILWACO

Long Beach likes to call itself the longest beach in the world, and 28 miles of sand is difficult to dispute. While all that sand is lovely today, it was less enticing to early sailors who looked upon the Ilwaco–Long Beach run with some trepidation. Many looked upon it with insufficient trepidation and paid the price for their incaution: more than 200 ships were swamped here to give these treacherous waters the sobering label "Graveyard of the Pacific."

Overlooking that watery graveyard is a promontory known as Cape Disappointment, where a beacon, warning of controlled but still tricky waters, is aided by the efforts of the state's largest Coast Guard search-and-rescue facility and the guard's only Motor Lifeboat School teaching rough-weather lifesaving.

After some slow years, Long Beach is coming back into its own with a small cranberry industry helping to offset the losses of fishing and logging incomes.

Neighboring Ilwaco, named after a local Indian chief, is bordered on its western edge by awesome headlands with names that reflect the dangers inherent here: Cape Disappointment and Dead Man's Hollow. That latter sobriquet dates back to the time when the *Vandelia* foundered here in 1853 killing all aboard. These days jetties help control the waters of the bar and are aided by the Coast Guard station and its search-and-rescue facility here. Cape Disappointment is home to Fort Canby State Park, where a Lewis and Clark Interpretive Center focuses on the 7,000-mile trek of the two explorers.

Another group of noted visitors: Trumpeter swans that spend their winters here.

GETTING THERE: Only one road reaches this region of Washington, **Wash. 103,** which branches off from U.S. 101, the coastal road in both Oregon and Washington. From the east Wash. 4 joins Wash. 401, which joins U.S. 101 to reach the Wash. 103 branch that runs up this peninsula.

VISITOR INFORMATION: The **Peninsula Visitors Bureau,** P.O. Box 562, Long Beach, WA 98631 (tel. 206/642-2400), has plenty of information they'll be happy to share with you.

USEFUL INFORMATION: For **emergency police or medical help,** call 206/642-4444. . . . The "Long Beach Peninsula Visitor's Guide" is a helpful publication filled with information on the what to see and do in the region. . . . You'll find a **self-service laundry** in Seaview at the corner of 49th Place and Pacific Way, open from 8 a.m. to 9 p.m. . . . Short Stop Store and Deli has **food and gasoline** and is open from 5 a.m. to 11 p.m. daily at U.S. 101 and Pacific Hwy. in Seaview.

WHERE TO STAY: In addition to a collection of small motels, you'll find a delightful country inn filled with brass beds and antiques.

We have to admit to negative feelings toward cookie-cutter hostelries where the wood is wood-grained Formica and the décor comes right out of an institutional catalog. On the other hand, a place that shows a little concern, a little ingenuity, and, wonder of wonders, a little decorative pizzazz just charms the socks off us.

That's why we fell in love with the **Shelburne Inn,** Wash. 103 and J Street (P.O. Box 250), Seaview, WA 98644 (tel. 206/642-2442). Miracles have been wrought here, turning this old house into a delight of beveled glass, with a cozy sitting room, bright colorful sleeping quarters, and a wonderful restaurant. A National Register home built in 1896, the Shelburne is a study in brass beds, homemade quilts, fringed lamps, and lace curtains billowing in the breeze. In 1911 a team of horses pulled the Shelburne across the road to join it to another building with a covered passageway. Now you'll find a regular maze of rooms, expanded in 1983 by owners David Campiche and Laurie Anderson. The art deco stained-glass windows were rescued from a demolished church in Morcambe, England, and have a new lease on life now as the focal point of this handsome inn. To reach the registration desk, you wend your way through a gift shop filled with antiques, a sitting room full of antiques, and on to your room, which is also full of antiques! If you covet one of the brass beds or carved nightstands for your very own, they'll sell it to you. That means no room stays exactly the same forever, but all remain delightfully decorated and cozy. Although it's not on the beach, the Shelburne is not far away and nobody seems to mind the walk. Some rooms share a bath; some have a private bath. Downstairs in the dining room, sunshine streams in the windows by day, candles glitter by night on crisp linens, and the food gets rave reviews—even from the late famed chef James Beard. Rates at the inn are $67 to $125 double, including breakfast.

The **Anchorage Motor Court,** one mile north of Long Beach on Wash. 103 (Rte. 1, Box 581), Long Beach, WA 98631 (tel. 206/642-2351), is a tiny, very quiet oceanfront spot with just ten rooms with queen-size beds; six of them have fireplaces stocked with firewood brought around by the management. There's a little play area for the kids and the Anchorage will even welcome Rover for an additional $3 charge. Rates range from $46.50 to $56.50 double for the largest quarters with four beds, $7.50 for each additional person.

The **Breakers,** 95th Street, at Wash. 103 (P.O. Box 428), Long Beach, WA 98631 (tel. 206/642-4414), is much larger, with 130 units, spacious quarters and in some, wood-burning fireplaces. Half the rooms here have kitchens; half are efficiencies. There's a heated swimming pool and whirlpool. Weekly rates are available and daily tabs are $45 to $52 double, up to $76 for the largest quarters.

With so much natural beauty around, one wonders why this long strip of sand isn't wall-to-wall with serenity seekers. But it isn't, and as long as it stays that way solitude will be one of its joys. You can discover a little about that solitude at **Klipsan Beach Cottages,** seven miles north of Long Beach on Wash. 103 (Rte. 1, Box 359), Ocean Park, WA 98640 (tel. 206/665-4888), a cluster of simple dwelling spots overlooking the ocean from amid a stand of pines. You're strictly on your own here: that is, you bring your own linens or rent them for $5 a cabin, do your own cleaning—but also sit in front of your own fireplace with wood provided and enjoy plenty of privacy and quiet. Cottages with one bedroom are $48 to $58 double; there are also cottages with two bedrooms and sleeping spaces enough for six.

Campers can find a space here at **Ilwaco KOA,** two miles east of town on U.S. 101 (P.O. Box 549), Ilwaco, WA 98624 (tel. 206/642-3292). Full hook-ups are available and there's a grocery supply, propane, ice, hot showers, and a children's playground at the campground, which charges $14 to $16 double.

WHERE TO DINE: The **Shelburne Inn** tops the list of dining spots, and a few rustic seaside spots tag along. We've already mentioned the beautiful surroundings in which you'll dine here (see "Where to Stay"). The menu may include local seafood or rabbit, wild mushrooms from the forests, pastas made right here, whole-grain breads hot from the oven, and wonderful desserts often incorporating local fruit. An outstanding wine collection offers surprises for oenophiles. Dinner prices are in the $12 to $18 bracket. Hours are 11 a.m. to 2 p.m. for lunch, 5 to 10 p.m. for dinner, Sunday brunch from 9 a.m. to 2 p.m., and a luscious English tea on Saturday afternoons. In winter months the restaurant is closed Wednesday and at lunch time.

In the village of Nahcotta, **The Ark,** on Peninsula Road three blocks north of town at Nahcotta Dock (tel. 206/665-4133), has acquired renown all the way to Seattle for its terrific seafood dishes. Served in picturesque surroundings in a postcard-pretty harbor across from a deserted island, those dishes feature oysters plucked right out of Willapa Bay waters. When salmon's running, that delicacy turns up here in several preparations, and when local cranberries are poking up out of the bog, those will appear in desserts. The desserts and fresh breads are the creations of an adjoining bakery which also uses local products such as blackberries and raspberries in sinfully wonderful ways. More than seafood is available, including chicken with a touch of Dijon mustard and cream and locally grown vegetables. Often special selections aren't listed on the menu, so it's always a good idea to ask what else might be cooking. As for prices: $10 to $15. Hours are 5 to 11 p.m. daily except Monday and Tuesday. On Sunday, brunch is 11 a.m. to 2:30 p.m. In winter from October to June the Ark closes at 9 or 10 p.m. on both Monday and Tuesday, and is shuttered completely for the month of January. Complete lounge here too.

Speaking of desserts, and aren't we always, **My Mom's Pie Kitchen,** at 12th St. South and Pacific in Long Beach, on Wash. 103 (tel. 206/642-2342), is not only an appealing name. From the ovens here pour wonderful flaky pies with fillings that range from blackberry to peach to apple and pecan. Mom Jeanne McLaughlin also produces a couple of other nondessert items like chili and salads, but the pies draw the raves. Prices are $7 to $9 for a whole pie, but you can also just buy a slice and consume it here. Hours are 11 a.m. to 6 p.m. Tuesday through Saturday and 12:30 to 5 p.m. on Sunday; closed Monday.

Milton York, Wash. 103 at 10th Street, Long Beach (tel. 206/642-2352), has been whipping up its own homemade ice cream incorporating local cranberries, for instance, and topping that off with homemade candy and chocolate for a century or so! There's also a restaurant here featuring breakfast all day, as well as lunch and dinner. Prices are in the $5 to $10 range. Hours are 7:30 a.m. to 8 p.m. daily, an hour later on Friday and Saturday.

In Chinook, the **Sanctuary Restaurant,** U.S. 101 and Hazel Street (tel. 206/777-8380), really is! Back in turn-of-the-century times the building was a church, as you will shortly realize when you see its ornate stained glass. Now it's a pleasant restaurant featuring the creations of chef Fernand Lopez, who whips up prime rib on Friday and Saturday nights, and chicken with spaetzle, Swedish meatballs, oysters Rockefeller, cioppino, fresh seafoods, and veals anytime. Entrees are in the $10 to $15 range. Hours are 5 to 10 p.m. daily.

NIGHTLIFE: Nights are pretty quiet hereabouts, but you might find some pleasant conversations at local lounges.

WHAT TO SEE AND DO: From a drive right on the sand to a look at Coast Guard lifesavers in action, this peninsular region offers some intriguing activities. You can drive your car on the sand at designated spots; you'll see the signs. These sandy strips are state highways, so you're obliged to maintain a 25-mph speed limit. There are a few other rules too: don't drive near the surf or on clam beds, and watch the tides, which move in and out every six hours.

Two of the oldest lighthouses on the coast are here, **North Head** and **Cape Disappointment.** Disappointment has been in operation since before the Civil War, and North Head has been shining since 1898. Before these lighthouses were built, the only navigational aids in these tricky waters of the Columbia Bar were a notched tree or a white cloth tied to a post by day, bonfires by night! You can visit the lighthouse exteriors anytime and arrange tours by calling the Coast Guard at 206/642-2382.

While you're talking to the Coast Guard you might ask them when they'll be taking boats out as part of their **Motor Lifeboat Surf School.** You can see the training in action on the North Jetty in Fort Canby or off Jetty A on Waikiki Beach, or visit the school Monday through Friday from 3:30 to 6 p.m. and on Saturday and Sunday from 9 a.m. to 5 p.m.

Fort Canby State Park, four miles southwest of Ilwaco on U.S. 101 (tel. 206/642-3029), is proud of its Lewis and Clark Interpretive Center, which gives you an idea how grueling were the thousands of miles traveled by this adventuresome duo. Medical treatment of the era, food, entertainment, and the contribution of the Indians to the success of the venture are all highlighted in exhibits here. Hours are 9 a.m. to 5 p.m. daily May to October. No admission charge.

The **Willapa National Wildlife Refuge** includes 23,400 acres of marsh and tidal lands covered with cedar trees that are home to deer, bear, elk, beaver, and the like. Admission is free, and you'll find a refuge headquarters 8½ miles north of the junction of U.S. 101 and U.S. 101A at Ilwaco (tel. 206/484-3482).

Rhododendrons like it here too, and bloom magnificently at the **Clarke Rhododendron Nursery** (tel. 206/642-2241). The best season to see the blooms is May, but you can take a look at the gardens, which also feature azaleas, any time of year from 8 a.m. to 4:30 p.m. Monday through Friday, free.

Washington State University operates the **Coastal Washington Research and Extension Unit** (tel. 206/642-2031), which specializes in cranberry production. You can take a free guided tour of the facility from 8 a.m. to 4:30 p.m. Monday through Friday, getting a look at blooms in June and watching the harvest in October. You'll find the center a mile north of Long Beach and three-quarters of a mile east on Pioneer Road.

Oysterville is a few miles north along this small peninsula. Now a sleepy little place, it was once home to highrollers who made fortunes from the oysters discovered here. In those days a plate of Shoalwater Bay oysters, reputed to have certain important powers, sold for $50 in gold in San Francisco! Many locals were said to have picked up $500 a day on their oyster sales, and that was pre-inflation! You can get a look at some impressive old Victorian homes, one of the best and most compact collections in the state, as well as other historic buildings, some in the process of restoration.

Shoalwater Storytellers offer you a little historical perspective on the region on Saturday afternoons at 4 p.m. in the Oysterville Church. Produced by the Pacific County Historical Society, the performances are on varying dates, so give them a call at 206/665-4716.

5. GRAYLAND, WESTPORT, AND TOKELAND

This is the land of whale-watching, and if you believe the charter fishermen, a chance to hook some whoppers almost as big as whales. While fishermen are wont to a bit of exaggeration, pictures don't lie. Hereabouts amazing photos of huge catches hold as important a place in some local wallets as any baby picture ever could.

When the whales wiggle by on their 6,000-mile journey from the Baja lagoon to their summer vacation homes in Alaska, whale-watching becomes a major industry. The first of the arrivals usually swims by in late February, Washington's Birthday or thereabouts, with the swim-in continuing through May. So popular has watching the big bruisers become, in fact, that researchers say the income from various watching operations from Oregon to Vancouver amounts to a whopping $5 million annually. The number of watchers has doubled each year in recent years.

Westport has been popular with sun-and-surf fans for more than half a century. Back at the turn of the century, fashionable socialites outfitted in swirling long dresses and parasols accompanied by snappily dressed escorts alighted gracefully from steam excursion boats that brought crowds downriver from Hoquiam and Aberdeen for a day or two of sea air. To give you an idea of how enterprising these beach dwellers are and always have been, an early hotel at Cohassett Beach was built of railroad ties that dropped off a passing freighter and were washed onto shore. These days the steamers are gone, but many people hereabouts spend some of their time out searching the beach for tidal treasures.

Toke having acquired rather a different meaning in recent years, this town has to take a lot of ribbing, but they don't mind much as long as you bring and spend a little money in their cozy village. Which is not to say they're just out for your money, but it does help, now that logging is finished in the area: clams, crab, and oyster supplies have abated; and. . . . Well, they'll be real glad to see you. You'll be real glad to see a lovely National Register structure now a delightful hotel and restaurant.

GETTING THERE AND GETTING AROUND: The only route to the towns is **Wash. 105,** which departs in a westerly direction from U.S. 101 just north of Raymond.

Ferryboats operate between Westport and Ocean Shores from May through September, departing every 90 minutes from 9:15 a.m. to 7:45 p.m. for $7.50 round trip. Grays Harbor Transit Authority operates **buses** in the region with 25¢ to 50¢ fares.

VISITOR INFORMATION: The **Westport-Grayland Chamber of Commerce,** Wash. 105 (P.O. Box 306), Westport, WA 98595 (tel. 206/268-9422 or 268-0991), will be happy to get you started fishing, beachcombing, or just exploring these attractive seaside villages.

USEFUL INFORMATION: For **police or medical emergency** help, call 911. . . . For one-day **photofinishing,** try Twin Harbor Drug in Westport (tel. 206/268-0505). . . . If you do get stuck in the sand or need automotive help, call **Mike's Auto Repair,** Spokane and Montesano Streets in Westport (tel. 206/268-9791), open 24 hours.

WHERE TO STAY: Some small beachside motels are supplemented by a historic dwelling. Let's start with the motels, largest of which is the **Château Westport Motel,** South Forrest and West Hancock Streets (P.O. Box 349), Westport, WA 98595 (tel. 206/268-9101). Here a mile southwest of town and a little west of Wash. 105A, you'll find an attractive, gray mansard roof atop this four-story building. Large for these quiet beaches, the Château Westport has 110 units, many featuring balconies and fireplaces. About a third of the accommodations are efficiency units with kitchens. For playtime there's a heated indoor swimming pool and a whirlpool. Rates at the motel are $55 to $59 double, about $3 to $7 additional for kitchen units. Top floors have the best views.

The **Islander Motel** is two miles north of Westport on the jetty, 1 Westhaven Dr., Westport, WA 98595 (tel. 206/268-9166). The Islander has a nice view across the harbor channel and the fishing fleet that takes off early in the a.m. to get across the bar ahead of the tides. Some of the medium-size rooms have kitchens, but you'll have to bring your own utensils. Kids will like the pool and wading pool. Rates are $49.50 to $69.50 from May to October, dropping about $14 to $15 in other months. You'll find a dining room, cocktail lounge, and coffeeshop here open from early morning to the wee, wee hours and charging prices in the $5 to $9 range.

Campers can find full hookups at many rec vehicle parks in the region, including **Coho RV Park,** Nyhus Street at Float 12 (three blocks off Wash. 105), Westport, WA 98595 (tel. 206/268-0111); **Erin RV Park,** 613 Ocean Ave., Westport, WA 98595 (tel. 206/268-9614); in Grayland, **Twin Spruce RV Park,** 101 Schmid Rd., Grayland, WA 98597 (tel. 206/267-1275); and in Tokeland, on the beach **Bayshore RV Park,** Tokeland Road, Tokeland, WA 98595 (tel. 206/267-2625). Rates at any of the parks range from $10 to $15 double for full hookups.

WHERE TO DINE: A local favorite is **The Dunes,** Wash. 105, Grayland (tel. 206/267-1441), tucked away among the seagrass down at the end of a gravel road. A terrific view across the sand dunes to the ocean awaits you here. Salmon, local crab and oysters, shrimp, snapper, cod, and clams of all kinds are offered, supplemented by lots of fresh vegetables, served with dinner and as an appetizer, and fruit pies. Breakfasts are popular, and the restaurant also serves lunch and dinner from 9 a.m. to 9 p.m. daily from June to early September; same hours, but Thursday through Monday only, from February through May; closed November through January. Prices are in the $10 to $15 range easily.

Arthur's, Westhaven Cove, Westport (tel. 206/268-9292), is increasing its reputation for good, fresh seafood well and carefully prepared abetted by a lively lounge and some good steaks. Hours are 11:30 a.m. to 2 p.m. for lunch, 5 to 10 p.m. for dinner daily except Monday. On Sunday hours are noon to 9 p.m., and prices are in the $10 to $15 range.

Dee's Café, 203 S. Montesano St., Westport (tel. 206/268-9737), isn't much on atmosphere but that doesn't stop the crowds from filling this tiny restaurant. They're all after good fresh seafood simply prepared, pies, pastries, and breads. Prices are in the under-$10 range for many selections and gargantuan feasts. The hours are 7 a.m. to 11 p.m. May to October, 8 a.m. to 9 p.m. Tuesday through Sunday in other months.

In Westport, the **Pancake House,** 402 N. Montesano St. (tel. 206/268-9323), is a favorite for breakfast fans who come here to begin the day with one of 40 different breakfast selections from Swedish pancakes to German pancakes served with cranberries. Prices are in the under-$5 bracket, and the hours are 4 a.m. to 1 p.m. May to October.

Another Grayland restaurant, the **Lamplighter,** Wash. 105 (tel. 206/267-1144), is an interesting spot housed in a historic Grayland speakeasy. A Mexican Fiesta here can keep you stoked with chimichangas, burritos, enchiladas, tacos, and tamales for many a day to come and not set you back much more than $10. Hours are 8 a.m. to 8 p.m. daily, closing a half hour later on Friday and Saturday nights.

At Shoalwater Indian Reservation in Tokeland you can dine on Indian fry bread and some other more common sandwiches and burgers at **Chief Charley's,** Wash. 105, Shoalwater Indian Reservation (tel. 206/267-8232). Prices are in the $5 bracket, and the hours are 8 a.m. to 8 p.m. daily.

The **Islander,** Westhaven Drive in Westport (tel. 206/268-9166), is both hostelry and restaurant with a view, serving seafood, steaks, and prime rib from 4 a.m. to 2 a.m. daily in summer, opening at 6:30 a.m. in winter. Those early hours accommodate fishing fans, who must leave long before sunrise to cross the sand bar at high tide. Prices are in the $10 to $15 range for dinner.

NIGHTLIFE: In a word, quiet. In two words, very quiet. Local lounges are the main after-dark scenes, so you might begin at **King's Le Domaine Restaurant,** 105 Wilson St., Westport (tel. 206/268-0312), which often has music in its lounge on weekends. Frivolity goes on to 6 a.m. here.

The **Islander** (see "Where to Stay") has a lounge open to 2 a.m. that features live entertainment and dancing nightly.

The **Knotty Pine Tavern,** on Dock Street in Westport (tel. 206/268-0591), and **Sourdough Lil's,** down the way on Dock Street (tel. 206/268-9700), are two get-down spots serving hamburgers; at Lil's there's honky-tonk banjo music, sawdust, and other assorted laughs.

WHAT TO SEE AND DO: Fishing, fishing, and more fishing. To help you get out there reeling in the big ones, here are the names of just a few of the charter boat operators in this region: **Cachalot Charters,** across from Float 12 (tel. 206/268-0323, or toll free 800/562-0141); **Deep Sea Charters,** across from Float 6 (tel. 206/268-9300, or toll free 800/562-0151); and **Westport Charters** (tel. 206/268-9120, or toll free 800/562-0157 May through August). Prices for a fishing trip range from $50 to $60 for six to ten hours of bottom fishing, equipment included, to $150 to $250 for one- and two-day albacore tuna fishing expeditions.

If it's whale you want to see, try **Whales Ahoy** (tel. 206/268-9150, or toll free 800/562-0145 in Washington after March), which schedules trips each Saturday and Sunday from March through May. Departure point is Ocean Shores and Westport docks, and tours leave at 9:30 a.m. and 1:30 p.m. with seminars at 12:30 p.m. The price of the trips is $25 per person, $15 for children under 12. Other companies offering whale-watching trips are **Deep Sea Charters,** across from Float 6 (tel. 206/268-9300); **Sea Horse** (tel. 206/268-9100, or toll free 800/562-0171 May to October); and **Westport Whalewatch** (tel. 206/268-9144 or 268-0169).

You can also go fishing from a new bridge across the boat basin at Westport across from Float 20 or drop a line from the jetties around Grays Harbor. Or try surf casting along North Cove and Grayland beaches during east winds, at Washaway Beach in north winds, and at Half Moon Bay or South Jetty in Westport during south or west winds.

If you're a photography buff, head for the **Westport Viewing Tower** at the end of Westhaven Drive in the Westport dock area for a look at scenery and waves spraying over it.

SPECIAL EVENTS: You can enter your beachcombing treasures in a popular spring **Beachcombers' Driftwood Show** in Grayland on the third weekend in March. The show's been going on for more than 25 years now. In mid-June the cranberry crowd gets together at the **Cranberry Blossom Festival,** during which you can tour the bogs, developed by Finnish settlers, and attend the Cranberry Ball. In July the **Grayland Beach-and-Bog Jog** lures Washington runners for a beach run.

BEACHCOMBING: Hey, you're here, might as well try it. Among the most-coveted treasures tossed up by the waves are Japanese glass floats, many of which make their appearances on the beaches all over the Pacific Northwest in winter, when tides and storms wash them up. Most Japanese fishermen use plastic floats these days, but some still use the colorful glass balls that come in every size and shape, most commonly round green or blue ones. They get here on the Kuroshio Current from Japan, and many are picked up by offshore fishermen so you have to be both keen-eyed and lucky to find them. Here's a tip: Begin your search in Tokeland, where the road ends a healthy distance from the spit so your only competition will be other die-hard seekers.

Driftwood floats up in abundance during winter months. Best time to go looking is after a storm, when winds have been blowing from the west or northwest for at least 15 hours. If you see kelp on the beach, there's a good chance you'll also find floats, and driftwood is a sure thing. Just don't play around the logs. Sturdy as they seem, logs can be easily rolled over on top of you by a sudden wave.

Agates also are washed onto the beaches here and come in all colors from red to yellow and white. Best searching beach is South Jetty in Westhaven State Park. Best searching time is on an outgoing tide when the sun is low and strikes through the clear stones, making them sparkle enough to be visible among the gravel.

Some people also find hatch covers from ships, boxes with Japanese or Russian writing on them, bottles, colored rocks, shells, of course, and one year the tides even brought in a carload of apples, Christmas trees, and English muffins washed off a container ship!

SHOPPING: The **Pacific Center for the Arts and Crafts,** Wash. 105 (tel. 206/267-1351), occupies an old red schoolhouse in Grayland where you will find paintings, wood sculpture, and the work of local artists. In summer a group of potters, ceramicists, and painters get together to form a cooperative gallery called **Westport Galleries,** Westhaven Drive (no phone) near the docks.

You'll find quite a number of **antique shops** on the Wash. 105 loop drive from Westport to Aberdeen. A book listing 600 antique shops in the Northwest can be purchased for $7 from Mapbook of Antique Shops, P.O. Box 501, Snoqualmie, WA 98065 (tel. 206/888-0647).

CHAPTER XV

WASHINGTON'S OLYMPIC PENINSULA

□ □ □

1. ABERDEEN AND THE BEACHES
2. LAKE QUINAULT, KALALOCH, AND FORKS
3. PORT TOWNSEND
4. PORT ANGELES
5. OLYMPIC NATIONAL PARK

To *say* "wilderness" is one thing, to *see* one is quite another. Here on this rugged spit of land, split from Canada and the rest of Washington by glacial ruptures that created the Strait of Juan de Fuca, the grandeur of nature is teamed with an unusual array of biologic and geologic forces.

This remote peninsula sits stolidly in the Pacific, looking every bit like a tomahawk gripped by the rest of Washington. Along this coastline it rains just about every day, the west winds bringing almost 200 inches each year to produce a dense, fern-filled, moss-covered rain forest that is tropical in every way but temperature.

As the Olympic Mountains rise from the sea to heights of 7,000 feet, it snows—some 40 feet every 365 days! North, along the straits, those rainclouds dissipate so rapidly that the north-coast village of Sequim is a virtual desert, its land so dry that the May Day celebration hereabouts is called Irrigation Day. In between, at Port Townsend, rose gardens behind the picket fences of colorful, turreted Victorian houses make do with a mere 20 inches of water from the skies each year.

Spread out between remote and lonely western beaches and a fanciful fairyland of Victoriana architecture on the north coast are more than a million acres of wild, uncharted backwoods and remote valleys visited only by mountain goats and wandering elk. Highways circle the magnificent Olympic Mountains that fill the center of the peninsula, but they don't begin to penetrate them. Roads skirt the edges of the Pacific beaches but rarely touch them, instead staying well inland, hugging the fringes of the rain forest, only a few byways venturing near the lonely, windswept sands dotted with craggy, upthrust hunks of rock.

This peninsular isolation is reflected in place names that have not changed despite the momentous arrival of the white man in these woods once peopled only by Indian tribes. You'll find places like Humptulips, Duckabush, Liplip, Mats Mats, Quilcene, Queets, Quinault—a geographer's delight of place names reflecting the effort of white tongues to roll around the Indian dialect. Translated, those Indian names are, in fact, much lovelier and more descriptive than the pioneer interlopers' groping pronunciations: Quilcene came from a word meaning saltwater people, Duckabush were reddish-faced cliffs, Sekiu (pronounced "*Seek*-you") told of quiet waters, Liplip of "boiling" waters, and Mats Mats warned of the opening and closing seas that we mundanely call tides.

But those pioneer newcomers added some interesting names too: Alcohol Loop Road, named for an ill-fated attempt to distill decent hooch from molasses (thus using up what the area had more than enough of in those lumbering-fortune days—sawdust); Port Townsend's Egg and I Road, a name that stuck over the bitter opposition of a local family that claimed it was satirized by *Egg and I* author Betty MacDonald in her amusing life-on-a-poultry-farm novel that went on to film fame. Perhaps those objectors would have preferred the simplicity of the moniker given to another local lane—No Name Road!

Many place names in the region hint at the death and misery occasioned by conflict between white newcomer and native Indian, but few do so as poignantly as Destruction Island. On two different occasions—once in 1775 when Spanish Capt. Juan Francisco de la Bodega y Quadra anchored just off the Hoh River, and again a hundred years later in 1887, when English Capt. Charles W. Barclay sent a party to explore the Hoh—Indians made their territorial feelings known simply but effectively: they massacred every man jack of the landing parties that set foot on their sacred ground. Those displays of territorial imperative gave rise to the river's name, Destruction, later changed to honor the Hoh tribe, but the island named Destruction remains, a vivid reminder of how vicious and heartrending was the battle for supremacy in these majestic lands.

On the lighter side, it's not at all difficult to imagine the dolorific, not to mention odorific, moment that led to someone's name for one local islet: Skunk Island. Tying up this package of wilderness, lushness, and biological perversity is a gray macadam ribbon called U.S. 101, the loop highway that runs all the way around the peninsula and back to Olympia to complete a full circle that can be driven in a day—or a month—of exploration.

At Aberdeen the region's logging life comes alive at a glitzy lumber king's fancy called Hoquiam's Castle, while over on the beaches of Pacific Beach and Ocean Shores, engines roar and lures soar as fishing fans go after the big ones. Then it's on to the depths of the rain forest. At Lake Quinault an excursion down the road to this deep blue, glacier-fed lake may reward you with a glimpse of a passing herd of elk, who think the weather here is just fine, thank you. Along the way you pass moss-draped trees five centuries old, their massive girths rising to a green canopy.

From Kalaloch north, Olympic National Park enfolds Quinault, Ozette, and Makah Indian Reservations and claims some of the most remote beaches in the nation, many accessible only by foot. Bears still feed along the beaches there, watched by migrating whales and sea lions. Here the Hoh River flows to the sea, carving out a valley where the near-constant drip of rain nourishes a never-ending cycle of life and death and rebirth. The trees are massive here, and their harvest has spawned many a legend, including an amusing one known as "The Iron Man of the Hoh."

It seems that one day deep in the forest, timber workers heard in the distance

334 ☐ FROMMER'S DOLLARWISE NORTHWEST

a rumbling, banging clank. Shortly there lumbered out from among the trees a massive, muscled logger bearing a pack on his back, in it an iron kitchen stove, a kind of early-logging-days bauble for his hard-working wife. Well, when those tough lumberjacks saw this apparition emerging from the forest, even they were amazed enough to put down their huge axes and admit this sight was something out of the ordinary. Finally one could stand his curiosity no longer.

"Isn't that heavy?" he inquired.

"Nah," came the terse reply. "It's not heavy. It's just a little hard keepin' mah balance on the logs when the hundred-weight sacks of flour shift inside the oven."

That's the kind of story you'll hear plenty of up here in this rugged Paul Bunyan country, where roughshod loggers wearing cleated shoes called "caulks" still have to be reminded with signs that on polished floors "no caulks allowed."

At the very tip of this peninsula you can walk across the most northwestern point of land in the continental U.S. At Neah Bay's Cape Flattery, the Makah Indian tribe has dwelt for thousands of years and can prove it: one of their ancient villages, buried for generations by a preservative mud slide, was unearthed recently, its 500-year-old artifacts proudly displayed in a tribal museum.

Back on U.S. 101 and shortly civilization, as we have come to know it, begins. At Port Angeles a ferryboat chugs across 18 miles of the Strait of Juan de Fuca to Vancouver Island and the veddy, veddy British enclave of Victoria, capital city of the Canadian province of British Columbia. Here, too, is the easy way into the fringes of the vast Olympic Mountains, ranges that stretch the length and breadth of the peninsula.

Less than an hour on a road from strait-side Port Angeles and you are at Hurricane Ridge. Here the massif of endless mountains stretches as far as you can see. Glaciers send torrents down tortuous paths to the sea. At this awesome display of natural forces, the hushed silence of onlookers is almost palpable.

Back on the strait and narrow road and you're in charming Port Townsend, where the railroad's demise proved a godsend. When the locomotives located elsewhere, hundreds of Victorian mansions that surely would have fallen to the march of debatable Progress remained, preserved forever, because nobody cared enough to demolish them. Now everybody cares, and cares so much that practically the whole town is a national historic site, and everyone in it is dedicated to the continued health and welfare of these delightful, furbelowed leftovers of whimsical Victorian fancies, these huge turreted mansions painted in every color of the rainbow. Indeed, history seems to have come full circle in Port Townsend, and the phrase "living history" comes to life in these Victorian homes-turned-inns, where you will be welcomed as guests today just as you would have been a century ago.

Beyond Port Townsend, in the irrigated desert land of Sequim, clamdiggers chase the elusive geoduck (pronounced, would you believe, "gooey-duck") clams that can burrow their two-foot-long necks into the ground in seconds. Other seekers dig with rubber-tipped forks for the less-elusive but equally epicurean-treasured Dungeness crab.

A quite peculiar peninsula indeed!

1. ABERDEEN AND THE BEACHES

Lumber put this town and its neighbor, Hoquiam, on the map and kept them there for generations. That's why the most interesting sight here is a towering edifice built to pander to the pretensions of a lumber baron. It's called Hoquiam's Castle, which overstates the case by only a bit. Beyond that and a park or two, Aberdeen is a just-passing-through spot unlikely to claim much of your attention.

GETTING THERE AND GETTING AROUND: You'll get here on **U.S. 101** from any point on the peninsula. That main highway runs straight through town, where it breaks into north- and southbound one-way sections called Wishkah Street northbound and Heron Street southbound.

VISITOR INFORMATION: In Aberdeen workers at **Grays Harbor Chamber of Commerce,** 2704 Sumner Ave. (P.O. Box 450), Aberdeen, WA 98520 (tel. 206/532-1924), are waiting with a smile and plenty of information on visiting the peninsula.

WHERE TO STAY: If you're staying over here, choices are limited to pretty standard motels. The **Red Lion Motel,** 521 W. Wishkah, Aberdeen, WA 98520 (tel. 206/532-5210), has an adjacent restaurant and coffeeshop, cable color television, in-room movies, phones, and radios, and prices are $41 to $52 double.
   The **Nordic Inn,** 1700 S. Boone St., Aberdeen, WA 98520 (tel. 206/533-0100), has quite large rooms in its 66-unit building, plus a dining room, coffeeshop, and nightly entertainment, for rates in the $28 to $44 bracket.

WHERE TO DINE: The most popular dining spot in town is **Bridges Restaurant,** at 1st and G Streets (tel. 206/532-6563), which was recently remodeled to become a light, airy spot with a pleasant greenhouse addition. You can always find a wide array of fresh seafood on the menu, seasonally anything from razor clams to steamer clams and scallops St. Jacques, as well as steaks, interesting chicken preparations, pastas, and some great salads. Dinner prices fall easily into the $10 to $15 range—and that includes freshly baked rolls, vegetables, and soup or one of the restaurant's really quite superior salads. Bridges' hours are 8 a.m. to 10 p.m. Monday through Friday, 9 a.m. to 11 p.m. on Saturday, and 9 a.m. to 9 p.m. on Sunday.
   A favored meeting spot in town is **Billy's Bar and Grill,** 322 E. Heron St. (tel. 206/533-7144), a place that like many buildings in this city can trace its history back many years. These days it's a rather sophisticated drinking spot that also serves good sandwiches from 11 a.m. to midnight weekdays, an hour later on weekends, and from noon to 10 p.m. on Sunday.

WHAT TO SEE AND DO: While you're here, have a look at **Hoquiam's Castle,** 515 Chenault Ave. (tel. 206/533-2005), built in 1897 for lumber millionaire Robert Lytle, who didn't spare any cost. For $3 for adults, $2 for children under 16, you can tour the 20 restored and furnished rooms of this turreted mansion that features golden oak columns, Viennese and French cut-crystal chandeliers, a rosewood piano, and Tiffany windows. Hours are 11 a.m. to 5 p.m. daily mid-June through Labor Day, on Saturday and Sunday only in other months; closed in December.
   A second historic home, this one with even more rooms—26—was built by lumberman Arnold Polson and is now a museum and part of **Polson Park and Museum,** 1611 Riverside Ave. (U.S. 101), in nearby Hoquiam (tel. 206/533-5862). Hours are 11 a.m. to 4 p.m. Wednesday through Sunday June through Labor Day, but on Saturday and Sunday only in other months. Admission is free. There's also a pretty picnic area here and a display of steam logging equipment, complete with a 1903 Shay locomotive.
   If your interest in trout goes beyond the platter, you can get a closeup look at those greedy little fellows being hatched and reared at the **Aberdeen Trout Hatchery,** U.S. 12 at Lake Aberdeen Road (tel. 206/533-1663), open daily from 8 a.m. to 4:30 p.m. and free.

VISITING THE BEACHES: A short drive from Aberdeen will take you to the region's most popular beaches, all of them small towns that are centers for fishing and clam digging. When the tides are right, thousands of clam-hungry types come roaring into the villages of Moclips, Pacific Beach, Copalis Beach, and Ocean City, armed with digging equipment. If you'd like to get in on the action, or just watch it, follow U.S. 101 north out of Aberdeen to its junction with Wash. 109, which runs along the coast as far as the settlement of Taholah on the Quinault Indian Reservation, where the road ends. For a loop drive that will take you along the beach and back to U.S. 101, take the Neilton Road west from Moclips.

As for what you'll see here: **Ocean Beach** has, or had, delusions of Hollywood grandeur but has backed off to something more in keeping with the rusticity of the landscape; **Copalis Beach** is more of the same long stretch of beach that meanders along for 25 miles of sand; while **Pacific Beach** and **Moclips** have a bit more ruggedly dramatic scenery with rocks looming over the dark sands.

Where to Stay and Eat

If you're staying over here, **Ocean Crest Resort,** a mile north of the Pacific Beach bypass at the junction of Wash. 109, Moclips, WA 98562 (tel. 206/276-4465), occupies a pleasant location overlooking the ocean from a bluff. Many rooms here have fireplaces and balconies; some have refrigerators. There's a large heated indoor pool, sauna, and whirlpool.

Ocean Crest has a good dining room specializing in home-cooked steaks and fresh seafood. The views over the ocean are nice too. Prices in the dining room are in a reasonable $9 to $14 range. Hours are 9 a.m. to 2 p.m. and 5:30 to 9:30 p.m. daily. Rates at Ocean Crest are $44 to $82, depending on size, amenities, and location of room.

2. LAKE QUINAULT, KALALOCH, AND FORKS

Wild, remote beaches line the Pacific side of this peninsula, ocean crashing against rocks and foaming across sands visited only by the occasional fisherman, razor-clam digger, or hiker.

The most traveled route in the region is U.S. 101, which heads inland from Aberdeen to skirt the Quinault Indian Reservation, then winds back to the coastline for a short distance before once again curving inland toward Olympic National Park.

Hikers love this land and are really the only ones who can see its raw, rugged beauty. Only four roads run to the beach: Wash. 109 from Aberdeen to the coastal towns of Ocean City and Pacific Beach; a county artery that takes off through the Quinault Indian Reservation to the sea; a county road that leaves U.S. 101 just north of Forks to meet the sea at La Push; and Wash. 112, which branches off U.S. 101 at Sappho to travel to the tip of the peninsula at Neah Bay. While you will find dramatic scenery at the ocean end of those roads, getting there is difficult and accommodations are rudimentary.

VISITOR INFORMATION: In the more remote sections of the Olympic Peninsula the people who can help you most are those at the **Olympic Peninsula Travel Association,** P.O. Box 625, Port Angeles, WA 98362 (tel. 206/437-2277).

A number of chambers of commerce are also operating in the region, including: the **Ocean Shores Chamber of Commerce,** P.O. Box 382, Ocean Shores, WA 98569 (tel. 206/289-2451); the **Washington Coast Beach Chamber of Commerce,** P.O. Box 562, Copalis Beach, WA 98535 (tel. 206/289-4552); and the **Fork Chamber of Commerce,** P.O. Box 1249, Fork, WA 98331 (tel. 206/ 374-2281).

WHERE TO STAY: There are two good places to settle to explore the backwoods and byways of this coastline. Both, as it happens, are operated by the same owners. One is an elaborate inland resort, the other a seaside hostelry.

The inland resort is attractive **Lake Quinault Lodge,** South Shore Road (P.O. Box 7), Quinault, WA 98575 (tel. 206/288-2571, or toll free 800/562-6672). Built half a century ago, this imposing lodge forms an eyebrow arch around lawns that slope down to the glittering lake. A massive fireplace flanked by French windows is the focal point of a beamed lobby outfitted in antique wicker furniture. Big windows in the dining room take full advantage of the view, charming at sunset on quiet summer evenings. Rooms in the main lodge are the most atmospheric, some even have fireplaces, but not all have private bath. Some rooms have a view of the lake and naturally cost a bit more than those without a view.

Rooms in the modern wing are spacious and accommodate queen-size beds, but lack the historic atmosphere of the main lodge. The new rooms, however, have a view of the lake through glass doors and from private balconies, and all have private bath. Lake Quinault Lodge features a heated indoor swimming pool, sauna, and whirlpool. Boats can be rented for expeditions around the pine-trimmed lake to see its beautiful scenery. From mid-June to October the lodge is often solidly booked a month or more in advance. Depending on view, lodge rates are $68 to $85 for two.

If there's no room at that lakeside inn, try sister property **Kalaloch Lodge,** on U.S. 101 (HC 80, P.O. Box 1100), Kalaloch, WA 98331 (tel. 206/962-2271). Pronounced "Kah-*lay*-lock," the property is a cluster of cottages anchored by a main lodge. Kalaloch Lodge sits on a bluff overlooking a gray sand boulder-strewn beach, over which the surf splashes. As the classiest act along this coastline, Kalaloch Lodge is also booked well in advance of the busy summer season.

A variety of accommodations range from attractive rooms in the main lodge to log cabins and a modern motel. Of those options, we like the lodge rooms best, particularly those with a view of the ocean, which can be quite dramatic in fall and winter months. In spring and fall you have a particularly good view from this clifftop vantage point when the whales spout by. Rooms in the motel, called Sea Crest House, are attractive, particularly those featuring fireplaces or private balconies with ocean views. Cabins range from rustic to new but have the advantage of private surroundings quite separate from the rest of the resort.

Naturally enough, seafood is featured in the lodge's dining room, but there are steaks and continental preparations on the menu as well, for prices in the $10 to $15 range or less. Cozy cocktail lounge here too.

For accommodations at Kalaloch, which is located on U.S. 101 about 30 miles from the turnoff to Lake Quinault Lodge, you pay $45 to $90 double, with a two-day minimum in effect on weekends.

WHERE TO DINE: Other than the two hotels we've just mentioned, there are few other dining spots. If we were looking for a dramatic view and some decent basic cooking, we'd select **Kalaloch Lodge,** where the surf views are wonderful. You'll pay $10 to $15 for dinner, with local salmon, razor clams, perhaps ling cod or halibut the best choices. Hours are 7 a.m. to 9 p.m. June to October, 8 a.m. to 8 p.m. in other months. Open daily.

For serenity we'd choose **Lake Quinault Lodge,** where prices (about $12 to $17 at dinner) and menu are about the same. The view differs dramatically, however: here it is a great sweep of lawns, lake, and pines, with an occasional canoe gliding past the windows of the glass-walled dining room. Once again seafood is the best option, simply because there is so much of it around, ensuring freshness. Steaks are available. Later, we'd find a seat in the unusually decorated lounge and see how close we could come to the bemused looks of the deerheads mounted on the ceiling beams. Hours at the lodge are 8 a.m. to 10 p.m. daily.

One other popular local spot is the **Smoke House Restaurant,** on U.S. 101 one mile north of Forks at La Push Junction (tel. 206/374-6258), a cannery that also cooks. What they cook most of for hungry diners is salmon, smoked over an alderwood fire. Plenty of other seafood is available too, plus prime ribs and a salad bar, for prices in the $8 to $15 range. Hours are 11 a.m. to 10 p.m., to 2 a.m. weekends in the bar. Open daily.

WHAT TO SEE AND DO: At Lake Quinault you can visit deep river valleys where water often pours down from above in the form of rain and just as often pours down from above in the form of mountain streams. Put the two together and you have the northernmost rain forest in the nation, an awesome place in which Douglas fir grow 300 feet tall and 9 feet in diameter! Scenery is the attraction along this side of the peninsula, and it ranges from wild waves tossing driftwood onto shore during winter storms to gentle forests and quiet valley lakes. In the midst of it all is a dense rain forest created by more than 140 inches of rain each year.

There are three ranger stations in the Lake Quinault/Kalaloch/Forks region to help you: (1) an **Olympic National Park Visitors Center for Kalaloch,** HC80, Box 2200, Forks, WA 98331 (tel. 206/962-2283), actually located at a settlement called Clearwater just off U.S. 101, can help you out with details of that quite long hike or shorter portions of it; (2) a joint U.S. Forest Service and National Park Service office at **Soleduck Ranger Station,** five miles north of Forks on U.S. 101 (Star Rte. 1, Box 5750), Forks, WA 98331 (tel. 206/374-6522); and (3) a ranger outpost at **Quinault Ranger Station,** South Shore Road, Quinault, WA 98575 (tel. 206/288-2525), can lead you to hiking trails in the rain forests and explain some of the flora and fauna you may see in the district, including, if you're lucky, lordly Roosevelt elk.

Rialto Beach and adjoining **La Push,** reached via a side road branching west just north of Forks, are the center of beach activities. In Rialto smelt runs occupy many minds, while in La Push salmon is the primary lure. You can often see Indians paddling dugout canoes in and around La Push.

Beaches in the region are numbered (Beach One, Beach Two, etc.). First Beach begins at La Push; Second Beach, reached by a trail from the road into La Push, is scenic and features a huge offshore rock called Teawhite Head. Around Teawhite tidepools form an interesting place to observe tidal life, particularly when dense fogs dim the light and tidal creatures forget to go out with the tide. Third Beach is reached by a mile-long trail; Beach Four is known for its smelt; Beach Two is a favorite with driftwood collectors.

Two of the more interesting sections of rain forest are along a gravel road that parallels the Queets River and departs east from U.S. 101 about five miles south of Queets and a few miles from the ranger station at Clearwater. Admission to the rain forests and to Olympic National Park is free.

Among the most dramatic sections of the park is **Hoh Rain Forest,** reached on a marked side road that turns east off U.S. 101 about ten miles north of Ruby Beach. Along a scenic drive that parallels the Hoh River, you will wander right through the center of the rain forest.

Port Angeles recently acquired a fine art center, the gift of a retired publisher. Dubbed the **Port Angeles Fine Art Center,** 1203 E. 8th St. (tel.

206/457-3532), shows the work of Northwest and national artists and has quiet walking trails among native flora. Hours are 11 a.m. to 5 p.m. Thursday through Saturday.

If you'd like to get a look at what happens to some of the huge trees that grow in this region, stop in at the **Forks Timber Museum,** on U.S. 101 at the edge of the village of Forks (tel. 206/374-9663), where logging and its interplay with pioneers and Indians is outlined. In the museum's gift shop you'll find some interesting work by Northwest artists and crafts workers. You can even get a photograph of yourself dressed in pioneer outfits. Hours are 10 a.m. to 6 p.m. Tuesday through Friday and 1 to 5 p.m. on Saturday and Sunday from May through October.

SIDE TRIPS: An interesting side trip in the region, albeit a long one, is to **Neah Bay.** First, so you'll know what we mean by long: Neah Bay is about 85 miles from Kalaloch, about 45 miles from Forks. To get there, follow U.S. 101 to Sappho, where Wash. 112 branches off to Clallam Bay, Sekiu, and finally to Neah Bay.

Neah Bay is headquarters of the **Makah Indian Reservation,** which is also home to **Cape Flattery,** as far northwest as you can go in the Pacific Northwest and in the continental U.S. Two hikes in the district take you to Cape Flattery, about a 30-minute walk (no roads accommodating automobiles) and a three-mile trek to Shi-Shi Beach, one of the few beaches in the nation that is still a wilderness. On the last weekend in August the tribe celebrates its 1931 citizenship grant with games, a canoe race, traditional dances, and a salmon bake.

A mysterious and intriguing sight here is the **Makah Cultural and Research Center,** Wash. 112 in Neah Bay (tel. 206/645-2711). Chronicled in the museum are the lives of the Indian tribe that has lived on this land for more than 2,000 years. Five hundred years ago their homes, including a 50-foot cedar longhouse, their canoes, their baskets, and baubles, were interred beneath a mudslide that buried the village. Wet clay that slid over the village sealed houses and artifacts from decay for generations, but in 1970 tidal erosion uncovered the village of Ozette about 15 miles south. Archeologists moved in to spend 11 years re-creating the lives of those who had lived there so long ago. You can see the best of what was uncovered at the Makah Cultural and Research Center. Photographs taken in the early 1900s show you how the dugout canoes, baskets, amulets, and tribal artifacts were used. A replica of a 60-foot cedar longhouse and canoes sailed on the oceans by the Indians, who hunted whale and seals from them, are on display daily from 10 a.m. to 5 p.m. June to mid-September, Wednesday through Sunday the remainder of the year. Admission is $3 for adults, $2 for students over 4.

To get the closest—and best—look at this wild section of the state, you must hike across the land and beaches, for roads are few. To hike part of it you can begin at Neah Bay, within the Makah Indian Reservation, and walk south across the beach and around Lake Ozette land to the villages of La Push and Rialto Bay. Again, those ranger stations we mentioned earlier can help you get organized for that lengthy trek.

3. PORT TOWNSEND

You can stay in other places along this coastline, but with Port Townsend just sitting there waiting for you in all its Victorian magnificence, why would you stay anywhere else? We find it difficult to tear ourselves away from this town and harder yet to stop thinking about it. We think you will too. Why the world isn't jamming in here we can't imagine, but we certainly rate Port Townsend as one of the gems of the Northwest.

One of the oldest cities in the state, Port Townsend gained fame and fancy homes at the turn of the century when, as the gateway to Puget Sound, it was a very important place indeed. Then railroads became very important, and the nearest one just plain passed this pretty town by. Their loss, our gain, for the railroad's bypass meant no one bothered to tear down the magnificent Victorian homes that surely would have gone the way of what people like to call progress.

None of that "progress" happened, however, and pretty little Port Townsend stayed just the way it was: filled top to tea kettle with Victorian furbelows.

These days you can spend many a day exploring what you're not sleeping in, for surely you will want to stay in one of these elegant old homes. Many, many of them are now beautifully restored, and once again filled with antiques much as they would have been in their heyday and once again ringing with the sounds of guests and laughter. So with little (we'd never say no) further ado, let's take a look at some of the wondrous places in which you can dream dreams of parasols and long gloves, top hats and tails, fancy carriages and manners as elaborate as lace trim.

GETTING THERE AND GETTING AROUND: The most interesting ways to get here from Seattle are by ferry or on a drive around this scenic and historic peninsula.

The **closest airport** is Seattle's Sea-Tac International. For information on airlines flying in there, see Chapter II on Seattle. San Juan Airlines flies into Port Angeles from Seattle and Victoria Island, B.C.

Sorry, Amtrak's closest stop is Tacoma or Olympia.

Washington State Ferries (tel. 206/464-7800, or toll free 800/542-7052 or 800/542-0810) connect Port Townsend with the town of Keystone on lovely Whidbey Island. If you have a free afternoon or are going on in that direction, the ferry trip is scenic and fun. Avoid summer Fridays and Sundays, however, when the traffic can be terrific, and we don't mean wonderful.

Greyhound Lines has scheduled service to Port Townsend from Seattle, connecting with Jefferson Transit, located at 1615 Sims Way. In Port Townsend call **Jefferson Transit** (tel. 206/385-4777) for information and schedules. Fares are 50¢ for adults (children under 6, free); a daily pass costs $1.50.

By car take **U.S. 101,** which loops around the peninsula from Aberdeen to Olympia. You can get to Aberdeen from Olympia on U.S. 12 to make a full circle trip around the peninsula.

Port Townsend Taxi (tel. 206/385-3434) and **Totem Taxi** (tel. 206/385-6920) will get you from place to place in Port Townsend. Fares are $1 a mile.

VISITOR INFORMATION: You'll find the **Port Townsend Chamber of Commerce** occupying cozy quarters at 2437 Sims Way, Port Townsend, WA 98368 (tel. 206/385-2722).

USEFUL INFORMATION: For emergency police or medical help, call 911. . . . **Don's Pharmacy,** 1151 Water St. (tel. 206/385-2622), is open to 8 p.m. weekdays, to 6 p.m. on Saturday; closed Sunday. . . . Two service stations on Sims Way can help you out with gasoline or automotive problems. One is **Harper's Super Service Station,** 2611 Sims Way (tel. 206/385-1240); the other is the **Texaco Service Station,** 1531 Sims Way (tel. 206/385-5682). . . . To find a local **doctor,** call 24-hour physician information and referral service, at 206/479-3388 or toll free 800/552-7114. . . . For **veterinary help,** call Dr. Harold Sherwood, 2201 Sims Way (tel. 206/385-0512, 385-3341 for emergencies).

WHERE TO STAY: If you're ever going to splurge on something wonderful, this is the place to do it. Ideally, we'd have a book just for Port Townsend but, alas, we'll have to cut the rhetoric back to just a few enraptured pages in which we'll tell you of just some of the restored—and restorative—wonders awaiting you in Port Townsend's unmatchable collection of hostelries. We need to add here that, for the most part, these are bed-and-breakfast inns, albeit quite elegant ones, so some may have rooms without private bath. We have indicated in each case what you will find in the way of private or shared baths. Few of these small inns have televisions or telephones in rooms, although both are always available somewhere in the house. Some also frown on smoking inside the house for obvious reasons. You might also keep in mind that the winter season is definitely not crowded here, although holiday weekends may be, so some inns may drop rates during winter months. Ask.

One more note: You can take a look at just about every hostelry in town free or by paying a small admission fee—50¢ or $1. Homes, even Manresa Castle, are open during posted hours—the chamber of commerce has a list—and owners will be happy to show you around at that time.

One's home is one's castle so they say, although it certainly isn't true for us. So let's begin with, what else, a castle. Here in Port Townsend a fellow named Charles Eisenbeis thought he'd worked hard enough to deserve a castle, so in 1892 he simply went out and built himself a fanciful one designed along the lines of those he remembered from his Rhineland childhood. For many years the castle sat empty and forlorn on its lofty peak overlooking the sound, then it became a Jesuit school and was renamed to honor the Spanish town in which the Jesuit movement began. Today **Manresa Castle,** 7th and Sheridan streets (P.O. Box 564), Port Townsend, WA 98368 (tel. 206/385-5750, or toll free 800/732-1281 in Washington), is a delightful hotel with all the comforts. Here you'll be greeted in a big sitting room where wing chairs, a fireplace, and a chandelier set the tone for what is to come. A cozy breakfast room next door features ceilings that seem to go on forever, tall windows, beautiful wainscoting, and a view over a formal garden. Down the hall a way is another dining room, a galleried two-story room with fountains in the center. On to your room, which can be one of the glamorously elegant bay-windowed quarters. In those you'll find a king-size bed decked out in a lace comforter and set into the bay window so you can stretch out in these luxurious surroundings and look down at Port Townsend. Clever designers have created a small sitting room in these very large rooms too, so you can also curl up on a couch or in a chair and contemplate the shining antiques around you. Each room is a delight of antiques or reproductions, ruffles and lace, marble and polished oak. But you can see for yourself: the hotel opens its rooms daily as part of the city's self-guided Victoriana tour. Rates at the Manresa, where all rooms have private bath, phone, and color television, are $65 to $80.

Lizzie's, 731 Pierce St., Port Townsend, WA 98368 (tel. 206/385-4168), certainly numbers among the most luxurious Victorian bed-and-breakfast homes in town. Its owner named this home after the original owner, Lizzie Grant, wife of a tugboat captain, who bought this imposing house in an era when women rarely owned their own property. The bedrooms are outfitted in a wondrous collection of antiques, refinished in velvets, laces, and plenty of polish. Each of the rooms, with one exception, bears the name of one of the ladies of this house, including Daisy, who signed her name on the wall in 1894! Lizzie's room is the showplace, with a half-canopy bed, fireplace, a bay window sitting area outfitted in velvet, and a private bath with clawfoot tub. Every room is a stunner, many of them huge, some less so, but all so cleverly decorated that small becomes cozy. For Lizzie's room you pay $85, while the others range from $45 to $69.

Be sure to get a look at the newest addition here: out in the backyard is a quarter-scale replica of the house, perfect in every detail. Its resident occupant is a very lucky dog named Goliath, who occasionally throws a bone to his owner, Bill Wickline, new owner of this Victorian wonderland.

To stay in the bridal suite of the **James House,** 1238 Washington St., Port Townsend, WA 98368 (tel. 206/385-1238), is to be pampered by such luxuries as a towering walnut-burl headboard, a velvet reclining couch, fabulous cabbage rose wallpaper, a fireplace, a beautiful view, and a cozy private sitting room. As one of the first bed-and-breakfast guesthouses in the Northwest, James House inaugurated a delightful tradition with this 1891 Victorian treasure. From the gingerbread trim on the porch to the antique pot-bellied stoves, this shingled home is a beauty. Two of the house's accommodations are two-room garden suites, while a garden cottage has twin beds and private bath. Those, along with the bedrooms in the main house, are furnished in period antiques and feature terrific views of the mountain or the sea or both. More private baths are being added. Breakfast, which includes poppyseed muffins, scones, or coffee cake, is served on an oak table. Not all rooms have private bath, so specify which you want. Prices for two are $85 for garden suites, $105 for the bridal suite, and $60 to $68 for bedrooms.

Hastings House Inn, 313 Walker St., Port Townsend, WA 98368 (tel. 206/385-6753), is a study in burgundy and white on the outside, a glory of beautiful colors inside. A master bedroom in one of the characteristic Victorian turrets of this beautiful home has two double beds and full bath. But the Lavender Room, all in that shade, also is beautiful, the Rose Room is a cheery spot, the third-floor Ivory Tower Room is complete with its own little circular sitting room and curved windows overlooking the sound, and in the Silk, Lace, and Gable Rooms glamour reigns. What more can we say? Most rooms have at least a half bath, but a few share baths, so specify what you want. Breakfast is included in the prices of $48 to $89.

Once upon a time, **Starrett House,** 744 Clay St., Port Townsend, WA 98368 (tel. 206/385-3205), was a place you couldn't miss—it was painted a riveting shade of purple! Owners said they dug through many layers of paint to discover the house's original zappy color. A fabulous Victorian house with dozens of unusual touches both inside and out, Starrett House fell upon some sad days and was closed for more than three years before lifesavers in the form of new owners Edel and Bob Sokol came along. Although the house, in its new cream-and-green incarnation, may not be quite as shocking as the Victorians liked their color schemes, it's every bit as lovely, all trimmed out in fancy furbelows. Inside you find five elegantly appointed rooms with private bath, four with shared baths, each sporting a bevy of antiques. There are two parlors in the house and a delicately lovely frescoed ceiling. You'll see a three-tiered free-hung staircase that leads to a widow's walk with another frescoed ceiling adorned by cavorting maidens depicting the four seasons. This ceiling is domed and features ruby-red stained glass so carefully placed that as the sun shines through the red glass an arrow of light points to the appropriate season. Beat that! Rates at this fascinating antique home include full breakfast and range from $55 to $80, depending on the size and sumptuousness of your quarters.

We didn't get to see the inside of **Irish Acres,** P.O. Box 466, Port Townsend, WA 98368 (tel. 206/385-4485), down a graveled country lane behind an open pasture, but we did meet one of its operators, Jo Monahan, who was babysitting another local inn. She proved so pleasant and welcoming that we couldn't resist mentioning her tiny country guesthouse of cedar, stone, and mortar. Each room has a private bath and outside entrance, breakfast is whenever you want it (there's no set schedule), and the atmosphere is serene. Rooms are $40 to $50 a night from March through September. In other months the price drops some. You'll find the cottage by taking Wash. 20 to Jacob Miller Road and turning left on Gun Club Road past the pasture and onto the graveled lane.

Port Townsend's residential section, high on the bluff overlooking the water, is so head-turning in its Victorian magnificence that one forgets it is surrounded by farmland and open countryside. If you like a wide open space, seek out the **Arcadia Country Inn,** 1891 S. Jacob Miller Rd., Port Townsend, WA 98368 (tel. 206/385-5245). It's a little tricky to find on this country road, but once there you'll be charmed by a sprawling country home down a long drive flanked by pastures. Built in 1908, the home was a roadhouse and later an inn, then a speakeasy and also a you-know-what, thanks to its location just 100 yards outside the city limits. Amusingly, the house got its water line free from city fathers, who wanted the ladies around but just didn't want them too visibly around. So they offered a little free city H_2O to the, ahh, lady of the house, if she'd just transplant her establishment outside city limits—but not too far outside.

These days the house is quite respectable, with 70 acres of woods and pasture to jog along and plenty of backcountry roads for biking or hiking expeditions. Quarters are done in upbeat country décor. Leif's Room shares a bath with adjoining Maia's Room (great for families) and has a small balcony. A Garden Room with a private entrance, Victorian private bath, and an outside deck is a delight in blue-dotted Swiss brass, and a bright-blue clawfoot tub. Prices, including breakfast and complimentary champagne, are $52 to $80. Once again, some rooms have private bath, some don't, so ask for what you want.

In downtown Port Townsend yet another historic old building has been converted into the **Palace Hotel,** 1004 Water St., Port Townsend, WA 98368 (tel. 206/385-0773, or toll free 800/961-0741). Not only is it beautifully decorated with antique-filled rooms of amazingly high ceilings but it's right in the middle of the fascinating architecture of the main downtown streets. Marie's Room has a water view, private bath, kitchenette, fireplace, and cable color television. It is matched in amenities by Capt. Tibbals' Room. Prices are $44 to $79 double, some with private bath, some sharing. Single travelers pay $5 less. All rooms here have television.

Now here comes a real departure. If you've ever wanted to be in command of all you survey, hie on over to the **Officers' Quarters at Fort Worden State Park,** P.O. Box 574, Port Townsend, WA 98368 (tel. 206/385-4730). Here the park service will rent you one of the imposing Victorian homes once occupied by the fort's top officers. Built in 1904, the houses are all in a row. It's easy to imagine the officers on the wide verandas, viewing imaginary troops mustering on the lawn. Inside you'll find old fireplaces and ornate high ceilings, big bedrooms, and some reproduction antique furnishings. Although the park service has not been financed well enough to permit them to do justice to these wonderful old homes, visitors with a little imagination can have a rollicking good time. Wonderful for families, the homes have big kitchens, big dining rooms, and up to six (!) bedrooms. Because they are so unusual and are part of a wonderful park with a beach and plenty of jogging, boating, biking, and fishing areas, these homes are very popular, often booked months in advance. Refurbished houses have carpeting and reproduction oak furnishings, often queen-size beds and fireplaces. Linens and towels are provided, but you do your own housekeeping. Unrefurbished houses have beds and all the architectural interest but are not as spiffy in décor and sometimes downright sparse. Rates for the whole house range from $62 a day for a two-bedroom refurbished house to $100 for three bedrooms, $163 a day for a six-bedroom. Unrefurbished houses run $76 to $133.

Full-fledged resorts are few and far between in this region, but there is one, quite simply called **The Resort at Port Ludlow,** 60M no. 3 Paradise Bay Rd.,

Port Ludlow, WA 98365 (tel. 206/437-2222, or toll free 800/732-1239). Winner of a national magazine's top rating as a family resort, Port Ludlow features a dramatic golf course, a glass-enclosed swimming pool and Jacuzzi, plus an outdoor pool overlooking the sound. Seven tennis courts lure players, while kids are treated to a supervised outdoor program. The resort's pleasant Harbormaster Restaurant has plenty of good steaks and seafood on hand. After dinner, swap a few got-away stories at the Wreckroom Lounge. A 197-unit condominium resort once known as the Admiralty Resort, the Resort at Port Ludlow overlooks a saltwater swimming lagoon and features apartments with living room, fireplace, fully equipped kitchen, dining room, and private deck. Many have good views of the sound. All quarters at the resort have twin or queen-size beds, telephone, and color television, plus private bath, of course. In summer months, from May to October 15, rates are $90 to $100, depending on view, for rooms; from $126 for one- to four-bedroom apartments. From October 15 to May, rates are about $20 lower. Port Ludlow is 18 miles from Port Townsend.

If you're **camping** in the area, **Fort Worden State Park,** Port Townsend, WA 98358 (tel. 206/385-4730), has 50 waterside sites available for $9.50, but advance reservations in summer are important as the campgrounds are often full.

WHERE TO DINE: A quite diverse array of dining spots, from Victorian home to waterside dining await you in Port Townsend.

Head for the upstairs tables at **Lido Restaurant,** 925 Water St. (tel. 206/385-7111), so you'll have a view through French doors out across the water. Quite a chic spot in décor and service, the Lido prepares an outstanding menu in a tiny kitchen where talented chefs whip up interesting preparations with mussels, clams, crab, and other seafood ingredients. Quite reasonable prices prevail: in the $9 to $12 range for dinner. Hours are 11 a.m. to 10 p.m. Open daily.

Dinner at **Manresa Castle,** 7th and Sheridan Streets (tel. 206/385-5750), was for many years one of the culinary delights of a trip to this furbeloved part of the world. In 1988 the restaurant was closed but it is expected to reopen in 1989. In anticipation of that happy moment we're going to describe this chic spot, but it would be wise to call the hotel and inquire about the dining room before you get your taste buds in a frenzy. So here's what you'll find here. Fountains tinkle in a dark and intimate room lined with private little alcoves. Upstairs an equally sophisticated bar has a view down through the fountains to the dining room below. Good continental cookery of steaks, prime rib, and seafood put this restaurant on local culinary maps and is likely to continue doing so. Add to those temptations a chance to look over this odd, old home-turned-hotel. Prices traditionally were in the $12 to $17 range and hours are likely to be 5 to 9 p.m. daily except Monday, closing an hour later on weekends.

The **Water Street Deli,** 926 Water St. (tel. 206/385-2422), is perfect for light meals and better than perfect for desserts. Clam bisque and other homemade soups join do-it-yourself sandwich choices, both to be followed by such irresistibles as chocolate fudge cake, chocolate or cherry cheesecake, and pecan pie. Eighteen kinds of beer, and hot cider too. You'll pay quite reasonable prices, $5 or so, and hours are 10 a.m. to 5 p.m. daily.

Elevated Ice Cream Co., 627 Water St. (tel. 206/385-1156), was named for an elevator cage the shop once occupied. You can sample yummy chocolates, fruit sherbets, gourmet coffees, or espresso, all with more than 40 kinds of homemade ice cream ranging from a cool raspberry made with local fruit to mocha to their special, amaretto hazelnut, served on a water-view deck. You'll pay a reasonable couple of dollars for something sinful but not regrettable. Hours are 11 a.m. to 10 p.m. daily.

Mexican flavors are always a treat, both in taste and in price. In Port Townsend you can fill up on tacos, margaritas, Mexican beers, and some seafood—everybody serves seafood in Port Townsend—at **La Fonda,** 2330 Washington St. (tel. 206/385-4627), for prices in the $10 range or less. Hours are 11:30 a.m. to 9 p.m. weekdays, 4 to 9:30 p.m. on Saturday and Sunday.

Salal Café, 634 Water St. (tel. 206/385-6532), is run by a cooperative that serves lunch but specializes in wholesome breakfasts with toast from a local bakery, home-fried potatoes and onions, omelets, freshly squeezed orange juice, or cheese blintzes. You dine at a community table in front, at a solarium out back. Prices are in the $5 range or less, and hours are 7 a.m. to 2 p.m. daily; breakfast is served all day Sunday.

Old-fashioned sodas are an endangered species these days, but you can find one at the **Plaza Soda Fountain** in the back of Don's Pharmacy, 1151 Water St. (tel. 206/385-2622): real cherry Cokes, folks, vanilla ones too, or something called a green river (must be a local egg cream). Prices are in the under-$5 bracket. Don's is open from 9 a.m. to 4 p.m. daily except Sunday.

The **Sea Galley,** 116 Taylor St. (tel. 206/385-2992), is a nautically themed restaurant and lounge. Nice woodsy atmosphere and waterside location supplemented by decent seafood selections, simply prepared, make this a favorite hangout. Prices are in the $10 to $15 range, and the restaurant is open from 9 a.m. to 11 p.m. weekdays, to midnight on weekends and with music in the lounge. You can dine outside on the deck too.

NIGHTLIFE: Nights are pretty quiet in Port Townsend, but there are a few bright lights to pursue. One of those is **Lanza's,** 1020 Lawrence St. (tel. 206/385-6221), which features an outdoor beer garden and live entertainment in the form of jam sessions on weekends and Wednesdays. It's open every night until the wee hours or what passes for wee here.

The **Sea Galley,** 116 Taylor St. (tel. 206/385-2992); **Town Tavern,** Water and Quincy Streets (no phone); **Hilltop Tavern,** Sims Way and Howard (tel. 206/385-0101); and **Russell's Back Alley,** Tyler and Water Streets (tel. 206/385-6536), can usually be counted on for entertainment on weekends and are meeting spots for local funseekers most any night.

Manresa Castle (see "Where to Dine"), 7th and Sheridan Streets (tel. 206/385-5750), has a very pleasant lounge designed for quiet conversation.

WHAT TO SEE AND DO: You can spend days, perhaps weeks, just roaming the historic streets of this small town and that certainly is one of the most interesting things to do here—but there are others.

Folks at the chamber of commerce can provide you with a free **visitor's guide** that outlines 70 historic homes and points of interest in town! We haven't seen them all yet, but we're trying. Most intriguing architecture is downtown or up on the hill in the area appropriately known as uptown.

Uptown was more than just a status designation, although it was certainly that too. In those days respectable ladies simply did not rustle their petticoats down on the waterfront, where every manner of rogue, rough lady, and heathen foreigner hung around. No, no, nice ladies comported themselves uptown and merchants shortly followed, naturally.

Rothschild House, Taylor and Franklin Streets (tel. 206/385-2722), is not one of the more spectacular Victorian homes, but it is filled with classic craftsmanship. A stair banister is Honduran mahogany and much of the original furnishings remain, including an 1860 sewing machine. Rothschild was not one of the international banking Rothschild family, but he built in 1868 a quite respectable house typical of the period. Hours are 10 a.m. to 5 p.m. daily mid-April to mid-October, 11 a.m. to 4 p.m. weekends only in other months. Donation is $1.

At **Fort Worden** in the state park (tel. 206/385-4730), the commanding officer's headquarters built in 1900 have been restored and furnished with lovely antique furniture so that it looks much as it must have more than 80 years ago. Hours are 10 a.m. to 5 p.m. daily April through mid-October, and admission is $1 per person. All of Fort Worden is a historic place, so the fort has worked out a self-guided walk past some of the most interesting buildings. A loop trail is about a mile long and takes about 30 minutes to walk. Stop by park headquarters for a free map. Tours by appointment in winter.

Genealogy fans must stop at the **Jefferson County Historical Museum,** City Hall, Madison and Water Streets (tel. 206/385-1003), where bound editions of the local newspaper go all the way back to 1891. No admission charge. The **Jefferson County Courthouse,** at Walker and Jefferson Streets, was built in 1892 and is quite an eyeful of Romanesque, Gothic, and Peter Pan architecture.

SPECIAL EVENTS: Two very special events occur in May and September when Port Townsend's **Victorian homes** open to the public so everyone can have a look at these national treasures. Adults pay $7.50, children under 12 pay $4, to take a self-guided tour of one of the most notable collections of Victorian architecture in the nation. Everything from extravagant mansion to simple cottage, country inn, and hotel is open for your perusal. The hours are 10 a.m. to 5 p.m.; the spring tour is usually the first weekend in May, the fall tour the third weekend in September. Call the chamber of commerce or the Port Townsend High School Scholarship Foundation (tel. 206/385-3614) for exact dates.

Port Townsend's annual **Jazz Port Townsend Festival** in early June is followed by a **Fiddle Tunes Festival** in early July, a **Chamber Music Festival** in nearby Brennan in late July, a **dance program** through August, and an **International Folk Dance and Music Festival** in late August. All the musical activity changes from year to year so call the Centrum Foundation (tel. 206/385-3102) for specifics. Tickets are $3 to $10. A **Community Tree Lighting** in early December is a colorful event.

SPORTS: With so much of the life of this north coast of the peninsula tied to the water, sailing makes a pleasant way to spend a day or more. **Sailing trips** can be arranged aboard the schooner *Alcyone,* 712 Washington St. (tel. 206/385-5378), which takes you on breakfast cruises that last about three hours for $20 per person including champagne and croissants. Other four- and seven-hour daylight cruises, including snacks or lunch, are $30 to $50 per person. A five-hour dinner cruise that takes you across the inlet to a restaurant is available for prices ranging from $35 per person, $60 a couple round trip.

Golfers will find 18 challenging tees at the **Resort at Port Ludlow** (tel. 206/437-2222), where a 6,350-yard, par-72 course awaits. The **Port Townsend Golf Course,** 1949 Blaine St. (tel. 206/385-0752), is a nine-hole, par-70 course. Greens fees at either are about $9 for 18 holes.

Port Townsend's Parks and Recreation Department (tel. 206/358-6182) can guide you to any of nine **tennis courts** scattered about town.

Bicycle rentals are available at **Coast to Coast,** 1102 Water St. (tel. 206/385-5900). Rates vary according to the size of bicycles but figure about $12 a day.

You can rent a boat at **Port Ludlow Marina,** Port Ludlow (tel. 206/447-2222), or charter fishing boats at **Port of Port Townsend,** 2539 Washington St. (tel. 206/385-2355). Charter fishing is offered by **Island Charters** at Port Ludlow Marina (tel. 206/784-4404), where you can rent a 21-foot sailboat for about $100 a day, or larger skippered boats for more.

ARTS AND CULTURAL ACTIVITIES: At Fort Worden an art group called Centrum sponsors an annual season of music and dance activities. For information on what they'll be offering, stop by the chamber of commerce or contact **Centrum** at P.O. Box 1158, Port Townsend, WA 98368 (tel. 206/385-3102).

SHOPPING: Many artists and craft workers have settled in this serene seaside town in recent years, so shopping is interesting.

Among the places you might look are **Port Townsend Art Gallery Bookstore,** 725 Water St. (tel. 206/385-1926), featuring work of local and regional artists; **Sandra Seton,** 2326 Washington St. (tel. 206/385-1205), featuring archival prints from original glass negatives taken by a ship's captain who once made a living towing turn-of-the-century ships into port; **Folklore Ethnic Imports,** 633 Water St. (tel. 206/385-6550), featuring woolens and handmade clothing; and **Liz's Loft,** 1010 Water St. (tel. 206/385-0773), with lovely collages, paintings, and pottery.

As you would expect, there are plenty of **antique shops** in town. Among them are: **Very Victorian Antiques,** 940 Water St. (tel. 206/385-2697); **Heirloom Galleries,** Victorian Mall, 940 Water St. (tel. 206/385-7836); **Mandarin West Antiques,** 827 Water St. (tel. 206/385-1290); **Dis N Dat,** Chimacum Hwy., U.S. 20 (tel. 206/385-5306); and **Marian's Place,** 827 Water St. (tel. 206/385-2010).

Crafts on the Dock, sponsored by a local art guild, offers regular summer shows of handcrafts by the bank at the new ferry dock or by the dock at Pope Park Building. Call them at 206/385-3182 to see what's happening when and where.

Fancy Feather, 1004 Lawrence St. (tel. 206/385-5371), specializes in vintage clothing and collectibles.

4. PORT ANGELES

Once an important port, Port Angeles sits out on a spit of land called Ediz Hook that makes it a fine harbor. Today that harbor harbors logging ships, fishing boats, and direct ferry service to Victoria. Port Angeles is also the hopping-off spot for trips into the grandeur of Olympic National Park. While you're here, however, there are a few interesting things to see and do in town as well.

GETTING THERE AND GETTING AROUND: Port Angeles is just 50 miles west of Port Townsend, so it makes an easy day trip or a side trip that can be combined with a visit to the lovely very British-like city of Victoria, just 18 miles away. To get to Port Angeles, take U.S. 101 west from Port Townsend.

VISITOR INFORMATION: When you arrive in town, stop by the **Port Angeles Chamber of Commerce,** 1217 E. 1st St., Port Angeles, WA 98362 (tel. 206/452-2363). In summer the chamber operates visitor information booths across from the Coho ferry terminal and at the east entrance to town on U.S. 101.

For information about scenically dramatic **Olympic National Park** and the many things to do there, stop in at or write to 600 E. Park Ave., Port Angeles, WA 98362 (tel. 206/452-4501).

WHERE TO STAY: If you're staying over in Port Angeles, try the **Red Lion Bayshore Inn,** 221 N. Lincoln St., Port Angeles, WA 98362 (tel. 206/452-9215, or toll free 800/547-8010). You could hardly find a more convenient location: it's right across the street from the ferry dock, which means you also have a water view. A long, low gray building, the Red Lion is quite modern with king-

or queen-size beds in spacious, attractively decorated rooms, many of which have private balconies overlooking this busy harbor. You'll find a casual coffeeshop, a good restaurant specializing in seafood, and a well-equipped resort with its own heated swimming pool and even a strip of sand. Rates are $56 to $96.

A pretty bed-and-breakfast here is the **Tudor Inn**, 1108 S. Oak St., Port Angeles, WA 98362 (tel. 206/452-3138), which is filled with antiques and even serves a traditional English breakfast with bacon, eggs, fruit, juice, muffins, and jams. The inn has king- and queen-size beds; rates range from $45 to $68 double. No children, pets, or smoking here.

WHERE TO EAT: Top dining kudos in Port Angeles go to **C'est Si Bon**, 2300 U.S. 101 (tel. 206/452-8888). The view across the pleasant countryside to the Olympic Mountains is topped only by the classic French cooking of such selections as tournedos, topped with seafood and a light sauce, coquilles St-Jacques, salmon with herbs, and veal entrees. Prices are in the $13 to $19 range for most entrees, and hours are 5 to 11 p.m. daily except Monday.

WHAT TO SEE AND DO: The **Arthur Feiro Marine Laboratory**, city pier at the foot of Lincoln Street (tel. 206/452-9277), has intriguing "touch" tanks where you can play touchy-feely with marine creatures of the region. The lab is open daily from 10 a.m. to 8 p.m. mid-June to Labor Day; only on Saturday and Sunday from noon to 4 p.m. in other months. Admission is $1 for adults and 50¢ for children 6 to 12.

The **Clallam County Museum**, 223 E. 4th St. (tel. 206/452-7831), occupies a 1914 building that once served as the county's courthouse. Local history and genealogy are outlined in the museum, open from 10 a.m. to 4 p.m. daily except Sunday June to September, Monday through Friday only in other months. There is no admission charge.

Sequim

Nearby Sequim (it's pronounced "Skwim") means "bountiful creature comforts" in an Indian dialect. So perhaps it should be no surprise that in this small town 18 miles east of Port Angeles you will find a group of creatures living in considerable comfort at the **Olympic Game Farm**, 383 Ward Rd. (tel. 206/683-4295). Once owned by Walt Disney Studios, this attraction has welcomed visitors for over 30 years. You can get a close look at wild animals living in an environment that has starred in more than 80 films ranging from *Never Cry Wolf* to *Grizzly Adams* and *Nikki, Wild Dog of the North*. You can drive around two looping drives here. On a walking tour you'll learn a bit about attempts to protect endangered species and perhaps even get a close look at a future movie star jaguar, leopard, fox, coyote, bobcat, badger, or bearcub. Hours in summer from June to October are 9 a.m. to dusk, in other months from 9 a.m. to 4 p.m. Open daily. Admission is $6 for adults, $4 for youngsters 5 to 12. In winter months from October to June admission prices drop to $4 for adults, $3 for children for a combined walking and driving tour.

Eons ago primitive dwellers hunted nine-foot-high elephant-like creatures called mastodons right here among these towns and villages. The actual sight where the mastodons lived is now closed, but the bones from the Manis Mastodon Site are on permanent display at the **Sequim-Dungeness Museum**, 175 W. Cedar St. (tel. 206/683-8110), in Sequim. Exhibits span 12,000 years of local history from Ice Age man to the early Klallam Indians. Museum hours from May 1 to October 1 are noon to 4 p.m. Wednesday through Sunday; from October 2 to November 30 and mid-February to April 30, from noon to 4 p.m. on Saturday and Sunday only. Closed December to mid-February. Donations suggested.

If you're a bird lover, the **Sequim Natural History Museum,** 503 Sequim Ave. in the Peninsula Cultural Arts Center (tel. 206/683-8364), features dioramas of Olympic Peninsula birds and wildlife in natural environments. You begin at the saltwater beach and move up the climatic ladder to forests, swamps, and the subalpine zones of the Olympic Mountain. There's a hands-on display for children and a collection of African animals as well. Admission is free but donations are encouraged.

For a change of pace, visit a modern winery. In 1978 two wine lovers set about the business of producing wines. They bought an old log dairy building, restored and remodeled it. They outfitted it with wine-making equipment, oak barrels, and vats, and so created **Neuharth Wines.** You can visit them and try some of their product at Still Road in Sequim (tel. 206/683-9652 or 683-3706). You'll find an attractive stone-floored tasting room with a solid oak bar. Cellars are open from noon to 5 p.m. Wednesday through Sunday, but it would be wise to call ahead to be sure all is going as scheduled.

This land is also the home of the Dungerness crab, a delicacy that garners such high prices in most parts of the country. Sample it at **Three Crabs,** 101 Three Crabs Rd. (Rte. 9-F), five miles north of Sequim (tel. 206/683-4264). The best season for the house specialty is October to March, but at any time of year you can fill up on seafood from local geoduck clams to salmon to sole. Prices are in the $10 to $15 range or less. Hours are 11 a.m. to 10 p.m. daily.

Another interesting Sequim stop is **Cedarbrook Herb Farm,** 986 Sequim Ave. South (tel. 206/683-7733), where the air is scented with wonderful aromas from 150 varieties of spices, herbs, and plants of all kinds grown and sold here. The Herb Farm is open March 15 to October from 10 a.m. to 5 p.m. daily; October to January hours are 10 a.m. to 4 p.m. Monday through Saturday. Closed January and February.

SPORTS: Sporting types will know that with mountains, sea, and lakes everywhere, there's no end to the sporting possibilities here. Floating trips in Olympic National Park on the Elwha, Queets, or Hoh Rivers are offered from mid-May to mid-September. You'll float along the Elwha River past coyotes, bears, and deer at $25 for adults, $15 for children under 13. Trips leave from Elwha Resort, eight miles west of Port Angeles on U.S. 101 at 10 a.m. and 2 p.m. Trips on the Queets, Hoh, and Quinault Rivers are $50 for adults or children, including lunch and transportation. For details on longer trips, contact Elwha Resort at 464 U.S. 101 West, Port Angeles, WA 98632 (tel. 206/457-7011).

5. OLYMPIC NATIONAL PARK

It has taken 70 million years to build the towering peaks that are today the chief lure of this ecologically varied peninsula. The best place to see the majesty nature and time have wrought here is Hurricane Ridge. More on that ridge in a moment.

First, to give you a better idea of the ceaseless change that created and is still at work on what you are seeing, here's a brief look at the making of these mountains. This Olympic Peninsula at the edge of a continental drift has on its western side the Juan de Fuca plate, which has crawled along an inch or two a year for millions of years, its vast thicknesses of molten rock moving up from the ocean bottom, pushing the earth's crust toward the North American continental plate.

Over eons, this moving crust has slid beneath the continent, its top layers slowly, slowly building to become finally the awesome peaks of the Olympic range. What you are seeing today was actually once ocean bottom, its rocky masses now so changed by pressure and temperature that only a geologist would recognize its origins. Lava seeping up through huge cracks in the rock was cooled by ancient seas into pillowy masses or into the craggy, jagged rock formations you will see.

These mountains are the forces behind the weather here, creating deep-green rain forest as they create sere desert. Winds rushing east from the Pacific pick up moisture from the sea, then rise to get over the mountains. As the winds rise, they cool. Cooler air, unable to contain as much moisture as it did when it was warm, promptly dumps its load right over Mount Olympus, the wettest spot in the continental U.S. On that mountain precipitation in rain and snow is 200 inches a year! Yet just 40 miles east, the village of Sequim has, amazingly, just the opposite extremes: it gets as little as 17 to 20 inches of wet a year. October through March are the dampest times of year on the rainy side, with more than 75% of the total downpour occurring during those months.

Deserts and rain forest . . . and glaciers. Glaciers carved the massive Strait of Juan de Fuca, carved the valleys of the Olympic Mountains, and are still at work here, fed by the highest snowfalls in the continental U.S.—40 feet a year. On Mount Olympus, where the most snow falls, ice water pours from the Blue Glacier and 60 of its relatives. Those waters turn from streams into racing rivers that are home to steelhead, salmon, and cutthroat trout. Occasionally running waters slow a bit and pool into cold and steely-blue glacial lakes.

To see some of these powerful natural forces at work, begin with a visit to **Hoh Rain Forest** where the seemingly ceaseless rain creates a shadowy green cathedral. To visit the forest, look back in this chapter to Section 2 under "What to See and Do" around Kalaloch and Lake Quinault.

The most dramatic view of the Olympic Mountains is at **Hurricane Ridge,** reached from Port Angeles by following Race Street South from town to Heart O'the Hills Road. Complete information on where and how to get a look at the most dramatic sights is available by contacting the superintendent of this 900,000-acre park at Olympic National Park, 600 E. Park Ave., Port Angeles, WA 98362 (tel. 206/452-4501). Admission to the park is free. An **Olympic National Park Visitor Center** at 3002 Mt. Angeles Rd. in Port Angeles (tel. 206/452-9235), has exhibits explaining the amazing natural forces at work here. It's open daily from 8 a.m. to 8 p.m. July to September, closing at 4 p.m. in other months.

WHERE TO STAY: In summer many people are so enchanted with the views and hiking possibilities they move right into **Lake Crescent Lodge,** HC62, Box 11, Port Angeles, WA 98362 (tel. 206/928-3211), 20 miles west of Port Angeles on U.S. 101. Operated by the National Park Service, the lodge sits in the shadow of a peak named Storm King and on the shores of a lake 600 feet deep. Its cabins and small motel are not fancy accommodations, but the beautiful lakeside location makes up for what you give up in luxury. Lodge rooms are the least attractive and bathrooms for those are down the hall. Motel rooms have little private balconies and a '50s rustic look. Fireplace cottages with living room, bedroom, fireplace, and private bath are the best choices but also the most expensive. Prices begin at $40 double in the lodge, rise to $72 for one-room cottages with private bath and $62 to $72 for motel rooms, and peak at $86 for two people sharing a fireplace cottage.

Rec vehicle campers will find space here too, for $12 double a day, and camping sites are also available.

There's a restaurant at the lodge serving all three meals, including good basic dinner selections like steaks and seafood, oysters, prime rib, fresh breads, and pies for prices in the $10 to $15 range. There's a cocktail lounge too. Lake Crescent Lodge is open only from mid-May to late September.

Lake Crescent Lodge is, as you may have noted, on a different road from Hurricane Ridge, and to get to that popular lookout you must go back east to

Port Angeles and take another road. There are no overnight facilities at Hurricane Ridge, although there is a pleasant lodge there with a gift shop and restaurant, and in winter, ski rentals, lockers, a rope tow, and Poma lift.

Hurricane Ridge Lodge is open mid-May to mid-June from 9 a.m. to 8 p.m., mid-June to September from 10 a.m. to 6 p.m., repeating the 9 a.m. to 8 p.m. hours in September. The ski season runs from December to April, when the lodge is open on weekends only. In winter the road up to the lodge is open only in daylight hours and may be closed altogether if there's a heavy snowfall, so take the necessary measures with snow tires, shovels, and chains. You can find out how road conditions are by calling a 24-hour road report at 206/452-9235.

Let us overlay those chilly thoughts with some warm ones, at the same time giving you an idea just how geologically bizarre this country is. Not far away from Hurricane Ridge, as the eagle flies, is a resort famous for its hot springs! **Sol Duc Hot Springs,** P.O. Box 2169, Port Angeles, WA 98362 (tel. 206/327-3583), welcomes you for swimming in its 100° to 110° waters for $3.25 a day, whether or not you stay in one of the motel units or cabins the resort offers. While these accommodations are not palatial, they're clean, neat, and well kept, particularly the newer units, which also have a kitchen, bath, heating, and two double beds but, strangely enough, no dishes or cooking utensils. Rate for those is $53, with prices dropping to $38 for motel rooms with or without kitchens. Trailer hookups are $8 a day. There are hot mineral spring pools and a swimming pool. The resort is open from mid-May to October.

CHAPTER XVI

PUGET SOUND AND MOUNT RAINIER

□ □ □

This is the region of endings and beginnings: here ended the Oregon Trail and here began what was to become the state of Washington. Here those first stubborn and courageous pioneers finally called it quits after hundreds of grueling miles and many heartbreaking moments.

When they saw the Pacific Ocean glittering on the horizon, those road-weary travelers put down hoe and household and settled in for a lifetime stay. That means, of course, that you will see many historic buildings here, from the tiny cabins of early settlers to the multiroom mansions of the region's first millionaires.

Over it all looms snow-clad Mount Rainier, a quiescent volcanic mass so majestic it is known simply as The Mountain.

1. ORIENTATION
To get a look at that long and touching history, start in Tacoma, where you'll see pioneer homes lovingly preserved, the stories of their owner's lives carefully recorded in museums and forts. Then move along 30 miles to Olympia, where you will see the modern embodiment of that pioneer spirit, Washington state's capitol buildings, so awesome in size and so elaborate in construction they rival anything that the Washington with the D.C. initials can boast.

Washingtonians are proud of their capital city and for good reason: Olympia's complex of capitol buildings are, well, capital! Indeed they're nationally renowned for their beauty and are among the finest state buildings you'll see in the nation. In fact, Olympia's Legislative Building, with its great dome looming over Capitol Lake, bears a strong resemblance to that D.C. Capitol building. Truly Olympian, are these architectural monsters.

Surrounded by rolling green lawns and blossoms in all the colors of the rainbow, Olympia's capitol complex is lovely enough to make it seem *almost* worth it to become a State of Washington politico. After all, how many state politicians debate under glittering chandeliers and sneak off to a rose garden for private tête-à-têtes?

When those legislators pour in here to talk, the town booms. When they pour out again at the end of the legislative session, Olympia's streets return to a quieter but by no means sleepy existence. With about 30,000 residents, the city's a bustling place but one that has plenty of green spaces to distract you from the hooting-tooting activity.

Tacoma, on the other hand, is a busy place *all* the time, with traffic racing up and down its steep hills. Those hills begin (and end) at the city's active port, the region's deepest harbor, where you will see sailing traffic cruising off to ports around the world. Tacoma is just 32 miles from Seattle, so close in fact that the airport located between the two and serving both cities (and many others) is called Sea-Tac in honor of both cities.

Built on hills, Tacoma swoops and dips down to the sound and overlooks the city's busy port on Commencement Bay. Along the sides of that bay are the hundreds of factories that have made this a bustling industrial city producing everything from copper to chemicals to stationery. Despite its proximity to Seattle, Tacoma has been a rare stop for most touring visitors to the Pacific Northwest. It is, however, a frequent haunt of business travelers, who come to wheel and deal with the huge lumber, paper, and mining companies that thrive here. Commercial as it is, the city has 44 lovely pine-trimmed parks to distract the touring traveler—and perhaps the business traveler as well!

Downtown Tacoma met the same fate as many American cities when the suburbia boom left downtown areas barren and bedraggled. Change is on the way, however, as the city continues to pursue a major downtown renovation that has already led to construction of a beautiful new hotel and a pedestrian shopping mall. In an attempt to lure shoppers and strollers back to town, the city has even connected two hillside avenues with the nation's first city-owned escalators!

Tacoma also makes a good spot to stop before heading off on a trip to majestic Mount Rainier. And in the spring, neighboring Puyallup, famed for its tulips, iris, and other bulb flowers, is a blaze of golden daffodils performing on command for the annual April Puyallup Valley Daffodil Festival, an event celebrated enthusiastically—and florally—by Tacoma as well.

Waters called the Narrows separate Tacoma from the ragged coastline of neighboring Kitsap Peninsula. When you cross the Narrows here to journey over to the Kitsap Peninsula, you'll drive across a 5,450-foot span that was once a rickety old bridge known as "Galloping Gertie" in salute to the swaying ride it provided. Gertie collapsed one day to be upstaged by a quite solid replacement with a center span nearly 3,000 feet long, one of the longest in the nation. On the other side of that bridge, you'll find yourself in Gig Harbor, a handsome little town that's also a chic fishing and sailing getaway spot for Tacoma dwellers and an arts and crafts center.

You're now on the Kitsap Peninsula. This mass of land jutting out into the sound west of Olympia has, as its most famous resident, a sprawling U.S. Navy base at Bremerton that hosts the battleship *Missouri*. As you drive through this southern end of the Puget Sound region, you'll often see the blue waters of the sound peeking through pine trees and flowers while in the distance loom the snow-capped peaks of the Olympic Mountains on the west and the Cascades on the east. Because these three regions are so close together, we'll introduce you to them all at once, so when you're in the area you can go exploring.

GETTING THERE: You can get to the south Puget Sound area by bus, train, plane, car, and even by ferry.

Sea-Tac International Airport is coastal Washington's air gateway. Many national and international airlines serve the area (see Chapter II for a list).

Greyhound buses travel to the region, stopping at 107 E. Seventh Ave. in Olympia (tel. 206/624-3456), in Tacoma at 1319 Pacific Ave. (tel. 206/383-4621), and in Bremerton at 215 1st St. (tel. 206/377-3701).

Amtrak trains (tel. toll free 800/USA-RAIL) serve the area, stopping at 1713 Pacific Ave. (tel. 206/627-8141) in Tacoma, and at Rich Road and 83rd Street in East Olympia (platform only, no telephone).

Two **ferries** serve Tacoma. From Vashion Island on the north it's a 15-minute ride from Tahlequa to the end of Pearl Street on Point Defiance. Ferry costs vary, so contact them for exact fares. From the south the ferry leaves Yoman Dock on Anderson Island and 20 minutes later deposits you at Steilacoom. Continue on Steilacoom Boulevard for about three miles to Orchard Street; turn north for about five miles to 6th Street and west to Tacoma's center. Bremerton on the Kitsap Peninsula can be reached by ferry from Seattle. After a 60-minute crossing you debark beside the Puget Sound Naval Shipyard at 6th Street (tel. toll free 800/542-7552 for specific schedule information).

Travel by Car

By car Washington's scenic capital, Olympia, is an easy target from nearly every compass point. From the north and east I-5, the state's—and the West Coast's—major north-south artery swings west around Puget Sound's southern extreme to Olympia just south of the city center. Southbound, take I-5's "City Center" exit 105A. U.S. 101 joins I-5 at Olympia; exit to I-5 North, then travel approximately one mile to the I-5 "City Center" exit no. 105.

The city and port of Tacoma—Washington's third-largest city—dominates the south Puget Sound area and provides a web of interstate, federal, and state roads. From the northwest and the Kitsap Peninsula, traffic funnels south to Tacoma through Bremerton on Wash. 16, where it crosses into western Tacoma over the Narrows Bridge to join with I-5 in the downtown area. I-5 drops down from Seattle on the north, then swings west to cross into Tacoma from the east. Both Wash. 99 and Wash. 509 come into the city from the northeast, while Wash. 167 breaches the city boundary on the east just a few blocks south of the I-5 entry. Washington Hwy. 512 skirts the southern edge of the city and joins I-5 and Wash. 7 from the south. Traveling north or south, you'll take exit 133 to Tacoma Dome and city center.

Bremerton and Kitsap Peninsula travelers coming in from the north will turn south on Wash. 3, after crossing the Hood Canal toll road, to enter Bremerton on the west. Alternatively, a turn to the east on Wash. 308, then south on Wash. 303, will bring you directly into the center of the city.

GETTING AROUND: The distance to Tacoma from Sea-Tac is about 32 miles to the south; to Olympia, it's 61 miles south; to Bremerton, 25 miles northwest.

A number of rental-car companies operate in the area. You can find **Budget Rent-A-Car** at Sea-Tac Terminal (tel. 206/433-5243), or in Olympia at 728 E. Fourth Ave. (tel. 206/943-3852). In downtown Tacoma, Budget is located at 1305 Pacific Ave. (tel. 206/383-4944).

If you are headed for Olympia or Tacoma from Sea-Tac International Airport, you can get to major hotels, college campuses, and even to private homes, on the **Capital Aeroporter** (tel. 206/754-7113, 206/866-8660 in Olympia,

206/572-9544 in Tacoma). Other times the company plies a regular schedule, which they'll be happy to send you or outline for you by telephone. Call to determine pickup hours. The ride to Olympia takes about 90 minutes; to Tacoma, about 35 minutes. Prices vary by distance from $10 to $17. To Bremerton from Sea-Tac International the **Bremerton-Kitsap Airporter** (tel. 206/876-1737, or toll free 800/562-7948 outside of Bremerton, open from 7:30 a.m. to 6 p.m.) runs a regular schedule daily. Prices vary according to your destination on the peninsula, but fares to Bremerton, for instance, are $16 for adults, $24 for a couple, $4 for children over 5, 10% less round trip.

Taxi service is provided by **Red Top Taxi** (tel. 206/357-3700), or **Tri-Cities Taxi** (tel. 206/357-4949) in Olympia; **Yellow Cab Co.** (tel. 206/472-3303) in Tacoma. Figure $1.50 a mile.

Pierce County Transit operates buses throughout the region for prices beginning at 35¢ in off-hours and 60¢ at peak periods (25¢ for senior citizens and free to children under 5). Call them for route information (tel. 206/593-4520).

2. OLYMPIA

Olympia got its start in the 1850s as a lumbering capital, but really got into business when it became the state capital. Since then it has, like many small capital cities, frequently fought off those who would like to change the location of the capitol—to *their* city.

History is important to Olympians, and they have preserved it with care. You can get a glimpse of the city's past in the capitol buildings, the historic Old Capitol Building, and several restored homes dating back more than a century.

In nearby Tumwater you'll find more history preserved, plus a crashing waterfall that forms the central core of a beautiful state park.

ORIENTATION: Although Olympia spreads itself around the inlets, bays, and lakes at the southern edge of Puget Sound, it's easy to find your way. Understandably its main street is called **Capitol Way**; it runs from the marina at Budd Inlet on the north to I-5 on the south, where it becomes Capitol Boulevard. **Fourth Avenue** divides Olympia north from south. The city center lies largely south of Fourth Avenue, west of East Bay Drive, north of I-5 and east of Capitol Lake. Avenues north of Fourth are named, while those south are numbered, progressing from north to south. Streets distinguish themselves with the names of early presidents and historical figures of Olympia.

GETTING AROUND: Intercity Transit travels between Olympia, Tumwater, and Lacey, stopping at several hotels and major points of interest in the area including Tumwater Falls Park, Olympia Brewery, the Capital Mall, and shopping plazas. Fares are 35¢ for adults, 25¢ for children. Day passes are available at 75¢ for adults, 50¢ for children. Buses operate from 6:30 a.m. to 10 p.m. Monday through Friday, to 6 p.m. weekends. Fare, route, and schedule information is available at 206/786-1881.

Rental-car companies include **Budget Rent-A-Car,** 722 S. Olympia Way (tel. 206/943-3852), and **A1 Rent-A-Car,** 722 Capitol Way (tel. 206/943-6990).

USEFUL INFORMATION: For **emergency police** help, dial 911. . . . Olympia's **hospital** is at 413 Lilly Rd. NE (tel. 206/491-9480). . . . For intercity **bus information,** call 206/753-8107. . . . To reach the **city bus station,** call 206/357-5541 or 352-8451. . . . **Washington State Visitor Information**

Center is at the Henderson Company House Museum, 602 N. Deschutes Way (tel. 206/753-8583), open from 8 a.m. to 4:30 p.m. daily in summer.

TOURIST INFORMATION: Find out what to see and do in the area by contacting the **Olympia Area Visitor-Convention Bureau,** 1000 Plum St., Olympia, WA 98501 (tel. 206/357-3370); or the **Olympia / Thurston County Chamber of Commerce,** 1000 Plum St., Olympia, WA 98501 (tel. 206/357-3362). Either can provide you with a handy local information pamphlet called the *"Thurston County Visitor Guide."* At the **State Capitol Information Center,** State Capitol Campus (Parking Division), Olympia, WA 98504 (tel. 206/753-3269), you'll also find plenty of informational materials. **Guided tour information** is at 206/586-8687.

WHERE TO STAY: If you'd like to settle in here to have a look and a listen at what's going on in the state capital, here's a rundown of some places where you might settle. Add 10.8% tax to rates.

Westwater Inn, 2300 Evergreen Park Dr., Olympia, WA 98502 (tel. 206/943-4000 or toll free 800/551-8500), isn't the easiest spot in the world to find, but it's worth the looking. Built high on a hill overlooking the city and just on the edge of town, the Westwater has some of the most gorgeous views in the area: off in the distance the pristine arch of the Capitol dome, and right outside your window, deep-green forests. You'll find 194 rooms at this recently renovated hilltop hotel, eight suites with Jacuzzi whirlpools, a heated outdoor pool and Jacuzzi, and everywhere those beautiful green woods for jogging, bicycling, or just meditating. Westwater's restaurant, Ceazans, has a lovely view of the Capitol dome and a lounge that will give you a clue on how to get to this resort—it's called Exit 104 Lounge. There's also a coffeehouse. To get here, take exit 104 from I-5, then take the Cooper Point Road exit off U.S. 101. Rates are $56 to $63 double, about $6 less single, for large, attractively decorated rooms with balconies overlooking those views.

The **Tyee Hotel,** 500 Tyee Dr., Tumwater, WA 98502 (tel. 206/352-0511, or toll free 800/648-6440 in Washington), is three miles south of the city. As well known for its top-rated dining room, Sutter's, as for its accommodations, the Tyee features entertainment, spacious rooms with contemporary décor, a swimming pool, and tennis. Long low buildings with house large, attractively decorated rooms overlooking green lawns where birch trees rustle in the breeze. There's a swimming pool on the grounds too. Room rates here are $52 to $125 double, depending on the size of the accommodations.

If you like central locations, you can't get much more central than **Governor House Hotel,** 621 S. Capitol Way, Olympia, WA 98501 (tel. 206/352-7700), a high-rise building a few minutes' walk from the Capitol. Smack in the middle of downtown, this hotel is a favorite with legislators and has all the comforts of home (perhaps *more* than home) in one building: attractive modern décor, a cozy cocktail bar, swimming pool, and a booth-lined restaurant called Sylvester's. Rates here are $48 to $52 double, $42 single.

The **Aladdin Motor Inn,** 900 Capitol Way, Olympia, WA 98501 (tel. 206/352-7200, or toll free 800/528-1234), is part of the reliable Best Western chain. It also occupies a downtown location close to the Capitol buildings. A comparatively small hotel with just 100 rooms, the Aladdin also houses a very well-known restaurant, Arnold's. Rooms here are of average size with queen-size beds, color TVs, and direct-dial phones. For amusement there's a heated pool or a seat in the lobby, where you can watch the movers and shakers on their way to and from lunch or dinner at this popular dining spot. Rates are $47.50 to $52.50 double, about $5 less single.

For a change of pace in Olympia, sink into the lace-curtained, columned magnificence of the **Harbinger Inn,** 1136 East Bay Drive (tel. 206/754-0389). Built in 1910 of concrete blocks made from sand unearthed from the cellar and worked to resemble stone, this three-story gray mirage sparkles with white trim and soaring white columns that create a very dramatic mien indeed. There are just four rooms at the inn, all of them on the second floor, two with views of Budd Inlet and two facing a waterfall behind the house. There are no telephones or televisions in your room, but you can wander the house at will night or day, including a beautiful second-floor balcony that runs all the way across the front of the inn creating a similar porch below. Decorated with dramatic élan, the inn also serves full breakfasts with options like blueberry crêpes or fancy egg concoctions or continental breakfast, you decide. Rates at the inn, which will serve you breakfast in your room or family-style in the inn's dining room, are $37 to $63 double, depending on the room and breakfast you select.

A budget spot in the area is the **Golden Gavel,** 909 Capitol Way, Olympia, WA 98501 (tel. 206/352-8533), where you'll find smallish but attractive rooms in a basic downtown motel charging $33 double for a room with queen-size bed, $36 for a room with two doubles. Extra persons sharing a room are $3 each, and prices are about $3 cheaper for single travelers.

If you're **camping,** try **Deep Lake Resort,** 12405 Tilley Rd. South, Olympia, WA 98502 (tel. 206/352-7388). Located about ten miles south of Olympia, the campground is on the shore of a 66-acre, spring-fed lake stocked with rainbow trout. You'll find boats, a camp store, games room, and horseshoe courts. Rates are in the $11 range, double, for a hookup. A few cabins, some with fireplaces also, are available at prices from $30 to $50. You furnish linens and pots. The camping resort is quite close to the Conservation Corps area at Millersylvania State Park and features log buildings constructed in 1935 set amid 841 acres of forest.

Another campground in the area is **American Heritage/KOA,** 9610 Kimmie St. SW, Olympia, WA 98502 (tel. 206/943-8778), where 100 campsites are available along with rental cycles, free evening movies, hayrides, and outdoor games. Take exit 99 from I-5 and drive east. Open Memorial Day through Labor Day, KOA charges $18 double for full hookup.

WHERE TO DINE: Many a political decision is made over breakfast, lunch, or dinner, so you can be sure you'll find some good restaurants in this legislative city. Here's a look at some of the options.

Arnold's, in the Best Western Aladdin Motor Inn, 900 Capitol Way (tel. 206/352-7200), is on the list of most Olympia visitors—and residents. Operated by a top chef, Arnold's is quite a pretty place too: hurricane lamps, fresh flowers on linen-topped tables, and skylights. Mirrors play such tricks with this comparatively small dining room that we were there for an hour before we discovered just how small it really is. On the menu at dinner you'll discover such unusual treats as filet of beef tips Malayan prepared in a light curry and chutney sauce. You'll also find all the old standards like prime rib and coquilles St-Jacques. Prices for dinner entrees are in the $10 to $15 range, about $4 to $7 for lunch. Arnold's is open Monday through Saturday from 6:30 a.m. to 10 p.m. and on Sunday from 7 a.m. to 2 p.m.

For more than 60 years Olympians have been going to the **Olympia Oyster House,** 320 W. Fourth Ave. (tel. 206/943-8020), to stock up on luscious oysters plucked right out of the waters of the sound. You'll dine here overlooking the water for prices in the $10 to $15 range. The Oyster House, which has been in business since 1925, is open from 11 a.m. to 10 p.m. Monday through Thursday, an hour later on weekends, and from noon to 10 p.m. on Sunday.

You can't beat the view from the **Falls Terrace Restaurant,** at the foot of the Olympia Brewery, 106 Deschutes Way, Tumwater (tel. 206/943-7830). At a window seat here you can look out over the dramatic Tumwater Falls and dine on prime beef and fresh seafood in the $10 to $17 price range. Falls Terrace is open from 11 a.m. to 10 p.m. Monday through Thursday, to 10:30 p.m. on Friday and Saturday, and from noon to 9 p.m. on Sunday.

When you're suffering a taco attack, head for **Migel's,** 4611 Tumwater Valley Dr., Tumwater (tel. 206/352-1575), for a fix of yummy Mexican goodies. Prices are in the quite moderate range, say $5 to $10 a person, maybe less. Migel's is *abierto* from 11 a.m. to 9 p.m. Monday through Thursday, to 10 p.m. on Friday, to 11 p.m. on Saturday, and 10 a.m. to 2 p.m. and 3 to 9 p.m. on Sunday.

If you're touring the Capitol Mall, stop into **Charlie's Bar and Grill,** 205 Capitol Mall (tel. 206/754-9767), and rub elbows with legislators who, like you, will be chowing down on some of the restaurant's 60 offerings, ranging from steaks to sandwiches and seafood. Dinner prices are in the $10 to $15 range. Charlie's is open Monday through Saturday from 11:30 a.m. to 11 p.m. and from noon to 9 p.m. on Sunday, later hours in the lounge.

If you ever had an urge to walk into a library and *raise* your voice, here's your chance. It's called **Carnegie's,** 302 E. Seventh Ave. (tel. 206/357-5550), and it is really in a library, built in 1914. Naturally aged meats are a feature of this interesting spot, but seafood lovers will find salmon, oysters, and more on the menu. Carnegie's is open from 11:30 a.m. to 2 p.m. Monday through Friday for lunch ($5 to $10) and from 5:30 to 10 p.m. for dinner, opening a bit earlier on Saturday and Sunday. Prices are in the $10 to $20 range. There are 10,000 books here too.

Fleur de Lys, 901 Legion Way SE (tel. 206/754-6208), creates French and nouvelle culinary treats in a handsome old home with a view of the city's stately Capitol Building. Long one of the city's favorites, the Fleur de Lys can be counted on for top-notch French dining focusing on seafood and veal. You'll pay $15 to $20 for dinner at this elegantly plush dining spot which is open from 11 a.m. to 2 p.m. weekdays and 5:30 to 9 p.m. on Thursday, Friday, and Saturday only.

Who could resist a spot called **Jo Mama's,** 120 N. Pear St. (tel. 206/943-9849)? A great monicker for a popular spot that seems to have gotten a lock on the tastebuds of Olympia's pizza lovers, Jo Mama's specializes in whole-wheat pizzas and fresh ingredients for toppings. Lasagne is another house favorite, and you can also chow down on some hearty soups and sandwiches in a cozy setting here. Prices are in the $10 to $12 bracket or less, and hours are 11 a.m. to 11 p.m. daily, opening at 4 p.m. on Saturday and Sunday and closing an hour or so later on weekends.

Ceazan's, in the Westwater Inn at 2300 Evergreen Park Dr. (tel. 206/943-4000), is like the inn itself, a place of spectacular views. Below, the dome of the Capitol building curves handsomely across the horizon and in the distance snow-capped mountains beckon. Well-prepared steak and seafood from all over the south Puget Sound area are specialties. Prices are in the $12 to $18 range. The restaurant is open weekdays from 11:30 a.m. to 1:30 p.m. for lunch and 5:30 to 10 p.m. for dinner. Saturday hours are 5:30 to 11 p.m. and a Sunday champagne brunch runs from 10 a.m. to 2 p.m., closed for dinner that day.

In Tumwater **Sutter's,** 500 Tyee Dr., in the Tyee Motor Inn (tel. 206/352-0511 or 754-6695), serves up seafood and beef in a garden atmosphere. There's frequent entertainment here for listening or dancing. Dinner prices are in the $12 to $17 range. Open Monday through Friday for lunch from 11 a.m. to 2 p.m. and for dinner from 5 to 10 p.m., on Saturday for dinner only, and on Sunday from 10 a.m. to 2 p.m. for brunch and from 5 to 10 p.m. for dinner.

Tucked away in Buck's Fifth Avenue store, 209 E. Fifth Ave. (tel. 206/352-9301), is **Chattery Down,** where you can sip high tea and lunch on delicate little things as you do what the name suggests. Open Monday through Saturday from 8:30 a.m. to 5:30 p.m. You'll spend only $5 or so for lunch.

Northwest wines are a specialty at **La Petite Maison,** 2005 Ascension St. NW (tel. 206/943-8812), where the cuisine features the most popular continental dishes. A restored farmhouse, this handsome spot always manages to come up with something different, so you might find pork stuffed with fruit or chicken prepared with unusual herbs. Dungeness crab prepared as a salad and roast beef with sour cream are two house specialties at lunch. Evening meals are limited to just a few choices, but each is carefully planned right down to the grand finale desserts. Price for a multicourse dinner at this sophisticated, outstanding restaurant is $13 to $15. Open weekdays from 11:30 a.m. to 2 p.m. and 5 to 10 p.m. (an hour later on Friday) and from 6 to 10 p.m. on Saturday; closed Sunday.

If pizza pangs have struck, **Dirty Dave's Gay 90's Pizza Parlor,** 3939 Martin Way (tel. 206/456-1560), offers those cheese- and tomato-laden pies in a memorabilia-filled atmosphere that's downright fun. Prices are in the $5 to $10 range for pizzas, and there are some good pastas available too. Open Monday through Saturday from 11 a.m. to 11 p.m. (an hour later on weekends) and from noon to 11 p.m. on Sunday. A good family spot.

Gardner's Seafood and Pasta, 111 W. Thurston (tel. 206/786-8466), takes all the best—and the most unusual—of Puget Sound seafood and combines it with unusual pastas to come up with some delightful treats. Prices are in the $7 to $15 range for dinner. Gardner's is open daily from 5 to 9 p.m. No smoking; reservations advised.

3. TACOMA

Tacoma likes to call itself the "City of Destiny," and certainly it has been the destiny of many a millionaire industrialist and lumberman who settled here. But it has also been the destiny of "just folks" who work together to keep this city a happy, friendly, and very active place.

Things have been going that way for nigh onto 200 years now since explorer George Vancouver stopped by in 1792. Others of his inquisitive ilk followed, including the Hudson's Bay Company, which set up a fort and trading post in the area in 1885. That fort on the Nisqually River is now Point Defiance Park. Commencement Bay got its name from another explorer, Capt. Charles Wilkes, who began surveying Puget Sound at Tacoma, dubbing his starting point, naturally enough, Commencement Bay.

First of those to settle here, however, were lumberman Nicholas De Lin and railroad buff Job Carr. Fifteen years or so after they moved in, the town, once called Commencement City, was officially dubbed Tacoma, meaning "Mother of Waters" in the local Indian language. By 1872 Tacoma had a lumber mill, two stores, a saloon, a hotel, jail, blacksmith, and all of 100 people to patronize those establishments. In 1873 the Northern Pacific Railroad dropped in for a permanent stay and the boom was on.

You won't find a raft of razzle-dazzle activities in Tacoma, but you'll find 44 diverting parks and some beautiful views. You'll see some of those, by the way, on a stroll through the downtown pedestrian shopping mall up high on a hill.

ORIENTATION: Tacoma spreads inland from Dash Point on Puget Sound, flows around Commencement Bay to the tip of Point Defiance, then moves south along the Narrows to the tip of Day Island.

On entering the city Wash. 16 becomes Olympic Boulevard, then joins Sixth Avenue, which in turn joins Division Avenue, thus forming the route that generally divides Tacoma north from south. Pacific Avenue divides Tacoma east from west. As a rule streets are numbered progressively from Division Avenue out. Lettered streets and named avenues run north and south.

GETTING AROUND: Pierce County Transit will get you around Tacoma for fares of 35¢ during off-peak hours and 60¢ before 9 a.m. and from 4 to 6 p.m. Telephone 206/593-4520 for route information.

Taxi service is available from **Yellow Cab** (tel. 206/564-2650). Rates are $1.25 at the flag drop and $1.10 per mile.

USEFUL INFORMATION: For emergency police and fire help, telephone 911. . . . For events of the day, the *Tacoma News Tribune* is the largest newspaper. . . . Send telegrams at 2209 Pacific Ave. or by telephoning 206/627-8898. . . . You'll find a 24-hour restaurant at the Quality Inn, 9930 S. Tacoma Way.

TOURIST INFORMATION: The Tacoma / Pierce County Visitor and Convention Bureau, 735 St. Helens, Tacoma, WA 98401 (tel. 206/627-2836), will help you out with information about the area and some pamphlets on area activities. In nearby Puyallup, contact the friendly folks at the **Puyallup Valley / Eastern Pierce County Chamber of Commerce,** 2823 E. Main Ave., Puyallup, WA 98372 (tel. 206/845-6755).

WHERE TO STAY: Let's take a look at some of Tacoma's stopping spots. Most accommodations in Tacoma are on the outskirts of town, but a sleek, new hotel that opened in the spring of 1984 bodes well for the renaissance of downtown Tacoma.

This new, top-of-the-line hostelry is the chic **Sheraton Tacoma Hotel,** 1320 Broadway Plaza, Tacoma, WA 94802 (tel. 206/572-3200, or toll free 800/325-3535, 800/268-9330 in western Canada, 800/268-9393 in eastern Canada). Go no farther than the lobby and you'll know you're somewhere special. A four-story skylit atrium occupies center stage with a raised lobby lounge set off by potted palms. The décor features muted shades of teal blue offset by pale pinks and trimmed with pink brass (we don't know how it gets pink, but it's lovely). Very friendly workers will tell you everything you want to know about their city, and what they don't know, they'll go and find out—at last, professionalism in tourism. Rooms vary from large to very large, and all are done in the latest colors and furnishings with oversize beds (king- or queen-size), plush carpeting, televisions, clock radios, and telephones, of course. Prices for a great deal of luxury in a city with few luxurious accommodations are quite reasonable: $82 to $110 double for quite amazing views. On "concierge floors" (24 and 25), you're treated to continental breakfast, even hors d'oeuvres, newspapers, and turn-down service. All rooms are about $10 less single. For dining the hotel's rooftop Rose Room has prices in the $12 to $17 range for a variety of steak and seafood choices, and the Wintergarden Café is a light-meal stop. That lobby lounge, by the way, is called the Music Room in salute to the piano renderings there daily. Parking at the hotel is free (a welcome extra in this parking-difficult town). You'll find a Jacuzzi and sauna here, and if you want a workout, the hotel will treat you to complimentary use of the YMCA a block away.

On the outskirts of town you'll find a very nice, moderately priced **Quality Inn,** 9920 S. Tacoma Way, Tacoma, WA 98499 (tel. 206/588-5241, or toll free 800/228-5151, 800/642-8700 in Nebraska, and 800/268-8990 in Canada, except 416/485-2600 in Toronto). From I-5 take exit 127 to South Tacoma Way. Spacious rooms are decorated in floral spreads and have glass doors opening on to a balcony or terrace, contemporary dark-wood furnishings, tweedy chairs, and a separate dressing area. The inn is housed in attractive two-story buildings trimmed in dark woods and stone and set well back from the highway. In the center of several buildings is a big plot of grass that's a perfect place for the kids to romp off some of that energy. A moderately priced restaurant will curb the hunger pangs, and there's a lounge. Rates at this spot, from which you can see Mount Rainier floating in the distance, are $65 to $75 double.

Just off I-5 at exit 137, you'll find the **Best Western Executive Inn,** 5700 Pacific Hwy. East, Tacoma, WA 98424 (tel. 206/922-0080, or toll free 800/528-1234). It provides such amenities as an indoor skylit swimming pool, a health spa with Jacuzzi, sauna, and exercise room, and an attractive restaurant, lounge, and coffeeshop. Rooms in the four-story building have big picture windows and are attractively decorated. Rates range from $53 to $58 double all year.

Another Best Western here, the **Best Western Tacoma Inn,** 8726 S. Hosmer (I-5 at the South 84th Street exit, exit 129), Tacoma, WA 98444 (tel. 206/535-2880, or toll free 800/528-1234), is quite an attractive place amid a cluster of motels. Opened in 1983, it has a gray-and-pink lobby dominated by a black stone fireplace and fitted out in a gray-and-pink color scheme accented by pink silk flowers. Those pink hues are carried into spacious rooms which feature chic brown-and-pink spreads. In 1984 the hotel added several new wings with similarly handsome décor. Rates at this lovely motel are $50 to $60 double, $6 per additional person. Commercial rates are $4 to $5 less.

At the South 84th Street exit (129) from I-5 (the exit sign says South 72nd and South 84th Streets if you're coming from the north, exit 128 from the south), you'll find two other attractive possibilities: the Sherwood Inn and Nendel's Motor Inn.

Sherwood Inn, South 84th Street and I-5, Tacoma, WA 98444 (tel. 206/535-2800), has large and airy rooms and a pretty pool—heated—surrounded by wood decking. Amenities include a beauty salon and barbershop, coffeeshop plus a more formal dining room. Rates are a reasonable $32 to $34 double, no charge for children under 12. Extra persons are $4 each and the inn permits pets but charges $3 for them.

Nendel's, 8702 S. Hosmer, Tacoma, WA 98444 (tel. 206/535-3100, or toll free 800/547-0106), is tucked away among pine trees where a greenthumber has created a rock garden and planted colorful roses. A small pool graces this attractive building, which is finished in dark woods and brick. Rooms have floral décor. The main building houses a contemporary 24-hour restaurant called Rocky's. Rates are $39 single, $44 double, for rooms with one or two queen-size beds. Rooms with king-size beds are also available. Suites measuring a lordly 12 by 29 feet are $45 single, $50 double.

WHERE TO EAT: Tacoma has plenty of restaurants so here's a look at a few.

Sebastian's Restaurant, 928 Pacific Ave. (tel. 206/272-0300), serves up fresh Northwest seafood and good steaks for lunch and dinner and has a lively happy hour from 4 to 7 p.m. with half-price drinks. Daily lunch specials, including soup, salad, and sandwiches, are in the $5 range; dinner entrees are $10 to $15 or so. Open from 11 a.m. to midnight weekdays, from 5 p.m. on Saturday; closed Sunday.

Towrys Le Snack Café Expresso Restaurant, 322 Tacoma Ave. South at 4th Street (tel. 206/272-5937), is a cozy little spot that specializes in its sumptuous Sunday brunch and in European cooking with Mediterranean overtones. That translates to such continental treats as steak au poivre coated with cracked black peppercorns; chicken Grecque sautéed with olives, white wine, and Greek feta cheese; turos Csusza, a Hungarian concoction of bacon, onions, noodles, cheese, and sour cream. New owners Dale and Marcy Towry have also introduced vegetarian options and such intriguing selections as Slovak sauerkraut soup with sour cream, sausage, and sauerkraut. Swiss raclette, potatoes smothered in melted cheese and served with an assortment of pickled vegetables, is not to be missed. Romanian and Polish dishes also appear on the menu here, as does wild game and seafood specialties. Prices rarely top $5, including soup and salad, for lunch, and are $8 to $16 for a changing array of dinner entrees. Brunch is served on Saturday and Sunday from 8 a.m. to 2:30 p.m. and dinner is served from 5:30 to 9 p.m. only on Thursday and Friday nights. Tuesday through Friday the restaurant offers breakfast—orange French toast or a German pancake, for instance—from 7 to 10:45 a.m. and lunch from 11 a.m. to 2:30 p.m.

The **Tacoma Salmon House,** 2611 Pacific Ave. (tel. 206/627-0141), is a nautical spot specializing in scrumptious alder-smoked salmon, a not-to-be-missed specialty of the Northwest. Open Monday through Saturday from noon to 10 p.m. The Salmon House has been around for umpteen years so it has been pleasing many most of the time. There's piano music from 6 to 9 p.m. Prices are in the $10 to $15 range.

You can have water views at several establishments in this water-fringed city, including the **Bay Co.,** 3327 Ruston Way (tel. 206/752-6661), a chic spot serving beef, lamb, and the like in healthy portions. The Bay Co. is open for lunch weekdays from 11:30 a.m. to 2 p.m. and for dinner from 4:30 to 10 p.m. Monday through Thursday, with slightly later closing hours Friday through Sunday. Dinner prices are in the $12 to $17 range.

Yet another waterfront spot is **Johnny's Dock,** 1900 E. D St. (tel. 206/627-3186). Johnny's is open beginning at 11 a.m. daily (at 9:30 a.m. on Sunday) and closing at 1 a.m. daily (an hour later on weekends and 10 p.m. on Sunday). Figure $10 to $15 each for dinner.

If you love ogling beautiful old homes, why not have dinner in one at **E.R. Rogers,** 1702 Commercial St., Steilacoom (tel. 206/582-0280)? In a mansion built in 1891 on a bluff overlooking Puget Sound, this slightly out-of-town spot features eastern corn-fed beef and Northwest seafood from 5:30 to 10 p.m. daily, longer hours on weekends. Prices range from $10 to $15 for dinner; Sunday brunchers congregate from 10 a.m. to 2 a.m.

Oyster fans should head straight for **Shenanigan's,** 3017 Ruston Way (tel. 206/752-8811), where the city's largest oyster bar dispenses quantities of the bivalves from 11 a.m. to 2 a.m. Monday through Saturday (from 10 a.m. on Sunday), plus a Sunday brunch and a Monday-night crab feed. Shenanigan's claims to have Puget Sound's largest deck for dining and cocktails. On it you can gaze at beautiful bay views as you dine on seafood and steaks. Later you can dance the night away in an equally bedazzling atmosphere at one of the region's hottest nightclubs, Club Rio, which sports sweeping views of Commencement Bay. Comedy and dancing to oldy-goldy selections are the order of the night here. Fresh seafood and steaks are the mainstays of the menu on which prices fall in the $11 to $16 range for dinner.

Cliff House, 6300 Marine View Dr. (tel. 206/927-0400), is yet another water-view spot, this one serving some fine continental specialties for lunch and dinner. There's music and dancing in the lounge and Sunday brunch in the dining room. Cliff House is open Monday through Friday from 11:30 a.m. to 10:30 p.m., with slightly later hours on weekends and closing at 9 p.m. on Sunday. You'll pay prices in the $10 to $16 range here for a wonderful dinner in a wonderful atmosphere.

If you're traveling with a hungry family, try the **Old Spaghetti Factory,** 1735 Jefferson St. South (tel. 206/383-2214), where all manner of tummy-filling pastas are served up in an eclectic atmosphere. Prices are very low—in the $5 to $8 range—and the Factory is open from 5 to 10 p.m. Monday through Thursday, to 11 p.m. on Friday and Saturday, and 4 to 9 p.m. on Sunday.

Grazie Caffe Italiano, 2301 N. 30th St. (tel. 206/627-0231), is proud of what it calls its classic old-world setting. You'll find homemade sauces and freshly rolled pasta, an espresso bar with sinful Italian pastries, and a location near downtown and the waterfront. Prices are in the $10 to $15 range, and the restaurant is open from 11 a.m. to midnight daily.

Much loved by the locals for its seductive atmosphere—it was once voted the most atmospheric restaurant in the region in a magazine readers' poll—**Lobster Pot South,** 4013 Ruston Way (tel. 206/759-2165), makes for a delightful getaway some afternoon or evening. Northwest seafood prepared in some quite innovative ways are the trademark of this Tacoma restaurant. You'll pay $15 to $20 for dinner entrees at this crustacean which is open from 5:30 to 9:30 p.m. weekdays, later on weekends, and 9:30 a.m. to 1:30 p.m. on Sunday.

Harbor Lights, 272611 Ruston Way (tel. 206/752-8600), sizzles with the best in steaks, chops, veal, and fresh seafood served in a rustically nautical décor. There's a lovely view from this restaurant. You'll pay $10 to $15 for many dinner entrees, more for some rarer creations. Hours are 11 a.m. to 11 p.m. Monday through Friday, later on Saturday, and 2 to 9 p.m. Sunday.

Stanley & Seafort's Saloon & Grill, 115 E. 34th St. (tel. 206/473-7300), is a favorite for business lunches but many sneak back later for dinner and beyond. Overlooking the city, S&S charges prices in the $15 to $20 bracket for dinner and is open from 11:30 a.m. to 2 p.m. weekdays and 5 to 9:30 p.m. daily except Sunday when hours are 4:30 to 9:30 p.m. On weekends hours are stretched to 11 p.m. or beyond.

WHAT TO SEE AND DO: Tacoma does offer some interesting things to see and to do. To get a look at much of what the city has to offer, make your way to **Fireman's Park** at 9th and A Streets, where a giant totem carved from a single tree signals the beginning of the **Klahowya Trail** (that means "welcome" in the Chinook Indian language). Designed to show you the high spots of Tacoma, the trail winds through the city past **Wright Park,** where the **Seymour Botanical Conservatory** is housed in a Victorian-era greenhouse (open from 8 a.m. to 4:20 p.m. daily; tel. 206/591-5330). That trail continues on past the city's major historic landmarks and parks and takes about two hours to drive.

Point Defiance Park (tel. 206/591-5335 or 591-3690) leads the pack of parks that dot this city. Largest of the lot, Point Defiance, at North 54th and Pearl Streets, covers almost 700 acres of ground on a peninsula that separates Commencement Bay from the Narrows. Here the scent of hundreds of roses permeates the air and you can stroll through a **Japanese garden,** masses of rhododendron, and a fascinating aquarium and **zoo** open year round. Admission to the zoo and aquarium is $3.50 for adults, $2.25 for teens, $1.75 for youngsters 5 through 12, and 50¢ for toddlers. Point Defiance Zoo and Aquarium are open daily April to October from 10 a.m. to 7 p.m., varying hours in other months. New at the zoo is a tidepool exhibit and a Marine Discovery Lab. Elsewhere in the park there's also now a **boathouse** and waterfront complex where you can rent boats and motors and obtain fishing licenses and salmon punch cards.

Meanwhile, those youngsters who can't stop to smell the flowers can be entertained at **Never Never Land,** which depicts 32 fairy tales in a wooded setting and also has mazes and slides. Never Never is always-always open from 10 a.m. to 5 p.m. daily April to September, weekends only in March and September. Admission is $3.50 for adults, $1.75 for children. Occasionally the zoo has a free admission day so check to discover when that may be occurring. Hours are 10 a.m. to 4:30 p.m. weekdays, closing at 7 p.m. on weekends.

Other attractions at Point Defiance include parts of the first steamship to sail in these waters, an operating steam locomotive, original and reconstructed buildings of old **Fort Nisqually** built here in 1833 by the Hudson's Bay Company. You'll find **Camp Six,** the old bunkhouse of early loggers here too. It's been converted into a museum of logging complete with pictures and antique tools. To get to Point Defiance Park, take Pearl Street north to the park entrance. Admission is free, and the park is open daily from 10 a.m. to dusk Memorial Day to Labor Day, 11 a.m. to dusk in other months, weather permitting.

Historians should pencil in some time in the **Old Town Historic District** where restored turn-of-the-century buildings are still in use. Among the historic sites you can tour on a drive around the city are: **Union Station,** one of the city's best-loved landmarks at 1713 Pacific Ave.; the 1906 **Rust Mansion,** 1001 N. I St. (tel. 206/572-2828); the turreted **Stadium High School,** once a hotel, at 111 N. E St.; **Engine House No. 9,** a museum-tavern at 611 N. Pine St.; the **Weyerhaeuser Mansion,** also called Haddaway Hall, at 4301 N. Stevens St.; and the **Job Carr Cabin** at 1200 Pacific Ave., built in 1865 by a pioneer whose tiny cabin in the woods became the first house in Tacoma and later the city's first post office.

The **Fort Lewis Military Museum** (tel. 206/967-7206) is 16 miles south of Tacoma off I-5 exit 120. The museum, on one of the army's largest permanent posts, occupies an old inn built in 1918. Exhibits of uniforms, equipment, and large field pieces are arranged and designed to teach you a little about war from the early history of the Pacific Northwest to and through two world wars and the Korean War. Admission is free, and the museum is open Tuesday through Sunday from noon to 4 p.m.; closed holidays. It's located in Lakewood just north of I-5; take exit 120 and follow the signs.

The **Washington State Historical Museum,** 315 N. Stadium Way (tel. 206/593-2830), is housed in a five-story building erected in 1911. Here you can see a vast collection of exhibits on the Indians and pioneers of the Pacific Northwest—the largest such collection in the Northwest, in fact. Admission is free. The museum is open Tuesday through Saturday from 9:30 a.m. to 5 p.m.; Sunday hours are 2 to 5 p.m.

This historic accent goes on and on, right into the neighboring villages of Eatonville, Puyallup, Tenino, and Steilacoom. Take a look at the **Pioneer Farm Museum,** Ohop Valley Road four miles west of Eatonville (tel. 206/832-6300). At this 1880 Ohop Valley homestead you can try your hand at some of the homesteading skills once necessary for survival and see how good a pioneer *you'd* make. Stop by the **Ezra Meeker Mansion,** at 321 E. Pioneer St. in Puyallup (tel. 206/848-1770), a three-story, 17-room Victorian mansion built in 1890 by pioneer Ezra Meeker, a lively fellow who in his 70s retraced the Oregon Trail in a covered wagon pulled by two oxen. Open Wednesday through Sunday from 1 to 5 p.m. Admission is $2 for adults and $1 for children.

Finally, the nearby village of **Steilacoom,** which was the first incorporated town in the Washington Territory, is a veritable museum of Victorian structures painted in pretty pastel colors. To get to Steilacoom, take I-5 south to the 84th Street exit, onto Tacoma Way, then turn south to Steilacoom Boulevard SW. Stop in at the 1895 Bair Drug and Hardware Store, Main Street, where you can order a soda at the store's 1906 fountain!

Tenino is a small town about 39 miles from Tacoma on Wash. 507. Here you can visit a pioneer museum in an antique railroad station called the **Tenino Depot Museum.**

Northwest Trek is a 600-acre plot of pine-strewn ground on which people are the intruders, animals the ones that belong there. You ride; animals roam free. Now you can prowl the park's new Cat Country where lynx, cougar, and the like pad silently about their forest home. In the spring of 1988 the park opened a barn owl exhibit right in a barn and the Cheney Discovery Center, a hands-on activity center where the youngsters can also cozy up to small reptiles and aquatic insects. There are also five miles of nature trails. Although the park is officially part of Tacoma's park system, it's actually quite a little distance out of town, 27 miles south of Puyallup. However, it is quite close to Mount Rainier so it's an easy—and fascinating—stop on your way to the mountain. You'll find the park six miles north of Eatonville on Wash. 161. Admission is $5.50 for adults, $1 to $3 for children depending on age. The park is open daily from 10 a.m. to dusk mid-February through October, but Friday through Sunday only from November through mid-February.

ARTS AND MUSIC: Tacoma is proud of its cultural programs. One of its top stars is the **Pantages Center for the Performing Arts,** 901 Broadway Plaza (tel. 206/591-5890), a historic building opened in 1913 and part of the chain that once hosted the performances of Bernhardt, Cohan, Sousa, and the like. These days touring companies and performers of international renown are stage center here. The **Tacoma Art Museum,** 12th and Pacific Avenues (tel. 206/272-4285), offers a look at a wide range of artwork from Early American furnishings to the art of Andrew Wyeth.

The **Tacoma Symphony Orchestra** performs in various locations and offers many free concerts, often with international guest artists. Call them for times and places (tel. 206/756-3396). The city is also proud of its **Tacoma Philharmonic Orchestra,** 909 Broadway (tel. 206/272-0809).

Two resident dance companies, **Balletacoma** (tel. 206/272-9631) and **Tacoma Performing Dance Company** (tel. 206/759-0782), feature a wide variety of programs. One more musical offering: the **Commencement Bay Jazz Society.** You can find out where the mellow sounds are playing by calling 206/759-7977.

Tacoma Actors Guild provides professional theater productions, and a number of colleges and universities in the area offer amateur productions. **Freighthouse Theater,** in Lakewood Playhouse, Village Plaza (tel. 206/588-0042), is a repertory theater with three plays performed each night Tuesday through Saturday in rotation with the Lakewood repertory company. Plays range from avant garde to classic.

SPECIAL EVENTS: Festive activities have long been key attractions in this part of Washington. Two big annual events are the **Western Washington Fair,** held in nearby Puyallup every September for more than 80 years, and the **Puyallup Valley Daffodil Festival,** in the spring when Tacoma also has a floral parade, the third largest such parade in the nation.

At the Western Washington Fair, sometimes called the Puyallup Fair—and often known as "doing the Puyallup!"—you can see more than 15,000 exhibits of the best the state has to offer in agricultural products, crafts, flowers, hobbies, everything from blue-ribbon pies to prize lamb chops on the hoof—and don't miss the fair's food specialty, raspberry scones. For information on the fair, contact P.O. Box 430, Puyallup, WA 98371 (tel. 206/845-1771).

SPORTS: Few places in the world offer the sports-minded so wide a choice or so many places in which to do them as south Puget Sound. Here's a look at a few, just to give you an idea and perhaps to tempt you.

Tacoma Dome is both a tourist attraction and a sports spot. Here in the world's largest wood-dome arena you and 26,000 other people can see everything from horse and ice shows to concerts, football, and baseball. Tacoma Dome is 15 stories high and 530 feet in diameter. You'll find the dome off I-5 at 2727 E. D St. (tel. 206/272-3663).

If you like to be a spectator, you can see the **Tacoma Stars** soccer team, the **Tacoma Tigers** baseball team, which is an Oakland As' farm club, and the **Pierce County Bengals,** semi-pro footballers, at various locations. Check local newspapers like the *Tacoma Tribune News* for information on locations.

Golfers new to the area can choose from several public clubs: **Brookdale Golf Club,** 1802 Brookdale Rd. East, Tacoma (tel. 206/537-4400), offers 18 holes at par 71, a clubhouse with food, etc., a pro shop, and cart rentals. Greens fees are $13. The **North Shore Golf Course,** 4101 N. Shore Blvd., Tacoma (tel. 206/927-1375), has a complete clubhouse and pro shop facilities to go along with a par-72, 6,015-yard course. Greens fees in the same range.

In addition to the multitudes of other recreational facilities it operates, the **Pierce County Parks and Recreation Department** runs 40 parks including two **public golf courses** and multitudes of **tennis courts.** To find out what's near you, call 206/593-4176.

In summer beach buffs head for **Owen Beach** or the shores of one of a multitude of lakes that dot the area.

In winter Tacoma's snow bunnies come out of hiding and head for one of eight skiing sites which offer 20 slopes. Among those are **Alpental** (tel. 206/623-3414), **Crystal Mountain** (tel. 206/663-2265), **Pacific West** (tel. 206/633-2460), **Ski Acres** (tel. 206/434-6671), **Snoqualmie** (tel. 206/434-6161 or 322-5450); **Stevens Pass** (tel. 206/973-2441), and **White Pass** (tel. 509/453-8731). Information on downhill and cross-country skiing in the region is available from the chamber of commerce (tel. 206/627-2175).

An outfit with the irresistible name **Frick and Frack Charters** has all kinds of boats available. The company features a "Cruise-N-Dine" evening with dinner at Johnny's Dock restaurant, a "Sea-N-Ship" cruise with a shopping stop in Gig Harbor, a salmon dinner cruise, and charter fishing daily at 7 a.m., returning 1 p.m., with bait and tackle included. Trip prices vary according to length, so give Frick and Frack a call at 206/582-0051.

SHOPPING: Large and diversified are the key characteristics Tacoma area shoppers want, and that makes it easy for you to find what you want.

Tacoma Mall is the number-one shopping spot. It claims to be the largest enclosed shopping center in the Pacific Northwest. Certainly there's no debating this is a very large mall with 150 shops anchored by Bon Marché, Federick & Nelson, Nordstrom's, J.C. Penney, and Sears stores. It's quite pretty too, with fountains, tropical plants, and sitting places. To get to the mall, take I-5 to the South 38th Street exit (exit 132) and follow 38th Street west.

Downtown, **Broadway Street** is now a pedestrian mall closed to traffic. You can combine the old with the new by shopping at the boutiques that now inhabit Tacoma's renovated **Old City Hall** at South 7th and Commerce Streets; across the street is another intriguing historic sight, the Northern Pacific Railroad headquarters.

NIGHTLIFE: In Tacoma nightlife mostly involves a trip to Seattle, but you can usually find something happening at **Cliff House,** 6300 Marine View Dr. (tel. 206/927-0400), which often has music for dancing; and the **Bay Co.,** 3327 Ruston Way (tel. 206/752-6661), is a pubby spot. You might also want to check out **C.I. Shenanigan's,** 3017 Ruston Way (tel. 206/752-8811), and the **Tacoma**

Salmon House, 2611 Pacific Ave. (tel. 206/627-0141), where a pianist plays nightly.

4. KITSAP PENINSULA / BREMERTON

About 25 miles northwest of Seattle, across Puget Sound, is Bremerton, largest town on the Kitsap Peninsula and gathering ground for the troops that inhabit the U.S. Naval Base here.

As home to hundreds of navy families, the region tends to be more a family spot than a rip-roaring tourist resort. The city and its environs provide tennis courts, three golf courses, the Kitsap County Fairgrounds, and finally, what most people come here to see, the U.S.S. *Missouri,* on whose decks the United States and Japan signed the treaty that ended World War II.

ORIENTATION: In Bremerton, Wash. 304 is known as Kitsap Way and forms the city's major east-west artery. Washington Hwy. 303, called Wheaton Way here, and Central Valley Road are the two major north-south roads.

TOURIST INFORMATION: If you are going to stop in the Bremerton/ Kitsap area for a few days, contact the **Bremerton–Kitsap County Visitor and Convention Bureau,** Enetai Plaza, 120 Washington Ave., Bremerton, WA 98310 (tel. 206/479-3588). You can also write to the folks at the **Bremerton Area Chamber of Commerce,** P.O. Box 229, Bremerton, WA 98310, or talk to them at 837 4th St., Bremerton (tel. 206/479-3579).

WHERE TO STAY: Bremerton, like Tacoma, is a popular place for conventions and for commercial travelers, so you won't find many big resorts here. If you're traveling through, however, there are a few attractive places to spend a day or two.

One of those is the **Bayview Inn,** 5640 Kitsap Way, Bremerton, WA 98312 (tel. 206/373-7349, or toll free 800/255-5022, 800/422-5017 in Washington). Here you'll find an elaborate hotel situated across a bluff overlooking forests and the waters of Oyster Bay. Behind it rise the snow-clad Olympic Mountains. Activities are nonstop here, from a morning swim under the dome of an indoor swimming pool to nightly dancing and musical entertainment, video games, and first-run movies in the resort's twin theaters. So numerous are the entertainments dreamed up for visitors, you'll be presented with a calendar list of them all when you arrive. For dining the Brass Unicorn is an attractive two-level restaurant with gorgeous views inside and out and a bountiful buffet. Bayview's 150 rooms are quite large, some with glass sliding doors opening onto balconies overlooking a smashing view. Some even have Jacuzzis, and all have televisions and telephones. Rates at the Bayview Inn begin at $48 double; suites are $85.

Another attractive spot, although sadly *sans* view, is the **Dunes Motel,** 3400 11th St., Bremerton, WA 98310 (tel. 206/377-0093). Located well off the road, the Dunes is an attractive three-story, wood-sided motel with big windows and a cedar-shingle mansard roof. You'll find medium-size clean rooms, simply but attractively decorated with telephones, in-room coffee makers, refrigerators, cable television, and queen-size beds. Rates are $33 to $36 for two.

Across the street and down a few doors, the **Hearthstone Inn** at 4312 Kitsap Way, Bremerton, WA 98312 (tel. 206/377-5531), is well known for its excellent restaurant. Simply decorated rooms at this roadside stopping spot have a pretty view out over the water and mountains. Rates are $38 to $41 for two.

WHAT TO SEE AND DO: An occasional sight on the peninsula is the historic **U.S.S. *Missouri,*** where the treaty that ended World War II was signed by the Japanese. You can see the room in which that war officially ended, but you can't visit much more of the ship. The *Missouri,* which also played a starring role in the film *Winds of War,* sometimes docks at the Bremerton ferry docks. Check with the local chamber of commerce for information on the ship. Admission is free.

Everyone wonders about the Indians of our nation—what are they like, how did they live in years past after they were uprooted and cast out of the lands they had known so well? On the **Suquamish Indian Reservation,** at the Suquamish Museum, you can get a remarkable look at just what was going on at this Indian tribe's lands as told through pictures and reminiscences of its elders and craftsmen. Here, beautifully displayed, are basketwork, a dugout canoe, and many implements the Indians used. You can also visit the grave of Chief Seattle, ancestor of these Indians and the man after whom Seattle was named. Ole Man House, an Indian longhouse, the Suquamish Fish Hatchery, historic **Port Gamble,** and the Scandinavian community of **Poulsbo** are all interesting stops in or around the reservation. You can also ride the oldest operating steam vessel on Puget Sound, the *Virginia V,* which stops at Kiana Lodge for a traditional salmon meal. For seasonal sailing information call 206/624-9119. The Indian reservation is open daily from 10 a.m. to 5 p.m. and admission is $3 for adults, $1.50 for children under 12. To get there from Bremerton, take Wash. 303 north to Wash. 308, which branches to the west to Wash. 3, which heads north again. Washington Hwy. 305 to Poulsbo branches off Wash. 3 and goes through the reservation and over to Bainbridge Island. Poulsbo is about ten miles from Bremerton. You can also get to the reservation by ferry from Seattle to Winslow, seven miles south of the reservation.

SPORTS: You'll find public **tennis courts** just off Wash. 3 and a bit south of Kitsap Way. **Rolling Hills Golf Course** at 2485 N.E. McWilliams Rd., Bremerton (tel. 206/479-1212), offers 18 holes with a 68 par. Greens fees are $12. **Beach** lovers will find plenty of stretch-out-on sand, including silica, at **Twanoh, Belfair, Scenic Beach,** and **Kitsap Memorial State Park,** all on Hood Canal. Oyster searchers abound on the pebbly shores at **Belfast State Park** and there are nearly 200 campsites there as well. At Puget Sound on the other side of the peninsula there are **beach parks: Kopachuk** is off Wash. 16 near Gig Harbor; **Illahee** is on Wash. 306 three miles north of Bremerton; and **Fay Bainbridge State Park** is on Bainbridge Island, which you can reach by continuing on Wash. 305 from Poulsbo. All have campsites and picnic grounds too.

5. MOUNT RAINIER

So loved and so famous is this awesome peak that here in Washington it is known, simply, as The Mountain. At 14,410 feet Mount Rainier is among the world's most majestic peaks. Rainier's stretch into the sky creates dramatic cloud halos that make it snow and is one of the reasons there are so many "wet" jokes up here in the Northwest. Rainier's proclivity for a foggy disappearance makes all the more spectacular that moment when the clouds part. Suddenly before your eyes appears this towering cliff, floating on the horizon like a white-cloaked mirage, visible for a hundred miles in any direction.

Its superlatives come not only from awed spectators but from people who record the world's -ests. Mantled in glacial snow every month of the year, the mountain is in winter buried under prodigious snowfalls deep enough to entomb a three-story building. It is, in fact, in line for a *Guinness Book of World Records* listing for the deepest snowfall ever recorded: 93½ feet! Mount Rainier has the biggest single glacier and largest glacier system in the lower 48 states. No fewer than 27 glaciers spread their icy fingers across 35 square miles of the mountain, increasing the visual impact of this lofty peak. Circling its slopes are dense forests of Douglas fir, red cedar, and western hemlock, monster trees soaring more than 200 feet above moss-covered rock. On the mountain you are less than 75 miles from Tacoma, 103 from Seattle, yet light-years away. Here silence reigns over pastoral valleys and forests so dense you must play hide-and-seek with the mountain's peak as you wind around the sides of this massif.

Seasons meet here. Alpine flowers butt up to deep snows; meadows turn lushly green in July and August as little by little the snows melt, sending hundreds of cascades down the sides of the mountains. In fall the process reverses as tip-top snows move inexorably down the mountainside turning forests into a blazing rainbow of autumnal hues. Quiet as they may look, these glaciers are active creatures, site of avalanches of ice, snow, and rock dangerous to climbers. Mud often flows down their sides, suddenly gushing from beneath a weakened sector. Believed to be extinct, Mount Rainier is nevertheless still a volcano, its two summit craters mute testimony to once-powerful forces at work here. Along the rims of the craters, caves carved by heat from deep in the earth are heated by steam that has more than once saved the lives of climbers caught in a sudden mountaintop ice storm.

EXCURSIONS TO MOUNT RAINIER: You can spend a pleasant day on the mountain, departing from Seattle or Tacoma in the morning and returning the same day. The best way of all to do that is to stop at Enumclaw in the valley at the foot of the mountain to stock up on some of the homemade breads, good wines, desserts, and gourmet picnic supplies.

Then ride up the side of the mountain, stopping at one of the many small campgrounds or picnic areas that dot the sides of the mountain. At any of them you will find a couple of tables near the road, but it's fun to penetrate deeper along forest trails to find a private spot beside a rushing stream. Audacious chipmunks come chattering for a handout, birds provide background music, and if you're very patient, a curious deer may stop by to see what you're doing. Mountain goats can sometimes be seen in the park, and furry marmots burrow among the rocks to whistle at you from afar.

One road up the mountain remains open all year: Wash. 706, the road to Paradise from the Nisqually entrances to Mount Rainier National Park. Other park entrances are closed from about late November to June or July.

Hiking in the park is a popular pursuit but has its hazards. If you're interested in joining the throngs of backpackers who walk the mountain, stop first at Hiker Information Centers at Longmire or White River Visitor Centers, where you can also get a booklet of hiking advice called "Fragile, Handle with Care."

Permits are required for **overnight backpacking** and can be obtained from ranger stations and visitor centers. Rainier is quite a dangerous mountain to hike —many hikers have been killed here. Some parts are more dangerous than others, so a stop at one of the visitor information centers is mandatory, not only for your safety but because you must register at a ranger station before beginning a hike.

Unless you and your fellow hikers can convince rangers that you are capable of hiking the mountain alone, you must be accompanied by a guide from **Rainier Mountaineering,** Paradise, WA 98397 (tel. 206/627-6242), a park-approved guiding outfit. They can also outfit you with equipment and maps and can be reached in winter months at 201 St. Helens, Tacoma, WA 98402.

Interpretive programs, nature walks, and slide shows are presented by the Park Service from late June through Labor Day with schedules posted in visitor centers and on campground bulletin boards.

You'll find self-guided nature trails at Longmire Meadows, Sourdough Ridge, Nisqually Vista, Emmons Vista, Ohanapecosh, Hot Springs, Grove of the Patriarchs, and Carbon River.

Camping is permitted in designated sites. Campgrounds with running water and flush toilets are at Ohanapecosh, White River, and Cougar Rock. Sunshine Point, near the Nisqually entrance to the park, is the only campground open all year. Reservations are not accepted. Fees are $5 to $6.

Administered by the National Park Service, **Mount Rainier National Park** covers 378 square miles. Information about the park along with a good topographical map are available from the National Park Service, U.S. Department of the Interior, Star Route, Ashford, WA 98304 (tel. 206/569-2211), or by contacting **Mount Rainier Guest Services,** P.O. Box 108, Ashford, WA 98304 (tel. 206/569-2275), which operates the Paradise Inn (tel. 206/569-2413), open from late May to early October. Paradise Inn is a must-see spot constructed of huge log beams with stone fireplaces and parquet wood floors. Handcrafted Indian rugs and western décor add to the rusticity of the place. Four of the 35 original rooms in the lodge have private baths and the rest have sinks, but there are many modern quarters in this 126-room hotel. Brunch in Paradise is a treat—you dine surrounded by majestic, snow-capped mountains, soaring pine forests, and a rainbow of wildflowers. It's served from 11 a.m. to 3 p.m. Paradise is open from mid-May to early October. Rates are $47 to $84.

Second of the two operations is the National Park Inn at Longmire, which has 16 rooms, some with private bath, some with shared facilities. In June and September the Paradise Inn has a two-night, money-saving deal including lodging and meals. National Park Inn is open year round. Rates are $38 to $72.

Admission to the park is $5 per car per day.

GETTING THERE: From Seattle, we recommend taking I-5 south to Wash. 164, which departs from I-5 just north of Tacoma. Washington Hwy. 164 heads east to and meets Wash. 410 at Enumclaw. Take Wash. 410 from there, following the loop drive outlined below.

From Tacoma Wash. 7 joins Wash. 706, leading to the Nisqually entrance to the park and the Paradise Visitor Center, the only visitor center in the park open all year.

Or take Wash. 410 which, like Wash. 7, departs from I-5 at Tacoma, goes east toward Auburn and on to Enumclaw. Washington Hwy. 410 circles the foothills of Mount Rainier past the Sunrise entrance and over Cayuse Pass. When Wash. 410 and Wash. 123 meet, stay on Wash. 123 to its junction with Wash. 706. To complete a loop back to Tacoma, take Wash. 706 toward Ashford, joining Wash. 7, which heads northwest at Elbe.

Stop in Enumclaw at Baumgartner's, on Wash. 410 just east of town (tel. 206/825-1067), for those picnic provisions we mentioned. (You can munch here too, in a country-kitchen atmosphere at several small tables.) Stock up on sausages, cheese, imported beer and wine, fresh breads, and croissants. They even sell fancy picnic baskets to put it all in, for a classy picnic.

If you're coming down from Seattle, leave I-5 at this same exit, Wash. 164 to Enumclaw, where you follow White River Road to the White River entrance and Sunrise Visitor Center. If you return on our suggested route, you'll turn off Wash. 410 at its intersection with Wash. 706 to Ashford, continuing on Wash. 7 back to I-5 at Tacoma.

Yakima, 103 miles away, is joined to the park by U.S. 12, which meets Wash. 123, running along the Ohanapecosh River to Stevens Canyon Entrance and the Ohanapecosh Visitor Center.

In winter get the latest word on **road conditions** by calling 206/569-2343.

CHAPTER XVII

VANCOUVER

□ □ □

Chic, cosmopolitan, and very, very today, Vancouver is the most sophisticated city in the Pacific Northwest. Sleek glass-and-steel buildings streak skyward, their hard edges softened by birch trees and waterfalls.

So tied to the sea is Vancouver that seaplanes are routinely docked at the door of major office buildings and take off from the town center.

Yet as you stand in the center of this pulsating city with cars and buses zipping about, a new monorail rapid-transit system and a world's fair under its belt, you are on the threshold of a province so large you could tuck Washington, Oregon, and California away here and still have space left over. Four times the size of Great Britain and bigger than all but 30 nations of the world, this province other Canadians call the Left Coast contains huge wilderness areas that are traversed by few roads. Its most remote regions are rarely or never seen by even the most adventurous explorer.

Dozens of nationalities blend here with little ethnic antipathy. Provinciality gets the boot quickly here, tossed aside by a let's-get-on-with-it attitude. Home to the second-largest Chinatown in the western hemisphere, Vancouver also has Greek, Japanese, Italian, and Indian neighborhoods, each with its distinctive sights and sounds, and the aromas of exotic cookery.

Vancouver has been around for generations, but to see it today is to think it must have sprung up overnight. Its angular architecture is a study in Skyscraper 101. Yet careful attention to street-level humanization of towering steel-and-glass edifices is a delight to the urban eye. In the center of it all, a complex of parks, offices, and shops called Robson Square is a study in concrete form softened by falls of water and cascades of greenery.

Even the staunchest Vancouver boosters admit that the weather here can be, to put it mildly, damp, although temperatures are surprisingly temperate for a city that occupies such a northerly spot on the map. That frequent rainfall is why you'll find much of the city underground in big, beautiful malls beneath office buildings and hotels. For the weather-conscious among us, Vancouver's temperatures rarely drop below the 30s in winter, so golfers can plan on teeing off even in that season. In spring temperatures in the 60s are the rule. Rarely do summer temperatures rise above the 75° level. So temperate are temperatures, in fact, that roses often bloom here in December! Yes, it does rain a great deal, up to 17 days a month in the dead of winter when the rainfall is heaviest, but enough drizzles down even in summer to make raincoats a staple of Vancouver closets.

Geographically, the city could hardly be more beautifully endowed. Plunked down on a spit of land bordered by the waters of the Georgian Strait and wedged between the Burrard Inlet and English Bay, Vancouver is view without end.

In summer a sunny day slows the city's fast pace to a shuffle as everyone who can come up with a passable excuse for absence takes to the beaches and the hills by car, bus, boat, bicycle, and foot. In winter a good snow on suburban Grouse Mountain has a similar effect, as one and all pack up the skis and head for slopes just a 20-minute drive away. Meanwhile, back in town there's likely to be no snow at all.

Despite its emphasis on its sparkling downtown skyline, Vancouver is proud of its history too. A bit of that has been preserved in a whimsical section of town once known as Skid Road, after the place at which logs were skidded into the river. Painted and prettied, that section is today called Gastown in honor of a bodacious publican named Gassy Jack, who earned his monicker only from, we hasten to add, his gift for gab! A most fitting folk hero, we think, for this brash outpost-turned-metropolis.

1. GETTING THERE AND GETTING AROUND

GETTING THERE: As one of Canada's major cities and the nation's vital West Coast port, Vancouver is easy to reach by plane, train, bus, or car.

Airlines flying into **Vancouver International Airport** (tel. 604/666-7593) include Air BC, Air Canada, British Airways, Burrard Air, Cathay Pacific, CP Air, Japan, Lufthansa, Pan Am, Quantas, San Juan, United, and Wardair. To get from the airport, which is on Hwy. 99 or Grant McConachie Way, to area hotels, take the **Airporter bus** (tel. 604/273-0071) which operates from 6 a.m. to midnight every 15 minutes from the airport, about every half hour from major downtown hotels. The fare is $5.75 ($4.50 U.S.), while a taxi ride to the airport will cost about $10 ($8 U.S.) to $15 ($12 U.S.).

VIA Rail Canada pulls into the station at 1150 Station St. (tel. 604/687-3837), bringing passengers here from points east.

Greyhound and **Pacific Coach Lines** both serve the city from points east, west, north, and south, pulling into a depot at 150 Dunsmuir St. (tel. 604/683-9277 or 683-8133).

Rental-car companies operating in the city include Budget, which often features discount coupons on regional activities and restaurants as well as some terrific weekend deals, at one time as low as $12 ($9.50 U.S.) a day! The **Budget** outlet is at 450 W. Georgia St. (tel. 604/685-0536), and at the airport. Others operating in Vancouver include **Avis,** 757 Hornby St. (tel. 604/682-1621);

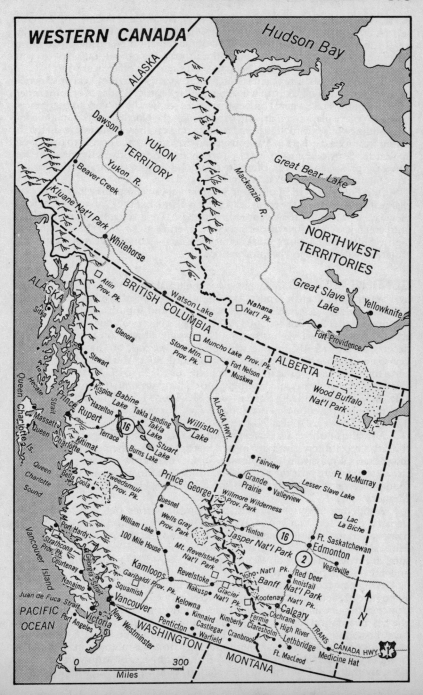

WESTERN CANADA

Hudson Bay

ALASKA

Dawson

YUKON
TERRITORY

Yukon R.

Beaver Creek

Kluane Nat'l Park

Whitehorse

Mackenzie R.

Great Bear Lake

NORTHWEST
TERRITORIES

Great Slave
Lake

Yellowknife

ALASKA

Sitka

Atlin
Prov. Pk.

BRITISH COLUMBIA

Watson Lake

Nahana
Nat'l Pk.

Fort Providence

Glenora

Muncho Lake Prov. Pk.

Stone Mtn.
Prov. Pk.

Fort Nelson

Muskwa

ALBERTA

Wood Buffalo
Nat'l Park

Stewart

Kispiox Babine
Lake
Hazelton
Terrace

Takla Landing
Takla
Lake
Stuart
Lake
Burns Lake

ALASKA HWY.

Williston
Lake

Prince Rupert

16

Queen Charlotte Is.

Massett
Queen Charlotte

Hecate Strait

Kitimat

Queen
Charlotte
Sound

Bella Coola

Tweedsmuir
Prov. Pk.

Prince George

Fairview

Grande
Prairie

Valleyview

Lesser Slave Lake

Ft. McMurray

Lac
La Biche

Quesnel

Wells Gray
Prov. Park

Willmore Wilderness
Prov. Park

Port Hardy

Strathcona
Prov. Pk.

Courtenay

Vancouver Island

Nanaimo

William Lake

100 Mile House

Kamloops

Garibaldi Prov. Pk.

Revelstoke

Mt. Revelstoke
Nat'l Park

Hinton

Jasper Nat'l Park

16

Ft. Saskatchewan

Edmonton

2

Vegreville

Georgia Strait

Squamish

Vancouver

Juan de Fuca Strait

Victoria

Port Angeles

New Westminster

PACIFIC
OCEAN

Kelowna

Nakusp

Glacier
Nat'l Pk.

Yoho Nat'l Pk.

Banff
Nat'l Park

Red Deer

Innisfail

Kootenay
Nat'l Pk.

Calgary

Cochrane

Kinnaird
Penticton
Castlegar
Warfield

Kimberly

Claresholm

Fermie
Cranbrook

High River

Lethbridge

Ft. MacLeod

Medicine Hat

TRANS

CANADA HWY.

WASHINGTON

MONTANA

N

0   300
Miles

Hertz, 666 Seymour St. (tel. 604/688-2411); **Dollar Rent A Car,** 497 Robson St. (tel. 604/688-2233); **Tilden Rent A Car,** and **National Car Rental,** both at 1140 Alberni St. (tel. 604/685-6111). Some rental-car companies have more than one office in the city—at hotels, the airport, and other locations—so you might check the local telephone book to see if there's an office near you.

In passing let us note that it is much more expensive to rent a car in Vancouver and drive it to the U.S. than it is to rent one in Seattle, Portland, or some other large city in the U.S., where competitive forces seem to be at work to keep prices down. If you're planning a driving trip through the Northwest, you might consider finding your way to Seattle and picking up a car there. One way to do that is to rent a car for a day here in Vancouver and drive it over the border to drop it off in Seattle. Seattle seems to have a particularly competitive environment for rental-car prices, so you can often strike a good bargain if you mention you're expecting to rent for a week or more.

One final note: In Vancouver most rental-car companies levy a dropoff charge if you're leaving the car in Seattle or Portland; but they will waive that fee if they have a Seattle car they want returned there. We'd suggest you keep calling until you find a company with a car they want returned. Dropoff charges can be as high as $50 or $60. Be sure to ask about these cars—none of the rental-car representatives will volunteer the information.

GETTING AROUND: Vancouver has the usual buses but here they even go over water! **B.C. Transit Operating Co.,** 1200 W. 73rd Ave. (tel. 604/261-5100), provides bus service all over Vancouver and suburbs. But B.C. Transit also operates the **Sea Bus** (tel. 604/324-3211), a cheery orange ferryboat that is actually part of the city's bus system. No cars are allowed on this ferry, which departs on an every-15-minute schedule from the foot of Granville Street to Lonsdale Quay on the North Shore of Burrard Inlet. You need exact change. Fares for either ferry or bus in nonpeak hours are $1.25 ($1 U.S.) for adults, 65¢ (50¢ U.S.) for students and children 5 to 11, and unlimited transfers are available. A $3.50 ($2.75 U.S.) Sunday pass ($1.75, or $1.50 U.S., for children) offers unlimited travel on that day and holidays. For route information, call 604/324-3211. Passes are sold at 7-11 stores.

A small aside here, Sea Bus is not only fun to take, it also departs from one of the city's most impressive buildings, a huge red-brick behemoth lined with no fewer than 14 massive white columns. Inside, trees grow in huge pots, ceilings rise to somewhere near the sky, and boutiques vie for attention. There's even a food purveyor who's hung an irresistible monicker on his shop: Franks for the Memory.

A different ferry system, **British Columbia Ferries** (tel. 604/669-1211), departs daily for Vancouver Island's Swartz Bay and Departure Bay; to Tsawwassen in the Gulf Islands; and to Nanaimo and the Sunshine Coast from Horseshoe Bay about 15 miles west of town. A central service called British Columbia Ferries Information Centre (tel. 604/669-1211) can outline schedule and fare information for you.

A big new **rapid-transit system** opened in Vancouver in time for the 1986 Expo here. Called **Skytrain,** it is designed to move 100,000 people through the center of the city in minutes, connecting to ferry and rail service. Stations are at the Sea Bus station on the waterfront, at Burrard Street, Granville Street, and near the stadium on Beatty Street—15 in all, with 13 miles of track, two- to six-car trains operating 5- to 12-minute schedules from 5 a.m. to 1 a.m. The system operates with cars 75 seconds apart. A branch connects downtown and the airport, another goes from the Sea Bus station to downtown stops in 60 seconds flat. Skytrain is a delight. Off-peak fares are the same as the bus fares, about 30% higher during rush hour.

Taxis operating in the city include **Advance Cabs** (tel. 604/876-5555), **Black Top** (tel. 604/681-2181), **B. C. Radio** (tel. 604/683-6666), and **Yellow Cab** (tel. 604/681-3311). Rates are $1.40 ($1.10 U.S.) at the drop, 90¢ (70¢ U.S.) a mile.

ORIENTATION: If you're driving in Vancouver, you'll find that streets and avenues downtown bear names you will just have to memorize. Many are one way. Streets running east and west are numbered, while those running north and south are named. Numbers begin at Ontario and Carrall Streets for east-west numbers and at Powell and Dundas Streets for north-south numbers. To get to West and North Vancouver, head for Lions Gate Bridge and Second Narrows Bridge. Burrard and Granville Bridges connect downtown to western Vancouver. U.S. 99 comes into the city from points south, becoming Oak Street here. From the east, Trans-Canada Hwy. 1 and Hwys. 1A and 7 head straight into town. Use the First Avenue or Hastings Street exit from the Trans-Canada Hwy. to get downtown.

A note on speeds: Canada has jumped wholeheartedly into the metric system, so posted speed limits here appear in kilometers per hour. To help you read them: 50 km/h is about 30 mph; 80 km/h, about 50 mph. Gasoline is purchased by the litre and one U.S. gallon is about 3.8 litres. Seat belts are *mandatory*, and the fine for failure to use them is high.

2. TOURIST AND USEFUL INFORMATION

There are plenty of people just waiting to help you out whatever information you're seeking.

TOURIST INFORMATION: Tourism Vancouver and Tourist British Columbia are separate promotional organizations, but here in Vancouver information on both the city and the province are available at **Tourism Vancouver,** 1055 Dunsmuir St., Bentall Four Bldg., Vancouver, BC V6E 4C8. There, Peter Chettle and his troupe of enthusiastic workers can fill you in on everything you ever wanted to know, and perhaps more, about both the city and the province. Theater tickets and a wide variety of other services also are available here. Hours at the center are 8:30 a.m. to 7 p.m. (occasionally later) daily from June to September, 9 a.m. to 5 p.m. Monday through Saturday in other months.

If you want to know what kind of sports activities are going on in town, contact **Sport BC,** 1760 Broadway, Vancouver, BC V6Z 2C6 (tel. 604/737-3000), an umbrella organization representing amateur sports groups there. BC's **Outdoor Recreation Council,** Suite 170, 1200 Hornby St., Vancouver, BC V6Z 2E2, also can fill you in on sports activities in the region.

If you're looking for train or ferry schedules, contact **B.C. Rail** at B.C. Rail Passenger Department, P.O. Box 8770, Vancouver, BC V6B 4X6 (tel. 604/984-5246); or **British Columbia Ferries,** at 1112 Fort St., Victoria, BC V8V 4V2 (tel. 604/669-1211, or 604/685-1021 for schedule information).

British Columbia's parks are one of the province's prides. For details on national parks, contact **Environment Canada,** Parks, Western Region, P.O. Box 2989, Station "M," Calgary, AB T2P 3H8. Provincial park information is available from the **Ministry of Environment and Parks,** Parks and Outdoor Recreation Division, 4000 Seymour Pl., Victoria, BC V8V 1X5.

Newspapers in town include the morning *Province* and the afternoon *Sun.* A useful publication for tourists is *Key to Vancouver,* available at most hotels, and the seasonal *YVR* (that's the airport code for Vancouver) magazine, which publishes an annual guide to the city.

USEFUL INFORMATION: For police or emergency medical help, dial 911; for non-emergencies, call 604/665-3321. . . . For general information on practically everything, call 604/439-3311, which has a number of extensions delineated in the telephone book. At those extensions are information on everything from highway conditions to ski possibilities and weather conditions throughout Canada and many U.S. cities. It's quite an amazing information source. . . . For a local doctor, call 604/683-2474. . . . For dental help, call 604/874-9848. . . . Telecommunications services are available at 175 W. Cordova St. (tel. 604/681-4231). . . . The Vancouver telephone area code is 604.

3. WHERE TO STAY

Vancouver has an extensive hotel roster ranging from lavish establishments to compact apartments. Weekend rates are often great money-savers, dropping as much as $20 ($16 U.S.) or more in luxury hotels.

CANADIAN CURRENCY AND EXCHANGE RATES: Canada denominates its currency in dollars and cents, just as we do south of the border—but with a pleasing difference: $1 Canadian is currently worth approximately 80¢ in U.S. currency (give or take a few points' daily variation), but costs have not increased proportionately. This means that by exchanging your U.S. currency (banks and major hotels will give you the best exchange rate) and paying for your purchases in Canadian dollars, you'll get about $1.25 (U.S.) value for each $1 (U.S.) you spend—a saving of about 25%!

In this chapter, prices are cited in Canadian currency, with the U.S. dollar equivalents following in parentheses.

LUXURY HOTELS: Vancouver has some elegant old hotels and some sleek and flashy new ones. We've picked out some of the best, defining luxury as hotels with prices of $100 ($80 U.S.) and up.

Our hands-down favorite in Vancouver is the **Hotel Vancouver, 900** W. Georgia St., Vancouver, BC V6C 2W6 (tel. 604/684-3131, 416/366-2214 in Toronto, or toll free 800/223-9869, 800/268-8136 in Canada), a hotel that is more than just a hotel—it's a landmark. The Hotel Vancouver's night-lighted copper roof, now mellowed to a pale green, is the first thing you'll see if you arrive by sea or air. Just as some people acquire mature beauty, so some old hotels age into classic elegance, and no upstart glitz-and-schmaltz hostelries can match them.

Such a place is the Hotel Vancouver: it's now more than 40 years old and doesn't show a day of it. Hallways are as wide as thoroughfares, and the ceilings are 10 to 12 feet high. Rooms are huge, some of them downright sybaritic with a separate sitting room as large as the bedroom in which a king-size bed barely makes a dent. A marble bathroom is bigger than many motel rooms. Beautiful ceiling moldings trim walls a foot thick. If it's available, no. 926 is a particularly gorgeous room, with white carpet, Wedgwood-blue-and-white-sprigged draperies, a big scalloped valance, and handsome furnishings.

At the elevators light streams through tall windows over deep wing chairs and glowing woodwork to highlight massive bowls of fresh flowers. On one side of the lobby a leathery/tweedy bilevel lounge is the scene of elegant white-linen buffet breakfasts. Later in the day the room is transformed for equally sophisticated cocktail hours at which well-trained servers present drinks on silver trays and power brokers sit happily ensconced in velvet wing chairs. There is no more clubby, cozy spot in town for that particular hour. These days the Hotel Vancouver, like many hotels, concentrates on the business traveler, providing amenities such as good telephone service, color television and radio, one- to four-bedroom suites, same-day laundry service, plenty of business services if you need them, currency exchange, and a raft of guest shops, beauty and barber shops, dress and jewelry shops, florist and specialty shops, and indoor parking.

Dining options range from the rooftop restaurant and dancing center called the Panorama Roof, where you can look down on the world from skyhigh windows; Timbers, serving grilled steak and salmon among other choices, in a rainforest atmosphere of heavy logs; to the Spanish Grill, a pleasant and satisfyingly intimate coffeeshop.

If you get the idea we think this is a very special place, well, you get the idea. Rates at the Vancouver, which also offers complimentary limousine service from the airport, are $135 ($108 U.S.) to $200 ($160 U.S.) double, lower from November to April.

The **Four Seasons Hotel,** 791 W. Georgia St., Vancouver, BC V6C 2T4 (tel. 604/689-9333, or toll free 800/828-1188, 800/462-1150 in New York State, 800/268-6282 in Canada), dropped a bundle to produce some of the flashiest public rooms in town. Most knock-'em-dead of all is the Garden Lounge, where a two-story atrium is filled with flowers and tall trees and lined with a soaring wall of glass, and ivy trails from huge ceiling-hung planters. At lunch a toque-topped chef serves. There seem to be lounges and restaurants everywhere: a Terrace Bar with low butterscotch leather chairs; the Grill Room upholstered in rich navy blue; and the Harvester, an airy light-green room trimmed with plants; and the elegant Le Pavillon, dominated by a wall-size oil painting of a snowy castle scene and furnished with burgundy highbacked velvet chairs and white linens, glittering crystal, cool marbles. Really a small city of its own, the Four Seasons has dozens of shops, its own pâtisserie, even a branch of the Holt Renfrew department store. Naturally rooms here are equally elegant, no. 1208 a smashing example of a suite with a deep-brown couch, chairs, two double beds, loads of space, and very sophisticated décor. All the accoutrements, of course, from white-gloved bellmen to color television, free shoeshines, 24-hour room service, an indoor-outdoor pool, sauna, and whirlpool. Rates are $160 ($128 U.S.) to $240 ($192 U.S.) double.

In 1984 the **Wedgewood Hotel,** 845 Hornby St., Vancouver, BC V6Z 1V1 (tel. 604/689-7777, or toll free 800/223-9868, 800/387-1338 in eastern Canada, 800/663-9582 in western Canada), opened brand-new doors to welcome travelers to a new kind of hotel in Vancouver, a classic French look, small and cozy. You'll see what we mean when you get a look at tall arched, small-paned windows, a light blue canopy, and a doorman in a matching vest, flowers and greenery streaming from flower boxes at the windows, a marble fireplace, cozy furnishings, and polished wood floors. That interesting combination of European atmosphere and cool contemporary colors is backed by rooms that are large and stylishly decorated. You'll find, for instance, bedspreads in pale green with pink roses, thick carpets, big windows, handsome wood furniture that tucks a television out of sight; some rooms have small settees, private bars, fireplaces, or attractive views over the city's law court square.

Special touches make this subtly glamorous hotel even more welcoming: continental breakfast, morning newspaper, evening shoeshine and turn-down service, and 24-hour room service—all are included as standard services. More beautiful colors and designs are found downstairs in a dining room and cocktail

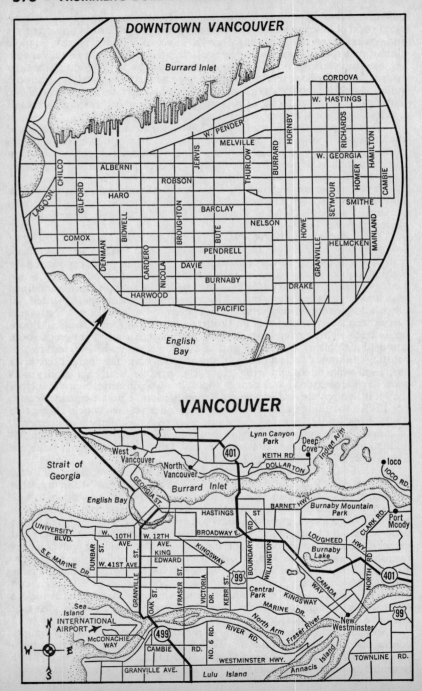

DOWNTOWN VANCOUVER

VANCOUVER

lounge with rattan furnishings and potted palms. Wainscoting, moldings, French doors, and antiques mark the Wedgewood with an understated elegance unlike any other hotel in the city. Rates are $115 ($92 U.S.) to $165 ($132 U.S.) double, higher for larger quarters and a penthouse suite.

We'd heard another stunner, the **Coast Georgian Court,** 773 Beatty St., Vancouver, BC V6B 2M4 (tel. 604/682-5555, or toll free 800/663-1144), had opened in Vancouver, but we were unprepared for quite as much glamour as we encountered. A sleek modern exterior with lots of brass, smoked glass, marble, and glitter is backed by an old-world interior lined with more marble and decorated in jewel tones. Behind the elegant façade is yet more elegance plus pampering touches ranging from terry robes to morning newspapers, an in-room mini-bar, three telephones in each room including a speaker-phone, all in 180 very spacious quarters outfitted in fine woods and soothing color schemes. A sauna and exercise room await, as does a slick neon-lighted disco called Regney's. The doorman is decked out in gray tailcoat. In a quiet corner of the hotel the Georgian Club, a private club for guests, is a soothingly handsome spot with floor-to-ceiling bookcases and two rooms of classic English-library furnishings. The William Tell Restaurant, a study in arches, moldings, crystal chandeliers, and elegantly subdued décor, was already famous in another location and has maintained its preeminence here as one of the city's top dining rooms. The Georgian Court is near BC Place Stadium, making this a most convenient hotel as well. Rates here are $100 ($80 U.S.) to $180 ($144 U.S.) double.

The **Ramada Renaissance Hotel,** 1733 Comox St., Vancouver, BC V6G 1P6 (tel. 604/688-7711, or toll free 800/228-9898), seems to set its sights on the active set, catering to them with a racquet club, indoor pool, saunas, and a roomful of exercise equipment. Certainly you see plenty of tennis racquets in the lobby here and in the attractive wicker and greenery lounge. A short distance from the middle of the downtown area in a quiet, tree-lined neighborhood, this tall hotel has 267 rooms in a high-rise building, fronted by flowers, fountains, and a reflecting pool. In each room you'll find quite attractive modern furnishings plus a color television, refrigerator, coffee maker, balconies, and in some suites, fully equipped kitchens. Atop the building on the 35th floor is a handsome restaurant with views that go on forever. If you're looking for tranquility but want to keep your options open, this seems the perfect retreat. The added attraction here is a small shopping mall, a movie theater, and complimentary downtown limousine service and airport transportation. Rates are $115 ($92 U.S.) to $160 ($128 U.S.), with highest figures buying you a one-bedroom suite, not bad in this pricy town.

The **Westin Bayshore,** 1601 W. Georgia St., Vancouver, BC V6G 2V4 (tel. 604/682-3377, or toll free 800/228-3000), occupies a pretty spot overlooking Burrard Inlet and a marina. Doormen decked out in British Tower guard costume usher you into the lobby, where impressionistic wall-size fiber sculptures set the atmosphere. Right at the edge of Stanley Park, the hotel is a massive place with a cavernous lobby. Set on a large tract of land, the Westin Bayshore is really more resort than hotel, with a big round outdoor swimming pool overlooking the inlet, an indoor pool and whirlpool, an exercise room, a masseur, pool table, even a bar that specializes in yogurts, fruit salads, and fresh juices, and a long row of posh specialty shops. The rooms are outfitted in chic modern furnishings, including a wardrobe that hides a swiveling television behind cabinet doors. Dining options range from the ubiquitous Trader Vic's to the Garden Restaurant and Lounge overlooking the pool and the inlet beyond. Rates in the hotel's main building or an adjacent high-rise tower are $150 ($120 U.S.) to $200 ($160 U.S.) double. Children under 18 sharing a room with their parents are free.

The **Delta Place,** 645 Howe St., Vancouver, BC V6C 2Y9 (tel. 604/

687-1122, or toll free 800/223-6800), is among the newest showplace hotels in town. This one was once part of the world-famous Mandarin chain, its first North American hotel. Here is a hotel one would guess will be a lodging legend: a lobby area rug is so thick it actually sinks an inch or so when you step on it; a cream-and-caramel blend of color covers a small raised seating area elegantly trimmed with brass, glass, and Oriental touches; marble floors and walls are set off by a splash of burgundy. Pure luxury is everywhere you look in this hotel opened in spring 1984. In the rooms you'll find silk flowers; a décor of brown Regency chairs and rose and brown prints; behind sliding doors, an unusually large bathroom with separate tub and shower areas; leather tops on oak writing tables; stocked refrigerator and bar; terrycloth bathrobes; and brass doorknobs. A serenely elegant dining room features French cooking, and the Captain's Bar sports brass tabletops and Empire armchairs in a clubby atmosphere. The hotel has snappy brass elevators, a library, billiards room, health club with pool, racquetball court, whirlpool, sauna, and masseurs. For this chic sophistication you pay $195 ($156 U.S.) double, from $210 ($168 U.S.) higher for suites.

Chandeliers glitter at the **Hyatt Regency Vancouver,** 655 Burrard St., Vancouver, BC V6C 2R7 (tel. 604/687-6543, or toll free 800/228-9000), a showy hotel in the middle of a large shopping complex in the middle of downtown Vancouver. A three-story lobby gleams with massive tiered crystal chandeliers. Up a few steps from the brick-trimmed lobby a chic restaurant, Peacocks, offers a buffet lunch with such delicacies as salmon Wellington or pheasant broth served in a setting of low tables, tub chairs, a soft pastel décor. Peacocks is the hotel's sophisticated candlelit dining room, where entrees are in the $18 ($14.50 U.S.) to $20 ($16 U.S.) range. The Café is a very elegant coffeeshop on the mezzanine level with lots of windows. A 34-story building, the Hyatt Regency offers great views of the busy waters hereabouts and the mountains beyond them. Spacious rooms are beautifully decorated and have electric blankets, digital clock-radios, refrigerators, color televisions with in-room movies, and good soundproofing. In carpeted bathrooms you will find special shampoos, fluffy towels, and a sewing kit. Rates at Hyatt are $150 ($120 U.S.) to $175 ($140 U.S.) double.

Hotel Georgia, 801 W. Georgia St., Vancouver, BC V6C 1P7 (tel. 604/682-5566, or toll free 800/663-1111), has an enviable center-city location across from the Vancouver Art Gallery. Behind a brass plaque at the door: beamed ceiling, fireplace with cozy seating area, gilded, carved wood, a sleek bilevel lounge with tapestry chairs and brass rails. The Georgia's been around for over 50 years, and its George V Pub is quite a popular place with décor as English as the menu, plus lively sing-alongs. Upstairs, rooms are handsomely decorated, many featuring attractive contemporary colors and beautiful wood moldings—721 an especially large one. Updated in 1986, rooms feature chandeliers, gilt trim, brass plaques on each door, different colors on each floor. All in all, jolly good: prices are $114 ($91.25 U.S.) to $134 ($107.25 U.S.) double, lower in winter months.

An outlying hotel on trendy Granville, offers very zippy accommodations in a community that is rapidly becoming the place to be in Vancouver. That hotel is the **Granville Island Hotel,** 1253 Johnston St., Granville Island, Vancouver, BC V6H 3R9 (tel. 604/683-7373). Quite an architectural departure, the Granville Island Hotel combines pink stucco with a glass atrium and corrugated iron, drawing it all together into a flashy spot filled with the latest in colors and fabrics. In the lobby, dusty pinks, purples, and forest greens, and in the atrium the hotel's whimsical trademark, the Cyrus P. Windless Kite Flying Machine, is a bizarre and amusing gizmo. A small hotel, the Granville Island has just 57 rooms, each decorated attractively in quiet colors with plenty of wood and shutters opening onto small balconies. For dining the hotel has a popular plant-filled restaurant called

Pelican Bay, with prices in the $12 ($9.50 U.S.) to $17 ($3.50 U.S.) range. BB's Bistro, with its big copper espresso machine, is another popular gathering spot. If you have a boat, you can dock right at the door of this waterside spot; if you don't, you can rent one here, along with surfboards and kayaks. Rates are $90 ($72 U.S.) to $130 ($104 U.S.).

The chief focal point of the **Château Granville,** 1100 Granville St., Vancouver, BC V6Z 2B6 (tel. 604/669-7070, or toll free 800/663-0575), is a riveting ceramic mural that covers one lobby wall in shades of orange. A multistory hotel, the Château Granville has an attractive upper-level BT's Restaurant, very chicly decorated in gray banquettes and contrasting pink napery backed by a wall of trellises. Another wall is made of smoked glass, and there's lots of hanging greenery. An adjoining lounge offers dancing and entertainment amid striking burgundy décor. In the main hotel accommodations are suites, each with a living room, bedroom, and small screened-off bar. Some have balconies. We prefer accommodations in an adjoining section of the hotel, a two-story town-house conclave called the Courtyard. An old-worldy strip of bay-windowed buildings facing each other across a central courtyard, the Courtyard is lined with globed, antique gas-lamp replicas. Rooms are a bit fresher looking in this addition and have the advantage of being far off the aging, rather depressing street on which the main building is located. Rates at Château Granville, now a Best Western, are $70 ($56 U.S.) to $90 ($72 U.S.) double.

The **Pacific Palisades Hotel,** 1277 Robson St., Vancouver, BC V6E 1C4 (tel. 604/688-0461), soars high over Robson Street, its straight-up gray lines softened by arched windows at street level. The Palisades turns its back on the street, however, to aim its lobby squarely at a pretty little courtyard where a swimming pool and small flower-bedecked garden beckon. Inside is one of the city's best-loved and pubbiest restaurants, Puffins's, as well as some very attractive quarters decorated in up-to-the-minute colors and furnishings. Studio suites and larger are quite spacious, with big windows overlooking nice city views or gardens filled with bright-blue hydrangeas, hanging baskets of blooms, and colorful rhododendrons. The location is nice, close enough to town but far enough away to avoid most of the worst central traffic. Rates are $125 ($100 U.S.) to $165 ($132 U.S.) double for studio or one-bedroom suites, higher for executive suites and penthouse apartments.

The **Abbotsford Hotel,** 921 W. Pender St., Vancouver, BC V6C 1M2 (tel. 604/681-4335), is a snug little spot with a great wood-lined Bull and Bear Pub and an opulent Victorian atmosphere in the Bombay Bicycle Club Restaurant. These cozy basement dining spots and watering holes are in fact the chief lure of this small, convenient downtown hotel. Quarters here come in sizes from medium to less. They're clean and attractively decorated in bright fall colors. Nothing elaborate, you understand, but the convenience in both location and in-house facilities make this a winner for the price. The Abbotsford also has same-day laundry service, a desk open 24 hours, telephones, and cable color television, plus Muzak and radio in rooms and room service. The lobby is tiny, as is most everything about this hotel, but it has an undeniable charm. Rates are $85 ($68 U.S.) to $60 ($48 U.S.) double, $75 ($60 U.S.) for a suite.

The **Barclay Hotel,** 1348 Robson St., Vancouver, BC V6E 1C4 (tel. 604/688-8850), was, when we first wrote this book, a basic spot undergoing some minor renovations. Whew, what a difference a couple of years make! Now aiming at becoming one of the city's four-star hotels, the Barclay has been redone top to toes in European style so it's now a study in glittering chandeliers, shining brass, polished woods, and Glamour, capital G. There's an antique-y feel about the place and a genuine European ambience from marble foyer to elegantly furnished rooms which offer twin, double, or queen-size beds decked out in pretty pastel shades. Rates are $69 ($55.25 U.S.) to $89 ($71.25 U.S.) at this small but significant hotel that occupies quite a convenient downtown location.

MODERATELY PRICED HOTELS: For all its size and sophistication, Vancouver offers a number of downtown hotels with moderate prices.

Our vote for poshest and loveliest medium-priced hotel in the city goes to the **Park Royal Hotel,** 550 Clyde Ave., West Vancouver, BC V7T 2J7 (tel. 604/ 926-5511). In West Vancouver just a few minutes' drive from the center of downtown is an enclave so serene and so insular you may just skip downtown. That could be done easily enough for some of the most interesting sights in Vancouver—sprawling Stanley Park, the Capilano Bridge—are right here on the western edge of the city. Perched alongside a river, the Park Royal's ivy-covered Old English buildings are surrounded by beautiful gardens in which a profusion of blooms scent the air. Just 30 elegantly decorated rooms are in this two-story building, which also houses one of the city's most acclaimed restaurants and a comfortable pubby downstairs lounge. This is a place for those who know quality. It's very popular so reservations are mandatory. Quarters are spacious, those overlooking the river particularly so. Many have brass beds, polished wood furniture, a writing desk, and a small sitting area with a couch. Diamond-paned windows add to the Old England look and feel of the place. Best news of all are the prices, which are $85 ($68 U.S.) to $106 ($84.75 U.S.) double, higher for suites.

Running a close second—and unrivaled in the airport area—is the **Abercorn Motor Inn,** 9260 Bridgeport Rd., Richmond, BC V6X 1S1 (tel. 604/270-7576, or toll free 800/528-1234 or 800/633-0085). This delightful Tudor Inn lookalike greets you with diamond-paned windows on a handsome, low two-story building set well off the expressway yet only a few minutes from the airport. The Abercorn is just as beautiful inside, with large rooms with comfortable chairs. Big windows offer a view of lovely rolling lawns. Rooms overlooking the mountains offer ever-prettier views. In the cozy Inglenook restaurant downstairs, good-looking wing chairs give the room an English-library ambience that's most appealing. The food is good too, and the chefs place great emphasis on the use of pure ingredients. The cooking is not fancy, but it's quite satisfactory, and prices for steaks and seafood are in the $13 ($10.50 U.S.) to $17 ($13.50 U.S.) bracket. Some suites are available, and a few rooms have whirlpools. The Abercorn has free airport transportation too, and the price is $80 ($64 U.S.) to $90 ($72 U.S.) double, often cheaper on weekends.

BUDGET HOTELS: We've defined budget hotels as those that fall roughly in the $50 ($40 U.S.) to $76 ($60.75 U.S.) bracket.

Most charming budget find in Vancouver is the **Sylvia Hotel,** 1154 Gilford St., Vancouver, BC V6G 2P6 (tel. 604/681-9321). Many people have discovered the joys of the ivy-covered hotel across the street from an awesome sweep of sand on arcing English Beach so you'll have to book well in advance to find a room here. That ivy we mentioned runs from cornerstone to roofline of this stone building melding it into the tree-lined boulevard so skillfully it looks as if it grew there. Clever people here have turned the front of the hotel into a pubby enclave that's a popular watering spot with a great view of the beach and bay. Handsome wing chairs make this such a cozy haven. Friendly help will show you to simply decorated rooms. One large one-bedroom suite with separate bed-sitting room and kitchen has such a sublime view that the importance of fancy furnishings pales in significance; it rents for $104 ($83.25 U.S.). Close to downtown yet well away from the bustling throngs and five minutes from Stanley Park, the Sylvia is just plain wonderful, particularly in light of the rates, which are $45 ($36 U.S.) to $75 ($60 U.S.) double, higher for a one-bedroom or two-bedroom suite.

The **Shato Inn Apartment Hotel,** 1825 Comox St., Vancouver, BC V6G 1P9 (tel. 604/681-8920), is a small but attractive motel located in a quiet neighborhood just a few blocks from English Bay Beach. On streets all around highrise condominiums loom, but here among a riot of blooms this good-looking wood-sided building is a serene spot. Spacious quarters are simply but attractively decorated and come in several configurations, ranging from rooms with double beds to accommodations with kitchenettes in a small alcove and a sitting area. Some rooms have a balcony, and all have large windows. Rates are $70 ($56 U.S.) to $90 ($72 U.S.) double.

The **Kingston Hotel,** 757 Richards St., Vancouver, BC V6B 3A6 (tel. 604/ 684-9024), shares a Tudor-y look with the Rose and Thorne next door. Definitely a bargain, the Kingston is not far from Gastown and Chinatown. It's brightly decorated and clean, although oddly mixed colors and patterns are a bit jarring. Rates are $30 ($24 U.S.) to $60 ($48 U.S.) double for rooms with a bath, about $10 ($8 U.S.) to $15 ($12 U.S.) less for singles, and a few dollars less for rooms that share a bath. No elevator, but a sauna and laundromat on the premises.

The **Burrard Motor Inn,** 1100 Burrard St., Vancouver, BC V6Z 1Y7 (tel. 604/681-2331), seems to be a comfortable friendly place with a pretty, plant-filled, beamed-ceiling Greenhouse restaurant just off the small stone-walled lobby. Big windows light colorful, simply furnished rooms with bright printed drapes. Many of them have two double beds and some overlook an outdoor patio garden. All have televisions, phones, and soundproofing. Parking is free at the motor inn, which charges $50 ($40 U.S.) to $68 ($54.50 U.S.) double.

Bosman's Motor Hotel, 1060 Howe St., Vancouver, BC V6Z 1P5 (tel. 604/682-3171), is a four-story downtown motor hotel with parking and a small coffeeshop. Big-windowed rooms overlook the street and have adequate furnishings with lively color touches. A heated swimming pool provides splashing space. Rates are $57 ($45.50 U.S.) to $69 ($55.25 U.S.) double.

Best Western O'Doul's, 1300 Robson St., Vancouver, BC V6E 1C5 (tel. 604/684-8461, or toll free 800/528-1234, 800/633-0085 in Canada), reopened in grand new form just in time for Expo '86. Redone from sidewalk to suites, O'Doul's is now a very modern spot with king- and queen-size beds, remote-control televisions with complimentary sports and movie channels, stocked mini-bars, an indoor swimming pool and whirlpool with exercise facilities, and around-the-clock room service. Occupying quite a convenient location, right in the heart of the Robson Street area, the hotel is walking distance from Stanley Park and downtown Vancouver. You'll now find 130 rooms here ranging in price from $115 ($92 U.S.) to $195 ($156 U.S.), that latter price for one-bedroom suites. Children under 13 are free in their parents' room.

Apartment hotels seem to be quite popular in Vancouver. The **Riviera Motor Inn,** 1431 Robson St., Vancouver BC V6E 1C5 (tel. 604/685-1301), has 40 units, some with really lovely views over the harbor, mountains, and city—nos. 802 and 902, for instance. Apartments have full kitchens and a tiny dining area. A separate bedroom in one has a frilly white spread while living room furniture is basic but comfortable. The Riviera's a little rough around the edges, but it does offer spacious and clean apartments and some wonderful views. Televisions and telephones too. Rates are $60 ($48 U.S.) to $78 ($62.50 U.S.) double a day.

The **Greenbrier Apartment Motor Hotel,** 1393 Robson St., Vancouver, BC V6E 1C6 (tel. 604/683-4558), is yet another apartment hotel in downtown Vancouver. This one has some quite large apartments with separate bedrooms, full but small kitchens, and often some antiquated furniture in rather haphazard combinations. Still, for rates of $40 ($32 U.S.) to $48 ($38.50 U.S.) double, that's a lot of space for the money. Cable color televisions and phones in all rooms, covered free parking, and daily maid service.

If you turn off immediately at the thought of a room in a **Hotel YWCA,** 580 Burrard St., Vancouver BC V6V 2K9 (tel. 604/662-8188, or toll free 800/663-1424), think again. Let us quickly add here that both families and couples are accepted at the Y, as well as female voyagers. Vancouver's Y is liberated indeed, liberated from the idea that the Y must be clinical and spartan. Redecoration has turned ten floors of this central city building into attractive quarters with pretty carpets, matching bedspreads, and drapes in muted colors. Downstairs a recently redecorated café called the Vagabond serves meals in the $5 ($4 U.S.) range. Open to couples and families as well as women travelers, the Y charges just $31 ($24.75 U.S.) to $36 ($28.75 U.S.) single, $46 ($36.75 U.S.) to $50 ($40 U.S.) double for its comfortable rooms.

If you're staying a little longer than a day or two, the **Sunset Inn Apartment Hotel,** 1111 Burnaby St., Vancouver BC V6E 1P4 (tel. 604/684-8763), may be just what you're seeking. Its location is lovely, in a quiet, tree-lined residential neighborhood near English Beach. These are full apartments with living/dining room, with wood couch and chairs, plus a separate bedroom with dresser and bright bedspread and carpeting. Glass doors lead to a balcony and there's a small tiled bath and small completely equipped kitchen. Furnishings are basic but put together with care. The rate is $58 ($46.50 U.S.) to $88 ($70.50 U.S.) daily, quite a lot of space for the money.

Vancouver's **YMCA,** 955 Burrard St., Vancouver, BC V6Z 1Y2 (tel. 604/681-0221, or toll free 800/633-1424), is in a yellow-brick building in which you'll find a huge open not-very-appealing communal lounge. Beyond that, not bad. Rooms are kept scrupulously clean and are brightly if simply decorated. Best part of the YMCA are the sports facilities, which range from a rooftop running track to exercise rooms, a racquetball court, and a swimming pool. A small coffeeshop closes after lunch. The Y is close to town and convenient, and costs just $25 ($20 U.S.) to $43 ($34.50 U.S.) double. Rooms here are for men or women only, no couples. Weekly rates are $114 ($91.25 U.S.) single.

In summer when students are vacationing, the University of British Columbia rents dormitory rooms to all comers. The rooms have single beds with shared baths. There are also 60 suites on campus, located 15 minutes from downtown Vancouver. Rates at the **University of British Columbia Conference Center,** 5959 Student Union Mall, Vancouver, BC V6T 1K2 (tel. 604/228-2963), in the Walter Gage Residence, which rents space from May to September, are $40 ($32 U.S.) to $55 ($44 U.S.). There's an indoor-outdoor swimming pool too.

BED-AND-BREAKFASTS: Canada's bed-and-breakfast movement is growing in popularity, so several firms in the Vancouver area are now specializing in B&B listings. Among those are **Born Free Bed and Breakfast Agency,** 4390 Frances St., Burnaby, BC V5G 1C7 (tel. 604/298-8815); **Town and Country Bed and Breakfast,** P.O. Box 46544 Station G, Vancouver, BC V6R 4G6 (tel. 604/731-5942); and **Western Comfort Bed and Breakfast,** 180 E. Carlsbrooke Rd., North Vancouver, BC V7N 1M9 (tel. 604/985-2674). Rates are $40 ($32 U.S.) to $75 ($60 U.S.).

CAMPING: Campers can find space at **Capilano Mobile Homes Park,** 295 Tomahawk Ave., North Vancouver, BC V7P 1C5 (tel. 604/987-4722), for $15 ($12 U.S.) to $20 ($16 U.S.) for a full hookup.

4. WHERE TO DINE

As one of the busiest ports on the West Coast, Vancouver has become home to a multiplicity of nationalities and, through them, has acquired some outstanding restaurants. In a city that boasts the second-largest Asian community in the nation, Oriental cuisine abounds, of course, but you'll also find the sauces of France, the exotic herbs of India, the earthy spices of Italy, and even the rare flavors of Africa.

We divided restaurants up by culinary specialties as much as possible.

The prices you'll see quoted here are in Canadian dollars, with the U.S. dollar equivalents following in parentheses. As this book went to press, the exchange was $1 U.S. equals about $1.25 Canadian.

SEAFOOD: Plenty, of course. When you say **Salmon House on the Hill,** 2229 Folkstone Way, West Vancouver (tel. 604/926-3212), you have pretty much told the story of this cliffside restaurant that specializes in Pacific Northwest salmon grilled over alderwood. As for the view, well, to call it spectacular is to understate. Sunday brunch is both good and very popular, so plan accordingly. Prices are in the $14 ($11.25 U.S.) to $18 ($14.50 U.S.) range for dinner entrees. Hours are 11 a.m. to 2:30 p.m. and 5 to 10 p.m. daily, 11 a.m. to 2:30 p.m. for Sunday brunch. No reservations are taken here. To find the place, make your way to Horseshoe Bay and turn at 21st Street in West Vancouver.

A Kettle of Fish, 900 Pacific (tel. 604/682-6661), is a bright and shiny spot topped by a huge skylight and filled with plenty of plants in big terracotta pots. Fresh fish offerings are written on blackboards for your perusal. In the caviar bar downstairs you can have just a tad of caviar, a glass of wine or bubbly, one oyster. The restaurant works hard to prepare fresh fish, simply and lightly cooked and served with terrific vegetables also very lightly cooked. You'll pay light prices too, in the $10 ($8 U.S.) to $16 ($12.75 U.S.) range. Hours are 11:30 a.m. to 2:30 p.m. weekdays and 6 to 10:30 p.m. daily.

The Amorous Oyster, 3236 Oak St. (tel. 604/732-5916), is a happy neighborhood restaurant with a chuckly name. You may or may not emerge from the Oyster amorous, but you'll have dined well on a lunch or dinner of good fresh seafood, perhaps teamed with pasta, homemade soups, and creamy cheesecakes topped with fresh fruit. As you might expect, oysters are the specialty of the house and here they are fat and sassy fellows, prepared mornay or Rockefeller or topped with green chili pesto, black beans, or Cajun spices. Three big, meaty Pacific oysters are $4.50. You'll feel loverly when the bill arrives: nothing in this pleasant restaurant tops $14 ($11.25 U.S.). Hours are 11:30 a.m. to 10 p.m. daily with brunch on Sunday from 11 a.m. to 3 p.m.

VIEW-TIFUL PLACES: Vancouver loves its views and serves many of them with dinner. **Jonathon's Seafood House,** 1333 Johnston St., Granville Island (tel. 604/688-8081), provides lovely interior views while an outdoor patio and all that water amply provide for exterior looking. Seafood is the specialty here and comes in a variety of creative preparations from mussels steamed in wine to escargots and scallops with snow peas. You don't have to pay the piper an exorbitant amount for the scenery either: prices are in the $12 ($9.50 U.S.) to $15 ($12 U.S.) range for most entrees. Jonathon's is open from 11 a.m. to 2 p.m. and 5:30 to 10 p.m. six days and 10 a.m. to 2 p.m. on Sunday.

The Cannery, 2205 Commissioner St. (tel. 604/254-9606), specializes in its view of Burrard Inlet. The atmosphere is quite nautical upstairs where the view is also a bit better. Once again all that water outside seems to influence the kitchen, which specializes in seafood, particularly mesquite-grilled fish. You'll find the restaurant just off Victoria Drive on Commissioner. Prices are in the $10 ($8 U.S.) to $15 ($12 U.S.) range and hours are 5 to 10 p.m. daily for dinner.

Ferguson Point Teahouse, Stanley Park (tel. 604/669-3281), lets you take a look at this wonderful city park, rated one of the finest in North America, and enjoy some water views as well. Located in a restored building bright with skylights and a glassy conservatory, Ferguson Point Teahouse is a tropical delight with wicker furnishings and lots of palm trees. French fare predominates in choices like steak au poivre and coquilles St-Jacques. Entree prices fall serenely in the $14 ($11.25 U.S.) to $17 ($13.50 U.S.) range for dinner. Brunches are served on weekends too. Hours are 11:30 a.m. to 2:30 p.m. and 5:30 to 10:30 p.m. daily, closing an hour earlier on Sunday. Brunches begin at 10:30 a.m. on Sunday, an hour later on Saturday.

Bridge's, 1551 Johnston St., Granville Island (tel. 604/687-4400), spreads all the glitter of Vancouver out before your eyes. A very romantic waterside spot at which you are liable to forget what you're consuming as the views opposite consume your attention, Bridge's pub, bistro, and dining room feature lots of glass and flash and serve goodies from nearby Granville Market so you can be sure the vegetables, fish, steaks, and dessert fruits are fresh. Hours are 11:30 a.m. to 1 a.m. daily and prices are in the $14 ($11.25 U.S.) to $25 ($20 U.S.) range.

English Bay is one of Vancouver's most beautiful neighborhoods and has survived the city's growth pretty much intact. That's why we always head out to the **English Bay Café,** 1795 Beach Ave. (tel. 604/669-2225), when we want to revel in the scenic beauty. And you will find good seafood simply cooked, plenty of steaks, rack of lamb, and beef brochette. The dining room is upstairs and the bar also has a lovely view so you might consider a nightcap here. Prices are in the $14 ($11.25 U.S.) to $21 ($16.75 U.S.) range, and hours are 11:30 a.m. to 2:30 p.m. weekdays and Saturday, and 5 to 11 p.m. daily. On Sunday the restaurant serves brunch from 10 a.m. to 3 p.m.

There certainly is no higher view in Vancouver than the one at the **Grouse Nest,** atop Grouse Mountain (tel. 604/984-0661). Summer or winter the view of a miniaturized Vancouver glittering far below you and the waters spreading out beyond is too spectacular to bear. On the menu are selections of seafood, prime rib, and steaks in a price range of $13 ($10.50 U.S.) to $24 ($19.25 U.S.). Your ride up here on the cable car, an event in itself, is free when you have dinner or brunch reservations. Hours are 11 a.m. to 10 p.m. daily, plus Sunday brunch from 10 a.m. to 2 p.m.

FRENCH: In simple surroundings or complex ones, French food is a favorite in town. A dearly loved haven for Gallic treats is the **Café de Paris,** 751 Denman St. (tel. 604/687-1418). There's a homey, welcoming atmosphere here, a casual simplicity about its marble-topped tables and walls lined with etchings. Backing up those comfortable surroundings is fine cooking that produces an outstanding coq au vin, salmon with basil sauce, mussels baked with garlic and a touch of tomato, among other of the best-known French preparations. Prices are in the $14 ($11.25 U.S.) to $17 ($13.50 U.S.) range for entrees, which are accompanied by beautifully cooked vegetables. Café de Paris is open from 11:30 a.m. to 2 p.m. Tuesday through Friday and 5:30 to 10 p.m. daily except Sunday.

Running close, however, is **La Côte d'Azur,** 1216 Robson St. (tel. 604/685-2629), a really lovely restaurant occupying a small white house trimmed in sky blue and set on a little rise overlooking Robson Street. Inside, owners have recreated a bit of French countryside via a big fireplace trimmed with copper pots. Atop linen tablecloths are white lace coverings. Many little touches will catch your eye here, things like a case full of ornate meerschaum pipes. A small bar occupies the front of the restaurant while the cozy dining spaces are in back. On the menu are duck, salmon, veal, and beef specialties, supplemented by whatever seafood looks good in the marketplace—Dover sole's a feature each week. La Côte d'Azur is open Tuesday through Friday from about 11 a.m. to 2 p.m. for lunch, from about 5 to 11 p.m. Monday through Saturday for dinner; closed Sunday. Rather casual attitude toward opening and closing hours here, one of the joys of owning your own restaurant, we suppose. Prices are in the $15 ($12 U.S.) to $20 ($16 U.S.) range for dinner.

The **Beach House,** 2099 Beach Ave., Vancouver, in Stanley Park (tel. 604/681-9951), is an award-winning and very lovely restaurant in a handsome home with a decidedly European ambience. Rave reviews here go to lapin de Bourgogne and a roast pheasant with truffles and champagne. A most impressive wine cellar adds yet another touch of sophistication to one of the city's most outstanding restaurants. Hours are 11 a.m. to 2 p.m. and 5 to 11 p.m. daily. Dinner entrees run $10 ($8 U.S.) to $15 ($12 U.S.).

Chardonnais, 800 W. Hastings (tel. 604/684-1511), is wowing them in Vancouver with its airy green Key Largo-ish décor and excellent menus, which are likely to feature such innovative treats as tournedos Moscovite with juniper berries, peppercorns, pine nuts, and caviar garnish. Skylights and big windows make this bilevel room a glowing spot by day, but by night the ambience changes to sophisticated elegance. Entrees are in the $10 ($8 U.S.) to $16 ($12.75 U.S.) range, and hours are 11 a.m. to 11 p.m. weekdays and 5 to 10 p.m. weekends.

Dubrulles Brasserie, 747 Thurlow St. (tel. 604/681-3818), is a most comfortable dining spot and wine bar quite near many downtown hotels. What makes it so comfortable is its unpretentious décor, along the lines of a simple country French bistro. Plain rung-back chairs are set on ceramic tile floors, and from the ceiling fringed hanging lamps cast a yellow glow over mirrors, paintings, and bibélots. If you're seeking an intimate corner, try the small, brick-walled side room. Fare is familiar French specialties—steak Diane, au poivre, or provençal with a tomato-and-garlic sauce, coquilles St-Jacques, and filet of boeuf dijonnais in a mustard cream sauce. Dinner, about $12 ($9.50 U.S.) to $16 ($12.75 U.S.). Hours are 11:30 a.m. to 3 p.m. and 5:30 to 11 p.m. daily except Sunday.

Restaurant Suisse La Vaudoise, 1812 Broadway, at Burrard (tel. 604/734-0414), is the city's preeminent Swiss spot, serving four kinds of fondue. A house specialty is raclette, a delectable concoction featuring potatoes surrounded by tiny vinaigrette vegetables and topped with steaming just-melted cheese. Among the other entrees are such tempters as braised escalope of salmon in a chive sauce, roast monkfish in a cream of pistachio sauce, rack of lamb, and roast duck. Fresh pasta "perfumed with citrus fruits" sounds interesting too. Hours at this restaurant, housed in a handsome old Vancouver home with a pretty solarium room, are 11:30 a.m. to 2:30 p.m. for lunch weekdays, 6 to 10 p.m. for dinner six days; closed Sunday. Prices fall in the $15 ($12 U.S.) to $20 ($16 U.S.) range.

AFRICAN: We tantalized you with that mention of African cuisine, so now we produce it at **Kilimanjaro,** 332 Water St. in Le Magasin Building (tel. 604/681-9913). Seems the Indian owner of this interesting restaurant saw some ominous handwriting on the walls of Uganda, and wisely picked up stakes and moved to Vancouver to open this Gastown eatery. Animals of the veldt join you via paintings that adorn the walls of this up-a-floor dining room. Admittedly, most of Kilimanjaro's flavors are Indian, with specialties including meat-stuffed samosas, curries, and Indian breads, but those exotic flavors are married to African herbs,

□ FROMMER'S DOLLARWISE NORTHWEST

peppers, peanuts, coconuts, and plaintains. You'll find an upstairs dining room here, where African drummers occasionally perform on African Music Nights, a bistro called Amyn's downstairs, and in summer a sidewalk café. Prices are in the $12 ($9.50 U.S.) to $20 ($16 U.S.) bracket. Some very interesting dining here from 11:30 a.m. to 4:30 to 11:30 p.m. daily.

ITALIAN: Sooner or later, spaghetti fever strikes. From the kitchen at **Caffè de Medici,** 1025 Robson St. (tel. 604/669-9322), come ten different kinds of pastas topped by fettuccine della casa, rich with prosciutto, chicken, and peas in a cream sauce. Or begin with spaghettini carbonara and follow that with veal piedmontese sautéed in wine and topped with fresh tomato and mushroom sauce. Or try carré d'agnello alla menta, a rack of lamb with mint and mustard, topped by a sauce steeped in the flavors of Martini & Rossi. Veal fans might order scalloppine alla friuliana to sample the ham, fontina cheese, and marsala wine medley of that region of Italy. Adventuresome types can tuck into pollo a sopresa with shrimp stuffed inside chicken basted in a wine sauce. Consuming is done in very attractive surroundings of forest green, light woods, candles in brass holders, handsome Oriental carpets, tapestries, carved wood ceiling, fresh pink carnations, and lighted oil paintings of Renaissance types like the Medicis. The restaurant is in the back corner of Robson Galleria, a tiny courtyard shopping area on Robson Street. You'll pay $20 ($16 U.S.) to $35 ($28 U.S.) for full dinners. Hours are noon to 2:30 p.m. weekdays, 6 to 11 p.m. daily.

Massimo, 1355 Hornby St. (tel. 604/688-1916 or 688-3934), produces more than a dozen kinds of pastas, some unusual antipasto selections like quail eggs, and very good and innovative veal selections, all carefully cooked and served in a sleek contemporary atmosphere that is as lovely as it is dramatic. There is nothing here that is not done competently yet with flair. You'll pay $12 ($9.50 U.S.) to $14 ($11.25 U.S.) for entrees, and the restaurant is open from 6 to 10:30 p.m. daily except Sunday.

Prego, 1090 Howe St. (tel. 604/684-5000), has been around for 18 years, carefully seeing to the needs of a loyal clientele that keep coming back to the fine flavors and warm welcome here. Occupying a handsome old yellow house trimmed in green, the restaurant has several small cozy rooms. Nicole Berardi oversees preparation of a lunch- or dinner-of-the-day plus other specialties. You pay reasonable prices in the $8 ($6.50 U.S.) to $16 ($12.75 U.S.) range for entrees, and the restaurant is open from 11:30 a.m. to 2:30 p.m. weekdays and 5 to 11 p.m. daily except Sunday.

LIGHT DINING/TRENDY SPOTS: Vancouver likes to attend the trend.

Old Bailiff, 800 Robson St. (tel. 604/684-7448), is another Robson Square spot, this one featuring jail bars at the entrance and plenty of British flavor—and flavors—behind the bars. London mixed grill and a carvery serving up succulent roast beef top the bill of fare. In summer most habitués take to the outdoor tables to absorb whatever sunshine turns up and to imbibe specialty coffees. Prices are in the $10 ($8 U.S.) to $14 ($11.25 U.S.) range for dinner entrees, including salad bar, and hours are 11:30 a.m. to 11 p.m. weekdays, an hour later on weekends; closed Sunday. Free parking here after 6 p.m. at Howe and Nelson Streets.

Austrian drapes set the tone at **Mozart's Tea Room,** 800 Robson St. (tel. 604/688-6869), a little bit of Vienna set down below Robson Square. That namesake music master would have been right at home here, dining on a sandwich of Black Forest ham and horseradish, bratwurst, Bavarian meatloaf, weisswurst, schnitzel, or perhaps a croissant with hot or cold fillings like the Normandy—with apples and Camembert. Prices are in the $7 ($5.50 U.S.) to $10 ($8 U.S.) range, and hours are 10 a.m. to 10 p.m. every day.

O'Doul's, 1300 Robson St. (604/684-8461) is a light, airy spot with tall windows and skylights. Loads of plants grow happily in all that light. The fare runs to fat burgers and sandwiches at lunch, salmon filet with hollandaise, crepes, fish and chips at dinner. Prices are in the $5 ($4 U.S.) to $10 ($8 U.S.) range for many selections, so the price is right too. The lounge here is open to midnight or 1 a.m. daily. Dining hours are 11 a.m. to midnight weekdays, later on weekends, and from 10 a.m. to 10:30 p.m. on Sunday.

Ping Pong, 1030 Denman St. (tel. 604/683-5341), is the place to head when an ice cream attack strikes. All the ice cream is homemade, and specialties include such unusual Italian offerings as meringata, zuccotto, arancia ripiende, and—are you ready?—spaghetti ice cream (relax, it's topped with coconut). You'll pay $3 ($2.50 U.S.) to $5 ($4 U.S.) for some of the creamy specialties, and hours are 9:30 a.m. to 11 p.m. daily.

If you've ever been to Spain, you've been introduced to the interesting cocktail-hour tradition of "tapas," a raft of little tastes designed to tide you over until Spain's late dinner hour arrives. You can taste that tradition at **Las Tapas,** 760 Cambie (tel. 604/669-1624), which offers up its tapas in delightful surroundings of a fireplace and hefty but delicately upholstered country furnishings in a bright sunny room—great at the close of a long day. Prices are under $5 ($4 U.S.) for many things. Hours are noon to 10 p.m. weekdays, 5 to 10 p.m. weekends.

ORIENTAL: Vancouver's large Chinatown guarantees some top Oriental cuisine.

Jinya, 567 W. Broadway (tel. 604/873-5040), lines 'em up at the sushi bar where fine—and very beautiful—sushi creations are whipped up by the chef who will be happy to explain the meaning of his designs. Key ingredients, of course, are the freshest of fish. Cool fish flavors may be offset by a spicy sauce, a touch of crunchy sesame, or a few drops of sake. You can also perch in a tatami room for a platter of various selections presented so beautifully you hate to ruin it all by consuming them. Tempura, teriyaki, and sukiyaki are also available. Open from 5 to 11 p.m. daily except Monday, closing an hour earlier on Sunday. Prices are in the $20 ($16 U.S.) to $25 ($20 U.S.) range for dinner.

Some days nothing sounds as good as a tempura or sushi or sashimi dinner. When one of those days hits, head for **Ichibankan,** 770 Thurlow St. (tel. 604/682-6262), to choose from a number of interesting Japanese offerings including salmon teriyaki. Most prices are in the $9 ($7.25 U.S.) to $15 ($12 U.S.) range. Ichibankan, by the way, means "number one gathering place" in Japanese, and many people seem to agree—a sushi counter is often filled. Hours are 11:45 a.m. to 2:15 p.m. for lunch weekdays and Saturday, 5 to 11 p.m. daily for dinner. Ichibankan is in below-ground quarters in a handsome brick-lined building dolled up with antique street lights and wood beams.

Down the hall a few steps from Ichibankan, **Kamei Sushi,** 811 Thurlow St. (tel. 604/684-5767), offers quite similar Japanese surroundings and menu, same price range and same hours, so if one's busy, just walk a few doors down to the other.

STEAKS/CONTINENTAL: As the all-time favorite, steaks are well represented in Vancouver. **Hy's Encore,** 637 Hornby St. (tel. 604/683-7671), is exactly what a great steakhouse should be: dark, candlelit, wood paneled, quiet, sophisticated, and brimming with good steaks, seafood, and salad. From filet mignon to New York strips and top sirloin, top-quality beef reigns. Seafood selections like king salmon with hollandaise sauce or several shrimp preparations are supplemented by whatever appears in the market. Substantial spinach and Caesar salads are favorites, and dinners include hearty soups, salad, a basket of toasts, and a choice of three kinds of potatoes. Special pastas each evening are worth trying, particularly the tortellini with meat and spinach, summer sausage, and tomato sauce. Finale options include chocolate mousse, crème caramel, and hazelnut cake. As sleekly handsome in atmosphere as it is in good cooking, this bilevel, columned dining room is lined with oil paintings. Hy's is a prime choice in Vancouver and has been for more than 25 years. Prices are in the $15 ($12 U.S.) to $25 ($20 U.S.) range for a full dinner. Hours are 11:30 a.m. to 2:30 p.m. weekdays and 5 to 11 p.m. daily.

Not too long ago Hy bought a beautiful old home in the west end of town near English Bay and turned it into a marvelous second restaurant, featuring many of the selections that had made the original Hy's a mainstay of local dining. This second Hy's, called **Hy's Mansion**, 1523 Davie St. (tel. 604/689-1111), is a real showplace and a national heritage residence. Prices are in the same general range, but the mansion is open for dinner only from 6 to 11 p.m. daily.

William Tell, 765 Beatty St. (tel. 604/688-3504), is a very sophisticated restaurant with a resounding reputation for quality. Outfitted in light-green armchairs and serene mauvey shades with brass columns and plenty of marble, the William Tell focuses on traditional French cookery very capably prepared. An occasional nouvelle cuisine touch is just enough to keep the interest piqued. Pâtés are fabulous, soups perfectly done—baked onion is not to be missed here—and such standards as veal Cordon Bleu, lamb teamed with basil, and seafoods united with delicate combinations of spices. Prices are high, but this kind of quality is worth it. You'll pay $17 ($13.50 U.S.) to $28 ($22.50 U.S.) for entrees served from 5 to 10 p.m. daily.

Puffin's, 1277 Robson St. (tel. 604/688-0461), is particularly beloved by meat-and-potatoes diners who come here for good steaks and chops. In its pubby bar many a deal is made, and in its dining room you're greeted with heraldic flags fluttering from the ceiling, dark cozy furnishings, wine-rack dividers, and a clubby atmosphere much loved at happy hour. Crêpes, omelets, and veal are featured at lunches, when prices are in the $6 ($4.75 U.S.) to $8 ($6.50 U.S.) range; quail, rack of lamb dijonais, prime rib, steaks, and salmon at dinner, when the tab rises to the $14 ($11.25 U.S.) to $20 ($16 U.S.) range. Hours are 11:30 a.m. to 2 p.m. weekdays for lunch, 5:30 to 10 p.m. Monday through Saturday for dinner; the bar's open to 1 a.m.

The Keg Downtown, 1122 Alberni (tel. 604/685-4388), is a very popular place. That popularity is warranted too, for the restaurant provides interesting surroundings, plenty of juicy steaks, an extensive salad bar, and sourdough bread at reasonable prices in the $12 ($9.50 U.S.) to $13 ($10.50 U.S.) range for dinner. Atmosphere is the primary lure, translated here to stained and leaded glass, old photographs, acres of wood tables and beams, a lively bar, fringed fabric lamps that offer the maximum of dark and intimate, without turning off the kilowatts altogether. Very popular with the young, trendy set. If you're looking for the maximum in serenity, ask for a seat in the library-like back room. Snacks and some dinners here are offered at ever lower prices. Hours are 11 a.m. to 11 p.m., later on weekends and in the bar. Open daily.

READERS' RESTAURANT SELECTION: "We found **Bishops,** 2183 W. Fourth Ave., (tel. 604/738-2025), where the entrees are $12 ($9.50 U.S.) to $18 ($14.50 U.S.), to have unpretentious décor, excellent food and service, all of which made this accidental discovery a pleasant plus to our trip. It is a restaurant worthy of being passed on to your readers" (Mr. and Mrs. M. Rudoltz, North Bellmore, N.Y.). [*Authors' Note:* Bishops is open from 11:30 to 5:30 p.m. weekdays, from 5:30 to 11 p.m. daily, closing at 10 p.m. on Sunday.]

5. NIGHTLIFE

Some sailing friends of ours, who always seem to find the action, swear by the glories of **Richards on Richards,** 1036 Richards St. (tel. 604/687-6794). A very lively spot, Richards is plenty big enough to permit frequent changes of scenery, if you get our gist.

Nite Lites, 1022 Davie St. (tel. 604/521-0721), is a showy brass-trimmed spot with a big blue canopy. Always lots of action here, some top bands featuring a variety of music.

Panache, 364 Water St. in Gastown (tel. 604/681-0541), flashes with silver and mirrors, features funk, soul, and rhythm-and-blues on a great sound system. It's jammed on weekends.

Other busy spots are **Sneaky Pete's,** 595 Hornby St. (tel. 604/681-3820), a top party spot; and **The Metro,** 1136 W. Georgia St. (tel. 604/684-1733), a Vancouver rock-and-roll center.

Systems, 350 Richard St. (tel. 604/687-5007), claims to be the largest dance club in western Canada and remains to date unchallenged. An urban tunnel entrance introduces the laser-video world that is to follow.

Kits Pub, 1424 W. Broadway (tel. 604/736-5811), is a lively spot.

A pubby spot with the downright wonderful name of **Jolly Taxpayer Pub,** 828 W. Hastings St. (tel. 604/681-3574), is a dark, wood-paneled establishment that must do a land-office business on April 15.

Every major hotel in town has some kind of entertainment. Some of the largest—Hotel Vancouver, Hyatt, Westin, Four Seasons—have several different entertainment areas. The **Roof Restaurant and Lounge** of the Hotel Vancouver, 900 W. Georgia St. (tel. 604/684-3131), is a particularly lovely spot for dancing, with glittery views over the city lights from high on the lighted roof of this landmark hotel.

Vancouver is hot on jazz, so you'll find several jazz clubs in town, among them **Hot Jazz Society,** 36 E. Broadway (tel. 604/873-4131); **Classical Joint,** 231 Carrall (tel. 604/689-0667); and **Anabelle's,** in the Four Seasons Hotel, 670 Howe St. (tel. 604/689-9333).

6. WHAT TO SEE AND DO

In 1986 Vancouver celebrated its 100th birthday in style: as home to Expo '86, a world exposition focusing on mankind's accomplishments in transportation. This green city continues to offer many ways to spend your days.

A LOOK AT THE PAST: Vancouver has a long and interesting history, trackable from prehistoric days to Victoriana at several museums. Most interesting of those is the **University of British Columbia Museum of Anthropology,** a soaring glass-and-concrete building housing a collection of the monumental work of the Northwest Coast Indians. One of the world's top collections and presentations of Indian totemic work, the museum has a fascinating collection of smaller things as well—intricate jewelry, sculpture, and ceremonial objects in silver or gold, bone or wood. You'll find the museum at 6393 N.W. Marine Dr. (tel. 604/228-5087, or 228-3825 for taped message). It's open from 11 a.m. to 5 p.m. daily except Monday, closing at 9 p.m. on Tuesday. Admission is $2.50 ($1.85 U.S.) for adults, $1 (80¢ U.S.) to $1.50 ($1.25 U.S.) for students and children, free for children under 6, free for everyone on Tuesday, $7 ($5.50 U.S.) for families.

At **Vancouver Museums and Planetarium,** in Vanier Park, 1100 Chestnut St. (tel. 604/736-7736 or 736-4431, or 604/736-3656 for planetarium information), is a trifaceted complex housing two museums and the planetarium.

Here is a good place to begin your look at the recorded history of this city. Exhibits range from the pioneer days of the fur traders to the Victorian era that spawned Gastown. Admission to Vancouver Museum is $4 ($3.25 U.S.) for adults, $1.50 ($1.25 U.S.) for children under 12, and hours are 10 a.m. to 5 p.m. daily. Third resident of the museum complex at Vancouver Museums is the **Maritime Museum,** which features an Arctic Patrol Service schooner, the *St. Roch,* first vessel to sail through the Northwest Passage from west to east and back. Admission is $3 ($2.50 U.S.) for adults, $1.50 ($1.25 U.S.) for children, and hours are 10 a.m. to 5 p.m. daily, closing at 9 p.m. on Sunday. At the **planetarium** you can zoom through zillions of years from past to future in this world and others. Admission is $4 ($3.25 U.S.) per person, $10 ($8 U.S.) for families, and no children under 8 are permitted at the evening shows. Show times vary, so give them a call for information.

The **Burnaby Village Museum,** 4900 Deer Lake Ave., Burnaby (tel. 604/294-1231), is about nine miles out of town and offers a look at a working turn-of-the-century village. Blacksmith, printing presses, bankers, trolley cars, all banging and clanging away with workers dressed in period costumes. Hours are 11 a.m. to 4:30 p.m. daily, but Sunday only from mid-October to mid-November. Admission is $3.50 ($2.75 U.S.) for adults, $2.50 ($2 U.S.) for children over 6; $8 ($6.50 U.S.) for families.

The **Old Hastings Mill Store Museum,** 1575 Alma Rd., at Point Grey Road (tel. 604/228-1213), was the first store on Burrard Inlet, built in 1865. Somehow it managed to survive Vancouver's Great Fire in 1886 and now houses pioneer and Indian artifacts. It's open daily from 10 a.m. to 4 p.m. June to September; weekends only, from 1 to 4 p.m. in other months. Admission is free, but a donation is requested.

IT'S A GAS: Vancouver was named after perfectly respectable Capt. George Vancouver, but these days the city's folk hero is a rowdy roustabout named Gassy Jack. He liked to talk—gas—with anyone who'd listen. Gassy Jack is said to have beached his canoe here in 1867 and gone immediately into business as a publican (smart man!), and it wasn't long before the region became known as **Gastown.** Wild living has its rewards, but rarely does the real estate benefit. So it was in Gastown, where a disastrous fire that swept through Vancouver in 1886 burned Gassy Jack's pub and everything else to the ground. The buildings you see today date from about 1887, when Vancouver managed to put the pieces back together with a little help from the Canadian Pacific Railroad, which steamed into town that year, linking eastern and western Canada. Gastown was a pretty spiffy place, with big hotels and fancy buildings, but before long the action moved elsewhere, and it became a slum. In the 1960s, however, a group of entrepreneurs and local artists rolled up their sleeves and rolled away the grime. That preservation project is now known as Gastown. The ornate old turn-of-the-century buildings have been revamped and are a conglomeration of interesting little boutiques and restaurants. The main streets in Gastown are Water, Alexander, Powell, and Carrall. Gassy Jack gets his due here too: there's a statue dedicated to him at the Globe Saloon in Maple Tree Square.

To take a look at this once-rowdy district, stroll east from Harbour Centre at Seymour and Cordova. At Richards Street, West Cordova and Water Streets merge. Stay on Water Street to Gassy Jack's statue in Maple Tree Square, then go another half block along Alexander, heading south on Columbia and west on Cordova to complete a loop journey. A favorite sight for visitors and residents alike is the **Steam Clock,** at the corner of Water and Cambie Streets, once officially known as Skid Road, the spot at which logs were skidded into the water. That clock blows its top every 15 minutes, shooting steam into the area and banging out a rather strange version of Westminster chimes. While you're watching the clock, look at the buildings on the south side of the next block. They were once wooden waterfront saloons. At Maple Tree Square, where Water Street becomes Alexander Street, is the Hotel Europe, an example of an architectural style known as flatiron. Just off the square between Water and Cordova are a couple of alleyways with some interesting brick façades, wrought-iron terraces, and two rough-and-tumble names: Blood Alley and Gaoler's Mews. Gassy Jack would have been pleased.

A SQUARE CENTER: With an eye toward a little European ambience, Vancouver has named part of Robson Street **Robsonstrasse** and tried to generate a little of that European village square atmosphere. Pastry shops and sausage shops help, but this multilevel, fountain-trimmed, landscaped concrete cityscape is a bit too contemporary to pull off much Old Europe. It doesn't matter, however, for the street makes interesting walking and looking, sitting and sometimes listening, when local brass bands perform at open-air luncheon concerts. You'll find Robsonstrasse between Hornby and Bute Streets.

Right along here you'll also find **Robson Square** (between Hornby and Howe Streets south of the 800 block of Robson), where lectures, ice skating, concerts, and art exhibits often take place.

ABACUS TWO, THREE, FOUR: Vancouver is home to the second-largest Chinatown in North America (San Francisco is first), an exotic enclave centered on three blocks of West Pender Street between Carrall and Gore Streets. Chinatown's streets are lined with herb shops, Oriental groceries, restaurants, and boutiques purveying everything from silks to ivory, jade, rattan, bamboo, kites, brass, and brocade.

A strange aside here: At the corner of Pender and Carrall Street is a building Ripley's "Believe It or Not" dubbed the world's thinnest office building. It's five feet two inches wide!

MORE THINGS TO SEE AND DO: In Vancouver you can sway on a suspension bridge, ride up a mountain in a cable car, or visit a whale.

Crossing the **Capilano Suspension Bridge,** 3735 Capilano Rd., North Vancouver (tel. 604/985-7474), is one of those things you'd like to do if you get up enough nerve. One of us did, one didn't. There has been a bridge across this awesome gorge since 1899. The first one was a *real* terror, built of wood and hemp and called the "laughing bridge" by the Indians—guess you laughed if you made it. These days the 450-foot, century-old span is made of sturdier stuff, and takes you across to a wooded park and a 200-foot waterfall. Cowards among us can spend their time in a jam-packed gift shop specializing in animal hides and lots of trinkets. Hours are 9 a.m. to dusk every day from May to September, closing at 5 p.m. in other months. Admission is $4.25 ($3.50 U.S.) for adults, $3 ($2.50 U.S.) for students 13 to 18, and $1 (80¢ U.S.) for children 6 through 12.

Grouse Mountain, at the end of Capilano Road (tel. 604/984-0661), is open daily in summer for rides up to the mountaintop in a cable car that slowly rises 3,000 feet to a pretty chalet restaurant and a cluster of shops. On the way you'll have some smashing views of the city and harbor way down below. Fare is $9 ($7.25 U.S.) for adults, $5 ($4 U.S.) for children 6 to 16. You can walk up or down the mountainside with the aid of a map provided by the Vancouver Visitors Bureau (tel. 604/984-0661). Grouse Mountain, despite its proximity to the city, is a wild and rugged place: when we visited, park personnel were sharing a joke about one of their own who'd been chased into a shelter by one of the bears that hangs around looking for a handout. Rides up the mountain run from 10 a.m. to 10 p.m. daily.

Vancouver's **Aquarium,** in Stanley Park (tel. 604/685-3364 or 604/682-1118 for a recorded message), is home to an amazing assortment of animals ranging from killer whales to a collection of Amazon creatures living in a jungle-like environment. Sharks, moray eels, and tiny sea horses will all come out to play with you at this attraction. Tickets are $5.50 ($4.50 U.S.) for adults, $4.50 ($3.50 U.S.) for children under 12. Hours are 9:30 a.m. to 9 p.m. May to September, from 10 a.m. to 5 p.m. in other months. Open daily.

Harbour Centre Complex, 555 W. Hastings St. (tel. 604/689-7304), has a 25-minute multimedia show describing Vancouver's past and present and there's also a breathtaking view of the city. You'll also find a revolving restaurant here and a shopping mall. Hours are 10 a.m. to 10 p.m. Sunday through Thursday, to midnight on Friday and Saturday. The skylift elevator is $2.50 ($2 U.S.) for adults, $2 ($1.50 U.S.) for children under 12. Show admission is $2 ($1.50 U.S.) for adults, $1 (80¢ U.S.) for children.

The **University of British Columbia** has many exhibits other than its best-known one, the anthropology museum (see "A Look at the Past"). You can also visit an Asian or Aquatic Center and stop in at a Geology Museum guarded by dinosaurs. Information on hours and locations of each of the museums is available by calling 604/228-3131. UBC is at the west end of Marine Drive at Westbrooke Street.

An interesting hands-on place is **Science World,** 1455 Quebec St. (tel. 604/687-8414). You can see a microcomputer lab in operation, find out if white light is really white, learn how stereo works, and watch your voice on an oscilloscope, even blow a square bubble! Hours are 10 a.m. to 5 p.m. daily, opening at 1 p.m. on Sunday. Admission is $5 ($4 U.S.) for adults, $3 ($2.50 U.S.) for children 5 to 12.

TOURS: If you'd like to see everything but on your own time and at your own speed, you can pick up a **self-drive tour** on cassette tape, turn it on, and drive blithely around the city on a two-hour narrated trip. Tapes are available at record shops in the city or by calling Cantrav West at 604/669-0900. The cost is $20 ($16 U.S.).

Those who want to leave the driving to them can call **Gray Line** (tel. 604/681-8687), open 24 hours, which departs daily year round on a full schedule of sightseeing trips around the city of Vancouver and to Victoria. Prices begin at $26 ($20.75 U.S.) for adults, $13 ($10.50 U.S.) for children under 12 for city tours, rising a few dollars for optional excursions. One- to six-day tours of Victoria or Moraine Lake and Valley of the Ten Peaks in the Canadian Rockies are also available. Tickets and information are available at booths in the Hotel Vancouver, 900 W. Georgia St., and the Hyatt Regency, 655 Burrard St. Gray Line will also arrange free parking for you in downtown Vancouver while you're on a tour.

A fascinating way to spend a day and see Vancouver by both land and sea is on a six-hour **boat/train trip** on the M.V. *Britannia*, a sleek white steamer that leaves Vancouver at 9:30 a.m., stops at the picturesque village of Squamish, where you board a burgundy-and-black steam train to huff and puff past beaches and mountains, around hairpin turns, and chug back to your starting point by 4:30 p.m. Combination tours operate from late May to early September and depart from Vancouver's Coal Harbour by boat or from the railroad station in North Vancouver with connecting bus transportation to get you back where you started. Tickets are $42 ($33.50 U.S.) for adults, $38 ($30.50 U.S.) for students 12 to 18, and $25 ($20 U.S.) for youngsters under 12, and are available from

Harbour Ferries, docked at the north foot of Denman Street, off West Georgia Street (tel. 604/687-9558), or from **Royal Hudson,** British Columbia Railway, 1311 W. 1st St., North Vancouver (tel. 604/68-TRAIN). You can also take either journey separately.

Other tour companies include: **Town Tours,** Miramar Hotel, 1160 Davie St. (tel. 604/733-4711); **Maverick Coachlines,** Palisades Hotel, 1277 Robson St. (tel. 604/255-1357); and **Mini-Bus Tours,** 1414 Pemberton Ave., North Vancouver (tel. 604/980-4744).

An enterprising lady named Clasina Van Bemmel operates a company called **Circle Nature Adventures,** 2091 E. Sixth Ave. (tel. 604/254-5015), which will take you on a walk along a forest trail, through a subalpine plateau, into a canyon, or along cliffs where you can bask in the ocean spray. Tours are $25 ($20 U.S.) for a half-day adventure or $69 ($55.25 U.S.) for an all-day excursion May to mid-September.

You can see the city from above aboard **Vancouver Helicopters, Inc.,** 5455D Airport Rd. South, Richmond, for fares beginning at $60 ($48 U.S.) to $120 ($96 U.S.) per person. A North Shore Discoverer trip to snow-capped mountains is $125 ($100 U.S.) per person. Call them at 604/270-1484 or 525-1484, a 24-hour telephone line, for details of the tour. **Harbour Air** offers a seaplane trip at Vancouver International Airport (tel. 604/278-3478) to several outlying cities. Prices vary.

Victoria is such a charming old town, you really shouldn't miss it. **Air BC** and **Gray Line** have teamed up to offer a bargain that includes pickup at your hotel, followed by a ferry ride to Victoria, a city tour, a visit to Butchart Gardens, and later a limousine ride to Victoria airport and return home by plane for $65 ($52 U.S.) per person. Tours leave at 8:30 or 9:30 a.m. from late June through early October, return on any of four 25-minute flights after 6 p.m. All admissions are included in that price too.

GARDENS AND PARKS: Thanks to plenty of rain and a mild climate, Vancouver is practically one big garden. King of all the city's parks is **Stanley Park,** 1,000 acres of recreational facilities and one of the finest parks in North America. Activities range from a pitch-and-putt golf course to beaches, tennis courts, a zoo, aquarium, summer theater under the stars, jogging course, and a lagoon where trumpeter swans glide. You'll find Stanley Park at the tip of the city. Georgia Street cuts right through the middle of the park. To tour the park, follow the Scenic Drive signs that begin at Georgia Street. For a complete rundown on specific dates and hours of park activities, call 604/738-8535 or 681-1141. Stanley Park is home to the city's aquarium as well (see "More Things to See and Do").

Van Dusen Botanical Gardens, 5251 Oak St. (tel. 604/266-7194), are almost an insiders' secret in Vancouver. Everybody knows they're here, of course, but their flaming beauty is less frequently visited than some of the more hyped garden displays. On 55 acres is one of Canada's largest collections of ornamental plants, thriving happily in mild temperatures. Each section of the garden has a theme. A Sino-Himalayan Garden, for instance, salutes the flowers and designs of the Himalayas with a display that mimics a mountainscape. Our favorite's an Elizabethan hedge maze. Free guided tours are scheduled on Sunday at 2 p.m., and there are electric carts for those with walking difficulties. A new feature of the gardens is a five-acre perennial garden that's a blooming spectacular in July but very, very lovely in other months too. In a shadehouse are hundreds of hanging baskets overflowing with blossoms, and from mid-December to January the garden is a glittering wonderland of twinkling lights. Daily hours are 10 a.m. to 8 p.m. in summer, closing at 4 p.m. in winter. Admission is $3.70 ($3 U.S.) for adults, $1.75 ($1.50 U.S.) for students, $7.90 ($6.25 U.S.) for families.

Queen Elizabeth Park, 33rd Avenue and Cambie Street, harbors ornamental and rose gardens in two former stone quarries. There are lots of tennis courts here too. **Bloedel Conservatory** (tel. 604/872-5513) grows plants under a huge dome and will welcome you for a look from 10 a.m. to 5 p.m. daily, to 9 p.m. in summer months. Admission is $2.20 ($1.75 U.S.) for adults, $1.10 ($90¢ U.S.) for students.

Exhibition Park, bounded by East Hastings, Renfrew, Wall, and Cassiar Streets (tel. 604/253-2311), is the site of the annual Pacific National Exhibition in late August each year. There is an amusement park here called **Playland,** at Renfrew and East Hastings Street (tel. 604/255-5161), with rides, a roller coaster, and games. It's open from March to September at varying hours.

SPECIAL EVENTS: From Shakespeare to hogs, sandcastles to polar bears, Vancouver celebrates. Each summer from mid-June to September the city presents the **Vancouver Shakespeare Festivale,** at Festival Tent, Vanier Park, Cornwall and Arbutus Streets (tel. 604/687-4444 or 734-0194). In a fall a grand parade kicks off the annual **Pacific National Exhibition** (tel. 604/253-2311), with contests between loggers and hog growers, bull raisers and horse racers. It's an Exhibition Park in late August and September. In January a hardy group hits the waves in the **Polar Bear Swim** each New Year's Day and the city's Chinese population celebrates the **Chinese New Year** with dragons and street dancers, firecrackers, and colorful costumes.

7. SPORTS

When the sun comes out, Vancouver goes nuts, trying to make up in minutes what exercise they missed in days of rain. You can swim, bicycle—a mania here—ride, run, or just rack out on a stretch of green parkland in a leafy bower. The **Vancouver Board of Parks and Recreation,** 2099 Beach Ave. (tel. 604/681-1141), stands ready and waiting to help you find any kind of recreational activity in the city.

Golfers have many choices, among them **Fraserview Golf,** 7800 Vivian Dr. (tel. 604/327-3717); **Langara Golf Course,** 290 W. 49th Ave. (tel. 604/321-8013): and the **McCleery Golf Course,** 7170 MacDonald St. (tel. 604/261-4522). Greens fees on 18-hole courses are in the $12 ($9.50 U.S.) to $20 ($16 U.S.) range, up to $30 ($24 U.S.) at private courses.

There are 20 **tennis courts** in Queen Elizabeth Park. Call the Board of Parks and Recreation and they will point you to 200 more.

Vancouver Aquatic Centre, 1050 Beach Ave., offers a big, indoor, heated, saltwater swimming pool with sauna, whirlpool, exercise equipment, gymnasium, and diving tank. Give them a call at 604/665-3424 for information on hours, which vary. Admission is $2.15 ($1.75 U.S.) for adults, $1.05 (85¢ U.S.) for children.

From June to September **beaches** at English Park, Stanley Park, and other locations are open daily from 11:30 a.m. to 9 p.m. They're free, and location and lifeguard information is available at 604/738-8535.

You can rent **bicycles** at Stanley Park from **ABC Rentals,** 676 Chilco St. (tel. 604/681-5581), for $4 ($3.25 U.S.) to $6 ($4.75 U.S.) an hour up to about $12 ($9.50 U.S.) a day plus a refundable deposit. There's a bike trail in Stanley Park.

Dozens of companies organize white-water trips, among them **Whitewater Adventures,** 1620 Duranteau St., Granville Island (tel. 604/669-1100), which also plans other kinds of trips, ranging from ballooning to gray whale-watching. One-day rafting trips on the Thompson are scheduled from late April through September and leave at 10 a.m. from various points. One-day trips are $79

($63.25 U.S.), higher for trips on weekends in July and August. Longer tours are proportionately higher.

Fishing trips of all types leave from Sewell's Landing, 6695 Nelson Ave., Horseshoe Bay, in West Vancouver (tel. 604/921-7461). Rental and **charter boats** are available from $10 ($8 U.S.) to $15 ($12 U.S.) an hour to about $350 ($280 U.S.) a day. Sewell's Landing is about a 20-minute drive from Vancouver. **Windsure Windsurfing School,** 1768 W. Georgia St. (tel. 604/687-SURF), will teach you how to get boat, sail, and wind going in the same direction. Board rentals are available at **English Bay Beach Bath House** (tel. 604/669-SAIL), **Kits Beach** (no phone), and **Jericho Sailing Center,** foot of Discovery Road (tel. 604/224-4177) for $10 ($8 U.S.) an hour, six hours for $100 ($80 U.S.). They'll rent you accessories and wetsuits too, and teach you how for $30 ($24 U.S.) an hour including board rental.

In winter all thoughts turn to **skiing.** Grouse Mountain is a 20-minute drive up the hill from Capilano Suspension Bridge at the end of Capilano Drive (tel. 604/984-0661). Lift tickets there are $22 ($17.50 U.S.), for adults, $11 ($8.75 U.S.) for children, and hours are 10 a.m. to 10 p.m. daily. Lift tickets drop in price before 10 a.m. and after 4 p.m.

SPECTATOR SPORTS: B.C. Place Stadium is a popular tourist attraction as well as the site of the city's major sporting events. Seating 60,000, the stadium features a massive Teflon-coated fiberglass roof and artificial turf. Guided tours are at 11 a.m., 1 p.m., and 3 p.m. (tel. 604/661-2300), from Gate A on Beatty Street, and are $3 ($2.50 U.S.) for adults, $2.50 ($2 U.S.) for students 13 to 18, and $1.25 ($1 U.S.) for those under 12. Tickets to all events at B.C. Place Stadium are available by calling 604/280-4444 in Vancouver, or toll free 112-800-663-9311 elsewhere in British Columbia. Gamesters playing at B.C. Place Stadium include the **British Columbia Lions football team** for the Canadian Football League and the **Vancouver Whitecaps soccer team.** Tickets vary widely in price, but you can figure to pay $15 ($12 U.S.) to $25 ($20 U.S.) for most seats.

The **Vancouver Canadians baseball team** plays at **Nat Bailey Stadium,** 4601 Ontario St. (tel. 604/872-5232), and the **Canucks** of the National Hockey League play at **Pacific Coliseum,** Exhibition Park (tel. 604/253-2231).

Gamblers can try their luck on the ponies at **Exhibition Park,** East Hastings and Cassiar Streets, which is open from mid-April to mid-October (tel. 604/254-1631). Post time is 6:15 p.m. on Monday, Wednesday, and Friday, 1:15 p.m. on Saturday and Sunday. Admission is $4.50 ($3.50 U.S.) to the grandstand and $2.50 ($2 U.S.) to the clubhouse; tables for two are $6.50 ($5.25 U.S.).

Auto racing takes place at Westwood Track in nearby Coquitlam (tel. 604/687-3333). Admission is $7 ($5.50 U.S.).

8. ARTS AND CULTURAL ACTIVITIES

Vancouver has a fine art gallery housed now in a lovely old 1910 building, and the city's art, theater, and musical groups are active.

ART: The **Vancouver Art Gallery,** at 800 W. Georgia St. (tel. 604/682-8621), features major paintings of Canadian artist Emily Carr and art from the 17th century to modern days. Outside the gallery, fountains and lights adorn this interesting architecture. Hours are 10 a.m. to 6 p.m. daily except Monday, remaining open until 9 p.m. on Friday, and opening at 1 p.m. on Sunday. Admission is $2.50 ($2 U.S.), but the museum is free on Tuesday. Free guided tours of the gallery are available daily on request.

THEATER: Vancouver loves theater and has many performing groups. The **Arts Club Theater,** 1181 Seymour, Granville Island (tel. 604/687-1644), has year-round professional theater performances of hit London and Broadway productions, while the **Queen Elizabeth Theatre,** 600 Hamilton St., at Georgia Street (tel. 604/280-4444), offers opera, dance, Broadway shows, and pop and rock concerts, among other popular attractions. The **Orpheum Concert Hall,** Smyth at Granville (tel. 604/280-4444), features symphony, classical, pop, choral, and chamber concerts. The **Vancouver Playhouse,** Hamilton at Dunsmuir (tel. 604/280-4444), plays live theater, dance, and choral concerts in an intimate atmosphere.

Other playhouses include the **Firehall Theater,** 1800 E. Cordova St. (tel. 604/684-5311), specializing in mime and experimental theater; the **City Stage,** 751 Thurlow St. (tel. 604/688-7013); the **James Cowan Theatre,** Gilpin and Canada Way (tel. 604/291-6864); the **White Rock Playhouse Theatre,** 1532 Johnston Rd. (tel. 604/532-7535), operating October to June; and **Presentation House/Studio Theatre,** 333 Chesterfield Ave., North Vancouver (tel. 604/986-1351).

MUSIC AND DANCE: The **Vancouver Symphony Orchestra** (tel. 604/875-1661, or 604/280-3311 for tickets), plays in a renovated theater called the Orpheum, Smythe at Granville. Symphony supporters also sponsor a series of **ballet** performances throughout the year at Queen Elizabeth Theatre, 630 Hamilton St. (tel. 604/280-4444). Tickets are in the $8 ($6.40 U.S.) to $25 ($20.00 U.S.) price range. The **Vancouver Opera,** 111 Dunsmuir St. (tel. 604/682-2871), features a quartet of operas from about October to May each year.

9. SHOPPING

Underground, above ground, and even, it would seem, in a netherworld between the two, Vancouver provides plenty of places for you and your wallet to do business. Let's start with the city's most famous market place, the **Granville Island Public Market.** You'll find it under the Granville Street Bridge. Open daily, the market is at its liveliest on Saturday, when all the world turns out to buy fresh produce, meats, fish right out of the sea, and all kinds of treasures and nontreasures. Entertainers show up to get in on the act too.

The **Harbour Centre Observation Deck** tops a big shopping center and has a revolving Harbour House Restaurant (tel. 604/689-0421) atop it. It's all at the west end of Gastown between Cordova, Seymour, and Richards Streets.

Lots of Vancouver is underground. Among the blocks of underground shopping spots are the **Pacific Center Mall** connecting with the Bay, Eaton's, and the Four Seasons Hotel; and the **Vancouver Centre Mall,** at Georgia and Granville. Those two malls are below Granville Mall, home to several movie theaters.

You'll find **Royal Centre Mall** below the Hyatt Regency Hotel on Burrard off Georgia Street, and **Harbour Centre Mall** below Simpson-Sears at Hastings and Richards.

The **Park Royal Shopping Center** (tel. 604/922-3211) features more than 170 shops anchored by Eaton's and Woodward's department stores. The mall even has a free shuttle service to help you see it all. Everything here from Eskimo artifacts to an exercise center.

Savvy Vancouver shoppers swear by the bargains at Japanese-operated stores which seem always to be open when every other store in town is shuttered tight. Furs are a specialty of the Japanese-owned shops. With the dollar at its current price levels, you can find some real steals in any kind of fur in any length from scarf throw to full-length mink.

10. SIDE TRIPS

You can't say Vancouver doesn't offer diverse attractions: within 100 miles you can play in snow pouring down from the clouds or in hot springs rushing up from beneath the ground. Harrison Hot Springs provide the hot stuff; Whistler, the ski slopes.

Whistler is 75 miles north of Vancouver. In winter the slopes are the lure, of course, but Whistler is popular in summer too, for riding, hiking, swimming, golfing on an 18-hole Arnold Palmer course, and tennis. Here you stay in condominium-style lodges with sunken living room, dining room, fireplace, full kitchen with dishwasher, color television, bath with whirlpool, handsome décor, and triangular bay windows. Special packages offer prices of $50 ($40 U.S.) per person daily, including golf in summer, while in winter you're likely to pay $90 ($72 U.S.) to $150 ($120 U.S.) a day for accommodations. Among the lodges in the region are **Mountainside Lodge,** P.O. Box 488, Whistler, BC V0N 1B0 (tel. 604/932-4511), which offers those sunken-living-room loft apartments with whirlpool baths that we mentioned; **Delta Mountain Inn,** 4050 Whistler Way, Whistler, BC V0N 1B0 (tel. 604/932-1982); **Blackcomb,** 4220 Gateway Dr., Whistler, BC V0N 1B0 (tel. 604/932-4155); and the **Whistler Village Inn,** Sundial Place, Whistler, BC V0N 1B0 (tel. 604/932-4004). All are in that price range we mentioned. In summer prices drop to $65 ($52 U.S.) to $95 ($76 U.S.). Whistler, by the way, gets its name from the whistling noise made by the marmots that occupy these slopes when the ski bunnies are off tanning.

The opposite extreme is **Harrison Hot Springs,** about 78 miles east. Here thermal spas lure soakers to lazy days of splashing interspersed with hiking in snow-clad mountains, lake sports, golf, waterskiing, tennis, and horseback riding. The main hotel in town is the **Harrison Hotel,** Harrison Hot Springs, BC V0M 1K0 (tel. 604/796-2244 or toll free 800/663-2266), a handsome place and famous resort on the shores of Harrison Lake. Accommodations are in suites, bungalows, and hotel rooms, and the rate is $70 ($56 U.S.) to $100 ($80 U.S.) year round.

CHAPTER XVIII

VICTORIA

□ □ □

Set in waters that unite Canada and the U.S., Vancouver Island is 280 miles of jagged Pacific coastline, studded with mountains and dotted with forest-trimmed lakes.

Warm winds spawned by the Japanese Current flow across miles of tranquil pastureland and lonely beaches, then run smack into a range of peaks that split the island like a bumpy backbone. Clouds and mountain collide, dumping so much liquid sunshine that the western half of Vancouver Island has become a deep rain forest, lined with massive age-old stands of red cedar, hemlock, and Douglas fir. East of the mountains the sheltered city of Victoria revels in a temperate climate with enough rain to keep its lawns emerald green and temperatures warm enough to keep visitors coming here to play.

Nature and man work together here: massive logs felled in the forests of the island leave the harbor bound for ports around the world; fish pulled from the seas here end their days as star of many a Pacific Northwest menu. So good is the fishing, in fact, that whales and sea lions come here to get in on the action, bringing with them human groupies who want to get a look at those big sea fellows at work and play.

Set down in the middle of all this environmental action and reaction is a city that makes its own rules—and the rules of all the province of British Columbia. Victoria is the capital of British Columbia and quite a capital place at that. Massive Parliament buildings are the scene of much pomp and circumstance: a costumed sergeant-at-arms bears a golden mace and the speaker sits on a gilded throne. At night, Parliament's dome and the steep green-copper roof of a neighboring behemoth called the Empress Hotel drop their pretension and light up like Christmas candles, their distinctive architecture twinkling with all the whimsical glitter of a Canadian Tivoli.

Sparkling blue waters, green lawns, a riot of roses, baskets of blooms dangling from old-fashioned gas lamps, and whimsical Victorian architecture are the lures here, a siren's call answered by hordes of tourists who flock here each summer and in all three other seasons as well.

Victoria's entrepreneurs are no dummies. They took a long look at what they had to offer and set out to enhance it and to enchant with it. Merrie Olde Englande comes to life here as it probably never did in merry old England. Victoria's veddy British overlay may be Madison Avenue–inspired, but beneath the surface, dedication to tradition remains.

If you ring someone up at 4 p.m. and get no answer, just hang up and head for a tea room. There, as likely as not, you will find your missing colleague, musing over a cuppa and a crumpet. At that time every day, Victoria contains its crises for a moment and nips out for a pot of tea. A tradition as firmly rooted here as it is in the Mother Country, tea time is a sacrosanct half hour of placidity amid the haste. It's also a custom you might as well mimic, since you won't get much accomplished anyway when Victoria goes to tea.

What's more the social strata here in the "colony" comes close to being as rigid as it is in the Motherland, give or take a duchess or two. Friendships are not made lightly, but once made they last forever. You will rapidly discover that these folks are a rather straitlaced, form-fitting lot with every right to announce proudly: "I'm Victorian." But bite your tongue, you must certainly not respond: "Oh, I understand, dear. I'm quite conservative myself."

Still, even with all its hype and hoopla, on a soft summer night in a small quiet lane that has hardly changed for a century, you will be charmed at the sight of a mob-capped, pinafored lass sweeping silently along, looking for a brief eye-popping moment every bit like a ghostly 18th-century apparition. Victoria is that kind of city, a place that can carry its British antecedents to ludicrous extremes yet somehow never fail to charm you with its devotion to heritage.

1. GETTING THERE AND GETTING AROUND

Both getting there and getting around are easy and fun in Victoria.

GETTING THERE: Airlines flying into **Victoria International Airport,** located about 45 minutes north of town, include Air BC, Air Canada, CP Air, Burrard Air, Lake Union, Otter, Pacific Western, and San Juan Airlines. The **Airporter** (tel. 604/383-7311) takes you from the airport to the Empress Hotel with a few intermediate stops for $9 ($7.25 U.S.) for adults, $6 ($4.75 U.S.) for children. Give them a call for details of transfers. **Taxi** fares are about $25 ($20 U.S.) one way.

Greyhound and **Pacific Coach Lines,** 710 Douglas St. (tel. 604/385-4417 for either), drive their buses right onto ferries that sail to Victoria from Vancouver and can be boarded on the island at Nanaimo or Victoria, on the mainland at Vancouver, or on the ferry.

Ferries are the most interesting way to get here. Several connect Victoria to points east, north, and south to Seattle. The **British Columbia Ferry Corp.,** 818 Broughton, has service between Victoria (Swartz Bay) and Tsawwassen (South Vancouver) and between Departure Bay (Nanaimo) and Horseshoe Bay (North Vancouver). Call them at 604/386-3431. Fares between the mainland and the island are about $4.50 ($3.50 U.S.) for adult passengers (children 5 to 12 are half price), about $21 ($16.75 U.S.) for car and driver. The **British Columbia Steam-**

ship Co. operates the *Princess Marguerite* on a daily scheduled run between Seattle and Victoria, leaving Seattle at about 8 a.m. each morning, departing Victoria at cocktail hour. Call 604/386-1124 or 388-7397 (or 206/441-8200 in Seattle) for exact schedules, which vary by season. Fare is $40 ($32 U.S.) for a car and driver, $22 ($17.50 U.S.) for other adults, $16 ($12.75 U.S.) for children. Round-trip tickets save you a bit.

Black Ball Transport, Inc. (tel. 604/386-2202) operates the Coho ferry from Victoria to Port Angeles, Washington, year round but more frequently in summer. Sailing time is about 90 minutes, and the cost is $22 (U.S.) for car and driver, $5.50 (U.S.) for each adult passenger. Finally, **Washington State Ferries,** Empress Hotel (tel. 604/381-1551, or 656-1531 for a taped message), joins Anacortes to the port of Sidney near Victoria daily. Fare is $32 ($25.50 U.S.) for a car and driver, $7.60 ($6 U.S.) for adult passengers; children are charged half price. Connecting bus service is available to Seattle (tel. 604/624-5813) and in Victoria (tel. 604/384-4146). If you're considering the scenic ferry rides, remember that in summer *everybody* is considering the same thing, particularly on weekends when the boats are jammed. Make reservations.

Rental-car companies in Victoria include **Budget,** which has offices in both Victoria and Nanaimo and often has discount offers and special deals on meals and lodging. Offices in Victoria are at 843 Douglas St. (tel. 604/388-5525) and at the airport (tel. 604/656-3731). Other rental-car operations include **Hertz,** 901 Douglas (tel. 604/388-4411), and at the airport (tel. 604/656-2312). You can rent mopeds at **Moped Rental,** 270 Government St. (tel. 604/383-4424), which will deliver the scooters to you.

In town, **Metro Transit buses** (tel. 604/382-6161) cover the city and suburbs, charging 85¢ (70¢ U.S.). You get on at the front, get off at the side of the bus. A special tourist daily-rate ticket is available from the driver for $3 ($2.50 U.S.).

Taxis will get you around town for $1.40 ($1.10 U.S.) at the drop, $1 (80¢ U.S.) a kilometer. You can hail one, but calling one is easier and more likely to be successful. Among the taxicab companies operating in the city are **Bluebird Cab** (tel. 604/382-4235) and **Victoria Taxi** (tel. 604/383-7111).

2. TOURIST AND USEFUL INFORMATION

Small as it is, this neat-as-a-bandbox city has honed the business of tourism to a fine edge. Victoria's Visitor Centre knows just what you need to know and will provide you with such quantities of information, you'll soon feel you're an island in an ocean of pamphlets. Victoria has been playing to SRO crowds for many a year now, and folks at the Greater Victoria Visitor Information Bureau are among the most professional greeters we've met anywhere in the world. Stop in to see what a slick operation they're running at **Tourism Victoria,** 812 Wharf St., Victoria, BC V8W 1T3 (tel. 604/382-2127). In peak summer between mid-June and September, the office, which is right in the middle of the downtown area inside a historic tower smack across the street from the Empress Hotel, is open until midnight!

Tourism Victoria now has a **reservation service** for tourists at no extra charge. Telephone 604/382-1131 to book accommodations, transport, tours, charters, and restaurants, and to rent vehicles and make nightclub reservations. The office also carries British Columbia tourist information.

USEFUL INFORMATION: For **emergency police** or **medical help,** call 604/383-1313 or 383-1193. . . . If you need to send a **telegram,** stop in or call

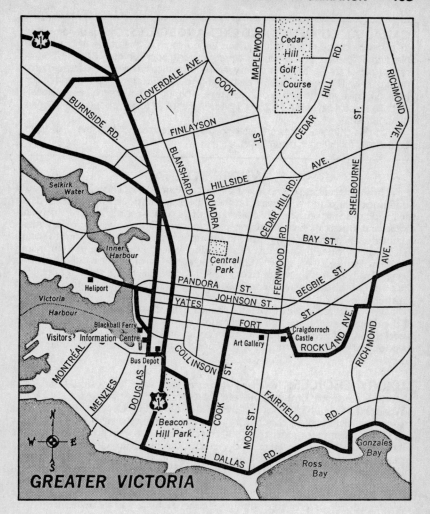

GREATER VICTORIA

CN/CP Telecommunications, 530 Fort St. (tel. 604/384-7174). . . . For a **highway report,** call 604/387-3192. . . . If you want to know **weather** or not it's going to rain today, call 604/656-3978. . . . If you have been out of the U.S. for more than 48 hours, you are permitted to return with $400 per person in purchases duty free; after that 10% duty is levied. . . . To change kilometers to miles, multiply by six and drop the final digit. . . . To change Canada's Centigrade temperatures to Fahrenheit, multiply by 9, divide by 5, and add 32. . . . Pedestrians have absolute right-of-way at all crosswalks, so you *must* stop for walkers. . . . Seatbelt use is mandatory in Canada, and fines for failing to wear one are stiff. . . . Local **newspaper** is the daily *Colonist Times.* . . . You'll find the **post office** at 1230 Government St. (tel. 604/388-3141). . . . The **U.S. consulate** can be reached at 604/685-4311.

CANADIAN CURRENCY AND EXCHANGE RATES: Canada denominates its currency in dollars and cents, just as we do south of the border—but with a pleasing difference: $1 Canadian is currently worth approximately 80¢ in U.S. currency (give or take a few points' daily variation), but costs have not increased proportionately. This means that by exchanging your U.S. currency (banks and major hotels will give you the best exchange rate) and paying for your purchases in Canadian dollars, you'll get about $1.25 (U.S.) value for each $1 (U.S.) you spend—a saving of about 25%!

In this chapter, prices are cited in Canadian currency, with the U.S. dollar equivalents following in parentheses.

---

3. WHERE TO STAY

Those British ties so well loved by the city extend to its hotels as well. You'll find Tudor beams and whitewash on the outside and antique four-poster beds on the inside of some of the more elaborate hotels, at least some kind of British architectural touch on practically every place in town. Downtown Victoria, with its quaint alleyways and colorful Inner Harbour, is what most people want to see, so that is where you will find most of the higher-priced hostelries and a surprising number of budgetwise stops. Many wallet-watching motels are lined up along Gorge Road, an area that likes to call itself Motel Village. It's about a mile from the center of the downtown area, so you'll have to allow some time for traffic and parking.

We've selected some of what we think are the most convenient and prettiest of the thousands of hotel and motel rooms in tourist-conscious Victoria. We've listed them in descending price order. A brief note on that breakdown: Despite its popularity, Victoria is not as outrageously expensive as cities of similar popularity.

LUXURY CHOICES: It's hard to imagine a more imposing hotel than Victoria's landmark **Empress Hotel,** 721 Government St., Victoria, BC V8W 1W5 (tel. 604/384-7121, or toll free 800/268-9411). On any given day, this massive ivy-clad, turn-of-the-century hotel overlooking the city's Inner Harbour is a vacation home for more than 800 travelers and a stop-in spot for thousands who drop by to ogle the huge lobby, elegant dining room, clubby bar, and delightful Garden Café. Opened in 1908, the hotel symbolizes elegance and oldtime upper-crust living. In the cavernous lobby are no less than two huge fireplaces. Tall columns rise to an elaborately carved ceiling. Light streams through tall windows festooned with heavy drapes. On both sides of a central entrance corridor a dozen or so cozy groupings of couches invite you to meditate on these elegant surroundings. Many changes have been wrought here recently, $32 million worth as a matter of fact. That's the size of the facelift this venerable lady received in 1988 when everything from the lobby to the 1920s Palm Court and from the massive crystal chandeliers of the elegant Crystal Ballroom and the bloomingly beautiful gardens were spiffed up to make this quite lovely hotel even lovelier. You'll now find an exercise room, a Jacuzzi, a larger Garden Café, and 50 new rooms which were added in spaces not used in prior years. At tea time you can join the throngs who come here to sup where the likes of Winston Churchill, Teddy Roosevelt, and even the King of England have been.

You can visit here for serious dining in one of several dining rooms, the most dramatic of which, the Empress Room, boasts an elaborately carved mahogany ceiling in a candlelit setting. On the menu are such choices as medallions of veal with oyster mushrooms, cream of watercress and spinach soup, and escargots with basil sauce. Entree prices are in the $20 ($16 U.S.) to $25 ($20 U.S.) range, but you should probably figure $35 ($28 U.S.) to $40 ($32 U.S.) a person to cover the tempting extras you won't be able to resist. Breakfast, brunch, lunch, and lighter meals are served in the Garden Café, open from 7 a.m. to 9 p.m. If nothing else, stop by for a drink in the plushy Library Bar or in the Bengal Room, where a Bengal tiger skin is the focal point.

If you're as intrigued as we were with the luxury and elegance offered by this grande dame of hotels, you can have an attractive room here for $135 ($108 U.S.) to $155 ($124 U.S.) double. Rooms in a southerly wing are larger and more serenely decorated than those in the north or central parts of the building. If you're visiting here in the off-season (from October through April), ask about the hotel's two-night package program, which offers you a room, including some meals and a double-decker bus tour, at lower prices.

As long as we're discussing historic hostelries, let us tell you about the **Captain's Palace,** 309 Belleville St., Victoria, BC V8V 1X2 (tel. 604/388-9191). Without a doubt one of the smallest hotels you will read about in this book, the Captain's Palace has just four accommodations for rent in the main house. But what accommodations! This charming Victorian mansion offers three two-room suites with bedroom, sitting room, private bath, and balcony, and one double room. When you want service, you may just grip the bell pull and ring for the smiling maid in mobcap and pinafore. Filled with antiques, the suite even has a small parlor in which you may order your dinner sent up from the wonderful restaurant below. Rates for these charming quarters in this rose-and-lattice-trimmed, perfectly maintained old home are $110 ($88 U.S.) to $135 ($108 U.S.), including full breakfast and a bottle of wine. Another ten rooms are available in an annex building, but we much prefer the original mansion where the pace is more tranquil and the surroundings more like what you'd expect in this lovely old city.

Tradition, despite all the demands it makes upon one, is an important part of the **Oak Bay Beach Hotel,** 1175 Beach Dr., Victoria, BC V8S 2N2 (tel. 604/598-4556). This magnificent Tudor-style seaside hostelry has not let its traditions be eroded by the pace of modern life. High tea, complete with crumpets, is still served each afternoon. You sleep among traditions too: furnishings include a high-backed antique mahogany bed, brass bedsteads, antique wardrobe, pretty flower prints, and elegant old-world colors. Best of the nook-and-cranny corners have balconies and an ocean view. A 50-year-old hotel built on the ashes of an earlier hostelry, Oak Bay was the focal point of community life in the 1930s and remains a very special place today. Its Snug lounge was once a spot frequented by the vicar, the local bobbie, and other folks who didn't care to have the whole neighborhood know they were downing a quick pint. You can get a look at some lovely—and mysterious—antiques, each with an intriguing history, on your way to the hotel's Tudor Room by the Sea, which in summer features a salmon barbecue dinner on the terraces, steaks and burgers for landlubbers. So complete is this hotel that it even has its own yacht! You can board it for sightseeing, fishing, or even private dinner cruises—and doesn't that use sound like the beginning of a very interesting evening? Rates at Oak Bay Beach range from $58 ($46.50 U.S.) to $168 ($134.50 U.S.), depending on the location and luxury of accommodations. Suites also are available. Two-night package rates, including some meals, can be a good buy here.

Now this next spot may be, for your taste, schmaltzy, but schmaltz-to-extreme can be fun. The **Olde England Inn,** 429 Lampson St., Victoria, BC V9A 5Y9 (tel. 604/388-4353), is fun and then some. What you have here is a whole village of half-timbered, gabled cottages clustered about a central inn, five acres of grounds, enough elaborate antiques and suits of armor to stock a city, and even a replica of Anne Hathaway's thatched cottage and a costumed staff. Despite the hokum, the rooms here are enchantingly romantic—one comes complete with a lacy, arched-canopy bed and a stone fireplace. Despite the Tudor style, however, all have modern bath. For amusement you can stroll down a re-creation of an old English lane, sip high tea, and dine on roast beef and Yorkshire, and tour the Hathaway House. It's weird, a little wacky, and really quite fun. Rates vary rather widely, from $57 ($45.50 U.S.) to $160 ($128 U.S.), with the higher prices buying you the fancy canopied bedrooms. From November to March your second night here costs half as much as the first. You'll find the inn by heading west on Pandora Street to Esquimalt Road and turning left at Lampson Street (the fifth traffic light on Esquimalt Road).

The **Victoria Regent,** 1234 Wharf St., Victoria, BC V8W 3H9 (tel. 604/386-2211), features the latest in contemporary concepts from its slick modern architecture to its brand-new way with rooms. You'll know what we mean about the architecture when you see the snappy curvilinear sweep and smoked-glass exterior of this attractive harborside hostelry. And you'll know what we mean about the Regent's way with rooms when you discover rooms are not rooms but suites, each with a balconied living room, dining area, a kitchen, and one or two bedrooms. Surprisingly, you'll pay about as much for all the extra space as you would for only an ordinary hotel room: $95 ($76 U.S.) to $215 ($172 U.S.) for a one- or two-bedroom suite. The Regent also offers weekly rates that treat you to seven days for the price of six. If you're of a self-indulgent bent, there's a fancy honeymoon suite with a fireplace in the living room and a whirlpool in the bathroom. There are also executive suites with fireplaces, dens, and whirlpools for $215 ($172 U.S.) to $550 ($440 U.S.).

Executive House, 777 Douglas St., Victoria, BC V8W 1B5 (tel. 604/388-5111), is a conveniently located hotel in the heart of the downtown area. You're greeted in a high-ceilinged lobby lined with beautiful wood paneling, woven wall hangings, and leather couches. Rooms are wallpapered in attractive prints and decorated in contemporary pastels, often sparked with deep contrasting colors. At the hotel's Bartholomew's Restaurant, English sherry trifle is a daily tradition. At cocktail time the veddy British pub is a popular place, as is the hotel's Doubles Oyster Bar, where shuckers flip open bivalves by the dozen. Later you can nip into Hy's for charcoal-broiled prime beef from Alberta Province or some seafood from the waters nearby. Figure $20 ($16 U.S.) to $25 ($20 U.S.) for dinner. You can choose standard hotel rooms with king-size, queen-size, twin, or double beds, or move up in the world to a one- or two-bedroom or studio suite, or even stay in a fancy penthouse suite with a Jacuzzi bath and private steamroom. Double rooms are $90 ($72 U.S.) to $110 ($88 U.S.), suites higher.

The **Dominion Hotel,** 759 Yates St., Victoria, BC V8W 1L6 (tel. 604/384-4136, or toll free 800/663-6101, 112-800/663-6101 in British Columbia), is our choice for those who love to live in historic surroundings. This beautiful old hotel fell upon some less-than-glorious days in past years but has been restored to her former glory, perhaps even better. You'll find 101 big, pretty rooms, simply furnished in contemporary styles and colors with ceiling fans and a faintly tropical air about them. Rooms have queen-size or double beds and some even sport steambaths. It is in the public rooms, however, that you will find the most impressive evidence of this hotel's impressive past. In the lobby, swagged drapes reach to an ornately paneled ceiling where crystal chandeliers glitter. A grandfather clock ticks at the entrance, and in the two-level Barbary Coast lounge, you will find shining mahogany paneling polished to a fare-thee-well, gleaming brass trim, brocaded bar chairs, and a gorgeous wooden bar glowing in the aura cast by a sparkling chandelier. The Dominion's Gaslight Lounge features dark velvety fabrics, carved oak paneling, and Victorian lamps. The Central Park Dining

Lounge serves up a tropical atmosphere of highbacked wicker chairs and lots of greenery. Rates at the Dominion are $69 ($55.25 U.S.) to $89 ($71.25 U.S.) double. Rates drop 50% from October to May.

The **Laurel Point Inn,** 680 Montreal St., Victoria, BC V8V 1Z8 (tel. 604/ 386-8721, or toll free 800/663-7667), is on a small peninsula that juts out into the Inner Harbour area. Across the water are the green domes of the Empress Hotel. Recent additions have brought the hotel's room count to 400, including some luxurious one-bedroom and penthouse suites. You'll have a lovely view of the city from most guest rooms and public rooms. Views inside are lovely too: a brick-lined lobby lighted by a gleaming and very contemporary ceiling fixture. On a brick wall hangs a tactile wool fiber sculpture, and in front of the fireplace is a cozy cluster of chairs. For relaxing moments there are tennis, a whirlpool with a view, jogging trail, and a glassed-in indoor/outdoor swimming pool with a glass roof that slides back on balmy days. There are still more beautiful views from the hotel's dining room and lounge. Rates are $140 ($112 U.S.) to $160 ($128 U.S.) double.

Near the harbor in which the Seattle and Port Angeles ferries dock is the large and attractive **Coast Harbour Towers,** 345 Quebec St., Victoria, BC V8V 1W4 (tel. 604/385-2405, or toll free 800/663-7555). You'll see the arched windows of its top story as you explore the quiet streets of this peninsula. The Coast Harbour Towers is filled with marble and brass in soft colors. A few nautical artifacts enhance the South Seas flavor of this attractive hotel. You'll find 183 large rooms here, decorated in handsome furniture with drapes and bedspreads in a matching modern print. Other amenities include an indoor swimming pool, a sauna, whirlpool, cocktail lounge, gift shop, and Raven's Dining Room. Rates at the Coast Harbour Towers are $125 ($100 U.S.) to $150 ($120 U.S.) year round, with one- or two-bedroom suites, VIP suites, and penthouse accommodations available.

There are two special features of the **Château Victoria,** 740 Burdett Ave., Victoria, BC V8W 1B2 (tel. 604/382-4221): the lofty view from the rooftop restaurant and the perfectly gorgeous lounge where you can sink into highbacked wing chairs and luxuriate in Old English surroundings. The rooms are straightforward and serviceable, nothing fancy, but some have balconies, others come with sitting room and kitchen. Rates are $99 ($79.25 U.S.) to $150 ($120 U.S.).

MODERATELY PRICED HOTELS: Victoria has some very appealing medium-priced hotels.

Who can resist those low-slung basset hounds with their floppy ears and sad eyes? Nobody, that's who, and few are able to resist the **Waddling Dog Inn,** 2476 Mount Newton Crossroad, Saanichton, BC V0S 1M0 (tel. 604/652-1146), named—what else?—after a beloved basset hound that became the inn's mascot. A three-story building with small-paned windows and lots of Tudor touches, the Waddling Dog's rooms have brass headboards on queen-size beds and wood ceiling beams—nice touches of Merrie Olde England. In the public rooms much of the design was done by British craftsmen. There's entertainment in the lounge on weekends, and good food in the attractive dining room lined with oil paintings. To tie up this very neat package, the setting 16 miles out of town on the road toward Buchart Gardens is woodsy and pleasant. Rates are $99 ($79.25 U.S.) to $125 ($100 U.S.) double in the height of the summer season from June to October, then dropping as much as $30 ($24 U.S.) to $40 ($32 U.S.) in fall. Despite the 30-room inn's tenderness for bassets, they will not welcome yours, sorry.

The **Inn on the Harbour,** 427 Belleville St., Victoria, BC V8V 1X3 (tel. 604/386-3451), occupies a very convenient site about two blocks from the Parliament Building and the Empress Hotel—it's right at the ferry dock. Heraldic

crests decorate the exterior of this long four-story building, and flags fly gaily
from its walls. Accommodations here are basic motel rooms with one or two
double beds in bright floral prints. A popular stop for auto travelers, this motel
features a pretty paneled dining room, named Swiftsure after the British frigates
that patrolled these waters a century ago. There's even a little sidewalk café open
in summer months. An outdoor pool offers entertainment for the youngsters
and for exploration-weary adults. Rates are $62 ($49.50 U.S.) to $93 ($74.50
U.S.) double year round.

Just a few steps away is the **Crest Harbourview Inn,** 455 Belleville St., Victoria, BC V8V 1X3 (tel. 604/386-2421). Like its neighbor, this is a simple spot
—three stories with rooms opening onto a shared balcony/walkway. Big picture
windows offer a view of the harbor area across the street. A big 60- by 30-foot
heated, glassed-in pool is tempting on a sunny Victoria afternoon. Crest's
Bayside Room restaurant is decked out in bright linens and open from early
breakfast to late-evening snacks. The rates at the Crest Harbourview, which has a
few kitchenettes, a launderette on the grounds, and plenty of free parking, are
$91 ($72.75 U.S.) to $96 ($76.75 U.S.).

On nearby Quebec Street, which runs parallel to Belleville Street, the harborside drive, is **Huntingdon Manor Inn,** 330 Quebec St., Victoria BC V8V
1W3 (tel. 604/381-3456), a really handsome spot. We could hardly drag ourselves away from the wainscoted Olde English library, where cushy, velvety, wing
chairs and a fireplace fairly beg you to linger. Windows overlook the tiny circular
garden filled with flaming roses and violet irises. In this four-story wood-sided
inn, you will find 116 accommodations, ranging from plush two-story penthouse suites overlooking the harbor and James Bay to rooms with romantic four-
posters. Oak furnishings are features of all rooms, from the gallery suites with
gabled ceilings to the simpler quarters. Family suites offer kitchens and convertible sofas. An indoor whirlpool and sauna lined with plants is a pleasant place to
while away a couple of hours. Summer rates range from $85 ($68 U.S.) to $110
($88 U.S.) for a double room or waterbed. In winter rates drop about $20 ($16
U.S.) for rooms, more for suites. Kitchen facilities are an additional $15 ($12
U.S.) as are rollaways and additional persons, but children under 12 are free.

A favorite sipping spot for both locals and travelers is the atmospheric Old
Bailey Lounge in the **Courtyard Inn,** 850 Blanshard St., Victoria, BC V8W 1B3
(tel. 604/385-6787). A very convenient downtown hotel, the Courtyard Inn
offers king-size beds or two doubles in attractively decorated rooms. There's a
beauty salon, an indoor pool, a sauna, and a launderette here too, but the cozy
wood-trimmed pub and the small Courtyard Restaurant are the biggest attractions. Rates are $79 ($63.25 U.S.) to $89 ($71.25 U.S.) double, lower October
through May.

Another downtown hostelry with comfortable and attractive accommodations is **Helm's Inn,** 668 Superior St., Victoria, BC V8V 1V2 (tel. 604/385-
5767). Located on a quiet, shady street just behind the Parliament Building,
Helm's Inn has large and simply furnished rooms, some with wood-rimmed balcony or terrace, some with small kitchenettes. Rates at this two-building, three-
story inn are $72 ($57.50 U.S.) to $96 ($76.75 U.S.) double.

Victoria's **Beaconsfield Inn,** 998 Humboldt St., Victoria, BC V8V 2Z8
(tel. 604/384-4044), is British to its 1905 core and handsome as a swan. A stolidly square Edwardian edifice all decked out in white with forest green trim, the
Beaconsfield Inn was once a beautiful old home given as a wedding gift by a millionaire to his very lucky daughter. After many a moldering year, this gem was
rescued by a local lawyer who turned it into this upmarket bed-and-breakfast
beauty. Open since 1984, the inn is named after a hideaway used by King Edward

VII for some of his less-than-licit romances. If you're saturated with Victorian furbelows, you'll love this tailored Edwardian architecture that quells the flamboyant and encourages the luxurious. You'll find wicker furniture, lots of potted plants to soften interior edges, etched glass, mahogany paneling, and a grandfather clock that chimes out the hour with subtle élan.

In the dozen rooms here you'll sink into down comforters, revel in antiques, brass beds, lace curtains, fringed lamps, lovely colors, beautiful old wardrobes. Doors to unoccupied rooms are left open to encourage you to explore. All that does, unfortunately, is tempt you to sleep your way around the entire building. Rosy stained-glass windows are the focal point of the Rosebud Suite, blue is the theme in the Blue Room, and the aerie Attic Room has a Jacuzzi. A room named for Lillie Langtry has an unusual wood-enclosed bathtub and shower while other rooms sport clawfoot tubs and steam-heated towel-drying racks. Rates range from $75 ($60 U.S.) to $150 ($120 U.S.) and include a sherry hour, a full breakfast with some elegant egg concoctions, scones, and fresh orange juice.

Bill McKechnie and his partner, Steward Lloyd, have another inn in the making: Humboldt House, a few steps down the street from the Beaconsfield Inn. It will have four most *intime,* private suites with breakfast served in your room. Stay tuned.

BUDGET CHOICES: Another very lively place in town is the **Strathcona Hotel,** 919 Douglas St., Victoria, BC V8W 2C2 (tel. 604/383-7137), a spot geared particularly to the very active nightlife-loving traveler, young or not-so-young. The public rooms here are very pretty places. The Forge is a 1920s cabaret decked out in stained-glass windows and Tiffany-look lamps. The Cuckoo's Nest is a restaurant and disco the Strathcona calls "zany," and who could disagree? Booths are trimmed in fur, curtained with beads, and decorated in Indian prints. Accommodations here can be simple or quite elegant, including one with a tall wooden bedstead and a small couch set in an alcove trimmed with wooden railposts and arched mirrors. All in all, the Strathcona is a little world of its own in which you will always find plenty of things happening. Rates are a mere $52 ($41.50 U.S.) to $67 ($53.50 U.S.), very reasonable for this downtown location.

An intriguing spot in the downtown area is **James Bay Inn,** 270 Government St., Victoria, BC V8V 2L2 (tel. 604/384-7151). Located near Beacon Hill Park just behind the Parliament Buildings, James Bay Inn is a cozy place with plenty of English atmosphere. There are just 54 rooms here, and some of them share a bath with a neighboring room. Some but not all have televisions. The friendly management will give you the latest word on walking tours in town. The rates are the reason most people choose this well-located hotel: prices begin at $36 ($28.75 U.S.) and rise to just $51 ($40.75 U.S.).

Call it motel village, motel road, or just "where all the motels are." It's Gorge Road, a motel-lined roadway a mile or so from downtown Victoria. We weren't particularly overwhelmed by the choices out here—most are just basic motels. If you think Gorge Road is for you, however, a few of the top choices are: the **Coachman Inn,** 229 Gorge Rd. East, Victoria, BC V9A 1L1 (tel. 604/388-6611), a mansard-roofed three-story building trimmed with ivy and featuring an indoor pool, twin saunas, a laundry, a cheery restaurant, a lounge and 74 newly refurbished rooms, with rates of $65 ($52 U.S.) to $96 ($76.75 U.S.) double; the **Budget Host Maple Leaf Inn,** 120 Gorge Rd. East, Victoria, BC V9A 1L3 (tel. 604/388-9901), boasting attractive wood trim, a heated outdoor pool and sauna, queen-size beds and waterbeds, kitchenettes, a laundromat, complimentary coffee, and rates of $44 ($35.25 U.S.) to $70 ($56 U.S.); and the **Scotsman,**

490 Gorge Rd., Victoria, BC V8T 2W4 (tel. 604/388-7358), a cheerful budget stop with free coffee, some kitchen units, and rates of $48 ($38.50 U.S.) to $78 ($62.50 U.S.) double.

CAMPING: Campers have plenty of options on this lovely island. You might try, for instance, **Victoria East KOA,** Box 129, Mount Newton Crossroad, Saanichton, BC V0S 1M0 (tel. 604/652-3232), about ten miles north of town near Butchart Gardens. An ocean view and beach are the lures here. Hookups are $15 ($12 U.S.) double.

BED-AND-BREAKFAST CHOICES: With so much Britishism in evidence, it is only natural to expect there will be some bed-and-breakfast establishments. Among those are **Campus View House Bed and Breakfast,** 1840 Midgard Ave., Victoria, BC V8P 2Y9 (tel. 604/477-3069), a friendly spot; and **VIP Bed and Breakfast,** 1786 Teakwood Rd., Victoria, BC V8S 5E3 (tel. 604/477-5604).

4. WHERE TO DINE

Surprisingly in a town that places such emphasis on its British antecedents, there is a wide variety of ethnic choices, ranging from Japanese to Greek with plenty of pubs and seafood houses. We've divided up the choices with an eye to the specialty of the house.

CONTINENTAL: Continental food is always a crowd-pleaser. The **Captain's Palace,** 309 Belleville St. (see "Where to Stay") (tel. 604/388-9191), spreads out through the delightful main-floor dining rooms of an 1897 mansion of surpassing beauty. Flowers in crystal vases adorn the lovely bay-windowed rooms with elaborate ceiling moldings and delicate pastel colors. Very good seafood preparations and beef are menu highlights. You'll pay $15 ($12 U.S.) to $20 ($16 U.S.) for dinner entrees, $6 ($4.80 U.S.) to $11 ($8.80 U.S.) for lunch. Hours are 7:30 a.m. to 10 p.m. daily.

Hy's Steak House, in the Executive House Hotel, 777 Douglas St. (tel. 604/382-7111), features sumptuous décor, great steaks, and good, fresh seafood in the $12 ($9.60 U.S.) to $28 ($22.40 U.S.) price range. Hours are 5 p.m. to midnight daily, closing at 9 p.m. on Sunday, and closed completely on Sunday from October through April.

Dingle House, 137 Gorge Rd. East (tel. 604/382-8721), offers candlelight, antiques, and formal and luxurious dining alcoves in a charming Victorian home. Add to that good prime rib, steaks, seafood, and rack of lamb to come up with a cozy, romantic hideaway perfect for special evenings. Prices are in the $12 ($9.50 U.S.) to $20 ($16 U.S.) range for set dinners, higher for à la carte selections. The hours at Dingle House are 5 to 10 p.m. daily plus Sunday brunch hours of 11 a.m. to 2 p.m.

It isn't unusual for a restaurant to open in an old home, but it is rather a departure for a home to take over a restaurant. That's just what happened at **Chantecler,** 4509 W. Saanich Rd. (tel. 604/727-3344), some years back, and many are those who bless the day. Throngs of the hungry swear by this fine restaurant, which features an interesting range of selections from beautifully prepared local seafood to unusual game selections presented in an elegant Tudor home. Prices are in the $14 ($11.25 U.S.) to $18 ($14.50 U.S.) range for dinner, and Chantecler is open from 11 a.m. to 2 p.m. weekdays for lunch, 5 to 10 p.m. daily for dinner, and from 11 a.m. to 2 p.m. on Sunday for brunch. There are even half-price specials that begin in the $8 ($6.50 U.S.) range.

Pablo's, 225 Quebec St. (tel. 604/388-4255), provides lovely, elegant surroundings inside a national heritage home built in the Victorian era. Tables tuck into bay windows here, lace curtains sway in the breeze, fresh flowers are everywhere, and lovely wainscoting and antique moldings trim rooms. On the menu are such treats as paella valenciana, rack of lamb imported from the nearby island of Salt Spring, and chateaubriand forestière. After dinner, wander up to the Loft Room for coffees. Try Pablo's special flaming coffee presentation. Prices are in the $13 ($10.50 U.S.) to $17 ($13.50 U.S.) range, and hours are 5 to 11 p.m. daily.

SEAFOOD: As an island Victoria is bound to have good seafood. **Chauney's,** 614 Humboldt St. (tel. 604/385-4512), is a stunner in both décor and cuisine. Swirly art nouveau lines are featured here in a room with burgundy ceilings, brass, and glass. Seafood is the specialty. Get into the spirit of things with oysters Florentine or Dover sole, perhaps take a crack at a whole cracked Dungeness crab, lobster, or some fresh British Columbia salmon. Steamed clams are a favorite. For a very satisfying dinner in smashing surroundings, you'll pay $15 ($12 U.S.) to $30 ($24 U.S.), perhaps less. Chauney's is open from 11:30 a.m. to 2:30 p.m. weekdays, from 5 to 10 p.m. daily, and for Sunday brunch from 11 a.m. to 2:30 p.m.

There are few things better than seafood treated to French culinary techniques. You can see what we mean at **La Ville D'Is,** 26 Bastion Square (tel. 604/388-9414). You can also hear an intriguing story about the ville that gave this restaurant its name: Seems eons ago off the coast of Brittany a willful princess crossed swords with local spirits. A god turned himself into a handsome prince, appealed to her vanity, managed to get the keys to the water-gates, opened them, and *voilà!* she and the island were gone. Today they say this French Atlantis is still out there in the Atlantic at the end of five underwater roads.

Begin here with shrimp in a rosemary mayonnaise, move on to lobster soup or oyster chowder, try an asparagus mousse followed by pan-fried trout topped with a beaujolais sauce, lobster soufflé, or beef tenderloin in a burgundy sauce. Finish with a taste of flaky pastries and a special coffee. There's outdoor dining here in summer. You'll pay $14 ($11.25 U.S.) to $20 ($16 U.S.) for entrees here, including soup, salad, potato, and vegetables, but you'd better figure on a little more in case your will fails. Hours are 11:30 a.m. to 2 p.m. for lunch, 5:30 to 10 p.m. for dinner, daily except Sunday.

Chandler's Seafood, 1250 Wharf St. (tel. 604/386-3232), occupies an old ship chandler's quarters and serves up good seafood simply cooked or grilled over mesquite wood. This is a trendy spot with prices in the $12 ($9.50 U.S.) to $15 ($12 U.S.) range. Hours are 11 a.m. to 11 p.m. daily.

FRENCH: French food is surprisingly popular in this city. **Chez Ernest,** 4496 W. Saanich Rd. (tel. 604/479-2123), backs its Swiss chalet décor with all the favorites of French cooking to come up with a winning mix indeed. Try starting with duck pâté sprinkled with hazelnuts or fresh oysters glazed with garlic, parsley, and anchovy butter. Move on to spinach or Caesar salad and follow with an entree of rack of lamb rubbed with garlic, mustard, and herbs, or poached local salmon topped with white wine sauce, shrimps, scallops, and mushrooms, or roast pheasant topped with a sauce of raspberry vinegar and blueberries. Complete dinners of salmon or pheasant or filet bordelaise, plus soup, salad, vegetables, and a dessert of chocolate mousse topped with Grand Marnier, are $15 ($12 U.S.), while entrees themselves range in the $15 ($12 U.S.) to $24 ($19.25 U.S.) bracket. Chez Ernest is open from 5 to 10 p.m. daily except Tuesday.

Another local favorite is **Chez Pierre,** 512 Yates (tel. 604/388-7711), where wrought-iron gates welcome you to a casual but charming restaurant decorated with copper pots in a country French mode. Classic French cooking produces such favorites as rack of lamb with herbs, duck with a light orange sauce, veal in a mushroom cream sauce, and a good seafood selection. Prices are in the $10 ($8 U.S.) to $20 ($16 U.S.) range, and hours are 6 to 10 p.m. daily.

Folks at **Le Café Français**, 1635 Fort St. (tel. 604/595-3441), may take cooking seriously but turn a little humor on themselves: "ze only cheap classy joint in town," the restaurant advertises. There's some truth to that: with a sophisticated décor featuring acres of polished wood, fresh flowers, and shining crystal. Furnishings are particularly attractive 18th-century design in serene colors. Specialties of the house include a hearty pâté, good hot and cold soups, stuffed clams, and excellent bouillabaisse. Always some sinful desserts, of course, and all of it for prices in the $11 ($8.75 U.S.) to $18 ($14.50 U.S.) range for entrees. Hours are 5 to 10 p.m., with a lighter late-evening menu served after 10 p.m. for the European diners among us.

ORIENTAL: Several attractive restaurants in town offer Oriental specialties.

Maiko Gardens, 940 Fort St. (tel. 604/383-3421), is a really lovely Japanese dining room with a tiny garden surrounded by private tatami dining rooms closed off with shoji screens. The food is just as lovely, served on lacquered platters. You might try prawns tempura or a selection called batayaki, which mixes sliced beef, onions, mushrooms, and green peppers, or perhaps have a go at salmon teriyaki. A sushi bar turns out wonderfully artful creations, and a seafood platter gives you a chance to try several different fish, including abalone. Many entrees are in the $8 ($6.50 U.S.) to $10 ($8 U.S.) range, including salad, soup, dessert, and green tea; some are in the $10 ($8 U.S.) to $15 ($12 U.S.) bracket, that platter a dollar or so higher. Hours are 5 to 10 p.m. daily except Sunday, with opening at 6 p.m. on Friday and Saturday.

Ming's, 1321 Quadra St. (tel. 604/385-4405), is quite a showplace with a massive red dragon gate and loads of plants. Worth a try for Chinese food enthusiasts. Prices are in the $10 ($8 U.S.) to $15 ($12 U.S.) range, and hours are 5 p.m. to 1 a.m. daily, closing at 10 p.m. on Sunday.

Yokohama Japanese Restaurant, 980 Blanshard St. (tel. 604/384-5433), has a very popular sushi bar where you can try many colorful and delectable treats for $1 (80¢ U.S.) or so each, nibbling your way as far as appetite and wallet will take you. Tempura, sushi, and other treats are in the $10 ($8 U.S.) to $12 ($9.50 U.S.) range. Yokohama is open from 11:30 a.m. to 2 p.m. weekdays and from 5 to 9:30 p.m. daily except Sunday.

Koto Japanese Restaurant, 510 Fort St. (tel. 604/382-1514), is a simple spot with wood booths and kimono-clad waitresses serving a variety of sukiyaki and teriyaki selections for prices in the $10 ($8 U.S.) range. Hours are 11 a.m. to 2 p.m. weekdays for lunch, 5 to 10 p.m. daily for dinner.

INDIAN: India's exotic flavors are on tap too. Somehow the **Taj Mahal**, 679 Herald St. (tel. 604/383-4662), has managed to create an exterior that evokes memories of its fabled namesake love-temple. Behind the minarets is some fine Indian cooking doing full justice to Indian herbs and spices. Tandoori treats are prepared in a genuine tandoor (clay oven), or you can feast on lamb and chicken biryani, fiery beef vindaloo, or prawn masala. Prices are in the $13 ($10.50 U.S.) to $17 ($13.50 U.S.) bracket, and hours are 11 a.m. to 2:30 p.m. Monday through Saturday and 5 to 10 p.m. daily.

GREEK: Moussaka fans have their selections too. Greeks love to have a good time, as you will see at **Periklis**, 531 Yates St. (tel. 604/386-3313), now here for more than a decade. A lively, cheerful place, Periklis is an attractive bilevel spot with red-checkered tablecloths and a corner on the copper market. On the menu are some unusual Greek treats like saganaki, a dish of fried Greek cheese flamed with brandy, shrimp Santorini prepared as the islanders do with tomatoes, wine, and feta, and the house specialty, arni sti souvlas, spit-roasted lamb. You can even try them all with a Periklis Platter for two. Prices are in the $11 ($8.75 U.S.) to $20 ($16 U.S.) range for most selections, and hours are 5 to 11 p.m. daily, closing at 9 p.m. on Sunday.

GERMAN: The **Rathskeller Schnitzel House,** 1205 Quadra St. (tel. 604/ 386-9348), is a pleasant, simply furnished dining room. On the menu are plenty of good, solid German specialties: sausages, six different schnitzel preparations, Hungarian beef goulash, hearty cabbage rolls, beef rouladen, and for the undecided, a Rathskeller plate with a little of everything. Top it off with a slice of apple strudel or Black Forest cake. You'll pay prices in the $9 ($7.25 U.S.) to $16 ($12.75 U.S.) range. Hours are 11 a.m. to 10 p.m.

TEA: It's tea time. Tea's a delightful custom in Victoria, so even if you're not usually a tea drinker, give high tea a try here. Just about every place in town serves tea, including the **Empress Hotel** (see "Where to Stay"), which does so in rather considerable style, but usually to packed audiences. Try the **Gazebo Tea House and Gallery,** 5460 Old W. Saanich Rd. (tel. 604/479-7787), where afternoon tea includes scones with jam and cream, crumpets, fruit salad, fresh strawberries or raspberries, tiny sandwiches, and homemade cakes. Lunch is a joy too, with homemade beef pies. Prices are in the $5 ($4 U.S.) bracket, and hours here are 11 a.m. to 6 p.m. daily from June to September, closed Monday in other months, but call ahead.

Other tea houses in Victoria include **Four Mile House,** 199 Island Hwy. (tel. 604/479-2332), open from 1 to 5 p.m. Tuesday through Sunday; **The Gables,** 1181 Fort St. (tel. 604/382-4213), open from 11 a.m. to 4 p.m. daily except Sunday; and the **Tudor Rose Tearoom,** 253 Cook St. (tel. 604/382-2225), open from 10 a.m. to 5 p.m. daily. **Murchie's** at 1111 Government St., at Fort Street (tel. 604/383-4181), is not properly a tea house but a restaurant that serves afternoon teas; hours are 8 a.m. to 4 p.m. with afternoon tea served from 2:30 to 4 p.m. and dinner from 5:30 to 11 p.m.

ITALIAN: If pasta makes perfect for you, Victoria provides. Try the **Prancing Pony,** 1311 Gladstone Ave. (tel. 604/383-6722 or 383-8512), a pizza specialist, which also features pastas and even a selection of vegetarian specialties. Pizzas —feta cheese is among the choices—are in the $7 ($5.50 U.S.) to $12 ($9.50 U.S.) range.

5. NIGHTLIFE

There is life after dark in Victoria no matter what you might have heard. Several theaters operate in the city including the **Belfry,** 1291 Gladstone Ave. (tel. 604/385-6815), a serious playhouse; and the **Bastion Theatre,** Bastion Square (tel. 604/386-8301), performing at McPherson Playhouse. Many top entertainers performing in Victoria go on stage at the **McPherson Playhouse,** 3 Centennial Square (tel. 604/386-6121), or at the **Royal Theatre,** 805 Broughton St. (tel. 604/386-6121).

The **Vancouver Symphony** (tel. 604/385-9771) schedules two dozen performances between September and April at the Royal Theatre (tel. 604/383-9711) and the **Pacific Opera Society** (tel. 604/385-0222) performs here. **Vic-**

toria Jazz Society (tel. 604/592-5222) can tell you what's jamming on the jazz scene. What's happening where appears in the *Daily Colonist* newspaper or in the *Visitor's Guide,* available at hotels and in the visitor center.

Victoria's atmospheric English-style pubs are the city's most interesting places after dark, but there are some other evening diversions as well, ranging from disco to cabarets. Among the pubbiest spots in town are **The Beaver,** a nautically themed place in the Empress Hotel, 631 Humboldt St. (tel. 604/834-8111); the **Old Bailey Pub** in Courtyard Inn, 850 Blanshard St. (tel. 604/385-6787); the **Public House,** 4680 Elk Lake Rd. (tel. 604/658-8202); the **Six Mile House,** 494 Island Hwy. (tel. 604/478-3121); and **Spinnakers Brew Pub,** a waterside watering hole that occupies a lovely old house and also is the only four-star microbrewery on the West Coast.

Surely, we don't need to mention that today's hot disco is tomorrow's warehouse, do we? Good. Here's what was still extant on a recent visit. In the **Strathcona Hotel** (see "Where to Stay"), 919 Douglas St. (tel. 604/383-7137), are four spots with terpsichorean foci, the Cuckoo's Nest, Max Headroom, the Forge, and the Sting, each offering its own kind of diversion. **New York, New York,** 860 Yates St. (tel. 604/381-5442), calls itself the most outrageous club on the West Coast, a claim you can check out for yourself, and **The Thatch** in the Royal Oak Inn, 4680 Elk Lake Rd. (tel. 604/658-5266), offers dance music Tuesday through Saturday. The **Dixieland Lounge,** 1140 Government St. (tel. 604/388-9166), can be counted on for jazz adventures.

In Canada some dance spots are called cabarets, which doesn't seem to indicate much of anything except a different kind of liquor license. Among the livelier cabarets in Victoria are **Harpo's,** Bastion Square (tel. 604/385-5333), and **Merlin's Nightclub** in Hartwig Court, 1208 Wharf St. (tel. 604/381-2331).

The **Barbary Coast,** 759 Yates St. (tel. 604/384-4136), is a two-level lounge featuring Gold Rush–era décor; **Bayside Lounge** in Crest Harbourview Inn, 455 Belleville St. (tel. 604/386-2421), has a lovely view; the Empress Hotel's **Bengal Room,** 721 Government St. (tel. 604/384-8111), is an unusual lounge; and the **Gaslight Lounge** in the Dominion Hotel, 759 Yates St. (tel. 604/384-4136), is a study in carved solid oak paneling. **Paul's Upstairs Lounge,** 1900 Douglas St. (tel. 604/382-9231), has nightly entertainment, and **Impressions Café,** 345 Quebec St. (tel. 604/385-2405), features an Indian theme. At Oak Bay Beach Hotel, 1175 Beach Dr. (tel. 604/598-4556), **The Snug** gives permanent space to the mugs of regular patrons and considers them entertainment enough.

6. WHAT TO SEE AND DO

While there are quite a number of official things-to-see-and-do in Victoria, the best of them is Victoria itself, a green and pretty city, surrounded by sparkling seas, dotted with rolling green lawns, and trimmed with monumental buildings. At night tiny klieg lights and huge floodlights turn Victoria into a Canadian Tivoli. Be sure to plan some time just to wander the lanes and byways of this neat-as-a-bandbox city.

GOVERNMENT STREET AND ENVIRONS: You might start your wanderings with a self-guided **walking tour map** that the city's conveniently located Visitor Information Centre will be happy to provide for you. That will help you find your way to Government Street, which runs straight through the middle of Old Town where you will find **Bastion Square,** once a rowdy, howdy-ma'am kind of spot that attracted the hoi-polloi and other assorted characters, some of whom ended up on the gallows, which were placed right here to keep things simple. Today Bastion Square is a snappy shopping mall lined with antique buildings. As you stroll Government Street, you'll come across **Trounce Alley,** once another rough spot where miners and sailors spent their moola with considerable fanfare. It, too, is now a delightful little cluster of boutiques trimmed with gas lamps.

Major sight, of course, is the one you cannot miss: the **Parliament Buildings** at Government and Belleville Streets. Opened in 1898, the Parliament Buildings are the meeting place of provincial legislators who still participate in a great deal of pomp and circumstance to get things going each legislative session. A golden throne is seat for the speaker, and the doorman, called the sergeant-at-arms, carries a golden mace. At the Parliament Buildings you can go on a guided tour daily from May to September, weekdays the rest of the year. Tour times vary, so call 604/387-3046 for details. A carillon here plays hour-long concerts daily at 3 p.m. from July to mid-September, at noon on holidays.

In the same complex of governmental buildings you will find the **Provincial Museum,** 601 Belleville St. (tel. 604/387-3701), with three floors of exhibits on the history of British Columbia. Some are hands-on exhibits featuring sounds and smells. Hours are 10 a.m. to 9 p.m. daily July to October, closing at 5:30 p.m. in other months. It's $5 ($4 U.S.) for adults, $3 ($2.50 U.S.) for children. The Provincial Archives in the Heritage Court here will give you a look at documents dating back to the first days of the colony. Open weekdays from 9 a.m. to 5 p.m. and free.

While you're here, be sure to take a look at the **totempole** at Thunderbird Park, corner of Douglas and Belleville Streets (tel. 604/387-3504), and watch the carvers at work on more.

Conducted walking tours are sponsored by the Greater Victoria Visitors Bureau each day at 9:30 a.m. and 1:30 p.m. from about June to September.

GARDENS AND PARKS: Butchart Gardens may very well be Canada's most famous garden; certainly it is western Canada's most revered expanse of grass and flowers. These lovely gardens cover 50 acres and are located about 13 miles from the city on Hwy. 17. Here you can see a Sunken Garden, an English Rose Garden, a Japanese Garden, an Italian Garden, and a Lake Garden. Every Saturday night in July and August fireworks erupt over this fabulous collection of greenery. Butchart Gardens are open from 9 a.m. to 11 p.m. daily July to September, closing at 9 p.m. from May to July and in September. From March to May and in October hours are 9 a.m. to 5 p.m., closing an hour earlier in other months. Admission is $8 ($6.50 U.S.) for adults, $4 ($3.25 U.S.) for children 13 to 17, and $1 (80¢ U.S.) for children 5 to 12; under 5, free. Restaurants here, too, so you can make a day of it.

The **Crystal Garden,** 713 Douglas St. (tel. 604/381-1213), brings the tropics north to this conservatory filled with exotic tropical flora. Hours are 10 a.m. to 8 p.m. daily from July to September, closing at 5:30 p.m. in other months. Admission is $4.50 ($3.60 U.S.) for adults, $2.50 ($2 U.S.) for children 6 to 16, and families may enter for $9.50 ($7.60 U.S.).

Government House Gardens, 1401 Rockland Ave. (no telephone), are every bit as large as Butchart Gardens, with thousands of heather, azaleas, and rhododendrons spread over formal lawns that also include a sunken rose garden and lily pond. Hours are dawn to dusk daily all year and admission is free.

FROM CURIOSITY TO A CASTLE: Victoria has more than enough odd and intriguing sights, but the best of them are architectural treasures given loving care for generations and open now for you to discover what life was like before we all began living in closets. Let's open with **Anne Hathaway's Cottage,** 429 Lampson St. (tel. 604/388-4353), part of an amazing collection of jolly Olde

416 ☐ FROMMER'S DOLLARWISE NORTHWEST

English architecture and armor. Guided tours begin at 9 a.m. and continue to 9 p.m. daily from June to October, closing at 4 p.m. in other months. Admission is $4 ($3.25 U.S.) for adults, $2.50 ($2 U.S.) for children 8 to 17.

Moving right along now, don't miss the castle, called **Craigdarroch Castle,** 1050 Joan Crescent St. (tel. 604/592-5323). Built in the late 1880s by Scottish immigrant Robert Dunsmuir, who found his way to riches (coal) and renown (scads of money) in Victoria, this mass of stone was a little bauble for his wife, Joan. A famous Canadian family, the Dunsmuirs spawned a son who married a daughter of Virginia's Byrd family and became a Canadian premier; a daughter, who married Irish royalty; and a son honored by California, which named the town of Dunsmuir there after Robert. Although the home has served the city in many capacities in recent years, it has now assumed its rightful place as a beloved city landmark. Original stained-glass windows, mosaics, and paintings have been restored and furnishings replaced to re-create the original look of the place as closely as possible.

Its massive stone façade is quite something. A dancing hall on the top floor is large enough to contain a three-bedroom house; and a double drawing room has two fireplaces and twin chandeliers, and is 50 feet long and 24 feet wide! Hours are 9 a.m. to 9:30 p.m. daily June to October and 10 a.m. to 5:30 p.m. in other months. Admission is $3 ($2.50 U.S.) for adults, $2.50 ($2 U.S.) for students.

Back in the mid-1800s when this community was a pretty rough-and-tumble place, the Hudson's Bay Company wheeled and dealed with Britain over control of the land. One of the deals they made required the fur-trading company to establish a colony here in exchange for control over the land. That colony, founded in 1853 and named Craigflower Farm, was a collection of small farms operated by laborers, artisans, and farmers. Each committed himself to five years' labor in exchange for an annual allowance and a land grant of 25 to 50 acres at the end of the contract. Families recruited in Scotland and England made the six-month journey around Cape Horn to find here only rough, bare-essentials shelter and 900 acres of recalcitrant wilderness.

Today you can get an idea how demanding those early days must have been for those first settlers with a visit to **Craigflower Heritage Site,** 110 Island Hwy. (Hwy. 1A) (tel. 604/387-3607). A restored Georgian-style farmhouse is on display, as is the colony's schoolhouse, a big barn of a place modeled after England's early school buildings. Craigflower is open from 10 a.m. to 3:45 p.m. Wednesday through Sunday year round; closed on holidays. There is no admission charge.

Another historic home is **Point Ellice House,** 2616 Pleasant St. (tel. 604/385-3837), a century-old and beautifully furnished place. Hours are 10 a.m. to 5 p.m. daily except Monday from mid-May to mid-September. At other times of year the house is open Tuesday through Friday from 10 a.m. to 4 p.m. It's free.

One more historic site, **Helmcken House,** built in 1852, was the home of Hudson's Bay Company's doctor, J. S. Helmcken. One of the city's oldest homes, the small four-room house is the repository of many antiques, including medical instruments. Open year round from 10 a.m. to 3:45 p.m. Wednesday through Sunday, the house is at 638 Elliott St., and you get to it by walking south half a block from the Empress Hotel just east of the Provincial Museum. It's free.

Christ Church Cathedral, 912 Vancouver St. (tel. 604/383-2714), looks a great deal like England's Gothic churches and is one of the nation's largest cathedrals. You can visit daily from 9 a.m. to 5:30 p.m., free.

KID STUFF AND OTHER ASSORTED SIGHTS: Victoria's **Chinatown** is small but interesting, its entrance topped by a massive gilded red Torii gate. Inside you'll find restored streets, some so narrow that outstretched arms bump walls on either side. You'll find the district halfway between Government and

Wharf Streets between Fisgard and Pandora. Be sure to seek out Fan Tan Alley, once notorious for opium dens and gambling houses, now a crafts enclave.

Sealand, Beach Drive at Oak Bay Marina (tel. 604/598-3373), lets you dive beneath the sea without getting wet, then watch those sea fellers through big viewing windows. Up above, seals and sea lions, as well as a friendly killer whale, leap and lollygag around for your amusement. Sealand is open from 10 a.m. to 5 p.m. daily. Admission is $5 ($4 U.S.) for adults, $4 ($3.25 U.S.) for students 12 to 18, and $2 ($1.50 U.S.) for youngsters 5 to 12.

Miniature World, in the Empress Hotel at the Humboldt Street entrance (tel. 604/385-9731), features two huge dollhouses and presents a historical program on the city's past using sound and light. All the little folks' furniture is on display daily from 8:30 a.m. to 10 p.m. May to October, closing at 5 p.m. in other months. Adults pay $5 ($4 U.S.), students 12 to 18 are charged $4.50 ($3.50 U.S.), and children 5 to 12 pay $3.50 ($2.75 U.S.).

Just across the street from the pier at which the *Princess Marguerite* docks, a group of ten diversions have joined to call themselves the **Victorian Village,** 321 Belleville St. (tel. 604/384-3232). Here you can play a round of miniature golf on two 18-hole courses, visit an Enchanted Garden trimmed with dozens of flower baskets, get a look at an irresistible dollhouse collection and a miniature railroad, creak through the passageways of a haunted mansion, then recover at the Cricket Grill amid a display of cricket player memorabilia. There's a currency exchange here, a bike-rental shop, a Christmas House gift shop open all year, a camera shop, Tickles Gift Shop, and even a bed-and-breakfast home, Belleville House Bed and Breakfast. One thing or another here is open from early morning to late at night, and if you play a round of miniature golf you can visit the Enchanted Village free.

Now here's a strange one: **Fable Cottage Estate,** 5187 Cordova Bay Rd. (tel. 604/658-5741). Every stick of furniture here was made by hand, and it took 11 years to do it! These handmade furnishings are supplemented by pretty, but odd, gardens filled with tiny gnomes who move about right before your wondering eyes. To top it off, a 2,000-pound flower basket revolves. Fable Cottage is open and provides guided tours daily from 9:30 a.m. to dusk April through October. Admission is $6 ($4.75 U.S.) for adults, $3.75 ($3 U.S.) for students, and $2.75 ($2.25 U.S.) for children 4 to 11.

At last, we wrap up this whole ball of wax: **Royal London Wax Museum,** 470 Belleville St. (tel. 604/388-4461). Eeeeek, it's the chamber of horrors . . . and 50 other all-too-lifelike scenes of people who have played their part on history's stage. The museum is open from 9 a.m. to 9 p.m. daily May to October, closing at 5 p.m. in other months. Adults pay $5 ($4 U.S.) admission, students 12 to 18 pay $4 ($3.25 U.S.), and youngsters 5 through 11 pay $2.25 ($1.75 U.S.).

TOURS: You can tour this water-rimmed city by car, plane, or boat. **Gray Line Tours** takes you around the city in cherry-red double-decker buses that visit all the top sights downtown and around the island. Prices vary from $5.25 ($4.25 U.S.) to $10.50 ($8.50 U.S.).

Much of the life of Victoria is now and always has been tied to its harbor. To see what that harbor looks like, hop aboard **Harbour Tours** (tel. 604/383-6824 for tickets or 604/381-1511 for information), which sails from the kiosk bearing its name on Government Street across from the Empress Hotel. Tours operate every day from about 11 a.m. to 6:30 p.m. mid-May to mid-September, from 11:15 a.m. to 5:15 p.m. in early May and from mid-September to mid-October when the service stops for the winter. For the 75-minute trips you pay $9 ($7.25 U.S.) for adults, $3 ($2.50 U.S.) for children.

You can tour the **Inside Passage** on B.C. Ferries, 1045 Howe St., Vancouver (tel. 604/386-3431 in Victoria). Accommodations are a bit on the spartan side, but the scenery is magnificent going on stupendous. One-way fares for the inside passage journey to Port Hardy / Prince Rupert are $62 ($49.50 U.S.) for adults plus $191 ($153 U.S.) for the car.

E & N Dayliner *Nanahat,* 325 Esquimalt Rd. (tel. 604/383-4324, or toll free 800/665-8630), chugs 135 miles north on this big island to the villages of Nanaimo and Courtenay. You can take all or part of the trip for prices that begin at $8 ($6.50 U.S.) one way for the short trip to Duncan and top at $30 ($24 U.S.) for the journey to Courtenay.

And finally by hoof: **Tallyho,** 180 Goward Rd. (tel. 604/479-1113), lets you sit in, shall we say, Victorian splendor up on the seat of a rubber-tired carriage decked out in a gaily striped awning and drawn by two draft horses. Trips leave every 15 minutes or so from 10 a.m. to 7 p.m., and commentators tell you some amusing stories about this city. The fare is $7 ($5.50 U.S.) for adults, $3.50 ($2.75 U.S.) for children.

7. ART AND CULTURAL EXHIBITS

Victoria has its own art gallery, fittingly called the **Art Gallery of Greater Victoria,** 1040 Moss St. (tel. 604/384-4101). Permanent exhibits include a fine one of Japanese art as well as Canadian and European prints. Temporary exhibitions change frequently. Housed in a historic mansion, the gallery has a charming tea room, craft shop, Japanese gardens, and a miniature dollhouse. You can visit the art gallery from 10 a.m. to 5 p.m. Monday through Saturday (until 9 p.m. on Thursday), but only from 1 to 5 p.m. on Sunday. In winter months it's closed on Monday. Admission is $2 ($1.50 U.S.) for adults, $1 (80¢ U.S.) for students older than 12, but free to everybody on Thursday evenings.

Emily Carr is perhaps the most famous of Canadian artists, certainly she is western Canada's most respected artist. At the **Emily Carr Gallery,** 1107 Wharf St. (tel. 604/387-3080), you can see some of the hundreds of her paintings of totempoles, done in an attempt to preserve a record of these national treasures. Hours are 10 a.m. to 8 p.m. daily from mid-May to September, Tuesday through Saturday from 10 a.m. to 4:30 p.m. in other months. There is no admission charge.

8. SPORTS

Fishing is the big lure here, but there are plenty of other sports opportunities available. If you have **fishing** on your mind, any one of a number of charter boats operate from the docks at the inlet across from the Empress Hotel. On board a 65-foot cruiser docked at 1327 Beach Dr. (tel. 604/598-3366), you'll pay about $150 ($120 U.S.) for a boat and captain to search for the big ones. Fishing guides in Victoria include **Juan de Fuca Salmon Charters,** Sunny Shores Resort, Hwy. 14 (tel. 604/642-4933 or 642-4107), and **Magna Charters,** 902 Deal St. (tel. 604/598-4213). Rental boats are $10 ($8 U.S.).

Water babies will love **All-fun Waterslides and Recreation Park,** Hordon Road (tel. 604/474-4546 or 474-3184), about eight miles from Victoria. Corkscrewing slides, miniature golf, go-karts, a snackbar, and electronic games are all here and open from 10 a.m. to 9 p.m. but times vary (i.e., waterslides only in summer), so give them a call to check. Fees for the various amusements range from $5 ($4 U.S.) to about $10 ($8 U.S.).

Elk Lake Sports, 5411 Hamsterly (tel. 604/658-5721), rents canoes, windsurfing boards, and small sailboats for prices from $5 ($4 U.S.) to $20 ($16 U.S.) an hour, depending on the size of the craft.

Rockhaven Ranch, Finlayson Arm Road (tel. 604/478-3023), will get you up on one of their steeds for $20 ($16 U.S.) for a two-hour ride.

Hikers should get in touch with **Coastal Outdoor Recreation,** P.O. Box 316, Lantzville, BC V0R 2H0 (tel. 604/758-1451), which has guided eight-day hiking tours all summer long for $395 ($316 U.S.), including equipment and food.

Cedar Hill Municipal Golf Course, 1400 Derby St. (tel. 604/595-2823), is an 18-hole, par-67 public course. You'll find nine holes of golf at **Henderson Park,** 2291 Cedar Hill Crossroad (tel. 604/595-7946). Greens fees are in the $12 ($9.50 U.S.) to $15 ($12 U.S.) range for 18 holes at public courses, higher at private clubs.

Tennis courts are at Beacon Hill Park on Cook Street, and Recreation Oak Bay, 1975 Bee St. (tel. 604/595-7946). For other locations call the city's Parks Department at 604/385-5711. **Racquetball** courts are at Courts West, 1756 Island Hwy. (tel. 604/474-3544), and Sussex Squash Club, 740 Discovery St. (tel. 604/382-8623).

Beaches are at Willows Beach in Oak Bay along Beach Drive; Thetis Lake Park, Hwy. 1 at the foot of Malahat; and Beacon Hill Park, Douglas Street and Dallas Road.

In winter there is **skiing** at Mount Washington (tel. 604/334-3424 or 338-1386), about 132 miles north of town, where two double chairs and a triple chair take you to the top. Lift tickets are $24 ($19.25 U.S.) a day for adults, $15 ($12 U.S.) for children. The ski season runs from about December to April, and all facilities are available at the mountain.

Skating rinks are open at Juan de Fuca Parks and Recreation, 1767 Island Hwy. (tel. 604/478-8384), and Recreation Oak Bay, 1975 Bee St. (tel. 604/595-7946).

9. SPECIAL EVENTS

In mid-May the city turns out for a big celebration of **Victoria Days** topped by a Victoria Day Holiday Parade. So important is this festival that most dates in the city are reckoned from it. In mid-May the massing of a rainbow-hued fleet of sailing boats, moored gunwale to gunwale, marks the start of the **Swiftsure Classic Sailboat Race.** Of course, **Canada Day** is celebrated all over the nation on July 1, and in winter the city schedules an **international skating** event in late October and **ice curling championships** in early March.

10. SHOPPING

Victoria is one big shopping mall—with municipal incorporation papers. You'll have no difficulty finding your way to the shops lined up cheek-by-jowl along Government Street and all the intersecting side streets and alleys. Other shopper thoroughfares are Fort, Douglas, and Yates Streets.

Among the more interesting purchases in town are elegant one-of-a-kind furs from **Scuby Furs,** 911 Government St.; handcrafted and contemporary quilts and soft sculptures from **Satin Moon Quilt Shop,** 106 Johnson St.; and heavy hand-knit Cowichan Indian sweaters from the **Bay,** Douglas and Herald Streets, or **Sasquatch,** 1233 Government St.

More? Yes, indeed: **antiques** from any one of ten or more dealers whose shops line Fort Street; menswear from **Knickerbockers,** Harbour Square, 910 Government St.; Canadian handcrafted work from **Hand Loom,** 625 Trounce Alley; kitchen knives and cutlery from **International Knives,** 1306 Government St.; lambskins, knitting and spinning yarns, and handmade knits from **Alcheringa,** 616 Trounce Alley.

CHAPTER XIX

CRUISES FROM THE PACIFIC NORTHWEST

□ □ □

1. ALASKAN PORTS OF CALL
2. SHIPS THAT SAIL TO ALASKA

Our friend Bernice, a wilderness and wildlife enthusiast, recently listened patiently through all our enraptured sighs over the Pacific Northwest. When we'd wound down, she had only one question: "Yes, but how was Alaska?"

For her and for many another adventurous traveler, the single most wondrous part of the northwest corner of the nation is snowy, solitary Alaska, so awesome in size and isolation that it gives a whole new meaning to the word wilderness.

Regrettably, it also requires new meaning for the word "dollarwise." Alaska can be, and usually is, outrageously expensive — $90 a night in a small motel, for instance. It is also amazingly difficult to reach.

There is, however, a way to visit the most remote sections of this remote state with ease and in pampered comfort. That way is on a cruise to Alaska. Conveniently enough, nearly all the cruises to fjords and glacier-rimmed bays of the 49th state begin right here in the Pacific Northwest, most at Vancouver, a few at Seattle.

To give you an idea of what's available and what you'll be seeing if you take an Alaskan cruise, here's a brief look at the ports visited by most cruise ships and a few details on what ships are sailing there.

Here comes the plus: it just so happens we have written another book — *Frommer's Dollarwise Cruises* — that will give you the *complete* lowdown on prices, departure dates, and the like.

But first, that always-important question: cost. Cruise ships, like any other form of transportation these days, vary widely in price, but you can expect to pay fares that begin at about $1,000 each for a seven-day cruise.

Now that may seem a hefty hunk from the wallet, but consider that for your money you're buying *every* bite of food you can consume. You're also buying your hotel room, transportation, a steady round of entertainment day and night, and a guided tour of some fascinating scenery and ports. Quite a bargain, no matter how you figure it!

Right after money comes the second most important question about Alaska: weather. Answer: good in summer. Despite its frigid image, Alaska is quite pleasant in summer, ranging from an average high of 41° to 47° Fahrenheit in April to averages of 63° to 72° in July, 53° to 55° in September.

As for what you'll see, well, wondrous indeed!

Blue-white glaciers glittering in the sun. Eagles soaring overhead. A school of whales crashing and blowing its way north. A flapping, honking group of sea lions, a lumbering grizzly bear swiping at a salmon, perhaps an elk munching sedately amid a rainbow of alpine flowers.

Up here in a land that dismisses all the rest of the U.S. as "the lower 48," folks and fauna are a diverse lot indeed. On a recent Alaskan cruise we were greeted in Sitka by a group of red-skirted lasses in babushkas whirling their way through intricate steps of folk dances taught to them by Russian ancestors who settled here when this land was still a Russian colony.

On another occasion we watched as adventuresome sailors clad in yellow slickers sailed off into half-frozen waters to chip off a tiny corner of a massive glacier. Later we sipped drinks chilled by that very piece of rock-hard ice as we watched a fiery sunset turn snowy ice into a rosy wonderland.

1. ALASKAN PORTS OF CALL

Although a few Alaska cruises depart from Los Angeles or San Francisco, by far the majority sail from Vancouver.

Some stop in **Prince Rupert,** a small totempole-lined town way up on the north end of British Columbia.

Many a ship cruises through **Misty Fjords National Monument,** a place as beautiful as its lovely name. Those mists lift early to give you a look at deep blue waters and white snows.

Ketchikan likes to call itself the "Salmon Capital of the World," so one of the favorite port excursions is an open-fire salmon bake. In this city famous for its totempoles, you can learn to read them, each of which tells a little story of clan history, including a little "Dallas"-like scandal! Don't miss Creek Street, where former bawdy houses are now boutiques.

Sitka is a very small town but it's big on the list of best-loved ports. Once known as the "Paris of the Pacific," Sitka was once the capital of Alaska and it was here that proprietorship of Alaska was turned over to the United States in 1867. A landmark is St. Michael's Cathedral, a handsome Russian Orthodox church adorned with glittering goldleaf, ornate chandeliers, and priceless icons. In Sitka you will also see the New Archangel Russian Dancers.

Juneau, capital city of Alaska, is a highlight for shopper-cruisers. Top port visit here is a raft ride past Mendenhall Glacier just a short distance out of town. Everyone, but everyone, but absolutely *everyone* who visits Juneau also strides through the doors of the Red Dog Saloon, which has for generations been welcoming the free-thinkers and pioneering spirits that make their way to this outpost of civilization.

Another popular port is **Skagway,** gateway to the Klondike goldfields and once home to 20,000 rip-roaring miners. You will have no trouble getting an idea what the place was once like, however: most of the downtown has been designated a National Historic Park, its false-fronted stores and boardwalks maintained just as they were way back when.

Glacier Bay National Monument is perhaps the best-known bay in Alaska and a spot nearly every ship visits. This is fjord country at its finest. As you sip a mid-morning mulled wine, you'll watch great masses of ice "calve" from the main glacier and send floating "pups" out into the main stream. A naturalist comes on board every cruise ship sailing Glacier Bay to tell you a little about the evolutionary processes you see going on here.

Largest city in Alaska is **Anchorage,** a landlocked spot you reach by train on a three-hour ride from the port at Whittier. Quite a cosmopolitan place for all its remote location, Anchorage is home to Denali National Park and Preserve. One of the nation's most dramatic national parks, Denali is spread across 5.6 million acres of wilderness surrounding Mount McKinley, the tallest mountain in North America. Here you'll see all manner of birds and beasts showcased in dramatic scenery.

2. SHIPS THAT SAIL TO ALASKA

Here, then is a look at some of the ships that sail in Alaskan waters. Cruises begin in mid-May and end in mid- or late September.

Best known of the land tour operators offering conducted tours in Alaska is **Westours,** a company that has been taking hundreds of thousands of travelers to this snowy corner of the globe for many years. The variety of its Alaska experiences was expanded a few years ago when Westours was purchased by **Holland America Line,** 300 Elliott Ave. West, Seattle, WA 98119 (tel. 206/281-3535 or 206/281-1970, or toll free 800/426-0327), a cruise line that has been sailing for generations.

In summer the line's flagship, the 1,111-passenger *Rotterdam* sails on weeklong cruises from Vancouver. It is joined there by Holland America's newest ship, the 1,214-passenger *Noordam* and the three-year-old *Nieuw Amsterdam,* which also sail from Vancouver to Alaska on seven-day voyages.

Exploration Cruise Lines, 1500 Metropolitan Park Building, Seattle, WA 98101 (tel. 206/625-9600, or toll free 800/426-0600), operates several small but interesting ships in northern waters. What's most interesting about them is a movable bow piece that lifts to allow passengers to step ashore and walk right out onto a glacier!

Explorer Starship, North Star, and *Great Rivers Explorer,* three of the line's several ships, head for Alaska in mid-April to spend the summer based in Ketchikan, sailing from there to some unusual ports including Wrangell, Tracy Arm Fjord, Petersburg, and Le Conte Glacier among others.

Another ship in the line, the *Pacific Explorer,* sails up the Columbia and Snake Rivers between Washington and Oregon from mid-May through September, calling at Astoria (Ore.), The Dalles (Ore.), several dams along the Columbia River, Lewiston (Id.), and Kennewick (Wash.).

Cunard Lines, 555 Fifth Ave., New York, NY 10017 (tel. 212/880-7500, or toll free 800/221-4770), owns one of the world's most famous ships, the *Queen Elizabeth 2,* but it is one of the line's other ships that visits Alaska.

That ship is the 750-passenger *Cunard Princess,* which sails on seven-day journeys that go from Vancouver to Whittier, gateway to Anchorage. *Cunard Princess* turns around at Whittier and spends another seven days returning to Vancouver, visiting some different ports. You can book either a 7- or 14-day cruise on the ship or get off at Whittier, spend two weeks touring Alaska, then catch the next ship back.

Cunard has also bought the ships of another line and formed **Cunard/ Norwegian American Cruises** (same address and telephone numbers as Cunard Lines). Now you'll find the elegant gray *Sagafjord* sailing from mid-May to September on 10- and 11-day Alaska cruises from Vancouver to Whittier and back.

Costa Cruises, 1 Biscayne Tower, Miami, FL 33131 (tel. 305/358-7325, or toll free 800/462-6782), an Italian line with seven cruise ships in its fleet, sends its 16,330-ton *Daphne* north to Vancouver each spring to sail every Friday on week-long cruises.

Another cruise line, **Admiral Cruises,** 520 Pike St., Suite 2200, Seattle, WA 98101 (tel. 206/467-8200, or toll free 800/222-5505), has come up with an unusual plan for its Alaska cruises. If you're interested in driving through some of the 49th state, you can wheel your car onto a 27,000-ton former ferryboat called *Stardancer,* and cruise for three days before you leave the ship to explore Alaska in your car. Later you can return to Haines to catch the ship on its four-day return journey. You can stay on board for all seven days too, of course.

World Explorer Cruises, 550 Kearny St., San Francisco, CA 94108 (tel. 415/391-9262, or toll free 800/854-3835, 800/222-2255 in California), operates a single ship, the *Universe,* which has a 12,000-volume library (the ship is chartered by a university in winter) and a bevy of lecturers aboard. *Universe* features 14-day Alaskan cruises offering an extensive look at these northern waters.

Sitmar Cruise Lines, 10100 Santa Monica Blvd., Los Angeles, CA 90067 (tel. 213/553-1666, or toll free 800/421-0880, 800/252-0301 in California), is another line that has been visiting Alaska for many a season. Carrying 1,212 passengers, Sitmar's *Fairsky* and *Fairsea* sail from San Francisco and Vancouver on varied-length sojourns that include stops in Victoria and Vancouver.

Royal Viking Lines, 1 Embarcadero Center, San Francisco, CA 94111 (tel. 415/398-8000, or toll free 800/422-8000), is another Scandinavian-run line with some very handsome ships, one of which, the *Royal Viking Sky,* spends the summer sailing in Alaska on 11-day cruises from San Francisco.

Everyone has sailed the Love Boat if only in imagination! That television show that makes cruises look so tempting was filmed on the ships of **Princess Cruise Line,** 2029 Century Park East, Los Angeles, CA 90067 (tel. 213/553-1770, or toll free 800/421-0522, 800/252-0158 in California).

If you think this is your summer for a Love Boat experience, you can combine it with a look at Alaska aboard Princess's newest ship, the *Royal Princess,* a 45,000-ton ship carrying 1,200 passengers on ten-day cruises round trip from San Francisco with a stop at Vancouver on the way to Alaskan ports.

Three sister ships, the *Island Princess, Sun Princess,* and *Pacific Princess,* are based in Vancouver from June through September sailing on seven-night Alaska cruises.

Regency Cruises, 260 Madison Ave., New York, NY 10016 (tel. 212/972-4774, or toll free 800/457-5566), sails one of its two ships, the *Regent Sea,* in Alaska from about May to October on week-long cruises from its summer home port in Vancouver.

Index

Newport (OR), 287–91
Nippon Kan Theater (Seattle), 61
North Head (Long Beach), 326
Northwest Trek (Tacoma), 365

Oak Harbor (Whidbey Island), 76
Oaks Amusement Park (Portland), 199
Oceanside (OR), 297
Oddfellows, International Order of (Ashland), 259
Ohme Gardens (Wenatchee), 85
Old Church (Portland), 198
Old Hastings Mill Store Museum (Vancouver, BC), 392
Old Town (Portland), 197
Olympia (WA), 355–9
Olympic Game Farm (Sequim), 348
Olympic National Park (Port Angeles) 349–51
Olympic Peninsula (WA), 331–51
  Aberdeen, 334–6
  beaches, 336
  Lake Quinault, Kalaloch, Forks, 336–9
  Olympic National Park, 349–51
  Port Angeles, 347–9
  see also Port Townsend
Omnidome Theater (Seattle), 60
Ontario (OR), 137–40
  excursions from, 140–1
Orcas Island (WA), 78–9
Orcas Island Historical Museum, 80
Oregon:
  coast of, 267–312; map, 270; orientation, 268–9; tourist information, 268–9; transportation to and within, 268; see also specific places
  map, 25
  southwestern, 245–62; caves, 264–5; Crater Lake, 262–4; map, 248; nightlife and entertainment, 260; orientation, 246–7; Redwood National Park, 265–6; shopping, 262; sights and attractions, 261–2; sports, 261–2; tourist information, 246–7; transportation to and within, 246–7; see also Ashland; Jacksonville
  tourist information, 11
Oregon, University of (Eugene), 225–6
Oregon City (OR), 207–8
Oregon Historical Society (Portland), 197
Oregon Museum of Science and Industry (Portland), 195
Oregon Trail (OR), 136–52
  orientation, 137
  riding the, 150–1
  see also specific places
Oswald State Park (near Cannon Beach), 303
Owyhee Lake (near Ontario), 139
Oxbow Studio (Bend), 239
Oysterville (near Long Beach), 327

Pacific Northwest, 420–3
Pacific Science Center (Seattle), 57, 61
Pasco (WA), 160, 161
Pendleton (OR), 147–52
  accommodations, 147–8
  nightlife and entertainment, 149, 151–2
  restaurants, 148–9
  riding the Oregon Trail, 150–1
  shopping, 152
  sights and attractions, 149–50
  sports, 151
  tourist information, 147
  transportation to, 147
Pendleton Woolen Mills, 150
Peninsula Park's Sunken Rose Garden (Portland), 196
Perozzi (Domingo) House (Ashland), 259
Phillips Lake (near Baker), 144–5
Pike Place Market (Seattle), 63, 67
Pine Mountain Observatory (near Bend), 240
Pittock Mansion (Portland), 197
Plamer (John) House (Portland), 198
Point Defiance Park (Tacoma), 363
Point Elice House (Victoria, BC), 416
Polson Park and Museum (Hoquiam), 335
Poneer Farm Museum (near Eatonville), 364
Port Angeles (WA), 347–9
Portland (OR), 176–203
  accommodations, 181–7; bed-and-breakfast, 187; budget, 186–7; camping and hosteling, 187; Jantzen Beach, 183–4; luxury, 181–4; moderately priced, 184–6
  excursion to Vancouver, WA, 208–9
  history of, 176–7
  map, 180
  nightlife and entertainment, 194, 199
  orientation, 179, 181
  restaurants, 187–94; Continental/steaks, 188–9; French, 190–1; Italian, 191–2; light dining, 193–4; miscellaneous, 192–3; seafood, 188; trendy, 190
  shopping, 202–3
  sights and attractions, 194–200; art and cultural, 199; for children, 198–9; historical, 197–8; parks and gardens, 194–6; special events, 199–200; touring rivers and roses, 196–7; wine country, 205–6; zoo, 194–5
  sports, 200–2; skiing, 203–5
  tourist information, 181
  transportation to and within, 177–9
Portland Art Museum, 199
Portland International Airport, 163, 177–8
Portland Police Historical Museum, 198

Skiing:
Ashland, 260–1
Cascade Mountains, 90
Oregon Trailore, 144
Portland, 203–5
Seattle, 66–7
Sun Valley, 133–4
Snohomish (WA), 91
South Slough National Estuarine Reserve
(Coos Bay), 281
Space Needle (Seattle), 57
Spokane (WA), 98–115
accommodations, 101–5; budget,
103–4; camping, 104–5; luxury,
101–2; moderately-priced, 102–3;
ski condos, 103
excursions from, 114–18
history of, 98–9
map, 100
nightlife and entertainment, 107–8,
112
restaurants, 105–7
shopping, 112–13
sights and attractions, 108–12; architectural, 108–9; art and cultural,
112; historical, 108–9; Mount Spokane, 115; parks and gardens, 111;
Riverfront Park, 108; special events,
111–12; wineries, 110–11
sports, 113–14
tourist information, 101
transportation to and within, 99
Spokane House Interpretive Center, 110
Spokane International Airport, 99
Spokesmen-Review Building (Spokane),
109
Stanley Park (Vancouver, BC), 394,
395
Startup (WA), 91
State Capitol Building (Salem), 215
Stehekin (WA), 84
Steilacoom (WA), 364
Sultan (WA), 91
Sumpter Valley Railroad (Baker), 143
Sun Valley, 119–35
accommodations, 123, 125–9; bed-
and-breakfast, 128–9; budget, 127;
camping, 127; condominium rentals, 127–8; luxury, 123, 125–6;
moderately-priced, 126–7
history of, 120–1
map, 124
nightlife and entertainment, 131–2
orientation, 122–3
restaurants, 129–31
shopping, 135
sights and attractions, 132–3; special
events, 133
sports, 133–5
tourist information, 123
transportation to and within, 122
Suquamish Indian Reservation (Kitsap
Peninsula), 368

Tacoma (WA), 359–67
accommodations, 360–1
excursions to Mount Rainier, 369–70
nightlife and entertainment, 366–7
orientation, 359–60
restaurants, 361–3
shopping, 366
sights and attractions, 363–5
sports, 365–6
Tenino Depot Museum (WA), 364
Tillamook (OR), 297–9
Tillicum Village (Seattle), 59, 63
Tokeland (WA), 327–31
Transportation:
air travel, 20–1
buses, 23–4
cars and driving, 24, 26
ferries, 26
trains, 21, 23, 24
see also specific places
Trevitt (Victor) Memorial (The Dalles),
166
Tri-Cities (WA), 160–1
Trojan Nuclear Power Plant (Rainier),
206
Trounce Alley (Victoria, BC), 415
Turnbull National Wildlife Refuge (near
Spokane), 114–15

Underseas Gardens, Oregon (Newport),
290
U. S. National Bank (Baker), 143

Vancouver (B.C.), 371–99
accommodations, 376–7, 379–84;
bed-and-breakfast, 384; budget,
382–4; camping, 384; luxury,
376–7, 379–82; moderately priced,
382
currency, 376
map, 378
nightlife and entertainment, 391, 398
orientation, 375
restaurants, 385–90; African, 387–8;
Continental/steaks, 389–9;
French, 386–7; Italian, 388; light
dining/trendy, 388–9; Oriental,
389; readers' selection, 390; seafood, 385; with views, 385–6
shopping, 398
side trips, 399
sights and attractions, 391–6; art and
cultural, 397–8; gardens and parks,
395–6; historical, 391–3; museums
and planetarium, 391–2; Robson
Square, 393; special events, 396;
tours, 394–5
sports, 396–7
tourist information, 375–6
transportation to and within, 372,
374–5
Vancouver (WA), 208–9
Vancouver, Fort (Vancouver, WA), 208

NOW, SAVE MONEY ON ALL YOUR TRAVELS!
Join Frommer's™ Dollarwise® Travel Club

Saving money while traveling is never a simple matter, which is why, over 27 years ago, the **Dollarwise Travel Club** was formed. Actually, the idea came from readers of the Frommer publications who felt that such an organization could bring financial benefits, continuing travel information, and a sense of community to economy-minded travelers all over the world.

In keeping with the money-saving concept, the annual membership fee is low—$18 (U.S. residents) or $20 U.S. (Canadian, Mexican, and foreign residents)—and is immediately exceeded by the value of your benefits which include:

1. The latest edition of any TWO of the books listed on the following pages.
2. A copy of any Frommer City Guide.
3. An annual subscription to an 8-page quarterly newspaper *The Dollarwise Traveler* which keeps you up-to-date on fastbreaking developments in good-value travel in all parts of the world—bringing you the kind of information you'd have to pay over $35 a year to obtain elsewhere. This consumer-conscious publication also includes the following columns:
   Hospitality Exchange—members all over the world who are willing to provide hospitality to other members as they pass through their home cities.
   Share-a-Trip—requests from members for travel companions who can share costs and help avoid the burdensome single supplement.
   Readers Ask . . . Readers Reply—travel questions from members to which other members reply with authentic firsthand information.
4. Your personal membership card which entitles you to purchase through the club all Frommer publications for a third to a half off their regular retail prices during the term of your membership.

So why not join this hardy band of international Dollarwise travelers now and participate in its exchange of information and hospitality? Simply send $18 (U.S. residents) or $20 U.S. (Canadian, Mexican, and other foreign residents) along with your name and address to: Frommer's Dollarwise Travel Club, Inc., Gulf + Western Building, One Gulf + Western Plaza, New York, NY 10023. Remember to specify which *two* of the books in section (1) and which *one* in section (2) above you wish to receive in your initial package of member's benefits. Or tear out the next page, check off your choices, and send the page to us with your membership fee.